p. 45

Teaching Choral Music

DON L. COLLINS

Professor of Choral Music Education
University of Central Arkansas
Conway, AR

Prentice Hall
Englewood Cliffs, NJ 07632

Library of Congress Cataloging-in-Publication Data

Collins, Don L.
    Teaching choral music / Don L. Collins.
        p.   cm.
    Includes bibliographical references and index.
    ISBN 0-13-891490-7
    1. Choral singing--Juvenile--Instruction and study.   2. School
music--Instruction and study.   I. Title
    MT930.C58   1993
    782.7'07--dc20   92-46700
                                                      CIP
                                                      MN

Editorial/production supervision and interior design: Jordan Ochs
Acquisitions editor: Bud Therien
Editorial assistant: Lee Mamunes
Copyeditor: Kathleen Lafferty
Prepress buyer: Herb Klein
Manufacturing buyer: Robert Anderson
Cover design: Patricia Kelly

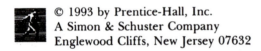 © 1993 by Prentice-Hall, Inc.
A Simon & Schuster Company
Englewood Cliffs, New Jersey 07632

Printed in the United States of America
10 9 8 7 6 5 4 3 2 1

ISBN   0-13-891490-7

Prentice-Hall International (UK) Limited, *London*
Prentice-Hall of Australia Pty. Limited, *Sydney*
Prentice-Hall Canada, Inc., *Toronto*
Prentice-Hall Hispanoamericana, S.A., *Mexico*
Prentice-Hall of India Private Limited, *New Delhi*
Prentice-Hall of Japan, Inc., *Tokyo*
Simon & Schuster Asia Pte. Ltd., *Singapore*
Editora Prentice-Hall do Brasil, Ltda., *Rio de Janeiro*

Contents

Part I   Building Foundations

Part II   Teaching

Part III   Administering

Preface

This book has been written for choral music teachers in secondary schools and for those who are studying to become part of our noble profession. It is written in textbook format with features that enhance that purpose, but its value to the practicing professional was constantly on my mind as I wrote. In fact, I tell the traditional students in my secondary choral methods classes that the book will be much more helpful to them after they have taught for a year or two than it is as their current text, because at this point in their lives, they really understand very little about the magnitude of skill and information necessary to be successful master teachers.

The book is divided into three parts: The first helps you to build strong foundations for success; the second relates to the nuts and bolts of the profession (how to teach) and the third aids you in structuring your responsibilities so your tenure as teachers will be long, complete, and satisfying (administration and organization).

At the end of each chapter you will find some *Thoughts for Contemplation and Discussion* that are questions for which there may be no specific answers in the chapter but which provide kindling for the fires of meditating, pondering, contemplating, reflecting and discussing. Some of them may be sources for major research projects.

Finding enough time to teach all the information students need to know to be prepared to be choral directors is always a problem for professors of choral methods. Part I and Chapter 15 and 16 of Part III are appropriate for separate introduction to music education courses for both choral and instrumental majors. If all the information in the text must be covered in one semester, due to limited class time, professors may desire to devise ways (reading, special research projects and so forth) to cover some of the material outside of class, possibly that in Part I. Chapters 15 and 16 have basic information about how to organize the choral curriculum. Students will have a better perspective for understanding the information in Part II and the remainder of Part III if those two chapters are studied before approaching Part II.

Each chapter has a comprehensive bibliography to be used for further reading and research. Each bibliography includes current books about information in the chapters and those books which have served as war horses of the profession for years.

Choosing the exact word to communicate a thought or concept is always a challenge to a writer. I must clarify my concept of one word which is used throughout the text. When many music educators read or hear the word *adolescent,* they think about a student who is pubescent. That is a common understanding of the word. Although I deal with adolescence in detail in Chapter 7, I must reiterate here that my use of the word is much more encompassing. I think about adolescents as being from pre-pubescence (fifth or sixth grade) to those in their first year or so in college. Experts cannot agree as to exactly when adolescence ends, but there is a basic consensus of opinion that students are no longer adolescents when they take on adult responsibilities such as marriage, full-time employment, and so forth. In this book, I differentiate between early adolescents (middle-junior high school students) and older adolescents (senior high school students). The book addresses the needs of all adolescents.

It is easy to understand the frustration Tevye experienced in *Fiddler on the Roof* when at the marriage of each of his daughters, in giving his permission, it became necessary for him to choose between "tradition" and "change." Tradition is important. Change is inevitable. One of the most difficult considerations when one writes a book is the choice of writing style. Traditionally, textbooks have been written to share information and to teach. When writing for college or university students and practicing professionals, it is expected practice to write in the third person, be direct and to the point, choose words which mean exactly what the author desires to say, be relatively formal, and not be overly flamboyant or decorative in the language. It is important for the author to set a good example of legitimate writing style so that aspiring student-writers may follow suit. Such is the importance of tradition.

I have been a teacher of choral music and related subjects on the university level for over twenty years. I have stood semester after semester in front of classes of real students, a few of whom were frustrated, others naive, some bored, many excited, and all desiring a degree. To turn these students on to the wonderful profession of music teaching has been my constant challenge and in most cases one of my greatest satisfactions. When I think about the students who will be using this text, I realize they, too, are real students with the same approach to the classroom as the multitudes of young people I have encountered day after day. When I write, I want to be able to say, "*I* have something important to tell *you*," not, "this author desires to share the following with the reader." Therein lies the importance of change.

Now, do you see the frustration I share with Tevye? I have decided to handle the frustration in the same way Tevye handled it—through compromise. Most of this book is written in traditional textbook style. However, there will be occasions, particularly at the beginning of various chapters, where I will break from tradition and speak to you one on one—when I have something *I* really want to say directly to *you*. Those passages are printed in **bold type.**

Finally, I must acknowledge the massive amount of time and effort expended by Dorothy Sahlmann, former Assistant Professor of Music at the University of Central Arkansas. She served as proofreader, grammarian, stylist, supporter, and friend. Without her and the encouragement of my wife, family, and faculty collegues, this project would never have come to fruition.

Don L. Collins
University of Central Arkansas
Conway

1

The European Roots of Choral Music

As a teacher of singing, it is essential for you to have a thorough foundation in the history of the choral art. Because the American culture is relatively new compared to its European, African, or Oriental ancestors, it is difficult for Americans to understand the significance of tradition and history fully. Even though we may feel great pride in standing in Independence Hall in Philadelphia, visiting the old Spanish fort in St. Augustine, Florida, or seeing the site of the Pilgrim's landing in Plymouth, Massachusetts, we should realize that much of what we are as a people and the thought processes that govern our lives are derived from the European cultures and even the earlier Greek, Roman, and Hebrew cultures. Regrettably, many Americans do not realize this, believing we are the way we are and we think the way we think simply because we are Americans. For you to be totally effective in the classroom, you must recognize the great historical events, sacrifices, traditions, and failures that preceded you. It is this understanding that enables you to challenge your students to fulfill their cherished responsibility of making a significant contribution to the choral art. Your understanding of choral history affects the manner in which you approach your students, the type music you choose, the teaching techniques you employ, and the aura of professionalism that will establish the proper attitudes about music your students will carry with them once they have left your care.

This chapter traces the development of the choral art from Greek, Roman, and Hebrew cultures to its practice in the European culture of the twentieth century. It is an intriguing story. After studying what has been presented here, you might want to read further in the books and articles delineated in the chapter bibliography to get a more thorough understanding of the parts that interested you the most.

SINGING IN THE GREEK, ROMAN, AND HEBREW CULTURES

Greek Influences

From research in ancient Greek culture it is evident that music was a vital part of the lives of the people. It was included in many public religious observances, marriage and funeral rites, harvest and vintage festivals, and banquets and other festive occasions. Instruction in singing and playing the lyre (a stringed instrument of the harp class with a small sound box made from the shell of a turtle) was a standard part of the education of the free citizen. Performance practice was not limited to professional musicians. The public was musically educated to the point of not only being able to judge good and bad performances but also being participants in singing hymns, paeans, dithyrambs, parthenias, and dramatic choruses.

Evidence indicates that choral singing was combined with dancing as well. These singing and dancing ensembles included men performing together, women together, men and women together, or men with boys, all of whom performed unison or octave/unison choruses. Of the many types of choral dances, three emerge that are significant:

The paean:	an invocation to Apollo, the god of manly youth and beauty, poetry, music, oracles, and healing. It was first mentioned in *The Iliad* (c. 850 B.C.).
The parthenia:	a chorus for all women composed of Spartan virgins introduced c. 650 B.C.
The dithyramb:	a choreographed representation of the adventures of Dionysus, god of fertility (c. 600 B.C.). This chorus resulted in the great Greek tragedies and comedies of the fourth and fifth centuries B.C.

Greek choruses are thought to have been quite large, possibly numbering as many as 600. Dithyrambic choruses were conventionally composed of fifty boys and men arranged in a circle around a player of the aulos, a popular Greek double-reed oboe-type wind instrument of Oriental origin.

Scholars disagree about the size of the choruses that performed in the

Greek dramas of the fourth and fifth centuries B.C. It is believed there were twelve participants in the dramas of Aeschylus and fifteen in those of Sophocles. The Greek comedies may have consisted of as many as sixty singers.

Robinson and Winold shed some light on one's understanding of the role of the chorus in Greek dramas:

> To appreciate the importance of choral participation in the dramatic presentations in ancient Greece, we must realize that these celebrations were not private undertakings intended for the amusement of the public, but festivals of a semireligious character which were considered essential to the political and moral welfare of the nation. The organization of the choruses was provided by law. If a poet wished to mount a dramatic production, he had to apply to a magistrate. If his request was granted, the best singers in each district were sought out and given an examination. Once the singers were chosen, wealthy citizens furnished the financial support necessary for the sustenance, instruction, and equipment of the choir. The singers were generally trained by a chorus master who was assisted by the leader of the orchestra. On certain occasions the poet chose to perform this duty.[1]

Roman Influences

Since the great Roman Empire contributed so much to modern-day civilization, it is difficult to believe that it contributed almost nothing to the choral art, but such is the case. In fact, it seems that the cultivated classes tolerated music, but in a bit of contemptuous manner. As an example, Cato, a great Roman statesman, provided as proof of the worthlessness of one of his political opponents the fact that he was a singer. The music-making process was not considered to be part of the educational procedure of the upper class, and the status of professional actors and musicians was very low.

Evidently, choral performances were popular in Rome but these came about strictly through Greek and Oriental influences. It may be concluded from literary evidence and inscriptions on various monuments that music was part of the popular life of Rome, particularly in public celebrations. During the reign of Julius Caesar it is recorded that 12,000 singers and instrumentalists assembled in Rome for such a celebration.

The Romans undoubtedly assimilated much into their culture from the Greeks and other cultures, but without extant musical documentation it is difficult to ascertain exactly what indigenous contributions were made.

Jewish Influences

There is little question that the performance of music in the medieval church was most greatly influenced by performance practices in Jewish worship before and after the death of Christ. In fact, one might be so bold as to say that Christian musical performance was patterned after Jewish worship at least until the development of organum and beyond. Granted, modern notation and music

[1] Ray Robinson and Allen Winold, *The Choral Experience* (New York: Harper's College Press, 1976), p. 9.

theory have their roots in the Greek culture, but performance practice is definitely of Jewish origin.

Singing, mostly in small groups, dominated performance practice in both traditions. One of the best sources to understand the origin of singing in these cultures is the Bible, both Old and New Testament writings. The first recorded song in the Bible was sung by Moses on the banks of the Red Sea after the rescue of the children of Israel from Pharaoh's army. The second song mentioned in the Bible is the one sung by Miriam, on the same occasion, as sort of a refrain to Moses' song. Singing occurred at the battle of Jericho and at David's victory over the Philistines, and even while in captivity in Babylon the Israelites sang a song of their homeland.

One of the more ambitious musical presentations is recorded in Second Chronicles 5:12–14 where singing and playing of instruments marked the dedication of Solomon's Temple. In fact, when David ascended the throne of Israel he appointed the Levites to be the official musicians (singers and players) of the temple (First Chronicles 15:16); they included women in David's temple and young boys in Herod's temple.

The book of Psalms, often referred to as the hymnbook of the Hebrew people, represents the largest body of biblical songs. Interestingly, they have become a staple for singing in Christendom as well. This will become evident as their influence is examined throughout the development of choral music.

Recorded examples of singing in the New Testament include the *Annunciation* (Luke 1:30–33), the words of the angel Gabriel to the maiden Mary; the *Magnificat* (Luke 1:46–55), Mary's response to being chosen to be the mother of God; the *Benedictus* (Luke 1:68–79), the outburst of Zacharias on the birth of his son John; the *Gloria in Excelsis* (Luke 2:14), the song of the hosts of angels as they sang to the shepherds in the field at the coming of the Christ child; the *Nunc Dimittis* (Luke 2:29–32), the words of Simeon, the devout servant, upon seeing the Christ child at the temple; the *Triumphal Entry* (Luke 19:38 and Matthew 21:15), the songs of praise of the disciples upon the entry of Christ into the city of Jerusalem at the beginning of Passion Week; and the *Last Supper* (Matthew 26:30), sung by the disciples around the table in the upper room as was the custom at Passover. Paul and Silas sang while in prison (Acts 16:25), and there are other references to singing of psalms and lyric songs in Ephesians 5:19, Colossians 3:16, Acts 4:24–30, and James 5:13.

In Jewish worship, evidence indicates singing was antiphonal (the singing of a chant as a refrain to the verses of a psalm) and responsorial (the performance of the congregation and choir in alternation) between a leader and the choir and congregation. It is believed that in these ancient times the congregation seldom joined in the singing except for one word responses such as *Amen, Halleluyah, Hoshahnna* (Oh help!), or *Aneau* (Answer us!). Somewhat later there is an indication that the Psalms may have been sung in a sort of dialogue between the leader and the choir and/or congregation.

What were the melodies like? There are present-day Jewish church musicians who insist that much of the original character of their chants is still maintained. Some musicologists believe that early Christian chants were patterned after early Jewish melodies; therefore certain traditions in Eastern Orthodox worship are reminiscent of these original melodies. Suzanne Haik Vantoura, a French musician and scholar, promotes the theory that mysterious signs found above and below some of the Hebrew scriptures is a type of music notation. Over a period of several years she has deciphered these signs and arrived at specific rhythms and melodies. She has transcribed and recorded approximately three hours of early Hebrew music.[2]

As previously stated, the Eastern and Western medieval church maintained significant ties to Jewish music, particularly as far as worship and performance practice was concerned. It used the concept of yearly cycle of services, with each day ranked according to its importance. It retained Bible reading and psalm singing as major elements of worship. The performance characteristics of antiphonal and responsorial singing, and of soloistic virtuosity in an improvisatory style, were used. Some of the actual melodies, particularly those used in psalm singing, can be found in parallel Jewish and Christian worship versions. Also, like the Jews of the synagogue, the Christians generally employed only vocal music within their liturgy.

Accepting the above premise, one is able to close the 600-year gap between the New Testament singing practices and the emergence of monophonic plainchant of Pope Gregory I (590–604).

SINGING IN THE EUROPEAN CULTURE

Antiquity and Medieval Singing

Other than the premise that music in the early Christian church was based on Jewish practices, extant evidence is unavailable about singing procedures in worship services in the first three centuries of the Christian Church. In a letter to the Corinthian church (A.D. 96), Clement of Rome refers to the *Sanctus* (Holy, Holy, Holy), usage of which was acceptable practice in worship for Jews and Christians. Pliny, governor of Bithynia (c. A.D. 111–113), in a letter to the Roman emperor Trajan, referred to Christians as "meeting on a fixed day before daylight and reciting responsively among themselves a hymn to Christ as a god, and that they bound themselves by an oath not to commit any crime. . . . When they had performed this it was their custom to depart and to meet together again for a meal, but of a common and harmless kind."[3]

Extant examples of worship practices in the second and third centuries do not include specific references to singing, but since singing was a part of worship before the second century and after the third century, there is reason to believe that it was also included in the intervening centuries. References to antiphonal and responsorial singing occur in Eusebius' (c. 260–340) *Historia Ecclesiastica*.

[2] Suzanne Haik Vantoura, *La Musique de la Bible Revelee* (Paris: Dessain et Tolra, 1978), p. 364.

[3] T. S. Garrett, *Christian Worship* (London: Oxford University Press, 1961), p. 47.

Responsorial psalmnody was mentioned by Tertullian (c. 155–222). Indications are that antiphonal and responsorial singing practices were common to Eastern and Western churches alike by the end of the fourth century. Specific examples of orders of worship recorded in *The Apostolic Constitutions* (c. 380) verify that Christian worship practices had become highly developed by the fourth century. Constantine the Great's Edict of Milan of 313 gave official status to Christianity as a recognized religion allowing worshipers to practice their faith openly and freely, no longer hiding in their homes or in underground catacombs. Evidently it was a very exciting time for the Christians. The new faith spread quickly. Congregations were established so rapidly that it was difficult to train the new converts fast enough for these new congregations to have pastors. To suffice, bishops wrote down acceptable worship materials for the untrained (but ordained) leaders to read. Depending on the sizes of the congregations, buildings (some were quite large) had to be erected, and worship was organized and designed to meet their needs. For fear of heresy creeping into the faith, the practice of assigning the worship practices (including singing) to the clergy became more and more accepted. Ultimately, the church bishops became the new nobility of the empire, adopting the symbolism of the state that was now available to them because of their power and control over vast buildings, properties, glorious furnishings, vestments, and impressive pageantry.

St. Sylvester, pope from 314 to 336, founded the first *Schola Cantorum* as an institution for training apprentice choir singers. The Schola is a very important entity to the choral musician because it represents the first official school for training vocal musicians in the medieval world. The Schola at Rome, which preserved its identity and organization unbroken for almost 800 years, had the double aim of sustaining a group of ecclesiastical musicians capable of producing and singing music of the liturgy and capable of supporting or aiding schools to train a continuous supply of singers. The Schola was further developed during the fifth century by Popes Celestine I, Hilarius, Sixtus II, and Leo I. Popes Sixtus II and Leo I are thought to have established monasteries that practiced psalmnody. Pope Hilarius (461–467) organized a group of seven ecclesiastical singers (also called Schola Cantorum) who were responsible for all services, wherever held, at which the bishop officiated.

In 595, Gregory the Great issued a decretal forbidding deacons to fill the office of chief singer at Mass and confining music responsibilities to lesser orders of the ministry. Then Gregory took action to supply enough singers needed to fulfill requirements of the decretal. To have enough singers he organized two more schools (Schola Cantorum) and further developed the two previously existing ones. The seminarians who studied there were required to memorize both words and music for the major part of the church's services. The musical responsibilities of the inferior orders such as lectors, cantors, and subdeacons were undertaken by younger men who were also trained at the Schola.

Realizing a further need to supply singers for church services of the future, Gregory founded and endowed two houses for the express purpose of training orphans in duties of the Schola Cantorum and other allied bodies of singers that were appointed for the church's use. These orphans, evidently all boys, were given a general, musical, and religious education by members of the Schola Cantorum. So successful was this foundation in supplying competent religious musicians that the Schola Cantorum itself came to be popularly called, after the orphanages, the *orphanotrophium*. These orphanages may be loosely connected to the conservatories in Naples and Venice of the sixteenth century that were also orphanages to which Vivaldi was so closely related.

During the following century other branches of the Schola Cantorum were organized in England and various points of Europe. In 596, Gregory sent to England a group of forty missionaries led by Augustine (later canonized as St. Augustine) of Kent, a Benedictine monk who began a singing school that flourished greatly. These institutions fostered new and vital creative activity that enriched the world with a fresh treasure of musical devotion. This widespread diffusion of musical ideas and practical plan of organization for putting them into practice was of immense service to the Christian world. As a result, liturgical choral music became an integral part of the devotional and intellectual life of many countries in Europe during the Middle Ages.

With the foundation of monasteries, by the eleventh and twelfth centuries, Schola were incorporated into monastic and cathedral schools. While these institutions originally came into being for the purpose of training churchmen, doors were later opened to laymen. The cathedral schools moved music education from the contemplative atmosphere of the cloister experienced in the monastic schools to the bustle of the developing urban centers. They educated choristers and young clerics primarily, but their secondary reponsibility included the education of a rising civil servant class. In these urban centers young men flocked to the cathedral schools to study both the *trivium* (grammar, dialectic, and rhetoric) and the *quadrivium* (arithmetic, geometry, astronomy, and music) and, in some cities, to study the professional subjects as well, such as law and medicine. It was from this relatively stable student population that the university emerged.

The training of monks and boys in the Schola Cantorum and the monastic and cathedral schools affected singing in two ways. First, it affected the style of the chant. No longer were they simple syllabic works. Chants became much more difficult and elaborately melismatic. By the eleventh century much of what remained simple were single-tone chants. These single-tone chants were of two types: the lection tone, for singing long sections of prose texts and the *psalm tone*, for singing the poetry found in the Psalms. These psalm tones were formulas consisting of a *reciting tone* punctuated by an elaborate system of intonations and cadences grounded in the eight melodic modes. Some chants sung by both priests and scholarly singers had more elaborate musical/textual relationships: *syllabic, neumatic,* and *melismatic.* They were distinguished from lection tones and psalm tones in that when they were employed, the music was written out in full and was associated with only one text at a time. Among these styles the simplest settings are the syllabic chants, and the most important of the early ones are the hymns. Neumatic chants are more elaborate, and the most characteristic of them are the Mass and Office antiphons. Melismatic settings are the most complex and were usually performed by highly skilled soloists.

During the eleventh and twelfth centuries chant melodies continued to expand both horizontally and vertically. Horizontally, there were the additions of the *trope*, newly composed text and melody inserted into and used primarily with antiphonal chants of the Introit, Offertory, and Communion; the *sequence* or *prose*, a large, independent piece sung after the Alleluia in the Mass; the *prosula*, a smaller new chant created entirely by providing a new text for a pre-existent melisma; the *conductus*, a processional piece with a metrical text and a newly composed melody not based on the existing liturgical melodies; and the *versus*, a monophonic setting of regular rhyming, scanning poetry in strophic form. Vertically, there evolved *organum* or *polyphony* in which one or more new melodic lines were invented to be sung simultaneously with the original chant tune.

Second, the training of scholarly singers affected singing through performance practice. The simple syllabic chants were entrusted to the priests and congregation. The more elaborate ones were assigned to the choir that had embodied within it a separate group of soloists, highly trained virtuoso singers, who were given the opportunity to display their skills in responsorial performance. Many of the antiphonal chants involved these virtuoso soloists as well. By 1200, after organun emerged, only those portions of the responsorial chants sung by the virtuosos were set polyphonically. The choirs continued to sing in unison. Evidence indicates that this practice prevailed throughout the Middle Ages, and it was not until the middle of the fifteenth century that polyphony was assigned to the choir.

Medieval chant is so significant to the evolution of present-day choral music that it would be inappropriate to leave this time period without grasping an insight into the surroundings and daily life from which this great body of music emerged. Charlotte Roederer gives an intriguing description of such:

> The physical and spiritual center of the monastic community was the church, much larger than any of the other buildings grouped around it. Nearby was an arcaded cloister, a wonderful place to enjoy the out-of-doors in all types of weather. Living quarters for the monks included a dining hall and kitchen, supplied by a food cellar, brewery, and bakery. The dormitory was well designed, with the sleeping area on the upper level and the hearing apparatus on the lower. The novices had their own quarters, and the abbot his own house. Visitors of various ranks stayed in the guest houses, sometimes for extended periods of time; all who came were to be welcomed graciously as children of God.
>
> A farm surrounded and supported the establishment, orchards and vineyards, vegetable and herb gardens, were planted. There also were coops for chickens and geese, stables for horses, pens for sheep, and a sty for pigs. In fact, monasteries were often leaders in agriculture, building the land and developing new breeds of animals and methods of crop cultivation.
>
> Near the church were the library and the rooms where manuscripts were copied. From the end of the ninth century on, St. Gall was famous for its high quality production of manuscripts and for its manuscript collection.
>
> Elsewhere on the grounds were workshops for other monastic craftsman, e.g., goldsmith, blacksmith, saddlers, dyers, woodcarvers, and turners. Just about everything needed was at hand, and provision for the needs of everyday life often went hand in hand with the creation of objects of great aesthetic value. A sheep could be a source

not only for wool but also of meat and hide. Depending upon its quality, the fleece might be spun and woven into rough monastic habits or used to create beautifully refined altar cloths and liturgical vestments. A fine sheepskin might end up as a manuscript. Metalworkers provided hinges for books and reliquaries for the safekeeping and proper display of precious relics. These artisans could also fashion many items necessary for corporate worship, such as crosses, candlesticks, thruibles for the burning of incense, and various sacramental cups and plates. It was within such well-planned and self-sufficient communities that the great body of medieval chant evolved.[4]

As implied earlier, the churches and monasteries supported choirs composed of just men or of men and boys. Women were given the opportunity to sing choral music but only in the convent. By the end of the Middle Ages, the choirs usually consisted of four to six boys and ten to thirteen men. Also, by the end of the period, instruments that earlier had been completely eliminated from church services by decree of early church fathers were allowed to be used in worship. Many churches had organs; and string and wind instruments were used both in the church service and for processions and other events outside the church building. In fact, it is believed that instruments were used to double the voices or to substitute for certain voices that might not be available. This practice cannot be substantiated by extant documents, however, and definite descriptions by fourteenth-century witnesses indicate that the organ, for example, was played alternately with the voices and not simultaneously.

Choral Singing in the Renaissance Period

It is vitally important for the student of the choral process to realize that the Renaissance period represents the point of eminence in the history of singing. Regrettably, never before nor since has a majority of humankind held the choral process in such lofty esteem. Probably the largest body of choral (motets, masses) and vocal (madrigals, frottolas, chansons, lied, carols, and so forth) repertoire of all time has emerged from this period. Further, most of the great composers of the period (Dufay, Josquin Desprez, Willaert, Gombert, Clemens, Binchois, Palestrina, Victoria, Lassus, and others) were trained as vocalists, having begun their musical experiences as choirboys. Most importantly, the majority of the populace used singing as the principle form of musical expression. Even the instruments of the period took on vocal designations such as soprano, alto, tenor or bass viols, lutes, or recorders. Indeed, it was the singers' delight to have lived in that day.

Sacred choral literature of the early Renaissance was developed mostly in the form of the motet and mass by Johannes Ockeghem, Jacob Obrecht, Josquin Desprez, and others. Later in the period it was developed by Andrea and Giovanni Gabrieli and Adrien Willaert in their great polychoral works, and by Palestrina and Orlande de Lassus with their Counter-Reformation contributions.

Composers of the period in most cases worked as part of the royal or noble

[4] Charlotte Roederer, "The Middle Ages." Reprinted with permission of Schirmer Books, a division of Macmillan, Inc., from *Schirmer History of Music*, Leonie Rosenstiel, general editor. Copyright © 1982 by Schirmer Books.

chapels, the papal chapel, or a cathedral. The primary function of the chapel musicians was to prepare and present music for Mass, Daily Offices, and ceremonial occasions that involved sacred music. By the end of the period, the chapel became the principle arm of the aristocracy with kings, lords, and popes eagerly seeking the best singers and composers. Further, the best literature of every well-known composer was sought for aristocratic performances.

The important composers of the fourteenth and fifteenth centuries were chaplains who had been educated in a cathedral school or in one of the choir schools connected with noble chapels. They were trained as singers, and the most gifted became composers. Although some chaplains probably played instruments such as the vielle, recorder, or lute, these instruments were not used in the chapel. The only instrument with a place in the chapel was the pipe organ. It is likely that instruments were used to double voices in the sixteenth century. Chaplains were usually the gifted children of commoners, sent to choir school as an avenue for advancement. However, some of them were minor nobility and landed gentry. Composers who showed musical gifts as well as intellectual and administrative abilities soon accumulated wealth and privileges and had easy access to powerful rulers. The chaplains were allowed leaves of absence that gave them the freedom to join other establishments for short periods of time. Lords borrowed singers from various cathedral choirs and in turn loaned their own singers to other chapels and choirs. These exchanges were not always for purely musical reasons. A well-known educated musician was a useful ambassador since the entree to high places that his artistic capabilities permitted enabled him to glean valuable information. Chaplains received money, clothes, and food for their work, and the court paid for the copying and care of the chant and polyphonic music books.

Choir personnel in the chapels varied in number. The choir of the Sistine Chapel (the descendent of the Schola Cantorum) had sixteen singers in 1450 and had grown to thirty-two by 1625. The Burgundian chapel of Philip the Good consisted of about thirty men and boys, and in England sixteen boys and sixteen men made up the choirs of the collegiate churches of King's College and Magdalen College at Oxford.

The cathedral was not organized very differently from the chapel. Canons performed the Mass and Offices in chant with a small number participating in the singing of polyphony. French cathedrals record a surprisingly consistent number of polyphonic singers throughout the fourteenth and fifteenth centuries. At Cambrai the choir consisted of thirteen to sixteen men and about six choirboys.

At the beginning of the Renaissance, the practice of singing polyphonic music with solo voices and assigning the choir unison passages began to disappear. By the time of the rise of *monody* (solo singing with continuo accompaniment) in the early Baroque, the practice of unison choral singing was virtually gone. The choir developed into four specific voice parts with the range of the lowest to the highest about three to three and one-half octaves. The four polyphonic parts were contratenor bassus (since it had originally moved contrapuntally below the tenor), tenor (which literally meant "holding" since it had previously functioned as the holder of the preexisting material or cantus firmus), contratenor altus (it had moved contrapuntally above the tenor), and superious (the highest part). Each voice part was performed by several singers so these ensembles became choral in the truest since of the word. Soprano, alto, tenor, bass voicing, as it soon became known, did not limit the composers to writing only in four parts, however, since much of the literature is for five, six, or eight voice parts in various combinations. Many works were written for several choirs having up to forty voice parts as in Tallis's motet, *Spem in Alium*. The great polychoral works of the Gabrielis, Andrea and Giovanni, at St. Mark's Cathedral in Venice had several choirs and multiple voice parts. Guillaume Dufay, Antoine Busnois, Johannes Ockeghem, Jacob Obrecht, and particularly Josquin Desprez are the first composers whose music is associated with distinct voice parts as previously described.

During the latter part of the Renaissance (1560s), the *castrato* (castrated male singer whose voice did not change) appeared in the singing personnel of the Roman Catholic choirs. The practice of using male singers in the choirs prevailed throughout the period, and prior to the castrato's appearance, the soprano was sung by boys (and occasionally by men falsettists) and the alto by men (some natural singers who had very high voices, others falsettists) and boys, with the tenor and bass parts carried by changed adult voices. At first, castrati sang only the soprano part often assisting the boys, but occasionally singing the part without boys. Somewhat later, by the 1680s, some castrati were assigned to alto as well. Seemingly the practice of using castrati was prevalent in Italy, particularly Rome, but it is evident that they sang in choirs throughout Europe and as early as 1570 in Portugal and elsewhere. Their involvement came to fruition in the late eighteenth century when several hundred were employed in the churches in Rome. The Sistine Chapel continued to use them throughout the nineteenth century, with the last castrato retiring as late as 1913.

Much has been made about the Renaissance being the "golden age of a cappella singing," and it is true that some choirs, such as the Sistine Chapel choir, sang without instruments. There are indications, however, that choirs of the period performed more often with instruments than without, particularly during the sixteenth century. Melody instruments were used to play, either alone or doubling the singers, one or more of the parts of polyphonic works. There is little evidence that instruments were used as a separate entity to accompany the choir. Even sixteenth-century extant organ scores show that keyboard instruments consisted, for the most part, of a reduction of the vocal parts.

Even though the full effect of the Protestant Reformation was not manifest in choral music until the seventeenth and eighteenth centuries, the seeds were sown and foundations set during the sixteenth century. A profound influence on Protestant church music was that Martin Luther was an amateur musician. He loved the great music of the mother church and the Latin text of the Mass. Josquin Desprez was his favorite composer. Consequently, Luther's first reformed liturgy, *Formula Missae et Communionis* (1523), outlines much of the historic Catholic service. One should be aware that this same Luther is the one who gave the German people the Bible and chorales (commonly thought about as being Lutheran hymns) in their own language. Theologically he recovered the doctrine of the priesthood of the believer and restored the sermon to its central place in worship. Therefore, that he maintained portions of the Latin worship service and text may be seen as a bit of a theological contradiction that can only be explained by his love for great music. By 1526, he had mellowed slightly, possibly through the influences of his associates, with a second liturgy, *Deutscher Messe*, in which many of the historic Latin songs were replaced by vernacular hymns set to German folk-song melodies. Throughout the sixteenth century, most Lutheran worship used a variant of one of these two liturgies. The *Formula Missae* was the norm for cathedrals and collegiate churches; the German mass (*Deutscher Messe*) was common in smaller towns and rural churches.

In the *Formula Missae,* the choir sang the traditional psalms, songs, and prayers in Latin to Gregorian chant or in polyphonic settings. They also led the congregation in the a cappella settings of the new chorales in German. These early Lutheran choirs still did not include female singers. Men and boys were trained in the cantorial tradition (J. S. Bach was a cantor). Although somewhat larger than their Catholic counterparts, they were probably less professional because their personnel often included the clergy, teachers, and other interested citizens. This tradition of choral worship is what inspired the great German motets, passions, and cantatas of the eighteenth century.

Because the Anglican church in England broke away from the Catholic church more for political reasons (so that King Henry VIII could divorce and remarry) than for theological tenets, choral singing in those churches was not altered greatly from practices in the Catholic church. Between 1536 and 1540, monasteries were dissolved and so seemed the fate of the choir schools of the collegiate churches and cathedrals. To preserve them King Henry VIII set up more than thirty regularly constituted and endowed cathedral and collegiate choral foundations. The Royal Chapel was retained and continued to attract to its services the finest of England's singers and composers. Cathedrals at Oxford, Ely, Petersborough, Bristol, Carlisle, Chester, Gloucester, Rochester, Canterbury, Durham, Winchester, and Worchester and Westminster Abbey all had men's and boy's choirs with approximately twenty to thirty personnel. Like their Catholic counterparts, these choirs often included instruments, such as recorders, viols, cornetts, and sackbuts, and by the end of the sixteenth century the organ began to take its place in the choral tradition of the Anglican church.

Initially then, and as the practice exists today, these men's and boys' choirs were divided into two equally balanced groups and were placed in the chancel facing each other. Antiphonal singing was encouraged and exploited in the works of many of the English choral composers of the Renaissance. This divided chancel approach allowed the development of the English verse anthem that consisted of contrasting sections (verses) between soloist(s) and choir.

Regrettably, choral music did not fare so well in other segments of the Reformation. Ulrich Zwingli, a reform leader in Zurich and predecessor to John Calvin, eliminated music completely from worship. Calvin himself, when he first preached and taught at Geneva, set his worship entirely without music. After his experience with French exiles in Strasbourg and through the influence of

Martin Bucer, a follower of Zwingli but advocate of psalms and hymns in worship, Calvin allowed unison congregational singing of metrical psalms. Because of his austere stance on music in worship, it was almost 200 years before choral music was sanctioned in the Calvinist churches (Presbyterians, Reformed, and so forth) of Switzerland, France, Germany, Netherlands, and Scotland.

It is believed that the Separatists, a radical sect of Puritans, had no music in worship initially, but eventually included only unaccompanied metrical psalms. The Anabaptists evidently had little or no singing. English Baptists (General Baptists, Calvinistic Baptists, Seventh-Day Baptists, and Particular Baptists) used only metrical psalms, if there was any singing at all. There is some indication that by the seventeenth century solo singing was included in Baptist worship.

The Roman church was not willing to stand by and allow a mass exodus of membership to the Protestant faith. They offered a counterattack (Counter-Reformation) in an attempt to regain membership. The attack came in the form of internal reform brought on by the outer pressures of the Protestant affront and the inner pressures of Catholic eccesiastics who demanded revival. During the years of 1545–1563 a general council met in the northern Italian city of Trent (the Council of Trent) to address these concerns. Musically, several recommendations emerged: Chant was to be promoted over polyphonic music (polyphonic music was not to be totally abandoned as has been advocated by some historians); the text was to be clearly intelligible in polyphonic music; excessive melismas were to be discouraged, both in chant and polyphonic settings; and secular influences on melodies were to be discouraged with the older cantus firmus melodies reemphasized.

Music of Giovanni Pierluigi da Palestrina, Tomás Luis de Victoria, Francisco Guerrero, and Orlande de Lassus became popular after the council's recommendations partly because there was an attempt on the part of the composers to incorporate the recommendations in their writing and partly because the recommendations coincided with their own artistic directions.

Choral Singing in the Baroque Period

Because of the advent of *monody* (Greek for "solo song"; a soloist accompanied by a chord-playing instrument) and the influence of the *Florentine Camerata* (a group of musical amateurs credited with planting the seeds that grew into opera), the dominant choral emphasis of the Renaissance shifted to a very strong, mostly vocal emphasis in the Baroque. Solo singers took their places of eminence in the world of music. In the early part of the seventeenth century the stage was set to bring about what was to be, by the end of the century, a phenomenon that was just short of worship of these great soloists. An understanding of how the scene changed from the choral emphasis to the vocal emphasis is important to the choral musician.

Near the middle of the sixteenth century music treatises began to appear, namely Ganassi dal Fontego's *Fontegara* (1535), Diego Ortiz's *Trattado de Glosas* (1553), and Adrianus Petit Coclico's *Compendium Musices* (1552), that placed much emphasis on the art of singing and resulted in singing becoming ornamented as was the existing practice in instrumental music of the period. The practice of ornamentation was employed in motets and other sacred works, but it was applied primarily to madrigals during that time.

Another factor that set the stage for the solo singer was the arrival of the female vocalist, particularly the soprano, on the secular music scene. Researchers postulate that many of the female singers were courtesans (prostitutes of the aristocracy), which accounts for the difficulty in verifying the presence of female singers in the financial records or in scholarly documents, but there is evidence beginning in the Middle Ages that women sang in performance of secular music. By the sixteenth century a number of important women of noble rank evidenced serious musical accomplishments. By the end of the century the madrigals were often designated *a voce mutata* (without women's voices) or *a voce piena* (for mixed voices), the latter of which often took the soprano part as high as G, first space above the treble clef, which was considered to be too high for male falsettists. Claudio Monteverdi, in his first book of madrigals (1587), begins almost every piece with the women's voices, not allowing the men to enter for at least eight measures. One could easily assume that this was Monteverdi's attempt to be in vogue with the new practice of using female singers and displaying their vocal quality.

The practice of ornamentation developed into an improvisatory skill that allowed singers to display their virtuosity, and it became even more popular when the high female voice began to participate. As is human nature, the practice soon became overly burlesque with each singer attempting to "out-decorate" the next. Soon the practice became so exaggerated and in such bad taste that complaining composers began to write the virtuoso element into the music itself.

Historical sources describe the Florentine Camerata as a group of musicians and literary figures led by Count Giovanni de' Bardi who met in the 1570s and 1580s to discuss the music of the ancient Greeks. Musically oriented members were Vincenzo Galilei, Piero Strozzi, and Giulio Caccini. Ottavio Rinuccini, the poet and librettist, was associated with the group, but there is some evidence that he may not have been a member. In 1592 Bardi moved to Rome and Jacopo Corsi became the leader. Corsi and composer Jacopo Peri set to music Rinuccini's *Dafne* (first performance, 1598), which is considered to be the first opera. Giulio Caccini is credited with setting the groundwork for monody through his work *Le Nuove Musiche* ("The New Music"), a compilation of monodic songs, in which he coined the term *Stile Rappresentativo* (writing that is free in rhythm and phrasing and characterized by frequent pauses, ornamentation, and the use of unusual intervals for emotional effect).

It should be noted that the composer Caccini was also a virtuoso tenor. *La Nuove Musiche* contains detailed information, even to the point of explicit notation, about how to initiate proper ornamentation. In view of the embarrassing ornamentation practices of madrigal singers at that time, one might postulate that there was a very practical reason the Camerata began to meet. The Camerata was opposed to the contrapuntal music of the period because the meaning of the words was hidden in the complex musical texture, but could it be that another reason they were meeting was because they were ashamed of the distasteful singing practices and desired to change them? Further, perhaps Caccini as a composer was upset with the way singers were adulterating his music. As a tenor virtuoso he did not want to discourage ornamentation, so he encouraged a new style of singing that needed only a solo voice and simple chordal accompaniment. This would allow properly performed ornamentation to thrive without destroying the meaning of the words.

A third factor that contributed to the prominence of the solo singer in the Baroque period was the emerging popularity of the castrato. The high female voice was making a significant impact on secular vocal music of the day, so to achieve a sound just as exciting, the church could no longer rely on boy trebles. Because only the castrato could provide the sound required, moral qualms pertaining to castration were disregarded. Composers of opera quickly recognized the superior vocal power of the castrati, along with the opportunity to have a male character with a treble sound, and capitalized upon their availability. The castrati reached the apex of their popularity between 1650 and 1750. They dominated the operatic stage during that time with the terms *primo umono* (leading person) and *primo musico* (leading musician) invariably referring to the castrato particularly in opera seria. They were mostly Italian but many achieved international reputations in England, the German-speaking lands, and to a lesser extent in France. They often behaved with the capriciousness of *prima donnas* (leading ladies), in many cases commanded high salaries, and had wide reputations as bad actors. Anecdotes abound concerning amorous adventures of every conceivable sort, and a few even attempted marriage. Castrati were probably mostly selected from among boy singers, either orphans or the children of poor parents who gave consent in return for payment or the hope of future honor. The practice was clandestine but widespread. Castration was performed on perhaps 4000 boys during the eighteenth century. The usual age for the operation was from six to eight years, rendering the victim infertile and suppressing development of secondary sex characteristics including changing of the voice. The last living castrato was Alessandro Moreschi, who was a member of the Sistine Choir from 1883–1913. In 1902–1903 he made a number of recordings and, in spite of the very poor recording technique and equipment of the time, the virile, masculine, power, and emotional content of the voice is obvious.

The fourth and final factor was the extended use of the *cadenza* by the vocal artists at the end of arias. A cadenza is best defined as a decorated cadence. At the final cadence of the aria, the performer would embellish the vocal line with an improvisatory (although it may have been prepared in rehearsal), decorative passage to display the agility, flexibility, and extreme range of the voice. Early in the period the cadenzas were usually quite short, but after the castrato stormed the scene they became greatly extended and gaudily dramatized.

As a result of the influence of the female soprano and castrato, vocal ranges began to be extended several notes higher than in literature of the Renaissance. There are a few Italian cantatas from the second half of the seventeenth century that take the soprano voice as high as C^3 (second ledger line above the treble clef). Since many of the castrati were promoted as being able to sing F^3 (fourth ledger space above the treble clef), and even though the literature does not bear it out, some historians believe that during the singing of the cadenzas castrati often displayed F^3 and possibly even higher pitches. By the early Classical period Mozart and others were including F^3 as written notes in the soprano literature.

Italy dominated the musical scene during the Baroque. Most of the important innovations in Baroque musical style—figured bass, opera, oratorio, aria, recitative, monody, basso ostinato, passacaglia, cantata, sonata, ritornello, concerto grosso, among many—were products of Italian composers. With a few exceptions, only in Italy were composers and performers regarded so highly as artists that they could demand and receive princely salaries and favored treatment from their employers. Elsewhere, composers, performers, instrument makers, and music printers were regarded primarily as artisans and were reimbursed accordingly.

In most cases music was written for a specific occasion and after such was discarded or refashioned into another work for a different occasion. Both Handel and Bach were particularly adept at resurrecting previously performed compositions and rearranging them for their own particular purposes.

To have a work published was exceptional; nevertheless, several composers became wealthy and famous through the printing of their music. The art of printing enabled a composer to live independently of a noble patron or to find new patrons; it was one of the many important factors in the breakdown of the patronage system of the Renaissance and early Baroque.

Composers often received their first training from their fathers if they were professional musicians. Others were students of choir schools. In contrast to the Renaissance emphasis on the voice as the primary instrument, Baroque composers were trained to play in orchestras; once they took a position of leadership, they were expected to play violin and harpsichord and direct an orchestra from either instrument. Amateur musicians from the nobility not only patronized their concertmasters or chapelmasters, they also studied with them because the concertmasters and chapelmasters were considered to be master teachers as well.

Regrettably, the tremendous growth of church and chapel choirs that had occurred during the Renaissance was not extended during the Baroque, even though unusually large choirs occasionally flourished as a result of strong patronage or special occasions in which two or more choirs were combined or a single choir was enlarged by employing additional singers. As a general rule, Baroque choirs were not as large as those of the Renaissance. In Germany choirs suffered a drastic shortage of adult male singers due to the Thirty Year's War (1618–1648). English choirs, already adversely affected during the Civil War (1642–1649), did not exist at all during the Commonwealth and Protectorate (1649–1690). By the end of the period, many patrons lost interest in support of the choral art. Church and cathedral choirs were able to maintain thirty to forty voices even though their maintenance was expensive.

This is not to infer that great choral singing disappeared. Bach maintained an exemplary choir in Leipzig with as many as thirty-six singers on special occasions. Dietrich Buxtehude employed a choir of about thirty in his Abend-music concerts at Lübeck. St. Mark's Cathedral in Venice continued its great polychoral tradition, even influencing Lutheran musicians such as Michael Praetorius and Heinrich Schütz. The Sistine Choir in Rome and the restored Chapel Royal of England persisted admirably.

With large choirs requiring expensive maintenance, the Baroque choral composer began to look for ways in which the smaller ensemble could be used that would result in effective sonorities. Contrast became an essential factor of consideration. The polychoral idea of the Renaissance expressed between two large choirs took on a more concertino/tutti complexion (that is, a small group pitted against a larger one). In some cases a soloist, or group of soloists, would be pitted against the choir, a practice found particularly in England and France. The Renaissance practice of having the instruments to double the voices began to disappear as the orchestra took its place of equality with the choir. By the end of the period many of the choruses were assisted by an orchestra of stringed instruments fulfilling a role of its own as an accompanying body. The two working together helped maintain a full sonority badly needed since the resonant polychoral sounds of many large choirs had ceased to exist.

A principle form of the period, although more important vocally than chorally, is *opera*. Loosely defined, opera is a musical dramatic work in which actors or actresses sing some or all of their parts. As indicated previously, it had its beginnings and roots in Italy, particularly with the Florentine Camerata. The term *opera*, the plural of the Latin term *opus*, literally means "work". The earliest operas in Italy at the turn from the sixteenth to the seventeenth century were basically courtly entertainments for aristocratic spectators. In an attempt to revive the ancient Greek drama, the results included a very simplified musical style that emphasized the solo voice punctuated with choral interludes. The form projected a libretto that was unencumbered by the music and easy to understand. The first opera, *Dafne*, by Corsi and Peri (first performed in 1598), is no longer extant. In 1600, *Euridice*, also by Peri, was performed and is considered by many to be the first opera since it is extant. However, there are those who say that the first opera of any significance is Monteverdi's *Orfeo* (1607) because he was able to achieve in it a much greater dramatic intensity through variations for strophic texts, clear melodic goals for phrases, powerful choral singing, and musically dramatic organization resulting from the repetition of pieces, especially instrumental ones.

By the 1640s opera had moved out of the court and into the public opera house and had taken on audience-appealing properties to sell subscriptions or tickets to the performances. In 1637 the first public opera house, Teatro San Cassiano, was opened in Venice by two Romans, Benedetto Ferrari and Francesco Manelli. Because the genre had to be self-supporting, the chief attraction was soon found to be a combination of virtuoso singing and spectacle. Venetian opera quickly became so successful that several theaters opened. Some were relatively small, lacking the resources for grand spectacle, while others were larger and more lavishly equipped.

By the end of the seventeenth century opera was popular throughout Italy. Griffiths described the situation:

> Rome and Naples offered valuable alternatives to the theatres of Venice, though Venice continued to produce many more operas per season than anyone else. The "star" system was now well established, the public tending to favour the upper voices, particularly castratos. To satisfy public taste, the aria now became lengthier, with the reprise of the *da capo* aria (though the rigid convention came later); there were therefore few opportunities for ensembles, and little chance for choral writing. However, the arias themselves covered a wide variety of moods and extended instrumental ritornello and concertante parts to simple songs based on dance rhythms. The orchestra assumed considerable importance, both in the overture (which could sometimes be a substantial piece) and in the accompaniment of the singers; indeed, in the later operas of Alessandro Scarlatti (the most influential opera composer of the period around 1700) arias are never accompanied solely by the continuo.[5]

The scene in France by the end of the century was somewhat different. French opera, using legendary and mythological themes, was still essentially part of the court. It preserved a certain courtly magnificence and formality with big choral numbers, ceremonial scenes, and less emphasis on the solo aria. Germany and England each imported Italian opera, but there were occasional attempts at opera written in the German language, particularly at Hamburg, and in the English language beginning with the operas of John Blow and Henry Purcell.

Another significant vocal and choral form of the Baroque period is *oratorio*. Most musicians understand what an oratorio is, and they are able to conjure an image of a work even though they may have never read a definition. Interestingly enough, however, it is very difficult to be definitive when one attempts to describe the work primarily because, unlike opera, oratorio has taken several varied forms as it has evolved. The oratorio may be defined as a major (although some are quite short) vocal and choral work (some do not include chorus) for solo singers (some have duets, trios, quartets, and ensembles as well) that tells a story (a story line is difficult to discern in some). The oratorio is dramatic in character (some lack a great deal of drama) but is intended to be neither staged (although some have been) nor performed in church (although some have been). Perhaps one can better understand if the evolution of the form is delineated.

In the mid-sixteenth century when the Roman Catholic church mounted its Counter-Reformation against the Protestants, Filippo Neri (1515–1595) became convinced that the spiritual well-being of the congregation would be enhanced if there were religious meetings provided in the vernacular with congregational participation. He decided that after vespers he would have an *oratorio vespertino* (little prayer service) in which a sermon would be given and there would be singing of motets and *laudi* (hymns usually sung in Italian). Some of the laudi told a story or were framed as a dialogue between two characters.

---

[5] Paul Griffiths, "Opera," *The New Oxford Companion to Music* (New York: Oxford University Press, 1983, p. 1249.

Simultaneously at the Society of Jesus in the German College in Rome, there were presentations of plays based on biblical stories or the lives of saints performed in the vernacular. These plays were provided as an alternative entertainment during carnival season. Some of them were spoken but others had some music.

In 1600 Emilio de' Cavalieri devised a play, similar to those presented at the Society of Jesus, in which many laudi were strung together to make a drama. It was performed shortly before Lent at one of Neri's *oratories* (artistically decorated halls where prayer was usually offered) with scenery, costumes, and dances. Soon published as *Rappresentatione di Anima e di Corpo (Representation of the Soul and the Body)*, it is considered to be the first work published in the new, monodic style of the Baroque era. Some say it is a sacred opera; others call it the first oratorio.

Next in the evolution of oratorio was the 1619 publication by Giovanni Francesco Anerio (c. 1567–1630) of what he called *spiritual madrigals*. As indicated in the dedication of this set, the dialogue texts told "stories from sacred scripture and praises of all the saints." Different voices took the parts of various participants with an ensemble and chorus singing the words of a group of characters or acting as narrator. Although voices were accompanied by continuo, the work included instrumental sinfonias and ritornelli.

In the 1620s and 1630s, elaborate musical presentations occurred at four oratories throughout Rome. These presentations probably used instrumental ensembles, choruses, and solo singers. Finally, in the late 1640s, works considered by most historians to be definite oratorios were written by Giacomo Carissimi and Luigi Rossi. Rossi's two extant oratorios, *Giuseppe* and the *Oratorio per la Settiman Santa*, are very operatic, telling stories largely by dialogue with a minimum of narrative. Each includes short arias, instrumental ritornelli, and a large chorus. Carissimi wrote oratorios in both Latin (*oratorio latino*) and Italian (*oratorio volgare*). His works are not as operatic as Rossi's and use a narrator to tell the story. Many of Carissimi's oratorios were written to be performed in pairs, one from the Old Testament, the other from the New Testament, and were to be presented before and after the sermon in the devotional meetings of Neri and his followers.

Because Carissimi had pupils scattered throughout Europe, the form as developed by him spread with them. Marc-Antoine Charpentier, a pupil of Carissimi, spread the form in France. Draghi and Caldara, Italian composers, exploited the form in Vienna in the latter part of the seventeenth century. In the 1670s oratorio appeared in Protestant Germany at the great opera house in Hamburg. *Der Blutige und Sterbende Jesus*, written by the opera composer Reinhard Keiser, was presented in 1704. It was followed by works of two better known composers, Johann Mattheson and Georg Philipp Telemann.

In Italy the form spread from Rome to Bologna, Florence, and Venice in the 1660s. In the period of 1660–1680, the development of the form in Italy followed that of opera. By 1700 a regular alternation of recitative and aria was usual, the arias being mainly extended and in *da capo* (ABA) form. The chorus was virtually abolished, although all the characters often joined in a finale. It was this oratorio structure, of which Alessandro Scarlatti was a master, that George Frideric Handel encountered when he was working and studying in Rome.

Handel was poised to become a great composer of oratorio. He encountered Reinhard Keiser and Johann Mattheson (he once fought a duel with Mattheson over a continuo part; neither was hurt) when playing second violin at the Hamburg opera house. He was influenced by Arcangelo Corelli, Bernardo Pasquini, and both Alessandro and Domenico Scarlatti while studying in Rome. He had years of experience writing opera, so when the operas he was producing in London ceased to remain popular, it was natural for him to turn to oratorio. Through the years of 1707 until a few years before his death in 1759, he composed and produced such great works as *Messiah, Susanna, Theodora, Saul, Belshazzar*, and *Samson*, among others. The oratorio as a form enjoyed its greatest hour at the hands of this great composer.

Another vocal and choral form that came to fruition during the Baroque, somewhat akin to the oratorio, is the *passion*. Actually, the idea of dramatizing the Passion of Christ during Holy Week dates back to medieval times. It was not until the sixteenth and seventeenth centuries that musical presentations of that period of Christ's life became popular with great composers. This was due to a renewal of devotion to the idea and the practice of setting biblical stories to music by Lutheran and other Protestant denominations. Even though the form is most often considered a Protestant form set in the vernacular, settings of the Passion story in Latin were also common for Roman Catholic churches. Like the oratorio, the musical design of the form is difficult to define since it was been handled different ways by different composers. The responsorial passions of Heinrich Schütz, although written around the 1660s, have a definite Renaissance flavor each with a composed cantus firmus and madrigalian counterpoint. By the early eighteenth century passions had been greatly influenced by opera and oratorio and were infinitely more Baroque in flavor. Works by Keiser (of Hamburg), Handel, Caldara, and Scarlatti are more operatic in style and the role of the chorus is small. The works of Telemann, forty-four in all, give a greater responsibility to the chorus and are more reminiscent of the oratorio. Probably the two best-known passions are those of J. S. Bach, *St. John Passion* and *St. Matthew Passion*. They are very much like the oratorio except that Bach included rich harmonizations of chorale tunes because of his association with Lutheran church music.

When oratorios, operas, and passions are performed nowadays, the size of the chorus and orchestra is often quite large, involving several hundred singers and players. This practice prevails because of the influence of the large orchestras and choruses employed in the great works of the Romantic period. In the recent past, the tendency was to apply the Romantic style and number of performers to the Classical and Baroque works. There is very little documentary evidence concerning the size and other physical characteristics of Baroque opera and oratorio choruses. When one considers the customs and practices of the day as recorded in history there is reason to believe that they were quite small. The early operas and oratorios are believed to have included only sixteen to eighteen singers. In fact, the designation "chorus" was sometimes used in early Italian operas to refer to an ensemble that was composed of only one singer for each part. In most cases, Handel's oratorio choruses numbered no more than thirty-eight, with an average size of around twenty-five.

There is also a question as to exactly when female singers became part of the opera, oratorio, and passion chorus. Evidence indicates that they appeared at the outset in solo roles. Further, women were serving as dancers as early as the 1680s in French opera. It seems reasonable to believe that they served as choristers by this time as well. However, it would appear that the Foundling Hospital performance of the *Messiah* consisted of all male singers in the chorus, thirteen adult males and six boy trebles, with three male and three female soloists.

Upon hearing the term *cantata*, another of the vocal and choral forms of the Baroque period, today's music educator often imagines a sacred, evangelical work performed by soloists, chorus, piano, organ, and possibly orchestra (or a prepared tape of an orchestra) at Christmas or Easter in a local church. If the educator is from a more liturgical church background, the image might be that of a Bach cantata based on a familiar chorale tune. Had the educator lived in Italy where the term originated during the Baroque period, neither of these images would have surfaced. In reality, the term was an all-encompassing one that literally meant a work to be sung as opposed to one that would be played (sonata). With the exception of opera and oratorio, the cantata was the most important and ubiquitous form of vocal and choral music of the period. The term first appeared in a work by Alessandro Grandi around 1620 entitled *Cantade et Arie*, a collection of three pieces similar to arias. In early Italian Baroque music, the term soon came to mean a work for one or more voices with instrumental accompaniment. Most Italian cantatas were for solo voice (usually soprano) and were predominantly secular. In the early part of the period they were quite simple, but by the early eighteenth century they consisted of several independent movements of contrasting recitatives, ariosos, and arias. The Italian composers prominent in developing the form were Luigi Rossi, Virgilio Mazzocchi, Giacomo Carissimi, Antonio Cesti, Alessandro Stradella, Agostino Steffani, G. F. Handel (during his Italian years), and Alessandro Scarlatti. These Italian cantatas were also fairly widely cultivated in France and to a lesser extent in England.

To the Baroque Protestant, particularly Lutherans, the term *cantata* meant a sacred work for soloists and chorus including movements ranging from simple chorale harmonizations to extended complex structures accompanied by continuo and/or orchestra. Works developed by Dietrich Buxtehude, G. P. Telemann, and J. S. Bach represent the Baroque cantata as it is most performed today.

A choral form that maintained some prominence during the Baroque, even though it enjoyed much greater acceptance during the Renaissance, was the *motet*. The Renaissance motet written in *stile antico* (old style) by Palestrina and others was to a small degree continued in the Catholic worship services during the seventeenth century. For the most part, however, the form evolved to adopt various musical characteristics associated with other Baroque music. In reality, in the seventeenth and eighteenth centuries the term came to mean any kind of vocal music that was associated with church worship. Those written for the Catholic service were in Latin and those written for the Protestants were in the vernacular.

Because the motet was a favorite form of Louis XIV in France, it was popular with some French composers, particularly Marc-Antoine Charpentier, Henry Du Mont, Michel-Richard de Lalande, and André Campra. There were two types of Baroque French motets: the *grand motet*, which typically included three five-part choirs (one of vocal soloists, one a full chorus, and one an instrumental choir), and the *petit motet*, which required only one to four vocal soloists and a continuo player. Both types were heard in church services throughout France during the Baroque period.

Protestant German composers employed the motet along with the vocal concerto (another all-encompassing term to mean about the same as motet) and the cantata as gospel commentaries in their services. Michael Praetorius, Johann Schein, Samuel Scheidt, and Heinrich Schütz all contributed significantly to these genre. The motet reached its apex with those of J. S. Bach, even though he wrote only six. Currently, Bach's motets are probably the most performed of all the Baroque motets.

A contemporary choral form that is used in most English-speaking Protestant churches is the *anthem*. Currently an anthem is viewed as a special choral presentation, either original or arranged from an existing hymn, chorale, spiritual, or gospel song that is designed to enhance worship. The term may be traced to the Church of England in the Baroque period. At that time it was basically the English analogue to the Latin, German, or French motet. In the early Baroque the predominant form was the *full anthem*, which was written in the style of a late Renaissance motet. It was replaced in the late Baroque by the *verse anthem* written in the style of the concertato motet. John Blow, Henry Purcell, and G. F. Handel contributed the best examples of this choral form.

Choral Singing in the Classical and Romantic Periods

Considering the development of new musical forms and the evolution of old ones during the nineteenth century, there is no doubt that instrumental music predominates. When one examines historical accounts, there is such a strong descriptive emphasis on the instrumental forms of the two periods that one might presume, with the exception of opera, that vocal and choral activity was kept to a minimum. There were very few new choral forms, but the existing ones from the Baroque and some from the Renaissance continued to flourish and expand. Further, performances of vocal and choral music (operas, masses, songs, cantatas, motets, and oratorios, among others) indeed prospered throughout Europe.

The ideas and ideals of romanticism affected the choral idiom, particularly in its secular context as was expressed in Ludwig van Beethoven's *Choral Symphony* and the ambitious Wagnerian music dramas. Churches officials attempted to regain guardianship of the choral expression, but the influence of the secular could not be discounted. The masses of Haydn, Mozart, and Beethoven as well as the liturgical works of Berlioz, Bruckner, and Verdi greatly resemble those composers' secular output and are vastly different from the sacred works of the Renaissance masters.

During the latter years of Handel's life his oratorios were enormously popular. "His death turned what had already become a cult almost into a religion."[6] In 1759, *Messiah* was performed for the first time in a cathedral whereas previously it only had been performed in secular buildings. During that same year there were Handel commemorative performances in London, Oxford, Cambridge and even in the small village of Church Langton, near Leicester, where a two-day festival was held. The 100th anniversary of his birth was celebrated by a large festival of his works in Westminster Abbey with 300 singers and 250 instrumentalists. This 1784 commemoration set a precedent that prevails to this day. Large choruses and broad effects continue to be emphasized when his works are performed. Handel festivals were held in successive years in Westminster Abbey and included 616 participants in 1785, 749 in 1786, and 806 in 1787, and in 1791 there were over 1000 participants. Joseph Haydn was present for the 1791 festival. There was a festival in York Minster in 1823 that had 465 participants and in Norwich in 1830 that included seventy boy trebles, thirty-eight countertenors, sixty-one tenors, and sixty-five basses.

Eventually, presentations of his oratorios spread to the continent with performances of German versions in Hamburg in the 1770s. One of the most important performances was given in Berlin Cathedral in 1786 with 305 singers and players and was duplicated later in the year in the university church in Leipzig. The first time *Messiah* was performed in Copenhagen was in 1786.

It was during this time that sacred music moved from the church into the theater. For instance, in 1771 a large chorus constituted as the Tonkünstler-Sozietät in Vienna, modeled after the Society of Musicians in London, was organized to give charity concerts to meet the needs of indigent members of the musical profession and their dependents. Their premiere performance in March 1772 was a work by Florian Gassmann entitled *Betulia Liberata* and was so successful that it was repeated twice in April. This resulted in annual performances of major works at Christmas and Easter in the Kärntnertortheater until 1783 and in the Burgtheater thereafter. Haydn composed a special work, *Il Ritorno di Tobia*, for the Tonkünstler-Sozietät, and his great oratorio *Creation*, which had been fashioned after the oratorios of Handel, became a standard part of their repertoire.

Continental choruses grew in response to special needs and occasions. In 1773 oratorios in Vienna were given by 400 performers; in Naples in 1774, 300 performed; in 1811, 700 performers were required for an oratorio in Vienna; and by 1812 over 1000 participated in the presentation of Handel's *Alexander's*

---

[6] Percy Young, "Chorus," *The New Grove Dictionary of Music and Musicians*, Vol. 3 (London: Macmillan Publishers, Ltd., 1980), p. 351.

Feast. This practice of using such large numbers of performers continued in Vienna until 1847.

In England, societies for the preservation of old music, such as the Madrigal Society (1741) and Ancient Consort (1776), and those to encourage the production of new music, such as the Noblemen's Catch Club (1761) and the Glee Club (1783), were becoming well established. By the early 1800s new choral societies were organized in almost every British town. Through the influence of the Sacred Harmonic Society (1832–1880) the scope of choral opportunities for women was broadened. Although women were not allowed to be official members of the society, they were invited to sing the soprano and alto parts; previously this had been the responsibility of the men of the cathedral choirs.

Beyond the realm of the professional and semiprofessional choral organizations, the nineteenth century was a great age for amateur part-singing groups designed primarily for social purposes. The female choir, which had its roots in convent music, was very popular, and most of the prominent composers of the time wrote for female voicing. The male choir was a great group for gentlemanly camaraderie, but it also served to support nationalistic and even revolutionary causes in many countries, including Russia and Scandinavia. Choirs flourished everywhere: In Czechoslovakia the Moravian Teachers' choral movement was recognized with high distinction; in Hungary the folk music and music education movement of Zoltan Kodály and Béla Bartok was expressed through many choirs and choral festivals; and in Germany during the years just previous to World War I, Wilhelm II instructed that a two-volume book of folk songs be published for male, female, and school choirs.

Most of the great Romantic composers wrote for various types of choirs. In the early part of the period the oratorio tradition of Handel and Haydn was continued with Felix Mendelssohn approaching their greatness. In the latter part of the period Liszt, Berlioz, and Elgar also made significant contributions to oratorio literature.

Haydn, Mozart, Beethoven, Cherubini, Rossini, Liszt, Gounod, and Bruckner contributed to the sustenance of the mass and particularly the *requiem* (mass for the dead). Contributions to the Latin motet were made by Mozart, Michael Haydn, Berlioz, Saint-Saëns, Fauré, Liszt, and Bruckner, and the German motet found contributions in the works of Mendelssohn and Brahms.

Ways in which vocal performers approached and utilized the voice changed in the first half of the nineteenth century. In opera, new voice types such as *tenore robusto, tenore di forza, heldentenor, Verdi baritone, falcon soprano, dramatic soprano,* and *lirico spinto* emerged. The size of the Romantic orchestra required singers to develop voices that produced much bigger sounds in order to be heard, voices that could resonate and project to the back of large concert halls. "In 1860 Wagner instigated a reorganization of the music school at Münich with the intention of cultivating voices suited to the heavier roles of his music dramas."[7] In the latter part of the century, even though the bravura style

[7] Owen Jander, "Singing," *The New Grove Dictionary of Music and Musicians,* Vol. 17 (London: Macmillan Publishers, Ltd., 1980), p. 343.

persisted in some quarters, there was an increasing appreciation of the subjective element in singing that yielded a new class of singer who specialized in recitals and oratorio. Even in opera, the French were somewhat critical of singing that manifested itself in massive sound and singing that lacked finesse. This attitude resulted in French singers who built reputations on acting ability rather than on vocal production.

Two types of opera, the dominant vocal form of the period, prevailed throughout the early 1800s: *opera seria* (serious opera) and *opera buffo* (comic opera). Serious opera, dominated by the castrati, was enjoyed by the upper classes, the nobility, and the royalty. Almost every Italian city enjoyed a stage reserved for the performance of opera seria, equipped with machinery necessary for spectacular stage effects. Comic opera (*opera buffo* in Italy, *singspiel* in German-speaking countries, and *opéra-comique* in France), on the other hand, with its propensity to a more national character and a simpler lifestyle, appealed to the middle class.

Throughout the nineteenth century Rossini, Donizetti, Bellini, Verdi, and Puccini preserved and contributed to the great Italian opera tradition while France, Germany, and other nations developed their own operatic styles. Italians wanted to hear great, full-throated singing. The French liked lighthearted, sentimental entertainment, and the Germans enjoyed dances, stories of folklore, tales about nature and the supernatural, and symphonic use of the opera orchestra as culminated in the great music dramas of Wagner.

It is important that teachers of choral music understand about the emergence of this full-throated style because it is a technique of singing with which choral conductors have had to deal from its arrival in the Romantic period until the present. Developed as a solo style, in many cases when used in a choral setting, it results in a deterioration of choral blend. Many choral teachers, particularly those who work with adults, shy away from inviting singers who have extremely large voices and full-throated style from singing in their groups.

Choral Singing in the Twentieth Century

"Immense changes brought about by rapidly developing technology and two global wars helped create ideas and attitudes toward life and art that are vastly different from those of preceding centuries."[8] These new attitudes have greatly influenced the way music sounds. One need not explore the effects of impressionism, expressionism, serialism, neoclassism, nor electronic and computer music to make this point. These effects are more greatly pronounced in instrumental music, but choral music has also experienced a metamorphosis.

The technique of *sprechgesang* (a specialized mode of vocal expression crossed between singing and speaking introduced by Arnold Schoenberg), *bocca chiusa* (a glissando and controlled shout), choral recitation, and other special effects are the principle results of twentieth-century choral writing. Young

---

[8] Faye-Ellen Silverman, "The Twentieth Century," *Schirmer History of Music* (New York: Schirmer Books, 1982), p. 723.

explains how the invention of the microphone and of techniques of electronic amplification have played an important part in introducing new singing styles:

> These techniques were first used in popular music and were generally frowned on elsewhere, but since the 1950s they have been increasingly used by 'serious' composers. In Crumb's *Ancient Voices of Children* (1970), for example, a soprano sings (or shouts) into an open piano and the sympathetic vibrations of the undamped strings are then amplified through a contact microphone. In Stockhausen's *Stimmung* (1968) the voices of six singers produce drawn-out sonorities that are manipulated electronically and fed into a ring of loudspeakers surrounding the audience. In Berio's *Sinfonia* (1968) a microphone is used to weave the kaleidoscopic sounds of a small chorus into larger orchestral fabric.[9]

However, modern electronic techniques have been useful beyond just the ways they have affected singing style. A comparison of the vocal production and style of Enrico Caruso as recorded in the early 1900s to that of today's singers would not have been possible without the invention of the gramophone. Further, one can examine the evolution of interpretation and style of a single singer by comparing the sound of the singer in early recordings to that of later ones. Today's society, and that of the future, would never have known how the castrato sounded had not the recordings of Alessandro Moreschi been made before he died.

Probably the most important innovation of the twentieth century is the trend to restore authenticity to choral performances. Modern performers attempt to make Renaissance music sound as if it were being performed in the sixteenth century, Baroque in the seventeenth, Classical in the eighteenth, and Romantic in the nineteenth, not only in style and interpretation but also in size and personnel of the performing groups. This trend has brought about a renewed interest in the countertenor, a voice type that had virtually disappeared in performance except in England, and is manifested in the work of Alfred Deller in the 1950s and 1960s and in that of the King Singers in the 1970s and 1980s. The boy's choir has found new purpose with the famous choirs in which old ecclesiastical standards are retained, such as those in Cambridge (and other British cathedrals), Copenhagen, Dresden, Leipzig, and Vienna and purely secular ones such as the Texas Boys Choir.

THOUGHTS FOR CONTEMPLATION AND DISCUSSION

1.   As an American, do you feel that we have a strong tradition as choral music educators? Why or why not?
2.   In your opinion, which of the three ancient cultures (Greek, Roman, or Jewish) had the greatest influence on the way choral music is today? Why?
3.   In your opinion, which of the six basic periods (Medieval, Renaissance, Baroque, Classical, Romantic, or Twentieth Century) had the greatest influence of contemporary American choral music? Why?

[9] Ibid., p. 344.

4. If the castrati had not disappeared from society, do you think they would have been as influential today as they were during the Baroque period? Why or why not?

5. The church has influenced choral music significantly throughout history. Do you think it is as influential today as it has been in the past? Why or why not?

6. Do you think that Romantic opera and the advent of vocal technique that requires the voice to project above a large orchestra was beneficial or detrimental to choral technique as we use it today? Why?

BIBLIOGRAPHY

ABELES, HAROLD F., CHARLES R. HOFFER, and ROBERT H. KLOTMAN. *Foundations of Music Education.* New York: Schirmer Books, 1984.

DOUGLAS, WINFRED. *Church Music in History and Practice.* New York: Charles Scribner's Sons, 1902.

ELLIS, ARTHUR K., JOHN J. COGAN, and KENNETH R. HOWEY. *Introduction to the Foundations of Education.* Englewood Cliffs, N.J.: Prentice-Hall, Inc., 1981.

GARRETT, T. S. *Christian Worship.* London: Oxford University Press, 1961.

GRIFFEL, L. MICHAEL. "The Romantic and Post-Romantic Eras." *Schirmer History of Music.* New York: Schirmer Books, 1982.

GRIFFITHS, PAUL. "Opera." *The New Oxford Companion to Music.* New York: Oxford University Press, 1983.

HUSTAD, DONALD P. *Jubilate! Church Music in the Evangelical Tradition.* Carol Stream, Ill.: Hope Publishing Company, 1981.

JANDER, OWEN. "SINGING." *The New Grove Dictionary of Music and Musicians,* Vol. 17. London: Macmillan Publishers, Ltd., 1980.

JONES, PERRY. "The History of Women's Liberation in Choral Music." *Choral Journal* 16, no. 6, 12–14.

KEITH, EDMOND. *Christian Hymnody.* Nashville: Convention Press, 1956.

LAZAREVICH, GORDANA. "From Preclassic to Classic." *Schirmer History of Music.* New York: Schirmer Books, 1982.

LEONHARD, CHARLES, and ROBERT W. HOUSE. *Foundations and Principles of Music Education,* 2d ed. New York: McGraw-Hill Book Co., 1972.

LINDGREN, LOWELL. "Music in the Baroque." *Schirmer History of Music.* New York: Schirmer Books, 1982.

MARK, MICHAEL L. *Contemporary Music Education,* 2d ed. New York: Schirmer Books, 1986.

McCOMMON, PAUL. *Music in the Bible.* Nashville: Convention Press, 1956.

ORNSTEIN, ALLAN C., and DANIEL U. LEVINE. *An Introduction to the Foundations of Education,* 3d ed. Boston: Houghton Mifflin Co., 1985.

ORREY, LESLIE. "Song." *New Oxford Companion to Music.* New York: Oxford University Press, 1983.

PLANCHART, ALEJANDRO ENRIQUE. "The Ars Nova and the Renaissance." *Schirmer History of Music.* New York: Schirmer Books, 1982.

ROBINSON, RAY, and ALLEN WINOLD. *The Choral Experience.* New York: Harper's College Press, 1976.

ROEDERER, CHARLOTTE. "The Middle Ages." *Schirmer History of Music.* New York: Schirmer Books, 1982.

RUSSELL, JAMES E. *German Higher Schools.* New York: Longmans, Green and Co., 1907.

SADIE, STANLEY. "Opera." *The New Grove Dictionary of Music and Musicians,* Vol. 13. London: Macmillan Publishers Ltd., 1980.

SILVERMAN, FAYE-ELLEN. "The Twentieth Century." *Schirmer History of Music.* New York: Schirmer Books, 1982.

SMITH, JAMES G. "Chorus: Antiquity and the Middle Ages." *The New Grove Dictionary of Music and Musicians,* Vol. 4. London: Macmillan Publishers, Ltd., 1980.

VANTOURA, SUZANNE HAIK. *La Musique de la Bible Revelee.* Paris: Dessain et Tolra, 1978.

WALKER, THOMAS. "Castrato." *The New Grove Dictionary of Music and Musicians,* Vol. 3. London: Macmillan Publishers Ltd., 1980.

YOUNG, PERCY. "Chorus." *The New Grove Dictionary of Music and Musicians,* Vol. 4. London: Macmillan Publishers, Ltd., 1980.

———. *The Choral Tradition.* London: Hutchinson and Co., Ltd., 1962.

2

Choral Music in America

In Chapter 1 we studied a brief, succinct treatise of our European choral music heritage. As important as our European choral roots are, understanding the immediate past in our American culture is of equal or more importance to the choral music educator because it represents a direct line to the traditional practices occurring in the classroom today. This chapter should help you grasp our wonderful choral heritage and give you a glimpse, if only slightly, of the direction in which it may proceed in the future.

CHORAL SINGING IN THE AMERICAN SOCIETY

The Beginnings

Music in America can be traced back to the indigenous inhabitants when Europeans first arrived. These "Indians," as they were called by Columbus when he arrived at what he thought was India, produced elaborate textiles and ceramics of all types that artistically depicted music making, dancing, and musical instruments. Indian music, however, did not amalgamate with those contributions of the early-arriving Europeans to have any significant influence on what was to follow. Not until several hundred years later did Indian music appear in published song books, enabling it to be considered part of American culture.

Around A.D. 1000, Leif Ericson and other Norsemen, believed by some to be the earliest Europeans to embark on the North American continent, set up temporary colonies in which dancing and playing pipes and drums occurred. Because their settlements were short-lived, they seem to have had no impact on the development of music in the New World.

Indians did function in the first acts of singing recorded in America. In the spring of 1564 three shiploads of Huguenots settled ten miles down the St. Johns River from what is now Jacksonville, Florida. These Calvinists were hearty psalm singers, and Indians came from all around to listen to them sing. Before long the Indians were joining in the singing of the French language learned by rote.

The Indians were also involved when the Franciscan friars arrived near St. Augustine, Florida, in 1603. In these friars' schools, the first students were Indians, who were taught vocal and instrumental music. The seventeenth century saw the spread of Franciscan education from the West Indies and Mexico to New Mexico and lower California and later to Texas and Louisiana. It is believed that approximately 60,000 Indians were being educated in New Mexico alone during this time.

Singing was also part of the curriculum of French Catholics in the Mississippi valley and the eastern coast from Maine to Nova Scotia and Quebec. These French Catholic missionaries were primarily responsible for the education of the Indians in those parts during the seventeenth and eighteenth centuries.

British influence on vocal education in America began with the arrival of English Protestants to Jamestown and the Pilgrims to Plymouth. The Puritans arrived with a manual of psalmody known as the *Ainsworth Psalter*. By 1640 an American rendition of the psalter appeared in the form of the *Bay Psalm Book*, which is considered to be one of the first books printed in America. Although the *Bay Psalm Book* came into being in 1640, not every singer and church adopted the new edition at once. The church at Plymouth, the first in New England, continued to use the Ainsworth version until 1692. The Ainsworth edition was used by both Pilgrims and Puritans. Eventually most of the churches were using the *Bay Psalm Book*, which appeared in seventy editions in America, Scotland, and England. The seventieth edition (1773) is considered by most scholars to be the last.

The Puritans of Boston and the Pilgrims of Plymouth were distrustful of music whether it was secular or sacred; therefore, congregational singing was not a priority activity in church worship. During the colonial period in America there was very little part singing in the churches, and most of the congregations only knew three or four tunes to which they sang the different psalm texts. "Lining out," a method of singing in which the pastor or a layman would sing a phrase or line and the congregation would repeat it in rote fashion, was practiced by most congregations since few, if any, of the members could read music. Apparently the singing was very uncultivated and somewhat stressing to the listener.

The Singing School Movement

Around 1720 several prominent New England clergymen, namely Cotton Mather, Jonathan Edwards, Thomas Symmes, Timothy Dwight, and John Eliot, among others, began a drive to improve the status of congregational singing in the church. They advocated what came to be known as "regular singing," which meant singing by note according to musical rules instead of the "old-style singing" that used lining out. Regular singing was not immediately accepted among the churches; in fact, a controversy emerged, but those who advocated regular singing prevailed. This launched the singing school movement. Advocates of old-style singing promoted some interesting excuses: (1) Regular singing was in an unknown tongue; (2) it was not as melodious as the usual way; (3) there were so many tunes that one could never learn them; (4) the new way made disturbance in churches, grieved good men, exasperated them, and caused them to be disorderly; (5) it was "popish"; (6) it would encourage the use of instruments in the church; (7) the names of the notes were blasphemous; (8) it was needless, the old way being enough; (9) it was only a contrivance to get money; and (10) it required too much time to learn it, made the young disorderly, and kept them from the proper influence of the family.[1] They sound similar to arguments which might be used by people today when new musical approaches are advocated by sacred choral musicians.

The earliest documented referenced to an American singing school was found in the diary of William Byrd (not the English composer) that indicated there was a singing school at Westover, Virginia, during December 1710 and January 1711. While this first known school existed in the South, it is relatively certain that most of the singing schools were held in New England initially. They were conducted by itinerant singing masters with William Billings, the well-known composer, being one of the first and ultimately the foremost embodiment of what was considered to be a typical singing master. The schools generally had around fifty students and lasted between one to three months. They were held in churches, meetinghouses, or taverns. The pupils were taught to sing in parts and to read music using *fasola* solmization (a method of music reading with shaped notes that first appeared in the ninth edition, 1698, of the *Bay Psalm Book* and later was advocated in a modified form by John Tufts in his *Introduction to the Art of Singing Psalm-tunes*, 1721, in which he eliminated the original shaped notes and placed the initial letters of the syllables directly on the staff). Attention was also given to vocal production, style of performance, and deportment. In most cases the school was concluded with a public demonstration. The most obvious purpose of the singing school was to teach those musical concepts and other precepts described above; however, they made an impact much more far-reaching than this immediate purpose. The first American music professional, the singing master, was a result of the movement. In fact, this was the only way an American could earn a living from music teaching during the eighteenth century. Singing schools also promoted music publishing because a large majority of the *tune books* (collections of sacred music with pedagological instructions) of this time period were written specifically for them. Further, most of the early American composers, including William Billings, Daniel Read,

---

[1] Lloyd Frederick Sunderman, *Historical Foundations of Music Education in the United States* (Metuchen, N. J.: The Scarecrow Press, Inc., 1971), p. 13.

Oliver Holden, Jacob French, Jacob Kimball, Jr., and Samuel Holyoke, were, singing school masters.

The Choral Societies

The enthusiasm of the singing school masters promulgated choral music in church and community choirs throughout New England after 1750. The Stoughton (Massachusetts) Musical Society, the oldest enduring community choral organization in the United States, was founded in 1786 because of the influence of the singing school. The Uranian Academy founded by Andrew Adgate in 1787 grew out of the singing school movement. In Philadelphia Adgate led a chorus of 230 singers and fifty instrumentalists in a program of sacred works including the "Hallelujah Chorus" from Handel's *Messiah* and Billings's *I Am the Rose of Sharon*. Similar concerts were held subsequently in New York and Boston. William Tuckey conducted Handel's *Messiah* in a reasonably complete form for its first performance in this country in New York City in 1770. These were exceptional events for public concerts in this period of American music history.

By the early nineteenth century, choral societies (often called singing societies) proliferated, particularly on the East Coast. Shortly after 1800 Dartmouth College had a Handel singing society. The Massachusetts Musical Society, organized in 1807, lasted three years. In 1814 the Handel Society of Maine was organized. One of the greatest choral societies in America was the Handel and Haydn Society in Boston founded in 1815, followed by the Musical Fund Society of Philadelphia in 1820. According to Sunderman, Haydn's *The Creation* was presented in America for the first time by the Musical Fund Society on June 10, 1822.[2] Robinson and Winold give a different date, indicating that it was premiered by the Moravian Collegium Musicum in 1811, two years after the composer's death.[3]

Choral societies were important to the development of American choral music because they set very high standards for other musically minded individuals and groups to emulate. Not only did they bring outstanding choral works before the public, but they also provided commercial and professional opportunities for concert singers (and amateurs as well) and conductors.

Early Church Choirs

Prior to the nineteenth century, development of the church choir was extremely slow. In New York City there was a crude form of choral training in the parish charity schools in 1709. By 1761 the Old Trinity Church choir had boys to sing the treble parts. By the end of the century churches were accustomed to seating those singers who could read music together, and in some cases they were

---

[2] Ibid., p. 24.

[3] Ray Robinson and Allen Winold, *The Choral Experience* (New York: Harper's College Press, 1976), p. 16.

invited to come to the front of the church to assist the congregation in hymn singing.

Ann Lee, founder of the Shakers, immigrated to America from Manchester, England, in 1774. There is some indication that she communicated several songs for the purpose of choral singing to her followers in an unorthodox notation that had been revealed to her in visions. J. Conrad Beissel, the leader of a Pennsylvania sect known as the *Ephrata Cloister*, organized choirs and singing schools for his followers, but the most significant contributions by a religious sect were made by the Moravians. In 1744 the Moravians founded a collegium musicum for performance of great choral works in Bethlehem, Pennsylvania, followed by a similar organization in Salem, North Carolina, in 1786. Their church has contributed a large body of very sophisticated choral music that compares favorably with classical European compositions. The Moravian archives in Winston-Salem, North Carolina, consist of approximately 10,000 manuscripts including some 7000 individual works, about two-thirds of which were written by composers connected with the Moravian church.

Choral Developments in the Nineteenth Century

Probably the person who influenced choral music the most in the United States during the early part of the nineteenth century was Lowell Mason. As a young man he showed considerable talent as a musician, learning to play the organ, piano, violoncello, and clarinet. His musical career began very early: Before he was sixteen he was the leader of his hometown band in Medfield, Massachusetts, by sixteen he was teaching singing in a singing school, and by twenty he had already been conducting a parish choir. That same year, his twentieth, he moved to Savannah, Georgia, where he performed as a violoncellist and singer. He also worked as a clerk in a local bank. This did not keep him busy enough so he organized a band and a community choir, conducted many community groups, and assumed the responsibilities of a large Sunday School in the First Presbyterian Church in Savannah. All the while he was composing church music. The crown of his young career came when in 1827 at the age of thirty-five he became president of the Handel and Haydn Society in Boston. This prestigious honor came about after the society had published a collection of his church music.

Thomas Hastings, William B. Bradbury, and Mason were instrumental in supplanting the singing school movement in the Northeast with what was commonly called the "better music movement." They criticized the unsophisticated compositions and performance practices of current singing school masters. They wrote a more dignified music, raised the performance standards in church choirs, founded new choral societies, and established "conventions" (instead of singing schools) that were short-term events and "normal institutes" for summerlong study programs. The choir that Mason conducted at the Bowdoin Street Church in Boston served as a model for the methods and techniques favored by the normal institutes.

The singing school movement prospered during the nineteenth century in the South and in the states that were experiencing western expansion. The fasola shaped-note system of reading music, introduced in the Northeast long before Mason's "better music movement," became extremely popular particularly in the South. Using only four pitch syllables (the major scale was fa, so, la, fa, so, la, mi, fa) and a different note shape for each (fa was a triangle; so, a circle; la, a square; and mi, a diamond), the system prevailed over the traditional tonic solfa (do, re, mi, fa, so, la, ti, do) recommended by the "better music movement" until just before the Civil War when the seven-note system became more popular. It was during the nineteenth century that the shape-note singing convention (a festive occasion of several days where religion and fellowship were of equal importance, also called "a Sacred Harp singing" from the song book, *The Sacred Harp*) became established in American culture; this practice still occurs in certain parts of the South today. After the Civil War, when religious music came under the influence of camp meetings, Sunday schools, spirituals, revivals, and gospel singing, the conventions adopted a seven shape-note system based on tonic solfa.

An aphorism of that day was "to the American frontier Methodism gave the circuit rider and to Methodism the frontier gave the camp meeting." Analogously one can say "to the camp meeting American hymnody gave the revival spiritual and to American hymnody the camp meeting gave a whole new direction." There is no question that after the advent of the camp meeting, American hymnody began a gradual development that is manifested in what is currently referred to as Christian contemporary music. This evolutionary process began with hymns from the genteel tradition of the early nineteenth century, spirituals and gospel songs, and Sunday school songs, and continued with revival songs of Dwight L. Moody and Ira David Sankey in the latter part of the nineteenth century. The more sentimental gospel hymns of Billy Sunday and Homer Rodeheaver followed in the early twentieth century, and the evolution continued through to the crusade gospel hymnody of Billy Graham and Cliff Barrows, folk musicals, urban pop gospel, and the sound of Amy Grant and her contemporaries in the latter part of the twentieth century. The hymn singing of most major Protestant denominations has been affected by this evolutionary process: Baptist, Methodist, Presbyterian, Congregational, Disciples of Christ, Church of Christ, Lutheran, Episcopalian (to a lesser degree), Nazarene, Assembly of God, and Pentecostal. It even affected the Roman Catholic church by contributing the folk mass and the usage of popular contemporary songs and choruses in congregational singing. American hymnody has had and continues to have a very special flavor, character, and uniqueness not found in European hymnody.

Choral societies continued to prosper during the nineteenth century. Wherever there was a large community of German-Americans, one could usually find a singing society of German immigrants affirming their cultural heritage. In New York it was the Deutsche Liederkranz organized in 1847. Others were found in Milwaukee, Chicago, and Cincinnati. Glee clubs styled after the British were also popular; the Mendelssohn Glee Club in New York (1866), the Apollo Club in Boston (1871), the Apollo Musical Club in Chicago (1872), and the Mendelssohn Club in Philadelphia (1847), to name a few, were prominent. Most German choral societies and English glee clubs were originally all male, but some grew into large choruses that included women and that featured mostly art music in their repertoire. The Handel and Haydn Society in Boston, mentioned previously, served as a model for similar groups that formed throughout the country: the New York Oratorio Society (1873), the Mendelssohn Society (1858) and Beethoven Society (1873) in Chicago, and the Bethlehem Bach Choir (1898) of Moravian tradition. The first of several choral societies associated with an academic institution included Oberlin Musical Union (Oberlin College, 1860), the University Choral Union of the University of Michigan (Ann Arbor, 1879), the Mozart Society at Fisk University (1880), and the Madison Choral Union of the University of Wisconsin (1893) also were formed.

Large choral festivals were sponsored by many of the singing societies. One of the first was the May Festival of German immigrant origin held in Cincinnati in 1873 that included a chorus of 800 and an orchestra of over 1000. The Handel and Haydn Society sponsored a festival for chorus and orchestra in 1856 that included 600 singers and seventy-eight in the orchestra. The largest festivals held in the United States in the nineteenth century were organized in Boston in 1869 and 1872 by Patrick S. Gilmore. Called Gilmore's Peace Jubilees, the 1869 affair included more than 10,000 choristers and 1000 instrumentalists only to be outdone by the 1872 festival with 20,000 in the chorus and 2000 in the orchestra.

The A Cappella Tradition

In the early part of the twentieth century the a cappella choir came into vogue. The first university choir to use that title was the A Capella Choir of Northwestern University, under the direction of Peter Christian Lutkin, which grew out of a need to develop singers who could demonstrate how music of Renaissance composers should be performed. In 1891 Lutkin joined the faculty to head the Northwestern Conservatory of Music. Under his influence the conservatory soon became a music department with Lutkin as its chairman and full professor. By 1895 he had developed a full music curriculum, and the department became a school of music with Lutkin as its dean. He organized the university choir in 1906, and by 1928 the members had achieved national prominence when they sang for the convention of the Music Supervisors National Conference.

Three other very prominent choirs emerged immediately: The St. Olaf Lutheran Choir (1912), F. Melius Christiansen, conductor; the Westminster College Choir (1925), John Finley Williamson, conductor; and the Paulist Choristers (first from Chicago, 1904, and later from New York City), Father William J. Finn, conductor. The first two of these choirs grew out of existing church choral organizations; the St. John's Church choir of Northfield, Minnesota, and the Westminster Presbyterian Church choir in Dayton, Ohio, respectively.

Christiansen, a Norwegian immigrant, joined the faculty at St. Olaf College around 1900 as director of the band, the Choral Union, and the St. John's Church Choir. In 1907 he organized a choir of students and faculty members to sing for a conference of the United Norwegian Lutheran Church. In 1910 he combined the male and female segments of the Choral Union into one choir that sang under the name of the St. John's Church Choir. In the spring of 1912 the choir's name was changed to the St. Olaf Lutheran Choir. By 1920 the choir had developed a national reputation, particularly after receiving excellent reviews from a tour of the eastern United States and New York City.

The St. Olaf choir set the standards that became the performance practices of the a cappella tradition in senior high schools and colleges throughout the country. The singers memorized their music in sectional rehearsals and were not allowed to bring their music to full rehearsal or performances. They took their pitch for each selection from choir members blowing pitch pipes during the applause from the previous number, giving the appearance of the members having absolute pitch. They worked extensively and in detail on every piece of music in approximately ten hours of rehearsal per week, performing only a maximum of twenty-five compositions a year. Their trademark was the straightness of tone achieved throughout the vocal range.

By the end of Christiansen's career he had trained literally thousands of senior high school and college directors to use his highly respected choral technique in two-week choir schools held each summer at Winona Lake, Indiana; Lake Forest, Illinois; and Chambersburg, Pennsylvania. He retired in 1942.

In 1925, John Finley Williamson founded the Westminster College Choir from the Westminster Presbyterian Church Choir of Dayton, Ohio. In the early 1930s the college and choir moved to Princeton, New Jersey. Williamson organized four choirs at the college: a chapel choir, an oratorio choir, a symphonic choir, and the Westminster Choir, the latter of which maintained the a cappella tradition throughout his tenure at the college. As a young man Williamson had been greatly influenced by Christiansen but gradually changed his ideas pertaining to choral tone. His ultimate approach included a very dark, full-throated sound characterized by full vibrato (some even called it a tremelo). A man with a magnetic and persuasive personality, he was able to contribute greatly to the a cappella tradition and to church music in general. Under his influence, most of the Westminster Choir College graduates prepared for positions as choral directors in churches.

Father William J. Finn founded a men's and boys' choir, the Paulist Choristers, in Chicago in 1904, that soon became known nationally and abroad. After moving to New York City, Finn carried out his choral art through radio broadcasts and concerts. Eventually he was engaged by directors of mixed choruses to share his choral expertise with them, resulting in five decades of professional influence on the art of choral singing.

Another prominent collegiate choir of that era was the Harvard Glee Club under the direction of Archibald Davison. Davison was able to take an all-male social society and turn it into a choral ensemble that performed well-prepared selections of art music.

The a cappella choir movement greatly benefited the cause of choral music in the senior high schools. Before its influence, senior high school choral music consisted primarily of casual auditorium singing, extracurricular glee clubs, or large groups for the purposes of singing oratorios. After the 1930s, the organization of a cappella choirs in senior high schools began to spread nationwide. Soon strong state organizations began to promote excellence in choral singing by sponsoring contests, festivals, and honor choruses at regional and state levels. By the 1950s, through the influence of Duncan McKenzie, Frederick Swanson, and Irvin Cooper, choral directors began to understand how to train students with changing voices so that choral singing began to improve in the junior high schools as well.

Other Choral Developments in the Twentieth Century

During the twentieth century there has been a shift of emphasis from the choral art of the singing societies to the music programs of colleges and universities. Students majoring in choral music have been able to prepare themselves sufficiently to be choral conductors by acquiring the necessary experience of singing in first-rate choral ensembles. Under the umbrella of academic freedom these organizations have been able to develop and explore all choral idioms. In many instances, singers from the community not enrolled in the university or college have been invited to participate in a "town-and-gown" ensemble thereby placing the university and college in the role of patron.

Coinciding with the university and college choral movement was the development of several excellent professional ensembles. The first of these groups was the Musical Art Society of New York City (1893) founded by Frank Damrosch for the express purpose of performing ancient and modern a cappella music. It was soon followed by the Choral Art Society of Boston (1902), the Cecilia Choir of Pittsburgh (1932), the Madrigal Club of Chicago (1900), and the MacDowell Chorus (1912), later to become the Schola Cantorum of New York City. Two choirs of black singers having great influence on American choral music were the Eva Jessye Choir (1927) and the Hal Johnson Choir (1930), which later became the Festival Negro Chorus of Los Angeles. By the middle of the century other distinguished professional choirs emerged, including the Fred Waring Glee Club (1923), the Robert Shaw Chorale (1947), the Roger Wagner Chorale (1945), the Norman Luboff Choir (1963), and the New York Pro Musica (1953). Probably the best-known groups of this nature from the latter part of the twentieth century are the Gregg Smith Singers and the Dale Warland Singers.

The twentieth century has seen the development of the uniquely American professional boys' choir. Traditionally the boys' choir has been associated with the church or the cathedral, and such is the case with many excellent boys' choirs in America. However, the best ones have been community organizations or live-in training organizations that have traveled throughout the country under the auspices of the Community Concerts subcription plan, which has been available since the 1950s. (Some of the following choirs were not part of this booking system but were booked independently or by other professional booking agencies.) Among these are the Apollo Boys Choir (in the 1930s), the Columbia Boys Choir (later called the American Boys Choir), the Texas Boys Choir founded and conducted for over twenty years by George Bragg, the

Tucson Boys Choir, the Phoenix Boys Choir, the Harlem Boys Choir, the Pennsylvania Boy Singers, and the California Boys Choir.

Currently, the strongest supporter of choral music in America is the American Choral Directors Association. Founded in 1959, it holds biennial meetings and publishes the *Choral Journal* each month (excluding summer months). Current membership in the association exceeds 15,000.

THE DEVELOPMENT OF PUBLIC SCHOOL VOCAL MUSIC

The Beginnings

Heinrich Pestalozzi (1746–1827) was a Swiss educator who had great influence on the American public school system prior to the Civil War. He advocated that the best education was that which was assimilated through the senses, and he was one of the first to differentiate clinical learning experiences from knowledge gained from a book. Pestalozzi urged educators to include vocal music as part of the public school curriculum. Therefore, in 1810 Hans Georg Nägeli combined the educational objectives of Pestalozzi with basic musical knowledge in his treatise *The Theory of Instruction in Singing*. This treatise influenced both William C. Woodbridge, one of the early American leaders in music education, and Lowell Mason, who is credited with beginning American public school music. Joseph H. Naef, a member of Pestalozzi's European staff before emigrating to America around 1806, made a presentation to the American Institute of Instruction at a meeting in Boston in 1830 in which he presented the basic tenets of the Pestalozzian/Nägeli system of teaching music. Those principles are:

1. to teach sounds of the music before the signs and to make the children learn to sing them before they learn the written notes or their names (a typical example of rote to note teaching);
2. to lead them to observe by hearing and imitating sounds, their resemblances and differences, their agreeable and disagreeable effects, instead of explaining these things to the children; in other words, to make them active instead of passive in learning;
3. to teach but one thing at a time (rhythm, melody, and expression are to be taught and practiced separately) before the children are required to attempt all at once;
4. to make them practice each of these entities separately, until they have mastered each, before passing to the next;
5. to give the principles and theory after the practice;
6. to analyze and practice the elements of articulate sound in order to apply them to music; and
7. to use the letter names of the notes as with instrumental music.[4]

---

[4] Harold F. Abeles, Charles R. Hoffer, and Robert H. Klotman, *Foundations of Music Education.* Reprinted with permission of Schirmer Books, a division of Macmillan, Inc. Copyright © 1984 by Schirmer Books.

in 1837 to observe how music was being taught in the schools. Convinced of the value of the Pestalozzian theory he observed in use there, he returned to America to begin teaching without pay in 1838 in the Boston public schools, hoping to incorporate music as a integral part of the curriculum. Because of his success, by the end of the year the school system employed him as the nation's first public school music teacher.

Mason believed that music contributed to the well-being of the individual: It united that person with God, created better homes, better citizens, and happier human beings. He deeply believed that everyone should enjoy music and that enjoyment could be achieved if children experienced a music education. Mason's strong convictions and dedicated effort prepared the American psyche to accept the tenet that "music is for everyone," not just for the so-called musically gifted, a belief that had been promoted for generations in the European culture. That every child should have an opportunity to study music in public school is still the most prominent tenet in American music education today.

Public school music received a big boost from the organization of normal schools, teacher-training institutions in the United States that served the profession for over sixty years. On July 3, 1839, the first state-supported teacher-training institution was opened in Lexington, Massachusetts. The first normal school building erected with state funds was constructed in 1846 at Bridgewater, Massachusetts. It was followed in 1848 by the Normal School of Philadelphia. By the latter part of the nineteenth century normal schools proliferated throughout the United States. After the turn of the century they ceased to be called normal schools and instead were called teachers colleges, and by the late twentieth century, almost all the teachers colleges had been granted university status.

The growth of public school music was slowed by the Civil War, but gained momentum after the war was over. The task of incorporating music into the curriculum of the schools was difficult because most school board members of that era still believed that music study should be reserved for the gifted. Evidently concerned parents and dedicated teachers prevailed because more and more schools added the study of vocal music on the elementary and secondary level to their curricula. The process was enhanced by increased activities of the choral societies, the formation of symphony orchestras throughout the country, the addition of music courses to the curricula of the institutions of higher learning, the emergence of community and professional bands nationwide, and a proliferation of various method booklets for all kinds of music instruction.

Recent Developments

After World War I, through the influence of John Dewey's emphasis on educating the whole child, public school music gained a more secure posture because the study of the arts was considered to be essential to produce a well-educated individual. The first half of the century saw tremendous growth in secondary education as a whole when the frequency of students attending senior high school increased from one in ten to three out of four. Since many of these students were planning to attend college, by 1940 seven out of ten senior high school students were involved in college preparatory programs that included music.

In fact, prior to World War II, school music programs grew so rapidly that there was insufficient trained personnel to meet the demand. Administrative officials turned for assistance to professional performing musicians who needed work due to the Depression and because their jobs in pit orchestras, theatre bands, and as organists were terminated when the silent movies were replaced by "talkies." This approach to hiring resulted in the music classroom experience becoming a rehearsal with emphasis on performance, a practice that is still prevalent today.

During World War II, because of such a strong emphasis on the war effort, trained music teaching personnel again became scarce. To alleviate the problem an attempt was made to provide the regular classroom teacher with sufficient skills to teach vocal music to the elementary students. Long after the war when the music specialists had returned, the practice prevailed of having the classroom teacher conduct music lessons on a daily basis with the music specialist acting as a consultant and/or appearing once or twice a week to introduce new skills. In many school systems even today, music professionals are still attempting to reestablish the position of music specialist in the elementary school as the prime source of music instruction.

In 1957 when the Soviets launched *Sputnik*, the United States became overly concerned with the pursuit of scientific knowledge. In an attempt to recover what was perceived to have been lost in the race for the moon, the U.S. government allocated much more money to the sciences than to the arts. The pursuit of excellence pervaded all disciplines, including music. Music educators took to the defensive to justify the place of quality music in the curriculum. They began to realize that people must be convinced of music's intrinsic aesthetic value, which is essential to humankind's well-being and which was not part of the curriculum just for the sake of performance, but because it was a fun activity or that it had admirable social benefits.

Fortunately, when an American was the first to stand on the moon, the inordinate concern for support of the sciences relaxed and a desire to educate the whole child was restored. In 1965 under President Lyndon Johnson's "Great Society" emphasis, Congress passed the Elementary-Secondary Education Act that provided renewed support for arts through cultural enrichment programs. During the 1960s, other events that strengthened the music education process occurred. These included the Contemporary Music Project for Creativity in Music Education, 1963 (a Ford Foundation and National Music Council project to place young composers in public school systems); the Yale Seminar, 1964 (a conference that ultimately recommended that the young people of America be exposed to what the conference considered to be as much "good" music as possible); the Manhattanville Music Curriculum Program, 1965 (students at all levels were given the opportunity to compose, perform, and analyze music to gain an understanding of music structure and process); and the Tanglewood Symposium, 1967 (a symposium of music educators, performing musicians, sociologists, labor leaders, scientists, educators, and representatives from corporations, foundations, and government that focused on the problems and potentials for music activities and musical development in American society).

Probably the single greatest contributor to the advancement of public school music (currently referred to as music education) over the years has been the Music Educators National Conference. The conference evolved from a parent organization, the Music Supervisors National Conference, which met for the first time April 10–12, 1907, in Keokuk, Iowa, at the Westminster Presbyterian Church. Initially, twenty-six music supervisors assembled to view a demonstration by the students of the Keokuk schools using the materials and teaching techniques of Philip C. Hayden, the music instructor. Although these supervisors attended annual meetings of the National Education Association (NEA), there was a feeling among some of those present, as a result of various informal discussions that were held while they were there, that it would be advantageous for them to convene on a regular basis to address problems related to music not specifically addressed by the NEA. From 1909 until 1926 the Music Supervisors National Conference met annually, and from 1926 until 1934 they met biennially with smaller regional meetings in the intervening year. The purpose of the meetings was to address problems in music education specifically, to hear and see new teaching techniques and materials, to promulgate new ideas to the profession as a whole, and generally to have a good time. In 1934 the organization broadened its perspective by changing its name to the Music Educators National Conference. The publication of *The Supervisors Bulletin* (their official magazine) began in 1914, changed its name to *Music Supervisors Journal* in 1916, and finally to *Music Educator's Journal* in 1934. In 1953 the organization added a second publication, the *Journal of Research in Music Education*.

Four important music educators from abroad have influenced music education in the United States in the latter part of the twentieth century: Emile Jaques-Dalcroze (actually Jaques-Dalcroze was introduced to the United States between 1910 and 1920 but only recently has received national attention), Carl Orff, Zoltán Kodály, and Shin'ichi Suzuki. None of the men was entirely original in developing his method of teaching, but all were able to focus international attention on their efforts. Jaques-Dalcroze developed a complex system of expression music through movement (eurhythmics); Orff emphasized the concept of creativity through a strong rhythmic base; Kodály centered in teaching musicianship (particularly rhythm and melody) through folk music and existing literature; and Suzuki stressed rote instruction, particularly at a young age, in learning to play the violin.

Abeles, Hoffer, and Klotman provide a fitting conclusion to this section when they say:

> The distinctive feature of music education in this country is that its programs are conceived and carried out in such a way they are designed to benefit all the children of each community. . . . It is the basic tenet of music education and its concern for each student that he or she may advance at a rate of speed consistent with his or her interest and ability.

Under the aegis of the American educational system music education was permitted to prosper and flourish in this country in a manner that has now become an exemplar for music training in schools throughout the world. This accomplishment has been the result of the combined forces of dedicated teachers, appropriate funding to permit installation of programs in schools, and finally establishment of realistic goals and objectives that enable the profession to make students informed and literate about music and the world around them. It is the ultimate goal of the profession that such individuals may participate in a musical society that is both vital and enlightened.[5]

THOUGHTS FOR CONTEMPLATION AND DISCUSSION

1. Do you think Pestalozzi affected the way you were taught to sing in choir? Why or why not?
2. Would choral music education in the United States be better or worse if we did not advocate that music is for everyone? Why or why not?
3. Would shaped notes (a different shape for each note of the diatonic scale) be a useful technique in teaching music literacy in our public schools today? Why or why not?
4. In your opinion, which of the choral pioneers of the a cappella tradition of the early twentieth century has influenced choral music in America the most? If you do not know enough about their techniques to form an opinion, ask your choral director's opinion and request an explanation.
5. In your opinion, which of the professional choral directors of this generation (Robert Shaw, Roger Wagner, Norman Luboff, Gregg Smith, or Dale Warland) has been the most influential on the choral technique used in your college/university choir? Why? Again, ask your choral director's opinion if you do not have one.
6. How have the American Choral Directors Association and the Music Educators National Conference affected your involvement in choral music education?

BIBLIOGRAPHY

CRAWFORD, RICHARD, and DAVID WARREN STEEL. "Singing School," *The New Grove Dictionary of American Music*, Vol. 4. New York: Grove's Dictionaries of Music, Inc., 1986.

ELLIS, ARTHUR K., JOHN J. COGAN, and KENNETH R. HOWEY, *Introduction to the Foundations of Education*. Englewood Cliffs, N.J.: Prentice-Hall, Inc., 1981.

HENRY, NELSON B., ed. *Basic Concepts in Music Education*. Chicago: The National Society for the Study of Education, 1958.

HUSTAD, DONALD P. *Jubilate! Church Music in the Evangelical Tradition*. Carol Stream, Ill.: Hope Publishing Company, 1981.

JOHNSTON, JAMES A., et al. *Introduction to the*

Foundations of American Education, 6th ed. Boston: Allyn and Bacon, Inc., 1985.

JONES, PERRY. "The History of Women's Liberation in Choral Music." *Choral Journal* 16, no. 6, 12–14.

KEENE, JAMES A. *A History of Music Education in the United States*. Hanover, N.H.: University Press of New England, 1982.

KEITH, EDMOND. *Christian Hymnody*. Nashville: Convention Press, 1956.

LEONHARD, CHARLES, and ROBERT W. HOUSE, *Foundations and Principles of Music Education*, 2d ed. New York: McGraw-Hill Book Co., 1972.

MARK, MICHAEL L. *Contemporary Music Educa-*

---

[5] Ibid., p. 26.

tion, 2d ed. New York: Schirmer Books, 1986.

ORNSTEIN, ALLAN C., and DANIEL U. LEVINE. *An Introduction to the Foundations of Education,* 3d ed. Boston: Houghton-Mifflin Co., 1985.

ROBINSON, RAY, and ALLEN WINOLD. *The Choral Experience.* New York: Harper's College Press, 1976.

ROSENSTIEL, LEONIE. "The New World," *Schirmer History of Music.* New York: Schirmer Books, 1982.

SMITH, JAMES G. "History of Choral Music," *The New Grove Dictionary of American Music,* Vol. 1. New York: Grove's Dictionaries of Music, Inc., 1986.

STEVENSON, ROBERT. *Protestant Church Music in America.* New York: W. W. Norton and Co., 1966.

SUNDERMAN, LLOYD FREDERICK. *Historical Foundations of Music Education in the United States.* Metuchen, N. J.: The Scarecrow Press, Inc., 1971.

3

Developing a Philosophical Basis for Teaching Choral Music

When I tell my students that we are going to study the philosophy of choral music, I often get a negative reaction. Many undergraduates think about philosophy as being the thought processes of great thinkers expressed in erudite language; therefore, the students expect to be unable to understand it when they read about it. Granted, much of the writing of great thinkers is difficult to understand. Luckily, most of those great thoughts have been studied, evaluated, and explained by writers of texts and service books in such a way that it becomes quite enjoyable to study them. It is usually easy to find great thought expressed in "everyday language."

Students who choose to go to graduate school will delve into the study of the philosophy of music education in detail. It is not within the purview of undergraduate study to deal with it extensively. An in-depth study of philosophy should be delayed until students have obtained some practical teaching experience. This is not to say that undergraduates should desist from deciding what they believe, nor is it to say that they should be inconsistent and unstructured about their beliefs. Due to their ability to think more deeply and creatively and because they have had experience teaching, most teachers' philosophies change as they get older, so graduate school seems to be the most appropriate time to give strong consideration to extensive study. For our purpose in this chapter, we are going to identify areas where you must decide exactly what you believe, take a brief look at relevant philosophical thought that affects music teaching, and then suggest ways of applying this philosophical

43

knowledge to choral music education to develop a philosophical foundation for effective teaching.

The study of philosophy should not be feared, and most of all, it should not be thought to be unimportant. The fact of the matter is that people have a philosophy about almost everything they do. Even young children and early adolescents have some type of philosophy of life. Usually it is manifest by innate reactions to situations. They do not know why they believe what they do and react the way they do, they just do. Their belief about and reaction to certain things is a result of genetic input combined with the experiences of their short lives. As they grow older, they are seemingly more greatly influenced by their life experiences and less by their genes.

You might feel, since you already have a philosophy pertaining to teaching choral music, that further study is not necessary. Thinking in that fashion is analogous to saying that since I like roast beef, it is not necessary for me to taste ice cream. You can go through life eating roast beef prepared in many different ways and brag about how fortunate you are to be able to enjoy roast beef provided in such culinary varieties. Since you have never tasted ice cream you do not know what you have missed. Those of us who have tasted roast beef and ice cream think you to be quite limited in your culinary experiences, particularly if the ice cream has been served in 101 different flavors. Before you realize it, not only will you be eating roast beef and ice cream but hamburgers and french fries as well. As your culinary experiences expand you might even learn to enjoy escargot and raw oysters.

The study of philosophy gives you some options. As a teacher you constantly make decisions and take actions based on those decisions. If your philosophy is limited, you may not be aware of the greater implications of those decisions nor how they will relate to future decisions. Keep in mind that your decisions as a teacher are far-reaching and they influence your students as well as yourself. If you have arrived at a comprehensive, systematic philosophy, it will serve as a guide for all your actions; then when frustrations and discouragements come (and believe me, they will come), your sound philosophy will carry you through.

Teachers who have taught for a few years often find that sharing knowledge is the easiest part of teaching. Motivating the students and getting them to react positively to that knowledge is the difficult part. Experienced teachers have found that the key to success in this matter is *consistency*. To be consistent you must have direction. A sound philosophy gives you direction.

Finally, one of the most important reasons that you need a definite philosophy is because you will constantly find it necessary to justify your position on curriculum, teaching techniques, after-hours rehearsals, contests, festivals, student teachers, or other aspects to students, parents, your supervisor of music, the principal, members of the board of education, and others. It has been almost 200 years since Lowell Mason established music as part of the curriculum in public schools, but today's teachers are still fighting the battle to keep it there. The most effective ammunition for the struggle is a strong, organized philosophy.

IDENTIFYING AREAS WHERE A STRONG PHILOSOPHY IS NEEDED

Before choral teachers take charge of their classes they should have given consideration to four basic questions to be secure in their teaching:

1. What shall I teach (subject matter and content)?
2. How shall I teach (methodology)?
3. How shall I treat my students, and how shall they treat me (student-teacher relationships)?
4. How shall I measure the students' progress (evaluation)?

Choral teachers also should be able to determine how they are going to relate to music itself. Here the pertinent questions are:

1. What is the meaning of music?
2. Why is music important to people?
3. What is good in music?

Before we can find answers to these questions, we must discover ways in which those who preceded us have dealt with them. Pertaining to the first four questions, we shall examine four established schools of philosophical thought and determine how they relate to educational philosophy. In dealing with the second set of questions, we shall examine past and current thinking in the field of aesthetic music education.

FOUR ESTABLISHED PHILOSOPHIES THAT RELATE TO CHORAL MUSIC EDUCATION

If contemporary philosophers were to read this section, they very likely might say, "Where has this author been for the last forty years?" because the philosophies discussed herein have not been in the mainstream of philosophical thinking for quite some time. However, since it takes several decades for philosophical trends to emerge and, further, since contemporary philosophy is so diversified, it is very difficult to give serious consideration to today's happenings until time allows them to amalgamate or the more dominant ones to spring forth. One must acknowledge further that from the understanding of basic philosophy has grown a number of modern educational philosophies (or theories), namely *essentialism, perennialism, progressivism, reconstructionism,* and *existentialism* (among others), the study of which is vital for all teachers.[1]

[1] Consider reading the following books to ascertain an understanding about these educational philosophies: (1) James A. Johnson et al., *Introduction to the Foundations of American Education,* 6th Ed. (Boston: Allyn and Bacon, Inc., 1985), pp. 368–391; (2) Allan C. Ornstein and Daniel U. Levine, *An Introduction to the Foundations of Education,* 3d ed. (Boston: Houghton Mifflin Co., 1985), pp. 184–214; and (3) Arthur K. Ellis, John J. Cogan, and Kenneth R. Howey, *Introduction to the Foundations of Education* (Englewood Cliffs, N.J.: Prentice-Hall, Inc., 1981), pp. 74–99.

It is not our purpose, however, to study these educational theories or philosophies per se, but rather to develop some philosophical basis that choral teachers might use to secure their teaching technique. I have chosen to do this by considering philosophical thought that is secure and well established, most of which has its roots in antiquity, and that which has proven the test of time by surviving in our society for generations.

Naturalism

Considered to be the oldest approach to occidental thought, naturalism can be traced back at least to the sixth century B.C. The leading proponents of naturalism are the Greek thinkers: Thales, Anaximander, and Anaximenes (sixth century B.C.); Leucippus and Democritis (fifth century B.C.); Epicurus (341–270 B.C.); Lucretius (96–55 B.C.?); and modern thinkers, such as Thomas Hobbes (1588–1679), Jean Jacques Rousseau (1712–1778), and Herbert Spencer (1820–1903). Simply put, advocates of naturalism contend that there is order in nature and that humankind can depend upon that order. The axiom that applies is "let nature take its course."

For the benefit of this study, educators who believe that naturalism is the proper approach to teaching believe:

1. Education should conform to the natural growth and mental development of the student.
2. Education should be pleasant and enjoyable.
3. Education should utilize a great deal of spontaneous self-directed activity by the students.
4. The acquisition of knowledge is an important part of education.
5. Education should include the body as well as the mind.
6. Learning should generalize from particular bits of information.
7. Punishments should be the result of natural consequences of doing the wrong thing, but the teacher should be sympathetic when this happens.[2]

Idealism

In the occidental world idealism, like naturalism, was conceived and developed in antiquity. Socrates (470?–399 B.C.) and Plato (427–347 B.C.) are the original thinkers and promulgators of idealism. Because both have their origins in antiquity, naturalism and idealism have always been interminable rivals in philosophy. Modern contributions to idealism include the writings of René Descartes (1596–1650), Baruch Spinoza (1632–1677), Gottfried Wilhelm von Leibniz (1646–1716), George Berkeley (1685–1753), Immanuel Kant (1724–1804), and Georg Hegel (1770–1831). Idealism is built upon the premise that reality is realized with the mind (an idea). Axiomatically, we associate "I think, therefore I am" with this thought process.

[2] J. Donald Butler, *Four Philosophies and Their Practice in Education and Religion* (New York: Harper and Brothers, 1951), pp. 100–103.

The teacher is central in the idealist's approach to education. Idealists believe that teachers should fulfill the following criteria if they are to be considered to be good teachers:

1. Teachers are the personification of reality for the students.
2. Teachers should be specialists in sharing information with the pupils.
3. Teachers should be excellent technicians.
4. Teachers should be the kind of people who command the respect of their pupils by virtue of who they themselves are.
5. Teachers should take a personal interest in the students.
6. Teachers should be people who awaken in the pupils the desire to learn.
7. Teachers should be masters at the art of living.
8. Teachers should be co-workers in the perfection of man.
9. Teachers should be ones who capably communicate the subject.
10. Teachers should be ones who appreciate the subject they teach.
11. Teachers who really teach are always learning simultaneously.
12. Teachers are apostles of progress.
13. Teachers should also be makers of democracies.
14. Good teachers should be a study in self-elimination.[3]

Realism

Even though the spirit of realism may be associated with Aristotle and traced through time to the present, as a calculated school of thought, it sprang from the twentieth century. Since there are many varieties of realism, it is difficult to establish a specific point of view. If one could find a common distinctive emphasis, it might be that most, if not all, realists agree that the idealist's approach to knowledge and the way the idealist determines reality is incorrect. Realists hold that life experiences are real autonomous facts of people's existence and are not changed by the thought processes (ideas) of any mind, finite or infinite. This world is a real world, not a world of an imagined fulfillment of notions. The mind is established in the body and is not affected by that which is beyond the perception of the senses. Truth is found through observation and scientific evidence. Realists are inordinately dependent on the expert (connoisseur) to determine what they consider to be great, real, or true. A modern-day maxim that could be applied to the realist's point of view might be, "What you see is what you get."

Until recently, it has been difficult to identify specific individuals as realists, yet great philosophers have lived who espoused the point of view of realism (along with other points of view) as it is defined today: Aristotle (384–322 B.C.), St. Thomas Aquinas (A.D. 1225?–1274), John Amos Comenius (1592–1670), René Descartes (1596–1650), Baruch Spinoza (1632–1677), John Locke (1632–1704), Immanuel Kant (1724–1804), Johann Friedrich Herbart (1776–1841), and William James (1842–1910).

[3] ibid., pp. 226–29.

In a nutshell, realists advocate these educational tenets:

1. The subject matter is important.
2. Teach what authorities deem to be important.
3. Having a direct experience with the material (such as performing it) is better than merely reading about it.
4. Specific information and skills necessary to function in society and in an area of work are important.
5. Whatever works in communicating the information to the students should be attempted.
6. Teachers have the responsibility of molding the students into productive and meaningful individuals.
7. Teachers, as in idealism, are important to the educational process. If they do not have the information, they should be able to tell the student where to go to find it.
8. Teachers rely heavily on testing and evaluation of the student.

Pragmatism

Pragmatism is a modern American philosophy; however, it too has its roots in the past. Its ancient roots may be traced back to Heraclitus (c. 540 B.C.) and to the Greek Sophists, Protagoras and Gorgias. Francis Bacon (1561–1626) and Auguste Comte (1798–1857) are considered pragmatic in their thinking. Traditional pragmatism as it is known today was established by the thoughts of Charles Sanders Peirce (1839–1914), William James (1842–1910), and John Dewey (1859–1952). Basically, pragmatists advocate the tenet that experience and scientific verification confirm reality and value in life. In applying an oversimplified understanding of pragmatism, one might say "that which works (that which is practical) is best."

Teachers who are pragmatists will approach education with the following tenets in mind:

1. Teach learning skills.
2. Know how to gather information.
3. Stress "how to learn" over "what to learn."
4. Apply what is taught (and learned) to life experiences.
5. Evaluate the success of what is learned or attempted, particularly in light of how it was achieved.
6. Be consistent.
7. Consider the students as individuals.

APPLYING THESE FOUR PHILOSOPHIES TO CHORAL MUSIC EDUCATION

To begin building a foundation for a strong philosophy of choral music education, let us apply the information delineated above to the four basic questions about the teaching process delineated at the beginning of this chapter.

What Shall I Teach?

Choice of music literature reaches the heart of the choral music education program. Since a large portion of the time is spent singing, choosing what to sing is vital. A good percentage of the director's time outside of class will be spent choosing music. What, then, is the criteria for choosing literature that best suits the program? Not all classes in a quality choral program will be choirs or singing classes. What shall be the choice of the other type of classes to be taught? Some of the choirs will be better than others. What type of training groups shall be established? What about general music or fine arts classes for all those students not interested in choral singing? What subject matter shall be taught in these nonchoral classes? These, and many others, are the questions that must be answered in dealing with the larger question: What shall I teach? How would a naturalist, idealist, realist, and pragmatist answer these questions?

Naturalists are very interested in pupil attitudes. They are not concerned with what is learned at a particular time. They believe that children learn best when they are interested in a subject. Therefore, teacher-prepared curriculum and courses find little favor with naturalists. Under these circumstances, directors with a naturalist bent would not be inclined to give serious attention to the type of music they select or the type of classes they teach. They would be more concerned with whether or not the students liked the class and if the students seemed to be learning anything (even though the teacher might not care exactly what was learned). The naturalists would probably choose music they thought the students would like to sing so that the students would have a positive attitude about class. They might even be inclined to allow the students to choose the music themselves. They would probably be inclined to recommend music that is simple and easy to sing, not complicated. Choral music classes would not be required; only those students who wanted to sing would be invited to do so. Music class would be strictly an elective.

Curriculum and course content are very important to idealists. They are eager for those aspects of music that are great and lasting to be learned. Much attention is given to the organization and planning of what the students are to learn. General knowledge is important to the idealist; therefore, general music and other arts curricula would receive priority consideration in scheduling. Music of master composers that has stood the test of time would be the staple literature for their choral classes. Music history, theory, and appreciation classes would be important. When working with specific selections, it would be important for idealists to teach those aspects of the music that have given it lasting quality: composer, form, historical period, theoretical aspects, the meaning of the text, and the piece's purpose in society. Their rehearsals and classroom responsibilities would be planned and organized well and initiated with precision. Lesson plans would be very important.

Curriculum and course content are also important to realists. They would function similarly to idealists except that they would depend on the connoisseur to establish the criteria for what should be taught. It would be important to them to know what literature and type of classes the best teachers in the district, state, and nation are teaching. Probably they would be diligent in attending all types of conventions and workshops to ascertain what the most highly recommended materials and methodology is.

Pragmatists emphasize the learning of how to acquire musical skills and gather information. More emphasis would be placed on "how to sing" rather than "what to sing." To pragmatists, having good musical experiences is the best type of learning, so the more time spent singing and performing the better. Pragmatists are also interested in the nonmusical outcomes of music study. Curriculum and course content might be similar to that of the idealists and realists, but the methodology in the classes could be significantly different. Pragmatists would choose literature that would help to solve vocal technique problems, build sight-reading skills, and teach good musicianship. They might also choose literature that would expose the student to a variety of styles, historical periods, and voicings with the idea of building a well-rounded individual, one who could contribute significantly to society as a whole.

How Shall I Teach?

Methodology is important to some and not so important to others. Generally, teachers' background and musical training are the greatest contributors to the development and use of their technical abilities, but their philosophical inclination can be influential. According to Butler, naturalists believe that the educational process should be enjoyable, should use spontaneous self-directed activity by the students, should emphasize the acquisition of knowledge, should teach through involving the body as well as the mind, and should use the inductive approach to learning where the students generalize from particular bits of information. Under these stipulations, the choral classroom would include learning and singing activities initiated by the students. Singing endeavors would include a great deal of body movement, perhaps the use of choralography or choreography. Songs and choral pieces might be analyzed through a process of allowing the students to rationalize concepts from specific facts shared by the instructor or, better still, gathered from other sources.

Naturalists tend to follow the student's natural maturation process; therefore, they would be very careful to consider the age of the student before they began to teach vocal technique. Probably, they would wait until after voice change when the voice began to mature before serious vocal study would be recommended. They might even be more prone to emphasize the natural singing quality of the voice and to discourage vocal study altogether.

Sight-reading skills probably would not be important to naturalists. They would be more apt to allow students to engage their innate music ability by attempting to read through nonstructured singing experiences. Their nonsinging classes would be of the "open classroom" format with emphasis on the natural curiosity of the student. The "discovery technique" of teaching would be accentuated. Folk dancing, eurhythmics, and other activities, such as those recommended by Emile Jaques-Dalcrose, that involve the entire body would be employed. Naturalists view themselves as "assistants," not as primary sources of information. Therefore, there probably would be no lecture classes; instead, great care would be given to devising classroom experiences that prompt learning through projects and hands-on undertakings.

Methods that are effective in achieving the learning of the material are the ones favored by idealists. The teacher is central in the idealist pattern of education, and self-realization is its ultimate aim. Much is taught through example set by the teacher. Dialogue is the principal methodology, and many questions that prompt thought are asked by the teacher. In some cases, lecture by the instructor is employed. Reading and studying are emphasized.

Obviously, idealist methodology is more easily applied to nonsinging classes such as music appreciation, music history, fine arts, music theory (to a degree), and general music (if it were a non-singing class, as it probably would be if an idealist were teaching it). In choral classes attention would be given to assuring that the student learned the material. Performances probably would be by memory as a result of the specific methods of memorization that are employed. Sight reading and vocal-choral techniques would be used to promote learning the material.

The philosophy of realism confirms the traditional conception that education is the acquisition of knowledge by the learner. Here again, realists are like idealists in their view of methodology. Whatever works in getting the material learned is favored. Realists, however, would be inclined to use tried-and-true methods of teaching. They would be inclined to use the same methods used by accepted masters of technique. They would look to their own choral teachers for advice. Workshops that feature well-known and established choral technicians would be frequented. Music supervisors of a realist propensity would bring in the nation's best teachers for their in-service training sessions. Master teachers are revered in the realists' world.

Since methodology is the central emphasis of pragmatists, teaching the students how to sing well would be of prime importance. Vocalises would dominate a good portion of the class period and polishing the literature might consume the remainder. Pragmatists are constantly looking for better methods and means of teaching. They feel that consistency is important to effective teaching; therefore, each rehearsal would unfold similarly and sequentially. Goals would be established and attained. The nonmusical reasons for being involved in choir or music class, such as espirit de corps, fellowship, good citizenship, developing a disciplined life, community service, and so forth, would be emphasized. To the pragmatist, being involved with singing is a lifelong pursuit with the idea that each year brings advancement.

How Shall I Treat My Students, and How Shall They Treat Me?

Good student-teacher relationships enhance the effectiveness of the teacher and the success of the student. Most good teachers respect and admire their students, and good students generally have a healthy regard for their teachers. How do the advocates of the various philosophies manage this important responsibility?

The activity of the student is most strongly emphasized in naturalism than in any other philosophy. Students and teachers work together as equals. The teacher is viewed as an enabler, not as a source of information. If at all possible, students design their own learning experiences and the teacher assists as the activities evolve. Ways are sought through student involvement to motivate the students, but control in the classroom, particularly with unmotivated students, is often difficult. Punishment should be the result of natural consequences of doing wrong, but the teacher should be sympathetic when this happens.

Student-teacher relationships are similar with idealism and realism. In both philosophies the teacher is the center of the learning process. The teacher and other prescribed sources (books, audiovisual aids, libraries, and so forth) provide the knowledge. Discipline is administered exactly so that students will learn. In realism, since the master teacher is so highly revered, every attempt is made to build a convincing respect and admiration for the teacher. In idealism, since the rational process is so highly revered, here again the teacher serves as the primary protagonist.

Pragmatists represent a compromise between the student-emphasized naturalists and the teacher-dominated realists and idealists. To pragmatists, since the learning process is so vitally important, both students and teachers are incorporated into the procedure. They believe that it is critical for students to be treated as individuals. They consider the influences (musical and nonmusical) on the individual that cause in each person to be treated as someone worthy of distinction and honor. Since learning is a lifelong process, each student must be molded into a seeker of knowledge in that student's own unique way. Giving the student the necessary skills to be a self-motivated learner is the ultimate goal of the pragmatist. Discipline (control over the individual) is considered by pragmatists, but it is not more important than the end result. They will use whatever means to reach their goal and if discipline interferes, it might be ignored.

How Shall I Measure the Students' Progress?

Choral teachers are often criticized for what is considered to be a weakness in employing structured methods to evaluate of their students. This stems from the fact that, to a degree, evaluation is innate in the choral process. If a student sings well or if a choir sounds good, obviously progress has been made. Therefore, in the eyes of some, formal evaluation is not necessary. Many believe, however, that a more in-depth understanding of exactly what has been learned is essential.

Naturalists are not very interested in evaluation of learning. Since goals and objectives often represent what society as a whole desires (naturalists have difficulty conforming to the needs of government and society), evaluation is not valuable to them. Evaluation (grading) encourages conformity and reduces individuality. Since learning is an individual matter, anything that diminishes personal interest is unsuitable.

Idealists are interested in evaluating students' progress. Although they might appraise the learning of precise information, internalizing knowledge that results in a change of behavior is more important to them. Students should have a "birds-eye view" of everything they learn.

Comparably, realists value evaluation except that they are more interested in the specific facts and skills. They believe that students must be able to function in society, so the more they know and the more competent they are, the better.

Because the process of learning is so important to pragmatists, they are most interested in evaluation. They are more concerned with testing to determine if students are acquiring learning skills rather than just knowing the facts. As mentioned earlier, teaching sight-reading skills and vocal technique would be very important to pragmatists.

AESTHETIC PHILOSOPHIES THAT RELATE TO CHORAL MUSIC EDUCATION

Before the process of building a strong foundation of choral music education philosophy is finished, critical information about the very nature of music itself must be covered. It will be difficult to develop a sound teaching philosophy if you do not have a thorough understanding about why music is important to people. Why do students enjoy singing? Why do people listen to music? Why does music intrigue people? What is the meaning of music? What is an aesthetic experience? Why should choral music be part of the curriculum? The answers to these questions are not easy to ascertain. Many books have been written that deal with the value of art in our society. Musicians have argued for years about the aesthetic experience: what it is, how to experience it, and why experiencing it is important when justifying the inclusion of choral music in the curriculum. It is to be hoped that these brief remarks will give you an insight, even if somewhat limited, to this intriguing subject. Most of all, perhaps they will help you to question your present understanding and challenge you to look at it in more detail.

Traditionally, people have viewed music from one of three perspectives: as *referentialists, formalists,* or *expressionists.*[4]

Referentialism

Referentialists believe that the value of music is found in the "references" beyond the music itself. Bennett Reimer explains the referentialist's point of view in this way:

The meaning and value of a work of art exist outside of the work itself. In order to find the art work's meaning you must go to the ideas, emotions, attitudes, events,

---

[4] Leonard B. Meyer, *Emotion and Meaning in Music* (Chicago: University of Chicago Press, 1956), pp. 1–6.

which the work refers you to in the world outside the art work. The function of the art work is to remind you of, or tell you about, or help you understand, or make you experience, something which is extra-artistic; that is, something which is outside the created thing and the artistic qualities which make it a created thing. In music, the sounds should serve as a reminder of, or a clue to, or a sign of something extra-musical; something separate from the sounds and what the sounds are doing. To the degree that the music is successful in referring you to a non-musical experience it is a successful piece of music. To the degree that the experience is an important or valuable one the music is itself important or valuable.[5]

Vocal music is popular with referentialists because the words communicate meaning that may or may not be enhanced by the music itself. In most cases they see the music as a vehicle for intensifying the meaning of the words. Others become involved with it because it makes them feel nostalgic, it brings back old memories. Most adolescents are referentialists because their involvement with music has strong social implications. They respond to it in the same fashion as their friends because it represents acceptance by their desired peer group.

Referentialists relate to instrumental music, too. Programmatic works designed to communicate extramusical meanings are important to them. Patriotic music is significant because it strengthens their love of country. Others like music because they desire to dance to it.

The message of the music does not always have to be so precise. It may express moods or suggest affective conditions. Deryck Cooke believes that specific feelings are communicated by various intervals and scales. To him, the minor second connotes "spiritless anguish"; the minor third, "stoic acceptance and tragedy"; the major third, "joy"; the sharp fourth, "devilish and inimical forces"; the major seventh, "violent longing"; the first five pitches of the ascending major scale, "an outgoing, active, assertive emotion of joy"; the first five pitches of an ascending minor scale, "an outgoing feeling of pain"; and the final five tones of a descending minor scale, "an incoming painful emotion, in a context of finality: acceptance of, or yielding to grief."[6] This interpretation of musical meaning represents the definitive referentialist's point of view.

Referentialists constitute the largest body of music lovers because it takes very little understanding about music to be able to relate to it in this fashion. For them, the study of music is not essential to enjoyment.

Formalism

A directly opposite point of view to the referentialists is that of the formalists, who believe that the meaning of the music is found entirely in the music itself. There are no extramusical meanings. They relate to the music because of the sounds. Edward Hanslick, the nineteenth-century aesthetician, writes: "Definite feelings and emotions are unsusceptible of being embodied in music. The ideas

---

[5] Bennett Reimer, *A Philosophy of Music Education*, 2d ed. (Englewood Cliffs, N.J.: Prentice-Hall, Inc., 1989), p. 15.

[6] Deryck Cooke, *The Language of Music* (London: Oxford University Press, 1959), pp. 90–133.

which a composer expresses are mainly and primarily of a purely musical one."[7] Clive Bell nails down the formalist's approach:

> . . . to appreciate a work of art we need bring with us nothing from life, no knowledge of its ideas and affairs, no familiarity with its emotions. Art transports us from the world of man's activity to a world of aesthetic exaltation. For a moment we are shut off from human interests; our anticipations and memories are arrested; we are lifted above the stream of life.[8]

Formalists approach music from an intellectual point of view. They believe that to really understand and appreciate music one must have studied it thoroughly. They find meaning in the tonal relations, form, rhythm, instrumentation, dynamics, structure, theoretical aspects, and so forth. University music professors in many cases are formalists. Music majors often begin study as referentialists and finish as formalists.

Expressionism

The third and most sophisticated approach to music is from the point of view of the expressionist. This approach is delineated in the writings of Suzanne Langer, John Dewey, Charles Leonhard, Bennett Reimer, and others. Expressionists relate musical experiences directly to ordinary life experiences. They believe that art symbolizes that which transpires in people's daily routine. To them, humans have a need to express these struggle-fulfillment activities (daily routine) in a subjective, indirect way, beyond the limitations of language; therefore, they express them through artistic endeavor.

Langer identifies the need to symbolize experience as a basic necessity distinctive to humankind and absent in other animals. She characterizes humans as symbol-making, symbol-using, symbol-responding creatures. To her, music is a symbol of human psychological processes and feelings.[9] She thinks of music as being the tonal analogue of emotive life.[10]

John Dewey believed that life experiences are ever changing as exemplified in the struggle-fulfillment comparison. ("One cannot step twice into the same river"—Heraclitus[11]). Dewey applied this philosophical precept to art by emphasizing that the basis for an aesthetic experience with music is established in the rhythm of ordinary creature existence:

> These biological commonplaces are something more than that; they reach to the roots of the esthetic in experience. The world is full of things that are indifferent and even

[7] Edward Hanslick, *The Beautiful in Music* translated by Gustav Cohen (Indianapolis: Liberal Arts Press, 1957), pp. 21 and 23.

[8] Clive Bell, *Art* (New York: G. P. Putnam's Sons, 1914), p. 25.

[9] Suzanne K. Langer, *Philosophy in a New Key* (Cambridge, Mass: Harvard University Press, 1942), p. 195.

[10] Suzanne K. Langer, *Feeling and Form* (New York: Charles Scribner's Sons, 1953), p. 27.

[11] Butler, *Four Philosophies*, p. 396.

hostile to life; the very processes by which life is maintained tend to throw it out of gear with its surroundings. Nevertheless, if life continues and if in continuing it expands, there is an overcoming of factors of opposition and conflict; there is a transformation of them into differential aspects of a higher powered and more significant life. The marvel of organized, of vital adaptation through expansion (instead of by contraction and passive accommodation) actually takes place. Here in germ are balance and harmony attained through rhythm. Equilibrium comes about not mechanically and inertly but out of, and because of, tension. Form is arrived at when a stable, even though moving, equilibrium is reached.[12]

As a person becomes more mature, the ability to relate to the expressionist's point of view becomes easier because experiences of tension and release, struggle and fulfillment, and the way they relate to music become more subtle and complex. The need to express these ordinary experiences through a symbolized artistic expression becomes more important. Undergraduate university students often have difficulty understanding this point of view because both the youth factor and the lack of oppressing life experiences serve as limiting determinants.

As a modified point of view, the *absolute expressionists,* championed by Bennett Reimer from Northwestern University, accept the formalists' contention that the value of music is in the music itself but reject their belief that the musical components are irrelevant to the rest of life. Absolute expressionists believe, as do the expressionists, that "the aesthetic components in a work of art are similar in quality to the quality inherent in all human experiences."[13]

Other Perspectives

Beyond the three traditional perspectives—referentialism, formalism, and expressionism—there are other reasons people love music. The factor that motivates many senior high school graduates to come to college to major in music is what Aaron Copland calls their "sensuous attraction to music."[14] This great attraction to music developed because of the experiences they had as music makers in senior high school choir, church choir, or other singing organizations. What is being described is the tingling of the spine, the cold chills, the rigor that ran through their body when their choir sang at its best. It is that feeling people get when they nudge a friend and say, "That sounds wonderful!" It is difficult to be a music lover and have never experienced it.

Once aspiring musicians develop acceptable singing technique, their love for music often becomes manifest in what is known as the *critical factor.* Singers become engrossed in admiration of flawless performances of soloists and choirs. Often they will listen for hours just to revere the singing technique and perfection of performance of their favorite singers or groups. Conversely, they often listen to criticize poor performances.

---

[12] John Dewey, *Art As Experience* (New York: Minton, Balch and Co., 1934), p. 14.

[13] Reimer, *A Philosophy of Music Education*, pp. 14–15.

[14] Aaron Copland, *What to Listen for in Music* (New York: McGraw-Hill Book Co., 1957), pp. 9–10.

The Aesthetic Experience

Finally, in attempting to develop a philosophy pertaining to the teaching of music, we need to contemplate the word *aesthetic*. What is an aesthetic experience? As a choral director, will you lead your students to relish aesthetic experiences? Will your audiences enjoy aesthetic experiences from listening to your groups perform? Most important, it is because of the aesthetic value of music that we justify its inclusion in the music curriculum. Therefore, if we do not fully understand about the "substance" and purpose of aesthetics in choral music education, we will never be able to rationalize and substantiate our reason for being music teachers.

Musicians, educators, and philosophers have disagreed about various aspects of aesthetics for quite some time. The definition of the word itself will vary according to the philosophical inclination of the one defining it. It is difficult to understand exactly what happens when one experiences an aesthetic occurrence. How does the feeling of an aesthetic experience differ from the feeling of a sensory experience; the feeling of a worship experience; the feeling of a sexual experience; or the feeling of loving something? Does it have to differ from these? Is there any sense of feeling at all? Does the quality of the art object or artistic endeavor with which one is involved affect the aesthetic experience? There are those who relate an aesthetic experience to the tingling of the spine or some other physical sensation that might occur while performing or listening to music. Is that an aesthetic experience?

Almost every author in the bibliography at the end of this chapter deals extensively with this subject. In their book *Foundations of Music Education*, Abeles, Hoffer, and Klotman delineate what they consider to be the characteristics of an aesthetic experience.[15] These should be food for thought for a more detailed investigation into this subject.

In most cases, people can agree that to have an aesthetic experience one must be involved with an art object or artistic endeavor. It is not necessary to agree upon exactly what is an art object (it might be a painting or sculpture for one, or a beautiful scene from a mountaintop for another) or artistic endeavor (this might be listening to a beautiful symphony for one, or making mud pies for another), but there must be something artistic present or occurring that initiates a response for one to have an aesthetic experience. With this thought in mind, we contemplate Abeles, Hoffer, and Klotman's reflections.

First, to them, an aesthetic experience has no practical or utilitarian purpose. (As Ralph Vaughn Williams once said, "Music is the most useless thing in the world; you can't eat it, sit on it, or make love to it."[16] He compared the common brick to a Schubert song and found the brick to have many more practical uses.)

Second, an aesthetic experience involves feelings. There is a response, no

[15] Harold F. Abeles, Charles R. Hoffer, and Robert H. Klotman, *Foundations of Music Education* (New York: Schirmer Books, 1984), pp. 63–65.

[16] G. Beglarian, *Comprehensive Musicianship: An Anthology of Evolving Thought* (Reston, Va.: Music Educators National Conference, 1971), p. 59.

matter how subtle, to what is seen or heard. The feeling may not be so strong that there is laughter or crying, but there will be some feeling present.

Third, an aesthetic experience involves the intellect. One must contemplate what is seen or heard. The mind has to be put into operation. It cannot be similar to the response of a person standing in a shower enjoying the water running over the skin but thinking about something else.

Fourth, an aesthetic experience involves a focus of attention. The person must concentrate on the work of art (visual or aural) to respond to it. A short stroll through an art gallery or working one's homework at a concert will not render a significant aesthetic experience.

Fifth, an aesthetic experience must be a firsthand encounter. Someone describing a painting or song to a person will not yield an aesthetic experience. Neither will listening to the last minute of a symphony.

Sixth, the result of aesthetic experiences is a richer and more meaningful life. The opposite of aesthetic might be considered to be "anesthetic," which means "nothingness, no life, no feeling, no humanness."[17]

Abeles, Hoffer, and Klotman also point out (1) that the quality of the aesthetic experience depends on the quality of both the object and the viewer or listener, (2) it is not limited to the intelligentsia or a special group of gifted persons, (3) one's cultural background influences conceptions of what is considered aesthetic, and (4) it is seldom a pure experience: All the previous experiences of an individual plus all the individual's inherent inclinations affect each experience.

It is also important to remember that the age of an individual affects each experience. Seemingly the older one gets, the less emotional and more intellectual is the content of each experience. Finally, and probably most important, the quality of the experience is more greatly enhanced as knowledge about the art object or artistic endeavor is increased. The more one knows, the greater the enjoyment.

Justifying Why Music Should Be Included in the Curriculum

With this understanding about the "substance" of an aesthetic experience, let us determine an answer to the question that affects music teachers most greatly. Why is it important for students to learn music?

In the recent past, music has been justified to be part of the curriculum mostly from a referentialist's point of view. Referentialists have indicated that music should be part of the curriculum because (1) it improves learning skills, (2) it strengthens moral character, (3) it fulfills various social needs, (4) it provides an outlet for repressed emotions, (5) it encourages self-discipline, (6) it is a good way to spend leisure time, (7) it helps to give focus to one's efforts, and (8) it improves health. Since almost all other disciplines also provide these same external rewards, over the last few decades many educators have come to realize that music should be justified because it is intrinsically music (it has aesthetic

---

[17] Abeles, Hoffer, and Klotman, *Foundations of Music Education*, pp. 62–63.

value). They have come to realize that there are contributions to life experiences that only music can make, and that is the reason music should be taught. From their perspective, that justification alone will assure its permanence in the overall school curriculum.

Charles Leonhard, a pioneer in the field of aesthetic music education, gives eleven practical reasons why the study of music is important, all based on the tenet of aesthetic education as justification for music teaching. Participation in the music program:

1. Inducts all students into a unique system of nonverbal symbols through which the noblest thoughts and feelings of human beings have been expressed and can be communicated.
2. Engages the imagination and creativity of all students and enables them to cultivate their imaginative potential that contributes greatly to the richness of living.
3. Enables all students to discover their level of musical talent.
4. Enables all students to develop their musical talent and musicianship to the highest possible level.
5. Reveals to all students the richness and breadth of our musical heritage.
6. Prepares people to participate meaningfully in the rites and rituals of the society.
7. Provides all students with the opportunity to develop resources for a rewarding personal life and for positive social interaction.
8. Provides a means to the development of self-confidence.
9. Provides a focus for disciplined effort.
10. Admits students to a creative mode by which they can enrich their lives through self-expression and response to the expression of others.
11. Enlivens the spirit of the students and the school as a whole.[18]

Paul Lehman, past president of the Music Educators National Conference, plainly says: "Music is intrinsically worthwhile. It needs no further justification. It is worth knowing. It is a field of study with its own special body of knowledge, skills, and ways of thinking. The study of music is valuable in itself. Every member of society should have the ability to perform, to create, and to listen to music with understanding. That basic rationale is simple and direct. And it ought to be sufficient."[19]

Often administrators who have control over the school's curriculum do not understand music's intrinsic value, however, so Lehman delineates several other reasons why the study of music is important to the school and to society:

1. The arts are an important part of our culture. Music is one of the most powerful, the most compelling, and the most glorious manifestations of our heritage.

[18] Charles Leonhard, *A Realistic Rationale for Teaching Music* (Reston, Va.: Music Educators National Conference, 1985), pp. 8–11.

[19] Paul R. Lehman, *Music in Today's Schools: Rationale and Commentary* (Reston, Va.: Music Educators National Conference, 1987), p. 8.

2. A primary function of attending school is to help individuals realize their full potential. Musical potential is one of the basic abilities that exists in every human being.

3. Music provides a much-needed outlet for creativity and self-expression. It enables us to express our noblest thoughts and feelings.

4. Music in the school provides an opportunity for success for some students who have difficulty with other aspects of the curriculum.

5. The study of music can help the student better understand the nature of humankind.

6. The study of music can increase the satisfaction that the student is able to derive from music and enable him or her to deal with more sophisticated and complex music. Formal study of music can sharpen one's perception, raise one's level of appreciation, and expand one's musical horizons.

7. Music is one of the most powerful and profound symbol systems that exists.

8. Much of the curriculum teaches implicitly that every important question has a right answer. On the other hand, living teaches that life is filled with ambiguities. Music and the other arts are different from the other basic disciplines of the curriculum in that they do not reflect a preoccupation with right answers and thus are nearer to true life experiences.

9. Music exalts the human experience. It enhances the quality of life. It transforms the human experience. It brings joy and pleasure to human beings in every society and in every culture.[20]

The Challenge

As a choral director your responsibility is to find suitable answers to the many questions delineated in this chapter, and they *do* need to be answered. Their answers will be part of your overall philosophy. Your degree of effectiveness as a teacher depends upon how completely you understand the answers to those questions. More important, your grounds for existence as a choral music educator might depend upon your finding the answers.

Following is my personal justification for why I teach music. Maybe it will be helpful as you ponder these things. Human beings are unique in the extent of their potential as individuals. They have physical, intellectual, ethical, religious, and aesthetic potentials. Past generations have understood this because they have emphasized the importance of exposure to all the liberal arts in which the many aspects of the human experience could be investigated and tantalized in an attempt to develop a truly educated person. In our age of specialization we have moved away from this approach in search of fame and fortune. We have become more concerned with going to a college or university to obtain a degree that will provide us with a license to make money. We may have lost sight of the true purpose of education.

People who are old enough to have developed the ability to engage in the "true art of living" have concentrated on developing the body for good health, the mind for intellectual gratification, moral and ethical standards for survival, religious understandings for justifying life, and aesthetic cognizance

---

[20] Ibid.; pp. 9–13.

for enrichment. If any of these potentials are neglected, they will not have attained their full stature as human beings.

I submit to you that it is your responsibility to provide a course of study that will help your students to begin to develop the aesthetic potential and specifically the choral music-making potential in their lives. Without this fully developed aesthetic potential, they will never realize total fulfillment in the human experience. They will never be able to be engrossed in the "true art of living." From my perspective, that should be your reason for being a teacher! That should be the reason why you teach choral music! And you have my permission to share these thoughts with your school administrators.

SUMMARY

The purpose of this chapter has been to help you as a choral teacher develop a teaching philosophy that will serve as a foundation for all you do. We took a brief look at each of four accepted and established philosophies: naturalism, idealism, realism, and pragmatism. Then we determined how each could affect one's philosophy of choral music education. We also examined traditional ways in which people view music: as referentialists, formalists, or expressionists. We looked at current thought pertaining to the meaning of music. Finally, we dealt briefly with the aesthetic experience and why music should be included in the curriculum.

The information contained herein is designed to "whet your appetite." As you engage in your daily teaching activities you will want to return to this chapter for inspiration. I hope you will find the need to investigate this entire area thoroughly, because I think you will determine, if you intend to be a master teacher, that you must begin with a strong teaching philosophy.

THOUGHTS FOR CONTEMPLATION AND DISCUSSION

1. Do you feel that it is useful for choral teachers to be familiar with the fundamental ideas of early philosophers? Why or why not?
2. Do you think that studying each of the four basic philosophical positions has helped you to establish your own philosophical base? If so, how? If not, why?
3. As a teacher, how will you answer the question, "Why is it important for students to learn choral music?" In other words, how are you personally going to justify your position on a secondary school faculty?
4. Does choral music make people more human? Is so, how? If not, why?
5. Do the words *aesthetic* and *beautiful* mean the same to you? Why or why not?
6. If you feel there is one, what is the difference in an aesthetic experience and an emotional experience? Sensual experience? Worship experience? Sexual experience? If you do not feel that there is a difference, how do you justify why you plan to teach choral music?
7. Can including choral music instruction in the schools be justified by its value to other academic disciplines? If so, how? If not, why?

8. Does a good choral program improve the attitude of the music students in other subjects? If so, how? If not, why?

BIBLIOGRAPHY

ABELES, HAROLD F., CHARLES R. HOFFER, and ROBERT H. KLOTMAN. *Foundations of Music Education.* New York: Schirmer Books, 1984.

BAKEWELL, CHARLES M. *Source Book in Ancient Philosophy,* rev. ed. New York: Charles Scribner's Sons, 1899.

BEGLARIAN, G. *Comprehensive Musicianship: an Anthology of Evolving Thought.* Reston, Va.: Music Educators National Conference, 1971.

BELL, CLIVE. *Art.* New York: G. P. Putnam's Sons, 1914.

BRUNER, J. S. *The Process of Education.* New York: Vintage Books, 1960.

———. *The Relevance of Education.* New York: W. W. Norton, 1971.

BUTLER, J. DONALD *Four Philosophies and Their Practice in Education and Religion,* 3d ed. New York: Harper and Brothers, 1968.

COMENIUS, JOHN AMOS. *The Great Didactic,* translated and edited by M. W. Keatinge, Part II. London: Adam and Charles Black, 1907.

COOKE, DERYCK. *The Language of Music.* London: Oxford University Press, 1959.

COPLAND, AARON. *What to Listen for in Music.* New York: McGraw-Hill Book Co., 1957.

DEWEY, JOHN. *Art as Experience.* New York: Minton, Balch and Co., 1934.

———. *Democracy and Education.* New York: Macmillan, 1916.

ELLIS, ARTHUR K., JOHN J. COGAN, and KENNETH R. HOWEY. *Introduction to the Foundations of Education.* Englewood Cliffs, N.J.: Prentice-Hall, Inc., 1981.

HANSLICK, EDWARD. *The Beautiful in Music,* translated by Gustav Cohen. Indianapolis: Liberal Arts Press, 1957.

HENRY, NELSON B., ed. *Basic Concepts in Music Education.* Chicago: The National Society for the Study of Education, 1958.

HOFFER, CHARLES R. *Introduction to Music Education.* Belmont, Calif.: Wadsworth Publishing, 1983.

JOHNSTON, JAMES A., et al. *Introduction to the Foundations of American Education,* 6th ed. Boston: Allyn and Bacon, Inc., 1985.

KOWELL, BONNIE C., ed. *Perspectives in Music Education, Source Book III,* Reston, Va.: Music Educators National Conference, 1966.

LANGER, SUZANNE. *Feeling and Form.* New York: Charles Scribner's Sons, 1953.

———. *Philosophy in a New Key.* Cambridge, Mass: Harvard University Press, 1942.

LEHMAN, PAUL R. *Music in Today's Schools: Rationale and Commentary.* Reston, Va.: Music Educators National Conference, 1987.

LEONHARD, CHARLES. *A Realistic Rationale for Teaching Music.* Reston, Va.: Music Educators National Conference, 1985.

LEONHARD, CHARLES, and ROBERT W. HOUSE. *Foundations and Principles of Music Education,* 2d ed. New York: McGraw-Hill Book Co., 1972.

MARK, MICHAEL L. *Contemporary Music Education,* 2d ed. New York: Schirmer Books, 1986.

MEYER, LEONARD B. *Emotion and Meaning in Music.* Chicago: University of Chicago Press, 1956.

ORNSTEIN, ALLAN C., and DANIEL U. LEVINE. *An Introduction to the Foundations of Education,* 3d ed. Boston: Houghton-Mifflin Co., 1985.

REIMER, BENNETT. *A Philosophy of Music Education,* 2d ed. Englewood Cliffs, N.J.: Prentice-Hall, Inc., 1989.

4

Applying Established Learning Theories to Choral Music Education

Years of research have gone into developing the theories of learning and other information contained in this chapter. What is more, a tremendous amount of information about how students learn music is completely ignored. There is also a wealth of knowledge yet to be determined. We are going to examine the contributions of many pioneers in this area, but it is not necessarily our purpose to determine how and why people learn music nor to study learning theory for the purpose of researching ways that people gain knowledge. It is our purpose to use this information as a springboard to evaluate and improve our ability to teach choral music to young singers. I have chosen these particular theories, many of which were researched and proven years ago, as points of reference in achieving our goal. Opportunities to be involved in studies that emphasize learning theories and current research in how and why students learn music will be available in graduate school or through individualized research. Since the early 1970s, Edwin Gordon, University of Iowa, has contributed significantly to the foundations established by Mursell, Seashore, Schoen, and others. Study about their contributions will have to wait for another time and place. The bibliography at the end of the chapter includes books that relate these many contributions.

To most of you, much of the information in this chapter may seem to be common sense, but what you will discover is that conjecture and speculation are removed from the teaching process when learning technique has been tested with research. No matter how gifted you are as a teacher, you probably will not have the ability to "sense" some of what you will understand from this information. Please do not minimize its importance.

The chapter deals with two major areas: (1) learning theory as applied to teaching technique and (2) motivation in the classroom. As you examine each of these areas, notice that we have attempted to promote clarification by applying most of the basic concepts to choral music or to a situation that might occur in the classroom. It is this feature that makes the study of learning theory relevant to choral music education. Without it, most of the information could be obtained by reading a basic educational psychology book. These applications appear in this type of bold print in the text. You may test your understanding of the learning theory as it is applied to choral music teaching by conjuring up a different application, concept or situation that might be exemplary of the same.

LEARNING THEORY

To attempt a brief résumé of these chosen learning theories is very risky business. For clear understanding, concepts as complex as these require extensive descriptions, definitions, and discussions that are not within the scope of a textbook such as this. However, if teachers are to comprehend how students learn choral music, the consideration of learning theory is important. To alleviate confusion, it might be beneficial for you to consult several of the sources in the chapter bibliography. A few extra hours invested in further clarification could pay valuable dividends once you reach the classroom.

Prevalently, among most learning theorists, *learning* is thought to be a change in people's behavior as a result of reacting with their environment. In school, learning is implied when students demonstrate knowledge and skills. A more formal definition is: "Learning is a highly general term for the relatively enduring change, in response to a task demand, that is induced directly by experience, or the process or processes whereby such change is brought about."[1]

How, then, do people learn? Finding the answer to that question has taken years of research and experimentation, and the process is ongoing. Educational psychologists use *theory* (a principle or generalization that explains phenomena) to establish an *hypothesis* (a theoretical statement designed to explain observed behavior) that they test in practical experiments to evaluate the validity of that theory. If the hypothesis proves valid, then the process of understanding how people learn has developed one step further. Basically, learning theory elucidates laws or principles that describe the conditions favorable for learning to occur.

Before World War II, learning theories were established on the findings obtained from experimental research with animals. Animals were used because it was easier to control the many variables that influence the learning process.

[1] H. B. English and A. C. English, *A Comprehensive Dictionary of Psychological and Psychoanalytical Terms* (New York: McKay Publishing Co., 1958), p. 289.

Since World War II, human subjects have been used because scientists are able to control those research variables more precisely. Interestingly enough, research using human subjects has verified much of the research originally done with animals. It has also provided in-depth understanding of the intricacy of human behavior and assisted educators to understand the learning process.

The Evolution of Learning Theory

Considerations about human behavior can be traced back to Socrates, Plato, and Aristotle. The Greeks perceived the mind to be similar to a muscle in the body that constantly requires exercise to remain healthy. They believed that the more the mind was used, the better people learned. To them, much of the intrinsic strength of an individual was centered in a healthy mind. The idea of the mind controlling the body was reinforced by St. Augustine (354–430) and St. Thomas Aquinas (1225–1274), who believed that disciplining the mind kept individuals from being evil. Jean Jacques Rousseau (1712–1778) and Heinrich Pestalozzi (1746–1827) promoted the tenet that people are free, have autonomy, are actively involved in their own development, and are responsible for the formation of their own potential. These notions about intrinsic mental strength have been a central concept pertaining to learning for over 2000 years.

Thomas Hobbes (1588–1679), John Locke (1632–1704), and other British empiricists believed that a proper environment was essential to learning. Knowledge was derived from life experiences, concepts and ideas were formulated, and learning occurred from reflecting on those experiences.

From Locke's reflections evolved the concept of *apperception* (relating newly learned information, skills, or feelings to existing ones), which was later developed and advanced by Johann Herbart (1776–1814). Herbart postulated two principles about learning: "the *principle of frequency*, which maintains that, the more often ideas enter the consciousness, the greater the chances of their remaining, and the *principle of association*, which holds that, when several ideas gather in the mind, their combined strength determines when they will enter consciousness."[2] Apperception (often called Herbartianism) was introduced by some American students who had studied in Europe in the 1890s. The theory subsequently spread throughout the United States and became important in teacher education. Some believe it to be the forerunner of stimulus-response psychology.

E. L. Thorndike (1874–1949) is considered to be the father of scientific experimentation in learning theory. In 1898 he began research with cats that showed the effect of a reward on a cat's behavior. His work proved there was a relationship or connection between a stimulus and a response (often referred to as S and R). *Stimulus-response learning* (the specific input of a response into the brain due to some external stimulation) holds a prominent position in learning theory today. *Associationists* (a term used to identify those who subscribe

---

[2] Hershel D. Thornburg, *Introduction to Educational Psychology* (St. Paul: West Publishing Co., 1984), p. 13.

to stimulus-response learning theory and technique) view learning as forming mental connections, developing habits, and changing behavior. Learning is perceived as combining elements in a cumulative or associative manner beginning with trial and error and building in a structured way toward complex behavior.

Approximately twenty years after Thorndike began his work, a German psychologist, Max Wertheimer, began to promote another theory he called the *Gestalt* (a configuration or pattern of a psychological phenomena that is a whole entity). Today, interpretations of this theory, in which are discussed mental procedures pertaining to perception, attitudes, and beliefs about people's environment, are called, collectively, *cognitive psychology* (the study of new patterns, knowledge, or ideas in dynamic and meaningful ways). *Cognitivists* (a term used to identify those who subscribe to cognitive learning theory and technique) view learning as a process of gaining insight. Learning is a process of reorganizing percepts and concepts and involves meaningful behavior of an individual in striving for a goal.

For years stimulus-response learning and cognitive learning were considered to be completely dissimilar, but certain modifications of the two systems, along with newer explanations about learning theory containing elements of both theories, have served to bring the two approaches closer together.

Stimulus-Response Learning

Various terms have been assigned to stimulus-response learning theory by different people, each contributing to the advancement of the theory as a whole. E. L. Thorndike used the term *connectionism* (the reinforced association of a stimulus and response in the mind). A Russian psychologist, Ivan P. Pavlov (1849–1936), and an American psychologist, J. B. Watson (1878–1958), are associated with the term *classical conditioning* (the substitution of a new, neutral stimulus for the stimulus that naturally elicits the response). Watson is also associated with the term *behaviorism* (change in behavior is indicative of learning). Edwin R. Guthrie (1886–1959) is most closely associated with the term *contiguity* (if two or more events occur in the same time frame, learning will result), but he actually extended the idea from premises of Pavlov and Watson. B. F. Skinner (1904–1990) contributed *operant conditioning* (response to the environment) as an outgrowth of the Thorndike tradition. Clark L. Hull (1884–1952) and Kenneth W. Spence (1907–1967) are associated with *reinforcement theory* (deals with habit as a factor in learning).

Thorndike's Connectionism   Connectionism is devoted to the association of stimulus and response and the factors that influence the making, retaining, and use of mental connections. Thorndike's theory emerged from his extensive and controlled study of animal behavior when he was a graduate student under William James at Harvard, the results of which were published in 1898 in a monograph entitled *Animal Intelligence* (actually this was Thorndike's graduate thesis). He determined that behavior which was, initially, trial and error through repetition appeared to be intentional. One of his experiments included placing cats in a box (he called it the "puzzle box") and observing their behavior as they attempted to free themselves to obtain food. At the beginning the cats might scratch, bite, claw, and move about as they attempted to escape. Eventually they would accidentally touch or move an escape mechanism that would allow them to obtain the food. With repeated observations, Thorndike discovered that the length of time it took the cats to free themselves to obtain the food decreased with each attempt. He deduced that the animals had "learned" to make the appropriate response. The cats had made the mental "connection" between the tripped mechanism and the food. As a result of his experimentation he formulated and refined numerous principles (or "laws") to explain how animals learn. Eventually these principles were extended to account for human learning in a three-volume series published in 1913 and 1914. The entire set is called *Educational Psychology* with volumes entitled *The Original Nature of Man* (Volume I), *The Psychology of Learning* (Volume II), and *Mental Work and Fatigue and Individual Differences and Their Causes* (Volume III). According to Thorndike, there are three major laws, the law of exercise, law of effect, and law of readiness, and several minor laws as discussed briefly in the following.

The first of these principles is what he called the *law of exercise* (repetition), which postulates that the more times a stimulus-response connection is repeated, the more apt it is to be repeated when the situation recurs. In other words, the more opportunities the cats had to trip the mechanism to escape the box, the more likely it was that the cats would trip the mechanism when the occasion presented itself. **The law of exercise is probably the most important law of learning applied to music. It simply means "practice makes perfect." Students are taught to sing correctly through practice.**

The law of exercise also includes Thorndike's minor principles of use (practice) and disuse. The *law of use* is in effect when a mental connection is made, such as in practice; it is more likely that response will be made again in the same situation. This is opposed to the *law of disuse*, which indicates that if a connection is not used, it will weaken and likely will not recur. If the cat is not allowed to continue tripping the mechanism, it will soon be unable to determine how to escape the box. **The law of disuse is the reason teachers have to spend several weeks at the beginning of the fall semester reviewing efforts practiced last spring. Over the summer, the students did not use what they learned; therefore, they lost part of their skills.**

His *law of effect* incorporates a pleasure and/or pain principle. If the connection is based on pleasure, then the connection is strengthened. If it is based on pain (annoyance), the connection is weakened. Reward results in repetition and learning, whereas punishment tends to reduce the likelihood of repetition and results in lack of learning. If, after the cats learned to trip the mechanism to obtain the food, they were to receive a slight electrical shock when they tripped the mechanism, they would more than likely choose to decrease the number of repetitions. **Simply stated, students tend to practice that which is a pleasure and avoid practicing that which is unpleasant. This is one of the reasons that students enjoy practicing some pieces more than others. With some selections they are not required to think, work, or put forth an exerted**

effort. With others, concentration is required. Naturally they choose to sing the easy ones over the difficult ones. Once the difficult ones are conquered, they might choose to sing them in preference to new ones that might be unknown.

The *law of readiness* is more physiological than psychological. It has to do with the biological readiness of a person's nervous system to provide connections between the stimulus and the response. In view of current knowledge about brain-behavior relationships, Thorndike's law of readiness is somewhat naïve. The law deals with the momentary readiness of "conduction units" in the nervous system to conduct neural impulses and the effects that this readiness can have on determining whether acts are experienced as satisfying or annoying. In other words, if people are annoyed, their nervous systems are not ready to respond. If they are satisfied, their nervous systems respond more eagerly. **This law can be applied to choral practice from the perspective that students learn more readily if they are mentally prepared to practice. If they are mentally annoyed, they learn less in practice than if they are mentally satisfied.**

Multiple response is a minor law pertaining to ways in which individuals initially respond in new situations. When first the cats were put into the puzzle box, they displayed a wide range of behaviors such as walking around the box, purring, scratching their ears, or rubbing and scratching at the wall. From this behavior Thorndike theorized that instead of persisting in only one response in a new situation, most people display multiple responses or varied reactions. The significance for learning lies in the possibility that each response preserves the opportunity for different connections to be strengthened if learning is to occur. **In the choral classroom, directors may choose several different methods of teaching rhythm, such as clapping, using rhythm syllables, counting, or speaking, each of which may be successful and may allow learning to occur.**

The *law of set or attitude* indicates that very little learning will occur unless the subject is disposed to learn. If the cats were tired or not particularly bothered by confinement in the box, they might not work very hard to get out. Therefore this law holds that people will act in any given situation in accordance with their "set," "attitude," or "determination" to make given responses. Students' energy level, motivations, and general determination will influence what responses are made, at least initially. **Teachers soon learn that there are days in which practice seems futile because of the circumstances of the hour, day, or season. It seems that there are times when students simply are not inclined to learn no matter how hard the teacher tries.**

The principle of *partial activity* is a response to the observation that some aspects of the learning situation may be more prominent than others and will elicit responses more readily. The cats did not always pay attention to every part of the box when they were put into it, and after a while certain influences of the situation seemed to be more significant in affecting their behavior. This law holds that a part of a situation may come to have special impact on people's behavior when they are involved in the situation. That part of the situation may become so predominant that some responses may become bound to the stimuli no matter what else is occurring in the situation. **If students become so intent** on learning one particular skill in a rehearsal (such as proper vowel formation), they might be unable to respond to other aspects of the rehearsal (such as producing a free, flowing tone). Intense concentration on one thing often closes the mind to other considerations.

Thorndike noted that current situations are not identical to those that perhaps occurred in the past, and yet people will use past experiences to confront new situations. His *law of assimilation or analogy* holds that, when confronted with a novel situation, subjects will respond similarly to situations they have encountered in the past. **When choristers are taught to sing Renaissance music stylistically correctly, they will use the same technique to sing Romantic music when first introduced to it. They soon learn that Romantic music does not sound well when sung in Renaissance style, and vice versa, therefore, they must develop different techniques to sing different styles correctly.**

Finally, in Thorndike's *law of associative shifting* he theorized that even complicated acts can be "shifted" from one stimulus to another without having the response disintegrate into its several parts. If the situation in which the cats were originally taught actually consisted of a combination of several stimuli, all of which were connected to a correct response, these stimuli can be phased out one at a time and replaced with new stimuli while maintaining the correct response throughout. **If students are taught to breathe correctly while standing with a raised thorax, straight back, and relaxed shoulders, they too can be taught to breathe correctly while lying of the floor in a fetal position with their knees tucked under them. Such might be the requirements while singing in a scene of an opera or musical. This can be achieved by replacing the standing position with each consecutive step of learning to breathe correctly while sitting, then kneeling, then lying on the back, and ultimately lying in the fetal position.**

In conclusion, Thorndike did not view learning in animals to be vastly different from learning in humans. Human learning still consists principally of selecting and strengthening connections. The basic difference lies in a lesser degree of specificity and increased responsiveness in human behavior. Human beings can react to a greater number of signals in various circumstances than animals can, resulting in a broader spectrum of learning experiences. A dog may not respond to an identical command when given by someone other than it's owner. A human, on the other hand, can learn to drive one car and continue the process when sitting behind the wheel of a different vehicle. In both cases, the behavior is habitual but the human's response is not controlled by the original training situation, as is the case with the animal.

Further, human beings are not as predisposed as animals to assimilate the whole of a situation indiscriminately, but are more apt to participate in selective learning of important factors. In order words, learning processes are more complex in humans than in animals. Thorndike believed, however, that it would not be possible to understand complex processes of humans if people did not understand the simple processes of animals.

Pavlov's Classical Conditioning   About the same time that Thorndike was researching animal behavior in the United States, Ivan P. Pavlov (1849–1936) began research with animals in Russia. He stumbled into stimulus-response research quite by accident. He had received the Nobel Prize in 1904 for his work with dogs in which he studied the effect of dog saliva on the digestive process. In the process of feeding the dogs to generate saliva for his experiments, he noticed, apparently strictly by happenstance, that the dogs, upon seeing the assistants who fed them enter the laboratory, would begin to salivate before the food was actually given to them to eat. They were reacting to a stimulus that was not physically present. He labeled the act of salivating when the food was present as an *unconditioned reflex* in that it was a natural reflex such that occurs when a blow on the patellar tendon results in a jerk of the lower leg or when the shining of a light in the eye results in pupil contraction. He labeled the act of salivating before the food was present as a *conditioned reflex*. In his research he would ring a bell each time the dogs were fed until eventually the dogs would salivate each time the bell rang, even though the food was not present. These experiments solidified his theory of classical conditioning.

In dealing with the relevance of Pavlov's classical conditioning with dogs to that of learning in the classroom, according to Snelbecker, three aspects should be considered:

First, Pavlov strongly felt that one should not lose sight of the fact that the investigator in natural sciences merely exposes nature to his view, and that he does not declare how natural (in this case, psychological) processes *should* operate.

Secondly, it was his contention that one can best discover the nature of complex learning processes by understanding first the most elementary forms of such processes. He considered the conditioned reflex to be a fundamental cortical reaction, and he viewed it as the most basic learning process.

Third, he visualized at least two ways in which the simple conditioned reflex could be extended to complex learning processes. A number of simple conditioned reflexes could be arranged sequentially in "chains" of stimulus-response associations to form more complex learning processes. Or, the concept of conditioned reflex could be used with words or speech (which Pavlov called the "second signal system") as well as with physical stimuli (the "primary signal system"). In his second extension, words are associated with other words through recognition of their meanings and the appropriate responses for them, similar to the way that Pavlov's dogs associated the salivating response with auditory and visual stimuli.[3]

Classical conditioning is evident in the choral classroom in the way that singers learn to read music with a structured system such as Tonic Sol-fa. In using the Curwen hand signs the singer learns to respond with the correct tone when shown the hand sign. Initially, the students must concentrate and, through the use of tonal memory, recall the pitches and assign them a name (*do, so, fa*, and so forth). In this fashion, the students are able to sing the correct pitches using the correct names. After several months of drill, however, the mental process changes. The singers no longer depend on tonal memory

[3] Glenn E. Snelbecker, *Learning Theory, Instructional Theory, and Psychoeducational Design* (New York: McGraw-Hill Book Co., 1974), pp. 69–70.

to recall the pitches. **They see the hand signs and the correct pitches and names emit from their mouths and voices almost completely as a reflex. They have learned to sing the pitch syllables in the same fashion that they learned to speak words and combine them into sentences. They do not have to recall or choose each word as they think; the words simply emerge as complete thoughts.**

People learn to type or to drive a car in the same fashion. These are conditioned reflexes applied to complex learning processes through *chaining* (as described previously in the quotation by Snelbecker). The students use Pavlov's *second signal system* in their conditioned response. **Later the students will be able to respond to reading the notes from the printed page using conditioned reflexes if they are drilled in the same fashion as they were when relating to the hand signs.**

One should not conclude a discussion of Pavlov's classical conditioning without looking briefly at the work of J. B. Watson (1878–1958), who was greatly influenced by Pavlov. Watson researched the behavior of rats as they ran through mazes. His best-known experiment, however, was carried out with an eleven-month-old infant named Albert. Watson applied Pavlov's classical conditioning "dog" experiment to a situation where he banged a hammer on a steel bar each time Albert reached to touch a white rat. In just over a week the child had been conditioned to cry and crawl away at the sight of the rat even though the rat had not threatened the child in any way.

Watson's conclusions led to the development of a branch of psychology commonly called *behaviorism*. According to Watson:

> Psychology as the behaviorist views it is a purely objective experimental branch of natural science. Its theoretical goal is the prediction and control of behavior. Introspection forms no essential part of its methods, nor is the scientific value of its data dependent upon the readiness with which they lend themselves to interpretation in terms of consciousness. The behaviorist, in his efforts to get a unitary scheme of animal response, recognizes no dividing line between man and brute. The behavior of man, with all its refinement and complexity, forms only a part of the behaviorist's total scheme of investigation.[4]

Watson believed that for psychology to be a science, its subject matter had to withstand the scrutiny imposed upon it by measured reliability. Explanations of behavior that involved mental processes were not allowed in the science of behaviorism since at that time they could not be measured. Introspection and talk of instinctive behavior and the human conscious or unconscious mind were forbidden. Since behavior is what can be observed, then behavior is what should be studied.

Similar to the rationale of John Locke (that the mind at birth is a blank piece of paper in which the world can write its impressions), Watson was an extreme believer in the influence of the environment over heredity in relating

---

[4] J. B. Watson, "Psychology as the Behaviorist Views It," *Psychological Review* (American Psychological Association, 1913), p. 158.

to the behavior of individuals. He believed that people are born with a few basic emotions (fear, rage, and love) and through classical conditioning these emotions (he called them reflexes) are paired with a variety of stimuli. He attempted to describe learning according to two basic principles: *frequency* and *recency*. The law of frequency is similar to Thorndike's law of exercise: The more frequently people respond to a stimulus, the more apt they will be to respond to that stimulus in the same fashion each time it is encountered. **This again reinforces the old adage, "Practice makes perfect."** The law of recency holds that the more recently a subject has made a response to a stimulus, the more apt that the response will recur. **A choral group will sing better if the performance comes soon after a rehearsal. This law also reinforces the need for a warm-up session before performance to refresh those responses that were learned in rehearsal.**

Guthrie's Contiguity Theory Edwin Ray Guthrie (1886–1959) was professor of psychology at the University of Washington from 1914 until his retirement in 1956. His *law of contiguity* served as the one principle on which he based all his theories about learning. He stated the law as follows: "A combination of stimuli which has accompanied a movement will on its recurrence tend to be followed by that movement."[5] In 1959 he revised the law to read: "What is being noticed becomes a signal for what is being done."[6] Simply stated, the law means that if people do something in a certain situation, the next time they are in that situation they tend to do the same thing. In reality, the law was not new with Guthrie since it can be traced back to Aristotle's law of association, but by accepting the law as a basic tenet, Guthrie devised an entire theory about how people learn.

Guthrie completely rejected the *law of frequency* (the strength of an association depends upon the number of times it has occurred) as endorsed in various ways by Pavlov, Thorndike, Skinner, and Hull. Guthrie said ". . . a stimulus pattern gains its full associative strength on the occasion of its *first pairing* with a response."[7] To him, learning was the result of contiguity (from the word *contiguous* which means "touching, near, or adjoining"[8]) between a pattern of stimulation and a response, and learning is complete (the association is at full strength) after only *one* pairing between the stimulus and the response. This "one-trial learning" depends on what Guthrie called the *recency* principle that we encountered in a slightly different form with Thorndike and Watson. The recency principle infers that whatever was done last in a situation is apt to be what people will do again in that same situation.

[5] E. R. Guthrie, *The Psychology of Learning*, revised edition (New York: Harper and Row, 1952), p. 23.

[6] E. R. Guthrie, "Association by Contiguity," in *Psychology: a Study of a Science*, Vol. 2, edited by S. Kock (New York: McGraw-Hill, Book Co., 1959), p. 186.

[7] E. R. Guthrie, "Conditioning: A Theory of Learning in Terms of Stimulus, Response, and Association," *The Psychology of Learning*, edited by N. B. Henry (Chicago: University of Chicago Press, 1942), p. 30.

[8] *Webster's New Collegiate Dictionary* (Springfield, Mass.: G. & C. Merriam Co., 1956), p. 180.

Since he rejected the law of frequency, which is the basic justification by other learning theorists for progress made as a result of practice, under the law of contiguity, how did Guthrie explain the "progress through practice" phenomenon? He used the idea of *chaining* as described in the discussion of Pavlov's classical conditioning and applied it differently. He said that pairing between a stimulus and a response results in *movement-produced stimuli* that are caused by the movements of the body. He explained it this way:

> When the telephone rings we rise and make our way to the instrument. Long before we have reached the telephone the sound has ceased to act as a stimulus. We are kept in action by the stimuli from our movements toward the telephone. One movement starts another, then a third a fourth, and so on. Our movements form series, very often stereotyped in the form of habits. These movements and their movement-produced stimuli make possible a far-reaching extension of association or conditioning.[9]

Movement-produced stimuli are combined to result in *acts* such as typing a letter, playing a piano, singing a song, reading a book, or throwing a ball. Ultimately these acts combine to produce a skill. **Singing is an act. Singing "Il Mio Tesoro" from *Don Giovanni* on the stage of the Metropolitan Opera is a skill.** In other words, the act of singing is just a result of combined movement-produced stimuli, but the art of singing developed from years of training is a skill that results from combining several different acts. That skill is influenced by the law of recency because each time singers practice, they are able to associate the responses (and acts) from the previous practice sessions. It is Guthrie's law of recency that supports the importance of *daily* practice. Associations are weakened when days lapse between practice sessions. They are strengthened when practice occurs on a regular basis at established times.

In the singing process, students often practice incorrectly and make the wrong associations. They learn to sing incorrectly. It then becomes necessary to "unlearn" or "break the habit." According to Guthrie, a habit is a response that has been associated with a large number of stimuli. In other words, people do something the same way time and time again until it becomes standard procedure. To break a habit, according to Guthrie, the cue that triggers a negative association must be found and replaced with a cue that triggers the correct association. The difficulty lies in finding the responsible cues that, in many bad habit systems, are extremely numerous. **If singers are producing a thin, anemic tone as a result of singing in that fashion for a period of years, the director must find the association cues that lead to that type sound. The causes might be numerous: poor breathing, poor posture, poor self-image, lack of energy, lack of interest in singing, poor singing role models, or the way the family and friends view singing, among many. Any one of these has a multitude of negative association cues that must be found to improve the tone.**

[9] E. R. Guthrie, *The Psychology of Learning*, p. 54.

Guthrie offers three ways to change behavior: (1) the *threshold method*, (2) the *fatigue method*, and (3) the *incompatible response* method. In the threshold method, individuals are introduced to a stimulus at such a low level that it will not cause a response. The intensity of the stimulus is increased but is kept beneath the threshold of response. He indicates that members of a family often use the threshold method in dealing with their housemates. If a mother wants her daughter to attend an expensive college, the idea is gently introduced to the father. The mother might first mention the college's advantages without directly confronting the issue, or she might criticize the father's choice of a school, at first so mildly that it will not trigger a defense. The mother prepares the father so that when the question is finally discussed, he does not make a scene over the expense. By the time he is familiar with the idea, there is no violent reaction.[10] **If choral directors decide that a thin, anemic tone is the result of poor images the singers have of themselves (they may not think of themselves as being good singers), they can choose the threshold method to begin to change those images, without the singers realizing it, by subtly pointing out the positive aspects of their personalities and praising them when they respond positively to the directors' teaching.**

The fatigue method can be explained in this way:

> To break a dog of the habit of chasing chickens, all you have to do is to tie a chicken around the dog's neck and let it run around and try to get rid of it. When the dog eventually becomes fatigued it will be doing something other than chasing in the presence of the chicken. The chicken has then become a cue for doing something other than chasing.[11]

The most obvious use of the fatigue method is in choral classroom when students do not desire to learn new literature. Directors can practice on the old literature so diligently and redundantly that the singers will implore them to be allowed to sing the new literature. The fatigue method is automatically effectuated immediately following regional and state choral contests when it has taken several months of practicing the same music to prepare for the events.

The third method of changing behavior is called the incompatible response method. Hergenhahn explains:

> With this method, the stimuli for the undesired response are presented along with other stimuli that produce a response which is incompatible with the undesired response. For example, a young child receives a panda bear as a gift, and the first reaction is fear and avoidance. On the other hand, the child's mother elicits a warm relaxed feeling in the child. Using the incompatible response method, you would pair the mother and the panda bear; hopefully the mother will be the dominant stimulus. If she is the dominant stimulus, the child's reaction to the mother-panda bear

---

[10] E. R. Guthrie, *The Psychology of Human Conflict* (New York: Harper and Row, 1938), pp. 60–61.

[11] B. R. Hergenhahn, *An Introduction to Theories of Learning*, 2d. ed. (Englewood Cliffs, N.J.: Prentice-Hall, Inc., 1982), p. 208.

combination will be one of relaxation. Once this reaction has been elicited in the presence of the bear, the bear can be presented alone and it will produce relaxation in the child.[12]

If singers produce thin, anemic tones because they do not like the sound of full, resonant tones, in using the incompatible response method to change their behavior directors should bring to rehearsals a role model the singers admire who produces a full resonant tone. If the singers admire that role model enough, they will also admire the full, resonant tone and desire to produce it.

Punishment is considered by some to be a controversial method of motivation. According to Hergenhahn, Guthrie believed that punishment works in changing behavior, not because of the pain experienced by individuals but because it changes the way people respond to certain stimuli. However, if it is not applied intelligently, the result may not be that which is desired. He used the example of the dog who chases cars. To restrain the dog from chasing cars, the driver should reach out and slap the dog on the nose as it is chasing. This punishment is likely to be effective. If, on the other hand, the driver reaches out and slaps the dog on the rear, the punishment is apt to be ineffective. Both slaps are equally painful, but the slap on the nose tends to make the dog stop and jump backward, whereas the slap on the rear encourages it to continue forward.[13] **In the singing process, some singers who are scolded because they are singing incorrectly might take the scolding as a challenge to improve. They view themselves as good singers and good singers should not sing poorly. Others singers, because they view themselves to be inadequate, may sing even worse as a result of the scolding because they feel that there is no hope for improvement.**

Guthrie maintained that if children learn to add two plus two at the chalkboard, there is no guarantee that they are going to know how to add two plus two when they return to their seats. He advised that people should practice the exact behaviors demanded of them under the same conditions in which they are going to be tested or evaluated. This strengthens the association between the stimulus and the response. **Choral directors should rehearse as much as possible in the performance hall if they expect their singers to respond identically in performance as they do in rehearsal.**

B. F. Skinner's Operant Conditioning   Considered by many to be the most influential psychologist of his time, Burrhus Frederic Skinner (1904–90) almost missed making his contributions to learning theory altogether. Under the influence of Robert Frost, the great American poet, Skinner decided that writing would be his chosen career. After authoring his first book and experiencing great frustration in his efforts to write, to the extent that he considered seeing a psychiatrist, he enrolled in Harvard University to study psychology. Skinner

[12] Ibid., p. 209.
[13] Ibid., p. 211.

taught psychology at the University of Minnesota (1936–1945) and Indiana University (1945–1948) before settling at Harvard to complete his career.

Taking his lead from Thorndike, Skinner developed what is known as *operant conditioning*. It grew out of his defining two types of behavior: (1) *respondent behavior*, elicited by a known stimulus (such as jerking of one's hand when stuck by a pin) and *operant behavior*, which is not elicited by a known stimulus but simply emitted by the organism (standing up and walking around or moving one's arms or legs arbitrarily).

Since Pavlov before him and several of those who came after him explored and developed classical conditioning as it is related to respondent behavior, Skinner focused on operant behavior out of which grew his ideas pertaining to operant conditioning. Two basic ideas govern operant conditioning. The first is that any response followed by a reward (Skinner called the reward a *reinforcer*) tends to be repeated. The second is that anything that increases the rate (speed of the frequency) of a response is considered to be a reward. The evidence of a change in behavior is the best test in determining if learning has occurred.

A *reinforcer* is any event or stimulus that increases the likelihood of learning (positive change in behavior). *Primary reinforcers* are those stimuli that are able to reinforce behavior without a person having had any previous experience with them. Primary reinforcers are food, water, sex, or acts of self-preservation. These are strong motivators in change of behavior in laboratory animals but are not nearly so powerful in the learning processes of humans. *Secondary reinforcers* such as acceptance, praise, privileges, money, and grades are much more important in promoting human learning. A *positive reinforcer* is any event that follows a response that is satisfying to the individual and increases the likelihood of the behavior (response) recurring. A *negative reinforcer* is the removal of an event that is perceived as annoying thus increasing the probability of a response recurring. In this case, negative is not the opposite of positive because both result in increasing the probability of behavior recurring. Positive and negative reinforcers are just two different ways to promote the prospect of a response recurring.

These concepts may be illustrated in the following two scenarios. In the first scenario, a teacher is standing before a classroom of choral students flashing the Curwen hand signs as the class responds to her requests by singing in unison her choice of different pitches. Each time the class sings the tones correctly the teacher praises their achievement. Each time they sing the tones incorrectly, the teacher sings them correctly for the students and then drills them further with the hand signs as they sing the pitches. In the second scenario, singers in a choral classroom have been drilling sight-reading skills that involve learning to sing different pitches. To provide an opportunity for individual singers to display their sight-reading skills, the teacher decides to divide the class into two teams ("The Kings" and "The Emperors"). The Kings line up on one side of the room and The Emperors on the other. In the fashion of a "spelling bee," using the Curwen hand signs, the teacher requests the students (one at a time) to sing two pitches (using the pitch syllable names) chosen from the tones that the students have been drilling. Each time the

tones are sung correctly, the team of which the singer is a member receives a mark on the chalkboard. Each time the tones are sung incorrectly, one mark is erased. As the game progresses the teacher adds more pitches and varies the order. After each student has had an opportunity to sing a preestablished number of times, the team with the most marks wins.

Some of Skinner's operant conditioning concepts may have been applied in the first scenario, but they have been applied more effectively in the second. Consider the two basic ideas governing operant conditioning. The first idea is that any response following a reward tends to be repeated. In the first scenario, each time the class sang the correct pitches, the teacher praised them (reward); thus the chances of their singing them correctly a second time were enhanced. In the second scenario, the reward was in receiving a mark on the board and winning the game; therefore, the motivation for learning is more intense (individual performance and competition), resulting in greater concentration on the part of each individual. Learning is more likely to occur when individuals focus their attention to a given task.

The second idea is that anything that increases the rate of a response is considered to be a reward. In both examples there were numerous rewards that promoted learning: praise, self-satisfaction, hearing one's own singing voice, competition, winning, and singing the interval correctly, to name a few. All these are examples of secondary reinforcers that Skinner believed to be the most influential on human learning.

Reinforcement Theory of Clark Hull and Kenneth Spence   One of the most prominent learning theorists during the first half of the twentieth century was Clark Hull, who was associated with Yale University most of his career. Hull radically changed the study of learning theory because he was the first to attempt to apply extensive scientific theory to the study of a complicated psychological phenomenon. He used Thorndike's law of effect as the basis for what he called *reinforcement theory* (often referred to as *drive theory*). His system centered on *habit* as the basic response in learning and changing behavior. He rejected Guthrie's idea of continuity or "one-trial" learning theory. Due to the scientific nature of Hull's work, it is not within in the scope of this chapter to describe it in detail. One of his contributions, however, is *primary reinforcement*, which is basically a restatement of Thorndike's law of effect. In Hull's primary reinforcement theory, reinforcers, which he specified as reducers of a *drive* (a basic psychological need), strengthen the stimulus-response behaviors they accompany.[14] Hull's concept of drive is summarized best by Donald A. Hodges:

> Drive, most simply, is an hypothesized state of arousal of the organism as a result of the presence of stimuli. Primary drives would result from deprivation, from unsatisfied physiological needs of hunger, thirst, sexual needs, or pain avoidance. Secondary drives would result from the presence of stimuli which have, through the learning

[14] C. L. Hull, *Principles of Behavior* (New York: Appleton Century Crofts, 1943), p. 223.

process, acquired drive strength and might include praise or material rewards. Drive, then is an activated state (temporary or prolonged) of the organism as a result of stimuli, these stimuli existing as a result of needs of the organism. Learning comes about as a result of reinforcement (both primary and secondary) and is explained in terms of drive reduction. If a response results in a reduction of drive or is associated in time with drive reduction, that response will likely be repeated and learned. Drive, then serves two functions—an energizing or activating function, and a source of reward when reduced. . . . It is not necessary that all drives be totally removed or reinforced for learning to occur. Partial drive reduction or reinforcement may occur and partial (or percentage in Hull's terms) learning may occur.[15]

Risking extreme oversimplification, one might say, according to Hull's principle of primary reinforcement, that learning occurs as a result of satisfying an intense urge, longing, or desire (drive) to accomplish a need. **Peer acceptance, individual recognition, the desire to be part of an excellent choir, and the need to please are all very strong adolescent drives. Choral teachers should realize that students have these needs or desires (drives), determine exactly which ones are the strongest with each individual, and use them to facilitate learning.**

A second principle is referred to as *habit-family hierarchy*. Hull viewed people as being born with a set of inherent habits that vary in their potential to occur. His hierarchy is the ranking of the responses by their greatest likelihood to occur. In other words, the stronger the drive and the more apt that a specific response will reduce it, the higher the response ranks on the hierarchy. **Master teachers, through personal encounters with their students, should be able to determine many of these "inherited priorities" in their students' lives and use them as motivative factors to enhance learning.**

Reinforcement theory was strengthened by the work of Kenneth Spence, a contemporary to Hull and his best-known student. The two have been connected because of the close association of their ideas and the influence they had on each other. Spence was a major spokesman for Hullian theory after Hull's death but later made several radical changes, and in doing so he created a learning theory that was basically his own.

Gestalt-Cognitive Learning

As mentioned previously, in 1912 Max Wertheimer (1880–1943) began his work on what became known as the *Gestalt* theory of psychology, which was extended by Kurt Koffka (1886–1941) and Wolfgang Köhler (1887–1967). Their work established a thought process that evolved into what has become known in education circles as cognitive learning theory. Current theories as exemplified by *discovery learning* of Jerome Bruner (1915–   ), *cognitive psychology* of David Paul Ausubel (1918–   ), and *information processing* of John Bransford complete the evolutionary process.

---

[15] Donald A. Hodges, ed., *Handbook of Music Psychology* (Dubuque, Iowa: Kendall/Hunt Publishing Co., 1980), p. 246.

The Gestalt Theories of Max Wertheimer, Kurt Koffka, and Wolfgang Köhler Although Max Wertheimer is considered to be the founder of Gestalt psychology, from the very beginning he worked closely with two men, Kurt Koffka and Wolfgang Köhler, who are considered by some to be the cofounders of the concept. All three men made significant and unique contributions to the Gestalt approach to psychology.

An event that occurred while Wertheimer was riding on a train on his way to the Rhineland for vacation evidently served to launch the movement. He observed that two lights blinking on and off at a certain rate gave the impression that one light was moving back and forth. He was so intrigued by the idea that he left the train, bought a toy stroboscope, and conducted numerous simple experiments in his hotel room. There, in his room, he authenticated the idea that had occurred to him on the train that if the eye sees something in a certain way, one perceives the illusion of motion. This illusion became known as the *phi phenomenon*, which was the basis for much of Wertheimer's research. The focal point of the idea is that, to Wertheimer, the mind perceives a situation as a whole and not as a sum of its parts. The sensation of motion could not be explained by analyzing each of the two lights flashing on and off; somehow the experience of motion emerged from the combination of the elements. Wertheimer objected to the breaking of thoughts into parts. He, along with Koffka, insisted that thinking consisted of whole, meaningful perceptions and not of a collection of associated images. Therefore, Gestaltists believe that in perception people add "something" to an experience that is not contained in the basic sensory data, and that "something" is organization (the German term for organization is *gestalt*). **When students sing a melody, they do not perceive it as a group of isolated notes but as a musical thought (as a whole).** In opposition to stimulus-response psychologists, who attempt to isolate the elements of thought that they believe are combined to produce complex mental experiences, the motto of the Gestaltists has become "to dissect is to distort."[16]

Wertheimer and Koffka arrived at six primary laws of organization that explain how perception operates. The *law of proximity* states that objects grouped together tend to be perceived as a unit **(four sixteenth notes beamed together)**. The *law of simplicity* indicates the tendency to perceive a group of objects as being organized in the smallest possible collection **(in a song of eight measures containing two four-measure phrases, there are four beats in a measure with two pulses for each beat)**. The *law of inclusiveness* declares that the object most likely to be seen is the one that includes the greatest number of stimuli. For instance, if a smaller figure is camouflaged within a larger one, people have a tendency to perceive the larger of the two **(beginning music readers often do not notice a dot beside a note, but they seldom fail to notice the note itself)**. The *law of common direction* asserts that there is a tendency for objects to be perceived as groups if they somehow exhibit a similar direction or an orderly series of events **(the musical sequence is exemplary)**. The *law of similarity* indicates that objects of similar features (shape, color, size) will likely be grouped

---

[16] Hergenhahn, *An Intro to the Theories of Learning*, p. 245.

together (**cue-sized notes are used by engravers to indicate reduced vocal scores that are to be played by the piano, whereas regular-sized notes are used for vocal scores that are to be sung by the singers**). The *law of closure* states that the more thoroughly something is perceived, the more apt it is to be considered complete. **In most cases, for a melody to be considered complete, it must have a cadence. If that cadence is a half cadence, the melody is perceived to be incomplete and something more is expected to follow. If it is a perfect authentic cadence, the law of closure takes effect: the melody is most assuredly complete.**

Köhler added to these six laws the idea of *insight*, which is a sudden awareness of relationships between objects or ideas that seemingly were unrelated. Insight is often called the "aha!" or the "eureka" phenomenon.[17] He developed this idea from his work with apes in which he placed two boxes in a cage with bananas hanging out of the reach of the animals. Eventually, the apes had the "insight" to place the boxes on top of each other and stand on them to reach the bananas. **The best musical example of insight is the observation of how much better a choral group is able to sight-read a piece of music if they have heard a recording of the piece before attempting to sight-read it.**

Gestalt psychology concludes that **it is more helpful for directors to present a new choral piece in its entirety when students are encountering it for the first time.** Gestaltists believe that students will have more success with a piece if they perceive the work as a whole before attempting to dissect its many parts. **If teachers will sing and/or play a piece on the piano, play a recording of the piece, or have the best sight readers read completely through it, the more insight the students will have as they attempt to learn it.**

Jerome Bruner's Discovery Learning   *Discovery learning* was first introduced by John Dewey, who emphasized learning by doing. He believed it was important that students solve as many of their own problems as possible by examining several possibilities and choosing the best solution. According to Bruner, effective learning occurs when students procure a basic understanding of a subject and see it as a related whole. They gain this understanding by building concepts, coding information, forming generalizations, and seeing relationships between things. As students internalize the basics of a subject, they begin to understand its governing concepts and rules. At that point they are able to solve problems and investigate the subject more thoroughly, ultimately creating new ideas and ways of doing things. **A musical example of this concept is illustrated by students' ability to learn the basic equivalencies of notation (four quarter notes equal two half notes). Once these are understood they are able to determine why all measures contain the proper number of beats.**

Jerome Bruner believes that information is demonstrated at three levels of complexity: (1) *enactive representation* (the ability to represent environmental phenomena through one or more of the senses), (2) *iconic representation* (an

---

[17] Thornburg, *Intro to Ed. Psychology*, p. 26.

awareness of the concrete representation of phenomena in the environment), and (3) *symbolic representation* (the ability to represent environmental phenomena through symbols, primarily language.)

Enactive representation refers to concepts people can grasp through the senses but that are demonstrated through physical actions. **Music teachers often use the four fingers and the thumb on one hand to represent the lines and spaces of a staff. By using the other hand to point to the end of a finger or a space between the fingers, they can communicate notes on lines and spaces. Another example can be seen in the Curwen hand signs used to communicate sol-fa pitches.**

Iconic representation is a stage of thought in which objects and events are represented in a concrete fashion. **Having a student draw a picture of a river flowing through the countryside while listening to Smetana's *The Moldau* is exemplary of iconic representation.**

Symbolic representation occurs when visual (or aural) images intermingle with language and the concrete object becomes symbolically represented. **Notes on a printed page are exemplary of symbolic representation. Printed notes represent aural sounds.**

According to Bruner, there are several advantages to discovery learning: (1) students' expectation of success increases, (2) it is self-rewarding; (3) at each discovery, new principles and strategies of discovering are learned; and (4) students are more apt to remember the things they discover.[18]

David Ausubel's Cognitive Psychology   Cognitivists view the human thought process as a data-processing and storage system. Individuals are able to retain information because they classify new data into categories that already exist in their minds. As previously discussed, Jerome Bruner's discovery method incorporates the student in an active role in discovering and categorizing the material to be learned. David Ausubel, another cognitivist, advocates a pedagogical approach in which the material to be learned is categorized in advance by the teacher.

Meaningfulness (the extent to which learning is useful or purposeful in a person's life) has become a key word in cognitive learning theory. Ausubel believes that material must have *logical meaningfulness* if it is to be learned. In other words, it must be within the limitations of a person's capacity to learn it. **This is the reason that music teachers do not attempt to teach counterpoint to most third graders. By age twenty, however, a student's capacity to learn counterpoint has developed.**

Ausubel also believes that learning is possible if learners sustain what he calls *potential meaningfulness*. That is the capacity to relate new learning to what the learner already knows. Further, learners must have the desire to relate the material to their own way of thinking. Ausubel refers to this desire as a *meaningful learning set*. **An adolescent boy who has had background in singing in a treble boychoir at an elementary age will have little difficulty understanding the**

---

[18] J. S. Bruner, *The Relevance of Education* (New York: W. W. Norton, 1971), p. 84.

falsetto because he is able to relate the head voice, which was his primary means of vocal production as an unchanged treble, to the falsetto of the male changed voice. An inexperienced adolescent boy who is attempting to sing for the first time as eighth grader, on the other hand, may find experiencing the falsetto most difficult because his understanding of his voice is limited to speaking in the chest area. This is an example of potential meaningfulness. Furthermore, the inexperienced boy's difficulty with the falsetto may be more greatly intensified because he sees very little need to use his voice in that manner. This exemplifies Ausubel's meaningful learning set.

Ausubel has provided several suggestions for teaching meaningful learning from his perspective: (1) Teachers should structure material in ways that increase the likelihood of student learning, (2) teachers should be precise in their presentation of information, and (3) teachers should point out the similarities and differences in ideas.[19] When presenting a new arrangement or composition to the choir, teachers will enhance the learning effort if they have analyzed the form of the piece (according to Ausubel, that would structure the material for better understanding). For instance, if the form is ternary design, they should point out how the first and last sections are similar and how the middle section differs. Attention to the recurrence of specific melodic phrases, rhythmic patterns, or harmonic progressions that are similar will certainly make greater understanding possible. Helping students to comprehend how one rhythmic pattern might have grown out of another, how one harmonic progression differs slightly from another, or how sequences and various motifs are combined within a melody will heighten their ability to relate to the piece. Using an overhead projector that shows the image of the score in such a way that the director may point to specific examples helps the students follow the details in the design of the piece (this provides the specificity to which Ausubel refers).

John Bransford's Information Processing   Seemingly, the essence of cognitive learning theory is centered around processing information in such a way that students will retain it and can recall it when necessary. This idea originated in experimental psychology and through the influence of computer technology. Processing information into *short-term* (the retention of learned material for a very specific purpose for a short duration) and *long-term* (the retention of learned material for an extended time through encoding of information into the mind) memory banks is the primary focus of John Bransford's information processing theory. Cognitivists speak in terms of *conceptual learning* (assimilating concepts or propositions through abstract verbal representation) and *complex learning* (the acquisition of information or skills that contain multiple components, thus multiple behavioral potential). Complex learning, Bransford's main interest, contains many components that must be integrated if they are to have meaning to the learner.

Bransford's research relates to complex learning and deals specifically with

---

[19] David P. Ausubel, "The Facilitation of Meaningful Verbal Learning in the Classroom," *Educational Psychologist* 12 (1977), 162–78.

how the mind processes information. Thornburg explains that, according to Bransford:

> We receive and register stimuli or learning materials in the sensory storage and represent information through verbal, visual, or tactile modes (Bransford, 1979). These representations decay if further processing does not occur. Because the sensory stores are temporary, information must be retrieved from them in order to enter short-term storage. We accomplish this by attending to it. We code items in short-term storage into some type of verbal (phonemic) or visual features or categories. The capacity for short-term storage is very small, and, without rehearsal, the information is often lost by displacement—that is, new material enters short-term storage and crowds non-rehearsed information out. Long-term memory has an unlimited storage capacity; so information that is highly meaningful or rich in semantic content may be rehearsed and subsequently organized into more complex memory structures. In this way, material leaves short-term memory and becomes part of the large response repertoire stored in long-term memory.[20]

Restated, one might say that people remember and share experiences and information verbally, visually, and tactilely. These experiences and information are forgotten if they are not brought back to mind right away or if other relative information is not added. Because people's ability to remember is temporary, information must be retrieved to remember it, and the more times it is retrieved, the longer it is remembered. If the information is not used, it will be replaced by other more important things learned. Information and experiences that are particularly meaningful will be remembered for a much longer period. Two well-known maxims easily summarize Bransford's research: **"If you don't use it, you will lose it" (short-term memory) and "the best way to remember something is to teach it" (long-term memory).**

Recent Contributions to Learning Theory that Include Both Associationist and Cognitivist Approaches

The introductory material to this chapter has shown that most current learning theorists believe that there is great value in incorporating the tenets of both associationist and cognitivist approaches to learning. Therefore, we are going to look briefly at three contributors.

Although Jean Piaget (1896–1980) is a developmental psychologist, his work concerns the issue of understanding how people learn. Included here is a description (or summary) of his achievements in cognitive growth as explained in his *stages of intellectual development*, particularly the stage of *formal operations* that focuses on those students who are eleven to fifteen years of age. Two more recent contributors are Robert Gagné (1916–   ), who developed *hierarchical learning* (the arrangement of acquired responses into a hierarchy from simple to complex), and Albert Bandura (1925–   ), who contributed *social learning* (the term used to describe the various processes by which he conjectures human learning occurs).

---

[20] Thornburg, *Intro to Ed. Psychology*, pp. 304–5.

Jean Piaget's Formal Operations Stage of Intellectual Development   Jean Piaget conjectures that humans develop through a series of specific maturational periods including sensorimotor (birth to two years), preoperational (two to seven years), concrete operations (seven to eleven years), and formal operations (eleven to fifteen years), the stage that is of primary interest to teachers of secondary age choral students. Even though ages have been assigned, the stages of development may vary according to the individual.

Abstract thinking is the basic characteristic of the *formal operations* stage. Further, this stage represents a transition from thoughts about "what is" (reality) to thoughts about "what might be" (possibility). The biological development of the brain reaches its apex during this stage. Thinking processes may change because of environmental influences, although the brain is capable of as much logic as it will ever develop, even as an adult. The ability to think about one's own thoughts (reflective thinking) is another major characteristic of this stage.

Piaget and H. Inhelder referred to two distinct substages during the formal operations period. During ages eleven through thirteen, adolescents will be in transition between concrete and formal operations. This substage is characterized by experimentation, hypothesis making, and synthesis and analysis of cognitive materials, but there still might be a need for environmental and concrete props. During ages fourteen through fifteen, synthesis can be done without the aid of environmental props and the mind seems to move through its final restructuring before its full growth potential is realized. **Choral teachers must remain cognizant of these two substages because they represent the difference in the cognitive processes of middle/junior high school students and those of senior high school students. Often early adolescents require a different choice of words, descriptions, analogies, and teaching approaches in the communicative process than those which might be chosen for older adolescents**.

Robert Gagné's Learning Hierarchy   Robert Gagné (1916–   ), who received his Ph.D. from Brown University in 1940, has been successful in structuring much of what is advocated by both associationists and cognitivists into a hierarchy of learning skills. Intellectual skills and concepts are arranged in a "bottom to top" order so that each subordinate skill is a prerequisite to the skill immediately higher in the structure. Gagné contends that people learn higher-level skills more readily if they first have learned the subordinate skills. In many ways, Gagné's work represents a composite of a portion of what has been presented in this chapter. His work seems to provide an organizational structure to some of the information about learning theory discussed previously. His hierarchy delineated from bottom to top follows.

LEVEL ONE: SIGNAL LEARNING

Gagné's signal learning begins when "the individual learns to make a general diffuse response to a signal".[21] Based on Pavlov's classical conditioning, the paragon example

---

[21] R. N. Gagné, *The Conditions of Learning* (New York: Holt, Rinehart and Winston, 1970), p. 63.

of signal learning occurred when dogs responded to a buzzer by salivating. **Students experiencing a rigor up the spine on producing a well-tuned, balanced, and exciting chord would be a good choral example of signal learning at an emotional level. At an educational level, the ability for students to assign letter names to dots (notes) on musical lines and spaces is representative of signal learning.**

LEVEL TWO: STIMULUS-RESPONSE LEARNING

Gagné identifies stimulus-response learning as happening when "the learner acquires a precise response to a discriminated stimulus".[22] This type of learning is based on Thorndike's connectionism and Skinner's operant conditioning. Making relatively precise movements of the muscles in response to specific stimuli or combinations of stimuli, **such as singing the syllable *so* when students see a note on the second line of the treble clef in the key of C major, is an example of stimulus-response learning.** Gagné is not exactly sure as to the relationship between level one and level two, although he suspects that level one is subordinate to level two. Stimulus-response learning is placed further up the hierarchy ladder than signal learning in the interpretations of Gagné's work provided by most psychologists and learning theorists.

LEVEL THREE: CHAINING

Chaining is learning to make a series of stimulus-response connections that result in a sequence of activities. **For instance, students singing the "Hallelujah" chorus from Handel's *Messiah* by memory employ the process of chaining.** Gagné derived the idea of chaining from concepts of Skinner and Guthrie.

LEVEL FOUR: VERBAL ASSOCIATION

Verbal association is similar to level three except that both stimulus and response elements are represented linguistically. An example of this would be the ability of students who speak French to express their thoughts in German. **An example from the choral classroom would be students who have learned Tonic Sol-fa to be able to perform melodies with numbers instead (*one* represents *do*, *two* represents *re*, *three* represents *mi*, and so forth).** Gagné cautions educators that Ausubel and others have expressed concern about the extent to which verbal association principles may be relevant to actual verbal learning.

LEVEL FIVE: DISCRIMINATION LEARNING

To Gagné, discrimination learning occurs when "the individual learns to make a number of different identifying responses to as many different stimuli, which may resemble each other in physical appearance to a greater or lesser degree."[23] Gage and Berliner explain that this is best exemplified when "a girl can see one car and call it a Chevrolet, and see another car and call it a Ford, not only for the models of one year but for those of a whole decade".[24] **Musically, to continue the sight-reading analogies, discrimination learning is the ability of students who have learned to**

---

[22] Ibid.

[23] Ibid.

[24] N. L. Gage and David C. Berliner, *Educational Psychology,* 3d ed. (Boston: Houghton Mifflin Co., 1984), p. 61.

sing melodies using pitch syllables in the keys of C, F, and G major to be able to sing melodies using pitch syllables in A-flat, B-flat, and E-flat major as well, and to be able to do so in both bass and treble clefs.

LEVEL SIX: CONCEPT LEARNING

According to Gagné, concept learning involves "making a common response to a class of stimuli that may differ from each other widely in physical appearance."[25] Here the learner is required to classify a group of stimuli that are similar in some way but also are obviously different. **Students learn that notes placed on every line and every space moving upward (or downward) comprise a scale.** *Scale* **is a concept. Then they learn that when all the notes are one step apart, except from** *mi* **to** *fa* **and** *ti* **to** *do***, which are only one-half steps apart, it is a major scale.** *Major scale* **is another concept.**

LEVEL SEVEN: RULE LEARNING

Rule learning (also called *principle learning* by some theorists) is the chaining of two or more concepts to give the student the ability to see relationships and understand the rules that govern those relationships. In other words, people apply rules as if they were general principles. **Extending the scale analogy described in level six, rule learning is applied when students are able to identify all the major scales by applying the step, step, half-step, step, step, step, half-step formula, no matter what the beginning note.**

LEVEL EIGHT: PROBLEM SOLVING

Problem solving involves using concepts and rules previously learned to generate new concepts and rules so as to find a solution to an unknown predicament. Hodges describes this level as *thinking*, that is, simply using the mind to solve problems.[26] Gagné describes it as the *scientific method* such as when students apply mathematical or scientific formulas to experiments to solve problems.[27] He also applies this level of learning to creative efforts, such as when composers immerse themselves in their music for long periods of time until *sudden insight* transfers "a problem situation into a solution situation."[28]

Albert Bandura's Social Learning Theory   Also called *observational learning*, Bandura's *social learning theory* establishes that learning occurs through observing the behavior of others. Bandura believes that observation of a model will induce several different options of behavior: (1) The observer (learner) may acquire new responses (behavior), (2) the observer may strengthen existing responses or may reduce the tendency to continue responding in some way (inhibition), or (3) the observer may recall or reestablish already learned or forgotten

---

[25] Gagné, *Conditions of Learning*, pp. 63–64.

[26] Hodges, *Handbook of Music Psychology*, p. 259.

[27] Gagné, *Conditions of Learning*, p. 215.

[28] Ibid., p. 228.

responses.[29] He believes that individuals learn much through imitation: "Almost any learning outcome that results from direct experience can also come about on a vicarious basis through observation of other people's behaviors and its consequences for them."[30] Thornburg summarizes Bandura's research and conclusions as follows:

1. Individuals learn from *symbolic models* as well as from real-life models. Bandura, Ross, and Ross used film-mediated models to show that children exposed to aggressive models learn and demonstrate the same behaviors without reinforcement.[31]

2. Bandura has demonstrated that "observational learning occurs through symbolic processes during exposure to modeled activities before any responses have been performed and does not necessarily require extrinsic reinforcement".[32] Reinforcement may accompany the modeling process but is not required in order for learning to occur.

3. *Self reinforcement* is important in modeling. Most stimulus-response explanations require external reinforcement. However, Bandura contends that self-reinforcement may be more important than external reinforcement, especially in older children and adults.[33] The ability to evaluate your own behavior and be satisfied or dissatisfied with it is part of the self-reinforcement process, a characteristic of human behavior that sets humans apart from animals.

4. Bandura uses social learning to explain the acquisition of attitudes (*affective learning*) as well as intellectual skills (cognitive learning). His is the first major system of learning that accounts for learning equally in these two areas.

5. Bandura has found that *proximal goals* serve in the development of self-perceptions of efficacy [competence, efficiency, or mastery]. Standards are needed against which people can judge their performance.[34] This aspect of Bandura's model also bridges some of the differences between more traditional reinforcement and cognitive positions.[35]

Bandura's research is important to choral teachers because it emphasizes the importance of the influence of teachers as role models. Students give attention to models with high status, competence, and expertise; therefore, it behooves the teacher to exhibit those characteristics. Teachers need to be cognizant that, particularly with early adolescents, role models receive so

[29] Albert Bandura, *Principles of Behavior Modification* (New York: Holt, Rinehart and Winston, 1969), and Albert Bandura, *Social Learning Theory* (Englewood Cliffs, N.J.: Prentice-Hall, Inc., 1977).

[30] Albert Bandura, "Behavioral Psychotherapy," *Scientific American*, 216, no. 4 (April 1972), 78–86.

[31] A. Bandura, D. Ross, and S. A. Ross, "Imitation of Film-mediated Aggressive Models," *Journal of Abnormal and Social Psychology*, 66, no. 12 (December 1971), 3–11.

[32] Bandura, *Social Learning Theory*, p. 37.

[33] Bandura, *Principles of Behavior Modification*, p. 114.

[34] Bandura, "Self-efficacy: Toward a Unifying Theory of Behavioral Change," *Psychological Review*, 84, no. 2 (February, 1975), 191–215. Also, Albert Bandura, "Self-efficacy Mechanism in Human Agency," *American Psychologist* 37, no. 9 (September 1969), 122–47.

[35] Thornburg, *Intro to Ed. Psychology*, p. 30.

much attention that their actions often become national fads. A nationally known actor's or actress's hair style may be copied by millions of young men or women. In 1980, when a popular television character took out a library card, it was estimated that library card applications from students ages nine through fourteen increased fivefold nationally![36] The model most admired in school may be the football player, the cheerleader, or the class clown. Teachers' understanding of this enables them to recruit, communicate, and motivate effectively in teaching choral music to adolescents.

MOTIVATION IN THE CLASSROOM

Discipline (control) in the classroom is one of the primary concerns of undergraduates who may be seeking a choral position for the first time. Because of their inexperience and young age, they may be worried that they will be unable to control their classrooms. The subject of how to control the classroom is addressed thoroughly in Chapter 14. Some music educators believe that classroom control is principally a matter of motivation. From their perspective, properly motivated singers are not discipline problems. A great deal of research has been done about the technique of motivation in the classroom; therefore, the psychology of motivation is examined in this chapter.

Most people are influenced by both *intrinsic motivation* (the internal desire to act) and *extrinsic motivation* (the desire to act if appropriate incentives are created within the environment). Intrinsic motivation is what students, as learners, bring with them to a learning situation. People preserve intrinsic motivation by being engrossed in activities that are internally satisfying. Students who are more internally controlled tend to receive more intrinsic satisfaction from external events. Extrinsically motivated students are motivated to accomplish certain tasks if the right incentives are initiated for them. **Intrinsically motivated choral students will gain satisfaction simply from working to produce a beautifully blended and balanced chord, whereas extrinsically motivated students need to be told what a great job they did in working to produce that beautiful chord.** It is generally assumed that intrinsic and extrinsic motivation working together produce the best results. **For instance, students who enjoy singing (intrinsic) and receive a grade of "A" for doing so (extrinsic) are the ones who become the best choir members.**

The early works of most stimulus-response (associationists) psychologists treated motivation from the point of view of *hedonism* (the tendency of an organism to seek pleasure while avoiding pain). Their concept of learning grew out of a belief that people learn (change behavior) through a need to reduce physiological needs. In other words, people's deprived physiological state obliged them to act. This was their motivation for behavior. Hedonism was actually an ancient Greek philosophy but it was conventionalized by Thorndike in his *law*

---

[36] *National Coalition on Television Violence*, NCTV News, July–August 1981.

of effect, which says that action is ensued by either a satisfying or an annoying situation. Several theories pertaining to motivation have grown from Thorndike's early work, including Kurt Lewin's *field theory*, Clark Hull's *drive theory*, and Abraham Maslow's *needs theory*. Hull's drive theory was discussed earlier in this chapter, so it will not be covered here.

Kurt Lewin's Field Theory

Although Kurt Lewin's field theory apparently does not carry much weight among contemporary learning theorists, it is important to choral musicians as they attempt to understand student motivation. Lewin (1890–1947) is considered by many to be a social psychologist rather than a learning theorist, but since his interest was in the psychology of motivation, his work initially had substantial impact on the work of learning theorists in both the cognitive and associative domains. Thus his contributions should be considered to be important.

Lewin introduced the concept of *life-space*, which represents the totality of individuals in their perceived physical and psychological environment at any given time. He believed that people live in a active field of forces that move them toward a goal. Learning depends on individual motivation and personality. To him, insightful learning occurs when goals are identified and dynamic environmental forces propel a person toward that goal. In simpler terms, the environment is composed of objects and events that are perceived to be important and these perceptions interact with their psychological condition to result in their behavior. To Lewin, human behavior had to be goal-oriented to be meaningful.

Lewin's research should help choral directors to realize that the learning environment is determined by the attitudes, contributions, and persona of the people (administrators, teachers, and other students) the students encounter. The physical attractiveness of the walls, floors, ceilings, and bulletin boards of the rooms in which they study (and the halls and restrooms of the school as a whole) are very important in the motivational process of helping students learn. Further, Lewin's work emphasizes the importance of setting demanding, yet reachable, goals that give direction, purpose, and motivation to the students' pursuit of knowledge and skill in the singing process.

Several components of the educational environment affect the learning process. Hunt and Sullivan suggest the following considerations to help identify these components: (1) cultural setting (includes national and community elements and values), (2) current school setting (includes culture of the school, class values, rural-urban-suburban locale), (3) school and classroom characteristics (includes size of school; number age and sex of students; number, age, and sex of teachers; and physical characteristics such as open architecture, and so forth), (4) school or classroom organization (includes power relations, decision-making patterns, division of labor, communication patterns, relations among staff, relations among students, peer influence, and so forth), (5) personal characteristics of teachers (includes teacher characteristics specifically oriented toward the teaching function, such as personality structure, religious attitudes, social attitudes, philosophy of life, and so forth), (6) student-oriented teacher attitudes (includes educational goals, concepts about the teacher role and the student role, attitudes toward teaching, acceptance or rejection of student, and so forth), and (7) teacher behavior (includes teaching practices, specific teaching techniques, response to student behaviors, changes in teaching strategies, and so forth).[37]

Studies by Lippitt and White (Lewin's students) examined the effects of democratic, authoritarian, and laissez-faire teachers on social climate and productivity of students. Basically, the results of the studies indicate that democratically operated classrooms were more motivating, produced more originality, and were more group-minded than the other classes, although they produced somewhat less work than the authoritarian-controlled classes. The authoritarian class generated more hostility, more dependence on the teacher, fewer individual differences, and more dropouts, while students in the laissez-faire social climate produced less work, and work of poorer quality, than either of the other two groups.[38]

Abraham Maslow's Needs Theory

The work of Abraham Maslow (1908–1970) has been of particular interest to music educators ever since he was one of the participants in the Tanglewood Symposium of 1967. Maslow developed what is known as *third force* psychology, which is a concept that emphasizes motivation, affect, creativity, and general fulfillment of human potential. In his *needs theory* he submits the idea that people's needs are learned. He believes that as people intermingle with the environment, they acquire certain needs that allow them to respond to life experiences. Therefore, when they are motivated by a need, they are responding to psychological circumstances that were procured through the learning process. Maslow conceived a hierarchy of needs that are basic to life. Individuals must satisfy the requirements in each rank of the hierarchy before moving up the ladder to the next set of needs. Beginning at the bottom with physiological needs and moving upward, Maslow's hierarchy of needs are:

PHYSICAL AND ORGANIZATIONAL NEEDS

1. Survival needs—needs of immediate existence such as nourishment, shelter, warmth, and so forth.
2. Safety needs—these include good health, security from harm and danger for self and the immediate family, and confidence in the future.

---

[37] D. E. Hunt and E. V. Sullivan, *Between Psychology and Education* (Hinsdale, Ill.: Dryden Press, 1974), pp. 89–90; and Harold F. Abeles, Charles R. Hoffer, and Robert H. Klotman, *Foundations of Music Education* (New York: Schirmer Books, 1984), p. 188.

[38] R. Lippitt and R. White, "The Social Climate of Children's Groups," in *Child Behavior and Development*, R. G. Barker, J. S. Kounin, and H. F. Wright, eds. (New York: McGraw-Hill Book Co., 1943); and Abeles, Hoffer, and Klotman, *Foundations of Music Education*, p. 189.

AFFILIATION AND SOCIAL NEEDS

3. Love and belonging needs—these needs are manifest in people's desire for acceptance within a group; their knowledge that others are aware of their existence. They are more strongly felt in close relationships such as family, sweetheart, spouse, children, and friends.

4. Esteem needs—recognition that self is a unique person with special abilities. These needs are manifest through a strong desire for achievement, respect of others, and self-respect.

ACHIEVEMENT AND INTELLECTUAL NEEDS

5. Need for knowledge—a need to have access to information; to know how to do things; and to want to know about the meaning of things, events, and symbols.

6. Need for understanding—a need for knowledge of relationships, systems, and processes that are expressed in broad theories, and the integration of knowledge and lore into broad structures.

AESTHETIC NEEDS

7. Need for order and beauty—a need to appreciate the order and balance in all of life and to develop a sense of beauty in and love for all.

SELF-ACTUALIZATION NEEDS

8. Self-actualization needs—these needs, at the top of the hierarchy, are apparent in people's attempt to realize self-fulfillment, to develop potential, and to make their behavior consistent with what they feel they are as individuals.[39]

Maslow contends that if people satisfactorily meet the demands of the first seven needs, the need of self-actualization is strong enough to become the prime motivator for all behavior. "The self-actualized person is one who is motivated by needs to be open and not defensive, to love others and self without giving into aggression or manipulative needs, to act in ways that are ethically and morally good for society, to express autonomy and creativity, and to be curious and spontaneous in interchange with the environment."[40]

If choral teachers are going to have students who are fully motivated learners, they must attempt to help the students to become self-actualized, which includes helping them to satisfy those psychological needs delineated by Maslow. This may be an impossible task when dealing with adolescent

[39] This hierarchy of needs is based on a formulation by Abraham Maslow, *Motivation and Personality*, (New York: Harper and Row, 1954) and modified by A. A. Root, "What Instructors Say to the Students Makes a Difference," *Engineering Education*, 61, no. 3 (March 1963), pp. 722–25.

[40] Abraham Maslow, *The Farther Reaches of Human Nature* (New York: Viking Press, 1971), p. 116.

students who may not have developed the capacity to become self-actualized at their young age. At least music teachers have a definite commission to help students fulfill their aesthetic needs (level seven). While the students are in the teacher's care, a primary goal should be to help them understand and accept the need for beauty, order, and balance in their lives. Working with music, a primary ingredient in aesthetic education, should make completing the teacher's commission a joy.

SUMMARY

For years choral directors have had a reputation for teaching by the "seat of their pants." We have taught through an inherent understanding of the teaching process or through what we have been able to observe about the work of other teachers. "If it works, do it" has been our motto. In this chapter, we have been introduced to several different learning theories and applied them to the choral process. We have dealt with motivation in the classroom, and in Chapter 5 we will determine how to develop an effective teaching strategy based on what we have learned. It is time for music teachers to remove the guesswork from the teaching process and establish their technique based on reliable research. In your quest to become a master teacher, your challenge is to become highly accomplished at understanding how students learn choral music; then apply that understanding to the teaching process. Great will be the results of your labor!

THOUGHTS FOR CONTEMPLATION AND DISCUSSION

1. Which do you think better defines the way we learn vocal-choral technique, the associationist or cognitivist approach? The way we memorize music? The way we read music? Why?

2. How does learning mathematics and music fundamentals compare? How do they differ?

3. Does musical giftedness affect the way we learn choral music? Is so, how? If not, why?

4. How does the *skill factor* affect the way we choose to make music? What affects the *skill factor* more, heredity or environment? Why?

5. How does student maturation affect the planning of the course curriculum in the choirs you will direct?

6. Which more acutely affects the success of choral singers: their intelligence quotient (IQ), their musical giftedness, or their motivation? Why?

7. Are child prodigies more greatly affected by IQ, musical giftedness, or motivation? Why?

BIBLIOGRAPHY

ABELES, HAROLD F., CHARLES R. HOFFER, and ROBERT H. KLOTMAN, *Foundations of Music Education*. New York: Schirmer Books, 1984.

AUSUBEL, DAVID P. *Educational Psychology: A Cognitive View*. New York: Holt, Rinehart and Winston, 1968.

————. "The Facilitation of Meaningful Verbal Learning in the Classroom," *Educational Psychology* 12 (1977).

BANDURA, ALBERT. "Behavioral Psychotherapy," *Scientific American* 216, no. 4 (April 1972).

————. *Principles of Behavior Modification*. New York: Holt, Rinehart and Winston, 1969.

————. "Self-efficacy Mechanism in Human Agency," *American Psychologist* 37, no. 9 (September 1969).

————. "Self-efficacy: Toward a Unifying Theory of Behavioral Change," *Psychological Review* 84.

————. *Social Learning Theory*. Englewood Cliffs, N.J.: Prentice-Hall, Inc., 1977.

BANDURA, ALBERT, D. ROSS, and S. A. ROSS, "Imitation of Film-mediated Aggressive Models," *Journal of Abnormal and Social Psychology*, 66, no. 12 (December 1971).

BEGLARIAN, G. *Comprehensive Musicianship: an Anthology of Evolving Thought*. Reston, Va.: Music Educators National Conference, 1971.

BELL, CLIVE. *Art*. New York: G. P. Putnam's Sons, 1914.

BRANSFORD, J. D. *Human Cognition*. Belmont, Calif.: Wadsworth Publications, 1979.

BRUNER, J. S. *The Process of Education*. New York: Vintage Books, 1960.

————. *The Relevance of Education*. New York: W. W. Norton, 1971.

————. *Toward a Theory of Instruction*. New York: W. W. Norton, 1966.

CHOATE, R. A., ed. *The Tanglewood Symposium, a Documentary Report*. Reston, Va.: Music Educators National Conference, 1968.

COOKE, DERYCK. *The Language of Music*. London: Oxford University Press, 1959.

COPLAND, AARON. *What to Listen for in Music*. New York: McGraw-Hill Book Co., 1957.

DEUTSCH, DIANA. *The Psychology of Music*. New York: Academic Press, 1982.

DEWEY, JOHN. *Art as Experience*. New York: Minton, Balch and Co., 1934.

————. *Democracy and Education*. New York: Macmillan, 1916.

ELLIS, ARTHUR K., JOHN J. COGAN, and KENNETH R. HOWEY, *Introduction to the Foundations of Education*. Englewood Cliffs, N.J.: Prentice-Hall, Inc., 1981.

ENGLISH, H. B., and A. C. ENGLISH. *A Comprehensive Dictionary of Psychological and Psychoanalytical Terms*. New York: McKay Publishing Co., 1958.

FADELY, JACK L., and VIRGINIA N. HOSLER. *Case Studies in Left and Right Hemispheric Functioning*. Springfield, Ill.: Charles C. Thomas, 1983.

FRIEDMAN, SARAH L., KENNETH A. KLIVINGTON, and RITA W. PETERSON. *The Brain, Cognition, and Education*. Orlando, Fla.: Academic Press, Inc., 1986.

GAGE, N. L. and DAVID C. BERLINER. *Educational Psychology*, 3d ed. Boston: Houghton Mifflin Co., 1984.

GAGNÉ, R. N. *The Conditions of Learning*. New York: Holt, Rinehart and Winston, 1970.

GORDON, EDWIN. *Learning Sequence and Patterns in Music*. Chicago: G.I.A. Publications, 1977.

————. *The Psychology of Music Teaching*. Englewood Cliffs, N.J.: Prentice-Hall, Inc., 1971.

GUTHRIE, E. R. "Association by Contiguity." *Psychology: a Study of a Science*, vol. 2, ed. by S. Kock. New York: McGraw-Hill Book Co., 1959.

————. "Conditioning: A Theory of Learning in Terms of Stimulus, Response, and Association." In *The Psychology of Learning*, ed. by N. B. Henry. Chicago: University of Chicago Press, 1942.

————. *The Psychology of Human Conflict*. New York: Harper and Row, 1938.

————. *The Psychology of Learning*, rev. ed. New York: Harper and Row, 1952.

HANSLICK, EDWARD. *The Beautiful in Music*, trans. by Gustav Cohen. Indianapolis: Liberal Arts Press, 1957.

HENRY, NELSON B., ed. *Basic Concepts in Music Education*. Chicago: The National Society for the Study of Education, 1958.

HERGENHAHN, B. R. *An Introduction to Theories of Learning*, 2d ed. Englewood Cliffs, N.J.: Prentice-Hall, Inc., 1982.

HILGARD, ERNEST R., and GORDON H. BOWER.

Theories of Learning, 4th ed. Englewood Cliffs, N.J.: Prentice-Hall, Inc., 1975.

HODGES, DONALD A., ed. *Handbook of Music Psychology*. Dubuque, Iowa: Kendall/Hunt Publishing Co., 1980.

HOFFER, CHARLES R. *Introduction to Music Education*. Belmont Calif.: Wadsworth Publishing, 1983.

HULL, C. L. *Principles of Behavior*. New York: Appleton Century Crofts, 1943.

HUNT, D. E., and E. V. SULLIVAN. *Between Psychology and Education*. Hinsdale, Ill: Dryden Press, 1974.

JOHNSTON, JAMES A., et al. *Introduction to the Foundations of American Education*, 6th ed. Boston: Allyn and Bacon, Inc., 1985.

KLAUSMEIER, HERBERT J. *Educational Psychology*, 5th ed. New York: Appleton Century Crofts, 1943.

KOWALL, BONNIE C., ed. *Perspectives in Music Education, Source Book III*. Ruston, Va.: Music Educators National Conference, 1966.

LEONHARD, CHARLES, and ROBERT W. HOUSE. *Foundations and Principles of Music Education*, 2d ed. New York: McGraw-Hill Book Co., 1972.

LIPPITT, R., and R. WHITE. "The Social Climate of Children's Groups." *Child Behavior and Development*, R. G. Barker, J. S. Kounin, and H. F. White, eds. New York: McGraw-Hill Book Co., 1943.

MARX, MELVIN H., ed. *Learning: Theories*. New York: Macmillan, 1971.

———. *The Farther Reaches of Human Nature*. New York: Viking Press, 1971.

MASLOW, ABRAHAM. *Motivation and Personality*. New York: Harper and Row, 1954.

MEYER, LEONARD B. *Emotion and Meaning in Music*. Chicago: University of Chicago Press, 1956.

MOULY, GEORGE J. *Psychology for Effective Teaching*. New York: Holt, Rinehart and Winston, 1973. *National Coalition on Television Violence*, NCTV News, July–August, 1981.

NODDINGS, NEL, and PAUL J. SHORE, *Awakening the Inner Eye*. New York: Teachers College Press, 1984.

ORNSTEIN, ALLAN C., and DANIEL U. LEVINE, *An Introduction to the Foundations of Education*, 3d ed. Boston: Houghton Mifflin Co., 1985.

PIAGET, J., and B. INHELDER. *The Growth of Logical Thinking from Childhood to Adolescence*. New York: Basic Books, 1958.

REGELSKI, THOMAS A. *Principles and Problems of Music Education*. Englewood Cliffs, N.J.: Prentice-Hall, Inc., 1975.

REIMER, BENNETT. *A Philosophy of Music Education*, 2d ed. Englewood Cliffs, N.J.: Prentice-Hall, Inc., 1989.

SERAFINE, MARY LOUISE. *Music as Cognition*. New York: Columbia University Press, 1988.

SLOBODA, JOHN A. *The Musical Mind*. Oxford: Clarendon Press, 1985.

SNELBECKER, GLENN E. *Learning Theory, Instructional Theory, and Psychoeducational Design*. New York: McGraw-Hill Book Co., 1974.

SNOW, R. S. "Intelligence for the Year 2001," *Human Intelligence International Newsletter*, 4, no. 2 (February 1974).

THORNBURG, HERSHEL D. *Introduction to Educational Psychology*. St. Paul: West Publishing Co., 1984.

WATSON, J. B. "Psychology as the Behaviorist Views It," *Psychological Review*. American Psychological Association, 1913.

Webster's New Collegiate Dictionary. Springfield, Mass.: G. & C. Merriam Co., 1956.

5

Developing a Strategy for Teaching Choral Music

In Chapter 4 the theories pertaining to how students learn were examined. Special applications were made that specified how students learn choral music in particular. Then, in an attempt to understand those influences that affect the interest (or lack of interest) students maintain when studying choral music, the subject of motivation was examined. The information in Chapter 4 was presented as a foundation for this chapter. Knowing the information that was examined is meaningless unless teachers develop an effective strategy for teaching choral music to the students. To be a master teacher, you must (1) identify the teaching-learning procedures that will be most effective in realizing the desired learning experiences, (2) organize what is to be taught (the basic body of knowledge, music, information, skill, and so forth) in such a way that it will be easy to understand and learn, (3) incorporate as many of the basic learning principles (all those theories we have discussed previously) as possible in the teaching procedure, (4) assess and understand the student differences in each of your classes, and (5) develop a system of evaluation that indicates if the present course is effective or if additional supplementary teaching should be executed.[1]

Further, master teachers must establish a teaching-learning environment that is conducive to learning choral music. According to Thornburg, there are four characteristics necessary to establish an effective teaching-learning

---

[1] Hershel D. Thornburg, *Introduction to Educational Psychology* (St. Paul: West Publishing Co., 1984), pp. 254–55.

environment: (1) determine the course content to be taught, (2) articulate the content to the students, (3) synthesize the content (pull together and demonstrate the interrelationships among its various aspects), and (4) be aware of the interactive effect of instruction (realize how teachers influence students, students influence other students, and students influence teachers).

AN INTERACTIVE INSTRUCTIONAL MODEL FOR EFFECTIVE TEACHING

Hershel Thornburg has proposed an instructional model that is a pragmatic framework for becoming an effective teacher. It includes (1) identifying student needs, (2) delineating instructional objectives, (3) devising teaching strategies, and (4) assessing the progress.[2]

Identifying Student Needs

Thornburg believes that students bring personal and performance needs into the classroom. These *personal needs* are their internal motives or reasons for being there. In a singing class, these personal needs (intrinsic motivation) are obvious. The students are there because they enjoy music and the creative process (or they are there because a friend, or prospective friend, took the class). Thornburg also believes students have *performance needs* that are the deficiencies or sufficiencies of the accumulated knowledge and skills that they bring to the classroom. In a singing class, the teacher's ability to identify the performance needs is very important. Students with more accomplished musical skills should not be combined with students with less accomplished skills. For this reason, it is important to have a training choir (similar to the "sophomore" choir in high school) and rehearse those students separately from those who are stronger musicians and who are qualified to be in the high-performance profile (a cappella) choir. To identify the performance needs of their students, most teachers accept members in the top choir by audition only.

Thornburg delineates five steps in identifying and meeting student needs (the comments in brackets are my statements that apply these reasons to the choral music class):

1. The teacher appraises prerequisite student learning to determine if it meets the requirements for the performance needs necessary to the tentative instructional objectives of the class. [Audition the students.]
2. After considering student performance needs and teacher goals, the teacher writes final student instructional objectives that specify desired learning outcomes. [Write the objectives and choose the music for rehearsal that will fulfill them.]
3. If learning deficiencies exist, the teacher instructs the student in supplemental

[2] Hershel D. Thornburg, *School Learning and Instruction* (Monterey, Calif.: Brooks/Cole Publications, 1973), pp. 22–76.

skills necessary to meet the prerequisite learning. [Practice choral technique and/or sight-reading skills necessary to learn and perform the music well.]

4. The teacher maintains ongoing assessment of performance needs. When student performance is below the stated objectives, reevaluation of the objectives in terms of student needs is necessary. [Periodically record the music for listening outside of rehearsal to determine if the learning of the music is on schedule or if alternate skill-building procedures should be effectuated.]

5. To align student needs and teacher goals, it may be necessary to restate objectives in more realistic behavioral terms. Further supplemental instruction or a change of strategy may be sufficient to meet the original goal. [Abandon certain numbers and choose different selections or incorporate additional skill-building procedures.][3]

Writing Instructional Objectives

"A *behavioral objective* describes what students will be able to do when they complete a teaching unit or instructional materials. Many educators and psychologists advocate their use because they help clarify how the teacher will aid student learning."[4] According to Thornburg, there are several good reasons for using behavioral objectives, including: (1) They help the classroom teacher prepare a teaching plan for the day, (2) they tell students what learning behaviors are expected, (3) they specify what learning behaviors students are responsible for, (4) they provide the teacher with a systematic basis for evaluating student learning, and (5) they align teacher behavior with student behavior.

Instructional objectives belong to one of three behavioral domains: (1) cognitive, (2) affective, or (3) psychomotor. B. S. Bloom, M. D. Englehart, W. H. Hill, E. J. Furst, and D. R. Krathwohl have prepared a taxonomy (henceforth referred to as *Bloom's taxonomy*) of education objectives for the *cognitive domain*. The cognitive domain is applicable to classes that are primarily academic, such as music appreciation, music history, fine arts, humanities, or music theory. The taxonomy is a classification of degrees of knowledge moving in a cumulative manner from the simplest level to the more complex levels. They include (1) knowledge, (2) comprehension, (3) application, (4) analysis, (5) synthesis, and (6) evaluation.

Knowledge includes "those behaviors and test situations that emphasize remembering (either by recognition or recall) ideas, material, or phenomena."[5] One consideration of Bloom's knowledge level is the ability to recall specific or isolated bits of information. Another consideration is the recall of terminology (remembering and understanding words) and specific facts such as dates, events, persons, and places. When teachers write behavioral objectives that speak to the knowledge level of understanding, the statements might be similar to these:

[3] Ibid., p. 251

[4] Ibid., p. 262.

[5] B. S. Bloom et al., *Taxonomy of Educational Objectives: Cognitive Domain* (New York: McKay Publications, 1956), p. 52.

1. The students will be able to sing the words to all stanzas of "The Star-Spangled Banner" by memory.
2. The students will be able to match the date and place of birth with each of the composers of the Romantic period to a 70 percent mastery.
3. The students will identify the letter names of each of the lines and spaces in both bass and treble clefs.

Comprehension includes "those objectives, behaviors, and responses that represent an understanding of the literal message contained in a communication."[6] It represents the ability to interpret information by using one's own words. Bloom indicates that there are three basic functions within the comprehension level: *translation* (reiterating a communication in a different form other than the original), *interpretation* (explaining a communication that is presented in a different form such as in a clef, chart, or graph), and *extrapolation* (extending or projecting information that is apparent but not included in the original communication). Examples of behavioral objectives written to the comprehension level are:

1. The students will be able to explain the events that led to the writing of Mozart's *Requiem*.
2. The students will be able to explain how word painting is used in Baroque compositions.
3. The students will be able to read (not necessarily sing them) the letter names of the notes in "The Star-Spangled Banner."

Application includes "those behaviors in which the student is applying the appropriate abstractions to a given situation without having to be prompted about which abstraction is correct or without having to be shown how to use it in that situation."[7] At the application level, "objectives include the use of abstractions as general ideas, rules, or methods that help the learner understand or solve a problem or situation."[8] Also, at the application level, information must be applied as well as be recalled (knowledge level) and understood (comprehension level). Examples of objectives written to the application level are:

1. The students will be able to harmonize (write down on paper, but not necessarily with correct rules of voice leading, and so forth) a folk melody using at least three different chords.
2. The students will be able to resolve properly a tritone in a given chord progression.
3. The students will be able to identify the pitches *do, mi, so,* and *la* as sung by the instructor in any key.

Analysis indicates the ability of students "to break down a communication into its constituent parts or elements and determine their relationships and

[6] Ibid., p. 89.
[7] Ibid., p. 20.
[8] Thornburg, *School Learning*, p. 265.

organizational principles."[9] Bloom includes three subheadings at the analysis level: (1) *analyzing elements* (separating and identifying various parts of a communication), (2) *analyzing relationships* (understanding the connections and relationships between various parts of a communication), and (3) *analyzing organizational principles* (understanding the structure or procedure that holds a communication together). Examples of objectives written to the analysis level are:

1. The students will be able to discern the texture (monophonic, homophonic, or polyphonic) of a composition by listening to the first eight bars of the selection.
2. The students will be able to analyze the harmonic structure of "The Star-Spangled Banner."
3. The students will be able to indicate the letter names of chords members in a composition as indicated by the figured bass.

Synthesis includes understanding how "to combine elements or parts to form a whole."[10] Bloom identifies three subheadings under synthesis: (1) producing a unique communication (attempting to write or otherwise convey ideas, feelings, and/or experiences to others), (2) developing a plan of operation (the ability to use rules in writing or composing), and (3) devising a set of abstract relations (the ability to formulate mathematical discoveries, project hypotheses based on analysis, and so forth). Instructional objectives written to the synthesis level are:

1. The students will compose and harmonize a new tune to "The Star-Spangled Banner" using all rules pertinent to correct theory practices for the chosen style.
2. The students will formulate a new method of composition based on the tritone.
3. The students will write a term paper with bibliographic references describing the differences in the true-to-life characterization of Mozart and that depicted in the movie *Amadeus*.

Evaluation is defined as the ability "to make value judgments about ideas, works, solutions, methods, or material in terms of specific criteria."[11] According to Bloom, there are two kinds of judgments: (1) those that are made in terms of the internal evidence, and (2) those that are formed in terms of external criteria. Behavioral objectives written to the level of evaluation are:

1. Based on the harmonic structure, the students will determine which is the best composition, "The Star-Spangled Banner" or the "Hallelujah Chorus" from Handel's *Messiah* and explain why.
2. The students will decide who was the best composer of contrapuntal style in the Romantic period and explain why.

[9] Bloom et al., *Taxonomy*, p. 144.
[10] Ibid., p. 162.
[11] Ibid., p. 185.

3. The students will be able to determine if a specific song should be sung staccato or legato.

The *affective domain* includes objectives that emphasize an emotion, an appreciation of tone or quality, or a value judgment. It also includes interest, attitudes, beliefs, motives, and values. These are objectives that more readily serve the teaching of the fine and performing arts, therefore, they are most useful to teachers in their choral classes and their performance activities in general music. D. R. Krathwohl, B. S. Bloom, and B. B. Masia have prepared a taxonomy for the affective domain that includes the levels of (1) receiving, (2) responding, (3) valuing, (4) organization, and (5) characterization.[12]

Receiving, the lowest level of the affective domain and one that provides the prerequisite behavior for the other levels, addresses the learners' awareness of phenomena or stimuli in the environment (that which is all about them) and their ability to attend to it. Examples of objectives written to the receiving level in the affective domain are:

1. The students will listen to the teacher's instructions and follow them explicitly.
2. The students will indicate interest in joining the choir.
3. The students will participate when the group sings together.

Responding goes slightly beyond attending (becoming aware of the environment) to making a low-level commitment to becoming involved. The responding is passive in the beginning but eventually evolves to willingness and then to satisfaction. Examples of behavioral objectives written to the responding level are:

1. The students will sing music of master composers when told to do so.
2. The students will stand for the warm-up exercises at the instruction of the director.
3. Without complaining, the students will sit in a mixed formation with the girls and boys alternating positions.

Valuing reaches the level of internalization where the students eventually choose to find value in aspects of their environment. This involves behavior in which they are not forced to comply, but do so willingly. Exemplary objectives are:

1. The students will choose to sing a composition by a master composer over one by a popular contemporary artist.
2. The students will stand with correct posture without being reminded to do so when a new song is being performed.
3. The students will care for their music and replace it properly after use.

---

[12] D. R. Krathwohl, B. S. Bloom, and B. B. Masia, *Taxonomy of Educational Objectives: Affective Domain* (New York: McKay Publications, 1964), p. 95

Organization is the level in which the students accept a set of values and organize them into a consistent system. As learners internalize and express values, they find it necessary to choose those values that have the most relevance to themselves. Therefore, they must structure their values, determine the inter-relationships among them and establish those that are dominant. Behavioral objectives at the organization level are:

1. The students will choose choral music over industrial arts class.
2. The students will choose to sing the "Hallelujah Chorus" from Handel's *Messiah* over the "Gloria Chorus" from Vivaldi's *Gloria Mass*.
3. The students will choose to listen to a recording of choral music in the presence of their friends who are not musicians.

In *characterization*, the highest level of the affective domain, the students have developed a generalized system of values that consistently guide them and characterize their behavior. Decisions regarding that which is right or wrong, important or unimportant, and other values are made without experiencing internal conflict. Objectives written to this level are:

1. For every rehearsal, students will arrive in the classroom, pick up their music, find their seats, and sit quietly until class begins.
2. Students will attempt to use good choral technique on every piece they sing.
3. Students will consistently listen to art music each time they place a disc in the compact disc player.

The *psychomotor domain* centers on objectives that emphasize muscular, motor, and/or verbal skills, manipulation of materials and objects, and neuro-muscular coordination. Several taxonomies have been devised for the psychomotor domain, three of which are presented here. Although singing seems to contain less psychomotor activity than playing an instrument, understanding this domain is still necessary because effective singing cannot be accomplished without efficient muscular coordination throughout the entire body. Further, since verbal skills are considered by some psychologists and educators to be part of the psychomotor domain, and since singing extends those skills beyond the realm of speaking, in some ways it includes more psychomotor prowess than playing an instrument.

Kibler, Baker, and Miles (henceforth called Kibler) have classified move-ments and skills of the psychomotor domain to provide a framework for identifying educational objectives. Their classification is not intended to be hierarchical, such as those of Bloom, Krathwohl, and Masia, but are directly related to child development. They divide the domain into four major areas: (1) gross bodily movement, (2) finely coordinated movements, (3) nonverbal communication, and (4) speech.

Gross bodily movement includes (1) movements involving the upper limbs, (2) movements involving the lower limbs, and (3) movements involving two or more body units. Finely coordinated movements includes (1) hand-finger movements, (2) hand-eye coordination, (3) hand-ear coordination, (4) hand-eye-ear coordination, and (5) other combinations of hand-foot-eye-ear movements. Nonverbal communication includes (1) facial expression, (2) gestures, and (3) bodily movements. Speech includes (1) sound production, (2) sound-word formulation, (3) sound projection, and (4) sound-gesture coordination.[13] Even though Kibler may not have intended to include choral sound production in the speech category (no. 4 in the previous paragraph), it is obvious that is where it belongs. Further research needs to be done to include the psychomotor aspect of how people perform and project musical sounds.

Elizabeth Simpson, a former home economics professor at the University of Illinois, developed a taxonomy of psychomotor skills that is organized according to complexity. The objectives at the lower levels of her taxonomy are considered to be easier to initiate than those at the upper levels. Her categories include (1) *perception* (the process of becoming aware of objects, qualities, or relations through the senses), (2) *set* (exhibiting a readiness for an action or experience), (3) *guided response* (actions developed under the guidance of a teacher), (4) *mechanism* (a habitual learned response), (5) *complex overt response* (effective performance of a complex motor skill), (6) *adaptation* (the ability to adjust a performance so it will be more useful), and (7) *origination* (ability to develop new skills).[14]

Level three, guided response, is of particular interest to choral instructors. Simpson indicates that there are two subheadings under this level: (1) *imitation* (executing an act after having observed someone else perform that act) and (2) *trial and error* (choosing an appropriate response after having tried several different ones). The use of imitation is a technique employed by many choral instructors when it is difficult to verbalize such things as tone production, style, or timbre. They sing what they want to communicate and ask the student to imitate them. Trial and error is employed by many students when they reach the practice room. For instance, when students are unable to experience the desired color of a vocal tone, they often experiment with several different colors before choosing the one they deem to be best.

Most perfected vocal skills fall at level five, complex overt response, which includes *automatic performance* (the ability to perform a finely coordinated skill with ease and muscular control). After students have perfected proper posture, breath control, resonance, and freedom in singing, the entire body must respond with tremendous finesse and control plus initiate whatever is being sung with rhythmic and intonation accuracy. These are definitely complex overt responses.

In 1963, R. H. Dave identified five different levels of psychomotor responses including (1) imitation, (2) manipulation, (3) precision, (4) articulation, and (5) naturalization.[15]

---

[13] R. J. Baker, L. L. Barker, and D. T. Miles, *Behavioral Objectives and Instruction* (Boston: Allyn and Bacon, Inc., 1970), p. 95.

[14] E. Simpson, *The Classification of Education Objectives, Psychomotor Domain* (Washington, D.C.: United States Office of Education, OE-85-104, 1966), p. 88.

[15] R. H. Dave, "The Identification and Measurement of Environmental Process Variables that are Related to Educational Achievement," Ph.D. dissertation, University of Chicago, 1963, p. 13.

Imitation, slightly different than Simpson's level three described above, relates the initial inner urge or desire to duplicate an observed action. The attempt to duplicate the observed action follows, but generally the first performance and its repetitions lack neuromuscular coordination and that which results is often unrefined, primitive, and undeveloped. Behavioral objectives written to the imitation level are:

1. The students will copy the notes on the lines and spaces of their papers as the teacher illustrates them on the board.
2. The students will sing "My Country 'Tis of Thee" as an audition selection for membership in the choir.
3. Each student will stand and take three deep breaths before singing.

Manipulation is the stage at which the learner is capable of performing an action according to instruction and directions given and not just on the basis of observation only. Here the emphasis is placed on being able to follow instructions, perform isolated psychomotor functions, and develop sound practice habits. Exemplary behavioral objectives are:

1. The students will copy the notes on the lines and spaces of their papers as dictated vocally by the teacher.
2. The students will stand with proper posture and sing "My Country 'Tis of Thee."
3. The students will take three deep breaths before singing and assure that the breath-band area expands completely around the body.

Precision includes proficiency of performance and reaching a higher level of accuracy and refinement in isolated psychomotor functions. Typical objectives for this level are:

1. The students will write an original melody using proper manuscripting skills.
2. The students will stand throughout the entire rehearsal using proper posture without having been told how to do so.
3. The students will breathe properly as they sing every phrase of an entire selection.

Articulation emphasizes the coordination of a series of actions and developing the ability to connect or "segue" from one to another. Objectives for this level are:

1. The students will write an entire original song using proper manuscripting skills.
2. The students will stand throughout the entire rehearsal using proper posture, correct breathing, resonant tones, and pure vowels without having been told how to do so.
3. The students will sing "My Country 'Tis of Thee" with correct choral technique in a sensitive, artistic fashion.

Naturalization indicates that the series of connected actions have reached their highest level of proficiency. The objective at this level is to make the actions seem routine and spontaneous with a minimum of expended psychic and mental energy. Behavioral objectives at this level are:

1. The students will compose a symphony using proper manuscripting skills.
2. The students will sing all the concerts on the fall tour using all aspects of correct choral technique.
3. The students will sing the *Liebeslieder Waltzes*, op. 52 by Johannes Brahms in German with correct choral technique in a sensitive, artistic fashion.

Devising Teaching Strategies

The third phase of Thornburg's instructional model is the actual teaching process, that is, deciding how the material will be taught. He suggests six steps to effective teaching.

1. *Student preparation*: The teacher directs the students' minds toward the learning tasks at hand.
2. *Stimulus presentation*: The deliberate presentation of specific, identifiable stimuli ensures more discriminated responses by the students.
3. *Student response*: Two crucial factors in teaching—give the students time to compose a response to a stimulus and give them feedback (reinforcement) as to the acceptability of the response.
4. *Reinforcement*: Planning for reinforcement, preferably positive, strengthens the tendency for students to learn a response and to maintain it when it is subsequently elicited.
5. *Evaluation*: Some assessment of the quality and rate of learning should be undertaken by the teacher. This makes both the student and the teacher aware of the effectiveness of the teaching-learning environment.
6. *Spaced review*: A crucial step in the teaching process is the periodic presentation of stimuli that will trigger previously learned responses. Such review ensures retention.

This model may be applied easily to teaching in the choral classroom. Consider how these steps may be used when teaching a new choral piece to the students.

1. *Student preparation*: Before Mrs. Alexander passed out the copies of the new selection for the forthcoming choral festival, she told the students, "In two months our choir will be going to the regional choral festival in Mayville where we will be adjudicated according to our performance abilities on three selections: "How Lovely Is Thy Dwelling Place" by Johannes Brahms, "The Road Not Taken" by Randall Thompson, and a folk song called "My Love is Like a Red, Red Rose." This will be the twenty-second year that our choir has participated in this festival and, as you know, we have received a superior rating eighteen of those twenty-two appearances. The students who have gone before you have established a precedent of high choral standards and a dedicated commitment to quality performance that we must strive to match

to continue this tradition. If we are to meet this challenge, each of us must be extremely diligent to the task at hand as we work each day. The music will not be easy. It will demand your very best in concentration, music reading skills, and choral technique."

At this point she distributed the music to the students and asked them to open it to the first page. "This piece is one of several movements from a larger work called the *German Requiem* that was written in commemoration of Brahm's mother who had just died. He also dedicated it to his good friend, Robert Schumann, a great composer and music critic, who too had died several months earlier. It is called a German requiem because it uses the German language (Brahm's native tongue) instead of liturgical Latin, the language of most requiem masses. We will sing an English translation of the work. A requiem mass is a memorial service for the dead. "How Lovely Is Thy Dwelling Place" is the best-known movement from Brahms's requiem mass and one that is well within the vocal capabilities of senior high school singers. You will find it to be a work with warm harmonies and beautiful melodies. Each voice part has an opportunity to sing a melody somewhere in the song. Once you have learned it, you will want to sing it again and again, and you will never forget it."

2. *Presentation of material*: Using the following behavioral objectives, Mrs. Alexander introduced "How Lovely Is Thy Dwelling Place" on the first day of rehearsal: (a) The students will listen to a recording of the piece to develop an understanding of the overall mood, texture, tempo, and style of the work. (b) Using the Kodály rhythm syllables, the students will chant the rhythm of the first section of the work, one voice part at a time. (c) Using the Kodály rhythm syllables, the students will chant the rhythm of the first section of the work, all voice parts together. (d) The students will clap the rhythm of the first section of the work, all voice parts together. (e) The students will chant the words in rhythm to the first section of the work, all voice parts together. (f) Using pitch syllables, the students will drill all pitches in the first section of the piece as they relate to each other in response to the teacher who will communicate those pitches with the Curwen hand signs. (g) Following the directed gestures of the instructor, the students will sing each of the pitches in their part with pitch syllables from the first section of the piece as they read from the printed page, but without the control of the rhythm, one voice part at a time. (h) The students will sing their voice part in rhythm with pitch syllables, one part at a time. (i) The students will sing their voice parts in rhythm with pitch syllables, all voices together. (j) The students will sing the words in the first section to the piece in rhythm, all voices together. (k) As time allows, the students will apply objectives *b* through *j* to the second and third sections of the work.

3. *Student response*: The students sang "How Lovely Is Thy Dwelling Place" according to the behavioral objectives related above and at the instructions of the teacher.

4. *Feedback/reinforcement*: Mrs. Alexander used both positive (praise when the students sang correctly) and negative (telling them when they sang incorrectly and drilling them until they were singing the proper pitches) reinforcement. She was careful to offer positive reinforcement intermittently so as to guarantee its effectiveness. If students are rewarded for every response, soon positive reinforcement becomes ineffective.

5. *Evaluation of progress*: Progress is apparent in a choral rehearsal because the desired sound emerges as the students work. To become more completely informed as to the student's weaknesses, Mrs. Alexander recorded some of

her rehearsals and listened to the tape in the quiet privacy of her office away from the external activity of the rehearsal. To determine if each singer was accomplishing the objectives, at various times she asked them to sing individually.

6. *Spaced review*: Mrs. Alexander maintained the same objectives for the next several rehearsals, following the appropriate teaching procedure. She began work on the other two selections for the contest and was careful to alternate rehearsal on each of them so the review would be effective when she returned to "How Lovely Is Thy Dwelling Place." As the group progressed, she developed new objectives that included vocal and choral techniques.

Assessment

The fourth and final part of Thornburg's interactive instructional model is assessing the progress of the teaching process. When students complete a unit (or a choral program), their work should be formally assessed to determine if the unit objectives were met. In structured music courses such as music theory, general music, music appreciation, fine arts, and such, this assessment provides the teacher with data that will be used to determine the grade. In choral classes, the final performance provides the data for assessment and, in a sense, the audience who attends the performance participates in the assessment process. A concert well received, music well performed, and students satisfied with their performance partially indicate that learning occurred. On the other hand, it is the teacher's responsibility to determine if the choir as a whole met the behavioral objectives specified before rehearsals began. The teacher must determine if each individual met those objectives. If such is the case, each individual in the choir has learned.

As part of the assessment process, the teacher should establish criteria that help the students understand their expected performance level. When individual students fall below that level, additional practice should be required.

In summary, two activities are necessary in assessing student learning: (1) Through evaluation with exams and/or observations, the teacher must detect whether students are progressing toward the goals specified within the instructional objectives and (2) student deficiencies are analyzed and steps must be taken to alleviate those deficiencies. In some cases teachers may determine that they have written inappropriate behavioral objectives or failed to administer adequate diagnostic testing. Possibly the teachers' teaching strategies were poorly designed. If this is true, it is essential that teachers evaluate each step of their teaching strategies in terms of student learning and take measures to correct them.

THOUGHTS FOR CONTEMPLATION AND DISCUSSION

1. Why is it important for you, as a choral teacher, to have clearly thought-out goals for what you want to accomplish?

2. Is student assessment in the affective domain harder than in the cognitive domain? Why or why not?
3. How would you justify the need for an interactive instructional model of learning as discussed in this chapter when a parent tells you, "I don't want James to be graded in choir. He's taking choir just for the fun of it"?

BIBLIOGRAPHY

BAKER, R. J., L. L. BARKER, and D. T. MILES. *Behavioral Objectives and Instruction.* Boston: Allyn and Bacon, Inc., 1970.

BLOOM, B. S., et al. *Taxonomy of Educational Objectives: Cognitive Domain.* New York: McKay Publications, 1956.

DAVE, R.H. The Identification and Measurement of Environmental Process Variables that are Related to Educational Achievement. Unpublished Doctoral Dissertation, University of Chicago, 1963.

KRATHWOHL, D. R., B. S. BLOOM, and B. B. MASIA. *Taxonomy of Educational Objectives: Affective Domain.* New York: McKay Publications, 1964.

SIMPSON, E. *The Classification of Education Objectives, Psychomotor Domain.* Washington, D. C.: United States Office of Education, OE-85-104, 1966.

THORNBURG, HERSHEL D. *Introduction to Educational Psychology.* St. Paul: West Publishing Co., 1984.

6

Characteristics of A Master Teacher

Some say that teachers are born, not made. The inference is that the ability to understand students, to communicate in ways they comprehend, and to motivate them properly is intuitive. We have all been influenced by teachers who seemingly had a knack for teaching. Whenever we observe a teacher who displays a skill that seems so natural, we do not know how much of that ability is innate or how much of it was the result of long hours of study and years of training and experience.

Ordinary teachers may be born, not made; but master teachers are made! Granted, the molding of master teachers seems to be easier with some individuals than with others. In some cases, the native ability to communicate, to be sensitive to what is happening in the classroom, to hold students' attention, and to "turn them on" to their subject greatly enhances teachers' chances to succeed. Master teachers will take that natural ability and augment it many times over by learning everything they can about the art of teaching.

What, then, are the characteristics of a master teacher? A definitive answer to that question is somewhat evasive. Teaching is a highly complex procedure that involves hundreds of actions and reactions both by students and teachers. One of the most inflammatory issues debated among teachers is how to measure quality teaching. Administrators on the university campus would like to find a conclusive way to deal with the problem so that their responsibilities pertaining to salary raises, rank, and promotion would be made easier. Elementary and secondary school principals are experiencing more and more pressure to expedite the procedure for awarding merit pay raises rather than just giving raises based on the number of years in the profession.

Almost everyone agrees that the teacher is the principal catalyst to an effective education process. Recent national polls on education indicate that John Q. Public perceives the improvement of the quality of teachers as the best way to improve the American public schools. According to Palonsky, the variables that affect the student's success as a learner are so many (to name three of the most influential ones: students' school and home environment, community and family expectations, and whether the class meets before or after lunch) that it becomes virtually impossible to determine the effectiveness of the teacher through standardized research.[1] If this is the case, then we must turn to empirical knowledge and the writings of those whom musical society deems to be great teachers to fashion a mental image of the master teacher.

THE MASTER TEACHER "IN A NUTSHELL"

Before attempting to delineate specifics, it might be wise to contemplate some general statements made by various music educators in their attempt to define the competent teacher. These are statements that project "in a nutshell" any unique ingredient(s) necessary to be a successful music teacher. On the surface, none of these statements may seem to be acutely profound but to the seasoned professional and to those who have pondered seriously each statement's philo-sophical base, they are pertinent indeed. All represent a fundamental approach used to define the successful teacher, which reaches to the core of the music teaching profession.

Although there might be those who would disagree with her, Gelineau believes that "love in your heart" is the most essential quality for excellence in music teaching:

> ... In my many years of classroom music supervision experience I have found that some of the best music comes from rooms where teachers can't sing. Their secret (a delightful one to share) is that they have a sincere desire in their hearts to bring joy into the lives of their children. So you see it's not so much what's in your head as what's in your heart.
> All that's really required for teaching music in the elementary classroom is a few musical teaching aids and love in your heart. And the greatest of these is love.[2]

In his junior high general music methods classes at Florida State University, Irvin Cooper said many times, "If a person is going to be successful as a junior

[1] S. B. Palonsky, "Teacher Effectiveness in Secondary Schools: An Ethnographic Approach," *The High School Journal* 61, no. 2 (1977), 45–51.
[2] P. R. Gelineau, *Experiences in Music* (New York: McGraw-Hill Book Co., 1970), pp. vii–viii.

high school music teacher he must believe totally and completely in what he is doing and have an undying love for the children."[3]

D. G. Ryans says:

> . . . warm, friendly, understanding teachers are more effective than those who aren't; businesslike and organized teachers are more effective than teachers who are careless and disorganized; and imaginative and enthusiastic teachers surpass in effectiveness those who are routine and dull.[4]

Charles Hoffer indicates that good teachers are those who utilize their strengths to the fullest to compensate for their weaker points:

> . . . with some teachers their strength is their ability to play piano, with others it is an ability to inspire students, and with others it is their knowledge of music and their intelligence. Each person develops somewhat different ways to fulfill the role of teacher.[5]

The authors of *Teaching Music in Today's Secondary Schools* believe that the music teacher's personality is the most important quality in determining effectiveness:

> The teacher's personality is probably the most important quality contributing to his success or failure . . . since the student who likes the teacher, and believes the teacher likes him, will learn more effectively.[6]

Ryans also corroborates those sentiments when he concludes that effective teachers are democratic, fair, alert, understanding, kindly, stimulating, original, attractive, responsible, steady, confident, responsive, and posed. Ryans characterized the ineffective teachers as being partial, autocratic, aloof, evasive, harsh, dull, uncertain, excitable, erratic, stereotyped, apathetic, unimpressive, and restricted.

Astin and Lee[7] and Biddle and Ellena[8] endorse "pupil performance" as the best measurement for good teaching. Master teachers are able to effectuate their intended music learning outcomes. To be effective, according to their research, a teacher must have both intent and achievement. Without intent, student achievement may be accidental rather than controlled. Moreover, beyond

---

[3] This quotation came from my class notes when I was enrolled in the class.

[4] D. G. Ryans, *Characteristics of Teachers* (Washington, D.C.: American Council on Education, 1960), pp. 360–61.

[5] Charles R. Hoffer, *Introduction to Music Education* (Belmont, Calif.: Wadsworth Publishing, 1983), pp. 15–16.

[6] Malcolm E. Bessom, Alphonse M. Tatarunis, and Samuel L. Forcucci, *Teaching Music in Today's Secondary Schools*, 2d ed. (New York: Holt, Rinehart and Winston, 1980), p. 5.

[7] A. W. Astin and C. B. T. Lee, "Current Practices in the Evaluation and Training of College Teachers," *The Educational Record* 27 (1966), 361–75.

[8] B. J. Biddle and W. J. Ellena, Editors, *Contemporary Research on Teacher Effectiveness* (New York: Holt, Rinehart and Winston, 1964).

intent, for the teacher to be considered effective, the student must have achieved the teacher's intended goals.

Charles Leonhard indicates that "passion" is that special ingredient needed to be a successful teacher:

> Perhaps the best summation of the necessary qualities teachers must possess has been given voice by Charles Leonhard, who throughout his career has called for "passion" in the teaching of music. Not just passionate attachment to music, and not just passionate caring for children, but also passionate commitment to ourselves and to our worth as a profession. Part of that commitment is the attainment of a deep understanding and ability to apply that understanding in education practice and the voicing of that understanding in educational policy.[9]

More recently, educators seem to rely on the mastery of a complex set of competencies such as teaching and rehearsing skills, musical knowledge, human relations techniques, and management skills (among many) as the best measures of effective teaching.[10]

Finally, here is a brief exposé by Shirley Mullins that takes the form of a personal experience. Although it is not expressed in definitive terms, it exemplifies exactly her assessment of a master teacher:

> My heart was beating with his. The little boy had been asked [in a master class] to play a scale. "He knows that scale perfectly," I thought. "He'll be fine." But there it was—the shaky tone that string players fear. It's the tip-off to nerves, like broadcasting it to the world.
> The master teacher watched and listened.
> "Young man, let's talk about the quiver in your bow."
> "But sir, my bow didn't quiver."
> "Good. Then let's talk about the bow that didn't quiver."[11]

SPECIFIC CHARACTERISTICS OF THE MASTER TEACHER

By now it should be relatively obvious that we are not going to be able to pinpoint the specific attributes of a master teacher. How can we, when even the experts cannot agree? Therefore, for the remainder of the chapter we are going to examine various ingredients that will be helpful in identifying the

---

[9] Ibid., p. 13.

[10] Consult the following sources to corroborate this approach: T. L. Good, "Teacher Effectiveness in the Elementary School," *Journal of Teacher Education* 30 (1979), 52–64; J. E. Brophy, "Teacher Behavior and Its Effect," *Journal of Educational Psychology* 71 (1979), 733–50; B. V. Rosenshine, "Content, Time, and Direct Instruction," in *Research on Teaching: Concepts, Findings, and Implications,* edited by P. L. Peterson and H. J. Walberg (Berkeley, Calif.: McCutchan, 1979), pp. 18–23; and D. K. Taebel and J. G. Coker, "Teaching Effectiveness in Elementary Classroom Music: Relationships Among Competency Measures, Pupil Product Measures, and Certain Attribute Variables," *Journal of Research in Music Education* 28 (1980), 250–64.

[11] Shirley Mullins, *Teaching Music, the Human Experience* (Yellow Springs, Ohio: Shirley Mullins, 1985), p. 27.

master teacher. Because of hereditary limitations, everyone cannot possess all these positive characteristics. In fact, it would be difficult to find any one master teacher who possesses them all. Nonetheless, one might imagine the ideal master teacher who could serve as a model to be emulated by those who are young and inexperienced. These ingredients are not necessarily in order of their importance.

Self-Honesty

There are two maxims relative to self-honesty that those who desire to be master teachers seriously need to consider: "Know thyself" and "To thine own self be true." The complete meaning of each of these maxims generally is not understood by the young. Life experiences are the essential ingredients necessary to find complete knowledge of one's self. Regrettably, there are those who have a wealth of life experiences but still do not know themselves. Further, life experiences are essential to determine how to be true to one's self. The implication of these thoughts is that age and experience are necessary to be a master teacher. Indeed they are. Should this reasoning lead the young to resign themselves to never becoming master teachers? Not at all. The age of youth is that fleeting period of opportunity in which the young choose those meaningful, significant, purposeful, and proper life experiences that result in the wisdom and technique of the master teacher. In other words, each moment of individuals' youth is important because decisions are being made that will determine how masterful they will be later in life. (Another maxim comes into play here that points out the tragic consequences of youth's inability to grasp this logic: "Experience is the best teacher." Many young people do not have enough confidence in themselves or their elders to believe it when they are told that they must take advantage of each moment and give careful thought to their daily decisions. They realize it when they get older and have experienced it, but, of course, by then it is too late: Their youth is gone. Those are the young people who often achieve very little, if anything at all, that is masterful in life.) Therefore, it is absolutely imperative for young and beginning teachers to set a course toward learning about themselves and then determine how to be true to what they have learned. They must set priorities, choosing to place at the top of the list those things that will make them better-informed, technically proficient choral teachers.

The first step towards self-honesty comes in the realization that it is possible to be self-dishonest. In other words, there are those who might not realize when their actions do not corroborate what they say. People often espouse one tenet or idea by the words they speak, but it becomes obvious by their actions that in their innermost being (their heart of hearts), they truly do not believe it. Suppose a young teacher announces to the choir that art (classical) music is the best literature for the choir to sing because it serves as the most suitable vehicle for students to learn good choral technique, but each time he introduces a new selection he begins his presentation with "you're not going to like to sing this piece but. . . ." That attitude automatically communicates to the singers that the teacher, in all reality, does not believe what he says or he would not apologize for the music he chooses. If he presents each new piece with a statement such as "you're not going to believe what a great piece of music this is," the students may not like singing it, but a least the teacher's actions support the tenets he espouses. If teachers are going to learn to be honest with themselves, they first must determine exactly what they believe and be true to that belief.

The most obvious portrayal of lack of self-honesty is evident in the actions of directors who make mistakes in rehearsal then blame the singers for the results of those mistakes. For instance, a director may cue the altos at a soprano entrance, then promptly say, "Sopranos, why didn't you come in?" Any respect students might have for a director will erode very quickly as a result of this type of behavior. The proper response should have been, "Oops, sorry sopranos—catch you next time." Another example of self-dishonesty is exemplified by directors who in general music class proclaim the importance of listening to symphonic music but never attend a symphony concert.

A Good Sense of Humor

Humor manifests itself in several different ways. Some people display a dry wit without cracking a smile; others have a more flamboyant expression of humor with a slap on the back. Some individuals display humor by telling a good story or joke; others emit funny words instantaneously, almost without thinking. There are those who appear to have very little innate wit, but they enjoy the humor of others and laugh hardily at a situation or comment. Having a good sense of humor, however it manifests itself, is an important characteristic of master teachers and is a vital ingredient in the music classroom. Teachers must be able to laugh at themselves. Those who display anger at humorous situations, particularly if they are directed at them, will eventually have difficulty in the classroom.

There are occasions when spontaneous humor for the sake of laughter is confused by the students with humor for the sake of drawing attention to one's self. Some adolescent students may have a tendency to interrupt the classroom procedure under the guise of humor because they want to draw attention to themselves. Teachers soon learn to keep the rehearsal or lesson moving, allowing spontaneous humor to occur without stopping the pace of the activities. If learning is impeded, students may need to be taught the difference.

Sarcasm and ridicule disguised as humor should be forbidden. If teachers create the process of controlling their classes with sarcasm and ridicule, severe repercussions usually result: Students soon determine that they must return the sarcasm with sarcasm and the ridicule with ridicule (even though the ridicule might not be in the presence of the teacher) to survive, and the classroom becomes a virtual battlefield of ridiculous wit. At that point, learning ceases.

Satisfaction in the Job

Most master teachers love what they are doing. Undergraduate music majors receive their greatest satisfaction through personal musical performance. In most cases, this is the reason they majored in music in the first place. Some students choose not to major in music education because they are fearful that they will miss the personal performance opportunities and they will not be fulfilled in teaching. When prospective music educators move from the role of student to the role of teacher, they should receive their satisfaction from the growth and musical expressions of their students and from the results of their preparation for choral music performances as conductors of the student choirs and other musical productions. If, as teachers, they find that the weaning away from personal performance is unbearable, they may desire to look for performance opportunities in a church choir, local opera company, community chorus, or some other similar organization. Some might seek full-time employment in personal performance and cease teaching altogether.

The point to be made here is that the music teaching profession does not need individuals who want to be professional performers but for one reason or another are unable to survive in that world. Teachers must be fully committed to the teaching profession. Commitment is essential to productivity and happiness. Young, prospective teachers who feel that full-time personal performance might be essential to their happiness should settle that question before taking their first teaching position.

Once young professionals are committed to teaching choral music, they must deal with another question relative to job satisfaction. Since music education involves the dimension of musical performance, educators must decide *how much emphasis* performance will receive in their overall curriculum. Performance activities in choral festivals, contests, and clinics serve as great motivators in the learning process. They represent the ultimate performance opportunity for most school choirs. Due to these two important factors, many teachers often find themselves committing a large portion of their teaching activity to achieving perfection in performance while other important activities necessary for a well-rounded and effective choral program fall along the wayside. For teachers who are committed to the "teaching process" instead of the "performance process," this serves as a constant source of frustration, particularly if they are confronted with undue pressure from principals, parents, and school boards to maintain an active performance schedule with their groups. Finding an answer to this nagging question is essential to satisfaction in their jobs: Which is more important, teaching or performing? The master teacher will be able to strike a nice balance between the two, finding daily satisfaction in each step of the learning process and heightened periodic satisfaction from "mountaintop experiences" through performance. Certainly, in the minds of master teachers, performance opportunities serve primarily as meaningful motivators but never as the sole reason for teaching.

Superior Scholarship and Musicianship

In the minds of some, the word *scholar* connotes an individual who is a bookworm. Most dictionaries define a scholar as, simply, a learner. There is no inference that the learning must necessarily come from books (even though learning from books is certainly an accepted practice). Peters and Miller make this point:

Teachers should be scholars. The idea sounds formidable, carrying images of dusty libraries, lonely rare-book rooms, and the like; however, modern scholarship rarely fits this stereotype. Scholarship . . . is more an attitude than a set of actions. You, as university students, are now afforded the rare opportunity to build in yourselves a set of scholarly attitudes that will serve you and your future students for the rest of your life. There are certain characteristics of a scholar that we hope will become a part of you, allowing you to deal with future decision making with much more ease.[12]

There is also a misconception that a scholar must exhibit a very high intelligence quotient (IQ). Still a further misconception among some people is that most musicians are not scholars. A better definition of a scholar would be one who has an open, seeking mind. That quality is crucial to be a master teacher. Master teachers, then, must be scholars. Master teachers should never cease to attempt to learn; their intellectual and technical growth should be ongoing and current. A "Renaissance person" is one who is enthusiastically and vigorously literary, artistic, and cultured, distinguished by an increasing pursuit of learning and by an imaginative response to broader horizons. Master teachers should be Renaissance persons in the truest sense. A "liberal arts person" seeks to develop the mind's general intellectual capabilities such as reason and judgment and is interested in all the liberal arts (humanities, languages, philosophy, history, literature, and the abstract sciences). Master teachers, even though displaying outstanding musical skills, should be liberal arts persons in the truest sense.

Not only must master teachers be scholars, they also must be good musicians. Preparation for teaching should include the study of music theory (including ear training), counterpoint, form and analysis, choral arranging, music history and literature, the attainment of a high degree of proficiency in performance in their major area (voice or piano), and the acquisition of basic keyboard skills for the vocalist and basic vocal skills for the pianist. Because they will be choral conductors, they must display knowledge of choral repertoire and performance practices and knowledge of voice production, conducting, and rehearsing, and they must possess communicative skills and leadership qualities. Finally, they must display a thorough knowledge of learning theory as applied to music making, adolescent growth and development, evaluation skills, technological hardware and software, and the basic philosophies governing music teaching.

A Great Communicator and Motivator

During his presidency, Ronald Reagan was known as the great communicator. What were Reagan's special communicative skills that warranted his receiving that special appellation? He did not display a vast vocabulary. He often stammered when he spoke. On occasions he even vacillated about what he said. He certainly was evasive in some of the answers he gave to very important

[12] G. D. Peters and R. F. Miller, *Music Teaching and Learning* (New York: Longman, 1982), p. 50.

questions. Why, then, was he such a great communicator? Probably it had to do with his sincerity. He truly believed what he said (he said it with conviction), and when he said it, people listened, even though they might have disagreed with him. Further, in all likelihood, it related to the way he looked at the listeners (or the television camera) when he spoke. Maybe people were drawn into his person and his message by his expressive use of the eyes and body language. Unlike some presidents, he went often to the people to explain his reasoning and to justify the decisions he made. He kept the people informed. Finally, he understood the medium (in most cases, this was the medium of television) that served as a vehicle to get his message to the people.

If teachers of choral music are to be good communicators, they too must be sincere, believe completely in what they have to say, display conviction when they speak, keep the students informed, and use the eyes and body language to draw their listeners to them. Most importantly, they must understand the medium (the conductor's podium) that serves as a vehicle to get their message to the students. Words are only one means of communication, and in the choral classroom they may be the poorest means. Choral conductors use an entire system of gestures and body movements to get their message to the students. A good choral communicator is one who is highly skilled in that system and is able to facilitate a rehearsal with a minimum of spoken instructions.

No matter how important the message, it is of little consequence to the ones for whom it is intended if they are not moved to action upon receiving it. Much is said about the art of motivation in other chapters throughout this book; therefore, the discussion here is brief. It must be related, however, that the ability to motivate is probably the greatest asset of the master teacher. Without motivation there is very little teaching. The first thing a young professional learns is that relating or emphasizing the message verbally is probably the weakest means of motivation. The master will devise nonverbal ways through organization, structure, goal planning, and incentives that will move the students to action. It is delightful indeed to observe a teacher who understands how to motivate. The students ostensively vibrate with enthusiasm for the subject and the activities of the class, and no threats are heard nor promises made.

Emotional Stability

Musicians are notoriously known to be temperamental. One only has to ask the principal of a school (the music teacher is often the one labeled as being difficult to please), the pastor of a church (organists and music directors may be the staff members requiring the most attention), or the dean of a college (the music faculty members frequently never seem to be able to get along) to verify this contention. Possibly artistic and highly creative individuals do display a greater degree of sensitivity on occasions, but in most cases, the elaborately tempermental musician is the one who has been influenced by the tyrant image portrayed by some of the great conductors and prima donnas of yesteryear, or they are under an inordinate amount of strain due to family problems and job stress. That type of behavior in the secondary classroom is absolutely taboo. If fits of temper and acts of frustration persist in the classroom, it is vitally important that teachers seek professional help. That behavior will destroy the esprit de corps of a choral organization and severely limit the learning process in the classroom. Out-of-control personal behavior generally conveys out-of-control classroom behavior. Everyone gets mad on occasions due to intolerable classroom situations, but losing one's temper certainly is not the proper way to deal with problems. There are better ways to prove to the class that teachers mean what they say, and "blowing the stack" only makes matters worse.

An Attractive Personality

Personality is the blending of people's personal traits so that they may be perceived to be who they are as individuals. The phrase "perceived to be" is used intentionally because there are times when observation and acquaintance over a long period reveal that people are not really who they are perceived to be, but are quite different indeed. How teachers are perceived by their students is important to teachers' success in the classroom. Teachers are perceived to be dull, stimulating, tolerable, funny, a nice guy, hard, weird and a multiple of other labels that students conjure up. In most cases, these labels are assigned due to teachers' personalities. According to Bessom, Tatarunis, and Forcucci:

> Successful teachers have variable traits, but often their personalities are marked by human understanding; tolerance; cooperativeness; democratic judgment; warmth and friendliness; a love of children; a deep interest in their work; a sense of involvement, dedication, and willingness; an informed outlook; intelligence; knowledge; a capacity for growth; talent and skill; a receptivity to new ideas and situations; organizational ability; clarity of thought and expression; emotional stability; good health; a neat, distinctive appearance; individuality; and creativity.[13]

After reading the above, the general consensus might be that teachers must be omnipotent, omniscient, and omnipresent as well, for only God could meet the requirements for such a complete list of personal traits. This points out how difficult it may be to become a master teacher. Young professionals should mark these traits in their minds and use them for inspiration as they work toward that goal.

Student/teacher relationships may be more important in the learning process than the actual selection, organization, and presentation of the subject matter itself. All teachers want to be liked, and as Bessom, Tatarunis, and Forcucci have said, "a student who likes the teacher, and believes the teacher likes him, will learn more effectively than the student who does not."[14] What is important is that teachers should not compromise their educational objectives by making decisions based on whether the students will like them. Conversely, teachers should never be so staunch and uncompromising in their educational goals that they take a position similar to "I don't care what the students think,

---

[13] Bessom, Tatarunis, and Forcucci, *Teaching Music*, p. 5.

[14] Ibid., pp. 5–6.

I'm going to make this course as hard as I can." A more satisfactory approach is one in which the teachers and students work together with mutual understanding and acceptance of the desired educational goals.

Because of personality conflicts, there always will be students whom teachers do not hold in highest regard, but the master teacher will look for ways to tolerate even the most unlikable student. Whenever statements such as "I love teaching, but I can't stand the kids" is bantered about in the teacher's lounge, it might be well to suggest to the proclaimers to take a long, hard look at why they are teaching. After all, teaching is not possible without students.

Uniqueness

Whenever young teachers first begin the teaching experience they often have a very high regard for one or more of the college or university professors with whom they have worked and studied. Often it is the university choral director because they have sung in the choir for four years, the director might have given them a scholarship for their services, or they know that person better than anyone else on the faculty because they have spent more time in that class. They often think, "Whenever I become a teacher, I want to be just like so-and-so." It is quite natural and even admirable to want to emulate someone who has influenced their lives so positively. There is a fallacy in this type thinking, however, because no one can be "just like" someone else. Their choral director's background, training, personality, taste in literature, and life motivations are different from theirs; therefore, to be like that person is impossible. This is not to say that students should discontinue to hold a special teacher in high esteem. They should always allow those standards and methods to motivate them to be the best teachers possible.

Individuals have personality traits that make each of them unique. Although not as complicated, there is a parallel between an individual's collection of personality traits and the deoxyribonucleic acid (DNA) in each cell of the body. From genome research it is known that each of the 100 trillion cells of the body contains all the biological characteristics of individuals, and the combination of cells makes the biological individuals who they are. People's personality traits are all combined to result in the psychological, sociological, and personal individuals who they are.

To mature into being the master teacher that you desire to be, use this formula for success: Look deep down inside yourself and determine those characteristics in your personality that make you UNIQUELY YOU; then develop, sharpen, mold, and hone the best of those characteristics to the best of your ability. A dry wit, tremendous energy, a keen sense of humor, or maybe an effervescent personality, to name a few, can all be used to develop your teaching skills. Just remember, you are the only person in the world who is uniquely you. Capitalize on it!

Self-Evaluation and Improvement

If teachers remain in the profession, chances are that they will teach for forty years. One of the characteristics of master teachers is their ability to remain fresh, vital, and interesting throughout their entire career. This is impossible without a plan of self-evaluation and improvement.

Most master teachers will attend at least one professional convention each year. They will also continue their educational efforts beyond the bachelor's level, at least seeking a master's degree and even a doctorate in some cases. If they do not work on a specific degree program, at least every other summer they will attend workshops and courses of study that will improve their teaching and rehearsal techniques. Many school districts require further study and will not give salary raises to teachers who neglect self-improvement.

The Music Educators National Conference has a professional certification program designed for teachers with eight or more years of experience who have demonstrated self-improvement as music educators. Those wishing to be certified must document their professional activities and provide letters of recommendations from administrators and colleagues. To reach the second level of certification, they must supply a videotape of their teaching prepared according to exact stipulations. Teachers must renew the certification every five years.

Others ways to prevent stagnant teaching are (1) to videotape lessons and rehearsals and after viewing them, write down specific ways the teacher could have improved them; (2) to ask colleagues to critique lessons and rehearsals (it is better if the colleague is a musician); (3) to ask the students periodically to write a critique of the course of study or choir; (4) to rewrite the class syllabus periodically; (5) to change textbooks every few years; and (6) to select intentionally new repertoire that teachers have never sung or conducted; even though they should choose certain choral repertoire standards.

Other Considerations

In 1980, Taebel and Coker asked 201 music teachers to rate a list of competencies in terms of their effect on student learning. The most important musical skills that emerged from the study were (1) detecting errors or problems in musical performance, (2) conducting skills, and (3) using vocal skills in illustrating various performance techniques.[15]

In 1982, P. B. Baker asked 119 music educators and general school administrators to identify those competencies they felt were essential to effective music teaching. These ten basic characteristics emerged:

1. Enthusiasm for teaching and caring for students;
2. Strong but fair discipline;
3. Observable student enjoyment, interest, and participation;
4. Communicative skills;
5. Sense of humor;
6. In-depth musicianship;
7. Knowledge and use of good literature;

[15] D. K. Taebel and J. G. Coker, "Teaching Effectiveness," 250–64.

8. Strong rapport with students individually and the group as a whole;
9. High professional standards for himself or herself;
10. Use of positive group management techniques.[16]

In 1975, C. Yarbrough examined the effect of "high-magnitude" versus "low-magnitude" conductors on mixed choruses. Four mixed choruses were all rehearsed under three different conductors: a regular conductor, a high-magnitude conductor, and a low-magnitude conductor. The study revealed that the chorus members were more attentive and performed better under the leadership of the high-magnitude director (not to mention that this conductor was also the most popular of the three conductors). Characteristics of the high-magnitude conductor included frequent eye contact, constant variation in volume and inflection of the speaking voice, frequent walking or leaning toward the chorus, extensive physical gestures and facial expressions, and a fast-moving and energetic rehearsal pace.[17]

In 1979, Ann Small determined that pacing and energy were important for effective music teaching in a general music class. Pacing refers to the amount of time allotted to each activity as well as the amount of time expended between each activity. To improve pacing, Small recommends spending more time on music and minimizing the necessary but nonmusical activities such as giving verbal instructions, walking from one place in the room to another, or writing on the chalkboard. She also indicated that having music materials and records in place prior to the lesson and limiting the amount of time spent on each activity further enhanced effective pacing.[18]

Recently in one of my classes a student was reporting on the attributes of a good teacher. In a rather creative fashion (by using the letters in the alphabet) he listed what he considered to be the characteristics of a good teacher. He said a teacher should:

have a positive **A**ttitude
be an **A**rtist
control **B**ehavior
be a **B**enevolent dictator
be a good **C**ommunicator
have good **C**lassroom management techniques
be able to **D**iscipline students
be **D**edicated
be **E**ffective

---

[16] P. B. Baker, "The Development of Music Teacher Checklist for Use by Administrators, Music Supervisors, and Teachers in Evaluating Music Teaching," Doctoral dissertation, University of Oregon, 1981, *Dissertation Abstracts International*, Vol. 42, 3489-A, University Microfilms No. 8201803, p. 205.

[17] C. Yarbrough and H. E. Price, "Prediction of Performer Attentiveness Based on Rehearsal Activity and Teacher Behavior," *Journal of Research in Music Education* 29, no. 3, 209–17.

[18] A. R. Small, "Pace Yourself," *Music Educators Journal* 65, no. 9 (1979), 31–33.

be **E**fficient
learn from past **E**xperiences
be able to **E**ndure
be **E**ager to teach
be **E**ncouraging
be **F**air
mold the **F**uture
be **G**enerous
be **G**enuinely concerned
be **G**ood-natured
be **H**ard-working
be **H**elpful
be **H**umble
be **I**mpartial
be an **I**nnovator
be **K**ind
always be **L**earning
be **M**ature
help students solve **P**roblems
be **P**roductive
behave as a **P**rofessional
always continue to **S**tudy
be **Z**ippy!

This list comes from the student's perspective, so since students are the most important half of the learning-teaching process, it would behoove all teachers to attempt to live up to these very challenging characteristics.

CONCLUSION

Being a master teacher is a way of life, a specific lifestyle. To Peters and Miller, it is a mind-set. Therefore, once young teachers embark upon this great journey in life in which they will be about the business of changing behaviors, they must begin to imagine themselves as being master teachers as defined in this chapter. Once the mind is set, the molding process, evolutionary in nature, will commence, and in due time from the cocoon of experience will emerge the finely honed, technically proficient, broad-minded, enthusiastic, and caring transformer of lives, the master teacher.

THOUGHTS FOR CONTEMPLATION AND DISCUSSION

1. After having read what the experts believe "in a nutshell" to be the attributes of a master teacher and after having studied in detail the nine attributes

described in the chapter, decide which *one* attribute is the most important. Why?

2. Do you agree with the statement; "Teachers are born, not made"? Why or why not?
3. What criteria would you like for the principal or music supervisor to use to evaluate your ability as a choral teacher? Why?
4. What are the strengths and weaknesses of annual "across-the-board" raises?
5. What are the strengths and weaknesses of merit raises?
6. What do you think Peters and Miller meant when they said that being a master teacher is a mind-set?
7. Think of characteristics of a master teacher other than those mentioned in the chapter that are important to your success as a choral director.

BIBLIOGRAPHY

ALLEN, TOM. "Identifying Behaviors of the Master Teacher." *Spectrum* 5, no. 5 (1987).

ASTIN, A. W., and C. B. T. LEE. "Current Practices in the Evaluation and Training of College Teachers." *The Educational Record* 27, (1966).

BAKER, P. B. "The Development of Music Teacher Checklist for Use by Adminstrators, Music Supervisors, and Teachers in Evaluating Music Teaching," (Ph.D. diss., University of Oregon, 1981. *Dissertation Abstracts International*, Vol. 42, 3489-A. University Microfilms No. 8201803.

BAKER, R. J., L. L. BARKER, and D. T. MILES. *Behavioral Objectives and Instruction.* Boston: Allyn and Bacon, Inc., 1970.

BESSOM, MALCOLM E., ALPHONSE M. TATARUNIS, and SAMUEL L. FORCUCCI. *Teaching Music in Today's Secondary Schools,* 2d ed. New York: Holt, Rinehart and Winston, 1980.

BIDDLE, B. J. and W. J. ELLENA, W.J., eds. *Contemporary Research on Teacher Effectiveness.* New York: Holt, Rinehart and Winston, 1964.

BLOOM, B. S. et al. *Taxonomy of Educational Objectives: Cognitive Domain.* New York: McKay Publications, 1956.

BROPHY, J. E. "Teacher Behavior and Its Effect." *Journal of Educational Psychology* 71, (1979).

COOPER, J. M., ed. *Classroom Teaching Skills,* 3d ed. Lexington, Mass.: D. C. Heath, 1986.

DAVE, R. H. "The Identification and Measurement of Environmental Process Variables that are Related to Educational Achievement." Ph.D. diss., University of Chicago, 1963.

EDELSON, EDWARD. *The Secondary School Music Program from Classroom to Concert Hall.* West Nyack, N.Y.: Parker Publishing Co., 1972.

ERBES, R. L. "Music Teacher Education: Toward the Twenty-First Century." In *Symposium in Music Education,* edited by R. Colwell. Urbana, Ill.: University of Illinois, 1982.

GELINEAU, P.R. *Experiences in Music.* New York: McGraw-Hill Book Co., 1970.

GOOD, T. L. "Teacher Effectiveness in the Elementary School." *Journal of Teacher Education* 30 (1979).

HOFFER, CHARLES R. *Introduction to Music Education.* Belmont Calif.: Wadsworth Publishing, 1983.

————. *Teaching Music in the Secondary Schools,* 4th ed. Belmont, Calif.: Wadsworth Publishing, 1991.

KEMP, A. "Personality Traits of Successful Music Teachers." *Psychology of Music* (1982).

KOWALL, BONNIE C., ed. *Perspectives in Music Education, Source Book III.* Reston, Va.: Music Educators National Conference, 1966.

KRATHWOHL, D. R., B. S. BLOOM, and B. B. MASIA. *Taxonomy of Educational Objectives: Affective Domain.* New York: McKay Publications, 1964.

LEE, RONALD T. "Would Your Students Give You a Passing Grade?" *Music Educators Journal* 71, no. 9 (1985).

LONG, JAMES D., and VIRGINIA H. FRYE. *Making It Till Friday.* Princeton, N.J.: Princeton Book Co., 1981.

MARPLE, HUGO D. *Backgrounds and Approaches to Junior High Music.* Dubuque, Iowa: Wm. C. Brown Co., 1975.

MILLER, KENNETH E. *Vocal Music Education,*

Teaching in the Secondary Schools. Englewood Cliffs, N.J.: Prentice-Hall, Inc., 1988.

MOULY, GEORGE J. *Psychology for Effective Teaching.* New York: Holt, Rinehart and Winston, 1973.

MULLINS, SHIRLEY. *Teaching Music, the Human Experience.* Yellow Springs, Ohio: Shirley Mullins, 1985.

NEIDIG, KENNETH L., and JOHN JENNINGS, eds. *Choral Director's Guide.* West Nyack, N.Y.: Parker Publishing Co., 1967.

PALONSKY, S. B. "Teacher Effectiveness in Secondary Schools: An Ethonographic Approach." *The High School Journal* 61, no. 2 (1977).

PETERS, G. D, and ROBERT F. MILLER. *Music Teaching and Learning.* New York: Longman, 1982.

ROE, PAUL F. *Choral Music Education,* 2d ed. Englewood Cliffs, N.J.: Prentice-Hall, Inc., 1983.

ROSENSHINE, B. V. "Content, Time, and Direct Instruction." In *Research on Teaching: Concepts, Findings, and Implications,* edited by P. L. Peterson and H. J. Walberg. Berkeley, Calif.: McCutchan, 1979.

RYANS, D. G. *Characteristics of Teachers.* Washington, D.C.: American Council on Education, 1960.

SIMPSON, E. *The Classification of Education Objectives, Psychomotor Domain.* Washington, D.C.: United States Office of Education, OE-85-104, 1966.

SINGLETON, IRA. *Music in Secondary Schools,* 2d ed. Boston: Allyn and Bacon, Inc., 1965.

SMALL, A. R. "Pace Yourself." *Music Educators Journal* 65, no. 9, (1979).

TAEBEL, D. K., and J. G. COKER. "Teaching Effectiveness in Elementary Classroom Music: Relationships Among Competency Measures, Pupil Product Measures, and Certain Attribute Variables." *Journal of Research in Music Education* 28, (1980).

THORNBURG, HERSHEL D. *Introduction to Educational Psychology.* St. Paul: West Publishing Co., 1984.

YARBROUGH, C., and H. E. PRICE. "Prediction of Performer Attentiveness Based on Rehearsal Activity and Teacher Behavior." *Journal of Research in Music Education* 29, no. 3, (1982).

7

Understanding the
Adolescent

A rumor persists in the teaching profession that adolescent students are the most difficult to teach because they are considered to be experiencing "the changing years." There is some truth as well as some falsehood in that rumor. Adolescents do have some unique physical, cognitive, emotional, and social characteristics that cause significant concern to some teachers. On the other hand, master teachers who are committed to working with adolescents, who understand and appreciate these unique characteristics, and who have a genuine love for students this age have tremendous success and receive abundant gratification from their jobs. As a matter of fact, every age group has unique characteristics, and any teacher who does not understand those peculiarities will have less success than those who do. Possibly, greater consideration should be given to the idiosyncrasies of the adolescent than other students, but professional satisfaction is well within the reach of teachers who are willing to commit themselves to meeting the challenges that greet them daily.

What is *adolescence*? Psychologists generally identify adolescence as being that period of time after childhood ends and before adulthood begins. Most agree that it begins with *puberty* (a series of physiological changes that signal reproductive capability and development of secondary sex characteristics), but exactly when it ends is much more difficult to discern. The arrival of adulthood is vague and variable but can be best defined in sociological terms as being when a person assumes adult roles.[1] Educators think about adolescence in terms of grade levels; generally the middle, junior high, and senior high school years. Their definition can be more encompassing because some students in middle and junior high school have not entered puberty, and senior high school students generally are not considered to be adults until they graduate, even if they are married and/or have a job.

In this chapter we consider those unique biological, cognitive, social, musical, and family relational characteristics of adolescents and attempt to determine how they affect the choral music-making process as well as how they affect your success as a teacher.

BIOLOGICAL DEVELOPMENT

During childhood a low level of sex hormones (*androgens, estrogens,* and *progestins*) is maintained in the body. At an appointed time late in childhood (why this occurs is not fully understood; body weight, athletic training and exercise, heredity, and nutrition appear to be the determinants), the *hypothalamus* (a control center in the brain regulating such states as hunger and thirst) relays a message to the pituitary gland, which then increases sevenfold the production of *gonadotropic* (growth) hormones. The *gonads* (testes in males and ovaries in females) respond to these growth hormones by increasing production of sex hormones, which stimulate the biological changes of puberty.

Growth of pubic and other body hair is stimulated by androgens produced by the adrenal gland in both males and females. *Menarche* (the first menstrual period) is an obvious physical indication of adolescence in women and the first ejaculation is indicative in males. The *adolescent growth spurt* (fast growth in height) defines the main characteristic of bodily growth during puberty.

Girls generally enter puberty about two years before boys, which results in the girls being taller than boys of the same age during those two years. Because voice change influences the choral classroom more significantly than any other biological occurrence, it is discussed thoroughly in Chapters 8 and 9.

The adolescent growth spurt often affects young singers adversely, particularly boys, in that they will appear clumsy and poorly coordinated, tripping over desks and other objects, and will be very maladroit in games, sports, and dancing. Some students (especially boys) may always seem to be fatigued and lethargic, complaining constantly about physical activity. Others, particularly those in the prepubescent stage, seemingly have an inexhaustible amount of energy that, much to their chagrin, constantly gets them in trouble. The choral teachers

---

[1] Roy J. Hopkins in his book, *Adolescence, the Transitional Years* (New York: Academic Press, 1983); Douglas C. Kimmel and Irving B. Weimer in their book, *Adolescence, a Developmental Transition* (Hillsdale, N.J.: Lawrence Erlbaum Associates, 1985), and Lawrence B. Schiamberg in his book, *Child and Adolescent Development* (New York: Macmillan, 1988) all agree on this definition of adolescence.

need to keep these characteristics in mind when engaging early adolescents in choralography or choreography, when playing musical games, or when providing other physical activities. The adolescent growth spurt often causes students to be very self-conscious about their appearance. In private they may admire themselves and be particularly observant of the physical changes, but in public they frequently stand and sit in ways that communicate an extreme self-awareness of what is happening to them. It is often difficult to persuade the girls to stand straight and hold their chests high because they are cognizant of their developing breasts. Boys' gangly arms and legs cause them to appear to have very poor posture, and often this is the case. Since proper posture is essential to effective singing, teachers must learn how to be sensitive yet productive in dealing with the students' physical appearance due to the adolescent growth spurt. Dealing openly and jovially (yet being careful not to ridicule) with these physical changes seemingly is the best approach. Once the students move beyond the stage of giggling about what has been said, they will attempt to alleviate any problems pertaining to posture and other conditions leading to effective singing.

Some girls may have their first menstrual period while in school. In most cases, parents have alerted their daughters about the forthcoming event and the girls are prepared for it. Occasionally, a girl may not know what is happening to her and it can be rather frightening. If this happens in a classroom where the teacher is male, the girl will be too embarrassed to approach the teacher. Male teachers should be cognizant of such a possibility and be ready to assist the girl to a female counselor or assistant if they suspect this biological occurrence.

COGNITIVE DEVELOPMENT

Just as adolescents experience the biological growth spurt, they experience an intellectual and cognitive growth spurt too. The changes that take place in adolescent intellectual growth are of both quantity and quality. Quantitative changes in thinking have to do with those alterations in the amount of development in a particular skill or ability. An example of this is the dramatic increase of verbal skills that occurs with many adolescents. Qualitative changes in thinking have to do with the process of cognitive functioning (the way one thinks), such as dealing with abstractions or drawing certain conclusions from given information.

Quantitative Changes

Adolescents are capable of internalizing more information at a faster rate than younger children. Sight-reading skills, for example, may be developed in two or three semesters, whereas it will take several years for elementary children to develop those same skills. During middle childhood, mental growth tends to be relatively even. However, during adolescence some abilities seem to develop more rapidly than others. Some students may develop a propensity for music while others appear to be better skilled in science or math.

It is difficult to separate sociocultural influences from actual cognitive development, but it appears that boys at this age develop scientific and mathematical skills to a greater degree and girls continue to develop verbal skills. Perhaps individual personality differences and sex-role stereotypes may be more instrumental in this phenomenon than the innate ability of the individual. Interestingly, since music requires both types of cognitive processes (verbal and scientific/mathematical), girls and boys have similar musical abilities. The sociocultural stigma that music is for girls and sports are for boys significantly affects their participation in choral music much more than their individual capabilities do.

Qualitative Changes

Adolescents may be termed as *scientific* thinkers, as opposed to individuals in middle childhood who may be considered to be *concrete* thinkers. Adolescents are capable of (1) reasoning in abstract as well as concrete terms, (2) considering several factors or variables simultaneously in solving problems, (3) considering probabilities, and (4) developing and testing hypotheses. Middle childhood individuals (1) are more limited to the here and now, (2) deal with problem solving as dictated by details of the problem, (3) limit thoughts to concrete objects and situations, and (4) focus on their own perspectives.[2]

Adolescents contemplate a problem before they attempt to solve it. Children begin to find solutions immediately. Instead of being limited to dealing with things as they are, adolescents have the ability to view things as they might be. For example, if the teacher lectures the choir on the importance of practice, younger children may realize that the music will not sound good if they do not practice, but adolescents may understand that their peers may laugh at them, that they will not get an "I" at contest, that Mom and Dad will be embarrassed, that the director's salary might be cut, and so forth. This may be inherent in their understanding without the director having to tell them (although many directors insist on emphasizing these points over and over).

This newly found cognitive ability of realizing the possible results of their future endeavors often leads to adult criticism because adolescents do not have the life experiences to understand the realities of a situation. They have ideals and dreams that might be considered to be unrealistic. They are often accused of living in a dream world and of not being down to earth. Master choral teachers are capable of directing many of those ideals and dreams toward music by planting seeds of consideration in the minds of their students. Students' imaginations often run wild when they consider themselves as professional singers. Although most will never realize such a dream, it is a wonderful motivational tool in the choral classroom for encouraging the young singers to be diligent about learning to read music and to sing with proper vocal technique.

Adolescents are capable of seeking more than one solution to a problem. Younger children often persist with their one solution to a problem even though the facts do not bear it out. They may even attempt to change or adapt the situation to make their solution work. For instance, when asked to learn to sing a given melody, elementary children may insist that the teacher sing the melody first. If the teacher refuses, they may seek a friend or a parent to sing it for them. To them, hearing someone sing the melody is the only solution to their problem of learning to sing it. Adolescents are capable of realizing that they may sight-read the melody; play it on piano; listen to it on a compact disk, cassette, or phonograph; or play it on the melody bells.

Adolescents are usually capable of abstract reasoning. They may be able to arrive at logical propositions, statements, or symbols that are derived from or based on reality. The most obvious example of this is adolescents' ability to work algebra problems where a symbol such as x represents a number. This concept is manifest musically in adolescents' ability to understand, for instance, how Bach used a musical motive to represent the letters in his name, whereas children might be unable to relate to such an abstraction. Another example is children's inability to understand how composers express political, social, and moral considerations in their instrumental music, whereas adolescents would be able to understand it, provided their life experiences were inclusive enough for them to deal with such factors.

Adolescents are more introspective than children. They are able to talk about their thoughts, beliefs, and commitments on a wide range of subjects usually in a very tactful manner, whereas children react more on an emotional level, unaware of the embarrassment of the moment.

Inasmuch as children may take things literally, adolescents tend to be able to understand the symbolic meaning of a parable or metaphor. They are able to understand the implications of proverbs and often provide some unique explanations to their true meaning. Some teachers are often unaware of this very important aspect of adolescents' cognitive process. This becomes evident when the literature for the students to sing is chosen. It is very important that the texts not be childlike in content. They need to be written from an adult perspective, yet be simple enough in vocabulary to be understood by the singer. Scriptural texts (although their use may be prohibited in some areas of the country), poems, proverbs, metaphors, and so forth are within the comprehension ability of most adolescents, particularly if the teacher takes a moment or two to explain their meanings.

There are differences in early and later adolescent thinking, so teachers should not expect middle/junior high school students to think just like senior high school students. David Elkind describes these differences as follows:

> By and large the young adolescent (twelve to sixteen years) tends to be rather flighty as a consequence of the rapid changes that have been occurring in him. Because the changes are new he is more preoccupied with them than he will be later when he is more accustomed to his enlarged body, deeper voice, and awakening sexual interest and curiosity. The young person has to adjust not only to the new changes in his body, but also to new changes in his thinking abilities. Certain phenomena of early

adolescents reflect this adjustment period. . . . The twelve and thirteen year old can now deal with possibilities and consider many new alternatives in any given problem-solving situation. Initially this is a somewhat terrifying experience because while the young person can see the many possible alternatives, he does not have the background or experience upon which to make a choice. It often appears, as a consequence, that young adolescents are hopelessly dependent and indecisive. . . . By the age of fifteen and sixteen, however, young people have more experience in decision-making and have a better idea of the relative importance of things.[3]

Often the parent is the first to suffer from adolescents' new cognitive skills. Elkind points out that to some adolescents "not only is the grass greener in the other person's yard, but the house is bigger and more comfortable and the parents are nicer."[4] Sooner or later their rationale affects the teacher as well. Children often evaluate teachers as to whether they are nice or mean. Adolescents can be very critical of a teacher's competence and personality. Older adolescents may shift that criticism to more general social issues, values, or institutions such as the church, school, or government.

How people emotionally respond to a situation depends on their individual interpretation of that circumstance. One may feel sad, another anxious, and still another happy about an identical state of affairs. The intellectual maturity of adolescents allows them to react emotionally different from the way children would react. Children take an event at face value and react accordingly. If someone gives them a present, they are happy. If someone calls them a name, their feelings are hurt or they get angry. Adolescents tend to look for the inner motive involved in a given event. If someone gives them a present, and they perceive it as a bribe, they will react differently than if it were given out of genuine affection. If someone calls them a name, they seek to understand why and then react accordingly. Here again, however, lack of experience often causes them to misinterpret true motives in people's actions. This often causes adolescents to fluctuate between depression and elation in unforeseeable patterns. These emotional fluctuations can happen almost instantaneously. In this emotional discontent the true patterns of adolescent behavior are manifest. In a way, adolescents are half children and half adults. One moment they may exhibit mature, adult demeanor and the next moment revert to childish pranks and demonstrations. The teacher must realize that these emotional upheavals are responsible for changes in behavior that are often negative and disruptive but can also be positive and beneficial when channeled in the right direction.

Adolescents often enjoy work that requires thinking and ingenuity. From an adult perspective their cognitive activities in the form of mind games seemingly have no practical purpose except to exercise the mind and develop powers of abstract thinking. The master teacher will be creative in presenting new material and challenging the students to think. Telling students directly may not be the best approach. They often learn more and retain it longer if the

---

[3] David Elkind, *All Grown Up and No Place to Go* (Reading, Mass: Addison-Wesley, 1984), p. 127.
[4] Ibid.

approach to communication of a concept involves their creativity and ingenuity. Teachers often fall into the trap of using their own communication skills in the same way day after day. It takes forethought, but it is important to vary the approaches to the ways they communicate during the choral rehearsal and other teaching experiences to ensure the students are receiving what they have to give.

Often students are interested in religion, particularly in matters pertaining to their destiny. They may accept or rebel against established formats of religious expression but will engage in philosophical and theological discussions that affect all humankind generally and themselves specifically. The constitutional right of separation of church and state does not allow teachers in public schools to take advantage of this adolescent cognitive characteristic. Certain moral concepts, civil rights, good citizenship, friendship, equal treatment of individuals, and so forth are concepts that interest adolescents, and it is considered by some to be well within the rights and responsibilities of vocal/choral teachers to assist their students in developing these positive personal attributes. Some believe the reason public school teachers do not have the respect and admiration they have enjoyed in the past (1940s and 1950s) is because they have ignored this responsibility by spending all their time teaching only the subjects in the curriculum.

Finally, adolescents are at an intellectual point in their lives when they can be taught most readily and effectively. They are generally intensely curious and eager to find solutions to the challenges that are offered them. Although they may display impatience with certain subjects and teaching methods, dislike memorization, and tire of drilling music over and over, they often can display more determination and singlemindedness than many adults. If they make poor grades the reason could be that their many varied interests prevent their dealing adequately with them all, just as easily as it could be that they lack interest or intelligence. Master teachers' success in working with adolescents is found in the ability to channel those varied interests toward music and the vocal/choral process.

SOCIAL CHARACTERISTICS

"Friendships are special relationships between two people who care for each other and who share important parts of their lives."[5] Children's friendships are often shallow and fleeting, whereas adolescents enter into special relationships with one or two people that occasionally develop by stages into lifelong alliances.

In late childhood and preadolescence, friendship takes the form of a close relationship with someone about the same age and sex. These friends become

---

[5] Kimmel and Weiner, *Adolescence, a Developmental Transition.* The social characteristics described in this section are discussed in detail in Kimmel and Weiner, including several case studies that verify their reliability (pp. 292–340).

inseparable, spend most of their waking hours together, and share many of their hopes and fears exclusively with each other.

As young people move through puberty and enter early adolescence, those relationships begun in childhood become an even more important part of their lives. The intellectual, physical, and social demands experienced by early adolescents require someone close with whom they can share intimate, personal concerns, someone who also is experiencing similar happenings. It is usually more important to share these things with another adolescent rather than with their parents because parents may be so far removed from their teen years that they are insensitive or unsympathetic to the adolescents' questions. Further, adolescents' desires to be self-reliant might cause them to hesitate to confide in their parents.

Early adolescent relationships are generally more intimate than childhood relationships, particularly in understanding each others' thoughts, feelings, and preferences. Intimate friends seldom keep secrets from each other, and they feel confident that whatever is shared will be kept in strict confidence. They know each other so well that they are often capable of predicting how their friends will react in certain situations. They know what each other likes, dislikes, wants, and fears. They develop a mutuality by treating each other fairly and by attempting to help each other whenever the need arises.

One of the tragedies of youth is the occasion for some friendships made in childhood to grow apart during adolescence due to the early physical development of one friend or the other. One friend might grow much bigger and physically mature, become more capable of thinking about abstract possibilities, and become more self-reliant or attracted to the opposite sex; the two soon have so little in common their friendship diminishes.

Because of the need for adolescents to have intimate friends and to be involved in peer-group activities, they often distance themselves from their parents. Since they have moved out of childhood but have yet to enter adulthood, adolescents find it necessary to establish a culture of their own that gives them a sense of belonging. It soon becomes evident that to be part of the youth culture they feel it necessary to be popular and to conform to the norms of the culture so they will have a sense of belonging. Peer pressure becomes extremely severe particularly during early adolescence (ages eleven through thirteen), decreases slightly during middle adolescence (fifteen through seventeen), and decreases even more among late adolescents (nineteen through twenty-one). However, it is present and effective completely throughout the adolescent period.

Even with the strong influence of the peer group, there are always individuals who choose not to conform. These are young people who have such a strong need for their own identity that they strongly resist thinking, looking, or acting similarly to other friends or peer-group members. In a reverse psychological way, this nonconformity may be their way of seeking acceptance among their peer group.

Other than the desire to be either a conformist or nonconformist, there are four other factors that seemingly affect how much peer groups influence the individual: (1) The amount of time spent with the peer group determines how much they influence each other; (2) the more determined adolescents become in their desire to separate themselves from their parents, the more they conform to the ways of their peer group; (3) in situations where the way adolescents should act or respond is an expected, customary occurrence, the affect of peer pressure is slight, but in circumstances where a typical response is not so obvious, adolescents seemingly rely upon the consensus of the peer group in seeking what to do; and (4) leaders in a peer group and, conversely, those who enjoy the least prestige in the peer group, are those least influenced by the group itself. This fourth point is true because the leaders set the standards so that they have to change very little, while the least prestigious feel they they cannot improve their social status no matter what they do. Therefore, those most greatly influenced by the peer group, are those in the middle status who conform with the hope of improving their social standing.

Being popular is a driving force among adolescents and is usually the reward of those with good social skills and attractive personality and appearance. In most cases students who were popular in childhood will remain so as adolescents, but occasionally the pace of developmental events produces significant changes in comparable popularity. Those who enter puberty extremely early or late are generally more adversely affected.

During adolescence the desire to make a good impression is constantly present; it is almost as if the students have an imaginary audience with them all the time. It seems as if they are constantly performing in order to impress their friends, even if their friends are not present. It is part of that great desire they have to be accepted and to find their place in the youth culture. Teachers must be very careful about inadvertently embarrassing the students by saying or doing something that causes them (from the students' perspective) to look bad in the presence of their friends.

The telephone becomes an important part of adolescents' lives. It may not be important because they use it as an instrument to obtain information or just to gossip; more than likely it is because being on the telephone for long periods indicates to others who receive the busy signal that a popular adolescent resides in that house. If adolescents indicate to callers they can not talk long because they are expecting a call from someone else, that action, too, may be a subtle indication to the callers that they are popular or they would not be receiving others' calls.

Another part of adolescent self-esteem has to do with being recognized and accepted in a crowd. When adolescents approach each other, it is important that they be acknowledged and greeted warmly. If they are snubbed or ignored by the one they approach, it is generally humiliating to them because they look inauspicious in the presence of those standing about or to that imaginary audience that is omnipresent.

Adolescents have a tendency to form cliques (small, tightly knit social groups) that are used by its members to enhance their self-esteem and impress those outside of the clique with the company they keep. Being a member of a clique communicates that the adolescents have special qualifications for acceptance into the group. Being excluded from a clique indicates to others that there is nothing special about the nonmember. This is a very important social characteristic to the vocal/choral teacher. Girls often form cliques based on their interest in choir; therefore, it is very easy to develop a good girls' chorus with a large membership. Boys, on the other hand, often form cliques based on other qualifications for acceptance. The master teacher will look for those boys who have assumed leadership roles among their friends and persuade them to enroll in choir. If this happens, it becomes the "in thing" to be in choir. In other words, boys, too, will form cliques based on membership in choir as a qualification for acceptance. Because most cliques are for all boys or all girls (mixed participation is rare, particularly with early adolescents), it has become accepted practice in many parts of the country to have all girls' classes and boys' classes (or choirs) in middle and junior high school. The success of such a practice is reinforced by the biological phenomenon that girls mature before boys and are therefore incompatible, to a degree, in a mixed situation.

Dating usually begins in early or middle adolescence and is begun for social reasons, not necessarily because a young person has entered puberty. In fact, the first dates generally do not occur because the adolescents are interested in the opposite sex or even enjoy their company, but because they want to impress their friends (of the same sex) that they dated a certain person. Early sexual encounters among middle/junior high school students result as much or more from a desire to impress their friends as they do from the actual physical desire.

Successful dating experiences soon become a crucial ingredient in promoting self-esteem and the feeling of being accepted by their peers. Those students who do not date often find that they are not taking part in the social activities of the school and may begin to develop a sense of inferiority.

Reasons for dating begin to change by the junior and senior years in high school. The students soon begin to date those whose company they really enjoy. It becomes less important to date those with whom they want to be seen and more important to date those with whom they are compatible and whose company they enjoy.

There seems to be acute loneliness for those adolescents (about 15 percent according to Rubin[6]) who for various reasons are unable to engage in those activities and participate in those groups that build self-esteem. The other 85 percent experience loneliness to a lesser degree and on just a few occasions. Adolescents are vulnerable to feeling lonely particularly if they change from familiar to unfamiliar surroundings. Poor social skills, being physically unattractive, feelings of inadequacy, and sensitivity to rejection often result in shyness that can become a lifelong trait. Luckily, older adolescents and young adults usually have positive social experiences that alleviate much of their shyness that might have developed in early adolescence.

---

[6] Zick Ruben, "Children Without Friends," in *Loneliness: a Sourcebook of Theory, Research and Therapy*, edited by L. A. Peplau and D. Perlman (New York: Wiley, 1982).

Because school is the principal center of social activity for the adolescent and, further, because choir and musical activities are very social endeavors, master teachers must maintain an undeviating awareness of the social relationships among their students. They must realize that the social characteristics of adolescents are responsible for a large portion of the students' behavior inside and outside of class. Creating situations and making demands that are contrary to those vitally strong social drives of adolescents will cause teachers many hours of concern. It is analogous to rowing a canoe upstream with a very short paddle. One might eventually get to the destination, but exhaustion is eminent. Much more will be accomplished by flowing with the current and devising ways to allow those characteristics to work to the teacher's advantage.

FAMILY RELATIONSHIPS

Today's families face a different set of social circumstances from those of several decades ago. These events have a direct influence on the family's adolescent members; hence, they also affect the secondary classroom. Current reports from the U.S. Department of Commerce indicate that between 15% and 20% of the U.S. population changes residence annually.[7] This type of mobility weakens the stability and influence of the neighborhood and community, which in turn affects the family. Uric Bronfenbrenner reminiscences about the character and influence of the neighborhood a generation ago:

> Everybody in the neighborhood minded your business. . . . If you walked on the railroad trestle, the phone would ring at your home, and your parents would know what you had done before you got back home. People on the street would tell you to button your jacket, and ask why you were not in church last Sunday. Sometimes you liked it and sometimes you didn't—but at least people "cared."[8]

Adolescents in the past twenty years have generally been influenced by a much different concept of community and neighborhood. A major change in family life has been the modification of the historical family pattern of the man as the exclusive wage earner and the woman as full-time housewife to a household in which both spouses work and the children are placed in the day care of a surrogate or the mother works and the father attends the children. A changing value system in which there is acceptance of a wide diversity of family structures including single-parent families, cohabitation, divorce, teenage pregnancy, homosexual parenting, and reconstituted families has impacted adolescent behavior. The adolescents in a modern-day classroom come to

---

[7] Bureau of the Census of the U.S. Department of Commerce, "Characteristics of American Children and Youth, 1980," *Current Population Reports*, No. 114 (Washington, D.C.: U.S. Government Printing Office, 1982), p. 23.

[8] U. Bronfenbrenner, *Two Worlds of Childhood: U.S. and U.S.S.R.* (New York: Russell Sage Foundation, 1970), p. 96.

teachers from these diversified backgrounds and family situations. It is the teachers' responsibility to mold them into a cohesive choral unit.

Coupled with the current social status of the family are the psychological concerns of early adolescents that are manifest in pressing needs for independence.[9] By age fifteen or sixteen adolescents are capable of procreation and they have accumulated considerable knowledge of the world around them; therefore, they feel that they are qualified to run their own lives and to be treated as adults. They take great satisfaction in exercising their capabilities and attempting adult roles. However, once they attempt to be on their own they are suddenly bombarded by incidents of the world such as handling their own money, following their own schedule, getting to appointments on time, applying for jobs, getting enough rest, and a multitude of day-to-day tasks. They may begin to vacillate and yearn for the carefree days of childhood rather than the practical matters of adulthood. This vacillation is particularly evident in early adolescents, as has been mentioned previously, where they alternate between mature and childish behavior.

Ambivalence is not only a characteristic of adolescents, but it is apparent in the actions of parents as well. Some parents want their children to grow up quickly, move from home, and become immediately independent. Others never seem to want to release them, remaining persistently overprotective. Problems emerge when the vacillating child encounters the ambivalent parent. Adolescents who are undercontrolled may feel good about the parent who gives them their freedom when they are desirous of it but resentful of the lack of concern when they seek the parents' advice and security. Adolescents who are overcontrolled usually feel good about their parents when they seek protection but resentful when they want their freedom. Most parents attempt to avoid the extremes of clutching to their child-rearing roles too long or emancipating them too quickly by finding a reasonable middle ground in which to operate. Because adolescence is a transitional period, informed parents will attempt to treat them like adults when they respond like adults, always being mindful that they periodically revert to childhood and need parenting.

Both parents and adolescents seemingly have a stake in the adolescent's developmental process. Obviously adolescents are concerned because they want to be the best individuals possible. Further, they want to be the principal contributor to their destiny. They are often torn between modeling themselves after their parents and seeking to be individuals in their own right. Parents are concerned because they have the life experiences to direct the adolescents in what they view to be the "straight and narrow." Parents want to contribute to a better life for their offspring than the one they experienced, one that brings more happiness and avoids the mistakes they made.

The previous information indicates that adolescents think, feel, look, and act differently from adults. Since they are from a different generation, have

---

[9] This concept and those about family relationships that follow are discussed in much greater detail in Kimmel and Weiner, *Adolescence, a Developmental Transition*, pp. 234–80.

distinctive tastes and attitudes, use their own language, favor their own dress, hair, and grooming styles, and prefer to pass the time differently, some observers have inferred that there is a "generation gap" between adolescents and adults. Studies show, however, that this gap is rather superficial, because when basic and essential commitments (a sense of values, a standard of conduct and decency, mutual love and respect, and the welfare of the family) are examined, adolescents and parents think alike.[10] Conclusions drawn from the studies indicate that (1) most young people get along well with their parents and share their sense of values, (2) most adolescents are not in rebellion against either the family or their society, and (3) poor family relationships and alienation from the adult generation are associated with psychological disturbance, not normative adolescent development. This provides hope for vocal/choral teachers, because even though the young people with problems require much time, it is consoling to realize that the majority are typical, well-adjusted teenagers who have good relationships with their parents. There is every reason to believe that this respect will transfer to teachers in their relationships with the adolescents.

MUSICAL CHARACTERISTICS

One of the encouraging considerations about teaching music to adolescents compared to younger children is that most children's ability to appreciate and understand the finer points of music is likely to reach a measurable level by ages eleven or twelve.[11] Most studies indicate that students' musical discernment continues to grow until ages twenty-one to twenty-three. The fastest rate of growth appears to be between ages ten and fourteen, with the rate slowing down in the years of fourteen through twenty-three. This means that most adolescents are approaching their capacity to deal with musical concepts. Experience indicates that adolescent singers are as capable of mastering musical concepts and technical difficulties as are adults provided that the material is within the vocal limitations of their young voices and that a sufficient amount of time is assigned to achieve the tasks.

Some teachers believe that girls are more musically astute than boys, although, on the whole, males tend to make about the same scores as females on musical ability tests. Some boys appear to be musically deficient, particularly in the area of exact pitch matching, but this can be attributed to the greater adjustments required from boys when dealing with vocal mutation. Since the boys' voice changes are more dramatic, it takes a longer period of time and more concentration for boys to accommodate their new vocal prowess than it does for girls.

Studies pertaining to music appreciation among young people reveal an

---

[10] These studies are delineated in Kimmel and Weiner, *Adolescence, a Developmental Transition,* pp. 269–74.

[11] Rosamund Shuter, *The Psychology of Musical Ability* (London: Methuen and Company, Ltd., 1968), p. 86.

overwhelming preference for popular music at all grade levels. Moreover, popular music is chosen to an even greater extent with increasing age (adolescence). Upper-class children tend to like classical music more than children from homes of lower socioeconomic status. Some vocal/choral teachers have taken these studies, coupled with the constant pressure exerted by their students to perform pop music, as a license to abandon all types of music other than pop. The studies do not show that students' music appreciation level cannot be broadened to include all types. Experience indicates that adolescents can appreciate and enjoy performing almost all types of vocal/choral music. Teacher preference is the most influential contributing factor as to what students sing and enjoy. If teachers like traditional art music, students will like it. If they infer, either directly or indirectly through what they say or do, that they enjoy pop music over classical, so will the students.

SUMMARY

In this chapter we have examined the biological, cognitive, social, musical, and family relational characteristics of adolescents. It attempting to find words that summarize the contents of this chapter, this quotation by Ira Singleton seems to recapitulate what has been said in a nutshell:

> The adolescent, then, is a curious mixture of youth and maturity, developing rapidly through various phases of physical and intellectual growth and exhibiting many and sometimes conflicting facets of character and conduct. Each is a distinct individual, does not fit readily into any generalized pattern, and requires individual attention and understanding from the teacher. He is inclined to be introspective, subject to fluctuations of mood and emotion, and finds it difficult to explain his inner feelings to others, adults in particular. Deprived of sympathy and understanding, he can become withdrawn and recalcitrant. Given appropriate attention and motivation, he can develop intense interests and display a large capacity for learning. Because of his unique make-up, the adolescent may be among the most difficult teaching problems in the public schools, but he is also the pupil who can respond wholeheartedly to effective teaching, providing deep satisfaction to the teacher interested in leading youth to new knowledge and insight.[12]

THOUGHTS FOR CONTEMPLATION AND DISCUSSION

1. How are you going to deal with correcting the mistakes of sensitive students who are inclined to get their feelings hurt?
2. How will you respond if one of your junior high choir members who already has been expelled from school twice suddenly stands up in class, points to another student, and yells in a loud voice, "I'm going to whip your xxx, you xxxxx (obscenities)!"?

[12] Ira C. Singleton, *Music in the Secondary Schools* (Boston: Allyn and Bacon, Inc., 1963), pp. 32–33.

3. How will your deal with a senior high choir member (one of your best singers) who tells you that her parents will not allow her to return to school in the evening for your choral concerts. Will you choose to eliminate her from the choir? Why or why not? If you keep her in choir, how will you reconcile her absences to the other choir members?

4. How will you respond when one of your best singers threatens to quit choir because he is upset with members of his section who do not take their responsibilities in choir seriously?

5. How will you respond when members of your junior high choir tease one of the girls because of her physical appearance and refuse to sit near her?

BIBLIOGRAPHY

BESSOM, MALCOLM E., ALPHONSE M. TATARUNIS, and SAMUEL L. FORCUCCI. *Teaching Music in Today's Secondary Schools*, 2d ed. New York: Holt, Rinehart and Winston, 1980.

BOYLE, J. DAVID, and RUDOLF E. RADOCY. *Measurement and Evaluation of Musical Experiences*. New York: Schirmer Books, 1987.

BRONFENBRENNER, U. *Two Worlds of Childhood: U.S. and U.S.S.R.* New York: Russell Sage Foundation, 1970. Bureau of the Census of the U.S. Department of Commerce. "Characteristics of American Children and Youth." *Current Population Reports*, No. 114. Washington, D.C.: U.S. Government Printing Office, 1982.

COLLINS, DON L. *The Cambiata Concept, a Comprehensive Philosophy and Methodology of Teaching Music to Adolescents*. Conway, Ark.: Cambiata Press, 1981.

COMMONS, MICHAEL L., FRANCIS A. RICHARDS, and CHERYL ARMON, eds. *Beyond Formal Operations*. New York: Praeger Publishers, 1984.

COOPER, IRVIN, and KARL O. KURSTEINER. *Teaching Junior High School Music*, 2d ed. Conway, Ark.: Cambiata Press, 1973.

EDELSON, EDWARD. *The Secondary School Music Program from Classroom to Concert Hall*. West Nyack, N. Y.: Parker Publishing Co., 1972.

ELKIND, DAVID. *All Grown Up and No Place to Go*. Reading, Mass.: Addison-Wesley, 1984.

HOFFER, CHARLES R. *Teaching Music in the Secondary Schools*, 4th ed. Belmont, Calif.: Wadsworth Publishing, 1991.

HOPKINS, ROY J. *Adolescence, the Transitional Years*. New York: Academic Press, 1983.

KIMMEL, DOUGLAS C., and IRVING B. WEINER. *Adolescence, a Developmental Transition*. Hillsdale, N.J.: Lawrence Erlbaum Associates, 1985.

KOWALL, BONNIE C., ed. *Perspectives in Music Education, Source Book III*. Reston, Va.: Music Educators National Conference, 1966.

MARPLE, HUGO D. *Backgrounds and Approaches to Junior High Music*. Dubuque, Iowa: Wm. C. Brown Co., 1975.

REGELSKI, THOMAS A. *Principles and Problems of Music Education*. Englewood Cliffs, N.J.: Prentice-Hall, Inc., 1975.

ROE, PAUL F. *Choral Music Education*, 2d ed. Englewood Cliffs, N.J.: Prentice-Hall, Inc., 1983.

RUBEN, ZICK. "Children Without Friends." In *Loneliness: a Sourcebook of Theory, Research, and Therapy*, edited by L. A. Peplau and D. Perlman. New York: Wiley, 1982.

SCHIAMBERG, LAWRENCE B. *Child and Adolescent Development*. New York: Macmillan, 1988.

SHUTER, ROSAMUND. *The Psychology of Musical Ability*. London: Methuen and Co., Ltd., 1968.

Singleton, Ira. *Music in Secondary Schools*, 2d ed. Boston: Allyn and Bacon, Inc., 1965.

STEVENS-LONG, JUDITH, and NANCY J. COBB. *Adolescence and Early Adulthood*. Palo Alto, Calif.: Mayfield Publishing Co., 1983.

8

Historical Approaches to Training the Changing Voice

Boys' and girls' voices change during adolescence; quite an obvious observation, but one that has far-reaching implications to the choral music educator. You will be greatly influenced by this occurrence. To be successful in working with these singers it is absolutely imperative that you have a thorough understanding of this phenomenon. Adolescent singers must believe that the choral experience is worthwhile and that they are making a meaningful contribution to the singing organization. Otherwise, they will be discontented and uninterested; they likely will be inattentive and will misbehave. Your understanding of the changing voice will enable you to select music for which the unique vocal limitations of these young singers have been considered. If they are able to sing the music well, they will feel that they are making a meaningful contribution. Further, your understanding of the changing voice will help you (1) to guide these young singers through the experience with a positive attitude, (2) to classify their voices correctly, and (3) to support them in their efforts to comprehend exactly what is occurring physically and emotionally.

Therefore, this chapter contains information about the approaches to the changing voice that have been used over the years, including the pioneer and current contributors to changing-voice phenomenon. More important, this chapter, and the one which follows, address how to deal with adolescent voices (unchanged, changing, and changed) in the choral classroom.

EARLY METHODS OF DEALING WITH THE CHANGING VOICE

Concern for consequences of the incidence of voice change in a young adolescent male can be traced back to Greek and Roman times. As early as 2000 B.C. the primary concern was in finding ways to keep the voice from changing. Deso A. Weiss reports that methods of castration were applied back then and continued until the latter part of the eighteenth century and, in a few isolated cases, even into the nineteenth century.[1]

After the practice of castration ceased, a more traditional approach emerged. Due to the influence of vocal training in boychoirs, the prevalent theory had been that when a young male entered puberty and the voice "broke," he should stop singing until the voice stopped changing. At that point he could reenter the congregation of song makers. This is commonly referred to as the *no-sing* theory. As early as 1885, Emil Behnke and Lennox Browne researched the attitudes of singing teachers and students in teacher training colleges. Their survey indicated that teachers and students believed that "the bulk of evidence most strikingly proves the injurious and even ruinous consequences arising from the exercise of the voice by singing during the period of change."[2] However, they also were cognizant of a surfacing attitude that perhaps singing through the change was not detrimental. They admitted that some believed the boy's voice may change "gradually and imperceptibly," in which case there is no break and singing "may possibly be continued, under the guidance of a competent teacher, without detriment."[3]

Forty-five years later the controversy was still alive. G. Edward Stubbs, a well-known New York organist, wrote in the *New Music Review*:

> The mere fact that the subject will not die out proves rather conclusively that it is not one-sided by any means, and that there is plenty of room for information, especially of a scientific kind. Choirmasters who train boys' voices are naturally interested in retaining the 'treble' as long as possible; yet there are few, we believe, who are willing to risk injury in doing so. As a rule boys who show danger of vocal strain are warned to sing very quietly, and leave top notes alone, allowing the voice to take its natural course towards tenor, baritone, or bass. But in a percentage of cases the treble voice never changes at all, and that this represents something unnatural has never been proved to the satisfaction of choirmasters of experience.[4]

Stubbs later wrote in *The Music Teacher* that he believed allowing the boy to sing through mutation is largely a matter of care and expert training on the part of the choirmaster:

[1] Deso A. Weiss, "The Pubertal Change of the Human Voice," *Folia Phoniatrica*, 2 (1950), p. 126.

[2] Emil Behnke and Lennox Browne, *The Child's Voice: Its Treatment with Regards to After Development* (London: Sampson Low, 1885), p. 25.

[3] Ibid., p. 26.

[4] G. Edward Stubbs, "Should Breaking Voices Be Rested?," *New Music Review*, July (1930).

... the average boy's voice, if properly handled and trained would gradually lower without any break whatever. The exceptions to the rule are too few to be taken into account.... There is nothing new in the no-break theory; it is as old as the hills. What is needed is more scientific recognition of a fact of importance, and more widespread knowledge concerning it.[5]

He indicated further that even the British (in the 1930s) were questioning the no-sing theory. This was highly unusual due to their traditions steeped in boychoir singing. Stubbs quoted an editorial by a Britisher in the *Musical Mirror* (London) as saying:

In recent years, at odd times, and from varying sources of information, a strong trend has been developing to allow a limited amount of vocal activity during the period of puberty, not only in the case of boys, but also of girls, the argument being that what is so pronounced in the male is identically followed in the female, only in a less strident degree. Naturally there are differences of opinion on the matter. So far the difficulty has been that musicians, choirmasters, and teachers of singing have mostly favored giving the singing voice a complete rest between the ages of fourteen and seventeen, and this notwithstanding the fact that history, physiology, and the science of phonology—not to speak of practical experience—were all ranged against them. *Grove's Dictionary* teems with the histories of great singers of the past (Santley, Reeves, Lloyd, Patti, Melba) who not only sang throughout the period of adolescence but who actually owed much of their success to the fact that they never ceased singing from early childhood.... One of the most striking peculiarities of the case is, that instead of their voices being damaged, they thrived upon what they were fed; those who had the 'nous' to keep on singing did not damage their voices one jot, as is so frequently prognosticated, but on the contrary, built for themselves vocal possibilities that advanced the flights of ages.[6]

A statement in 1932 by C. H. Moody, organist of Ripon Cathedral, advocating the no-sing theory brought an editorial response from Harvey Grace in the *Musical Times* (London and New York):

Dr. Moody's pronouncement against the singing of boys for three years after the breaking stage will, I hope, lead to something like a practical finding on the subject. We have to face the fact that every year many hundreds of enthusiastic choirboys end their singing careers forever. It will, I think, be agreed that the majority of these boys stop singing with regret; but during the blank period that follows, they lose their taste for singing and the majority are definitely lost to choral music. If perfect rest could be achieved there might be something to say for Dr. Moody's views, but we know that no power on earth can stop boys from shouting at their games, from singing raucously at scouts' camps and other gatherings. It is difficult to see how properly controlled and directed singing during the adolescent period could do a hundredth part of the damage that is done by uncontrolled shouting and yelling. I have heard of choirmasters who have tackled the problem by running a junior choirmen's class analogous to that of treble probationers. Perhaps some readers who have had practical experience of this, or any other method of retaining the musical interest of boys during the change-of-voice period, will give other readers the benefit of their experiences.... If the

[5] Ibid.

[6] From *Training the Boy's Changing Voice*, by Duncan McKenzie. Copyright © 1956 by the Trustees of Rutgers College in New Jersey. Reprinted with permission of Rutgers University Press.

present leakage of splendid choir material is unavoidable, there is nothing more to be said; but if the weight of evidence shows that the waste can be stopped, something ought to be done, and done promptly.[7]

In 1955, the controversy still raged because Duncan McKenzie in his book *Training the Boy's Changing Voice* quotes sources in England, China, Canada, and the United States who were trying to convince teachers of the safety of singing through puberty. By that time, however, the pendulum had swung toward the camp of believers in vocal training through puberty and against the no-sing mentality. Emerging in the 1940s and 1950s, three great American pioneers of changing voice theory have convinced, by the early 1990s, most teachers of singing and music educators of the safety and, in fact, the advantage of vocal training for mutational voices: Duncan McKenzie, Irvin Cooper, and Frederick Swanson.

DUNCAN MCKENZIE'S ALTO-TENOR PLAN

Duncan McKenzie taught in public schools in Montreal and was director of music in public schools in Toronto. Later he held posts as manager of the Music Department of Oxford University Press in New York for five years and director of Carl Fischer, Inc., in New York for twelve years. He was chairman of the Music Department of Douglass College from 1943 to 1952.

In his book *Training the Boy's Changing Voice*, he presents the *alto-tenor* plan for keeping adolescent boys singing in church and school choirs throughout the period when their voices are changing. The term alto-tenor was not original with him although he is not exactly sure of its origin. He stated:

> Eldridge W. Newton, for many years music editor for Ginn and Company, thought the term was first used about 1894: "The term referred to a part which might be sung by a girl alto or by an incipient boy tenor. I remember distinctly my first summer school for music supervisors in Boston in 1893. Luther Whiting Mason, George James M. McLaughlin, then his assistant in the Boston schools, and George Veazie, the Director of Music in Chelsea, Massachusetts, were there. All three used the term 'alto-tenor' in conversation, but in writing they used the term 'boy alto.'..."[8]

McKenzie believed that the first textbook to apply the rudiments of the alto-tenor idea was in a music text entitled *The Third Reader for Mixed Voices* from a series, *The Normal Course*, edited by John W. Tufts.[9] However, the term *alto-tenor* was not used nor was it established that the alto part that has the same range as the present-day alto-tenor was actually intended for changing voices. The earliest published music in which the word *alto-tenor* appears seems to be

---

[7] Ibid.

[8] Ibid.

[9] This series was published by Silver Burdett in New York in 1885.

the *Beacon Song Collection*, edited by Herbert Griggs.[10] The range of the third part, which was marked by three different nomenclatures throughout the book, alto-tenor, tenor or alto, and tenor-alto, keeps fairly consistently within the accepted range of today, G to G (treble clef). Here again, it is not clear that the part was intended for changing voices even though it was suitable for those purposes.

Ralph Baldwin, then director of music in public schools, Hartford, Connecticut, supplied McKenzie with the following information:

> I would not dare to say where the word originated, or who was the first person to use it. I began teaching public school music in Northampton, Massachusetts, in 1899. As soon as one of the schools was ready for part music, I put the boys with changing voices on the third part, the tenor part. These boys were called tenors. However, outside of school, in speaking of these voices or of the part they sang, I called the voice and the part "alto-tenor" so that it would not be confused with the mature tenor.[11]

According to McKenzie, use of the term *alto-tenor* as he projects it is:

> . . . the term used to describe and classify the boy's voice after it has lowered to the stage when the changed voice begins to develop. It was coined as the result of the need for a suitable designation for the third part of four-part voice music for adolescent boys in the upper grades of the elementary school, in the days before junior high school. The term was applied not only to the voice but also to the part. The voice is still alto, but it has lowered to the extent that the boy can sing in the tenor range; the quality, however, has not yet become masculine, that is, either tenor or bass.[12]

He further explains:

> With the advent of the junior high school movement at the beginning of the century, it became possible to experiment with the plan on a large scale and bring about its general use in America. The plan proved itself beneficial to the boy's future voice, not injurious to it. Hence, it can be said that the junior high school has been the proving ground for the acceptance of the modern theory about the boy's changing voice as opposed to the traditional theory [meaning the *no-sing* theory].[13]

McKenzie advocates that the voice change is a gradual process; that is, as the boy moves into the mutational process he will gradually lose the upper notes and add the lower notes until the voice settles. He believes the speaking voice is the best indicator of the onset of change; as it progresses downward, so does the singing voice. The singing voice will lower through each of the descending voice parts; first soprano to second soprano, then to alto. At that point it takes on a "youthy" quality that is neither a changed nor an unchanged sound. During this time, he should be classified alto-tenor. As the change continues the

[10] Published in New York by Silver Burdett in 1895.
[11] McKenzie, *Training the Boy's Changing Voice.*
[12] Ibid.
[13] Ibid.

unchanged boy voice gradually disappears until little of it remains. It then may be classified as tenor or bass. McKenzie believes that the voice change will occur more rapidly if the voice is destined to be a bass than if it is to be a tenor. When the lowering process is completed over the following few months, the voice will move back up by losing a few of the lowest notes and adding a few at the top. After this settling process the boy may be classified, according to adult categories; tenor or bass.

The range of the boy's voice during various stages of change as described by McKenzie are indicated as follows:

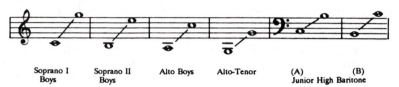

| Soprano I Boys | Soprano II Boys | Alto Boys | Alto-Tenor | (A) | (B) |
| | | | | Junior High Baritone | |

McKenzie refers to what he calls a comfortable range policy. The idea here is always to keep the boy singing in the area of the voice that is comfortable for him at each phase of change. This includes moving him down to the next voice part before the present part becomes too difficult to handle. It also includes keeping the young singer away from the extremities of his range (top and bottom) during the entire change process. He believes that moving the voice downward gives the lowest notes an opportunity to develop while the highest notes, being unused, will disappear. It is, however, very important not to force the lowest notes. If he is taught "to realize the importance of singing only in his comfortable range, he will never need to force, and with the music that is today available [1956] to suit the voice conditions in the junior high school, forcing is uncalled for."[14]

In his book he deals with various techniques including vocal exercises to assist the young singer to pass from the unchanged to the changed voice. He shows how to test the voice and indicates various tonal possibilities in the junior high school chorus.

FREDERICK SWANSON'S ADOLESCENT BASS THEORY

Frederick Swanson became concerned with changing voice problems in the late 1930s when he first started teaching music in a junior high school. In the 1940s he began keeping records of the vocal development of boys as they passed through mutation. In 1948 he organized the Moline Boys' Choir, and it was through his experience with them that he began to see the tremendous potential of young changing voices when properly trained. His doctoral dissertation entitled "Voice Mutation in the Adolescent Male" brought him to the forefront

[14] Ibid.

of expertise in this significant area.[15] His doctoral research, his practical experience over the years, and his genuine concern for the well-being of early adolescent male singers have resulted in Swanson's *adolescent bass theory*. Basically, Swanson believes:

1. The most useful indicators of voice change are the secondary sex characteristics such as the growth of pubic hair.

2. The rate of change is very rapid and can happen over a summer or even within a few weeks.

3. 30 percent to 40 percent of boys immediately become *new basses* with a range from A (first space, bass clef) to G (fourth space, bass clef), and it is not unusual for some of them to be able to sing low E (first ledger line below the bass clef); teachers aware of this kind of change and this kind of voice could train singers to be contra-basses through careful development of vocal *fry tones* (a range of fundamental frequencies below those of the modal, chest register);[16]

4. With some boys the area around middle C cannot be phonated in that the boy has the treble range (falsetto) and the full voice (chest) but there is a rather significant gap between the two voices in which the tones cannot be produced.

5. Greater success can be achieved when boys with changing voices are segregated from the girls and boys with unchanged voices; boys with changing voices should be trained in classes by themselves

6. Boys in the early stages of change before secondary sex characteristics appear have about the same range and timbre as boy altos and should be trained as unchanged voices.[17]

Swanson recommends training the changing voices as tenors and new basses in a class by themselves, singing first in octaves and later in sixths and using music with good melodies, particularly for the basses. The unchanged voices (including those boys in early stages of change) should be trained with the girls as boy altos. His recommended ranges for the three are:

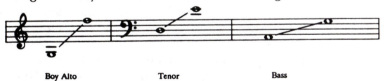

Boy Alto   Tenor   Bass

In recent years some of Swanson's concepts have been questioned. There is some doubt about his idea that rate of change is very rapid, sometimes within just a few weeks. Further research indicates that the rate of change in all boys is longer (even though the length of time does vary with individuals). It may

[15] Frederick J. Swanson, "Voice Mutation in the Adolescent Male: An Experience in Guiding the Voice Development of Adolescent Boys in General Music Classes," Ph.D. diss., University of Wisconsin, 1959.

[16] Frederick J. Swanson, "The Vanishing Basso Profundo Fry Tones," *Choral Journal* 17, no. 5 (1977), 5–10.

[17] Frederick J. Swanson, *Music Teaching in the Junior High and Middle School* (Englewood Cliffs, N.J.: Prentice-Hall, Inc., 1973), p. 188.

appear to be very fast in some boys, particularly if they are required to sing high treble parts until the voice cannot maintained proper phonation and suddenly moves explosively from chest to head voice (some people refer to this experience as the breaking or cracking of the voice). There is also some question about the feasibility of cultivating the fry tones to the point of developing contrabasses. It is generally accepted that the size and capability of the vocal folds are hereditary and are limited accordingly, even though the lower pitches eventually may be strengthened through exercise.

Swanson's most important contribution is the promulgation of the idea that in some voices the vocal folds are unable to phonate in the area around middle C. Experience has proven this to be true. It should be noted, however, when boys are allowed to sing literature that (1) keeps them singing in the comfortable area of the voice, (2) does not overextend the upper range, and (3) moves them gradually downward as natural maturation occurs, the incidence of the presence of this gap is significantly less.

IRVIN COOPER'S CAMBIATA CONCEPT

The approach to the changing voice that has received the greatest exposure, acceptance, and application is Irvin Cooper's *cambiata concept*. This is true for two reasons. First, Cooper supported his ideas with a choral literature of octavos and booklets that were used by thousands of adolescent singers in middle/junior high and senior high schools throughout the country during the 1950s and 1960s. Since that time a specialty publishing company, Cambiata Press, has received wide acceptance nationally by producing music based on the tenets of the cambiata concept.[18] Second, Cooper trained several disciples who have been prominent in providing workshops nationally since his death in 1971.[19] They have kept his concept alive both through promoting its use in secondary schools and churches as well as seeing it promulgated by various universities throughout the nation. The concept has been a part of the music education and church music scenes for fifty years or more.

Born in England, Cooper came to Canada after college to teach public school music. He received his undergraduate degree from the University of Manchester and began work in Montreal as a senior high school choral and instrumental director, where he worked for fifteen years. During his forties he became supervisor of music for the entire Montreal system and finished his

---

[18] Cambiata Press may be reached by writing P.O. Box 1151, Conway, AR 72032 or by calling a toll-free WATS number: 1-800-643-9967.

[19] Among others, these disciples are Don L. Collins, founder of Cambiata Vocal Music Institute of America, Inc. (1806 Bruce St., Conway, AR 72032), managing editor of Cambiata Press, and professor of music at the University of Central Arkansas in Conway; Wesley Coffman, dean of the School of Music at Hardin-Simmons University in Abilene, Texas; Eva Adcock, professor of music at Western Carolina University in Cullowhee, North Carolina; and David Riley, associate professor of music at Ithaca College in New York.

doctorate at McGill University, where he later taught as director of the McGill University Orchestra and the University Choral and Operatic Society. During his years as supervisor of music he became involved with early adolescent singers and changing voice problems. While supervising junior high classrooms he became aware that most of the boys were not singing but instead were having a study period during music class. This lack of involvement in music by the young singers led him to investigate ways in which their participation could be improved. Ultimately he engaged in an in-depth study of early adolescent voices.

He soon determined that the young men could sing completely throughout vocal mutation as long as they sang music written in accordance to their unique range and tessitura limitations. He felt that no attempt should be made to make the voice fit already existing music, but the music should be made to fit the voice.

Cooper spent the last thirty years of his life devoted to dealing with the early adolescent voice. Beginning with an intense study of the adolescent voice, he was to see, ultimately, his ideas promulgated throughout thirty states, Canada, England, France, and Hungary. His publications include twenty-two books of song collections arranged for changing voices; *Letters to Pat*, a professional book for middle/junior high school music teachers; *Teaching Junior High School Music*, a college textbook;[20] *The Reading Singer*, a sight-reading method for adolescents; and a movie, *The Changing Voice*, which was a blue ribbon winner at the American Film Festival. At the time of his death in 1971, he was chairman of the International Research Committee for the Study of Changing Voice Phenomena with the International Society of Music Education and he was establishing laboratory studies in England, Russia, and Japan. His tenure of twenty years as professor of music at Florida State University has resulted in his having students and disciples spread throughout the United States, Europe, and South America.

He took the term *cambiata* from the theoretical terminology *cambiata nota*, meaning "changing note" and adapted it to *cambiata voce* or *changing voice*. In the United States the term *cambiata concept* is recognized as a method of dealing with boys' changing voices, and originally it was indeed limited to this area. However, since Cooper's death, it has grown to encompass much more than that. It has been fashioned into a comprehensive philosophy and methodology of teaching choral music to adolescents.[21] The changing voice portion of the concept is covered in this chapter. Other aspects are addressed throughout the book.

Cooper worked with and classified over 114,000 adolescent voices in his lifetime.[22] From his research, the research of many of his disciples, and that great wealth of practical experience contributed by him and his disciples, the following tenets pertaining to adolescent voices have emerged.

Cooper believed that adolescent girls should not be classified as sopranos

---

[20] Currently distributed by Cambiata Press.

[21] Don L. Collins, *The Cambiata Concept, a Comprehensive Philosophy and Methodology of Teaching Music to Adolescents* (Conway, Ark.: Cambiata Press, 1981), p. 3.

[22] Ibid., p. 12.

and altos, but should be considered as having equal voices. He called them the *blues* and the *greens* to achieve this equality.

He indicated that there are four different types of boys' voices in middle/junior high school: (1) boys' unchanged, which he called sopranos; (2) boys in the first phase of change, or cambiatas (the plural form of cambiata is *cambiate*, but it is accepted practice to refer to a group of these boys as cambiatas); (3) boys in the second phase of change, or baritones; and (4) boys' changed voices, which he called basses (he considered this to be a rare voice appearing only occasionally at the middle/junior high school age).[23]

Ranges for these voices are shown here:

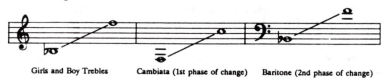

Girls and Boy Trebles   Cambiata (1st phase of change)   Baritone (2nd phase of change)

He warned that it is a gross error to assume that every voice in each category precisely fits the prescribed range boundaries. It is safe to assume that 90 percent of the singers in each category can maneuver vocally within the appropriate ranges designated above.

He further restricted the vocal parts by indicating that the music to be sung by adolescent singers should stay within a more comfortable area, which he called the *singing tessitura*. Tessitura is that portion of the vocal range in which it is comfortable to sing for a considerable length of time without tiring. He indicated that brief vocal excursions outside the tessitura can be very effective, but if the general line of any song lies outside the tessitura, vocal strain results. The following shows the tessitura within individual part ranges:

Girls and Boy Trebles   Cambiata (1st phase of change)   Baritone (2nd phase of change)

Cooper discouraged unison and unison-octave singing in middle/junior high school. When one examines a composite of all the ranges, it becomes apparent that to have successful unison or unison-octave singing one must choose a song with a compass of D (above middle C) to A (second space, treble clef) if the singers are to stay within the comfortable singing area of the voice.

Cooper avoided individual voice testing on the basis that, if given the opportunity, a young man will choose the most comfortable singing area of the voice thus literally classifying himself. Another important reason for not using individual voice testing was because Cooper believed it was vitally important for the student to have an exciting singing experience on the first day of class or

[23] Irvin Cooper and Karl O. Kuersteiner, *Teaching Junior High School Music*, 2d ed. (Conway, Ark.: Cambiata Press, 1973) p. 188.

meeting period. Time did not allow for individual testing. He wanted the students to leave the classroom after a thirty-to-fifty minute session having experienced four-part singing, which would certainly excite them about singing for the rest of the year. Therefore, through a special group classification procedure and by rote teaching of melodically oriented songs, he was able to achieve that goal.

To classify the voices quickly, he would meet the students at the door as they entered the classroom and instruct them exactly where he wanted them to sit. This not only placed the students properly for classification purposes, but it also established teacher authority and control at the first meeting of the students and their teacher. He placed the boys at the front of the room and the girls in the back, always assuring that there was enough room for him to move among them.

He began the class with a brief explanation (no more than three minutes) about the voice types that were present. He explained that in most classes in middle/junior high school there were four types of voices: boy sopranos, cambiatas, baritones, and basses (this type voice may not have been present, particularly in sixth and seventh-grade classes). Then he told the boys that he would determine quickly the type voice of each boy present. He assured them that they would not have to sing a solo but only sing together as a group. He told them he would pass in front of each of them while they were singing together. If he tapped the boy on the shoulder, the boy was instructed to stop singing. If he passed by him, he was to continue singing with the remainder of the boys.

During the years Cooper was classifying voices he used the song "Way Down Upon the Suwannee River" (nowadays, students are not acquainted with that particular folk song so usually either "America" or "Jingle Bells" is used). The boys were instructed to sing in the area of the voice that is most comfortable. (When "Jingle Bells" is used, the first time through choose the key of D or D-flat and have the boys sing only the chorus over and over.) As Cooper moved among the boys listening to them sing, he heard three things: boys singing in the octave above middle C (beginning on F or F-sharp in "Jingle Bells"), boys singing in the octave below middle C, and some boys who were unable to sing either octave (uncertain singers). When he passed in front of a boy who was singing securely in the octave below middle C, he tapped him on the shoulder to indicate he was to stop singing. If the boy was singing in an uncertain fashion or definitely singing in the upper octave, Cooper passed him by, indicating that he was to continue to sing. After he had eliminated all boys singing the lower octave, he asked the remaining boys to stop singing. He placed all those boys who had been singing the lower octave together on one side of the room. These were the baritones and basses. Then he asked the remainder of the boys to sing the song once more in a different key (if "Jingle Bells" is used, change the key to A-flat). This time as he passed among the boys he listened for those boys who were definitely singing the upper octave. These were the boy trebles. He placed those boy trebles together in a group near one of the girls' sections where they could sit with the boys but sing with the girls. Through the process of elimination, by finding the baritones and boy trebles he determined that the remaining boys were cambiatas or uncertain singers. He placed the uncertain singers with the cambiatas until a later period when he would have time to determine exactly which part they should sing regularly.

He divided the girls arbitrarily by assigning the number "one" or "two" to each girl, then grouped the "ones" together and the "twos" together in the back of the room. He placed the cambiatas (and uncertain singers) in one group and the baritones in another group, both in the front of the room.

At that point he was ready to teach a four-part (soprano I, soprano II, cambiata and baritone) song to everyone. Each part was taught by rote from a song chosen from one of his melody-part style song booklets. In no more than forty or fifty minutes, he had classified all the voices and taught the group to sing a four-part song successfully. This usually proved to be an exciting time for the young singers. Often they were unable to believe that they could be singing four-part music so easily and quickly.

In describing the timbre or vocal quality of the cambiata voice, Cooper used the term *wooly*. He said their voices are rich, undeniably masculine almost to the point of belligerency, and truly beautiful if the sound is controlled in volume and not permitted to become strident from sheer vocal exuberance. A perfect example of this sound may be heard in the very early recordings of Wayne Newton, the popular singer.

Cooper was concerned about the possibility of misclassification of the cambiata voice by teachers because of an aural illusion of its sounding an octave lower than is actually the case. He called this the *octave aural illusion*, which is due to the richness and depth of the tone quality. If cambiata voices are misclassified and required to sing a bass part, which actually will be sounding one octave higher than written, the resulting sound is quite unpleasant.

Cooper warned against placing the cambiata on a tenor part in Soprano, Alto, Tenor, Bass (SATB) music. In his view, the tenor part is too low, just as the alto part is too high. The cambiata needs a special part written specifically for him.

In providing a literature for young adolescent singers Cooper used a technique he called *melody-part style* writing. If one is particularly partial to harmonically oriented music, an approach favored by many composers and arrangers of music used in American schools, one may object to Cooper's style because of the cross-voicing, equal female parts, and contrapuntal voice leading. Cooper's style ensures that each part will be interesting for the singer, but more importantly, each young singer will be able to take advantage of the melodic characteristics of the music to remember the part and be secure in four-part singing. Often in harmonically oriented music, students attempting part singing finish the song by singing the original melody instead of their intended part. If the students have a part to sing that is, in fact, a melody, their ability to stay with it to the end is greatly increased. Cooper was willing to sacrifice a typical, homophonic sound for what to him was a greater educational purpose in writing.

Another significant consideration was the importance of choosing music appropriate for the young baritone voice (and some cambiatas) with their inability to articulate at an increased tempo. Melismatic passages should not be chosen for these boys to sing. Further, any part that requires an inordinate amount of articulation at an increased tempo should also be avoided.

Finally, and most importantly, it was imperative from Cooper's standpoint that middle/junior high school singers perform music written specifically for them. As mentioned, he discouraged placing cambiatas on a tenor part, because the tessitura was too low, or on the alto, because its tessitura was too high. He adamantly discouraged choosing SAB music for these young singers because he maintained that there was no part for the cambiatas to sing. Adult female parts are often too high or have a compass too wide for comfortable singing by adolescent females, and the same application can be made of bass parts for young baritones, particularly in the lower extremities of the voice.

The Cambiata Vocal Music Institute of America, Inc.

In the spring of 1979, eight years after Cooper's death, the *Cambiata Vocal Institute of America* was founded and incorporated as a nonprofit, state-chartered, educational institution.[24] The primary purpose of the institute is to train music educators in the comprehensive philosophy and methodology of the cambiata concept by providing sound basis for teaching vocal music to adolescents. The basic tenets of the concept promoted by the institute are:

> Music is a discipline and should be taught as such. Through structured curriculum individuals are taught (1) to understand and respond to the written language of music, (2) to sing with ease and beauty through proper vocal-choral technique, and (3) to communicate the message of the text and aural musical sound in an artistic and stylistic fashion.
>
> Vocal music is a gift or innate ability of all humans. Through discipline, it can be developed into a meaningful artform that heightens one's ability to judge the aesthetic value of certain life experiences.
>
> The four ingredients in music—melody, rhythm, harmony, and form (particularly harmony)—should be experienced as an aural art before one learns to deal with it in written form.
>
> The study of music not only prepares one for professional service, but, more importantly, it develops sensitive, artistic individuals with a greater ability to deal with life situations in a successful manner.
>
> Americans have an extensive music heritage that is disclosed in many facets. Vocalists should be able to experience and express themselves in as many of these as possible.

---

[24] I serve as founder/director of the institute. I was a student of Cooper's at Florida State University from 1967–1970 while working on my doctorate. Near the end of Cooper's tenure (he retired in 1971), he was chatting informally with me and another graduate student and the subject emerged about the future of the concept. Almost as if he were moved by divine guidance, Cooper somberly stated, "If the concept is to remain alive over the next several decades, it may well be left up to one of you." Mysteriously door after door has opened over the last twenty years that not only has kept the concept alive but has allowed it to be proliferated to thousands of music educators and church musicians throughout the world.

When one hears the term *music educator*, the listener immediately thinks about training teachers for service in the public schools. The scope of Cambiata Vocal Music Institute of America encompasses more than just public schools. It administers in five major areas:

Public and Private School Music Education: This is the traditional teacher training area.

Church Music Education: The safeguard of the country's church music heritage lies in teaching adolescents to express their faith in song. Ministers of music, church choir directors, organists, and so forth hold the key to that security, and they should be trained to cherish that responsibility and carry the torch high.

Private Vocal Studios: Due to the increase of privately funded elementary and secondary schools each year, the trend of the twenty-first century will be toward each family funding their child's education. In the music area, one will see more and more private studios being founded.

The Boychoir Tradition: There are very few institutions of higher education in the United States who specifically train directors of boychoirs. It is part of the American choral tradition that is becoming less and less active and it should be preserved.

Professional Early-Adolescent Choral Singing: This area includes the training of choral directors so that they may develop their adolescent choirs to such a high skill of level of performance that they may serve the needs of private business and entertainment on a professional basis.

Specific activities of the institute since its founding include sponsoring over 100 vocal-choral music workshops in thirty-one different states throughout the United States and overseas.

JOHN COOKSEY'S CONTEMPORARY ECLECTIC THEORY

The three pioneers, Duncan McKenzie, Irvin Cooper, and Frederick Swanson, brought about an educational awareness of the importance of caring and dealing properly with the changing voice and, moreover, proved that a boy can sing during mutation when allowed to sing proper literature either written or chosen for his particular, unique vocal limitations and capabilities. Research by John Cooksey while at California State University, Fullerton, has further crystallized the thinking of educators concerning this important subject.[25]

[25] Before going to California State University, Fullerton (CSUF), Cooksey taught choral music for seven years in the secondary schools of Tampa, Florida. While doing graduate work he was conductor of the Illinois Summer Youth Music Junior High School Choir for two summers and has extensive teaching experience with junior high school boys' choirs. At California State University, Fullerton, Cooksey, a very active teacher, conducted the Men's and Women's Choirs, taught a Choral Practicum course at Parlata Junior High School, Orange, and supervised student teachers. He was chairman of the American Choral Directors Association (ACDA) subcommittee on Children's and Boys' Choirs and a member of the ACDA Western Region President's Board of Officers. After extensive research pertaining to the changing voice, he wrote four rather extensive articles published in the ACDA *Choral Journal* from October 1977 through January 1978, providing scientific and empirical evidence of his conclusions about the boys' changing voices. In the ensuring years he held many workshops and clinics nationally, disseminating his findings. Following his tenure at California State University, Fullerton, he served as director of choral activities at Memphis State University. Currently he is teaching at the University of Utah.

Owing to the extent and detail of Cooksey's writings, it is impossible to present all of his research findings here; therefore a synopsis taken directly from the second of four articles published in the American Choral Directors Association *Choral Journal* from October 1977 through January 1978 is presented. He categorizes the boys' voices during mutation, giving the following ranges:[26]

| Boy Soprano | Midvoice I | Midvoice II | Midvoice IIA | New Baritone | Settled Baritone |

In a later research project, he submitted a revised set of ranges:[27]

| Boy Soprano | Midvoice I | Midvoice II | Midvoice IIA | New Baritone | Settled Baritone |

Here are his findings:

1. The individuality and uniqueness of the voice and person should be recognized during the period of adolescent voice mutation. Healthy concepts about singing arise from the young man's increased understanding about his vocal capabilities and limitations. He should be fully informed about the physiological aspects of mutation and its concomitant effects on range, tessitura, and voice quality.

2. In order to understand voice mutation, concomitant physiological changes related to sexual development, skeletal growth, increases in body height and weight, and basic metabolic fluctuations should be delineated. Mutational changes related to the organs of phonation during puberty must also be described.

3. The pubertal stages of sexual development closely parallel the stages of voice mutation. The most dramatic changes in the singing voice occur at the climax of puberty.

4. The speaking voice changes faster than the singing voice, but it is a fairly reliable indicator (timbre-wise) of the initial and high point phases of the singing voice mutation. The initial onset of change in the speaking voice precedes that of the singing voice.

5. The mean frequency pitch of the speaking voice lies near the bottom of the voice range, but more research is needed to confirm its exact relationship to the singing range during the most active phases of mutation.

6. Voice breaks do not occur more often during adolescence, unless the voice

---

[26] John M. Cooksey, "The Development of a Contemporary, Eclectic Theory for the Training and Cultivation of the Junior High School Male Changing Voice," *Choral Journal* 18, no. 5. (October 1977–January 1978).

[27] John M. Cooksey, Ralph Beckett, and Richard Wiseman, "A Longitudinal Investigation of Selected Vocal, Physiological and Acoustical Factors Associated with Voice Maturation in the Junior High School Male Adolescent." Research study resulting from the report from the American Choral Directors Convention, 1983.

is forced out of its normal singing range. If voice breaks are interpreted in terms of vocal quality variations (increased huskiness or use of the "fry"), higher incidents of this phenomenon can be expected during the first phases of vocal development.

7. Occurrence of voice breaks in the adolescent do not necessary signal the onset of voice mutation.

8. Singing voice mutation proceeds at various rates through a predictable, sequential pattern of stages. The onset of vocal development is also variable and is genetically predetermined, but some environmental factors (health, diet, and so forth) may also play an important role.

9. The changes in range, tessitura, and timbre follow a 5-stage pattern of development (as indicated by the ranges quoted previously).

10. The length of the period encompassing the most noticeable voice changes averages about 14 months.

11. For the majority of boys, mutation begins at 12–13 years of age, reaches its most active phase between 13 and 14, then tapers off between 15 and 17/18. The newly changed voice usually appears between 14 and 15, but "settles" for one to two years afterwards.

12. Triggered by hormone secretions, the first stage of voice mutation occurs at different times in different individuals. It is often difficult to detect at first. The upper range limit descends, but the timbre of the voice changes only slightly. There is also an increase in breathiness and strain in the upper extreme register.

13. There tends to be more stability and less individual variations in the lower range limits throughout the different stages of voice mutation. In the upper range limits there are great variations throughout the first three stages, but this stabilizes dramatically in Stage 4.

14. Age is not as reliable an indicator for voice classification as the pubertal stages outlined in this article. Neither is grade level . . . but both criteria are important. At any one grade level, one might expect to encounter boys experiencing any of the first four stages of voice mutation. The general tendency is as follows, however: (1) Grade 7: Boy sopranos and Midvoice I in the majority; (2) Grade 8: Midvoice I and II in the majority, with a significant increase in the spring of the newly changed baritone voice.

15. The quality of the singing voice can be differentiated in each stage of development. I. Rich soprano; II. Midvoice I, some alto characteristics, increasing breathiness on top notes . . . sound is somewhat darker; III. Midvoice II, approximates ingredients of treble and baritone sounds, but retains distinctive quality all its own; IV. Newly changed baritone sound, light, thin, and not yet truly settled; V. Early adult phase, voice is more powerful, resonant, and more closely resembles the adult baritone, bass or tenor sound.

16. The range limitation narrows significantly during the Midvoice II (Stage III) phase. Because its compass includes for the most part the lower register of the female voice, and the upper register of the newly changed baritone voice, unison singing is difficult to achieve . . . particularly in Grade 8 where the Midvoice II's are most numerous. Similarly, tenor parts in SATB music present problems since their range/tessituras are sometimes too low; likewise, the alto parts may be too high.

17. In Stages II–IV (Midvoice I—new Baritone), the voice loses some pitch/rhythmic/dynamic agility and flexibility. The rapid growth and extension of the vocal cords and surrounding muscle/cartilage structure has a lot to do with this.

18. Register definitions (modal, falsetto, whistle) become clear during the high mutation period (Stage III, Midvoice II).

19. In predicting future voice classifications, there is some evidence to support experts' claims that voices which mature early/quickly will become basses, and those which mature later and/or slowly will become high baritones or tenors. Some researchers say that the majority of voices will be baritones . . . and that true basses and tenors are rare. In any case, increased training and practice will not produce a certain type voice. This is primarily genetically predetermined. I might add that the upper register lift point may supply us with a better clue about voice classification. If the "gears shift" at middle C or D, the voice is probably a bass or baritone, but if the primary lift occurs at E or F (lower part of the treble clef), there are possibilities he will become a tenor.

20. The training and cultivation of the changing voice should begin with the comfortable singing range/tessitura which each individual has, regardless of the stage of mutation. It is important to consolidate the comfortable middle range through each state of mutation so that vocal problems and hyper-functional disorders will not occur. One should let the voice quality and flexibility develop gradually. The proper exercise of the voice in its comfortable range will eventually result in an extended range, but it will not speed up the mutation process! Proper exercise will also lead to comfortable register transitions.

21. Most laryngologists and speech pathologists say that private voice study should not begin before the male is 17 or 18 years of age. They believe that the voice should not be strained or overly worked before it has a chance to settle.[28]

22. Choral literature must be chosen to satisfy the vocal capabilities in each stage of mutation. Voices should not be taxed to problematic limits, especially in terms of breath support, range/tessitura, and volume/intensity.[29]

ANTHONY BARRESI ON ADOLESCENT VOICE

Anthony Barresi, professor of choral music education at the University of Wisconsin-Madison, has done a great deal to disseminate contemporary information about the adolescent changing voice, primarily through his videotape

[28] It is Cooksey's belief that the choral director must give some individual training to the voice as it develops; but in most cases, he believes, prolonged, intensive private study should not begin until the voice settles. I disagree with that point of view in that I believe private study is advantageous and, in fact, enhances the mutational process, provided the teacher is cognizant of the unique characteristics of the voice. Attempting to develop the voice from an adult perspective that includes training in such aspects as range extension, for example, produces negative results. Being taught to sing with proper breath control, resonance, and a free, relaxed tone are definitely positive factors in allowing a smooth voice change. My experience has been that boys who were using good vocal technique when they entered voice change experienced very little vocal uneasiness, discomfort, or limitations during the process. In fact, some hardly knew the voice was changing; it gradually lowered in a very natural manner. The vocal mechanism continued to function in the same manner as it had before the change and in the appropriate manner it should function after the change. Good vocal technique resulted in this phenomenon, in my opinion.

[29] John M. Cooksey, "Eclectic Theory," *Choral Journal* (November 1977), p. 14. Reprinted by permission of the American Choral Directors Association.

entitled *Barresi on Adolescent Voice*.[30] Barresi bases his understanding about early adolescent vocal mutation on his own research[31], the research of John Cooksey, and those pioneers who proceeded him. The tape is very helpful to the beginning teacher because it includes demonstrations by adolescent singers (both male and female) in various stages of vocal mutation. The stages and ranges he promotes are those advocated by Cooksey. Barresi has contributed further tessitura limitations to Cooksey's ranges, which are very helpful:[32]

| Pre-mutation | Midvoice I | Midvoice II | Midvoice IIA | New Baritone |

Barresi suggests some criteria that directors may use to evaluate choral literature for early adolescent singers.[33] Relative to technical demands, he advocates that directors should consider:

MELODIC CONTOUR

He says that "since characteristic growth patterns may limit the successful performance of certain kinds of melodic lines, pieces should be avoided that require the young singer to perform extended chromatic passages, lines with wide and rapid intervallic leaps, or melodies with rapid, angular pitch changes." He also feels that "choral parts which are written for areas of the voice where rapid register changes are required should be avoided since the minute vocal adjustments necessary for the successful negotiation of such passages are beyond the technical abilities of most adolescent singers." Finally, he points out that long phrases may be difficult to maintain, particularly with the boys, due to their developing breathing mechanisms. Music with florid passages and rapidly shifting harmonic passages should be avoided.

TEMPO AND RHYTHM

He advocates that adolescent girls, "because they are experiencing less dramatic effects of vocal change, are capable of performing parts in swift tempos," while

[30] This video is distributed by the Department of Continuing Education in the Arts, Division of University Outreach, University of Wisconsin-Madison, 726 Lowell Hall, 610 Langdon Street, Madison, WI 53703 (608-263-6322).

[31] Anthony L. Barresi and M. Goetsch, *A Self-instructional Module on the Adolescent Changing Voice* (Madison, Wisc.: Instructional Media Distribution Center, 1980).

[32] Anthony L. Barresi and Diane Bless, "The Relations of Selected Variables to the Perception of Tessitura Pitches in the Adolescent Changing Voice," *Proceedings of the Symposium on the Male Adolescent Changing Voice* (Buffalo, N.Y.: State University of New York at Buffalo, 1984).

[33] Anthony L. Barresi and Teresa Pamela Russell, "Criteria for Selecting Appropriate Choral Literature to Assist in the Developing of the Boy's Changing Voice," *Proceedings of the Symposium on the Male Adolescent Changing Voice* (Buffalo, N.Y.: State University of New York at Buffalo, 1984), 168–72.

changing voice boys "require parts that move at more moderate tempos." Very slow tempos also may be a problem in breathing because "the breathing mechanisms . . . are still developing. Difficult rhythm patterns (such as dotted eighth and sixteenth note patterns at a fast tempo) that occur on one syllable of a word should be avoided. Those same dotted eighth and sixteenth notes can be initiated if there is a different syllable or word on each note.

DYNAMIC MARKINGS

Fortissimos and pianissimos are difficult to initiate tunefully and with a pleasant tone quality for most adolescents, particularly in the extremes of the vocal ranges. Directors should work for mezzo fortes and pianos in the comfortable areas of their voices for successful, pleasant singing. They should choose literature that allows them to do so.

LENGTH OF COMPOSITION

"Because the adolescent vocalist in general does not have the physical and intellectual endurance to maintain good vocal production over an extended period of time, the total performance time of a piece to be performed should receive careful consideration."

Relative to textual and musical suitability, he suggests:

TEXT

"The selection of song texts is very important if students interest is to be heightened through topics to which they can relate. . . . Choral directors will have much more success with textual subject matter that is noble, heroic, religious, or humorous in nature." Easy foreign texts often stimulate interest.

MELODIC INTEREST

"Pieces composed in a quasi-contrapuntal style allow greater opportunities for the distribution of melodic ideas to each section of the chorus."

Pertaining to adaptability of voice parts, he relates:

STAGES OF CHANGE

"As part of the selection process, it is important to consider the adaptability of the choral parts to the change stages represented in the chorus. . . . For choruses containing singers in all the change stages [eighth and ninth grades], four—and sometimes three-part music—will meet the needs more adequately than unison or treble voicings.

UNISON SINGING

"Unison singing in choruses with 7th and 8th grade singers is, for the most part, impractical because the common pitches possessed by singers in all the change stages are limited in number."

OTHER VOICINGS

> Barresi advocates four parts for changing voice choirs, when possible: Soprano I, Soprano II, Cambiata, Baritone (SSCB); Soprano, Alto, Cambiata, Baritone (SACB); and Soprano, Alto, Tenor, Bass (SATB) voicings. He warns directors to be careful with Soprano, Alto (SA); Soprano I, Soprano II, Alto, (SSA); and Soprano, Alto, Baritone (SAB) because they may need to be edited to be functional.

Finally, relative to choosing music of worth, these statements by him may provide a framework for considering the musical worth of pieces under scrutiny:

1. "The work is by a composer or arranger with a reputation for fine musical craftsmanship."
2. "The work contains musical ideas and technical requirements which will contribute to the singers' vocal and musical growth."
3. "The text of the piece is well integrated with the music and is apt to evoke singer expressiveness and interest."
4. "The work will assist in the aesthetic growth of the singers by contributing to their awareness of the different styles and types of choral music."

Barresi has recommended several selections that he feels are appropriate for early adolescent singers. They are included in Appendix B and marked with a plus mark (+).

LYNNE GACKLE ON THE ADOLESCENT FEMALE VOICE

Recently, adolescent female voice change has become a topic of study and active research. Lynne Gackle, adjunct assistant professor at the University of South Florida in Tampa and formerly assistant professor of music education at the University of Mississippi in Oxford, has contributed significantly to current knowledge. Much of what she advocates was promulgated by Irvin Cooper and others pioneers of adolescent voice theory, but she has been successful through research to secure, safeguard, and alert music educators of the importance of proper educational principles in this strategic area of vocal consideration.

Gackle advocates that the adolescent female voice changes and goes through several stages of development just as does the adolescent male, even though the process and results may not be as dramatic.[34] She alerts choral directors to several indications that are symptomatic of female adolescent voice change: (1) insecurity of pitch, (2) development of noticeable register breaks, (3) increased huskiness in the voice, (4) decreased and inconsistent range capabilities, (5) voice cracking, (6) lowering of speaking fundamental frequency, (7) uncomfortable singing or difficulty in phonation, (8) heavy, breathy, "rough" tone production and/or colorless, breathy, thin tone quality, and (9) hoarseness.

---

[34] Lynne Gackle, "The Adolescent Female Voice; Characteristics of Change and Stages of Development," *Choral Journal* 31, no. 8 (March 1991), 17–25.

As Cooper indicated, Gackle verifies that adolescent females are neither sopranos nor altos in the adult sense of the term. She advocates relating to them as light sopranos or rich sopranos and treating them as equal voices by (1) vocalizing all girls throughout the full compass of the voice, (2) choosing music that has equal voice parts, and (3) switching parts in regular scores so that students have the opportunity to sing the two or three parts written for female voices, as long as the ranges are comfortable.

Gackle bases her information on ten years of working with and observing female adolescent voices. She indicates that girls pass through four specific stages of change in their development. She gives a chronological age for each stage, but she warns that they are only guides and certainly should not be used as definitive indications of each stage of change.

STAGE I—PREPUBERTAL (ages eight through ten or eleven):

> The singing voice is light and flutelike in quality, there are no apparent register breaks, and it is flexible and capable of managing intervallic skips. It is much like the male voice at the same age except the female voice is lighter in weight because the volume potential is generally not as great.

STAGE IIA—PUBESCENCE/PREMENARCHEAL (the onset of menstruation has not begun—during ages eleven through twelve or thirteen):

> This is the beginning of mutation with the first signs of physical maturation being breast development, height increase, pubic hair, and so forth. The singing voice may be described as breathy due to the appearance of the mutational *chink* (an inadequate closure of the vocal folds as growth occurs in the laryngeal area). The register breaks appears between G^4 and B^4 (in the octave above middle C). If the girls are not using chest phonation, there is an apparent loss of lower range around C^4 (middle C). Some girls have trouble producing chest voice at this time. Symptomatic signs include difficulty or discomfort with singing, difficulty in achieving volume (especially in the middle and upper range), breathy tone throughout the upper range (head voice), and a fuller tone in the lower range (chest voice) with an obvious *flip* into a breathy, childlike, flutelike voice at the transition from lower to upper registers.

STAGE IIB—PUBERTY/POSTMENARCHEAL (the months immediately following the onset of menstruation—during ages thirteen through fourteen or fifteen):

> This is the peak of mutation. It is a very critical time. Tessituras can move up or down, or sometimes they can narrow at either end yielding basically a five- or six-note range of comfortable singing. The register breaks are still apparent between G^4 and B^4 and also at D^5 to F-sharp^5. At times, lower notes are more easily produced, yielding an illusion of an alto quality. Singing in this range may be easier and can be recommended for short periods of time; however, singing only in the lower range for an indefinite period of time can be injurious to the young unsettled voice because of the tendency to overuse the lower (chest) voice. Symptomatic signs of Stage IIB are hoarseness without upper respiratory infection, voice cracking, difficulty or discomfort with singing, and lack of clarity in tone.

Adolescent Female Voice Ranges and Tessituras

Stage I (Pre-pubertal)   Stage IIA (Pre-menarcheal)   Stage IIB (Post-menarcheal)   Stage III (Young Adult Female)

(Whole notes designate range and quarter notes designate tessitura.)

STAGE III—YOUNG ADULT FEMALE/POSTMENARCHEAL (ages fourteen through fifteen or sixteen):

> In this stage the overall range capabilities increase.[35] There is greater consistency between registers, and the voice break (passaggio) is more apparent at D^5 to F-sharp^5, which is more typical of adult voices. The tone becomes deeper and richer but still not exactly like that of the adult female. Some ease returns in the singing process, a vibrato may appear, and there is a volume, resonance, and vocal agility increase.

SUMMARY

The various approaches to the adolescent changing voice in use currently and in the past have been thoroughly examined. How, then, may choral teachers in middle, junior high, and senior high schools use this information in practical application for their students? This is the subject of Chapter 9.

THOUGHTS FOR CONTEMPLATION AND DISCUSSION

1. Why do some directors of boychoirs still advocate the no-sing theory in dealing with adolescent changing voices?

2. Since voice change is such a natural occurrence, why is it necessary to give it such special attention?

3. Disseminating information about changing voices to college-university choral methods professors and persuading those professors to agree about how to teach students with changing voices are the two primary problems in achieving unified results in middle/junior high schools nationally. How would you suggest we solve the problems?

4. *Soprano, alto, tenor,* and *bass* are designations that have been used to classify adult voices since the Renaissance period. In view of the new information relative to vocal mutation that has come to light in the twentieth century, would you be in favor of widespread use of specific adolescent vocal designations that would more appropriately convey the phases of vocal development, particularly in published choral literature? If so, what designations would you suggest for male and female middle/junior high school singers? For senior high school singers? If you would not be in favor of the changes, explain why.

[35] According to Gackle, with some individuals the range does not decrease during the time of mutation. One characteristic of a quality singing voice is that it encompasses a large range. This does not imply that any voice is an alto at age fifteen to sixteen simply because those tones are within the singer's capability.

5. The terms *soprano* and *alto* infer highness and lowness in range and tessitura of female voices. Since the experts agree that these designations often create psychological barriers for adolescent singers, all of which have about the same range and tessitura, how would you suggest the profession deal with the problem?

BIBLIOGRAPHY

ADCOCK, EVA J. "A Comparative Analysis of Vocal Range in Middle School General Music Curriculum." Ph.D. diss., Florida State University, 1971.

AUBURN, CORISANDE. "A Survey of Pedagogic Methods and Materials Used in Teacher Training Institutions in Relation to the Widespread Lack of Teacher Understanding Concerning Junior High Vocal Phenomena and Their Choral Potential." Master's thesis, Florida State University, 1953.

BARRESI, ANTHONY L., and DIANE BLESS. "The Relations of Selected Variables to the Perception of Tessitura Pitches in the Adolescent Changing Voice." *Proceedings of the Symposium on the Male Adolescent Changing Voice*. Buffalo, N.Y.: State University of New York at Buffalo, 1984.

BARRESI, ANTHONY L., and M. GOETSCH. *A Self-instructional Module on the Adolescent Changing Voice*. Madison, Wisc.: Instructional Media Distribution Center, 1980.

BARRESI, ANTHONY L., and TERESA PAMELA RUSSELL. "Criteria for Selecting Appropriate Choral Literature to Assist in the Development of the Boy's Changing Voice." *Proceedings of the Symposium on the Male Adolescent Voice*. Buffalo, N.Y.: State University of New York at Buffalo, 1984.

BARRETT, HOWARD. "Choral Training in the Junior High School with Reference to the Changing Voice." Master's thesis, University of Arizona, 1935.

BEATTIE, JOHN, OSBOURNE McCONATHY, and RUSSELL V. MORGAN. *Music in the Junior High School*. New York: Silver Burdett and Co., 1930.

BEHNKE, EMIL, and LENNOX BROWNE. *The Child's Voice: Its Treatment with Regards to After Development*. London: Sampson Low, 1885.

COFFMAN, WESLEY. "A Study of the Incidence and Characteristics of Boys' Voice Change in Grades Four, Five, and Six, and Implications for School Music." Ph.D. diss., Florida State University, 1968.

COLLINS, DON L. *The Cambiata Concept, a Comprehensive Philosophy and Methodology of Teaching Music to Adolescents*. Conway, Ark.: Cambiata Press, 1981.

COOKSEY, JOHN M. "The Development of a Contemporary, Electic Theory for the Training and Cultivation of the Junior High School Male Changing Voice." *Choral Journal* 18, nos. 2, 3, 4, and 5 (October 1977–January 1978).

COOKSEY, JOHN, RALPH BECKETT, and RICHARD WISEMAN. "A Longitudinal Investigation of Selected Vocal, Physiological and Acoustical Factors Associated with Voice Maturation in the Junior High School Male Adolescent." Research study resulting from the report from the American Choral Directors Association Convention (1983).

COOPER, IRVIN. "The Junior High School Choral Problem." *Music Educators Journal* (November and December), 1950.

——. *Letters to Pat Concerning Junior High School Vocal Problems*. New York: Carl Fischer, 1953.

——. "Realizing General Music Outcomes Through Singing." *Music Educators Journal* (January), 1964.

——. "A Study of Boys' Changing Voices in Great Britain." *Music Educators Journal* (November and December), 1964.

COOPER, IRVIN, and KARL O. KURSTEINER. *Teaching Junior High School Music*, 2d ed. Conway, Ark.: Cambiata Press, 1973.

ELLIOT, AMBROSE. "Relationships Between Voice Ranges and Song Material in Grades Six to Nine," Master's thesis, University of Cincinnati, 1939.

FITZGERALD, JAMES B. "An Evaluation of the Problems of the Boy's Changing Voice in Public School Music." Master's thesis, University of Southern California, 1952.

FRIESEN, J. H. "Vocal Mutation in the Adolescent Male: Its Chronology and a Comparison with Fluctuations in Musical Interest." Ph.D. diss., University of Oregon, 1972.

GACKLE, LYNNE. "The Adolescent Female

Voice; Characteristics of Change and Stages of Development." *Choral Journal* 31, no. 8 (March 1991).

GEHRKENS, K. W. *Music in the Junior High School.* Boston: C. C. Birchard and Co., 1936.

GROOM, MARY D. "A Descriptive Analysis of Development in Adolescent Male Voices During the Summer Time Period." Doctoral diss., Florida State University, 1979.

GUSTAFSON, JOHN M. "A Study Relating to the Boy's Changing Voice, Its Incidence, Training, and Function in Choral Music." Ph.D. diss., Florida State University, 1956.

HAMLINE, FLOY. "Development of the Male Voice from Childhood through Adolescence." Master's thesis, University of Southern California, 1939.

HENNESSEY, MONICA MARY. "Problems of Selection and Arrangement of Songs for a Select Boy's Choir at the Later Intermediate Level." Master's thesis, University of Iowa, 1942.

HOLLIEN, H. and E. MALICK. "Evaluation of Cross-section Studies of Adolescent Voice Change in Males." *Speech Monographs,* 1967.

HUFF-GACKLE, LYNNE. "The Adolescent Female Voice (ages 11–15): Classification, Placement, and Development of Tone." *Choral Journal* 25, no. 8 (1985).

———. "The Effect of Selected Vocal Techniques for Breath Management, Resonation, and Vowel Unification on Tone Production in the Junior High School Female Voice." Ph.D. diss., University of Miami, 1987.

JOHNSON, CLAUDE E. *The Training of Boy's Voices.* New York: Oliver Ditson, 1935.

LUCK, JAMES THOMAS. "A Study Relating to the Boy's Changing Voice in Intermediate Church Choirs of the Southern Baptist Convention." Ph.D. diss., Florida State University, 1957.

MCKENZIE, DUNCAN. *Training the Boy's Changing Voice.* New Brunswick, N.J.: Rutgers University Press, 1956.

MELLALIEU, W. H. *The Boy's Changing Voice.* London: Oxford University Press, 1947.

PALMER, E. D. *The Boy's Voice at the Breaking Period.* London: Joseph Williams, 1892.

PITTS, LILLA BELL. *Music Integration in the Junior High School.* Boston: C. C. Birchard and Co., 1936.

RADTKE, ANOLA. "Positive Attitudes Toward Singing for Adolescent Boys." *Music Educators Journal* (January), 1950.

REDNER, ARTHUR. "The Missing Link." *Music Journal* (January), 1951.

RICHISON, S. R. "A Longitudinal Analysis of the Vocal Maturation Patterns of Individual Adolescents through Duration Periods of Eight and Nine Years." Ph.D. diss., Florida State University, 1971.

RORKE, GENEVIEVE A. *Choral Teaching at the Junior High School Level.* Chicago: Hall and McCreary Co., 1947.

RUTKOWSKI, JOANNE. "Final Results of a Longitudinal Study Investigating the Validity of Cooksey's Theory from Training the Adolescent Male Voice." *Pennsylvania Music Educators Association Bulletin of Research in Music Education* 16, 1985.

SORENSON, ROBERT ARTHUR. "The Changing Voice of the Boy." Master's thesis, University of Michigan, 1947.

STUBBS, G. EDWARD. "Should Breaking Voices Be Rested?" *New Music Review* (July), 1930.

STURDY, L. A. "The Status of Voice Range of Junior High Boys." Master's thesis, University of Southern California, 1939.

SWANSON, FREDERICK J. "The Changing Voice: An Adventure, Not a Hazard." *Choral Journal* (March), 1976.

———. "Changing Voices: Don't Leave Out the Boys." *Music Educator's Journal* 70, (January 1984).

———. *The Male Changing Voice Ages Eight to Eighteen.* Cedar Rapids, Iowa: Igram Press, 1977.

———. *Music Teaching in the Junior High and Middle School.* Englewood Cliffs, N. J.: Prentice-Hall, Inc., 1973.

———. "The Proper Care and Feeding of Changing Voices." *Music Educators Journal,* 48, 1961.

———. "The Vanishing Basso Profundo Fry Tones," *Choral Journal* 17, no. 7 (1977).

———. "Voice Mutation in the Adolescent Male: An Experience in Guiding the Voice Development of Adolescent Boys in General Music Classes." Ph.D. diss., University of Wisconsin, 1959.

———. "When Voices Change." *Music Educators Journal* (February and March), 1960.

TAYLOR, G. L. "The Problems of the Changing Voice and the Literature for Junior High School Mixed Chorus." Ed.D. diss., Colorado State College, 1966.

VINCENT, MABEL. "A Survey and Evaluation of the Junior High School Vocal Situation in

Schools of the State of Florida." Master's thesis, Florida State University, 1954.

WEISS, DESO A. "The Pubertal Change of the Human Voice." *Folia Phoniatrica* 2, (1950).

WILLIAMS, BONNIE BLU. "An Investigation of Selected Female Speaking Voice Characteristics through Comparison of Pre-Menarcheal to Post-Menarcheal Girls." Proposed Ph.D. diss., University of North Texas, proposed 1989).

WILSON, FRANK W. "Study of the Range of Boy's Voices at the Junior High School Level." Master's thesis, Temple University, 1946.

9

Dealing with Adolescent Voices in the Music Classroom

The college/university education of junior high and middle school music teachers/ conductors has been woefully inadequate from the standpoint of preparing the teacher for understanding the nature, care, and cultivation of adolescent changing voices. Often, only a cursory overview of basic range capabilities is given the beginning teacher in the choral methods class. If information is presented, it is often given in an impractical setting without the benefit of actually hearing young voices. Though a great deal of study has been given to the male adolescent voice, very little of this information is made readily available to the beginning teacher. . . . Our challenge is to help young voices develop to their fullest present potential for personal self-expression. We must facilitate their vocal future rather than hinder that development or contribute to lifelong feelings of vocal inadequacy. We must also help students to understand that each voice is unique—that it *grows* or develops uniquely.[1]

For the last two decades I have been traveling throughout the United States promulagating the message of how a lack of understanding about the adolescent changing voice affects *all* aspects of adolescent choral music education.[2] As the above quotation indicates, many music educators understand this, but we have found it difficult to capture the attention of those who stand in methods classes in our colleges and universities. Before classroom music teachers can have a genuine positive effect on the musical lives of their

[1] Lynne Gackle, "The Adolescent Female Voice—Characteristics of Change and Stages of Development," *Choral Journal*, 31, no. 8 (March, 1991), 17–25.

[2] Over 150 workshops and clinics relative to the adolescent changing voice have been provided in thirty-four different states.

students, they must be taught how to deal with their adolescent voices. Chapters 8 and 9 are among the most important chapters is this book. Study them and internalize them. When you practice what is taught in these chapters you will begin to change the status of early adolescent choral music education and the daily effect of your professional life.

The consensus of opinion from most of the experts presented in Chapter 8 is that voices change each in its own manner even though the voices may be grouped in various categories as they proceed through mutation. Such nomenclatures as treble, soprano, alto, alto-tenor, tenor, cambiata, midvoice, light baritone, new baritone, baritone, bass, and new bass have been used over the years to describe groupings in the phases of voice change. On what basis do teachers decide to group students for singing two, three, or four parts? What kind of success can be expected from part singing? How many parts should be included to administer most effectively to the needs of young singers? What type of groupings will yield the best choral results? These are the practical questions that should be answered if choral instructors expect adolescents to sing successfully.

The biggest mistake teachers can make is to apply adult terminology and nomenclature to adolescent singers. This only will lead to improper classification of the voices and misapplication of the voices to the literature. This is true no matter whether the changing voices are in middle/junior high or senior high school. There are no adolescents who are true sopranos, altos, tenors, or basses in the adult sense of those terms.

VOCAL REGISTERS

To administer successfully to the needs of adolescent singers, a teacher must have an understanding of basic phonation within the vocal instrument particularly in relation to the way the voice divides into registers, that is, chest voice or head voice.

Intentionally, a deeply detailed, scientific explanation of registers is not presented here. An attempt is being made to explain a very complex operation in simple lay terms. For a deeper, more discerning explanation, one may consult William Vennard's book, *Singing, the Mechanism and the Technic*,[3] particularly Chapter 4, or some other good book about the physiology of the voice.

Basically, all singers (male, female, child, adolescent, or adult) have two usable registers. There is a third in the extremely high area of the child and female voice called the *whistle register* and another in the extremely low area of the adolescent changed and adult male voice referred to as fry tones (note the previous discussion in Chapter 8 about Swanson's adolescent bass theory), but for practical purposes these are not very useful for singing. Some teachers avoid

[3] William Vennard, *Singing, the Mechanism and the Technic* (New York: Carl Fischer, 1968).

using the term *register*, particularly those who teach voice from a *resonance* point of view, because they want to discourage any inference that the voice is segmented. Their desire is to train the voice so that it sounds consistent from top to bottom. The use of the term here should in no way discourage the attempt to reach that same goal with adolescent singers. Some use terms that infer three usable registers, such as *normal* (or *modal*), *head*, and *falsetto* for the male and *chest*, *middle*, and *head* for the female. For purposes of this explanation, one must think about the high, light register (falsetto in men and head voice in women) as opposed to the heavier, lower register (normal or modal in men and chest in women). The head voice in men and the middle voice in women do not constitute a register (for the purpose of this explanation) but represent a mixture of the characteristics of the upper, lighter voice with those of the lower, heavier voice. Henceforth, the two primary registers shall be called head voice (upper, lighter) and chest voice (lower, heavier).

In lay terms, in using chest voice, phonation occurs throughout most of the length of the vocal folds (really a set of complex muscular fiber called *thyroarytenoids*) that become shorter and thicker than when they are not active. The *glottis* (the opening between the vocal folds) closes firmly and remains closed briefly during each vibration so that air pressure builds up below and bursts out. Each puff of air in each vibration opens the glottis in a rather explosive fashion. This makes the chest voice suitable for low tones, which are comparatively loud and rich in harmonic partials.

In the head voice (falsetto in the changed male voice), the inner part (farthest from the edge) of the vocal folds (thyroarytenoid muscular fiber) is almost inactive. The vocal ligaments that form the edge of the vocal folds are stretched and become quite thin. In phonation only the edges of the vocal folds (vocal ligaments) vibrate. If the pitches are low, even though the opening is narrow, the entire glottis is vibrating. In the higher frequencies the glottis only has time to vibrate at the forward end. The vocal instrument operating in this fashion results in a more flutelike tone with fewer partials.

In most cases singers are able to produce tones over a three-octave range. (Notice that the statement says "produce tones"; they cannot sing well throughout the entire three octaves.) The lower octave will be produced in chest voice, the middle octave may be produced in either voice, and the upper octave will be produced in the head voice (falsetto in the changed male voice). It should be understood that when the term *octave* is used, depending on the voice, these pitches may be more or less than eight tones. The black notes without stems in the example below indicate the area which can be produced in either voice.

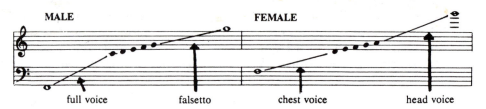

With young singers, the teacher should attempt to keep the female in the head voice in the upper two octaves, using the chest voice only on the lowest tones of the literature. Likewise, the teacher should attempt to keep the changing and changed male voice in the chest (normal/modal) area in the lower octave and most of the middle octave. Recommendations concerning the young male treble (unchanged voice) will be addressed later. With the changing voice and changed male voice, it is best to use literature that will keep them in the chest (normal) area most of the time. Please understand the importance of dealing correctly with the area indicated by the black notes. Using the wrong phonation with these pitches can be very detrimental to proper vocal production and good health.

At this point, for clarification purposes, the kinds of adolescent voices will be considered separately. Beginning with female voices, the discussion will proceed from the high to the low male voices including the various phases in the mutational process.

THE FEMALE ADOLESCENT VOICE

Adolescent girls are neither sopranos nor altos in the adult sense of the words. One might think about them as having a "tendency" toward alto or a "tendency" toward soprano. That is, some seem to sing in head voice more naturally, while others seem to be more comfortable using chest voice. As noted previously, the muscles controlling the vocal folds react differently when one sings in head voice as compared to when one sings in chest voice. Further, the resonating chambers seem to promote the use of head resonance more readily in some young voices, and in others, chest resonance seems to be more easily promoted. Therefore, it might be more nearly correct to think about young female singers as being natural *head singers* or natural *chest singers* rather than sopranos or altos. This is not to infer that these young voices should sing primarily in one area or the other. Quite the contrary, it is the teachers' responsibility to train both areas of the voice even to the point of bringing the two areas together, thereby resulting in a *middle* area (register), which contains characteristics of both head and chest resonance. In developing the middle register, the young singers learn to *mix* the registers; that is, to employ the phonation instrument in such a way that the sets of muscles that control the head and chest area function equally. Teachers should realize that many mature, trained singers have difficulty with this process, so it is probably rather idealistic to think that early adolescent females will be successful, but teachers should be cognizant of the ideal and work in that direction. More importantly, teachers should train the full compass of the voices except in the extremely high and low areas. Because the voices are growing, range extension should be reserved until a later time in the maturation process.

Some chest singers will have difficulty moving into the head area and may complain that they cannot sing above A (second space, treble clef). The problem is that in the singing process they have not experienced phonation in the head area and will need to be taught to pass through the *lift* or *break* (that place in the voice range where the folds change from one phonation process to another) into the head voice. They probably have experienced the head voice while yelling on the playground but simply do not realize that singing in the head voice and yelling require a similar production. Even after experiencing it, they often do not choose to use it because the lower part of the head voice is very weak and ineffective until it is trained and until students are taught to resonate properly in that area. Students must be led to realize that a stronger, more dynamic sound will result from head voice phonation as the muscles strengthen through exercise. It is important to keep a watchful eye on young, inexperienced female singers when they approach the break area because their tendency is to maintain phonation in the chest register far above where it is naturally comfortable. It is quite common for young chest singers to attempt to carry the chest voice as high as D (fourth line, treble clef) or occasionally E-flat (top space, treble clef), particularly if they enjoy singing gospel, rock, soul, or country music. All these styles are performed by various female singers who use mostly the chest voice, and it is only natural that young adolescent girls desire to emulate popular singers.

The vocal quality of the young female head singer in its natural state may be described as thin, breathy, and colorless. To realize full dynamic potential this voice generally requires greater stimulation than that of a boy or a female chest singer. Many times one hears the complaint by young teachers: "My girls just do not have any volume, and they are *so* breathy." The response of many educators is: "This is the way junior high or middle school girls are supposed to sound. Don't worry, they'll grow out of it." True, they will, but not until they are seniors in high school or older. By then they are out of middle/junior high school teachers' care having been replaced by another crop of breathy, colorless singers. It does not have to be middle/junior high school teachers' lot to be content with this type sound. With proper vocal technique (see Chapter 10) within about six months, the voices of young head singers will open up and they will be able to produce a fuller, almost mature, sound. At least it will be two or three times fuller, without forcing, than it was in its natural state.

Whether students are chest singers or head singers, it must be emphasized once more: It is the teachers' responsibility to train the full compass of their students' voices except in the extreme high and low areas so that head singers can use their chest voices on the lower notes and the chest singers can use their head voices most of the time except on the lower notes. This is done through proper vocal technique and by choosing music that relates to the instrument as a whole. Relative to choosing proper choral and vocal literature, it is important that both the soprano I, soprano II, and alto parts all extend into both areas of the voice and particularly into the head area. Many publishers are producing music for middle/junior high school that forces young females to sing only in their chest area. This is particularly true of much music in a contemporary popular style in which the typical range is A (below middle C) to A (one octave above). This never allows young adolescent females an opportunity to move into their head area. If the voice phonates primarily in the chest register and seldom in head register, those muscles controlling chest phonation become very strong and those controlling head phonation remain weak. The result is an obvious difference in the quality of sound between the two registers. The chest area will be loud and raucous and the head voice will be thin and colorless with a greatly pronounced break between the two voices. It is vitally important that the music being sung by young females involves both registers so that the muscles controlling both voices are allowed to develop equally in strength. Proper warm-up exercises and vocalises greatly enhance this developmental process.

From the discussion about Irvin Cooper and the cambiata concept it should be remembered that he wrote two equal parts for girls at this age. In his choral organizations he divided the girls into two groups that he called the blues and the greens. For example, in one song the blues would sing the soprano I part while the greens sang soprano II. In a different song he might reverse the process, with the greens on soprano I and the blues on soprano II. This gave all the girls the opportunity to use the full compass of the voice. Further, they experienced singing harmony, which is important for young singers. If girls are classified as sopranos or altos at an early age, sopranos often grow up singing nothing but the melody and altos nothing but harmony. Cooper's *equal voicing* alleviated this practice and gave the girls experience in both types of singing.

Music written for the cambiata concept in many cases will have parts for equal voices. Use of it is recommended in the promotion of healthy singing by young female voices. If music is chosen that is designated as soprano and alto, or unequal parts, it is suggested that different groups of girls be assigned to different parts in different pieces. This will allow all girls to receive experience singing the upper and lower parts. One word of caution against choosing music that takes young singers to the extreme areas (both high and low) of their ranges: The comfortable singing area for young female singers is D (above middle C) to D (one octave higher). However, they may be allowed to sing up to the F (top line, treble clef) or down to B-flat (below middle C). As to the nomenclature to be used for the two groupings, soprano I and II or treble I and II are recommended. If they are called sopranos or altos, help them to realize that these are adult terminology and that their voices will develop eventually to be more exemplary of the true meaning of those words. Just because they are called altos at present does not mean they will be altos as adults (the same is true of sopranos). At this point in their lives they are two equal groups of adolescent singers, and their voices need to be developed to full potential through proper training and the natural maturation process.

THE MALE TREBLE

Teachers in middle/junior high school and occasionally in senior high school will encounter male trebles. Many teachers view these young men as being unchanged voices and think about them as being in that specific category until their voices begin the fast growth process (adolescent growth spurt) during puberty. In reality these young men's voices are literally changing and maturing from birth, with each year of age bringing greater flexibility and agility to the singing voice. From about age nine or ten until they begin the fast growth process (mutation), they all have about the same range and may be categorized as unchanged voices. However, teachers who view young males to be always changing and growing until manhood will have a proper attitude for accepting and understanding the fast growth process that occurs at puberty.

In most boychoirs throughout the world where young male voices are trained extensively for singing, one finds that their trainers think about the vocal development of these boys as being an ongoing, changing process. Ten-year-old trebles certainly sound different in quality, range, flexibility, and agility than fourteen-year-old trebles. This is due partially to the four years' training the fourteen-year-old trebles have received, but it is mostly because the young men are further along in the maturation process, resulting in a more mature, effective sound.

The utopian situation would be one in which all young men experiencing voice change would have already received good vocal training as male trebles and also would have an extensive knowledge of the capability of the vocal instrument. Then they would experience mutation with very few vocal problems. Since utopian situations are rare, the approach by middle/junior high or senior high school teachers to the training of male trebles when they enter the teachers' care is greatly dependent on the young men's training in elementary school and how those young men understand their vocal instruments. If young men entering middle/junior high school have been singing in a boychoir or have had similar training in a church choir or the elementary classroom, they usually understand how to use their head voices well and are proud of their ability to sing high. On the other hand, if these young men's first vocal experience is in choir or general music class in middle/junior high school, they lack the understanding that is required for them to sing throughout the full compass of their voices. They generally consider the head voice to be the equivalent to that of the female voice, and they balk at the suggestion that they sing high. For the teacher to receive the cooperation of each young man, perhaps it is better that each be treated differently. The young men who like to use the head voice may continue to train as trebles by singing one of the soprano parts. They may feel more comfortable sitting with the rest of the boys but near the girls since they will be singing with them. It is important that teachers keep a constant surveillance on these young men's vocal development because they are approaching the age of puberty and possibly will need to move to a changing voice part in the near future. The young men who feel that it is "macho" to sing low and do not understand how to use the head voice will need to be approached differently. Even though they may not have entered the first phase of voice change, it may be well to place them with those boys who have, so they may use their chest voices predominantly. It is not detrimental for them to sing primarily in the chest area as it is with the practice of singing in chest voice with young females, because boys will continue to use the chest voice as their full singing instrument after vocal mutation. The head area will become their falsetto and will not be used except for special effects and on extremely high literature. These chest-singing young men will be singing with the proper group for their soon-to-arrive mutational process and will enter it without difficulty.

Teachers who are working with elementary male trebles, approximately ages six through eleven or twelve, should initiate a process of training in which the full compass of the voice (head and chest) is used. Vocal training at this early age greatly enhances young men's success when experiencing voice change. This tenet is supported by both scientific and empirical evidence. Experience in working with both treble and changing voices indicates that the voice change is much smoother and that young men encounter less difficulties in singing throughout mutation if they understand their vocal instruments and if at an early age they have trained those muscles controlling both head and chest voices through proper vocal technique and by singing literature that exercises the full compass of their voices.

Finally, in working with male trebles, it is a mistake to think about them as being similar in range and quality to young females at this age. Further, it is important for teachers to approach female treble voices differently from those of male trebles. As has been indicated, it is acceptable to train older male trebles who are inexperienced in using the upper voice as chest singers without detriment to the vocal instruments, because they use this part of their instruments when they become adult males. It is not acceptable, however, to train the female voices in this fashion, because they use the head voice as their principal singing instrument as adults and rely on the chest resonance only for special dramatic effects. Young females should be encouraged not to overdevelop the chest voice and to sing principally in the head area at all times except in very lowest notes of the literature.

THE MALE CHANGING VOICE IN MIDDLE/JUNIOR HIGH SCHOOL

Following the line of thinking that teachers should perceive adolescents not according to adult vocal categories but rather according to the specific phase of voice change, consideration is now given to those boys who have just entered the first phase of change. Cooper called them cambiata; McKenzie, alto-tenor; Swanson, alto; and Cooksey, midvoice I and II. In the North and East United States they are often referred to as sopranos and altos. In the South, Southwest, Midwest, and West they are most often called tenors. Most published music refers to their part as cambiata or tenor. In some music a term is not assigned, and the designation is simply a roman numeral such as "Part III." Often the part they are to sing is written in the treble clef to be sung at actual pitch. In other instances it is written in the bass clef, and in a few cases one will find the part written in the treble clef and designated to be sung an octave lower. Obviously, there is a considerable amount of confusion pertaining to the labeling of the part that is to be sung by boys in the first phase of change. The issue is further complicated by the inability of publishers, arrangers, and composers to agree as to where to score a part written for these voices. At the present time, probably the most commonly accepted term, nationally, for this voice is *tenor*. The problems in the use of this term are compounded by its association with the adult voices in addition to its being a "catch-all" term for those boys who might still be trebles, those who are in the first or second phase of change, or those who have changed voices. The term is not sufficiently specific for it to be meaningful to everyone. No matter what one calls boys who have just entered the first phase of change, it is important that teachers keep in mind those characteristics that include the range, tessitura, voice quality, and vocal limitations. Because there is a large body of music in print that utilizes the term *cambiata* and because the term does designate a specific time in the maturation process, for purposes of communication in this book it has been used when referring to the boy in the first phase of vocal change.

What, then, are those unique characteristics (including range, tessitura, voice quality, and vocal limitations) of cambiatas? How do those characteristics differ from those of boy trebles? What are the vocal limitations to the music chosen for them to sing? To deal successfully with early adolescent singers, teachers must know the answers to these questions.

To understand the characteristics of cambiata voices one must compare them to those of boy trebles. The vocal quality of boy trebles is clear and virile. When trained and singing together in a section, these young men can sing as low as F (below middle C) and as high as C (two octaves above middle C). As has been discussed, some are natural head singers and others natural chest singers, but the full compass of their voices should be trained. The period of time (as much as a year in some cases) before male trebles enter into puberty is truly a glorious time vocally for many of these young men, particularly if they are well trained. Their voices are rich, agile, and flexible, and they resonate comparably to adult females. Recordings of young soloists in the Vienna Boys Choir, the Texas Boys Choir, and others support this notion. As young trebles move into the cambiata range, they begin to lose some of their flexibility, particularly in the upper regions of their voices, and the lower notes become heavier with hints of a contralto quality. Cooper used the term *wooly* to describe their vocal quality. As days and months pass, the nice flexible sound of the boy treble begins to acquire the coloring of an adult male falsetto. They begin to complain of being uncomfortable when singing in the upper regions of the voice. They become more comfortable singing in the chest voice.

What part in the music should these young men sing? Swanson suggested that they continue to use the head voice and to sing in the alto section. Cooper wrote a special part for them that stayed basically between A above and A below middle C, which he called cambiata. McKenzie called them alto-tenors and suggested a part be written for them or that existing music be edited to allow them to be comfortable on the alto or tenor part of adult music. Cooksey divides the cambiatas into two separate categories called midvoice I with a range of G (below middle C) to D (fourth line, treble clef) and midvoice II with a range of E (below middle C) to C (one octave above middle C). He suggests that music be found in which these boys can sing any part (alto, tenor, or cambiata) that is most comfortable for them at any particular time in the mutational process.

Because of the female connotation, it is difficult to persuade these young men to sing alto, especially if they have a "macho" image of themselves. Further, if the alto part moves into unison with the soprano or above A (second space, treble clef), they will have difficulty dealing with it, particularly if they are inexperienced in using their head voices. A further problem with singing alto is that it constantly requires many of those in the cambiata section (depending upon where they are in the maturation process) to move back and forth through the break area between head and chest voice. As the voices become heavier in the lower regions, this break becomes more pronounced and the quality of the tone in the head voice (emerging falsetto) is dramatically different from that of the chest voice. The boys may feel uncomfortable since they will be clearly aware of the difference. Only those boys who have good breath control, proper resonance, and overall good vocal technique (and these are rare) will be successful in maneuvering back and forth through the break area with ease.

A tenor part must be carefully chosen or edited to keep the cambiatas from attempting to sing beneath their range and tessitura limitations. Even if a tenor part is found that lies within the A to A compass, the majority of the notes will be around middle C or lower, keeping them in the lower part of their chest voice. Singing in this area of the voice for cambiatas is analogous to adult tenors singing around C (below middle C) or adult sopranos singing around middle C. The part always feels low in the range to the boys and they cannot use the best part of their singing voices.

Since there is a rather significant amount of music on the educational market that has a special part written for cambiatas, it is suggested that teachers seek out those pieces that appeal to them and to their groups.[4] If other music is used, it is important that a part be found that stays basically between A above and A below middle C. If cambiatas sing in that octave they will use the best part of their singing instrument. Singing a cambiata part allows them to remain in the chest voice most of the time, thus avoiding the passing back and forth through the break area. Using music written specifically for them gives them a sense of belonging and being needed in the choir. Asking them to sing an alto part, tenor part, or some other designation relates the profession's inability to consider their needs, thus communicating to them that there is not a special place for them to contribute and that this time in life is bad for them as singers. This type of communication is definitely counterproductive. The most important consideration is to deal with the singers' needs. Find music they can sing. Offer them a sense of satisfaction in their work and contribution to the singing group in which they sing.

The length of time a voice remains in the first phase of change is unpredictable. For some boys it may be as little as two or three months, and for others it may be a year or more. Cooksey's research indicates that for approximately fourteen months they stay in what he calls midvoice I and midvoice II combined.

The second phase of change, baritone, is by far the most difficult with which to deal. Progressing from cambiata to baritone is a very individual matter and occurs in several different ways. Some boys move gradually downward by adding

---

[4] Contact Cambiata Press, Lawson-Gould Music Publishers, Plymouth Music Company, Cherry Lane Music Publishers, or Carl Fischer, Inc., for publishers who offer music written specifically for cambiata voices.

lower tones to the chest voice and by recognizing that the head voice is becoming more and more "falsetto-ish." (This type of change is corroborated by Duncan McKenzie.) These boys generally experience very few "cracking" problems. Some boys move into the second phase of change very rapidly, and because of the fast growth they experience considerable difficulty in controlling the voice, particularly when asked to sing above middle C. Even when they talk, they suddenly lose control and the voice "cracks" into the falsetto area. Still others completely lose the ability to produce any sound at all above A (top line, bass clef) other than falsetto, and it takes several months after the rapid growth period for them to be able to produce these tones at all. (This type of change is corroborated in Swanson's work.) Usually these adolescent boys have very strong low areas of their voices and often can sing down as far as two octaves below middle C. When singing falsetto, often they experience some freedom, but there is a wide gap between the falsetto and the full voice and they are completely unable to produce tones directly above and below middle C. As their voices settle, they usually move upwardly several tones before maturing. Often boys who experience this type of change have had very little singing experience before entering puberty or have been required to maintain total head voice phonation after they entered the first or perhaps even the second phase of change. This type voice change often occurs with young men who have been singing in a boychoir with an instructor who was reluctant to release them from singing treble.

With other boys going through the mutational process, there is a period of time in which the vocal range of the chest voice is extremely limited from middle C downwardly to F (fourth line, bass clef). These boys are generally referred to as being "light baritones" or "new baritones" (Cooksey's term). As the days and weeks pass they will continue to add pitches to the lower area of the voice until they become full-fledged adolescent baritones.

Cooksey indicates that there are three different stages or types of voices during the second phase of change: midvoice IIA with a range of D (below middle C) to A above, the new baritone with a range of B-flat (second line, bass clef) to G (above middle C), and the settled baritone with a range of A (bottom space, bass clef) to F (above middle C). These stages correspond to this author's understanding and description of how the voice moves from the cambiata to the baritone. The ranges of all boys as they proceed through the change will vary according to the individual. This results in the slight difference in ranges delineated by Cooper, McKenzie, Swanson, and Cooksey.

The above descriptions are the most common ways by which boys' voices enter the second phase of change. Again, the voice change is unique to each individual. When choosing literature for boys in the second phase of change, it should include a baritone part with the overall range of approximately B-flat (second line, bass clef) to F (above middle C). These are the maximum extensions of highest and lowest notes. Most boys will be much more comfortable singing within the octave of D (below middle C) to D above. Music with a part written specifically for a boy in the second phase of change should include optional notes when the part moves above middle C for those boys who are unable to produce those pitches. Conversely, when the part moves below F (fourth line, bass clef), there should be optional notes for the light baritone who yet has not added the lower tones. The greatest misconception held by music educators surfaces when they try to classify light baritones as cambiatas. This misconception often occurs because of light baritones' very narrow range of about middle C downwardly to F (fourth line, bass clef). These boys with the narrow range are definitely in the second phase of change and should be assigned to the baritone part even though they are currently unable to produce the lower tones. Classifying them as cambiatas is very unsatisfactory, particularly if they do not know how to use their head voices (emerging falsettos). Attempting to produce the upper tones of the cambiata part will create a great deal of tension, and the tone will be strident and tense. It is much more advantageous to put them on the baritone part to encourage development of the lower pitches. As they use the lower tones of the voice, they will become stronger. Also, they will add new lower tones very quickly with usage and in a short period of time be able to sing the full compass of the baritone part.

One rule of thumb should be used when deciding if it is time to move boys to the next section of the chorus as their voices change: *Always encourage the change.* When one senses that male singers are having difficulty producing the tones indicated in the part they are singing, move them down to the next part even though they might not be able to produce all the tones of that part immediately. There are times when this policy is very difficult to effectuate. Should the majority of the cambiata section in one's choral group suddenly begin to experience difficulty with the upper notes of the part, one would usually move them to the baritone part immediately. What happens if a performance is imminent? Obviously, for the sake of balance, the boys should continue singing cambiata until a time when they can make the change without disrupting the entire choral process. Keeping boys on the cambiata part beyond that time in the mutational process when it is obvious that they are emerging baritones is not recommended, but it is not necessarily detrimental if the voices are handled properly during those days. It is vitally important to encourage them to use the head voice (falsetto) whenever the production of the upper pitches creates tension and strain. Careful attention should be given daily to each boy as he sings. The director should be adamant about the necessity of using the head voice. The boys might complain that their volume output is greatly encumbered. Probably they will have a tendency to "belt" the tones even though it takes a great deal of effort. Watch them! Many improper production habits are acquired at this stage that will haunt the boys for years to come. The point must be made again: If at all possible, move them to the lower part and encourage the mutational process. This will ensure singing that is freer, more comfortable, and much easier to listen to in the years to come.

THE CHANGED ADOLESCENT VOICE IN MIDDLE/JUNIOR HIGH SCHOOL

Fully changed voices in middle/junior high school are rare. After boys have been in the second phase of change (baritone) for several months (Cooksey says the length of time is from one to two years), their voices begin to settle. They will begin to have greater control of their instruments, and the upper and lower limits of their ranges will become more secure. Remember that the voice continues to mature for several years and often does not reach its full performance ability until the late twenties or early thirties. Voices that show signs of settling should continue to sing the baritone part with those boys in the second phase of change. If the teacher recognizes that a voice is tending to mature toward bass quality, ask that boy to sing the lower octaves at cadence points in the music. This will give him a sense of pride in his newly developing bass instrument. If the teacher feels that the tendency of the voice is maturing toward tenor quality, use his voice in a leadership role on the higher notes of the baritone part. It is not recommended in middle/junior high school that boys be divided into tenor and bass sections (in the adult sense of the terms) because there will be so few of the maturing voices and such a predominance of the changing voices that the results will be counterproductive.

THE MALE CHANGING VOICE IN SENIOR HIGH SCHOOL

Some boys do not enter puberty until the ninth or tenth grade. There will even be a few, depending upon the part of the United States in which they live, who might even change as late as the eleventh or twelfth grade. Boys in the North tend to change somewhat later than those in the South. There is a question as to whether climate or heredity is the primary factor. Scandinavian and Germanic people settled in the North whereas the South and Southwest contain a large number of blacks, Latinos, and native Americans. Teachers should administer to the vocal needs of boys in the first and second phases of change. The practice of ignoring them or placing them on a tenor or alto part that might prove difficult for them to sing is strongly discouraged.

Teachers have a responsibility for the students' psychological well-being, and if they are content in their role in the choir teachers have fulfilled that responsibility. Taking particular care to find music in which those students can make a maximum contribution goes a long way toward ensuring the students' contentment. If SATB music is used, teachers should be careful to select that which administers to the needs of the cambiatas. If there are places in the alto or tenor part that move beyond the A-to-A octave recommended for the cambiatas' successful contribution, teachers should edit the part so that the students will be successful in singing it. Boys in the second phase of change (adolescent baritones) should receive careful consideration as well. Placing them on a tenor part that requires them to use the upper part of their range extensively will result in tension and misuse of the vocal instrument. Often the bass part lies too low for comfortable singing. Here again, if SATB music is used, teachers should take time to edit whatever part the adolescent baritones are singing for them to be able to sing in the comfortable area of their voices, the D-to-D octave.

A practice that is becoming more and more in vogue is the use of Soprano I, Soprano II, Cambiata, Baritone (SSCB) music for groups containing changing voices in senior high school, particularly if there is an abundance of girls and few boys. Since there will probably be only a few cambiatas, it is quite acceptable to place senior high school altos on the cambiata part to maintain balance. This is not detrimental to the young female singers, provided they are allowed to use their upper voices with other literature. The A-to-A octave is similar to many alto parts in Soprano, Alto, Tenor, Bass (SATB) music. It is important to continue to refer to the part as cambiata for the psychological well-being of those boys who might be singing it. Altos are not nearly as concerned about being asked to support the cambiatas as the cambiatas are about being called altos. The remainder of the girls are to be divided into first and second sopranos, and all the boys in the second phase of change (adolescent baritones) and changed voices (high school tenors and basses) will sing the baritone part that, with a few exceptions, stays within the D-to-D octave. Using SSCB vocal classification in senior high school for groups with changing voices and a preponderance of girls results in four-part singing with a much more satisfactory balance than using music voiced SATB or Soprano, Alto, Bass (SAB), but most importantly, it administers to the needs of the changing voices in the group.

MOTIVATING THE HESITANT SINGER

One of the difficulties beginning teachers face when attempting to teach a group of general music students or students in the beginning choir to sing is knowing how to deal with the hesitation the young singers display toward the vocal process. When early adolescents have not had experience singing in a church choir or elementary school music class, they may think that they are unable to sing or they will exhibit tremendous self-consciousness about the singing voice. They may even refuse to sing entirely. It is extremely frustrating for beginning teachers when the students either refuse to respond to their directions or the response is so anemic that the process is unfruitful. How does one persuade these fearful students to sing?

Historically there has been a mystique about the singing voice. The Romantics had a mind-set that promoted the misconception that only the highly gifted could sing. They believed it was a special ability that only "the chosen" enjoyed. Occasionally, particularly if students come from a family in which no singing occurs, they truly believe that they are "nonsingers," but in most cases it relates to their adolescent inhibitions (see Chapter 7). The best way to combat this self-consciousness is to begin to train their voices as described in Chapter 10. Before embarking on the process with general music students, however, one may need to break down the barrier of resistance by opening their minds and helping them to see that singing is an ordinary process that all people can enjoy.

When students take math class, they do not resist being taught how to deal with certain equations. In English they learn verbs, nouns, and pronouns with little resistance. The process of singing is no more mysterious than these other academic subjects. Singing in general music class does not require a highly defined degree of proficiency. The students should be brought to understand that the actual activity of music making is more important than worrying about how beautifully they sing. The more they sing, the more beautiful it becomes, particularly once they have been taught the correct way to do it. Teachers should do all they can to help the young singers to realize what a rewarding activity singing can be. Teachers might even want to devise a motivational presentation similar to the one they delivered to their choirs (see the section entitled "The Challenge and Rewards of Choral Singing" in Chapter 14) that will stimulate acceptance of the singing process.

TRAINING THE UNCERTAIN SINGER

Another difficulty beginning teachers encounter is deciding how to teach the "uncertain" singer. When students cannot sing certain pitches it is not an indication that they are tone deaf. The amount of talent, gift, or innate ability to sing tunefully varies only slightly among individuals. The capacity to make music vocally is inherent in everyone, just as the capacity to learn is inherent. How quickly and how early in life students learn to sing tunefully varies according to their capacity to make music. Educators now believe that children who become involved in the music-making process at a very early age have a greater capacity to make music as adults than those who begin making music later in life.[5] The vocal experiences students might have had before they were tutored by a certain instructor will affect their ability to sing tunefully at any particular time. To be an effective teacher of singing with adolescents, teachers must believe that all their students are capable of singing in tune and then transfer that belief to those with whom they work daily.

In most cases the inability to match pitch is a result of a lack of understanding about the singing voice. This is particularly true with the young baritone who has to learn to deal with his rapidly growing vocal apparatus that often reacts in a rather erratic manner. However, students who are inexperienced singers might have to be taught to understand and utilize their vocal instrument properly before they can sing tunefully.

After proper voice classification (see "Irvin Cooper's Cambiata Concept" in Chapter 8 for a quick, unique way to classify voices in a general music class), many inexperienced singers who might have been singing untunefully in the first session of choir or general music class will automatically begin to match pitch in a day or two, after being placed in the correct section where they are being allowed to use their comfortable singing tessitura. Instructors should make a mental note of which students were having trouble during the voice classification procedure. During the first several sessions together, teachers should pass in front of these students several times during each session to determine if they are in fact beginning to sing tunefully. If, after several sessions together, some

---

[5] Consult Edwin Gordon's *Learning Sequence and Patterns in Music* (Chicago: G.I.A. Publications, 1977).

of the students are still having trouble matching some of the pitches, it will be necessary to give them some individual attention. Teachers can do this best in several ten-minute segments alone with the student before or after school, during study hall, or at any time the student is available. Individual attention is essential at this point if the student has not caught on during the first few sessions with the group. Chances are that the student will never learn to match pitch without being taught individually. Obviously the success of the overall group sound is jeopardized until teachers deal with the problem. Observation of different choirs at choral festivals reveals that one of the most common mistakes choral directors make is to ignore the uncertain singers. An even more deplorable practice is to ask uncertain singers to "mouth the words" and not sing when they cannot sing tunefully. This approach is devastating to the morale and self-image of young singers who are having difficulty. This only camouflages the problem and does nothing for the self-assurance of the singers who obviously realize they are not performing well.

During the first ten-minute session with the individual students, explain that the difficulty is not their ability to sing in tune. Students must be assured that after they learn to use their vocal instrument, they will be able to make a fine contribution to the singing group. Be careful that they do not leave the session with the feeling they are a problem or the teacher's work will be much more difficult in the succeeding times together. Students should be led to understanding that learning to sing is like learning to count or to read. If they work hard and attend to their difficulties, they will learn to sing well.

It is difficult to believe that adolescents might not understand the difference in the simple concepts of up and down and high and low, but occasionally they do not. In the first session with the individual student, teachers should play or sing some high and low pitches and ascending and descending scales to determine if such is the case. If the concepts are confused, a few minutes of helping them to recognize the difference is generally all that is necessary to correct the misunderstanding.

Adolescents can learn to sing a melodic pattern easier than they can match isolated pitches that are not related to each other. Therefore, it is better to begin with a simple melodic pattern played or sung at different pitch levels than to play or sing a single pitch and ask the students to sing it. The simple childhood chant (*so, so, mi, la, so, mi*) is a good melodic pattern to use. Without any indication from the voice or piano, ask the students to sing the childhood chant where it is most comfortable in their voices. Sing or play the pattern back to them at the same pitch level, then move up one-half step, sing or play the same pattern, and ask the students to sing it. If they are successful in moving up one-half step, move up another and ask them to sing the pattern at that level. Continue to move up and down above and below the initial pitch that the students chose to sing. Each time they are successful, congratulate them. If the students are unsuccessful, ask them if what they sang was correct. They must realize when they are not matching the pitches. If the students do not realize that they have sung the pitches incorrectly, move back to an area where they are successful, then ask them to sing the pattern again and congratulate them when it is correct.

Continue this process until the students are able to tell the instructors each time they have sung correctly or incorrectly.

As long as teachers stay near the initial pitch level, the students will have success matching the pitches. As the teachers move upward, they will arrive at a pitch level in which the student is not using enough energy to match the correct pitches. At this point, instructors should take a different approach. The interval of an ascending fifth (*do* up to *so*) is a good interval to use to help students move into the area of the voice where they are tunefully uncertain. Place *do* in the area of the voice where they have been successful but where *so* will occur in the area of the voice that they have been unable to reach. Using the words *good morning* (*do, do, so*), sing or play the pattern to the student and ask them to sing it. It is best for both the students and instructors to stand. As the students attempt to sing the pitch *so* and the syllable *ing*, the instructors should press inwardly with their hand using a quick yet slight movement at the front of the breath-band area (just above the navel). The sudden impulse of air created by the quick movement will free the voice to produce the upper pitch. If the first attempt is not successful, try the exercise several times. After several attempts, students are usually successful in singing the upper pitch in tune. Once they have succeeded, following attempts will be easier. After the upper pitch has been achieved, maintain the pressure on the breath-band area and ask they to sustain the tone. Move the *do, do, so* pattern up one-half step and then another using the same technique until the students realize that they can sing the upper pitches.

Another method to achieve the same results may be used. Tell the students to cup both hands together about waist high, pretend the sounds are in the palms of the hands, and, with the leap to the second pitch of the pattern, lift both hands quickly above the forehead. The teacher should stand in front of the students and go through the same motion, which will provide a stimulus. Occasionally the students will overshoot the higher pitch, which is acceptable because the process will have freed the upper voice. Another method is the *siren* technique that is particularly helpful the assist the student in discovering the head voice or falsetto. Instruct the students to begin as low in the voice as they are able and imitate a police siren (use the old-fashioned straight single-tone effect, not the modern double-toned descending minor third), going as high as possible. As soon as a significant range movement is detected, transfer to the *good morn-ing* pattern.

One session with uncertain singers is insufficient. Instructors will find that the students will revert to the uncertain singing when they are put back with the other singers. It is essential to hold several sessions with the students, each time doing basically the same thing, constantly reinforcing the successes with praise, and questioning the lack of success until the students overcome their inhibitions and sing with confidence and energy on correct pitches.

Place the uncertain singers near the strongest vocalist in the section when they sing with the group. Often it is necessary to take those stronger vocalists into the instructor's confidence, explaining that the uncertain singer has been placed near them intentionally and asking them to assist in helping the uncertain singers find their voices. This is necessary because occasionally tuneful singers will ridicule untuneful ones and tease them about their untunefulness, particularly if the untuneful one is sitting nearby. Promoting the tuneful singers to serve as helpers discourages the teasing.

Due to the octave difference between females (and unchanged voices) and males whose voices have already changed, female instructors may have difficulty assisting male uncertain singers because the males may not relate well to the female pitch. If this proves to be a problem, it can be alleviated by inviting a male tuneful singer from the group to attend the sessions with the uncertain singer. Instead of demonstrating with the instructor's female voice, the tuneful singer may demonstrate with his voice. The uncertain singer soon learns to relate to the tuneful singer's voice because it sounds in the same octave and has a very similar timbre.

During the last several years as professor of music at Florida State University, Irvin Cooper conducted a chorus of all the students enrolled at the Blessed Sacrament School in Tallahassee. He would never exclude a student because of untunefulness and, believe it or not, he never had uncertain singers. Individual attention was the secret to success. It takes time and a good bit of extra effort on your part as a teacher, but the rewards are great! Early in my career I was working with an early adolescent girl who for the first time began to produce music with correct pitches. She stopped singing and after several seconds I turned around (she was standing behind me as I played the piano) to ascertain what was wrong. I observed large tears flowing down her cheeks. After years of untunefulness she was literally overwhelmed with her success as a music maker. Nothing is more satisfying to me than seeing the expression on the face of a youngster who is enjoying and appreciating music making for the first time.

SUMMARY

In Chapter 8 we examined how the changing voice has been handled from the time of the Greeks to present with particular attention given to pioneers in changing-voice phenomenon, Duncan McKenzie, Frederick Swanson, and Irvin Cooper, and the current contributions of John Cooksey, Antony Barresi, and Lynne Gackle. In this chapter the information has been applied to ways of working with changing-voice adolescents in the choral classroom.

To that can be added only that adolescents are great music makers. When you, as a choral teacher, understand your students' vocal limitations, use music in which those unique vocal limitations are considered, love those students for what they are and what they can be, and believe in your own personal capabilities, you are primed for some terrific musical experiences and the sky is the limit as to what can be done.

THOUGHTS FOR CONTEMPLATION AND DISCUSSION

1. Your junior high choir has been invited to sing for the regional meeting of the Music Educators National Conference. After a full semester of preparation for the concert, four of your seven cambiatas move into the second phase of voice change. The program is set for next week. They have begun to complain about discomfort when the parts move into the upper area of their voices. You are afraid of damage to their voices due to vocal stress. What should you do?

2. You have worked all year to convince the boy trebles in your middle school general music class to sing in their head voices, and at long last they are singing beautiful flutelike tones. One day a new student joins the class. He has had very little singing experience and does not understand how to use head voice phonation. He begins to tease the other boys about singing "high like girls" and calls them all wimps. Suddenly they all begin to complain about singing in their head voices and argue that it hurts to sing. What should you do?

3. Do you feel obligated to give special attention to the less talented students and uncertain singers? If you do, since the quality of your program may be evaluated by the strength of the musicians found therein, how much time should you allot to these students at the expense of the more talented ones? If you do not feel obligated, how do you justify ignoring them?

4. You have forty-five girls and six boys enrolled in your senior high intermediate choir. The boys are in the second phase of change or changed voices. You have been singing music voiced SATB but you are not happy with the balance; there simply are not enough boys to sing two parts. You could sing music with SAB voicing but you would prefer to continue singing four parts. What should you do?

5. You have fifty-four boys enrolled in an eighth and ninth grade all-male chorus. The enrollment includes six boy trebles whose voices are about to enter the first phase of change, twenty-one boys already in the first phase of change, seventeen boys in the second phase of change, and ten boys whose voices have basically moved through all phases of change. Would you choose to sing music that is voiced CCB, CBB, CCBB, TTBB, or SATB? Why?

BIBLIOGRAPHY

ADCOCK, EVA. The Changing Voice—The Middle/Junior High School Challenge, *Choral Journal* 28, no. 3 (October 1987).

BARRESI, ANTHONY L., and DIANE BLESS. "The Relations of Selected Variables to the Perception of Tessitura Pitches in the Adolescent Changing Voice." *Proceedings of the Symposium on the Male Adolescent Changing Voice.* Buffalo, N.Y.: State University of New York at Buffalo, 1984.

BARTLE, JEAN ASHWORTH. *Lifeline for Children's Choir Directors.* Toronto: Gordon V. Thompson, 1988. (Available through Oxford Press.)

BECKETT, R. L., N. J. BONSANGUE, and N. K. JONES. "An Investigation of the Anatomic, Physiologic and Acoustic Factors Related to Voice Mutation in the Adolescent Male." Presentation for the annual conference of the California Speech/Language and Hearing Association, Los Angeles, March, 1980.

BESSOM, MALCOLM E., ALPHONSE M. TATARUNIS, and SAMUEL L. FORCUCCI. *Teaching Music in Today's Secondary Schools,* 2d ed. New York: Holt, Rinehart and Winston, 1980.

BONSANGUE, N. J. "An Investigation of Selected Acoustical Factors Associated with

Voice Mutation in the Adolescent Male." Master's thesis, California State University, at Fullerton, 1981.

COLLINS, DON L. *The Cambiata Concept, a Comprehensive Philosophy and Methodology of Teaching Music to Adolescents.* Conway, Ark.: Cambiata Press, 1981.

———. "The Cambiata Concept of Boys' Changing Voices," *The Church Musician* 20, no. 2 (February 1969).

———. "The Cambiata Concept—More Than Just About Changing Voices." *Choral Journal* 23, no. 4 (December 1982).

———. "The Changing Voice—The Future Challenge." *Choral Journal* 28, no. 3 (October 1987).

———. "The Changing Voice—The High School Challenge." *Choral Journal* 28, no. 3 (October 1987).

EDELSON, EDWARD. *The Secondary School Music Program from Classroom to Concert Hall.* West Nyack, N.Y.: Parker Publishing Co., 1972.

EILERS, JOYCE. *Dealing with "Uncertain Singer" Problems through Careful Selection of Music.* New Berlin, Wisc.: Jenson, 1979.

FOWELLS, ROBERT M. "The Changing Voice: A Vocal Chameleon." *Choral Journal* 24, no. 1 (September 1983).

GACKLE, LYNNE. "The Adolescent Female Voice; Characteristics of Change and Stages of Development." *Choral Journal* 31, no. 8 (March 1991).

GORDON, EDWIN. *Learning Sequence and Patterns in Music.* Chicago: G.I.A. Publications, 1977.

GROOM, MARY D. "A Descriptive Analysis of Development in Adolescent Male Voices During the Summer Time Period." Ph.D. diss., Florida State University, 1979.

HOFFER, CHARLES R. *Teaching Music in the Secondary Schools*, 4th ed. Belmont, Calif.: Wadsworth Publishing, 1991.

GORDON, EDWIN. *Learning Sequence and Patterns in Music.* Chicago: G.I.A. Publications, 1977.

Marple, Hugo D. *Backgrounds and Approaches to Junior High Music.* Dubuque, Iowa: Wm. C. Brown Co., 1975.

MILLER, KENNETH E. *Vocal Music Education, Teaching in the Secondary Schools.* Englewood Cliffs, N.J.: Prentice-Hall, Inc., 1988.

NEIDIG, KENNETH L., and JOHN JENNINGS, eds. *Choral Director's Guide.* West Nyack, N.Y.: Parker Publishing Co., 1967.

RAO, DOREEN. *Choral Music Experience* (Twelve Volumes on Children's Choral Singing). Farmingdale, N.Y.: Boosey and Hawkes, 1987.

ROE, PAUL F. *Choral Music Education*, 2d ed. Englewood Cliffs, N.J.: Prentice-Hall, Inc., 1983.

RUTKOWSKI, J. "The Junior High School Male Changing Voice: Testing and Grouping Voices for Successful Singing Experiences." *Choral Journal* 22, no. 4 (December 1981).

SINGLETON, IRA. *Music in Secondary Schools*, 2d ed. Boston: Allyn and Bacon, Inc., 1965.

VENNARD, WILLIAM. *Singing, the Mechanism and the Technic.* New York: Carl Fischer, 1968.

10

Proper Vocal Technique
for Adolescent Voices

Vocal technique is probably the most controversial subject discussed by singers. There are as many opinions about it as there are teachers and singers. The primary point here is that you should not feel good about your teaching ability if you work or plan to work with adolescent singers and ignore proper tone production. You should take the responsibility to assist your students to be the best singers possible under your tutelage.

One conclusion upon which most singers and teachers usually agree is that whatever method is used to achieve whatever sound desired, it should be one that is not harmful to the vocal instrument. It should be one that allows the singer to produce sound over an extended period of time without causing hoarseness or extreme vocal fatigue. If after several hours of rehearsal or performance the singers are hoarse, perhaps the technique they have been taught is not good. Master teachers will constantly evaluate the results of the technique they are using, and if those results are bad, they will consider improving it. The reason adolescents become hoarse after several hours of rehearsal is because they may have not been taught any vocal technique at all; they just produce the tone the best way they know. Most teachers will give tips on forming correct vowels and adding crisp consonants and there may be some tutoring pertaining to blend and phrasing, but whenever it comes to sharing with the students exactly how to produce a correct tone, too often very little is said. These statements are a poor reflection on the choral teaching profession but because of inadequate training, pressing performance deadlines, heavy curriculum demands, and other reasons, many teachers do not teach vocal technique. Since teaching singing is choral teachers' primary responsibility, they should never ignore the one component that will yield the most positive results.

A specific, proven technique of proper tone production for younger and older adolescents is described here. For those who have not been teaching vocal technique at all, it can easily be understood, and with teaching experience and willingness it may be used to produce an exciting, vital tone with singing ease. If you have been teaching vocal technique but find your singers experiencing hoarseness, vocal fatigue, or intonation problems, consider this approach. If you have a group who sings tunefully, freely, and without vocal exhaustion, do not change; keep improving your present approach. Teaching proper tone production that results in unharmful singing is the most important consideration.

The beauty of the approach described here is its structure. Beginning with correct posture as the foundation, each cumulative step builds to the ultimate goal of a beautiful, free-flowing tone emitted through energized speech.

POSTURE

To teach correct posture instructors should consider first the feet of the singers and then move upward to the head. Singers should stand with the feet placed where the bend of one foot is directly beside the arch of the other. Both feet are rectilinearly beneath the hips. Therefore, one foot will be slightly forward, and if both feet are under the hips they will not be extremely close to each other nor will they be spread excessively far apart. The distance they are apart will vary with each individual due to the width of the hips.

The weight of the body should be equally distributed on the balls of the feet. The knees should never be locked. Singers should be able to lift either heel off the floor alternately without changing the shoulder height. Standing with the knees locked over a period of time may cause dizziness or even fainting. Encourage the singers to check the condition of their knees regularly by alternately lifting their heels off the floor. Their knees should bend and the height of the shoulders should not be affected. The lower abdomen (that frontal area below the navel) is retracted (pulled in) and held firmly in this position. The feeling should be as if the wall of the abdomen were glued to the backbone. The abdomen should not be released while singing. The thorax (the part of the body between the neck and the abdomen in which the heart, lungs, esophagus, and so forth, are situated) should be elevated. The sensation should be as if the singers were being lifted off the floor from beneath their armpits. The chest is high and there is a slight upward stretching of the spine in the small of the back between the hips and the lower floating ribs. The sternum (the compound bone and cartilage connecting the ribs in front of the thorax) seems as if it were suspended from the ceiling, allowing the chest to be heightened without tension. The chest remains elevated and expanded

FIGURE 10.1   Singing with Proper Posture

during inhalation and exhalation. In raising the thorax, the singers should be careful that the lower back remains straight and is not brought to a "swayback" position. This results in an exaggerated lifting of the thorax and will affect the breathing process.

The shoulders are back, down, and relaxed. The arms and hands hang loosely to the sides of the body. The neck and all muscles controlling its movement are completely relaxed and absolutely free of tension. The head is upright in a position in which it can easily swivel. The forehead is tilted slightly forward, pulling the chin imperceptibly downward. The singers should be careful not to move the chin downward too much as it will affect the position of the larynx and the quality of the tone being produced.

BREATHING

After the singer has been taught proper posture, breathing is the next considera-tion in the cumulative process toward effective singing. In the interim from birth to adolescence, the natural process of inhaling and exhaling, even though it occurs several times a minute, becomes affected by bad habits. The newborn baby breathes deeply naturally; the average adolescent breathes shallowly naturally. How did the change transpire? Possibly the many hours a student slouches in the classroom armchair desk cramps the breath-band area to the point that short, shallow breaths are taken expediently. Students do not use the proper sitting posture that allows the breathing mechanism to function correctly. Most adolescents must be taught to breathe properly, as when they were newborns, before they can sing the required musical phrases with correct breath control. Breath is the energy of the voice, so it must be used carefully. In most cases singers should never exhale breath while singing except that to produce tone. Everyone should breathe according to their needs. Long phrases require more breath than short phrases. Every breath should be taken and released with purpose. The concept is not how much breathe, but rather what kind of breath should be taken.

When inhaling, breathe through the vowel that is about to be sung. Form the vowel with the lips and tongue before the breath is taken. Breathe through the mouth and nose simultaneously. To discover the proper inhaling procedure, close the mouth and inhale completely through the nose. The in-rushing air will dry the nasal cavity and a cooling sensation will be felt just inside the nostrils. Next, hold the nose and breathe entirely through the mouth. The in-rushing air will create a cooling sensation in the back of the throat. The *cool spot* will be felt in the throat behind and beneath the larynx. With some experimentation students can determine how to inhale through the mouth and nose at the same time. When this happens, they will feel the cool spot above the roof of the mouth just behind the upper gum ridge. It is important to feel that cool spot at the correct place because later, in dealing with resonance, they will be instructed to direct the tone to that cool spot mentally. Inhaling in this manner and feeling the cool spot in the right area is essential to developing proper resonance and flexibility throughout the full range of the voice.

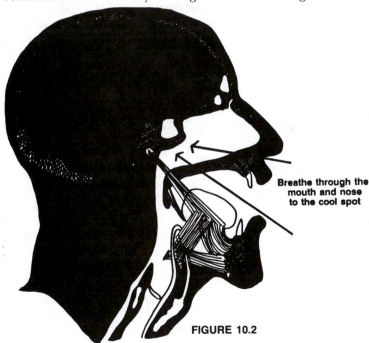

Breathe through the mouth and nose to the cool spot

FIGURE 10.2

The destination of the breath is to the *breath-band* (the area in the lower chest surrounded by the floating ribs). As the breath enters the breath-band area, it will expand all around and particularly in front. If proper posture has been maintained and the thorax has remained elevated, the breath will wind up naturally at the breath-band area.

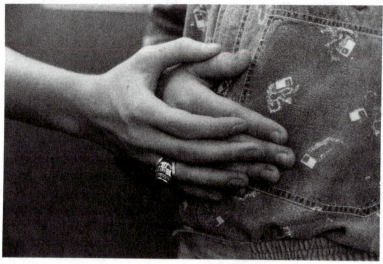

FIGURE 10.3

Release of the breath is the essence of correct vocal technique. The exhaling breath causes the vocal cords (or vocal folds, a more descriptive nomenclature) to vibrate and sound, and most importantly, it activates the *arytenoid cartilages* (a pair of ladle-shaped cartilages that provide the rear attachments for the vocal

Vocal folds at rest during inhalation

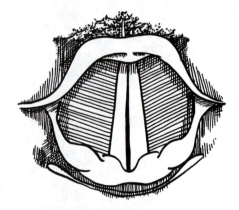

Vocal folds closed ready for exhalation and tone production

FIGURE 10.4

folds and control the opening and closing of the glottis) by reflex closing the *glottis* for tone production.

The glottis also can be closed with the swallowing muscles, which is incorrect. When the glottis is closed with the swallowing muscles the larynx shifts upward, the jaw locks, and the tongue becomes inflexible, making it impossible for the vocal mechanism to adjust properly for resonance and vowel formation. As the tone is produced, the act of *measured exhalation* (often called *support*) occurs when the muscles that control inhalation are applied against the muscles that control exhalation, with the latter exerting a slightly overmatching force. This state of tension (measured exhalation) activates the arytenoid cartilages, creating proper tone production.

The best way to experience measured exhalation (support) is to bark like a dog and then sustain the tone as when a dog howls. A more civilized manner, but one that is not so foolproof, is to blow tiny puffs of air through puckered lips. Note that the upper abdominal muscles controlling the puffing (or barking) move inward and upward. Another set of abdominal muscles that push downward and outward are used to move the bowels or to have a baby. These muscles are not used in measured exhalation. To safeguard against their usage, the singers should be reminded to keep the lower abdomen retracted as if it were glued to the backbone. Using measured exhalation allows the breath to be released gradually and uniformly with just enough breath to allow the vocal folds to sound. Singers should attempt to get the most sound from the least amount of breath. The upper abdomen is brought slowly, gently, and steadily inward and upward under the influence of measured exhalation while the lower abdomen is held firmly against the backbone. After the adolescents have experienced measured exhalation by barking or puffing, the next step is to experience it in a extended and controlled manner. First, they must inhale deeply. To begin the exhalation process with proper support, instruct them to start the breath flow with a gentle tug of the upper abdomen inward and

FIGURE 10.5

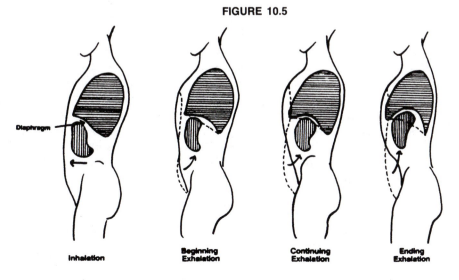

| Inhalation | Beginning Exhalation | Continuing Exhalation | Ending Exhalation |

upward, place a index finger in front of puckered lips, and blow against it as long as possible. They should repeat this process several times, each time attempting to extend the interval of time they blow against a finger. Using a watch with a second hand, they may be encouraged to extend the blowing time by calculating the length of exhalation with each repeat.

SINGING—RESONANCE

Singing is elevated, sustained, and energized speech. The students should speak the words energetically and then sustain the speech energy as they sing. The actual sound produced by the vocal folds is barely audible. The resonating chambers, which include the pharynx, the nasal cavity, and the mouth, amplify the tone before it leaves the vocal mechanism. The proper mixture of resonance from each of these areas is controlled mostly by the tongue. The lips are also used, particularly with some of the darker vowels. The object of proper resonance is to achieve a maximum sound with minimum effort. The throat remains open and tall inside. The jaw must always have a feeling of hanging loose with the singers allowing it to drop from the hinge just in front of the ears. However, it is not pressed or forced downward; it hangs freely. The tongue rides forward over the *hyoid bone* (a supportive cartilage located under and within the lower jaw). The tongue should never be pushed down at the back and the tip of it should rest touching the back part of the bottom front teeth. The position of the tongue when the students speak the vowel *ah* with the mouth wide open is correct. When the students have an opportunity to observe singers who display outstanding vocal production, they should notice that the tongue is always in the position described above.

Psychologically, the students should perceive the tone beginning in the middle of the body with a gentle tug to start the breath flow and finding its destination at the cool spot above the roof of the mouth just behind the upper gum ridge. They must have an open feeling all the way from the middle of the body to the nasal cavity. All vowels ring above and behind the hard palate at the cool spot. As the pitch becomes higher, nasal or head resonance becomes stronger. Lower pitches require more resonance in the pharynx area (chest resonance). The pitches in the middle area of the voice have a mixture of both. As previously stated, the tongue controls the type resonance a tone requires. Students control the tongue by mentally placing, directing, or thinking the tone to the desired destination. The higher the pitch, the farther forward toward the eyebrows the singer should place the tone. However, basic placement always begins by directing the tone toward the cool spot.

Energized speech is an important aspect of the singing process. Speech becomes energized by the use of exaggerated consonants and vowels produced through vibrant tones. It involves pronunciation, enunciation, and articulation, but most of all it includes a sense of vitality in the way the tone is emitted. Proper tone production is essential to a vibrant sound, but psychologically

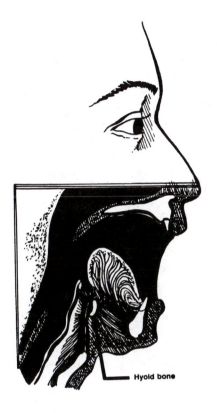

**Position of the tongue
for proper vowel formation**

singers also must have that sense of energy in their voices to be effective performers.

In summary, to sing well the adolescents have four basic responsibilities. They should stand correctly, breathe correctly, direct the tone to the proper resonance chamber, and utilize energized speech.

NONVOCAL AND SINGLE-TONE EXERCISES

Although this program of vocal technique works well in a studio environment, it is presented here to be used in a group situation such as a general music classroom or choral organization. As the students work together, they learn from each other. Viewing each other's breathing procedure and hearing the other singers experiment as they search for proper placement and freedom as they sing is part of that learning experience.

A unique aspect of this vocal technique program is the warm-up procedure that should be used at the beginning of each rehearsal or class period. It is unique in that each time the singers warm up, they review the entire cumulative method, and all the basic components of the technique are reinforced.

Initially, all aspects of the vocal technique should be explained in detail to the singers, including the reasons why each requirement is made. Adolescents have little difficulty accepting rigid requirements in singing, and they will give total cooperation if they feel the discipline will reap positive results. Their understanding of exactly why they are being required to participate in such rigid discipline is vital if their cooperation is expected. Asking them to become involved in what they might consider to be unorthodox procedures breeds rebellion if the only reason given is "just because it is good for them" or "because the teacher said so." They must be led through understanding to comply, not "made" to do so. Further, their understanding about the components of the technique and reasons for being involved allows the director to take advantage of the mental and physical abilities of each singer in reaching the desired goal and does not rely on the teacher's capabilities alone. The group and the director working together yield results much faster than when the director attempts the task alone.

In the beginning stages of teaching the technique, there will not be enough rehearsal time each period to use all the exercises. They should be introduced and sung in consecutive order. Instructors should present and sing as many of the exercises during the warm-up period as times allows. They should attempt to add one or two new ones each day until all of the exercises are used each warm-up period. After directors have taught all these exercises, they may choose others that will strengthen specific weaknesses of their group of singers.

Exercise 1—Correct Posture

It is best for the students to use a checklist of their body parts beginning with the feet and moving upward to the head so that they will not risk omitting an important posture requirement. The checklist may be delineated as follows. Feet: Is the arch of one foot directly beside the bend of the other? Are both feet directly under the hips? Is the weight of the body on the balls of the feet? Knees: Are they locked in? The teacher should ask the singers to check their knees to assure that they are not locked in by asking them to lift their heels off the floor without raising the shoulders. Lower abdomen: Is it tucked in against the backbone? Thorax: Is it elevated? To assist the students in obtaining an elevated thorax, the teacher might tell them to pretend that they have a string attached to the sternum and by pulling the string upward, they are attempting to lift themselves off the floor. Shoulders: Are they back, down, and relaxed? Arms and hands: Are they hanging loosely to the sides of the body? Neck: Is it completely free of tension? The teacher should ask the students to roll their heads around several times to develop a sensation of complete freedom in the neck and shoulder area.[1] Forehead: Is it tilted slightly forward? The students should have a sense of looking at the audience directly over their cheekbones, not down their nose (chin too high) nor under their eyebrows (chin too low).

---

[1] Some educators have indicated to me that rolling the head around is unsafe and therefore not recommended by physicians. In my years of teaching, none of my students have ever complained about any malady as a result.

Exercise 2—Deep Breathing

Ask the singers to place the left hand on the upper abdomen (the lower edge of the hand should touch the navel) and the right hand on the chest. If the thorax is high when they inhale, the left hand should move outward and the right hand should remain stationary. If the right hand moves outward and the left hand moves inward (this happens with many individuals), the breathing process is reversed and incorrect. Individual attention and instruction must be given to these students. Each singer should be breathing correctly before a unified sound will be forthcoming from the group as a whole. Those breathing incorrectly will not be able to sing long phrases nor will they have correct tone production, and the overall unified effect will be destroyed. After an extended period in which the singers have been taking multiple deep breaths, they might get too much oxygen in the blood. Some of them, particularly those who are thin, may have a tendency to feel dizzy. If this happens, ask them to sit down for a moment or two.

Exercise 3—Legato Exhalation

Keeping the left hand on the upper abdomen so that the singers will be aware of the breathing process, ask them to blow a gentle, continuous stream of breath against the index finger of the right hand placed about quarter of an inch from the puckered lips. The blowing process (exhalation) should begin with a slight tug of the upper abdomen inward and upward. This automatically tightens the proper muscles to assure measured exhalation. The purpose of this exercise is to see how long the singers can blow against the finger without stopping. They should blow a continuous stream of air but it should be as little breath as possible, making the blowing time to be as long as possible. Psychologically, to assist the process the instructor might tell the students to hold their breaths as they blow, even though this is physically impossible. The idea of holding their breath as they blow supports their efforts to maintain measured exhalation. The director may call out the passing seconds in five-second intervals so that the singers will know exactly how long they are able to blow. Then the director should repeat the process and challenge the singers to extend the blowing time at least ten seconds.

Exercise 4—Pulsated Exhalation

To practice using the breathing muscles that lift the breath to the vocal folds, the students should use a series of quick expulsions of breath, as if they were trying to blow out a candle. The teacher should tell the students to pretend that each finger and the thumb of the hand is a candle. Instruct them to puff out all the candles substituted by the fingers but leave the one substituted by the thumb burning. Each time they puff out a candle, they should inhale quickly (using the deep-breathing technique described in Exercise 2), then gently tug the upper abdomen inward and upward as they puff. They should repeat the inhaling and exhaling process as they blow out each candle. When they reach the thumb, the students should be instructed to inhale, then blow a continuous stream of air against the thumb as if they were only causing the flame of the imaginary candle to flicker (the same process described in Exercise 3). That final, legato blowing effort, as well as each of the four puffing efforts, should be initiated with a gentle tug inward and upward.

After practicing this several times, the students should be ready to perform it under the control of a beat. As the students perform the routine, the next step is for the instructor to count: one—puff, two—puff, three—puff, four— puff, five—blow (or instructors may use the word *hold* instead of *blow* if they desire). The students soon learn to inhale each time the number is spoken, then puff in rhythm each time the instructor speaks the word *puff*.

Exercises 5 and 6—The Pulsated and Elongated *ah*

In these exercises the teacher asks the students to replace the pulsated breath (four puffs and a blow) described in Exercise 4 with the spoken word, *ah*. The instructor may also use the counting routine with this exercise: one—speak, two—speak, three—speak, four—speak, five—hold *ah*. The students should be instructed to allow the jaw to hang freely, never forced down but certainly not closed. They should be able to place, simultaneously, the stacked index and middle fingers into the mouth between the upper and lower front teeth as they speak the word *ah*. When speaking the word *ah*, the students should be instructed to allow the tongue to lie in the bottom of the mouth with the tip of it touching the back side of the bottom front teeth. The tip nor the back of the tongue should be raised.

Exercise 7—The Elevated Sigh

To coordinate the breath throughout the overall vocal range, an elevated, vocalized *sigh* should be used. The sigh is the sound produced by individuals when they feel relieved that a task has been completed or a problem has been solved. Using the technique described in Exercises 4 and 5 to produce the pulsated breath and pulsated *ah*, ask the students to vocalize a sigh beginning in the upper area of the voice (male falsetto and female head voice), and move gradually downward to the lower extremities of the voice. The vowel to be used is *ah*. Instruct the singers to keep the placement forward and high, always directing the sound to the cool spot. The jaw continues to hang loosely. The teacher should point out to the singers how the breath is coordinated with the production of the tone. If they have conquered the previous breathing exercises, it should not be difficult for them to understand the connection between the two. The term *sigh* is used henceforth to mean three things: (1) coordinating the breath with tone production, (2) continuing the breath flow and tone production to the end of a musical phrase, and (3) allowing the students to sense a free, relaxed tone throughout the full compass of the voice.

To extend this exercise and to allow the students an opportunity to develop better breath control, the instructor may have the students begin the sigh in the lower part of the voice, sigh gradually upward as high as they are able, and then gradually back down again.

The six previous exercises should establish and reinforce thought patterns and patterns of coordination that are essential to proper vocal technique. The next four exercises (*hum, hum-ah, ah-eh-ee,* and *ah-oh-oo*) require definite pitches. When working with changing voice groups, the trebles (male and female) and cambiatas will be comfortable on D (directly above middle C). The baritones should sing A (below middle C). When using the exercises with older adolescents without changing voices, ask the boys to sing the A (below middle C) and the girls to sing the D (above middle C). When singing together, the open fourth should tune easily.

Exercise 8—The *hum*

The instructor should ask the students to prepare to sing the vowel *ah*. They should be asked to inhale through the mouth and nose simultaneously, feeling the cool spot above the roof of the mouth directly above and behind the upper gum ridge. Again, the jaw should be hanging loosely and the tongue should be lying in the bottom of the mouth with the tip of it touching the back part of the bottom front teeth. After they have inhaled according to the stipulations indicated previously, they should be instructed to close the lips so that they are barely touching. The jaw should close imperceptibly, if at all. Even though the lips are touching, it should continue to hang freely. The students should begin the hum, utilizing the slight tug inward and upward to start the breath flow and measured exhalation in order to maintain a consistent flow of breath under pressure as they sing. Remaining ever cognizant of control of the breath, they should be asked to hum until they have used all the breath. The director may call out the passing seconds in the same fashion as when the singers were blowing when practicing the legato breathing. Instruct the singers to direct the tone to the cool spot. The tongue should not touch the soft palate or the roof of the mouth, and the teeth should be parted. Each singer should work for as much vibrancy in the tone (often called "buzz") as possible. Psychologically, the students should think the tone is ringing or buzzing at the cool spot. In the early stages the group may sound very anemic, but as they are challenged to increase the vitality of the buzzing effect, the room will become alive as if it were filled with buzzing bees.

Exercise 9—The *hum-ah*

After the students have establishing a resonant hum, ask them to part the lips and sing the vowel *ah* on the same pitches used when humming. The object is to retain the buzz sensation at the cool spot as the *ah* is being produced. It is important that singers continue to allow the jaw to hang freely as they change from the *hum* to the *ah*. Some might have a tendency to push the jaw downward or possibly even to close it slightly. If the jaw is lowered, the focus of the tone has a tendency to move away from the cool spot and move back into the throat resulting in a very hollow, open sound which is incorrect.

Exercise 10—The Sustained *ah-eh-ee*

Using the singing and resonating techniques described previously, the teacher should ask the students to sing a sustained *ah* vowel, change to the *eh* vowel, and finally change it to the *ee* vowel all on the same, uninterrupted tone (pitches D and A). The vowels are produced in the pharynx and the mouth and they are changed simply by moving the middle and sides of the tongue upward and forward ever so slightly. The tip of the tongue should remain touching the back part of the bottom front teeth. The jaw should continue to hang loosely. The tendency to close the jaw on the *ee* vowel will need to be overcome. The jaw should move imperceptibly, if at all. The students should allow the tongue and the mind to create the vowel changes. The instructor should remind the students to incorporate the sigh into their singing (see the information in Exercise 7).

Exercise 11—The Sustained *ah-oh-oo*

Using the breathing and resonating techniques described previously, the teacher should ask the students to sing a sustained *ah* vowel, change to the *oh* vowel, and finally change to the *oo* vowel, all on the same, uninterrupted tone. Again the vowels are produced in the pharynx and the mouth, but they are changed by moving the lips gradually toward the puckered position. The jaw should continue to hang loosely as the vowels are changed. The tendency to close the jaw on the *oo* vowel will need to be overcome. As in Exercise 10, the jaw should move imperceptibly, it at all. There will be almost the same amount of space inside the mouth on the *oo* vowel as there was on the *ah* vowel. The lips and the mind should be allowed to create the vowel change. The students should be reminded to incorporate the sigh into their singing.

MULTIPLE-TONE EXERCISES

The following exercises all utilize different pitches. When they are used with groups containing changing voices, due to male and female students' inability to sing well in unison or in unison-octaves, each voice part should be given special consideration. The exercises are quoted here with an explanation that describes how they should be used with different voices. When the exercises are used with older adolescents where there are no changing voices, teachers may not need to be so careful with unison or unison-octave singing because changed voices have little difficulty in that area. Under those circumstances the teachers may disregard the special instructions directed specifically to those working with changing voices.

Exercise 12—The Sung *hum-ah*

The purpose of this exercise is to challenge the singers to maintain the buzz sensation and maximum oral (mouth) resonance as the pitch changes one-half step up and back down. Using the technique described in the single-tone *hum-ah* exercise (Exercise 9), the teacher should instruct the trebles (male and female) and cambiatas to begin on D (above middle C) and the baritones to begin one octave below. As indicated in the quotation below, the singers should move upward in one-half step intervals until the beginning pitch is F, a third above, and then return in one-half step intervals to the D. The teacher should encourage the students to incorporate the sigh into the singing process.

Hum - ah _____　　Hum - ah _____　　Hum - ah _____　*etc.*

Exercises 13 and 14—Singing *ah-eh* and *ah-oh*

The *ah* vowel should be produced in the same way as it was in the sustained *ah-eh-ee* and *ah-oh-oo* exercises (Exercises 10 and 11). In these exercises the singers will need to produce the correct *ah* vowel, and as they move up one step, change to the *eh* (or *oh*, as the case may be) and back to the *ah* as they move back down one step. When changing to the *eh*, only the tongue is moved (see Exercise 10). Move only the lips when changing to the *oh* (see Exercise 11). Trebles and cambiatas should begin on D (above middle C) as indicated below. The baritones should begin one octave lower. The exercises should move upward in one-half step intervals. When the beginning note is F-sharp (above middle C), ask the cambiatas to drop down one octave (F-sharp below middle C) and join the baritones. Continue upward until the beginning note in both octaves is D, then reverse the direction and move downward until the singers have returned to the original beginning pitch. The cambiatas should be reminded to jump up one octave when the beginning note reaches F-sharp as they move downward. The singers should always employ the sigh in their singing process.

1. ah - oh - ah - oh - ah　　ah - oh - ah - oh - ah　　ah - oh - ah - oh - ah
2. ah - eh - ah - eh - ah　　ah - eh - ah - eh - ah　　ah - eh - ah - eh - ah　*etc.*

Exercises 15 and 16—Singing *ah-eh-ee* and *ah-oh-oo*

Correct pronunciation and production of the vowels were explained in Exercises 10 and 11. These exercises extend the one sustained tone to a three-tone articulation. The teacher should remind the students to keep plenty of space between the teeth when phonation of the *ee* vowel is begun. It is not a French *ee*, which is very closed. Beginning pitches and voice differentiation are the same as in Exercises 13 and 14.

1. ah ____ eh ____ ee　　ah ____ eh ____ ee　　ah ____ eh ____ ee
2. ah ____ oh ____ oo　　ah ____ oh ____ oo　　ah ____ oh ____ oo　*etc.*

Exercise 17—The Staccato Arpeggio

The tempo of this exercise should remain very slow with inexperienced singers and when it is used at the beginning of technique study. The singers should be reminded to produce each tone with a slight tug inward and upward from the upper abdomen. After usage of the tug becomes coordinated physically, the tempo may be increased, but not until each individual tone is properly produced with a slight tug. The range and tessitura limitations of the voice should be kept in mind as the exercise moves up the scale and back down. It is best to vocalize the sopranos and baritones (in octaves) together, extending throughout the full compass of their ranges. The cambiatas should be vocalized together as a section but separately from the sopranos and baritones, and the instructor may vocalize them throughout the full compass of their range. At the beginning when the tempo is slow, the director should ask the singers to breathe between the production of each tone for the purpose of practicing coordination as the tug is incorporated. After the tempo accelerates, it becomes difficult to breathe between each note; therefore, the singers should be instructed to sing the arpeggio up and down on one breath.

Exercise 18—The Staccato Octave

The purpose of this exercise is to develop good physical coordination with the inhaling process and the slight tug inward and upward. The process is as follows: (1) inhale correctly, (2) begin the first pitch with a slight tug inward and upward simultaneously with the breath, (3) sigh to the upper octave and tug again slightly on the upper octave as it is released to obtain the staccato effect, (4) inhale again correctly, (5) sigh to the lower octave and tug once again with a slight tug as the tone is released, then (6) inhale and sigh as the whole note is produced for the full four beats. This is a rather difficult exercise for adolescents. The tempo must be very slow in the beginning. As they work, the physical coordination will eventualize.

Again the beginning pitch is D (above middle C) for the trebles (male and female) and one octave lower for the baritones. The cambiatas do not sing. When using this exercise with changed-voice groups, all girls begin on D and the boys begin one octave lower. All boys (except cambiatas) and girls move upward in one-half step intervals. When F becomes the octave pitch, the teacher should ask the baritones to stop singing and ask the cambiatas to begin singing (the octave pitch is F below to F above middle C). The cambiatas and trebles continue to move upward until the octave pitch is A. It is better not to return downward. The exercise may be repeated with a different vowel, if desired, but it is best to use open vowels only. When using this exercise, the teacher should remind the students that (1) the jaw should hang loosely; (2) the tip of the tongue should touch the back part of the bottom front teeth; (3) each time the octave is initiated upward or downward, the staccato should be produced with a slight tug inward at the breath-band area; and (4) incorporate the sigh as the longer notes are held.

Exercise 19—*moh-meh-mee*

In this exercise the singers must assure that the jaw hangs loosely; it should move as little as possible. The *m* is initiated by the lips. The jaw and tongue should not interfere. The instructor should keep the range and tessitura limitations of early adolescent singers in mind as the singers move up and down the scale. They should be dealt with in the same fashion as in Exercises 13 and 14.

Exercise 20—The Five-Tone Legato Scale

This exercise may be used with any open vowel. The teacher should vocalize the sopranos and baritones as a group together and the cambiatas as a group together. This is a wonderful exercise to develop a legato line and to open and build strength in the upper voice, particularly the head voice of the trebles. It is also a good exercise to help beginning singers (girls and unchanged boys) to discover and learn to sing in the head voice.

Exercise 21—The Controlled Sigh

The purpose of this exercise is to improve breath control and develop the use of the sigh. When the exercise is used for the first few times, it is important to set a moderate tempo. As the breath control develops over the weeks, the teacher may gradually lengthen the duration of each pitch until maximum control is mastered. The upper area of the voice is where all aspects of control and total concentration are required. The teacher must remind the students to drop the jaw completely. The sopranos and baritones may be vocalized as a group together, but the cambiatas should be vocalized as a group alone.

Applying the Vocal Technique to Choral Literature

If directors are going to be successful when using this technique, they should keep these stipulations in mind: (1) Use the exercises in consecutive order in each warm-up and (2) after the singers have learned the exercises, try to use as many as possible each rehearsal. The technique develops over a period of months, and the exercises, through consistency and concentration as the singers work, are the secret to the overall vocal development of each adolescent.

Obviously, for the singers to develop the technique, the basic tenets and approaches incorporated in the exercises should be applied to the choral literature that they will be singing in rehearsal daily. After directors have chosen a selection to be taught to the choir, if the students have not yet developed their sight-reading skills, one of the rote methods delineated in Chapter 13 should be chosen to teach the notes; or, even better, directors should teach the sight-reading method described in Chapter 11. Once the students can sing all of the notes to their specific parts, employ the following step by step procedure in applying the vocal technique to the choral literature. If the music is homophonic, the procedure may be applied to all parts at once. If it is polyphonic, directors will probably have to deal with each voice part, one at a time.

1. Directors should determine the exact phrases and mark them on their scores because they must apply the technique one phrase at a time. Later, after the students have been trained to allow the body to respond properly to each phrase, directors will be able to teach complete sections (and perhaps the entire piece) at one time.

2. Using correct posture, ask the students to hum the first phrase of the piece. Remind them:

    A. To inhale properly (as in Exercise 2) before beginning to sing,

    B. To begin the phrase with a *sigh* (see the three components of a *sigh* as described in Exercise 7) and continue it to the end of the phrase (remember to start the phrase with a gentle inward and upward tug of the upper abdomen with the lower abdomen glued against the backbone),

    C. To maintain as much vibrancy in the *hum* as possible (see Exercise 8).

3. Now, sing the phrase on the open vowel *ah* (directors may use *oh* or *oo* for pieces that require a less brilliant tone). Remind the students:

    A. To begin the phrase with a brief *hum*, then part the lips into the *ah*, maintaining the *sigh* to the end of the phrase,

    B. To refrain from moving the jaw or the tongue when changing from the *hum* to the *ah* so that the tone will continue to resonate at the cool spot (see Exercise 9),

    C. To apply stipulations A and B in explanation 2 above (humming) to the singing of the phrase with the *ah*,

    D. To remember to keep the tone as vibrant as possible (ringing at the cool spot) as the phrase is sung.

4. Read the text of the phrase to the students. Explain exactly what vowel sound is needed for each word (see "Diction" in Chapter 12).

5. Sing the phrase slowly using only the vowel sounds and the correct rhythm. Eliminate all the consonants. Directors should demonstrate the process to the students. To do so will be difficult at first, but the students will soon learn to initiate the phrases in this fashion. Remind the students:

    A. To apply stipulations C and D in explanation 3 above to the phrase,

    B. To move from one vowel to the next without moving the jaw and tongue (see Exercise 13 through 16 in this chapter and Exercises 1, 2, and 4 in Chapter 12),

    C. To remember to keep the tone as vibrant as possible as the phrase is sung,

    D. If diphthongs are present, to be aware of the two vowel sounds and initiate them properly (see Exercise 3 in Chapter 12).

6. Finally, sing the phrase with the words (both consonants and vowels). Teach

the students to throw the consonants in between the vowels in a quite, crisp fashion. Remind them:

A. Always to sing on the vowel keeping the jaw hanging; move the lips and tongue only when necessary to produce the consonant and always return to the correct formation for the vowel. Never allow the jaw to close. Always keep plenty of space inside the mouth.

B. To keep tone vibrancy, breathing, and sighing in mind as they sing.

7. Go through the above process for each remaining phrase in the song. The first time the process is effectuated, directors will need to use several rehearsals to get through it. After the students learn the process, the application will be much faster.

CONCLUSION

The vocal technique described in this chapter has a unique structure and tradition that makes it unusually applicable to adolescents, young and old. Several years ago, Ferdinand Grossman of Vienna, who was famous throughout Europe for his work with voices, was hired to train both choirmasters and choirboys of the Vienna Boys Choir. Grossman served as chorusmaster for the Vienna State Opera, and while working with the Vienna Boys Choir, he was also filling the post of Kapellmeister of the Imperial Chapel, the most revered post of Vienna's hierarchy of musical positions. One of Grossman's disciples was Romano Picutti. Picutti became director of the Men and Boys Choir of the Colegio de las Rosas (School of the Roses) in Morello, Mexico. Picutti went to the Colegio de las Rosas with the commission to organize a men's and boys' choir. After a rather arduous struggle to find proper personnel, he began to train the boys (mostly native Indian boys from the city) using the technique he learned from Grossman. After the men's and boys' first performance it was evident that the Colegio de las Rosas had one of the best choirs in all Mexico. Their reputation spread to Denton, Texas, where George Bragg was serving as founder/director of what was soon to become the Texas Boys Choir. During the early 1950s Bragg made several journeys to Morello with a few of his boychoir members to observe, to study, and be trained by Picutti. Bragg and the boys brought the technique back to the Texas group. The reputation of the Texas Boys Choir in America and abroad is remarkable. Their recordings on the Columbia label and bookings with the Community Concert circuit by Columbia Artists certainly place them among the ranks of the best of this generation.[2]

---

[2] It was my privilege to organize the Cambiata Singers of the Arkansas Boys Choir and serve as their founder/director for several years. During their first year, the Board of Trustees invited George Bragg to serve as a part-time consultant to the organization. Luckily, Bragg was able to come as a full-time consultant during the second and third years of operation. The three years I worked with Bragg proved to be extremely educational. Bragg not only taught me the intricate procedures of boychoir organization, but he reinforced and extended my ideas pertaining to vocal technique with adolescents. I had been teaching voice on the university level for several years, and there was very little about the technique with which I disagreed. Most of all, through Bragg's tutelage, I was able to organize and structure the information he gave me in a way that was most appropriate for adolescents. One of the purposes of the Cambiata Singers was to serve as an example of the cambiata concept in action. Under Bragg's tutelage, with the boys serving as living examples for training purposes,

The success of the Vienna Boys Choir, the Colegio de las Rosas Men and Boys Choir, and the Texas Boys Choir is an example of what can be done when this technique is taught in a consistent, concentrated manner. Most students who have been taught the technique over the years were no different than the most eager, full-of-life adolescents in classrooms throughout America. The leaders simply took time to harness that energy and turn it into productive and meaningful singing experiences.

THOUGHTS FOR CONTEMPLATION AND DISCUSSION

1. Think about your favorite vocal and choral instructors (without naming them). Which aspects of their vocal technique were beneficial and which were not?
2. Why do you think adolescents usually employ shallow, chest breathing?
3. How can individual choir members know they are producing the type tone the director desires?
4. Are physical exercises appropriate during warm-up? If so, describe some and tell how they are beneficial. If not, why?
5. Relative to vocal technique, compare the thought processes of a student who thinks like a musician with one who does not.
6. Do you feel that it is proper to teach middle/junior high school students to sound more like adults? Why or why not?

BIBLIOGRAPHY

BARTLE, JEAN ASHWORTH. *Lifeline for Children's Choir Directors*. Toronto: Gordon V. Thompson, 1988. (Available through Oxford Press.)

BESSOM, MALCOLM E., ALPHONSE M. TATARUNIS, and SAMUEL L. FORCUCCI. *Teaching Music in Today's Secondary Schools*, 2d ed. New York: Holt, Rinehart and Winston, 1980.

CHRISTY, VAN A. *Foundations in Singing*, 4th ed. Dubuque, Iowa: W. C. Brown Co., 1979.

COLLINS, DON L. *The Cambiata Concept, a Comprehensive Philosophy and Methodology of Teaching Music to Adolescents*. Conway, Ark.: Cambiata Press, 1981.

COOPER, IRVIN, and KARL O. KURSTEINER. *Teaching Junior High School Music*, 2d ed. Conway, Ark.: Cambiata Press, 1973.

EDELSON, EDWARD. *The Secondary School Music Program from Classroom to Concert Hall*. West Nyack, N.Y.: Parker Publishing Co., 1972.

EILERS, JOYCE. *Dealing with "Uncertain Singer" Problems through Careful Selection of Music*. New Berlin, Wisc.: Jenson, 1979.

HEFFERNAN, CHARLES W. *Choral Music, Technique and Artistry*. Englewood Cliffs, N.J.: Prentice-Hall, Inc., 1982.

HOFFER, CHARLES R. *Teaching Music in the*

I began using and teaching this unique technique that had passed from Grossman to Picutti to Bragg and now to me, with each man adding his own personality and interpretation as it evolved. The combination of attributes of the cambiata concept (the boys sang four-part music, two male treble parts, cambiata, and baritone) and the vocal technique resulted in a first-class singing organization in a very short period. The boys progressed so quickly that three short years after their beginning, they received national recognition by singing for the Music Educators National Conference annual meeting and the regional meeting of the American Choral Directors.

Secondary Schools, 4th ed. Belmont, Calif.: Wadsworth Publishing, 1991.

JIPSON, WAYNE R. *The High School Vocal Music Program*. West Nyack, N.Y.: Parker Publishing Co., 1972.

LAMB, GORDON H. *Choral Techniques*, 3d ed. Dubuque, Iowa: Wm. C. Brown Co., 1988.

MARPLE, HUGO D. *Backgrounds and Approaches to Junior High Music*. Dubuque, Iowa: Wm. C. Brown Co., 1975.

MILLER, KENNETH E. *Vocal Music Education, Teaching in the Secondary Schools*. Englewood Cliffs, N.J.: Prentice-Hall, Inc., 1988.

MOE, DANIEL. *Basic Choral Concepts*. Minneapolis: Augsburg Publishing House, 1972.

NEIDIG, KENNETH L., and JOHN JENNINGS, eds. *Choral Director's Guide*. West Nyack, N.Y.: Parker Publishing Co., 1967.

RAO, DOREEN. *Choral Music Experience* (Twelve Volumes on Children's Choral Singing). Farmingdale, N.Y.: Boosey and Hawkes, 1987.

ROBINSON, RAY, and ALLEN WINOLD. *The Choral Experience*. New York: Harper's College Press, 1976.

ROE, PAUL F. *Choral Music Education*, 2d ed. Englewood Cliffs, N.J.: Prentice-Hall, Inc., 1983.

SCHMIDT, JAN. *Basics of Singing*. New York: Schirmer-Macmillan, 1984.

SINGLETON, IRA. *Music in Secondary Schools*, 2d ed. Boston: Allyn and Bacon, Inc., 1965.

STANTON, ROYAL. *Steps to Singing*, 2d ed. Belmont, Calif.: Wadsworth Publishing, 1976.

TRUSLER, IVAN, and WALTER EHRET. *Functional Lessons in Singing*, 2d ed. Englewood Cliffs, N.J.: Prentice-Hall, Inc., 1986.

VENNARD, WILLIAM. *Singing, the Mechanism and the Technic*. New York: Carl Fischer, 1968.

11

Teaching Music Literacy: An Imperative

When I was in high school choir, I remember explicitly the instructions the choral director gave the group about how to read music. She said, "Watch the notes and when they go up, make the voice go up and when they go down, make the voice go down, and listen closely to the piano." Then she proceeded to "beat out the part" on the piano and each section sang, one at a time, until we knew how our part sounded and could sing it. After being exposed to this process for several years, if we, as singers, had any capacity for music-making whatsoever, we learned how to "read music" after a fashion. Actually, what we did was begin (1) to sense relationships between the tones in the diatonic scale, (2) to understand key relationships, (3) to understand how the highness and lowness of the tones felt in the voice, and (4) to sense how the tones fit in the various chords. We really did not know how to read music, but we were able to sing the correct notes most of the time through this "hit-or-miss" approach. Not until I had two university degrees did I really feel comfortable about my ability to read music. Eventually, I was taught a specific method (tonic sol-fa) and I soon learned that I did not have to rely so heavily on my innate ability to hit-or-miss the notes as I sang, because when I saw a note on a page, I heard a sound in my head and could sing it exactly.

One of the pitfalls for young singers is that singing is so natural that they can enjoy music making without being able to read the notes. Instrumentalists do not have that luxury because they cannot play an instrument without learning to read music (unless as a child they learned to an instrument "by ear," that is, in an improvisatory fashion as in jazz or country music). It is difficult to motivate instrumentalists who play by ear and singers who harmonize by ear because the desire to make music has already been fulfilled. They soon learn, however, that unless someone is present to sing or play the music first, they are unable to produce it. This is the advantage of the music-reading process. Printed symbols become aural sounds, what a wonderful happening.

The diversity of teaching music reading in American education is both a blessing and curse. Educators have the right, to a degree, to choose the approach they desire to use in teaching their classes. That is the blessing. On the other hand, singers who are exposed to several different teachers and approaches may become very confused and finish their tenure in secondary school unable to read. That is the curse.

Beginning teachers have many choices in the way they teach music reading. They may (1) approach it pentatonically or diatonically; (2) use numbers, letters, solfège, or intervals; (3) use a movable or fixed *do* system; (4) use hand signs or number signs; (5) use rhythm syllables, rhythm words, or a counting method; or (6) choose those aspects from many different methods that appeal to them specifically (the grab bag approach). They probably will begin by teaching it the way they were taught until they become experienced enough to find a way that produces the best results for them. Tragically, many young teachers do not choose to teach music reading at all because they feel inadequate in any one specific approach and they do not trust their ability to learn a method well.

Singers in secondary school must be taught to read music. It is an imperative. The ability to be self-sustaining music makers is their right as students in American public education. Teachers of singers must prepare themselves to provide their students that right.

There are two cardinal rules of skill building that teachers must follow. (1) For students to learn to sight-read they must be taught using a structured method that moves from the known to the unknown in a cumulative, sequential fashion. Any other approach will be haphazard and unproductive. (2) They must have time to learn to read through a series of exposures to and respites from the skill-building process. In other words, they must practice the material, then put it away, practice it, then put it away enough times so that the body learns to react responsively. To become completely proficient usually takes several years of exposure.

THE ADOLESCENT READING SINGER[1]

The writing and compiling of *The Adolescent Reading Singer* evolved from the need of music educators for a method in which the unique vocal limitations of

---

[1] Used by permission of Cambiata Press, P.O. Box 1151, Conway, AR 72032.

adolescent voices are considered. Several good sight-reading methods are available today, but many of them are directed to children in elementary school with unchanged voices or specifically for high school where most of the voices have changed. *The Adolescent Reading Singer* was written and compiled specifically to be used in secondary school. It may be used in middle/junior high or senior high school. One component, designed to facilitate effective use with early adolescents, is the consideration for their changing voices. Directors will find it more effective when used with the Beginning Choir (see Chapter 15). If students reach the Advanced Choir and yet have not been taught how to read, their chances of learning before graduation are slim, because musical literacy is developed over several years, more years than they will spend in Advanced Choir alone.

The Adolescent Reading Singer is based on the Kodály method of music education using the pentatonic scale (at the beginning), Curwen hand signs, solfège, and rhythm syllables as the basic components.

One dilemma in which directors find themselves is the constant battle between the need to teach music literacy and the ever-present deadline of preparation for performance. Using *The Adolescent Reading Singer* allows the teacher to do both. At the end of each phase of the method, the author has arranged selections for performance that use only those aspects of music reading that the students have encountered to that point in the method. This allows the directors to teach music literacy and to prepare for performance simultaneously. Teachers may find these selections in a booklet of choral literature or a series of octavos for each singer available from the publisher.

The teaching material and exercises included here are available from the publisher on transparencies to be used with an overhead projector. Teachers need to be able to point to significant aspects on each transparency to guide the line of vision of the students as they sing. Adolescents often get "tied up" in the printed music when it is in their hands. Quicker learning occurs when attention is directed to the teachers, whether they are using the Curwen hand signs or pointing to the transparencies (or screen). When the singers sight-read the choral literature, they can read from the printed page.

The rate of advancement through the method is quite flexible, depending on the singers. In the first two phases the author assumes that the singers have a limited knowledge about music reading, and by the end of phase seven the method brings the singers to complete musical literacy, including the use of chromaticism. This allows the singers to read atonal and polytonal music, if necessary. If the singers have been introduced to the Kodády method of music reading in their early years, it is advisable for the teachers to move quickly through the first two phases, using them only as a review. However, if teachers are introducing sight-reading to the singers for the first time, they should give much more time to the introductory phases because these beginning phases lay the foundation upon which the remaining phases are built. Teachers should allot about twenty minutes to sight-reading activities each time the singers are together, moving at a rate that allows them to be thorough without boring the students. Spending excessively long periods of time sight-reading is not nearly as helpful as several short periods. Putting the method away and returning to it enhances the rate of progress toward musical literacy.

The method is divided into seven phases with several exercises in each phase. There are three types of exercises: (1) preparation exercises provide new information and serve as the primary teaching tool, (2) application exercises allow the students to apply the knowledge they have learned to actual sight-reading activities, and (3) reference charts for instructors to use to assist the students once they are sight-reading from the printed page.

Phase One

Phase one introduces the basic musical elements and terminology the students need to know to be able to sing. In all phases of this sight-reading method except this phase, the students actually have to develop the skill of bringing the voice to react by impulse (habit) without rationalization. This, of course, is a more involved type of knowledge and capability than teaching basic facts or concepts. Therefore, teachers spend more time with these phases. Since phase one is just an introduction to musical terminology and basic concepts and only brings the students to an acquaintance level of learning, teachers may cover it quickly, probably within a maximum of two twenty-minute periods. It is *not* the teachers' responsibility at this point to explain the function of these musical symbols and terminology. Simply introduce them to the students so that they will know what they are and can identify them.

Preparation 1.1—Musical Symbols   Introduce the musical symbols found in Example 1.1 in the following order:

1. *Grand staff*: Four sets of five lines and four spaces are connected on the left by a single vertical line. The top two are further connected with a vertical line brace that indicates this music is to be sung by voices. The bottom two are further connected with a curved line bracket that indicates this music is to be played by a keyboard instrument.
2. *Treble clef*: The music found on this set of five lines and four spaces is to be sung by treble voices, which includes boys unchanged voices, female voices,

and cambiatas (boys in the first phase of vocal change). The cambiatas will sing this music at actual pitch. It is not to be transposed one octave lower as is the custom for adult males when they sing music written in the treble clef. Boys in the first phase of vocal change can more easily relate to the treble clef when they are singing at actual pitch than any other, since this is what they read when their voices were unchanged. However, they must also learn to relate to the bass clef because various publishers release music in both clefs. Some publishers even release music written in the treble clef to be sung by cambiatas one octave lower as high school tenors sing it. Having to relate to music published three different ways is somewhat problematic to directors. They must take time to explain to the young singers where the comfortable singing area of the voice occurs in each clef. When introducing new music to singers, taking a few moments to explain how to relate to the clef (in which the cambiata part is written) will be time well spent. Keyboard music found on lines and spaces following the treble clef is played with the right hand.

3. *Bass clef*: The music found on this set of five lines and four spaces is to be sung by the baritones (boys in the second phase of vocal change) and the cambiatas when closed scoring (hymn style) is used (exemplified in Example 1.1). In high school, tenors and basses read the bass clef. Keyboard music following the bass clef is played with the left hand.

4. *Key signature*: Following the treble and bass clefs is the key signature, which may contain as few as one or as many as seven sharps (point them out) or flats (point them out). One seldom finds both sharps and flats together in a key signature. For this reason, the flats have been placed in parenthesis to show how they would occur in a key signature.

5. *Meter signature*: This is the fraction following the key signature. Do not explain its function now. It will be explained later in the method. Point out that it also may be called a "time signature."

6. *Dynamic marking*: The *f* following the meter signature is the dynamic marking. It indicates loudness and softness of the music. It may be a *pp* (pianissimo, very soft), *p* (piano, soft), *mp* (mezzo piano, moderately soft), *mf* (mezzo forte, moderately loud), *f* (forte, loud), or *ff* (fortissimo, very loud). Instructors may choose to introduce the various dynamic levels as they occur in the music rather than all at once.

7. *Notes*: These are the symbols found on the lines and spaces. They communicate (1) how long a tone should be held and (2) what the pitch level (highness and lowness) of a tone should be. There is often a misconception among children when a note occurs on a line or space due to the way they were taught to print letters in elementary school. Children may consider these words to be written on a line. When a note is on a line, the line runs through the note. A note is written on a space whenever it sets between two lines. Be sure the students have this concept clear in their minds at this point. When notes occur vertically as shown here, they are to be sung simultaneously by different voices. In middle/junior high school, the top note in the treble clef is to be sung by first sopranos and the bottom note in the treble clef is to be sung by second sopranos (they may be called altos, if directors desire). The top note in the bass clef is to be sung by cambiatas and the bottom note of the bass clef is to be sung by baritones. In high school the notes are soprano, alto, tenor, bass, respectively. Rests are introduced later in the method.

8. *Bar lines*: The vertical line crossing the horizontal lines and spaces is called a bar. Two identical bars found together indicate the end of a section of a composition or music-reading exercise. One light and one heavy bar found

together indicate the end of the complete composition or music reading exercise.

9. *Measure*: The distance between two bar lines.

10. *Lines and spaces*: When referring to the horizontal lines and spaces, one should always count them from the bottom up, such as line 1, 2, 3, 4, 5, or space 1, 2, 3, 4. Lines added above or below either of the sets of five lines and four spaces are called ledger lines. Spaces between ledger lines are called ledger spaces. Point these out to the students. In this method, it is not essential to introduce the letter names of the lines and spaces for the students to read since they will be using the Sol-fa syllables. However, instructors may teach the students the letter names of the notes and use them for reference if they desire.

11. *Tempo/mood marking*: The word found above the grand staff is the tempo/mood marking. It indicates the pace of the beat note (that which receives the persistent pulsation that permeates the music) as well as the general feeling of the music. Often one will find a small note and a number (in this case, quarter note equals sixty) following the tempo/mood marking. This indicates the metronome marking of the beat note.

Preparation 1.2—Sol-fa Syllables   The purpose of Example 1.2 is to bring the students to a speaking knowledge of the proper order of the pitch (Sol-fa) syllables.

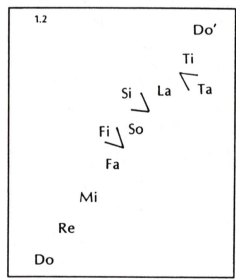

Instruct the students to chant the pitch syllables in order (ascending) to the following rhythm pattern:

D R M F S L T D
D T L S F M R D

Beginning slowly, as the students chant, constantly increase the tempo slightly until they are chanting them as quickly as they can enunciate them clearly. Point to the syllable names as the students chant. After they have become sufficiently acquainted with the ascending order of the pitch syllables, remove the syllables from the sight of the students and ask them to repeat the exercise described above by memory. If time allows, individual students will delight in chanting the pitch syllables alone.

Next, possibly at a different class period, repeat the preceding procedure, except this time, ask the students to chant the pitch syllables in reverse order (descending).

Teach only the diatonic scale with this chanting exercises. Tell the students there will be three other syllables (*fi*, *si*, and *ta*) with which they will become acquainted later. As the example shows, *fi* comes above *fa*, *si* above *so*, and *ta* below *ti*. The mark above *do'* indicates it is the upper octave, or high *do'*.

Keep in mind that the students are to speak the syllables only during this exercise. They are not to sing them now. Pitch relationships are established later in the method.

Preparation 1.3—Curwen Hand Signs Example 1.3 introduces the students to the

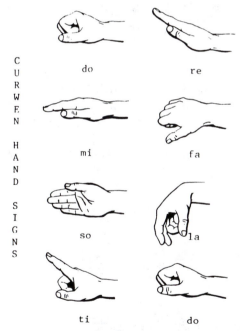

C
U
R
W
E
N

H
A
N
D

S
I
G
N
S

do   re

mi   fa

so   la

ti   do

Curwen hand signs. While making the sign with the right hand, point to each sign on the chart with the left hand. Then ask the students to make each sign with their hands.

Preparation 1.4—Finding So The Kodály presentation of pitches according to the pentatonic scale has been chosen for this sight-singing method. In phase two when the students begin to learn pitch relationships, the first three they learn are *so*, *la*, and *mi* followed by all members of the pentatonic scale (*so*, *la*, *mi*, *re*, and *do*) and finally the subpentatonic (*so, la, mi, re, do,* and *la* and *so* below *do*) before they are presented with the full diatonic scale (*fa* and *ti* added).

To read music from the printed page the students need to be able, in the beginning, to find *so* on the lines and spaces, since it is the beginning pitch of the first three pitches they learn. Later they will relate to finding *do* as they learn the pentatonic sounds. Example 1.4 shows them how to find *so*. The rule is simple. When there are sharps in the key signature, the line or space upon which the last sharp on the right occurs is the pitch syllable *ti*, as indicated by the plain arrows. If *ti* is on a space, *so* will always be on the space directly beneath it. If *ti* is on a line, *so* will always be on the line directly beneath it. In this case *ti* is the fourth line in the treble clef and the third line in the bass clef, therefore, *so* is the third line in the treble and the second line in the bass clef, as indicated by the crossed arrows.

When there are flats in the key signature, the line or space upon which

the last flat on the right occurs is the pitch syllable *fa*. If *fa* is on a line, *so* will always be on the space directly above it. If *fa* is on a space, *so* will always be on the line directly above it. In this case, *fa* is the fourth line in the treble clef and the third line in the bass clef as indicated by the plain arrows; therefore, *so* is the fourth space in the treble clef and the third space in the bass clef, as indicated by the crossed arrows.

When there are no sharps or flats in the key signature, *so* is always the second line in the treble and fourth space in the bass clef.

Reference 1.5—Key Signatures with Sharps   Example 1.5 shows where *so* is found in

all keys with sharps in the key signature. The note in parenthesis is the *so* students will find when they use the rule described in the narrative about Example 1.4. The other notes show *so* as it occurs on other lines and spaces in each key.

It is advisable to use this reference chart each time students are reading literature in sharp keys. It will help them to adjust their thinking toward the relationship between the various notes in the scale.

Reference 1.6—Key Signatures with Flats Example 1.6 indicates where *so* is found in

all keys with flats in the key signature. The note in parentheses is the *so* the students will find when they use the rule described in the narrative about Example 1.4. The other notes indicate *so* as it occurs on other lines and spaces in each key.

It is advisable to use this reference chart each time students are reading literature in flat keys. It will help them to adjust their thinking toward the relationship between the various notes in the scale.

Reference 1.7—Simple Meter Signatures There are three basic groups of meter

$$\frac{2}{8} \quad \frac{3}{8} \quad \frac{4}{8}$$

$$\frac{2}{4} \quad \frac{3}{4} \quad \frac{4}{4}$$

$$\frac{2}{2} \quad \frac{3}{2} \quad \frac{4}{2}$$

signatures: 8 on the bottom, 4 on the bottom, and 2 on the bottom. These bottom numbers tell the singers what type note receives (represents) the beat. The 8 represents the eighth note, the 4 represents the quarter note, and the 2 represents the half note. The students will be taught to recognize these notes later in the method. The top number indicates how many of those notes (or their equivalency) will be found in each measure.

As Example 1.7 indicates, there may be two, three, or four beats in various measures. Reading the meter signatures from left to right beginning at the top, one can see that in a measure of 2/8 meter will be two eighth notes; in a measure of 3/8, three eighth notes; in a measure of 4/8, four eighth notes. In the second group, in a measure of 2/4 meter will be two quarter notes; in a measure of 3/4, three quarter notes and so forth.

The second group (those with 4 on the bottom) are the most common meter signatures, and of those three, 4/4 (often called common meter) will be used the most.

Compound meter will be introduced later.

Phase Two

With the basic introductory material found in phase one behind them, the students are ready to begin reading music by sight. Unlike phase one, the remaining phases are student-activity (singing) oriented.

In phase two the students learn to react to three sounds: *so*, *la*, and *mi*. They will also learn to initiate three rhythm symbols: the quarter note, two eighth notes beamed together, and the quarter rest (all in 2/4 meter). Examples 2.1 through 2.5 are preparation exercises (for teaching new information). Examples 2.6 through 2.10 are application (sight-reading) exercises designed for the singers to read. After completing phase two, there are five compositions or arrangements in the student literature booklet and several octavos (available from the publisher[2]) that singers may read, using the same method, and perform in concert, if directors desire.

All the application (sight-reading) exercises in phases two and three are to be sung in unison. At the end of phase two, when the students begin reading the literature, they must sing in parts. However, all the parts are written in the treble clef. Each section of singers may read the parts one at a time and then put them together. Sight-reading more than one part simultaneously will come as the students feel more at ease with their newly attained musical skills. Part singing in different clefs is introduced in phase four.

Preparation 2.1—2/4 Meter, Stems, and Beams   Chant the words of Example 2.1 in rhythm for the students. After, chant it with the students, then point out what the text means:

1. The stem represents the quarter note, and in 2/4 meter the quarter note receives the beat. There will be two quarter notes (or an equivalent) in each measure.
2. A beam connects two eighth notes, and each of the two eighth notes are only half as long as a note with only a stem (quarter note); therefore, they move twice as fast. The two beamed eighth notes are equal to one quarter note (stem only).
3. The rests in measures 4 and 8 are quarter rests. As with the quarter note,

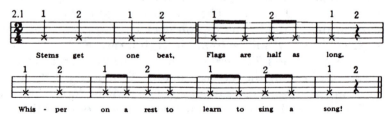

they receive one beat each. Students should whisper the word *rest* each time the quarter rest occurs. They must whisper rather than speak aloud the

[2] Don L. Collins, *The Adolescent Reading Singer Student Literature Booklet* (Conway, Ark.: Cambiata Press, 1977). Individual octavos are available from *The Adolescent Reading Singer Choral Series*.

word *rest* because the concept that notes are audible beats and rests are silent beats that must be considered is reinforced with the whisper.

Preparation 2.2—Ta *and* Ti ti   The students are introduced to the rhythm before

they combine it with the melody. Chant Example 2.2 for the students using the Kodály rhythm syllables as indicated. Point out the following information about the chant, then chant it with the students:

1.   The syllable *ta* represents the quarter note that receives one beat.
2.   The syllables *ti ti* represent the two beamed eighth notes that combined also receive one beat.
3.   Each time the quarter rest occurs, the students are to whisper the word *rest*. They will have a tendency to voice the word on occasions. Please keep them whispering because when they sing, rests communicate silence and notes communicate tones.

From this point on, whenever the students begin any of the exercises, they must *do something physical* on each beat. This physical movement is essential in learning to read music by sight. When students sing a selection for the first time, they must always give priority to the beat over the pitch. If they cannot hear a certain pitch, instead of stopping the beat to find it, they must skip that pitch and move on. After they have finished the exercise, go back and drill the pitches they were unable to sing. Giving the beats priority (allowing it to govern the music) enhances the learning process. Doing something physical makes the beat take priority.

Further, this physical action should be inaudible, such as nodding the head, tapping the ends of the fingers on the leg or the palm of the hand, or beating time with the arm. The inaudible physical movement is better than clapping, patschen (patting the thighs), or snapping the fingers because it allows instructors to maintain order in the classroom as well as speak to the students while they are keeping time.

As the students chant, check to see that their physical movement is on the rhythm of the beat (consistent pulsation) and *not* the rhythm of the melody (varies according to the note lengths).

On all the application exercises that follow, the beats have been included above each measure so that the students can see them as they physically feel them. When pointing to the exercise as the chant (or music) moves along, it is better to move the pointer to the rhythm of the beat as opposed to the rhythm of the melody. This allows the pointer to move more evenly and to direct the students eyes steadily across the exercise.

Preparation 2.3—Childhood Chant Using the words, sing the childhood melody found in Exercise 2.3 to the students, then execute the following:

1. Explain that this melody is often the first one that children sing at a very young age. It is very difficult to find a child who is unable to sing it at some pitch level. Due to its universal acceptance and understanding, it will be used throughout this sight-reading method. Each time new sounds are introduced, they will be related to this childhood melody (often called "the childhood chant").

2. There are three different sounds found in this childhood melody, *so, la,* and

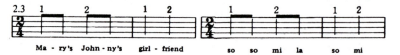

mi. Pitch *so* on F in the key of B-flat and sing the melody using the pitch syllables. Sing the childhood melody with the students and use the Curwen hand signs as they sing.

3. Ask the students to sing the childhood melody using the pitch syllables. Use the key of B flat when singing the exercise with early adolescents because it allows the sopranos and cambiatas to sing in unison while the baritones sing one octave lower. In high school, if there are no changing voices present, the key of D probably will be more comfortable.

Students should sing the childhood melody each time sight-reading activities begin. Singing the melody refreshes their tonal memory and pitch relationships. They also will use it to relate all of the new pitches they learn.

Preparation 2.4—Combining Rhythm and Melody The students are ready to combine

rhythm with melody. Pitch *so* on F and sing the words and melody to Exercise 2.4. The students will be able to relate to it what they learned in Exercises 2.1 and 2.2. Point out that the three sounds (*so, la,* and *mi*) are all that are included in the exercise. Then sing the exercise using the pitch syllables. Invite the students to sing it first with the words and then with the pitch syllables, mimicking what they have just heard sung. Always remind the students to do something physical, but inaudible, as they sing. Also, they should never be allowed to voice the word *rest.* They should whisper it as it occurs.

Preparation 2.5—Lines and Spaces The students are ready to read the combination of rhythm, melody, and words from the lines and spaces. Using the words, sing

the melody (instructor alone; students do not sing) in Exercise 2.5 (first introduced in Exercise 2.4), pointing to each of the notes as they are sung, then repeat it using the pitch syllables. Continue to point to the each of the notes, then explain to the students:

1. As the key signature indicates, the last flat on the right is on the fourth space. Therefore, all notes occurring on the fourth space should be called the syllable *fa*. Since *so* comes directly above *fa*, all notes found on the fifth line are the syllable *so*. The students will find, however, that these notes on the fifth line are very high in the voice, so it will be helpful to find a *so* that is lower. Since there are no notes in this exercise on the fifth line, speak the pitch syllables beginning with *so* and descending to *so* one octave lower. Point to each line and space as the descending syllables are spoken until low *so* is reached. Low *so* occurs on the first space.

    Teach the students this principle: *Henceforth, now, and forevermore* (these words are used for emphasis to help the students remember), if *so* is found on a space, *mi* will be on the space directly beneath it and *la* will be on the line directly above it. If *so* is on a line, henceforth, now, and forevermore, *mi* will be on the line directly beneath it and *la* will be on the space directly above it. In this case, since *so* is on the first space, *mi* is on the first space below the staff (the first ledger space) and *la* is the second line.

    Point to each *so* in the exercise showing the students that they are all on the first space. Do the same for the other two syllables.

2. When two dots are placed before a double bar, as shown in this exercise, the singer should repeat all the music between the double bars. If the repeat bars only occur at the end, singers should go back to the beginning and repeat what they have just sung.

Using the words, instruct the students to sing the melody. When they repeat it, as the repeat bars indicate, sing it with the pitch syllables.

Point to the *notes* as the students sing. Never point to the words. Teach the students to look directly at the notes and pick up the words with their peripheral vision. This is essential for students to become good sight singers. Since the students learned to read words before they learn to read music, looking directly at the words instead of the notes will be a difficult habit to break. They must be reminded constantly to look at the notes, particularly when they cease to read from the exercises and begin to read from the printed page.

Applications 2.6 through 2.10—Music Reading   Exercises 2.6 through 2.10 are application (sight-reading) exercises that incorporate the concepts and ideas presented in phases one and two.

Use the following seven-step procedure when presenting each of Exercises 2.6 through 2.10 to the class. For several weeks it is advisable to follow this routine conscientiously without deviation until the singers have achieved a competence that justifies elimination of one or more steps. If these seven steps appear to be too intense for the singers, create additional steps that will simplify the process even more.

1. **Instruct the students to chant the rhythm using the Kodály rhythm syllables**.
2. **Now that they know how the rhythm of the exercise sounds, ask them to clap it**. They will have more success at feeling the rests if they shake their hands (palms apart) on that particular beat. Clapping the rhythm allows instructors to see which children are missing certain rhythm patterns. It may be better to have the students clap and speak the rhythm syllables simultaneously, particularly if the students are having trouble with a certain part of the rhythm.
3. **Chant the words of the exercise in rhythm**. Instructors may prefer not to use the words of the exercise because they might want to keep the reading strictly musically oriented. Words often serve as a vehicle to help students remember melodies. Often, after a melody has been sung the first time with words, it ceases to be sight-singing and becomes melody-recall if they are asked to sing it on another occasion. On the other hand, since most music students sing has words, it is probably more helpful for them to learn to combine the music and the words as they learn to read music. If instructors choose not to use the words, the students may chant the rhythm of the exercise using a neutral vowel, such as *loo*.
4. **Using the Curwen hand signs, ask the students to sing Sol-fa syllables to arbitrary pitches in the key in which the exercise is written**. To keep from constantly moving to the piano when there is a need to refresh the tonal memory, use a pitch pipe to find the initial pitch. When a pitch pipe is used, there is no temptation to play the exercise on the piano. Remember, this is a sight-reading method, not a pitch-matching method. Do not incorporate any pitches in the hand sign warm-up that are not included in the exercise.
5. **Ask the students to determine on which line or space they will find the note representing** *so* (or *do*, if they are singing an exercise in phases three through seven). Relate all other pitches to it. **Point to isolated pitches in the exercise and ask the students to sing them using the pitch syllables.**
6. **Sing the exercise in rhythm using the pitch syllables**. Remind the students to do something physical, but inaudible, as they sing. Do not stop to correct the students when they sing an incorrect pitch. Sing the exercise from the beginning to the end once the beat has begun, then return to the trouble spots for isolated drill, using the Curwen hand signs or pointing to the pitches without being governed by the beat. The students must learn to keep the beat moving and simply skip sounds that do not come to mind as they approach them. This is essential for them to be good sight-singers.

   If the singers are unsuccessful singing step six, interject an intermediary step between steps five and six. Ask the students to speak (not sing) the syllable names of the pitches in rhythm. Once they have been drilled on what to call them, move to step six.
7. **Sing the exercise in rhythm using the words**. Remind the students to look directly at the notes and pick up the words with their peripheral vision. If instructors do not desire the students to sing the words, they may sing the exercise using a neutral vowel, such as *loo*.

The last exercise in each phase contains all the tonal patterns to which the students have been introduced at that point. Do not move to the next phase until the students can sing the last exercise correctly. If they cannot do so, repeat Exercises 2.6 through 2.10 until they are successful before moving to the next phase.

When using these application exercises with high school students, directors may desire to sing them in different keys than those in which they are written, if they do not have changing voices in their groups. A step, or even a minor third, higher will make the exercises easier to sing for the sopranos and tenors.

Phase Three

The rhythmic aspects introduced in phase three are the tie, slur, half note, half rest, whole note, whole rest, fermata, and 4/4 meter. The melodic aspects include the introduction of *do* and *re*.

After completing phase three, there is a series of compositions or arrangements in the student literature booklet and octavos that they may read and perform in concert. These choral selections include only the rhythmic and melodic aspects covered in the first three phases of the sight-reading method.

Preparation 3.1—More Rhythm Complexities   Point out the new rhythmic aspects of Exercise 3.1 to the students:

1. The tie is used to connect more than one note of the same pitch. The slur is used to connect more than one note of different pitches. When quarter notes are tied together, use *ta* to initiate the first quarter note and *ah* (a slight stress of the voice on the beat) on all other quarter notes as exemplified in measures 3, 7, 8, 15, and 16. When eighth notes are tied together, use *ti* to initiate the first eighth note and *i* (pronounced *ee*) on all other eighth notes that follow, as exemplified in measures 9 and 13. Slurs are initiated identically to ties.
2. In this exercise, for the first time, there is more than one quarter rest in a row. Whisper *rest* on each of them. If directors have performed the literature that accompanies this method, they will have already encountered more than one rest in a row at the end of phase two.

3. There are still two beats in each measure. Ask the students to do something physical, but inaudible, on each beat.

Now that the students have been instructed about the new aspects of this exercise, ask them to chant it, using the Kodády rhythm syllables.

Preparation 3.2—4/4 Meter Rhythmically, Exercise 3.2 sounds identical to Exercise 3.1, however, it is notated differently. Point out the following:

1. The meter signature is 4/4. There are four quarter notes (or an equivalent) in each measure.
2. Instead of having two quarter notes tied together, there is a new note, the half note (measure 2). It is initiated just like two tied quarter notes: *ta-ah*.
3. Instead of having two quarter rests, there is a new type rest, the half rest (measure 2). It sits on top of the third line and is initiated just like two quarter rests; whisper *rest* twice, once on each beat.
4. Instead of having four quarter notes tied together, there is a new note, the whole note. It is initiated just like four tied quarter notes (measure 4): *ta-ah-ah-ah*.
5. Instead of having four quarter rests in a row, there is a new type rest, the whole rest. It hangs beneath the fourth line and is initiated just like four quarter rests; whisper *rest* four times, once on each beat.
6. The symbol above the whole note in measure 8 is a fermata. The performers may hold the last beat of the note over which it is placed as long as they desire. If the singers are following a director, they should hold the last beat of the note over which it is placed as long as the director indicates. Another indication the note should be held is the short line (text indicator) found at the end of the last *ah*.

Now that the students have been informed pertaining to the new rhythmic aspects of this phase, ask them to chant the exercise using the rhythmic syllables. Notice that it sounds identical to the previous exercise, except it is notated differently. Remind the students to do something physical, but inaudible, on each beat.

Preparation 3.3—Re and Do   Exercise 3.3 introduces two new pitches, *re* and *do*. Sing the exercise to the students, pointing to each beat as it passes. After showing them the two new hand signs for these new pitches, explain the following:

1.   As they have already been instructed, remind them that when *so* is on a space, "henceforth, now and forevermore" *mi* is on the space directly beneath it. Notice further that if *so* and *mi* are on spaces, "henceforth, now and forevermore" *do* will be on the space directly beneath *mi*. The students now have been introduced to the tonic triad: *so, mi,* and *do*. The two most important pitches in the scale are *do* and *so*. The students should try from this point on to keep *do, mi,* and *so* in mind and relate the other pitches to them. In this case, while they are reading they should constantly remember the space, space, space relationship of *so, mi,* and *do*. As a result, their reading abilities will develop much more rapidly.

2.   *Re* is on the line between *do* and *mi*, in this case, the first ledger line below the staff. Always remember, if *so, mi,* and *do* are on spaces, *re* and *la* will always be on lines. Ask the students to sing the exercise using the pitch syllables.

Preparation 3.4—Notes on Lines   The importance of Exercise 3.4 is to point out the significance of *so* being on a line. If there are no sharps or flats in the key signature, the students should recall that *so* is on the second line in the treble clef. Since *so* is on the second line in this case, *mi* is on the line directly beneath it and *do* is on the line directly beneath that. The relationship of line, line, line is important, so the students should learn to relate to that concept. If *so, mi,* and *do* are on lines, then *re* and *la* will always be on spaces, *la* on the space above *so*, and *re* on the space between *do* and *mi*. Point out the notes for each of these pitches in the exercise to the students.

Ask the students to sing the exercise with the pitch syllables. If the whole rest presents a problem, it might be helpful to have them chant the rhythm syllables before trying to sing it with the pitch syllables.

Since all three members of the tonic triad have been introduced, instructors who learned to read music as it is relates to the diatonic scale rather than how

it relates the pentatonic scale may be more comfortable using *do* as the pitch to blow on the pitch pipe and then relating *mi* and *so* to it. Directors should continue to use the three-note childhood melody throughout this method because it is the foundation upon which the pentatonic scale is built. Teach the students to relate all new sounds to that three-note melody. The students should be able to practice sight-singing outside of class because all tones of the diatonic scale can be recalled if they are taught to rely on the childhood melody.

Applications 3.5 through 3.9—Music Reading   The students should sight-read Exercises 3.5 through 3.9. Use the seven-step music reading procedure delineated in the instructions following Exercise 2.5. In phase three, when step four is reached (which drills the students with the different pitches using the Curwen hand signs), begin the step with the following tonal sequence *so, so, mi, la, so, mi, re, do* in the key of the exercise. This sequence will renew all the pitches to which they have been introduced thus far in the method.

Exercises 3.5 and 3.9 each have two pages. Students should read both pages when sight-reading.

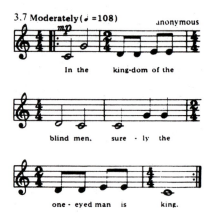

Exercise 3.9 contains all the tonal patterns introduced in the method to this point. Do not move to the next phase until the students can sing this exercise correctly.

Phase Four

The new rhythmic aspects of phase four include: the dotted half note, the flag, the eighth-quarter-eighth note pattern, bass clef, and 3/4 meter. The new melodic aspects include one new syllable, high *do'*. For the first time students begin to read more than one clef at a time.

After completion of phase four, please consult the student literature booklet or various octavos for a series of musical compositions or arrangements that the students may read and perform in concert. These choral selections include only the rhythmic and melodic aspects covered in the first four phases of this sight-singing method.

Preparation 4.1—3/4 Meter and More Rhythm Complexities Before the students chant the rhythm to Exercise 4.1, give them the following instructions:

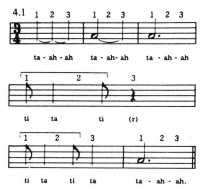

1. They already know to initiate three quarter notes tied together as *ta-ah-ah*. Another way to notate the same sound is to tie a half note (*ta-ah*) to a quarter note (*ah*), resulting in *ta-ah-ah*. There is a third way to get the same effect, the dot following the half note. When a dot follows a half note, it represents one more beat in length (three beats).
2. The flag is used when there is only one eighth note present, rather than two eighth notes beamed together. Since two beamed eighth notes receive one beat, one flagged eighth note will receive one-half beat. The rhythm syllable for one eighth note is *ti*.
3. Demonstrate the rhythm of the syncopated pattern of eighth-quarter-eighth using the rhythm syllables (*ti-ta-ti*), then ask the students to chant it. The students should perceive these three notes as a unit each time they encounter them in the music they sing. Point out to the students that the first *ti* always falls on the beat and never after it. The syllable *ta* always falls after the beat.
4. For the first time, students encounter 3/4 meter. Explain how there are three quarter notes (or an equivalent) in every measure.

After explaining these concepts, ask the students to chant the rhythm of the exercise using the Kodály rhythm syllables.

Preparation 4.2—High Do' Sing Exercise 4.2 to the students, using the pitch syllables (Sol-fa) and pointing out the new sound, high *do'*, then ask them to sing it together. Take precaution with the first two measures; they contain the familiar childhood melody, but the rhythm is different.

When using the Curwen hand signs, make regular *do* about waist level and high *do'* with the arm outstretched upwardly. Simulate the other pitches of the octave at the appropriate level between the waist and the upward outstretched arm, according to their highness and lowness.

When regular *do* is on a space, high *do'* will be on a line and vice versa.

Preparation 4.3—Bass Clef Exercise 4.3 is similar to the preceding one except that the key has been changed and it is slightly shorter. The purpose of this exercise is to introduce part reading with both treble and bass clef. The cambiatas and baritones (tenors and basses in high school) may read the bass clef for the first time. Point out to the students that when the voices reading the treble clef (girls)

are singing *so, mi,* and *do* on spaces, the voices reading the bass clef (boys) are singing *so, mi,* and *do* on lines.

The boys should be able to find *so* (or *do*) using the "last flat on the right" rule as when they were reading the treble clef. Once they know where *so* occurs, the other pitches should fall into place in the same fashion as when they were reading the treble clef.

The boys' part lies within a composite range so that both cambiatas and baritones may sing in unison. High school tenors and basses should be able to sing the part without vocal difficulty.

With all exercises that include part singing, the voice parts are designated I, II, III, and IV. In middle/junior high school, Part I is for Soprano I, Part II for Soprano II, Part III for Cambiata, and Part IV for Baritone. In high school, if Part III is written in the bass clef, the designation should be Part I for Soprano, Part II for Alto, Part III for Tenor, and Part IV for Bass. In high school, when Part III is written in the treble clef, the designation should be Part I for Soprano I, Part II for Soprano II and Part III for Alto (and any cambiatas who might be present). Part IV should be sung by both tenors and basses.

Applications 4.4 through 4.8—Music Reading The students should sight-read Exercises 4.4 through 4.8. Use the seven-step music reading procedure delineated in the instructions following Exercise 2.5. In phase three, when step four is reached (which drills the students with the different pitches using the Curwen hand signs), begin the step with the following tonal sequence: *so, so, mi, la, so, mi, re, do, so, do'*. This sequence will renew all the pitches to which they have been introduced thus far in the method. When singing the tonal sequence with middle/junior high school students, use the key of C as the sopranos and baritones sing together, then change to the key of A-flat and let the cambiatas sing along. High school students may sing together in unison in the key of C or D.

Exercise 4.6 encompasses two pages. It is designed to help those singing Parts I, II, and III to practice initiating the arpeggio. Exercise 4.7 is designed to assist Part III in initiating the octave jump properly. Exercise 4.8 is written in unison. Parts I, II, and III are to be sung at actual pitch. Part IV should sing one octave lower.

Phase Five

Rhythmic aspects introduced in phase five are four sixteenth notes, the eighth-two sixteenths note pattern, the two sixteenths-eighth note pattern, and the anacrusis. Melodic aspects include the introduction of two new sounds, *la,* and *so,* below *do.* With these two new sounds the students may sight-sing any pentatonic or subpentatonic melody.

After completion of phase five, please consult the student literature booklet or various octavos for a series of musical compositions or arrangements that the students may read and perform in concert. These choral selections include only the rhythmic and melodic aspects covered in the first five phases of this sight-singing method.

Preparation 5.1—More Rhythm Complexities   Before the students chant Exercise 5.1 with the rhythm syllables, point out the following:

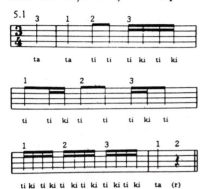

1. There is an incomplete measure at the beginning. Music often begins with an incomplete measure. Most of the time it will contain only one beat. Occasionally there are incomplete measures which contain one and one-half or two beats. In the last measure of the exercise the students will find only two beats, which makes it incomplete also. In most music that begins with an *anacrusis* (an incomplete measure) they should combine the beginning and ending measure to make one complete measure. In this case, the one beat at the beginning combined with the two beats at the end constitute the full three beats each measure contains in 3/4 meter.

2. The rhythm syllables for four sixteenth notes are *ti-ki-ti-ki*, which constitute one beat in the measure.

   The correct syllables taught by Kodály were *ti-ri-ti-ri*. Since Hungarian children flip the tongue when pronouncing the *r*, this sound was quite easily produced. Americans generally do not flip the tongue when pronouncing the *r*; therefore, they can more easily produce the *k*. Some American music educators have replaced the flipped *r* with a *d*, thus pronouncing four sixteenth notes as *ti-di-ti-di*, which sounds somewhat like the Hungarian flipped *r* in *ti-ri-ti-ri*. However, since the tip of the tongue is used to produce both the *t* and the *d*, singers can pronounce *ti-ki-ti-ki* more rapidly since they alternate between the tip of the tongue and the back of the tongue against the hard palate when pronouncing the *t* and the *k*.

3. An eighth-two sixteenth note pattern is pronounced *ti-ti-ki* and the two sixteenth-eighth note pattern is *ti-ki-ti*.

Ask the students to chant the rhythm of this Exercise 5.1 together using the Kodály rhythm syllables. Remind them to do something physical, but inaudible, as they chant. This particular chart is a great deal of fun to chant. The students will delight in attempting to chant it individually.

Preparation 5.2—La₁ and So₁ below Do   With the addition of *la₁* and *so₁* below *do*,

Exercise 5.2 includes the entire subpentatonic scale. Sing the exercise for the students after pointing out the presence of the childhood melody at the beginning with still a different rhythm (four sixteenth notes followed by two quarter notes). Use the Curwen hand signs while singing the exercise.

Next, sing the exercise with the students, using the pitch syllables. Students may tend to make eighth notes out of the two quarter notes in the first measure. Exercise precaution as it is chanted.

Since the exercise includes the span of a ninth between its highest and lowest pitches, some cambiatas may have difficulty singing the high B-flat, and some baritones may have difficulty singing the low A-flat. It is suggested that the cambiatas take the lower optional notes (those found in parenthesis) and the baritones take the upper optional notes.

Applications 5.3 through 5.7—Music Reading   The students should sight-read Exercises 5.3 through 5.7. Use the seven-step music reading procedure delineated in the instructions following Exercise 2.5. In phase three, when step four is reached (which drills the students with the different pitches using the Curwen hand signs), begin the step with the following tonal sequence: *so, so, mi, la, so, mi, re, do, so, do', so, mi, do, la,, so,, la,, do.* This sequence will renew for them all the pitches to which they have been introduced thus far in the method. When singing the tonal sequence with middle/junior high school students, use the key of D as the sopranos and baritones sing together, then change to the key of B-flat and let the cambiatas sing along. High school students may sing together in unison in the key of D or E-flat. If the students are beginning to feel confident in their sight-singing capabilities, some of the steps may be omitted, as desired. If the students cannot sing all the pitches correctly or if they miss the rhythm, go back and pick up some of the steps which were omitted.

Exercise 5.3 is the first one in which the students have encountered a minor key. This should not affect their approach to this melody whatsoever. It

should be taught just as if it were in a major key. It is optional whether or not to tell the students that the exercise is written in a minor key. They should be able to read it just as they have read the previous melodies. The additions of *la,* and *so,* below *do* (the subpentatonic) allows them to read minor melodies. They have been taught to think line, line, line or space, space, space for *so, mi, do.* They should also be taught to think line, line, line or space, space, space, for *mi, do, la,* when reading minor melodies.

Exercise 5.4 has two parts; however, both are written in the treble clef. When singing the exercise with middle/junior high school students, the sopranos and baritones should sing Parts I and IV and cambiatas should sing Part III. When singing the exercise with high school students, everyone should sing only the top line. The bottom line has been included to administer to the needs of the cambiatas' changing voices.

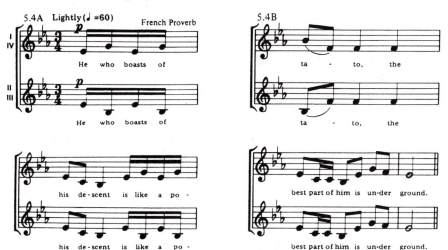

Applications Exercise 5.7A,B,C,D contain all the tonal patterns introduced in the method thus far. The students should not move to the next phase until they can sing these charts correctly. The ranges are wide due to the necessary tonal patterns so unison singing is not practical. Therefore, when using the exercise in middle/junior high school, the sopranos and baritones should sing Exercise 5.7A,B (key of F) and the cambiatas should sing Exercises 5.7C,D in the key of C. When singing the exercises in high school, sing only Exercise 5.7A,B.

Phase Six

New rhythmic aspects covered in phase six are the eighth rest, the quarter note tied to the eighth note, the dotted quarter note followed by the eighth, and the

eighth note followed by the dotted quarter. New melodic sounds include *ti* and *fa*, which now complete the diatonic scale. There are two types of major diatonic melodies: (1) authentic melodies where the range lies between *do* and high *do'* and (2) plagal melodies where the range lies between *so,* below *do* and *so* above *do*.

Whenever students are reading major diatonic melodies they should be taught to recognize the difference in those that are authentic and those that are plagal. This understanding will enable them to deal more securely with the melody they are singing.

One of the beautiful aspects of the use of Sol-fa syllables has to do with the proper tuning of the choral ensemble. The Curwen hand signs are the key to proper tuning because they indicate how the student should perceive each of the pitch syllables.

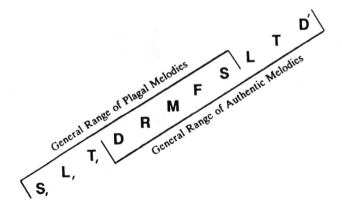

1. *Do* is the foundation sound (home base, security); thus the clinched fist, a symbol of security.
2. *Re* is tuned upwardly toward *mi* as is indicated by the upward tilted position of the fingers with the palm down.
3. *Mi* is the equalizer of the lower tetrachord; thus the palm down and level effect of the hand.
4. *Fa* is tuned downwardly toward *mi* and is indicated by the downward position of the thumb.
5. *So* is tuned upwardly toward *la* as indicated by the upward position of the thumb.
6. *La* is the equalizer of the upper tetrachord as indicated by the relaxed drooping of the fingers.
7. *Ti* (leading tone) is obviously tuned upwardly toward *do* as indicated by the pointed index finger in upward direction.

As students learn to maneuver their voices among the seven different sounds of the diatonic scale, they will be more successful if they are taught to think about the pitch syllables moving in the proper direction as indicated by the Curwen hand signs. This will also eliminate many of the tuning problems that often occur in choral singing.

After completion of phase six, please consult the student literature booklet or various octavos for a series of musical compositions or arrangements that the students may read and perform in concert. These choral selections include only the rhythmic and melodic aspects covered in the first six phases of this sight-singing method.

Preparation 6.1—More Reading Complexities Before the students chant Exercise 6.1, make the following explanation:

1. As the students have been taught, the pattern of a quarter note followed by two eighth notes is pronounced *ta-ti-ti*. The new symbol on the fourth beat of the first measure is an eighth rest. Whenever it occurs in place of an eighth note, students should whisper the word *rest* in place of the first *ti* in the *ti-ti* pattern. The students should initiate the last two beats of measure

1 (quarter note followed by an eighth rest and an eighth note) using the rhythm syllables as *ta-(rest)-ti*.

2. Again, as the students have been taught, the pattern of a quarter note followed by two eighth notes is pronounced *ta-ti-ti*. If the quarter note is tied to the first eighth note (first two beats of measure 2), the first *ti* becomes an *i* (pronounced *ee*) and the pattern is initiated *ta-i-ti*.

3. The dotted quarter-eighth note pattern is chanted identically to the pattern of the quarter note tied to the first of two eighths (*ta-i-ti*). After the students begin to feel the silent beat that falls on the *i*, they should omit the *i* and initiate the dotted quarter note-eighth note pattern as *ta-ti* in a galloping type rhythm. However, in the beginning they must feel the *i* (slight stress of the voice) so that they will assure that the silent beat is present. Take plenty of time drilling the students with the dotted quarter-eighth note pattern because it is one of the more difficult patterns for students to internalize.

4. Refresh the students about the syncopated eighth-quarter-eighth note pattern as exemplified in measure 4 (*ti-ta-ti*). Whenever the quarter note is tied to the final eighth note (beats one and two of measure 5), the students should replace the last *ti* with *i* (*ti-ta-i*). The eighth-dotted quarter note pattern is initiated identically: *ti-ta-i*. Finally, after the students feel the *ti-ta* effect, they may hold the *ta* through the *i* so that it vanishes away.

Preparation 6.2— Fa *and* Ti   Exercise 6.2 is written in two parts. The first part introduces the pitch syllable *ti* as it relates to the childhood melody, and the second part introduces *fa* as it relates to the childhood melody. Displaying the Curwen hand signs, sing each part separately to the students. Then the students may sing each of them.

Applications 6.3 through 6.6—Music Reading   The students should sight-read Exercises 6.3 through 6.6. Use the seven-step music reading procedure delineated in the instructions following Exercise 2.5. In phase three, when step four is reached (which drills the students with the different pitches using the Curwen hand

6.2

so　so　mi　la

so　la　TI　do.

so　so　mi　la.

so　FA　mi　re　do.

signs), begin the step with the following tonal sequence: *so, so, mi, la, so, mi, re, do, so, do', so, mi, do, ti,, la,, so,, la,, ti,, do, fa, mi, re, do, so, la, ti, do.* This sequence will renew for them all the pitches to which they have been introduced so far in the method. When singing the tonal sequence with middle/junior high school students, use the key of D as the sopranos and baritones sing together, then change to the key of B-flat and let the cambiatas sing along. High school students may sing together in unison in the key of D or E-flat.

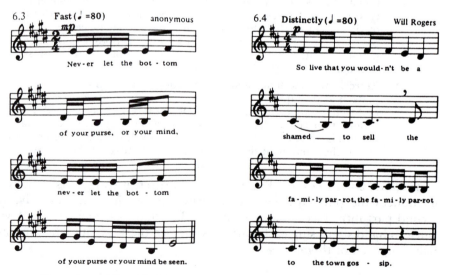

6.3　Fast (♩ =80)　anonymous
mp

Nev-er　let　the　bot-tom

of your purse,　or your mind,

nev-er　let　the　bot-tom

of your purse or your mind be seen.

6.4　Distinctly (♩ =80)　Will Rogers
p

So live that you would-n't be a

shamed ____ to sell　the

fa-mi-ly par-rot, the fa-mi-ly par-rot

to　the town gos - sip.

Exercises 6.5 and 6.6 encompass two pages. Exercise 6.6 contains all the tonal patterns involving *fa* and *ti* as they relate to the other sounds in the diatonic scale. The students should not move to the next phase until they can sing these pages correctly with confidence.

Phase Seven

The rhythmic aspects introduced in phase seven are simple meter, compound meter, mixed meter, the dotted quarter note as a beat unit, the triplet, the eighth note tied to the sixteenth note, the dotted eighth-sixteenth note pattern, the sixteenth-dotted eighth note pattern, and the sixteenth rest. The melodic aspects include three sounds not included in the diatonic scale, *fi, si,* and *ta.* These syllables are used primary for modulating to the key of the dominant and subdominant and for singing in melodic and harmonic minor keys.

After directors have covered phase seven they may consult the student literature booklet or octavo series for compositions or arrangements that students may read and perform in concert. The sight-reading method ends with phase seven. Upon completion, students should be trained to sing at sight most compositions designed for secondary students provided that they are written within the students' unique vocal range and tessitura limitations.

Preparation 7.1—Pulse and Beat in Simple Meter   Exercise 7.1 allows the students to take a more in-depth look at simple meter. Explain the following:

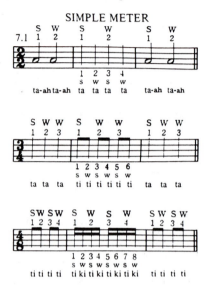

1. As a review, discuss the meaning of the top and bottom number of the meter signature again. The top number indicates the type note which will receive the beat. 2/2 tells the student that there will be two half notes (or any equivalent) in every measure; 3/4, three quarter notes; and 4/8, four eighth notes. Some beats are naturally strong and others are innately weak. In the example, the uppercase S and W indicate the strong and weak beats in each measure.

2. In any meter signature with the number 2 on the top, the first beat will be stronger than the second, as shown in the 2/2 example. The first beat will receive a natural accent.

3. In any meter signature with the number 3 on the top, the first beat will be stronger than the other two beats, as shown in the 3/4 example.

4. In any meter signature with the number 4 on the top, the first and third beats will be stronger than the second and fourth beats, as shown in the 4/8 example. However, the third beat is not quite as strong as the first. The first beat of any measure in any meter signature will always be the strongest.

5. In simple meter, each beat may be subdivided into two pulses, as exemplified in the second measure of the exercise. If the half note receives the beat, the quarter note will receive the pulse (subdivision) of the beat (2/2 example). If the quarter note receives the beat, the eighth note will receive the pulse of the beat (3/4 example). If the eighth note receives the beat, the sixteenth note will receive the pulse of the beat (4/8 example). When considering the two pulses in each beat, the first is always stronger than the second. The lowercase s and w indicate the strong and weak pulses within each beat in the exercise.

6. The uppercase C is another way to indicate 4/4 meter. It means *common meter*

and will be found in place of the fraction meter signature. It indicates that the quarter note receives the beat with four of them (or any equivalent) in the measure. The uppercase *C* with a vertical line running through it is another indication of 2/2 meter. It means *cut meter* and is often called *alla breve*. It indicates that the half note receives the beat with two of them (or any equivalent) in each measure.

    After explaining the exercise, ask the students to clap several measures of each type meter to experience the strong and weak beats.

Preparation 7.2—Pulse and Beat in Compound Meter   Exercise 7.2 introduces compound meter. Explain the following:

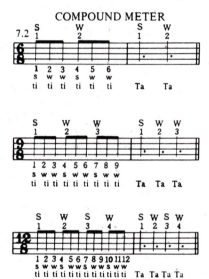

1. When reading compound meter, the meter signature has a different meaning than with simple meter. The top number in compound meter indicates the number of pulses (subdivisions) within a beat that will be in each measure. The bottom number indicates the type note that represents the pulse of the beat. Beats in simple meter are subdivided into two equal pulses. Beats in compound meter are subdivided into three equal pulses. The meter signature in simple meter refers to the number of beats in a measure, and the meter signature in compound meter refers to the number of pulses in a measure.
2. 6/8 meter indicates that there will be six pulses in a measure and the eighth note will receive the pulse of the beat. 9/8 meter indicates that there will be nine pulses in a measure and the eighth note will receive the pulse of the beat. 12/8 meter indicates that there will be twelve pulses in a measure and the eighth note will receive the pulse of the beat. Therefore, there will be six eighth notes (or any equivalent) in a measure of 6/8 meter; nine eighth notes (or any equivalent) in a measure of 9/8 meter, and twelve eighth notes (any equivalent) in a measure of 12/8 meter.
3. Since there are three pulses in every beat of compound meter, there will be two beats in a measure of 6/8 meter (two groups of three eighth notes), as shown in the second measure of the 6/8 example. The dotted quarter note

represents three eighth notes combined; therefore, the dotted quarter note represents (receives) the beat.

4. There will be three beats in a measure of 9/8 meter (three groups of three eighth notes), as shown in the second measure of the 9/8 example. The dotted quarter note also represents the beat as it does in 6/8 meter.

5. There will be four beats in a measure of 12/8 meter (four groups of three eighth notes), as shown in the second measure of the 12/8 example. Again, the dotted quarter note represents the three eighth notes combined.

6. In every beat of compound meter the first pulse is strong and the other two beats are weak, as demonstrated by the lowercase s and w in the examples. The beats within each measure of compound meter are strong and weak in the identical manner they are in simple meter. When there are two beats in a measure (6/8 meter), the first is strong and the second is weak. When there are three beats in a measure (9/8 meter), the first is strong and the other two are weak. When there are four beats in a measure (12/8 meter), the first and third are strong and the second and fourth are weak. These strong and weak beats are marked with the uppercase S and W, in the examples.

7. In compound meter, students should chant the Kodády rhythm syllable *Ta* for dotted quarter note (three pulses combined) in the same way they chanted the syllable *ta* for the quarter note (two pulses combined) in simple meter. The students will be able to differentiate between a *Ta* in compound meter and a *ta* in simple meter when they see them written in uppercase and lowercase letters, respectively.

After explaining the preceding information, ask the students to clap several measures of each type of compound meter to experience the three pulses in a beat and the strong and weak pulses within the beats and measures.

Compound meter with 4 on the bottom of the meter signature (6/4, 9/4, and 12/4) are not explained in detail in this method because they are rarely used in music performed by secondary students. If, perchance, students were to encounter a selection with these meter signatures, teachers should take a moment to explain that the quarter note receives the pulse of the beat. The dotted half note, which is the beat note, represents three quarter notes (pulses) combined.

Preparation 7.3—Mixed Meter   Mixed meter is introduced in Exercise 7.3. Explain the following:

1. Occasionally a composer desires to combine beats of simple meter (two pulses to the beat) and beats of compound meter (three pulses to the beat) in the same measure. This is called *mixed meter*. The duration of the pulse note should remain consistent in all mixed meter.

2. A measure of 5/8 meter contains five eighth notes (or any equivalent). Three of the eighth notes constitute a beat of compound meter (*Ta*) represented by the dotted quarter note, and two of the eighth notes constitute a beat of simple meter (*ta*) represented by the quarter note. Notice the 5/8 example in the exercise.

3. A measure of 7/8 meter contains seven eighth notes. There is one group of three eighth notes and two groups of two eighth notes (*Ta-ta-ta*). See the 7/8 example.

4. If 4 is on the bottom of the meter signature, the quarter note represents the

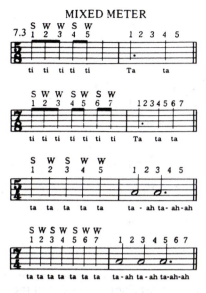

MIXED METER

beat. A measure of 5/4 meter contains five quarter notes (or any equivalent) combined into one group of two (*ta-ta*) and one group of three (*ta-ta-ta*), as shown in the 5/4 meter example. The half note represents the *ta-ta* of two quarter notes, and the dotted half note represents the group of three quarter notes. The duration of the quarter notes should remain consistent.

5. A measure of 7/4 meter contains seven quarter notes (or any equivalent) combined into two groups of two (*ta-ta ta-ta*) and one group of three (*ta-ta-ta*), as demonstrated in the 7/4 meter example.

6. The strong and weak beats and pulses are the same as they are with simple and compound meter.

Ask the students to chant the four different examples using the Kodály rhythm syllables. As the students chant, assist them in understanding the flow of mixed meter by having them to clap their hands on the dotted quarter and quarter notes in the meter with 8 on the bottom and on each quarter note in the meter with 4 on the bottom. The students understanding may be deepened by asking them to clap the rhythm as they chant the rhythm syllables in the exercise.

Preparation 7.4—More Rhythm Complexities   Please explain the following before chanting Exercise 7.4:

1. A *triplet* is one beat of compound meter superimposed into a measure of simple meter. In a measure that contains a triplet, the beat will remain consistent and the duration of the notes will vary depending on the number of pulses in the beat. Obviously, the pulse (subdivision of the beat) will be shorter in a beat which is divided into three portions (the triplet) than it will in a beat divided into two portions (as in a regular beat that is not a triplet). In simple meter where the half note receives the beat, such as in 2/2 meter, the triplet will be three quarter notes. The rhythm syllables for this type triplet are *ta-o-ta*.

2. If the triplet occurs in a measure of simple meter where the quarter note receives the beat, the rhythm syllables are *ti-o-ti* and the triplet will contain eighth notes as shown in the 4/4 example on the second line.

3. As explained in phase five, the eighth-two sixteenths note pattern is chanted as *ti-ti-ki*. The new symbol found on the second beat of the third line is called a sixteenth rest. It occurs in place of one of the sixteenth notes in an eighth-two sixteenth note pattern. It is chanted as *ti-(r)-ki*.

4. If in the same eighth-two sixteenth note pattern the eighth note is tied to the first sixteenth, it is chanted as *ti-i-ki* with a stress of the voice on the *i*. If a dot replaces the tied sixteenth note as shown in the fourth beat of the third line, it is chanted the same way, *ti-(i)-ki*. Eventually the (i) (a slight stress of the voice) may be omitted (but still considered), which results in a galloping rhythmic pattern (*ti-ki*).

5. As explained in phase five, the two sixteenths-eighth note pattern is chanted *ti-ki-ti*. If the second sixteenth note is tied to the eighth, it is chanted *ti-ki-i*. If the dotted eighth note replaces the tied sixteenth note, it is still initiated as *ti-ki-(i)*. The stress of the voice on the (i) may be omitted (but still considered) if desired resulting in simply *ti-ki*. The *ti* should always fall directly on the beat.

Ask the students to chant each of the first two lines separately since they are exemplary of different concepts. The last two lines may be chanted together. Repeat the exercise enough times that the students can perform each of the new complexities successfully.

Preparation 7.5—Fi *and* Si   Explain the following about Exercise 7.5:

1. A flat (♭) lowers a tone one-half step. A sharp (#) raises a tone one-half step. A natural (♮) returns the tone to its original pitch. If the tone has been raised, the natural lowers it. If it has been lowered, the natural raises it.

2. In the third measure of the first example, the pitches that originally were the syllables *fa* and *so* have been raised one-half step as a result of the natural

so so mila so mi   FI SI la

so so mi la   so mi   fi si la

so so mi la   so mi   fi si la

signs that precede them. The naturals raised the tones because they had been lowered due to the key signature. The singers must use the syllables *fi* and *si*, which are one-half step higher than *fa* and *so* when they sing those pitches.

3. *Fi* and *si* must be used in the second line because the first note in the third measure had been lowered as a result of the key signature. The second pitch in the third measure had not been raised in the key signature. To raise both of them a natural precedes the first note and a sharp precedes the second.

4. Also, *fi* and *si* must be used in the third example because the sharps that precede both of the notes raised them one-half step. They were not affected by the key signature.

Sing each of the three different examples demonstrating the sound of *fi* and *si* in the different keys. After, ask the students to sing the examples together. Point out how these two new sounds are related to the childhood chant as demonstrated in the exercise.

Preparation 7.6—Ta   Explain the following to the students:

so so mi la   TA la so   mi

so so mi la   ta la so   mi

1. *Ta* is the sound which is one-half step lower than *ti*.
2. In the first example, *ta* must be used because the flat preceding the quarter note in the first beat of the second measure lowers it one-half step.
3. In the second line, *ta* must also be used because the natural lowers the tone one-half step from the position it held as a result of the key signature.

Sing the two examples using the pitch syllables to the students, then ask them to sing examples together. Notice how the new sound (*ta*) is related to the childhood melody.

Applications 7.7 through 7.10—Music Reading   The students should sing Exercises 7.7 through 7.10. Exercise 7.7 challenges the students to sing *fi* and *si* in one spot immediately followed by *fa* and *so*. Exercises 7.8 utilizes both *ta* and *si* in a chromatic sense. It also contains mixed meter. Exercise 7.9 is written in parts using the triplet (*ta-o-ta*) and the melodic minor key. Exercise 7.10 involves 12/8 meter.

Reference 7.11—The Chromatic Scale Reference 7.11 includes all the syllable names for the ascending and descending chromatic scale. Use it as a reference whenever any of the chromatic sounds appear in the literature the students might be singing.

When a choir or class is performing atonal music, to sol–fa it successfully the singers should pretend that they are in the key of C and use the chromatic sounds the piece requires.

If a singing organization is singing polytonal music, the singers must analyze the various keys through which the music moves, then sol-fa it according to that key. There are several different methods for utilizing the Curwen hand signs with the chromatic scale as advocated by different music educators. The most practical way to indicate the chromatic sounds is to use the regular signs for the diatonic scale with the right hand, then place the left hand in an upwardly slanted *ti* position in front of the right hand to indicate one-half step higher and in a downwardly slanted *ti* position in front of the right hand to indicate one-half step lower. As an example, if instructors desire to indicate the syllable *si* with the Curwen hands signs, they would use the sign for the syllable *so* made by the right hand and then place the left hand in any upwardly slanted *ti* position in front of the right hand, indicating *so* one-half step higher.

References 7.12 and 7.13—Tonic Triads in All Keys   References 7.12 and 7.13 have been included to use as an aid for the singers so that each voice part may relate to the tonic triad in all keys. If teachers will use these charts before they sight-sing a new piece of music literature, the singers can more easily relate to the line, line, line or space, space, space concepts of the tonic triad.

THOUGHTS FOR CONTEMPLATION AND DISCUSSION

1. Relative to music literacy, compare the thought processes of a student who thinks like a musician with one who does not.
2. Do you recommend that students tap their feet as they sing? Why or why not?
3. Do you think eurhythmics would be helpful in learning to sight-read? Why or why not?
4. Which system of sight-reading do you think is best: Tonic sol-fa, numbers, or interval drills? Why?

5. Which system of sight-reading do you think is best: movable *do* or fixed *do*? Why?

6. What are the advantages and disadvantages of using a system to read music compared to learning notes by rote?

BIBLIOGRAPHY

BARTLE, JEAN ASHWORTH. *Lifeline for Children's Choir Directors*. Toronto: Gordon V. Thompson, 1988. (Available through Oxford Press.)

BESSOM, MALCOLM E, ALPHONSE M. TATARUNIS, and SAMUEL L. FORUCCI. *Teaching Music in Today's Secondary Schools*, 2d ed. New York: Holt, Rinehart and Winston, 1980.

COLLINS, DON L. *The Adolescent Reading Singer Teacher's Manual*. Conway, Ark: Cambiata Press, 1977.

COLLINS, DON L. *The Adolescent Reading Singer Student Literature Booklet*. Conway, Ark.: Cambiata Press, 1977.

COLLINS, DON L. *The Cambiata Concept, a Comprehensive Philosophy and Methodology of Teaching Music to Adolescents*. Conway, Ark.: Cambiata Press, 1981.

COOPER, IRVIN, and KARL O. KURSTEINER. *Teaching Junior High School Music*, 2d ed. Conway, Ark.: Cambiata Press, 1973.

EDELSON, EDWARD. *The Secondary School Music Program from Classroom to Concert Hall*. West Nyack, N.Y.: Parker Publishing Co., 1972.

HERMAN, SALLY. *Building a Pyramid of Musicianship*. San Diego: Curtis Music Press (Neil A. Kjos), 1988.

HOFFER, CHARLES R. *Teaching Music in the Secondary Schools*, 4th ed. Belmont, Calif.: Wadsworth Publishing, 1991.

JIPSON, WAYNE R. *The High School Vocal Music Program*. West Nyack, N.Y.: Parker Publishing Co., 1972.

LAMB, GORDON H. *Choral Techniques*, 3d ed. Dubuque, Iowa: Wm. C. Brown Co., 1988.

MARPLE, HUGO D. *Backgrounds and Approaches to Junior High Music*. Dubuque, Iowa: Wm. C. Brown Co., 1975.

MILLER, KENNETH E. *Vocal Music Education, Teaching in the Secondary Schools*. Englewood Cliffs, N.J.: Prentice-Hall, Inc., 1988.

NEIDIG, KENNETH L., and JOHN JENNINGS, eds. *Choral Director's Guide*. West Nyack, N.Y.: Parker Publishing Co., 1967.

ROBINSON, RAY, and ALLEN WINOLD. *The Choral Experience*. New York: Harper's College Press, 1976.

ROE, PAUL F. *Choral Music Education*, 2d ed. Englewood Cliffs, N.J.: Prentice-Hall, Inc., 1983.

SINGLETON, IRA. *Music in Secondary Schools*, 2d ed. Boston: Allyn and Bacon, Inc., 1965.

OTHER SIGHT-READING METHODS

ARKIS, STANLEY, and HERMAN SHUCKMAN. *The Choral Sight Singer*. Carl Fischer.

———. *An Introduction to Sight Singing*. Carl Fischer.

BAUGUESS, DAVID. *The Jenson Sight Singing Course: Vol 1 and 2 and Part Exercises* (in unison, two-part, and three-part using treble and bass clef). Jenson.

BOYD, JACK. *Teaching Choral Sight-reading*. West Nyack, N.Y.: Parker Publishing Co.

CARTER, JOHN, and MARY KAY BEALL. *Sol, Fa, So Good!* Somerset Press.

COLE, SAMUEL W., and LEO R. LEWIS. *Melodia— A Comprehensive Course in Sight Singing*, Vols. 1 and 2. Oliver Ditson.

CROWE, EDGAR, ANNIE LAWTON, and W. GILLIES WHITTAKER. *The Folk Song Sight Singing Method*. Oxford Press.

EDSTROM, RICHARD. *The Independent Singer* (for junior-senior high level). Curtis/Kjos Music.

EHRET WALTER. *See and Sing*, Vols, I, II, III. Pro Art.

HATCHER, W., and A. PETKER. *Choral Skills*. Fred Bock.

NELSON, RUSSELL C. *Visual Solfège*. Kjos Music.

OLVERA, JOHN. *The Ups and Downs of Music*. Kjos Music.

RODBY, WALTER. *Let's Sight-Sing*. Somerset Press.

STEUBING, CARL, and RUFUS WHEELER. *The Sol-*

Fa Book for Chorus and Choir. Scotia, N.Y.: Dickson-Wheeler, Inc.

STONE, LEONARD. *Belwin Chorus Builder, Parts 1 and 2.* Belwin-Mills.

THOMPSON, WILLIAM, and LEROY MCCLARD.

Developing Sightsinging Ability. Nashville: Broadman Press,

WHITLOCK, RUTH. *Choral Insights.* Kjos Music Co.

12

The Unique Sound of Adolescents Singing Together

Indeed, the choral sound of adolescents is different from any other vocal genré. As a current or future choral director in a secondary school, you must recognize and understand this uniqueness. You should not be guilty of carte blanche application of choral techniques recommended for either children or adults to the training of adolescent singers (grades seven through twelve). Many young, enthusiastic music educators take their first choral appointment with the sound of their college or university choir still ringing in their ears. They try to apply the same choral technique used by their revered college directors to their adolescent choirs, only to greet failure.

As there is uniqueness, there is common ground that is apropos to all choral organizations. In this chapter we shall consider some of the common ground and much of the uniqueness. Further, we are going to determine how to *apply* most of the common ground to that uniqueness.

After a few statements to establish the foundations for teaching choral technique, we will contemplate four major areas: (1) diction, (2) choral tone, (3) interpretive factors, and (4) style.

HEADING IN THE RIGHT DIRECTION

How does one become a master choral technician? The answer to that question is *direction*. Choral directors must have a mental image of the sound they want.

They must have the knowledge and experience to achieve that sound through a step-by-step process, and they must have the determination and patience to reach both their short and long-range goals (see Chapter 5).

To develop a mental image of how the adolescent choir should sound, directors should listen to recordings of adolescent singers. They will find it difficult to be successful with adolescent singers when they form their mental image of good choral sound by listening to recordings of adults and children or by singing in university choirs. While in college, undergraduates should observe and critique the secondary choral contests held in the region and the state, attend and critique choral concerts by public school choirs, and observe demonstration video-tapes of master teachers working with adolescent voices. Inexperienced teachers should buy the audio-tape recordings of the live performances of the selected adolescent choirs chosen to sing at regional and national American Choral Directors Association (ACDA) conventions.

Sequential structuring is the secret to success in perfecting the art of teaching. Choral teachers should acquiesce to the same organizational scrutiny when planning how they shall teach choral technique just as they do when teaching sight-reading skills or setting up the type of choral organizations they plan to teach. They should operate under the premise that in the sixth or seventh grade, students know absolutely nothing about choral technique, but by the twelfth grade they will be fully skilled to provide an artistic performance. With this in mind, teachers can formulate a step-by-step approach to successful teaching. This approach will also solve the problem of expecting too much from their beginning groups which is a pitfall for many inexperienced directors (see Chapter 15).

Adolescents learn good choral technique by practicing vocal exercises and then applying what they have practiced to the literature. Chapter 10 introduced a sequential approach that helps directors train singers' vocal instruments (and entire bodies) to produce the best possible individual sound. The approach in Chapter 11 helps directors to learn how to teach good musical skills. This chapter specifies how to train the students through a sequential approach to choral technique. Vocal exercises and descriptive processes are provided that train the students to execute correctly that which has been presented. Directors should introduce each area of choral technique to the students in the same order as introduced here.

The choral rehearsal first must include the exercises delineated in Chapters 10 and 11 or singers will not have the vocal prowess or musicianship to perform well those included in this chapter. Chapter 15 provides a structured approach to organizing and administering the overall choral program into Beginning, Intermediate, and Advanced Choirs. As the vocal exercises and descriptive processes in Chapters 12 and 13 are explored, often directors will find in **bold type,** and enclosed in parentheses, the choir for which the exercises and processes are best suited.

DICTION—THE CHOIR'S ABILITY TO COMMUNICATE THE TEXT

Secondary choral directors believe that good choral diction is essential to accurate choral singing. One must draw this conclusion because of the amount of rehearsal time many of them allot to its perfection. Attempting to improve choral diction probably consumes more rehearsal time than any other aspect of choral singing, possibly because lack of vowel unification and poor enunciation are usually the most obvious problems that beginning directors perceive they should correct. Understanding how to get results when dealing with the intricacies of good tone production takes much more teaching mastery, so directors, particularly those who have a keyboard background, often ignore vocal technique during the first years of their teaching and opt to teach diction instead. Further, improved diction yields the most obvious positive results toward good choral sound, particularly if the choir members are young and inexperienced.

Seasoned directors know they must teach diction, not because it is easy to learn, but because singing is a *vocal* art. The text not only enhances the emotional and intellectual content of the music, but, to many who attend concerts, it is the most important part of the listening experience. It behooves conductors to assure that the words are clear and understandable.

In the early occidental world of Gregorian chant, scriptures, not available in printed form, were wed to melodies so that the singers and the listeners could remember them. From that perspective, music was subservient to the text from the beginning. With the advent of polyphony, music soon dominated, but the Council of Trent intervened and declared that the text must be reemphasized. Several hundred years later, problems of communicating the text became pronounced once more with the arrival of the large nineteenth-century orchestras and dissonant compositional practices of the twentieth century.

There is little need for this conflict pertaining to the dominance of music over text, or vice versa. Both are important, and in the choral setting neither can exist without the other. Since the text is present, the listeners must understand it. Therefore, precise choral diction is a very important element in the choral occurrence.

Vowels

When people speak, unless they have been trained to do so they do not think individual syllables, but whole words. They are not aware of many of the hidden sounds in the words of the English language. Neither are they aware of the purity of vowel sounds. Due to regional dialects, many words are mispronounced.

When students sing, they must sing individual syllables instead of whole words or the listeners will be unable to decipher the distinguishable characteristics of the words, hampering their ability to understand the meaning of the text. Further, students must sing pure vowels, or the dialect of a particular region will be obvious.

The lips, jaw, and tongue play important roles in determining how singers form vowels. In all the following exercises, there must be no tension in the jaw or the tongue and there must be plenty of room inside the mouth.

Dropping the jaw enough to produce a pleasing, resonant sound can be difficult for beginning singers. Since speaking does not require much space inside the mouth, beginners are unaccustomed to complying with such a request when they sing. They may be self-conscious or they may not realize that they are not dropping the jaw. To assist them, directors should ask them to drop the jaw enough to place the index and middle fingers (the palm of the hand should be facing out, not down) between the front teeth. Occasionally, singers will force the jaw down too far, thereby creating tension in the throat or even causing the jaw to lock. This occurrence is rare; usually the opposite action happens in that they do not open the mouth enough.

The tongue should always be relaxed inside the mouth with the tip of it touching the back part of the bottom front teeth. Some singers have a tendency to pull the tip of the tongue down into the very bottom of the mouth causing the tongue to "bunch up" in the center. Others allow the tip of the tongue to rise up, away from the bottom teeth. Both of these actions will adversely affect the vowel sound and tonal resonance and will create unnecessary tension in the throat.

Primary Vowels   The primary vowel sounds are:[1]

ah	ay	ee	oh	oo
[a]	[ei]	[i]	[o]	[u]
ä	ā	ē	ō	o͞o
father	date	meet	obey	boot

Some directors prefer changing the *ay* and the *ee* vowel to *eh* and *ih* respectively.

eh	ih
[ɛ]	[I]
ĕ	ĭ
met	mist

If the striking brightness of the pure *ay* and the *ee* is unpleasing, altering them tends to give the choir a warmer and slightly darker sound. Some directors consider *eh* and *ih* to be primary vowels. These two vowels are introduced in the next section with the secondary vowels.

To train students (**Beginning Choir**) to establish the correct sounds of the primary vowels inside their heads and to learn to be consistent in producing them, use the following exercise:

Exercise 1—Establishing the Primary Vowels

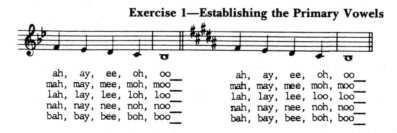

ah,   ay,   ee,   oh,   oo___   ah,   ay,   ee,   oh,   oo___
mah, may, mee, moh, moo___   mah, may, mee, moh, moo___
lah, lay, lee, loh, loo___   lah, lay, lee, loo, loo___
nah, nay, nee, noh, noo___   nah, nay, nee, noh, noo___
bah, bay, bee, boh, boo___   bah, bay, bee, boh, boo___

[1] One of the difficulties in communicating vowel sounds from a written text is the writer's inability to pronounce the proper sound for the readers. To minimize this

Since the exercise begins with the *ah* vowel, ask the students to drop and relax the jaw. The tip of the tongue is touching the back part of the bottom front teeth. When the singers move to the *ay*, they will think the vowel and move the middle portion and sides of the tongue upward and forward ever so slightly. The jaw and the tip of the tongue should not move. As the singers move to the *ee* vowel, the middle and sides of the tongue will move even further upward and forward. There will be a tendency for the jaw to close. The singers should attempt to produce the pure *ee* with the jaw still lowered. If it does move upward, it should be ever so slightly.

Moving to the *oh* vowel requires adjusting the tongue and the lips simultaneously. The tongue should return to the original position as when they sang *ah*. The lips should move to a minimally puckered position, rounding only enough to produce a pure *oh*. Finally, as they move to the *oo*, the lips will pucker even more, with the tongue remaining the same and the jaw still hanging in a relaxed fashion. Even though the *oh* and the *oo* are considered to be closed vowels, the singers should try to keep as much space inside the mouth as possible. Students should incorporate the *sigh* (see Chapter 10) as they initiate the *ah*, which begins each exercise.

If the Beginning Choir is a middle/junior high school choir, or an Intermediate Choir with changing voices, it will be better to vocalize the sopranos and baritones together beginning on the F octave above (girls) and below (boys) middle C, and moving upward by one-half steps to E-flat or F one octave higher. Then vocalize the cambiatas alone beginning on D (above middle C) and moving upward by one-half steps to A (above middle C). Senior high school choirs with no changing voices may vocalize together in unison-octaves beginning on the F octave above (girls) and below (boys) middle C and moving upward to F or G one octave higher.

It is very important for the students to master the purity of these primary vowels before moving to the remaining exercises, because all other vowels are modifications of these.

Secondary Vowels   The secondary vowels in the English language that have been altered slightly from the primary vowels described previously are:

aw	*eh*	*ih*	*a*	*oo*
[ɔ]	[ɛ]	[I]	[æ]	[U]
ô	ĕ	ĭ	ă	o͞o
Lord	met	mist	cat	took

Three other sounds may be considered to be secondary vowels:

---

difficulty, four different methods are provided to assure that the reader understands exactly what sound is desired: (1) a phonetic spelling of the sound, (2) the International Phonetic Alphabet (IPA), (3) the diacritical markings found in most dictionaries, and (4) a word example that contains the sound. Pertaining to the chart which follows, some singers promote the *I* as a primary vowel sound instead of the *AH*.

uh	*uh* (schwa)	*er*
[ʌ]	[ə]	[ɜ]
ŭ	ə	u
love	sofa	term

Some believe that none of these three vowels is a pleasant sound to the musical ear. Therefore, they do not use them, or if they do, they color them away from what they consider to be the inherent abrasive sound. For some, it is accepted practice to sing the *uh*, as in *love*, as if it were an *aw* (as in the word *lot*, except slightly darker).

The *uh*, or *schwa*, is a neutral sound that in always unaccented; therefore, when sung at the end of a word, it vanishes away, or when sung at the beginning of a word, the emphasis falls on the syllable which follows it. If singers must elongate the sound, and occasionally they do because it must be held over several beats, they most often treat it as if it were a dark *aw*.

Changing the *uh* sound to a dark *aw* is also a controversial practice. Many directors prefer the purity of the *uh* sound and will maintain it because they want the sung text to sound as much as possible like the spoken text. When encountering the following words, beginning directors must decide if they want their choir to sing:

an-ge*h*l or án-gu*h*l for the word *angel*
aw-gain or *uh*-gáin for the word *again*
áw-round or *uh*-róund for the word *around*
Christ-ma*w*s or Chríst-mu*h*s for the word *Christmas*
ex-cel-le*h*nt or éx-cel-lu*h*nt for the word *excellent*
gi-ve*h*n or gí-vu*h*n for the word *given*
hea-ve*h*n or heá-vu*h*n for the word *heaven*
judg-me*h*nt or júdg-mu*h*nt for the word *judgment*
king-da*w*m or kíng-du*h*m for the word *kingdom*
mo-me*h*nt or mó-mu*h*nt for the word *moment*
o-pe*h*n or ó-pu*h*n fo r the word *open*
pe-ta*w*l or pé-tu*h*l for the word *petal*
sad-ne*h*ss or sád-nu*h*ss for the word *sadness*
si-le*h*nt or sí-lu*h*nt for the word *silent*
ta-ke*h*n or tá-ku*h*n for the word *taken*
wood-la*w*nd or wóod-lu*h*nd for the word *woodland*

Using the same descending scale, beginning pitches, ranges and instructions as Exercise 1, sing each of five basic secondary vowels (**Beginning, Intermediate, and Advanced Choirs**):

The tongue, lips, and jaw should respond as they did in Exercise 1. The only difference will be the thought process. Think the modified vowels instead of the primary vowels.

Exercise 2—Establishing the Secondary Vowels

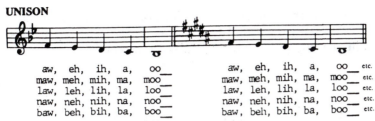

UNISON

aw,	eh,	ih,	a,	oo __	etc.		aw,	eh,	ih,	a,	oo __	etc.
maw,	meh,	mih,	ma,	moo __	etc.		maw,	meh,	mih,	ma,	moo __	etc.
law,	leh,	lih,	la,	loo __			law,	leh,	lih,	la,	loo __	etc.
naw,	neh,	nih,	na,	noo __			naw,	neh,	nih,	na,	noo __	etc.
baw,	beh,	bih,	ba,	boo __			baw,	beh,	bih,	ba,	boo __	etc.

The Troublesome R   The American *r* must receive special treatment. Untrained singers often treat it as a vowel, creating a very unpleasant sound. Directors often ask singers to omit it when it occurs as a final sound, such as in the word *winter*. They would sing the word *winter* as if it were *win-tuh*.

Flip the *r* (one turn of a trilled *r*) when it occurs in words or syllables beginning with *thr*, such as in *through, throw,* or *three*, or if it occurs between two vowels, such as in *the rain* or *occurring*.

Vowel Relationships

The following chart should be helpful to teachers in illustrating to their students how all the vowels are related beginning on the left (brighter, ringing, and more pointed vowels) with the *ee* vowel, moving to the right (darker, rounder, and richer vowels) and ending with the *oo* vowel. The chart will also be helpful if it is reproduced and placed as a poster in the choir room. Directors may refer to it as they deal with various vowel sounds in the literature the choir will be singing.

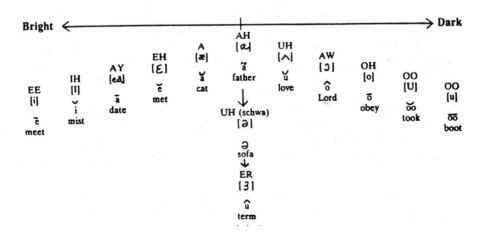

Diphthongs and Triphthongs

Diphthongs are vowels that contain two sounds: one that singers sustain and one that they allow to vanish away. In fact, two of the primary vowels may be diphthongs, depending on how they are used in a word:[2]

ay	*oh*
[ɛI]	[ou]
ā + ē	ō + o͞o
date	go
da-eete	goh-oo

In the word *go* the *oh* vowel is a combination of a sustained *oh* and a vanishing *oo*. That same vowel, *oh*, however, is a single sound when used in the word *obey*.

Actually, in the English language, singers use six different combination sounds. They are:

ah + oo	*ah + ee*	*ee + oo*	*aw + ee*	*oh + oo*	*a + ee*
[au]	[ai]	[iu]	[ɔi]	[ou]	[eI]
ä + o͞o	ä + ē	ē + o͞o	ô + ē	ō + o͞o	ā + ē
now	sigh	you	voice	know	rave
nah-oo	sah-ee	ee-oo	vaw-eece	knoh-oo	ra-eeve

In each of the above combinations, except the *ee + oo*, the first vowel sound is the one singers sustain when they are required to hold the sound over several beats. Notice that the *ee + oo* combination reverses the sound they sustain, requiring them to hold the second vowel sound. They should produce the short (vanishing) sound, *ee*, and then move immediately to the sustained sound, *oo*.

The neutral sound, *uh* [ə], as in the word *sofa*, occasionally serves as the vanishing part of a combination when replacing the *r*, as in the words *air* [ɛə], *ear* [Iə], and *sure* [Uə].

There are few *triphthongs* (three combinations of sound) worth noting. With most triphthongs, the first and last sounds vanish and the middle sound is sustained, such as in the words *yea* (ee-a-ee) [iei] and *wow* (oo-ah-oo) [uau].

Following is a short four-part song (**Beginning, Intermediate, and Advanced Choirs**) that, when practiced, will help the singers learn to deal proficiently with diphthongs. Middle/junior high or senior high school groups may sing it since the tenor part is within the comfortable singing tessitura of most cambiatas and the bass tessitura is high enough for early adolescent baritones. Since it is a contrapuntal selection, if there are no singers for one or more of the three lower voice parts, directors may omit them. There are two lines for each part. The top line is engraved in the way a singer would see the

---

[2] Pertaining to the following vowels, singers who use *I* as a primary vowel should note that it is also a diphthong. It is a combination of the sustained *AH* and the vanishing *EE*.

text and notes on the printed octavo. On the second line, the notation indicates how singers should think the individual syllables of diphthongs as they sing. The text contains all six of the possible combinations of diphthongs. It will be easier to learn if the singers will practice and memorize their parts by reading the upper line. After it is memorized, instruct the singers to sing the piece by reading the individual syllables and rhythms indicated in the second line of each part. It will become abundantly clear how important each syllable is when singing diphthongs. The song begins on page 258.

Consonants

There are two groups of consonants: those that are voiced (they have pitch) and those that are voiceless (they have no pitch).[3] The voiced consonants are:

b	*d*	*g*	*g*	*j*	*l*
[b]	[d]	[dʒ]	[g]	[dʒ]	[l]
big	done	gentle	gone	jump	love

m	*n*	*ng*	*r*	*s*	*th*
[m]	[n]	[ŋ]	[r]	[z]	[x]
money	nuts	bring	run	easy	those

v	*w*	*x*	*zh*
[v]	[w]	[gᶻ]	[ʒ]
voice	will	exempt	pleasure

Voiceless consonants are:

c	*c*	*ch*	*f*	*h*	*k*
[k]	[s]	[tʃ]	[f]	[h]	[k]
call	center	chosen	fiddle	how	kazoo

p	*q*	*s*	*sh*	*t*	*th*
[p]	[kw]	[s]	[ʃ]	[t]	[θ]
pep	quit	sing	ship	tiny	thin

wh	*x*
[ʍ]	[ks]
what	apex

Consonants add a sense of vitality and life to the music. Singers should exaggerate them, particularly when they fall at the end of a word. Often, generally when singing in legato style, singers drop the consonants when trying

---

[3] Some choral educators tend to subdivide the categories to indicate which consonants are (1) sustained voiced—*m, n, ng, l, r, v, z, zh, th* (as in *thee*), *w, y,* and *b* (when at the beginning of a word); (2) voiced explosives—*b, d, g,* and *j*; (3) voiceless explosives—*p, t,* and *k*; (4) sibilants—*f, s, sh, ch, th* (as in *thin*); and (5) aspirants—*h.* Others classify them according to the portion of the vocal instrument that generates them, such as (1) labial (lips)—*b, p, m, w,*and *wh*; (2) lower lip and upper teeth—*f* and *v*; (3) tongue and upper gum or teeth—*th, t, d, n, l, s, z, sh, r, j,* and *ch*; (4) back of the tongue—*k, g,* and *ng*; and (5) others—*q, u, h,* and *x.* Most secondary choral students seem to be able to deal with them more proficiently if they are lumped into two basic categories, voiced and voiceless.

Exercise 3—Practicing Diphthongs

Now Sigh With the Voice
So You Know the Crowd Will Rave
(SATB acappella)

Don L. Collins

to emphasize the legato line. An overused but very helpful cliché is: "Sing as long as you can on the correct vowels and add the consonants and vanishing final syllable of diphthongs in a quick, crisp, intense fashion."

When executing a consonant or the unsustained vowel of a diphthong that begins a word (such as the *ee* in the word *you*), students should place them slightly before the beat (similar to a grace note) so that the sound of the sustained vowel will fall precisely on the beat. Exceptions to this approach are those consonants which take only a microsecond to render (*k, t, p, b, d,* and *g*). They usually fall squarely on the beat.

Directors should listen closely to the sounds of the consonants *S* and *Z* because if the chorus is large or if the singers have a tendency to overemphasize them, the effect can be quite obnoxious. It may be necessary to ask all the singers to minimize their emphasis on those consonants. When there are an abundance of sibilant sounds in a piece, some directors will appoint a select group of singers to execute them. The remaining singers leave them out of the words completely.

Directors should place even greater emphasis on the consonants when the choir is singing marcato or staccato styles because, to be effective, both styles depend on distinct and precise articulation and accent.

Unique Practices That Will Improve Diction

In an attempt to assure that they are properly exaggerating the final consonants, some choral singers pronounce the final consonant on a word, such as the *d* in the word *Lord*, with an overstated *uh* on the end, resulting in the word sounding like *Lor-duh*. The word *wall* might sound like *wal-luh* or the word *tell* becomes *tel-luh*. In choral singing, this procedure is not necessary and is undesirable. With a little practice a singer can develop the ability to emphasize the *d* without making it sound as if it were an added syllable.

When singing legato style, students should push one sound into the next without leaving any gaps. Often directors admonish singers to put the ending consonant of one word on the beginning of the following word, such as in the phrase "Go tell it on the mountain." Singers should execute it as "Go tel li ton the mountain."

Gordon Lamb cautions directors about this practice, however, because sometimes it alters the meaning of the words. For instance, "her beautiful eyes" may sound as if the choir is singing "her beautiful lies" or the words "your ear" may sound like "your rear."[4] Along the same line Paul Roe points out that the phrase "help you" may sound like "hell pew," or "can't you" results in "can chew."[5]

When the same vowel in two different words must be repeated, such as in the phrase "so on we go," singers should separate them (*so* and *on*, in this case).

[4] Gordon H. Lamb, *Choral Techniques*, 3d ed. (Dubuque, Iowa: Wm. C. Brown Co., 1988), p. 135.

[5] Paul E. Roe, *Choral Music Education*, 2d ed. (Englewood Cliffs, N.J.: Prentice-Hall, Inc., 1983), p. 93.

If they do not separate the two *o's*, the phrase sounds like "sone we go," which does not make sense. These examples show that no matter how legato directors desire for their choirs to sing, they must teach them to separate the words in some cases.

Separation is also necessary on certain occasions so that the listeners will understand the meaning of the text, particularly when the singers repeat certain words in the sentence. In the text, "Sing alleluia, alleluia to the Lord," singers should stop the sound between the *ah* vowel at the end of the first *alleluia* and the beginning *ah* vowel of the second *alleluia*.

If a sentence speaks directly to someone, such as in the sentence, "Lord, God, Almighty, hear our prayer," singers should stop the tone between *Almighty* and *hear* to enhance clarity in meaning. It is not necessary, however, to separate the flow of the phrase between the words *Lord* and *God* nor between *God* and *Almighty*, unless there is a strong specified purpose for doing so or a need for special emphasis.

One of the most intolerable culprits of poor diction is the stressing of the wrong syllable in a word. This is very easy to do when the unaccented syllable of a word falls on the upper note of an ascending interval or if it falls on the strong, normally emphasized portion of the measure or beat. Choir members should read aloud in unison the text of any work they are performing to determine the natural flow of the words. This practice will help them to preserve properly accented syllables when they begin to sing.

Probably the best known example of improperly stressed word syllables are the first several measures of the "Hallelujah Chorus" from *Messiah*. Invariably, singers will sing the first two *Hallelujahs* with the accent on the *jah* (almost "popping" it). When singers speak the word, they find that the natural syllabic accent falls on the *lu*. In this case, the *lu* occurs on the third beat, which also is the where the strong musical accent occurs.

Some directors ask their choir members to either underline or place a check above or below the word (or syllable) in each measure that should receive the stress. This procedure unifies the choir's efforts and helps the choir to communicate the message of the text properly.

Special Problem Words

Here is a list of words that often are mispronounced, followed by a suggested proper pronunciation according to accepted practice:

WORD	INCORRECT PRONUNCIATION	CORRECT PRONUNCIATION	IPA SPELLING
a (before consonant)	*ay*	*uh*	[ʌ]
beautiful	beau-*tee*-fahl	beau-t*ih*-f*uh*l	[bIutIfʊl]
behold	b*ee*-hold	b*ih*-hold	[bIhoʊld]
believe	b*ee*-lieve	b*ih*-lieve	[bIliv]
Bethlehem	Beth-*lay*-ham	Beth-l*ih*-h*uh*m	[bɛxlIhəm]
can	kin	c*a*n	[kæn]
creation	cre-a-sh*ah*n	cre-a-sh*uh*n	[kriIən]

WORD	INCORRECT PRONUNCIATION	CORRECT PRONUNCIATION	IPA SPELLING
deliver	d*ee*-li-ver	d*ih*-li-ver	[dɪlɪvə]
dew	d*oo*	d*ih-oo*	[dɪu]
divine	d*ee*-vine	d*ih*-vine	[dɪvɑɪn]
emptiness	emp-t*ee-nehss*	emp-t*ih*-nuhss	[ɛmptɪnəs]
for	fur	f*aw*	[fɔə]
forget	fur-g*it*	f*awr*-g*eht*	[fɔəgɛt]
forgiveness	fur-give-nu*hss*	f*awr*-give-ni*hss*	[fɔəgɪvnɪs]
Galilee	Gal-*ih*-lee	Gal-*uh*-lee	[gæləli]
get	g*iht*	g*eht*	[gɛt]
glory	gl*aw*-ry	gl*oh*-ry	[glɔrɪ]
government	go-ver-ment	go-ver*n*-ment	[gʌvʌrnmɛnt]
honor	ho-n*ohr*	ho-n*uhr*	[ɑNə]
kindness	kind-nu*hss*	kind-ne*hss*	[kaɪndnɛs]
listen	lis-*ehn*	lis-*unn*	[lɪsən]
Lord	Lo*hr*d nor La*hr*d	La*wr*d	[lɔrd]
manger	man-g*ihr*	man-g*uhr*	[meɪndʒə]
Mary	M*ay*-re	M*eh*-ry	[mɛrɪ]
mountain	moun-'n	mount-*ihn*	[mauntɪn]
new	n*oo*	n*ih*-oo	[nɪu]
night	nite	n*ah-iht*	[naɪt]
our	are	*ah-oo*-r	[auə]
poor	p*ohr*	poor	[pʊə]
pretty	p*uhr*-*dy*	pr*ih*-tee	[prɪti]
redeemer	r*ee*-dee-mer	r*ih*-dee-mer	[rɪdimə]
remember	r*ee*-meem-ber	r*ih*-mehm-ber	[rɪmɛmbə]
repose	r*ee*-pose	r*ih*-pose	[rɪpoʊz]
roof	r*uh*f	ro*o*f	[ruf]
spirit	spear-*uht*	sp*ih*-ri*ht*	[spɪrɪt]
triumphant	tri-umph-*uh*nt	tri-umph-*ant*	[traiʌmfænt]
virgin	vir-g*uhn*	vir-g*ihn*	[vʌrdʒɪn]
wheel	we'll	*hw*eel	[ʍil]
when	win	*hw*ehn	[ʍɛn]
worship	wor-sh*uh*p	wor-sh*ihp*	[wʌrʃɪp]
your	*yoh-uhr*	*yoo-uhr*	[junə]

Latin Pronunciation

Much of the choral literature sung by secondary choirs will be in Latin. It is recommended that the introduction to Latin pronunciation begin with the **Beginning Choir** and that directors include some simple Latin selections in their repertoire, even if the students are middle/junior high school age. The study of the pronunciation of other languages (German, Italian, French, and Spanish) should begin in the **Intermediate and Advanced Choirs**. Pronunciation guides for these languages are not included in this text. Directors may refer to dictionaries that include foreign language pronunciations or to Robinson and Winold's text, *The Choral Experience*.[6] It provides a very succinct and easy-to-understand synopsis of those four languages.

[6] Ray Robinson and Allen Winold, *The Choral Experience* (New York: Harper's College Press, 1976), pp. 126–46.

Students must understand that the pronunciation of church Latin (Italianized), which they will be singing, differs from the classical Latin that they may be studying in Latin class (although, regrettably, very few students study Latin any more).

Some directors advocate that the singing of Latin should precede the singing of English. They argue that the vowels are purer and there are fewer consonant sounds in Latin. Therefore, it is simpler to pronounce and easier to sing correctly than the English language. Few question the premise that once choir members study and sing Latin, their English pronunciation and overall approach to diction improves.

Latin Vowels

There are only five Latin vowel sounds. Once the students learn them they need not concern themselves with secondary vowel sounds. Each time they see the written vowel they know that the sound is always the same.

a (ah)	e (eh)	i (ee)	o (aw)	u (oo)
[a]	ae (eh)	y (ee)	[ɔ]	[u]
ä	oe (eh)	[i]	ô	o͞o
father	[ɛ]	ē	dog	boot
Alleluia	ě	see	Gloria	Factum
	set	Christe		
	Hodie	Kyrie		
	saecula			
	coelestis			

Note that the sound *eh* may be written three different ways: *e, ae,* or *oe*. The sound *ee* may be written two ways: *i* or *y*.

Theoretically, diphthongs (vowels with one accented and one unaccented vowel) do not occur, but there are many words in which singers sound two vowels back to back, resulting in a sound similar to a diphthong except that both vowels receive equal emphasis when spoken. There are several different possible combinations. Here are examples of three:

au (aw + oo)	ua (oo + ah)	ii (ee + ee)
[ɔu]	[u ɑ]	[ii]
ô + o͞o	o͞o + ä	ē + ē
now	water	we eat
laudate	quam	filii

Consonants in Latin   Unlike the Latin vowels, many Latin consonants have more than one pronunciation, as indicated below. Singers pronounce those consonants not included in the following descriptions as they do in English, except the consonant *w*, which is not used in Latin.

C

C is pronounced as if it were a *k* in all cases except when is comes before *e, i, y, ae,* and *oe*. In those cases it is pronounced as if it were *ch* as in the word *church*. The *cc* (double *c*) is also pronounced as the *ch* in *church*.

G

G is always pronounced with a hard sound as in the word *get* except when it precedes *e, i, y, ae,* and *oe*; then it is pronounced with a soft sound as in the word *gentle.*

H

H is silent, never aspirated as in English, except in two words, *Mihi* and *Nihil,* where it is pronounced as a *k* (*Mee-kee* and *Neekeel*).

J

J is pronounced like the *y* in the word *yes* and is amalgamated into the vowel sound that follows it. The Latin pronunciation of the word *Jerusalem* is *yeh-roo-sah-lem.*

R,X,Z

R is always pronounced with a flip of the tongue. *X* is pronounced as if it were *ks* as in the word *excellent. Z* is pronounced *dz* as in the words *adzuki bean* (an annual bushy bean grown in China and Japan for food). The Latin pronounciation for *Lazarus* is *Lah-dzah-roos.*

EX

When *ex* precedes a vowel, it is pronounced *egs* as in the Latin word *exalto,* which sounds *egg-sahl-taw.* When it precedes a consonant, it is pronounced *eks* as in the word *excellent.* The Latin word *resurrexit* is pronounced *reh-soo-reck-seet.* Directors who instruct their choirs that the common Latin word *excelsis* is pronounced as in the English words *egg shells,* as *egg-shell-sees,* are disseminating misinformation. The correct pronunciation of the word is *eck-shell-sees.*

TI

TI is pronounced as if it were *tsee,* as in the words *tsetse fly,* when it is followed by a vowel and preceded by any letter except *t, s,* or *x.* An example is the Latin word *gratia,* pronounced *grah-tsee-ah.* When it is followed by any vowel and preceded by the letter *t, s,* or *x,* it is pronounced as it is in English with the common sound *t* as in the word *toe.* A Latin example is *modestia,* pronounced *maw-dehs-tee-ah.*

TH and CH

TH is always pronounced as a *t* since the *h* is silent. *CH* is always pronounced as a *k.*

GN

This is the same sound as the *n-yee* in the Spanish, language such as in the word *señor.* A close English equivalent is the sound in the words *dominion* or *canyon.*

The Latin example is *Agnus*, pronounced *Ah-ñoos*. The *gn* receives the *n-yee* sound except when it occurs at the beginning of a word, then it receives a hard *g* sound followed by an *n*. The pronounciation of the Latin word *Gnaeus* is sounded *Guh-neh-oos*.

SC

SC is always pronounced as an *sk* as in the word *skip*, unless it comes before an *e, i, u,* or *ae*; then it is pronounced *sh*, as in the word *ship*.

CHORAL TONE—THE CHOIR'S VEHICLE OF EXPRESSION

All choirs do not sound the same because directors can make preferential choices concerning areas of choral singing. On several aspects of choral sound, however, most directors agree. Directors want to avoid a breathy sound. They want the pitches to be in tune, the tone to be free, vital (at least to some degree) and supported, and the words to be uniformly pronounced. Beyond these agreements, that which is correct ceases to be absolute when one compares the many different ways in which choirs sing. There is debate concerning vowel color, vibrato, extremes in consistent loudness and softness, style, use of vocal registers, and which areas of choral technique should receive the most emphasis, among others. This section covers those aspects of choral tone that are accepted as necessary to good choral singing and some of the areas that are controversial. Directors will need to decide which of the preferred areas they want to emphasize and how to apply them to their specific choral needs.

Directors are somewhat limited in the type of sound they can expect and the type of literature they may choose to sing due to the inherent nature of the adolescent voices, particularly if some of the students are experiencing vocal mutation. Due to the *mutational chink*,[7] some adolescent voices will be breathy no matter how good their vocal technique. This is not to say that adolescents who sing with a breathy tone cannot improve their clarity; they can, with improved vocal technique.

The overall scope of the dynamic levels provided by adolescent choirs will be less than that of adults. Adolescents cannot produce a free, vital tone in the same degree of loudness or softness as older singers, no matter how good the vocal technique, even though the degree of freedom will ameliorate as the technique improves.

Adolescents should not try to sing the demanding vocal ranges, both high

---

[7] This is a natural occurrence in adolescent girls' voices, in which the front part of the glottis vibrates cleanly while the posterior ends of the vocal folds, bound by the arytenoid cartelage, do not close at all. This gap between the arytenoids is called a "mutational chink." It represents a weakness of the interarytenoid muscles (probably due to pubertal growth) and is indicated by the breathy quality typical of young girls' voices. See William Vernard, *Singing, the Mechanism and the Technic* (New York: Carl Fischer, Inc., 1968).

and low, required in some literature due to the immaturity of their voices. They should not sing works that require the massive sound needed to penetrate the output of a full orchestra unless the chorus is very large and the orchestra relatively small.

Although a natural vibrato appears in the voices of some adolescents who use good vocal technique, directors should not expect all their singers to sing with vibrato.

Well-trained adolescent choirs under the batons of competent conductors can handle most other aspects of good choral tone. Directors can expect artistic performances from their choirs, even those in the sixth and seventh grade, if they motivate them, teach them well, and give them enough time to rehearse.

Several different schools of choral thought (procedures of John Finley Williamson, Father William J. Finn, F. Melius Christiansen, Fred Waring, Joseph J. Klein, Douglas Stanley, John C. Wilcox, and Robert Shaw) that emerged with the a cappella tradition in the early part of the twentieth century (see Chapter 2) have influenced directors of American choral groups. Directly or indirectly, one or more of the originators of these approaches advocated most of what follows in this chapter. The information may be presented differently, but it still has its roots in their work. Few of them focused on the adolescent voice, but their shadows loom like enormous father-figures over the classrooms in junior and senior high schools everywhere. Secondary directors must learn to adapt these giants' choral techniques to the needs of adolescent voices. Certainly they cannot ignore them. The specific approach (or derivation of that approach) directors choose to teach will depend on their concept of choral sound and their personal preferences, but those choices were first promulgated by these choral giants. Howard Swan provides a detailed description of each of these schools of thought pertaining to choral tone in Chapter 1 of the second edition of *Choral Conducting Symposium*.[8] A careful study of that chapter is essential for the success of serious choral directors.

Blend and Balance

After you have taught the sequential approach to proper vocal technique (Chapter 10) and the exercises given in the diction section of this chapter, you are ready to unify the choral sound as the voices sing together. Singers' energetic, resonant, free, ringing tones (that they can control dynamically) are the results of good vocal technique. Since students progress at different rates, there will be times in which some have better technique than others. The utopian goal is for all the students to be equally competent vocally. If teachers reach this goal, all voices are equally strong and resonant, and the individual qualities of voices appear to dissipate when they are singing together. A good blend results without further concern. Since directors seldom reach that goal, they must devise ways to camouflage the sounds of certain singers whose voices might be brighter, harsher, more raucous, and less controllable due to lesser technical abilities.

---

[8] Harold A. Decker and Julius Herford, eds., *Choral Conducting Symposium*, 2d ed. (Englewood Cliffs, N.J.: Prentice Hall, Inc., 1988) pp. 7–68.

Some directors deal with blend and balance through audition. They intentionally do not choose singers who have large voices, unique vocal problems, or characteristically identifiable voice qualities. This approach may work well in a professional or university setting, but in secondary school, directors should involve as many students as possible in the choral program (see Chapter 15). This approach defeats that purpose.

Unified Vowel Color   In the section on diction much was said about the sound of vowels in the English language and how to pronounce and sing them correctly. Unified vowel formation effectively promotes good blend and balance. Directors should determine their preference in vowel colors then teach the students to perform them uniformly.

Exercise 4 (**Beginning and Intermediate Choirs**) will train students to achieve unified vowel color in four-part singing. Achieving pure vowel color is the principal purpose of this exercise, as it was with the first exercises in the section on diction. This four-part exercise allows directors to concentrate on the unification of vowel color with harmony rather than unison-octaves as in the earlier exercises. Voices on different parts and singing at different tessitura levels provide a different challenge to directors than when all the voices are singing unison/octaves. Teach each part by rote. After singing the exercise in the key of C as indicated, move up one-half step and sing it in the key of C-sharp. Continue this process until the choir has reached the key of A or B-flat then move back down by half steps to the the key of C. Ask the singers to sing the exercise in one breath and to keep it very legato. Set a tempo fast enough to complete one key level on one breath.

Exercise 4—Establishing Unified Vowels—Four Parts

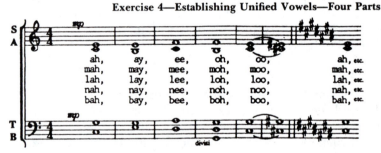

Arranging the Singers   For good blend among individual voices, directors should specify the standing (or seating) arrangement (**all three choirs**). Directors should arrange the singers in sections for both practice and performance unless they are intentionally choosing a scrambled (quartets) formation (see the section on seating and standing formations in Chapter 13)[9]. Due to certain timbre and acoustical phenomenon, some voices blend better standing by or between certain individuals than they do standing by or between others.

---

[9] Early adolescents (middle/junior high school age), unless they have received extensive vocal training as children, do not have the vocal skills nor musicianship to operate in scrambled formation (quartets).

To determine the proper formation, stand five singers from the same section side by side in a row. Counting from the left to the right, place the two singers who have the most prominent voices in positions two and four in the row. Ask the five of them to sing a neutral vowel (use a pure *ah* or *eh*) on a unison pitch. Choose a pitch in the comfortable area of their voices. Then, standing at least twenty feet in front of the singers, listen to determine how well the voices are blending. Next, move the two stronger voices to positions one and five and listen for the blend. Finally, place the two stronger voices in positions three and four and listen for the blend. It will be obvious after listening to the voices in the three different positions which position produces the best blend. Directors may use other position arrangements if they desire. Repeat the same procedure, except choose a pitch, to be sung forte, that is in the upper limits of the comfortable singing area of the voices. The results may change at that pitch level, causing some adjustment to the formation.

Directors should conduct this procedure with groups of five singers until they have arranged all members of the four sections of the choir. When placing the singers on the risers, directors may need to adjust the formations, but they can easily do so on the spot. If directors choose to stand in mixed formation (quartets), they may use the above procedure with each quartet.

Lack of Vocal Technique   When there are singers with weak vocal technique present, good blend and balance are more difficult to attain. This is particularly true if their part moves above their comfortable singing tessitura. Stronger voices or singers with unique vocal problems often protrude when the part they are singing is high. Until most of the singers' vocal technique becomes uniform and consistent, directors should choose choral literature with parts that are comfortable and easy to sing (**Beginning and Intermediate Choirs**).

Dynamic Changes   Dynamic changes often destroy good blend and balance. Some voices tend to crescendo more dramatically than others because forte for them is louder than forte to others. To train the singers to blend when gradually getting louder and when singing fortissimo, practice the following exercise (**Beginning and Intermediate Choirs**). As the singers practice this exercise, directors need to alert those students/sections whose voices "stick out" so that they will become sensitive to the problem and adjust at strategic points when they sing the literature. The ranges for this exercise are suitable for both junior and senior high school students. The high A may be too high for some junior high school girls. Sing it slowly and very legato.

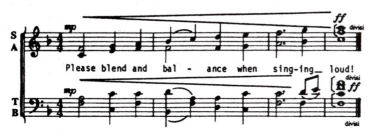

Exercise 5—Controlling the Crescendo

Misclassification of Voices　Misclassification of voices also will affect blend and balance. Older adolescents (senior high school) basses singing tenor and altos singing soprano will have the most obvious negative affect. Directors should be sure they have classified the voices properly. As delineated in Chapter 9, when dealing with singing groups containing changing voices, directors will find that boys in the first phase of change (cambiatas) and boys in the second phase of change (baritones) singing the same part will not blend well, although it is a common practice in much literature written for early adolescents. The vocal timbre of these two voice types is different, so each should have a separate part. With the same amount of boys, the balance in an SSCB setting will be better than with an SAB setting because the one part for boys places the cambiatas in the lower part of their range and the baritones in the upper part of their range, so neither group uses the best pitches of their voices. By dividing them into two parts written specifically for the comfortable singing area of their voices, they will balance the girls much better.

Section Size　Obviously, the number of singers in each section affects the balance of the group. The proper ratio of singers is controversial, however. Some directors recommend that each section have the same number of singers (should be considered only in the **Advanced Choir**). Others recommend that a choir have about three-fifths girls and two-fifths boys, or perhaps even two-thirds girls and one-third boys[10] (works better for the **Beginning and Intermediate Choirs**). The smallest section may be the tenors since they sing in the upper area of the modal voice much of the time. This produces a more powerful sound; therefore, fewer voices are needed. Most chamber or madrigal groups have an equal number of singers in each section, but since the best singers in the choral program are usually chosen to be in these groups, the dynamic quality and size of their voices are more nearly the same.

　　Unfortunately, with nonselect groups (and even some select groups) there are more girls than boys available from whom directors may choose singers. Directors have to select more girls than boys for their groups. Since boys' adolescent voices are stronger than girls' voices at the same age, this lack of equality in numbers may not adversely affect the proper balance in choral sound.

　　The general rule of thumb is that the better the vocal technique of the singers, the more likely it is that the number of singers in each section should be equal (**Advanced Choir**). If the vocal technique of the singers as a whole is not strong, probably there will need to be more girls than boys, more basses than tenors, more changing voice baritones than cambiatas (if it is an early

---

[10] Roe, *Choral Music Education*, p. 29.

adolescent group), and more sopranos than altos to achieve the best balance (**Beginning and Intermediate Choirs**).

Vowel Color and Modification

Uniformity of vowel color affects blend. Without it, good blend is but an illusion. Further, vowel modification in the upper regions of the voice helps camouflage the protruding voices and offers release from vocal tension, both of which are essential to good blend and balance.

Vowel color is one of those aspects of choral technique that is influenced by directors' preferences. It is not in the purview of this chapter to delineate all the different approaches to vowel color that choral musicians have propagated for the last six decades.[11] When directors use the approach to vocal technique described in Chapter 10, the results will be bright, ringing vowels with resonant, forward placement much akin to those produced by the Italian's singing style. This is true because the exercises begin with the open Italian *ah, eh,* and *ee* then proceed to the darker, more closed vowels.

Directors who desire a rounded, richer, and less brilliant color in vowels should choose to use the exercises in Chapter 10 with *oh* and *oo*. Some directors of children and adolescents desire the purity of the *oo* vowel and vocalize with it extensively because it produces a beautiful, flutelike tone conducive to training the head voice. It also promotes lightness in singing and enhances blend.

Since the natural quality of most adolescent voices, even though they may be using proper technique, is rather light and lacks the depth of adult groups, some directors desire to darken the sound slightly to make it have more depth. This is quite acceptable, particularly on more somber, legato passages and where a specific style dictates a darker sound. To do so, directors should color the pure vowels of *ah* toward *aw,* the long *i* toward *ah* (some consider the *i* to be a diphthong anyway, *ah* followed by *ee,* so it is easy to color it toward the *ah* vowel), *a* toward *eh, ee* toward *ih, oh* toward *oo,* and *oo* toward *uh* (as in the word *put*).

Higher pitches require vowel modification (change of vowel color) particularly in soprano voices. Singers must open the closed vowels (*oo, ee,* and *ih*) in the upper areas of the head voice or vocal tension will occur. Some directors teach their sopranos to sing an *ah* vowel on any pitch above F (top line, treble clef), no matter what word they are singing. Others take a more moderate view but require the lowering of the jaw (which immediately opens the vowel) when they produce tones above F.

When tenors sing in the upper area of the modal (full) voice, the tendency to yell the tone with a wide-open sound or to protrude the chin and "grab the tone with the throat muscles" often occurs. If the dynamic level is forte, some directors require tenors to modify the open vowels (*ah, oh,* and *eh*) slightly

---

[11] Study the different approaches to vowels and tone production that affect vowels as described in Decker and Herford, *Choral Conducting Symposium,* pp. 7–63. Note particularly the approaches that John Finley Williamson, Father William J. Finn, and F. Melius Christiansen took toward vowel color.

toward the *aw* or *oo*, and to produce the tone with a "grunt" sensation so the tone will be more pointed. By using the analogy that the tone should travel like a bullet instead of a shotgun blast and go to a specific point leaving a small hole instead of massive one, the wide-open approach to the vowel is often corrected. This approach is more beneficial for boys whose voices are mature. Teachers should not attempt to apply this special vowel modification approach to the upper model voice with boys whose voices have just changed. Teaching boys to sing falsetto (head) when tones seem too high and tensive is more advantageous with adolescent voices. Also, if the dynamic level is piano, the best solution in a choral situation to the wide-open sound or tensive high pitch is to use the falsetto voice no matter what the age or vocal maturity of the student.

To train male students to use the falsetto readily, vocalize them on descending (SFMRD) five-tone scales (begin with the *oo* vowel, advance to the *oh*, and progress to the *ah*), starting the exercises high in the falsetto and moving downward chromatically. Begin on E-flat, top space, treble clef, actual pitch. Do not begin around E-flat directly above middle C because some boys cannot readily experience falsetto in that area. They will attempt to produce the E flat above middle C with modal (full voice) phonation. Beginning an octave above that assures that they must use falsetto, since falsetto phonation is the only way the vocal folds will phonate in that octave of the male changed voice. Request them to maintain the falsetto as long as possible as they descend. They may be able to move downward to approximately A below middle C (if they sing very lightly) before they will, of necessity, have to produce the tones in modal voice.

Intonation

Teaching adolescents to sing in tune will demand many hours of the director's time. Before they try to teach the exercises in this section, they must have begun (and be well on their way) to teach the students musicianship (Chapter 11) and proper vocal technique (Chapter 10). Mastering musicianship and vocal technique will solve many of the students' intonation problems.

However, there are some specific tonal and nontonal factors that cause intonation problems. The non-tonal ones are:

1. Poor acoustics—Singing in a room that is too live may cause sharping, whereas singing in a room that is too dry may cause flatting.
2. Temperature—A room that is too hot and humid or too cold and damp may affect intonation. A stuffy and poorly ventilated room (lack of oxygen) will also affect intonation.
3. Inability to hear—The standing or sitting formation may affect the students' ability to hear all the pitches in a chord. This is particularly true if the room is too dry or too live.
4. Fatigue—Singing for too long a time, particularly if the tessitura of the music is high, or beginning a rehearsal with tired singers will generate poor intonation (usually flat singing).
5. Frustration—When most of the singers become frustrated for one reason or another the intonation will suffer. Directors should change pieces and return to the initial piece later when the mood of the choir has changed.

6. Tempo—When students try to read new music at a fast tempo, they must give so much concentrated attention to the notes and rhythm that they do not have time to contemplate intonation. Fast tempos often do not give enough time for the singers to find the pitch. Slow tempos, particularly if the dynamic level is piano, require more support and breath control. The sense of rhythmic drive is not clear, so the singers may go flat. Directors may desire to master the intonation of a piece at a moderate tempo and then gradually work toward the correct one.

7. Dynamics—Singing too loudly causes students to oversing or push the tone. This results in either sharping or flatting. Singing softly, unless the tone has vitality, often results in flatting. Directors should set up good intonation at a dynamic level less than fortissimo and more than pianissimo before attempting the ultimate (at which time vocal technique must be very secure).

8. Boredom—Directors who spend too much time drilling or singing one piece repeatedly will create intonation problems.

9. Director harassment—When choirs are not singing in tune, directors, through frustration, often resort to scolding or harassing the singers to make them work harder. This approach usually makes the situation worse, and good intonation will not result.

Several tonal factors also result in poor intonation. One is the inability to hear with one's inner ear that which is being heard with other's outer ear. Faulty tone production will cause students to hear a pitch inside their heads that will be sharp to the one the listeners hear. This usually occurs when the tone is not properly focused.

Using the piano as a teaching instrument rather than an accompanying instrument precipitates poor intonation. Students should learn to sight-sing and deal with harmony a cappella so that they will adapt to the natural tuning and tendencies of the pitches. The tuning of the piano is equal tempered. Students who rely on the piano to learn their music often sing on the underside of *re, mi, la, and ti* and slightly above *fa.*

The third of the chord is always the most difficult to tune. Note that *mi* is the third of the tonic chord, *la* the third of the subdominant chord, and *ti* the third of the dominant chord, and relate this to the mistuning described in the previous paragraph. Directors should keep this in mind when practicing homophonic (harmonically oriented) music and help the singers to adjust and learn to tune when necessary.

The tonal tendency is for *re* to tune upwardly toward *mi, fa* to tune downwardly toward *mi,* and *ti* to tune upwardly toward *do* (this occasionally causes some singers to sing *do* sharp). Directors should keep these tendencies in mind as they deal with polyphonic music or when the choir is singing in unison (or unison-octaves). Directors who use the Curwen hand signs as part of their rehearsal technique automatically remind the students about the tendency of these tones each time they use any of the signs for active tones, because the signs indicate the direction the tone should tune.

Robert Shaw and others (particularly French directors) advocate developing absolute pitch as a means to improving intonation. Shaw encourages choral singers to have a tuning fork on their person at all times, sounding it from ten to thirty times a day, each time attempting to sing the pitch before they "flog" (Shaw's term) the fork (**Beginning and Intermediate Choirs**). After developing pitch memory for one specific pitch, Shaw instructs them to follow the same procedure daily, except to produce a specific interval in relation to their memorized pitch (**Advanced Choir**). He encourages them to continue that process until they have mastered all the intervals. He might ask the choir to sing a chord in a particular key (such as the subdominant chord in E-flat) without first having heard it played on the piano (**Advanced Choir**) or to sing, without receiving any pitch at all, any dissonant or consonant harmonic interval of his choosing (**Advanced Choir**).

Singing whole-tone and chromatic scales will help develop good intonation habits. After the students have conquered the exercises in Chapters 10 and 11 as well as those already provided in this chapter (during their tenure in the **Beginning and Intermediate Choir,** in most cases), they should begin work on the following exercises (**Advanced Choir**). These exercise are not recommended for middle/junior high school students due to their difficulty and improper ranges. Cambiatas have difficulty singing a full octave scale because it moves too high when sung at actual pitch and too low when sung one octave lower. (Exceptions are the scales beginning on G, G-sharp, and A below middle C; those three scales are in most cambiatas' comfortable singing area).

Exercise 6—the Whole-Tone Scale

Do   Re   Mi   Fi   Si   Li   Do

Do   Ta   Lo   Sa   Mi   Re   Do

Quoted here is the ascending whole-tone scale followed by the descending form. When singing the scale, hold the first and last notes as indicated so that the singers can internalize those pitches since they will serve as an anchor for the purpose of tuning. Use the *Sol-fa* syllables because they will help them remember each specific pitch. Directors should use the following sequential approach in helping the students improve their intonation. Do not move to the succeeding step in the sequence until the current step is mastered. Always assign the beginning pitch of each scale the syllable *do*.

1. Practice singing the ascending whole-tone scale in unison (boys singing an octave lower than the girls) beginning on pitch C until the students can sing the proper syllables in tune by memory.
2. Practice Step 1 beginning on all semitones from B-flat up to F.
3. Practice singing the descending whole-tone scale in unison-octaves beginning of pitch C until the students can sing the proper syllables in tune by memory.
4. Practice Step 3 beginning of all semi-tones from F down to B-flat.

5. Practice singing the ascending scale followed immediately by the descending scale beginning on pitch C until the students can sing them in tune by memory.

6. Practice Step 5 beginning on all semitones from B-flat up to F.

7. Practice the ascending scale, singing it as a round between the girls and boys. Begin with the sopranos and altos. When they reach the syllable *mi*, have the tenors and basses begin on *do*. The girls should hold *high do* until the boys arrive at *high do*. At that point *high do* should be perfectly in tune. All intervals except the last two will be major thirds. Do not move from one third to the next until each interval is in perfect tune.

8. Practice Step 7 beginning on all semitones from B-flat up to F.

9. Practice the girls singing the descending scale against the boys singing the ascending scale beginning on pitch C. When they reach the fourth pitch, *sa* for the girls and *fi* for the guys, they should be singing a perfect octave. Be sure it is in tune before moving to the next interval.

10. Practice Step 9 beginning on all semitones from B-flat up to F.

Exercise 7—The Chromatic Scale

A similar sequential approach is required in mastering the intonation of the chromatic scale. Again, do not move to the succeeding step in the sequence until the current step is mastered.

1. Practice singing the ascending chromatic scale in unison (boys singing an octave lower than the girls) until the students can sing the proper syllables in tune by memory. If the students cannot sing the entire octave in tune, divide it into two segments. Practice singing chromatically from do to *so*. When they have mastered the intonation for those eight tones, practice singing from *so* to *high do*. When the intonation on the upper six tones is mastered, combine the two. Another technique is to have one group sing *do* and hold it while another group sings the chromatic scale against it. They should check each interval against *do* to assure that it is in tune before moving to the next interval.

2. Practice singing the descending chromatic scale in unison until the students can sing the proper syllables in tune by memory. Directors may use the same tuning techniques that were employed in Step 1.

3. Practice singing the ascending scale followed immediately by the descending scale until the students can sing them in tune by memory.

4. Practice singing the ascending and descending chromatic scale with the girls beginning on G (assign the syllable *do* to the pitch G) above middle C and the boys beginning on middle C (assign the syllable *do* to the pitch C). The results will be parallel fifths. The students should keep each harmonic interval perfectly in tune as they move from one semitone to the next.

5. Ask the girls to sing a descending chromatic scale in thirds against an ascending chromatic scale (also sung in thirds) by the boys. The sopranos begin on E (top space, treble clef) and the altos on C (above middle C) and descend chromatically to the lower octave. The basses should begin on C (below middle C) and the tenors on E (below middle C) and ascend chromatically to the upper octave. The scales are to be sung simultaneously. Assign each beginning pitch the syllable *do*.

Vibrato

Vibrato emerges in adolescent voices as the singers mature and as their vocal technique develops. It is not[12] uncommon to find singers in their third or fourth year of college who still sing with a straight tone. Conversely, occasionally one can find middle/junior high school singers who have a very natural, pleasing vibrato. There are those who believe that the presence of a vibrato at an early age is an indication that the singer is vocally gifted. Those who have it can sing naturally well, while those who do not may need extensive training to develop their vocal gifts.

Vibrato is an outcome of the fluctuation in energy, as dictated by intermittent nerve impulses, to the muscles that control tone production (cricothyroids). At one time singers believed that the diaphragm controlled the vibrato, but studies indicate that this is not the case.[13] Usually, the vibrato is visually apparent in the soft palate, tongue, and even the jaw, although a trembling jaw is evidence of lack of control.

Aurally, the vibrato is a fluctuation in pitch (variance of at least a semitone), intensity, and timbre. Unless, due to special training, the listener can hear the variation of pitch, the ear usually picks up a mean pitch that is in tune with the rest of the music. One perceives the other pitches as variance in vocal timbre and intensity. Most music makers and music lovers prefer a tone with vibrato. In fact, players of most orchestral instruments, particularly those of strings and winds, imitate the vocal vibrato.

The frequency of the vibrato is normally between six and seven times per second. When it becomes irregular, too wide, too fast, or too slow, it is offensive. Good vocal technique is the only cure for an offensive vibrato. Luckily, directors of adolescent choral groups usually do not have singers with offensive vibratos. The lack of vibrato in singers' voices is more likely to concern them. In most cases the maturation process and good vocal training (breath control) will alleviate that problem.

Some directors advocate that a straight tone promotes better intonation, particularly in the a cappella choral literature from the Renaissance period and in the dissonant harmony that dominates the Contemporary period. They also argue that it is more stylistically appropriate for the literature from those periods. Others believe that it may be vocally unhealthy to sing without vibrato

---

[12] The double negative—*not* and *un*—are used intentionally.

[13] Archie Wade and Clarence Sawhill, *The Anatomy of a Vibrato*, 16mm film, 12 min. with sound (Los Angeles: Radiology Department, Medical Center, University of California, 1960).

because it appears to be counter to the natural muscularity used in good vocal production. Apparently, there is no scientific evidence to support either argument. No one knows absolutely that the vibrato was absent in the voices of the adult singers in the Renaissance period. Nor is it clear that the performance of music from either period is aesthetically more pleasing or better in tune (as the ear perceives it) with a straight tone than with a vibrato enhanced tone. There are no apparent adverse consequences from singing with a straight tone, nor are there any scientific data to support such a premise. Some singers of country music and other popular styles who produce a straight tone often have vocal problems, but in most cases poor vocal technique and extreme vocal abuse cause these problems.

Traditionally, it is quite acceptable for early adolescent choirs and boychoirs to sing without vibrato due to the ages of the singers. College and university singers who continue this practice are criticized because the use of a straight tone limits their vocal potential in some ways. Although a straight tone may enhance the choral blend, intonation, and the ability to sing pure, controlled pianissimos, the sound usually suffers from lack of vibrancy, is often breathy, and contains very few thrilling fortissimos.

INTERPRETIVE FACTORS—THE CHOIR'S PERSONALITY

When choral teachers encounter a musical score, it is their responsibility, by using their imagination and expertise, to instruct and train their singers in such a way as to turn printed symbols and words into musical sounds. It is to be hoped that those sounds will be pleasing and inspiring to the listeners. The director's expertise in interpretation is the component that helps the choir communicate to the audience what the composer wrote. It is the director's imagination that creates a rendition of the selection that is unique, beautiful, exciting, inspiring, or meaningful (or any combination thereof). This section provides insight into those interpretive factors that help directors and students perform in a technically correct and aesthetically pleasing manner.

Dynamics

The degree of dynamic subtleties displayed by a choral group directly relates to the singers' vocal prowess. In most cases only those singers in the advanced choir will be vocally proficient enough to sing fortissimo or pianissimo well, and even some of them will be unable to do so. Trying to sing too loudly before the technique is secure results in a raucous, harsh, tensive tone, as trying to sing too softly results in a weak, anemic, thin, breathy tone that lacks vitality.

On a scale of one to ten with one representing pianissimo and ten representing fortissimo, directors should train students in the **Beginning** and **Intermediate Choirs** to sing between three and seven, never to singing a tone as loudly or as softly as they think they are capable of producing. By the time they reach the **Advanced Choir**, they may attempt dynamic levels between two and nine. Only as adults with excellent vocal technique will they be able to sing dynamic levels from one to ten.

Directors have three basic responsibilities pertaining to proper dynamics with adolescent singers: (1) to make the singers become cognizant of various dynamic levels in singing, (2) to teach them how to achieve those dynamic levels, and (3) to choose the best dynamic level for the style and markings of the piece they are singing.

Singers in the **Beginning** and **Intermediate Choirs** should deal with three dynamic levels. Referring to the levels by their designated names will help the students learn to respond effectively to proper dynamics.

1. *Free and easy*: the level in which all the singers are producing a free, vital, resonant tone—mezzo piano or mezzo forte.
2. *Loud and exciting*: slightly louder than level one—forte.
3. *Soft and vital*: slightly softer than level one—piano.

By limiting the singers to these three levels of dynamic contrasts, directors may run the risk of their **Beginning** and **Intermediate Choirs** being somewhat boring to the listener, but the beauty of choral tone and the security found in limiting vocal damage to their young voices is well worth the gamble.

Practice the following exercises with the **Beginning** and **Intermediate Choirs** to help them become aware of the three dynamic levels they should use and how to produce these levels. The ranges of each part are such that early or older adolescents may sing them. Teach the parts and words by rote. A choir will need to have them memorized so that they can concentrate on initiating the dynamic levels properly.

Exercise 8—Controlling Dynamics at Three Levels

Exercise 8A is written in the comfortable part of the singers' voices. The ability to sing each dynamic level will be easier with this exercise than with the two that follow.

A

In Exercise 8B the boys will have more difficulty than the girls controlling the dynamic level since they are singing in the upper area of their voices. They will need to be careful not to cover the girls at the "Sing loud and exciting" (forte) dynamic level. They may need to use falsetto phonation when singing at the "Sing soft and vital" (piano) dynamic level to produce a free and unconstricted tone.

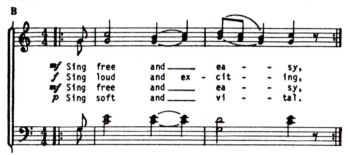

Exercise 8C places the girls in the upper area of their voices and the boys in a lower, more comfortable area of their voices. The girls will need to display more control on both the "Sing loud and exciting" (forte) and the "Sing soft and vital" (piano) dynamic levels.

By the time the singers reach the **Advanced Choir,** they should be skilled in five dynamic levels of singing.

1. *Free and easy*: the level in which the tone is free, vital, and resonant—mezzopiano or mezzoforte.
2. *Loud and exciting*: slightly louder than level one—forte.
3. *Strong, full and thrilling*: slightly louder than level two (but not as loudly as the singers think they are capable of singing)—fortissimo.
4. *Soft and vital*: slightly softer than level one—piano.
5. *Light, quiet, and stunning*: slightly softer than level four (but not as softly as they think they are capable of singing)—pianissimo.

Practice the following exercises with the **Advanced Choir** to help them to produce their five dynamic levels with good choral tone.

Exercise 9—Controlling Dynamics at Five Levels

Ensemble Precision

Ensemble precision is an aspect of choral singing that may require much attention and time, particularly if the ensemble is large. However, there are

three cardinal rules that can provide success almost immediately if directors train choral groups to respond to them. One rule addresses beginning together; another, staying together; and the third, ending together. The rhythm of the beat governs each of them.

Rule 1—Beginning Together   Directors should teach students *always to breathe together on the beat (or portion of the beat) that precedes the beat on which the choir (or section) enters.* In most cases entrances occur on the first or last beat of the measure. If the choir (or section) enters on the first beat of the measure, they should take a unison breath on the last beat of the preceding measure or on the director's cue beat if it is the initial entrance of a piece (see A, which follows). If the choir (or section) enters on the last beat of measure, they should take a unison breath on the beat that immediately precedes it (see B), which will be the first beat in duple meter, the second beat in triple meter, or the third beat of quadruple meter. On less frequent occasions when the choir (or section) must enter on the last portion (or pulse) of the beat (commonly called the offbeat), teachers should train them to take a unison breath on the first portion (or pulse) of the exact beat of which they enter (see C and D).

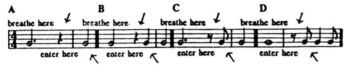

In most cases good directors will be able to give definite cue beats before entrances, particularly if the music is homophonic. If the music is polyphonic and the entrances are rapid and numerous, such as in double choruses or choruses accompanied by orchestra, it may be difficult for directors to cue each entrance. Then it is each section member's responsibility to be aware of the beat and to take their unison breaths without cue.

Rule 2—Staying Together   Directors should teach students *to internalize the persistent pulsation that permeates the music (the beat) and allow it to pervade their bodies and their beings.* When members of ensembles have difficulty singing together with precision, usually it is because conductors do not maintain a definitive, perpetual tempo of the beat or because students have not concentrated (centered in) on the tempo of the beat to the point that it has become a part of their "internal clock." It does not govern them as they sing.

Exercise 10—Internalizing the Beat

Directors should practice briefly the following exercise that helps students to internalize the beat as a warm-up before they perform a selection. Together the students conduct twenty silent measures without stopping, using the specific tempo of the selection they are about to sing as designated by the director. During the first four measures the students try to internalize the tempo of the beat as they conduct with the director. During the next twelve measures the students close their eyes and continue to conduct, feeling the beat they should have internalized. Finally, during the last four measures the students open their eyes and observe if their conducting pattern is identical to those about them.

When students perform this exercise initially and for several practices thereafter they will be unable to maintain a persistent beat throughout the twelve measures in which they close their eyes, finding they are not together during the last four measures. Eventually, after several weeks of practice, if the students are astute, they will open their eyes and find they are all conducting together. This accomplishment will enhance their ability to sing together throughout an entire selection, even if there are fermatas and rubatos present, because they will be able to return to the original tempo when they indeed internalize it. During the first several times the students practice the exercise, directors might desire to use fewer than twelve measures while the students close their eyes. The fewer the measures conducted with their eyes closed, the more apt the students are to be together during the final four measures.

This exercise also helps students to maintain steady tempos with pieces that have a tendency to gain momentum as they progress.

Rule 3—Ending Together   Directors should teach students *always to cut off directly on the beat or final portion (pulse) of the beat.* If the music *does not* require singers to reenter on the beat following the cutoff, they should hold the last note of the phrase its full value and cut off on the beat immediately following. For instance, if they are holding a half note the duration of the first two beats of the final measure, they should cut off on the third beat (see A, which follows). If they are holding a whole note the duration of four beats in a measure, they will cut off on the downbeat of the next measure (see B).

If the music *does* require the singers to reenter on the beat following the cutoff, they should hold the tone they are singing until the last portion (pulse) of the final beat of its value, release, breathe, and reenter on the following beat. For instance, if they are holding a half note the duration of the first two beats of a measure but must reenter on the third beat, they must hold the half note for one and one-half beats, cut off on the last pulse of the second beat, breathe in rhythm, and reenter on the third beat (see C). If they are holding a whole note the duration of four beats in a measure but they must re-enter on the first beat of the following measure, they must cut off on the last pulse of the fourth beat, breathe in rhythm, and reenter on the down beat (see D).

Once again, with or without the assistance of a conductor, students should follow Rule 3, which will enable them to render ensemble precision at the end of phrases. Teaching the singers to release and breathe in rhythm is the secret to success.

Phrasing

Phrasing, in this context, refers to the appropriate time for a choir to stop the choral tone. Further in the chapter, in the examination of mood in singing, the subject of how to turn a phrase is addressed. Effective interpretation and communication of artistic musical and textual thoughts are a direct result of effective phrasing.

Choirs must execute phrases together. It is terribly disconcerting when all singers take a breath together except one or two who "carry over" and do not breathe. Before singing, directors should ask the students to mark their music so that they understand where they should or should not breathe. When the music is homophonic and all four sections of the choir are singing the same text simultaneously, the choir should phrase as one large unit. When it is polyphonic, sections usually phrase individually.

Since musical and textual phrases may require different phrasing points, it may be difficult to determine which of the two is more important. Punctuation marks serve to guide proper phrasing. There are very few musical reasons to ignore a period in the text. A comma, on the other hand, may be ignored, particularly if stopping the tone to acknowledge the comma is musically awkward. Directors must be careful to preserve the legato line. Stopping the tone for every comma easily can destroy it. However, if preserving the legato line distorts or changes the meaning of the text, the musical meaning should yield.

Rhythmic Drive

American choral directors must credit Robert Shaw for pointing out the importance of rhythmic awareness and the effect of the *pulse* on the choral performance. "Rhythmic discipline is built first and surest upon the feeling of the smallest common rhythmic denominator. A chorus cannot hold a moderate 4/4 rhythm without a supreme awareness of the four sixteenth notes inherent in every quarter note."[14] Performances without this acute awareness of pulse lack a sense of energy, vitality, intensity, drive, and urgency currently expected by informed musicians as a result of the choral standard projected by Shaw. It is impossible to copy Shaw's technique. Many have tried and failed. Directors can learn from what he has done, however, and incorporate aspects of his choral technique into their rehearsals with positive results. The final product will not be the same as Shaw's, but a unique choral happening ensues from combining the technique, personality, expertise, and teaching ability of each director with the technique, personality, commitment and youthful vitality of the adolescent choir members.

Howard Swan provides an excellent description of Shaw's approach in *Choral Conducting Symposium*, edited by Harold Decker and Julius Herford.[15] It is advisable to study that work because it provides a more in-depth perspective to the approach presented here.

Earlier in this chapter reference was made to the student's "internal clock" when describing the importance of developing the ability to be governed by the rhythm of the beat to achieve effective ensemble precision. That internal clock (rhythmic awareness) should also effectuate the rhythmic drive and vitality inherent in any good choral performance. Each student should not only internalize the presence and influence of the beat (a quarter note in common time) but also the pulse (subdivision of that beat, the eighth note in common time) and its subdivision (the sixteenth note). Exercises 11 and 12 will assist students in executing a choral performance that has rhythmic drive and vitality.

---

[14] Howard Swan, "The Development of a Choral Instrument," in *Choral Conducting Symposium*, 2d ed., edited by Harold A. Decker and Julius Herford (Englewood Cliffs, N.J.: Prentice Hall, Inc., 1988), p. 38.

[15] Ibid., pp. 36–42 and 51–54.

Exercise 11—Developing Rhythmic Drive

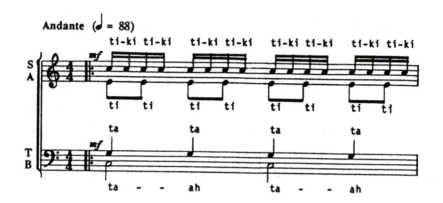

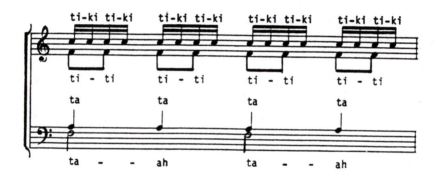

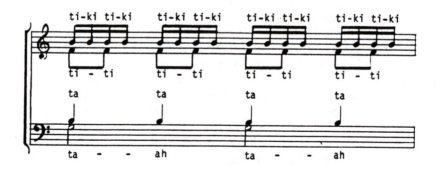

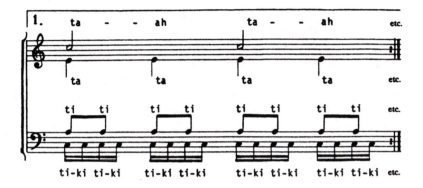

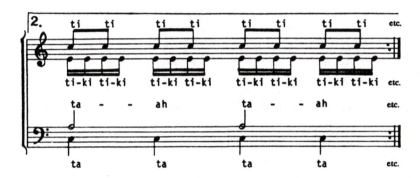

Directors may teach Exercise 11 by rote, one part at a time. Notice that at the first ending, baritone/basses are to render sixteenth notes; tenors/cambiatas, eighth notes; altos, quarter notes; and sopranos, half notes. Sing it again (each section sings the same pitches they sang the first time through). Continue the process by switching the note values to different parts until the choir has sung the progression four times, each time with each section performing a different note value. Directors may extend the exercise by singing the exercise over and over, each time moving up or down the chromatic scale until the parts become uncomfortable to sing. The students will have a tendency to rush the beat, so it might be advantageous to sing it with the metronome until they really begin to internalize the rhythmic drive.

After the choir has become acquainted with the exercise, directors should suggest to the singers that its purpose is not merely to *understand* there are four sixteenth notes inherent in a quarter note, but to *feel* that relationship inwardly (to internalize it) so that it results in a tone that becomes alive with rhythmic vitality and drive.

Directors should apply this technique of rhythmic drill to the literature they are performing. It is particularly appropriate with music that demands vitality and excitement in singing, but directors may also use it to awaken the rhythmic life inherent in slower, more legato pieces.

Exercise 12 is an example of how students should sing choral parts with each part subdivided so that they may experience the inherent rhythmic value of the pulse. In this case the subdivision is sixteenth notes. Directors may begin with larger or smaller note values, depending upon what type of note represents the beat and the ability and age of the singers. The upper line of notes in each part represent the original notes in the selection. The lower line of notes show the subdivision into sixteenth notes. The tune is Samuel Ward's "Materna," usually sung to the text "America, the Beautiful."

Tempo

One of the conductor's paramount responsibilities is to maintain a steady, even tempo, exclusive of ritards, accelerandos, rubatos, and other expressive markings. Even when these markings occur, conductors should be able to return to the original tempo. Serious conductors develop an inherent sense of correct tempo. They never have to use a metronome, even to set the tempo before they begin a piece.

The personality of the director may affect choirs who consistently and unintentionally accelerate or ritard tempos. Choirs conducted by directors with tensive, urgent personalities tend to rush whereas choirs with "laid-back," relaxed directors tend to lag. Further, tensive, uptight directors usually set faster tempos under the pressure of the concert than those practiced in rehearsal, while laid-back directors may set slower tempos in concert.

Keyboard accompanists also influence choirs' tempos. Accompanists may

Exercise 12—Developing Rhythmic Drive in the Literature

AMERICA, THE BEAUTIFUL
Tune - "Materna"

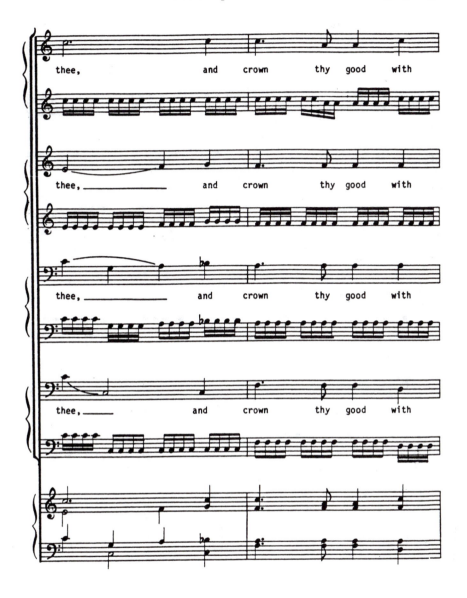

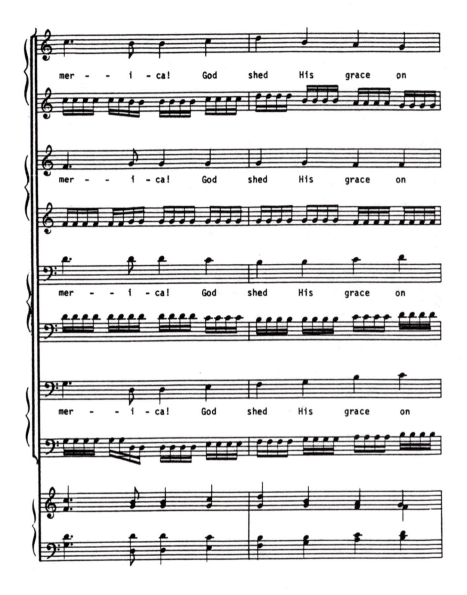

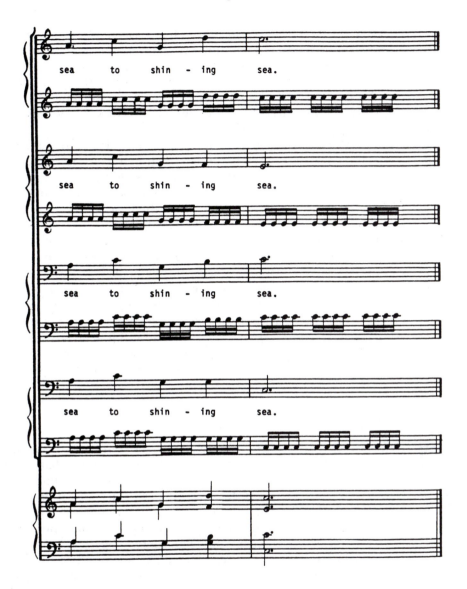

accelerate tempos if the music requires a strong sense of being "on task," that is, they have to work hard to execute the piece. If they can play the music with ease, the tendency to rush is not as prevalent.

Secondary students often associate dynamic level with tempo. When a dynamic level is pianissimo they automatically slow down the tempo, and when a tempo is fortissimo they accelerate the tempo. Directors should be aware of this tendency and maintain a steady tempo as necessary.

It is easy for choirs to rush or lag tempos due to the music's intrinsic rhythmic content. Accelerating tempos often occur when music contains reiterated eighth notes or dotted eighth and sixteenth note patterns. Retarding tempos result from singing repeated half and whole notes when choir members are not alert or when they are unaware of the subdivisions of the beat. Rehearsing Exercises 10, 11, and 12 will help choirs execute consistent tempos.

Additionally, choirs can develop a psychological sense (feeling) about the music they sing. Directors can teach them to execute a piece with a sense of holding back or relaxing to counter accelerating tempos, just as they can teach them a sense of moving forward or urgency to counter retarding tempos.

After several rehearsals where the choir has learned all the notes and rhythmic patterns and they have applied the proper choral technique, a selection will "settle in" on the desired tempo and the music will achieve a disciplined freedom from restraint. At that point the music becomes alive. It contains a type of free spirit and controlled intemperance inherent in an artistic and entertaining performance.

Modes of Choral Singing

There are four basic modes of choral singing. In this context, *mode* is not just a special means of articulation. It is an approach to the music that continues throughout the piece (or section of the piece) and results in a distinctive effect the choir achieves as they perform the work. If performed well it may create a notable ambience for the listener to enjoy while hearing it.

The first is the *staccato* mode. The choir achieves the detached effect by using a diaphramatic attack on each note. The singers separate more than one pitch on a single syllable of a word with the aspirated sound of the letter H. The aspirate may separate as few as two pitches on a syllable or as many as occurs in an extended melisma. The outcome of this mode of singing will be a light, buoyant, transparent sound. Clarity and cleanliness of tone is the goal in this mode of singing. Directors may use analogies such as "walking on eggs" and "dancelike tones" to convey the desired effect. Exercise 18, The Staccato Arpeggio, in Chapter 10 will train the singers to execute this style.

The second mode of choral singing is the *legato* mode. Smooth, peaked phrasing and constant intensity and energy of sound characterize this mode. Directors may relate the idea of a freight train with the engine in the rear pushing each of the boxcars as the train moves forward. Each note is analogous to a boxcar and the breath is the engine. Singers press each note value into the next. There is never a severance of tone even when they add the consonants.

The idea is for each singer to produce a beautiful, golden line of pure tone. It is the director's responsibility to decide where each phrase peaks in each voice part and lead the singers to reaching that peak together. Exercise 20, The Five Tone Legato Scale, and Exercise 21, The Controlled Sigh, in Chapter 10 are important in training the singers to perform in this mode.

The third mode is a *combination* of the staccato and legato modes that results in a light, yet connected sound. Music that demands peaked phrasing but does not seek the rich, beautiful, choral tone and intensity required by legato mode exemplifies this mode. Neither is the detached style of the staccato mode appropriate because of the chance of destroying the continuity of the text. Often the boys sing falsetto (head voice) to keep the intense sound of full voice from affecting the desired results. This is a particularly important mode of singing for early adolescent singers because it does not require the polished technique of the other two modes. Untrained adolescent singers may not have the ability to provide the detached clarity required for the staccato mode or the breath control required for the legato mode. Neither are they capable of producing the immense sound often required when singing in the legato mode. If directors implement either of the first two modes with young voices, they certainly should not require nor expect the mastery of effect produced by more mature voices.

The fourth and final mode is the *marcato* mode, which is similar to the staccato mode except that the tones are not totally detached and the pulses within the beat and beats within the measure are accented or marked. This is a very dramatic effect requiring excellent vocal technique. Directors should use this mode cautiously with adolescent voices because it can be vocally abusive when there is lack of breath control and support.

Appearance, Mood, and Facial/Body Language

Appearance   Not only must choirs sound good during performance, they also must look good. Listeners may perceive mediocre-sounding choirs to be outstanding because they look professional. Conversely, observers often perceive excellent-sounding choirs to be weak because their appearance and lack of uniformity in dress cause them to appear disheveled.

Some choirs portray a flashy, loud, ostentatious image by wearing bright colors and unorthodox styles in performance apparel. Others display the image of formality by dressing in black or dark, rich colors. Some are almost transparent because of the light, pastel colors and flowing styles. The physical appearance of choirs reflects the personality of their conductors or the image the conductors desire to portray.

Dressing uniformly also has a purpose beyond projecting the desired (or undesired) image of a choir. Uniforms (whether for performance or rehearsal) serve to inject a degree of oneness essential for unified purpose. In a society in which there is tremendous emphasis on the uniqueness of the individual, particularly where adolescents are concerned, the uniformity of dress may be essential to bring the choir together so that they will operate as a cohesive whole.

If choir members do not wear uniforms daily, directors should schedule a miniconcert early in the school year so that the students may see themselves in unified dress. In a positive way, this experience will affect how the students approach the choir rehearsal for the remainder of the year. After that first concert in which they all dress alike, they perceive, at least to a greater degree than before, how the choral unit operates.

Mood   Directors would like for their choral performances to have enough artistic content to provide an aesthetic experience for their listeners. Beyond that, most of them want their choirs to affect an audience emotionally when they sing. Even though, from one perspective, both are possible without the other, the perfect reality is for both to occur simultaneously. A performance may be technically correct and artistically fertile yet so emotionally sterile that it lacks audience appeal. On the other hand, it may contain deep, emotional content but if the choir performs the music haphazardly, members of the audience will criticize them for inadequate preparation.

Some will argue that one is inherent within the other: An aesthetic experience is emotional, and singers cannot project mood without technical skill and beauty in performance. Whichever the point of view, both are essential if a choir is to be successful in providing the audience a worthwhile concert experience.

The common cliché "to turn a phrase," in some quarters is a concept among musicians that relates to the sense of movement and relaxation inherent in most musical phrases. Often unintentionally, sensitive musicians approach the climax of a phrase with a sense of growing tension, resulting in an almost imperceptible increase in the tempo and a very slight crescendo (often musicians call this "leaning on" or "pressing" the phrase). Then they move away from the climax with a sense of relaxation (called "stretching" the phrase).

"To turn a phrase" also relates to a singer's ability to emote and express the meaning of the music and the text in a fashion that affects the listeners emotionally. In choral music, interpreting the text is an equal partner with executing the music. Singers will have difficulty "turning a phrase" (as it is used in the emoting sense) without internalizing the meaning of the text. The term *internalizing* deliberately was chosen instead of the word *understanding*. Often singers read and understand the meaning of the text (or if it is a foreign language, teachers explain it to them), but if they do not internalize it, they will be unable to communicate its meaning to the listener. Nothing is more bland than a technically proficient presentation of a phrase without musical meaning. Singers gain musical meaning by internalizing the text.

One way to teach singers to internalize the text is to require them literally to act out the message of the text in rehearsal. For instance, if they are singing about *exaltation*, ask them to raise their arms, shake their hands, and shout with joy and felicity. If they are singing about *damnation* have them to act out a scene where the building is on fire and they are unable to escape. Once they "experience" the text, they should be able to communicate it to their audience.

Facial/Body Language   Performance of an internalized text should cause singers' faces and bodies to respond with expression. Free body movement in a choral setting is a controversial subject. There are those who say it distracts from the effect of the singing. In most cases when distractions occur, they are a result of only one or two people moving while everyone else remains still. When choir members have internalized a text, appropriate movement is a result and each member of the choir will respond. When singers stand on risers, there should be enough space between each person to allow for extemporaneous expression. Directors should not stage or practice movement, it should be a genuine reaction to singing the text.

Since each singer has a different personality, the ability to communicate inward expression is easier for some than for others. Teachers should caution singers who display a proclivity for the melodramatic about overreacting. Although, because of personality, their reactions are truly genuine, if the response is obviously overdone, they will draw attention to themselves and away from the entire group. Since inhibition often restrains some people, those singers who innately communicate well have an added responsibility to help other classmates who do not inherit the ability to internalize and express easily.

One of the foremost barriers to uninhibited expression is the printed music. The singers must know the score thoroughly, almost to the point of memorization. Whether or not to memorize the music is another controversial subject among musicians. Without the music (which serves as a "security blanket"), singers run the risk of becoming completely lost or they may feel so inadequate that they affect the performance negatively. Performing with the music has the potential of having a similar negative impact because depending on it too much becomes a literal barrier to effective communication. Memorizing the music but holding it during performance is the most popular current practice. Some directors make a rule that the singers may not glance at one page more than twice. This rule should apply to the conductor as well. If everyone has freed themselves from relying on the music, then the exchange between conductor and choirmember and between choir and audience yields dynamic results.

When each singer's reaction from having internalized the music is genuine, the choir will pull the listeners into the concert experience and they will become an integral part, not just a group of detached observers. Then, if the concert is technically proficient, listeners will enjoy both an aesthetic and emotional experience.

STYLE—THE CHOIR'S AUTHENTICITY

The choral pioneers of the early twentieth century performed almost everything they sang in the style of the nineteenth century. They were engrossed with beautiful choral tone, singing technique, impressive sonorities, and mood, so they gave almost no attention to performing the music in the style of the period in which it was written. Since the middle of this century, choral directors gradually have become aware of authentic performance practices and style due to the amount of information that has surfaced through extensive research. Today most choral directors deem it unacceptable to perform all the music on a concert in the same style.

This quasi-obsession with authentic performance practices may leave you as a middle/junior high or senior high school choral teacher in a predicament. Since you are responsible for teaching and training adolescents who come to you only with exuberance and good intentions (and many of them do not even have those attributes), you have succeeded if you produce a musically literate choir who sings technically correct with choral artistry in one style. To teach the students to sing in several styles is virtually impossible.

We cannot accept, however, that because you may not have time to train students in several different styles, that you have the right to remain ignorant about them. Neither do I assume that students in my methods classes have that right. In this section, I examine the styles of each of the different periods. I discuss those styles which are appropriate for adolescents in greater detail than those that are more difficult or maybe impossible to perform for one reason or another.

As you grow in your teaching ability (even seasoned professionals must grow as long as we teach), you will find that you can produce an effective choral organization in less time than it took in the first years you taught. Therefore, you will be able to teach style in singing. For those of you who have arrived (or will arrive) at that point in your career, study Part IV of Robinson and Winold, *The Choral Experience*[16], because they present an excellent synopsis of much of the research about current performance practices. The bibliography of this chapter includes an extensive listing of other sources (some of them are original) to which you can refer for more information.

Chapters 1 and 2 provide an historical point of view and insight to forms and styles, so readers must review those chapters as they study this section. The discussion here is limited to specific performance practices and may not place them in historical perspective.

Those styles that are more appropriate for adolescent singers are presented first, then a brief synopsis of the others follows. Understandably, there will be selections from all periods that are inappropriate for various groups because they may be too difficult or the range and tessitura of the parts may be beyond the limitations of the singers' voices.

Renaissance (1450–1600)

Literature from the Renaissance period is particularly suitable for adolescent singers for several reasons:

1. Most of the music does not have extreme vocal ranges (neither in the upper nor lower areas), so it is particularly appropriate for the immature voice.

[16] Robinson and Winold, *The Choral Experience*, pp. 323–499.

2. Male singers who used very little vibrato performed most of the sacred music. As discussed, the natural vibrato is not as prevalent in adolescent singers as it is in older voices, so authencity is inherent within their voices.

3. Some of the music contains more than four parts. This makes it particularly appropriate for boys with changing voices because it makes it easier for directors to find a suitable part for each boy in the choir no matter which phase of vocal change he is experiencing.

4. The Renaissance period came before large operatic voices appeared, so the natural color of adolescent voices is possibly similar to that produced by Renaissance singers, although researchers can only surmise from viewing paintings and studying extant music as to how the singers sounded.

The problem with degree of authenticity is particularly acute when performing Renaissance music. A completely authentic concert is difficult to duplicate since performance conditions have changed.

1. Vocal ensembles often included instruments playing one or more of the voice parts, so the timbre was uniquely vocal/instrumental.[17] There was no distinction between the two and neither were the two pitted against each other as was the practice that emerged in the Baroque period. Today, it may not be possible to have authentic instruments that were part of the original Renaissance ensemble.

2. In most SATB choirs in the United States, women sing the soprano and alto parts although boys or adult male trebles sang those parts in the sacred music of the period.

3. The male castrato who was part of many of the Renaissance ensembles, with his distinctive vocal quality, has completely disappeared from today's musical scene.

4. The liturgical ensembles were small during the period, numbering as few as six to nine and no more than thirty by the sixteenth century. Historians assume that there were two to three performers on a part except parts sung by boys, which included a few more for proper balance. In a modern-day educational setting where the purpose is to involve as many participants as possible, it may be difficult to limit the ensemble size on all the Renaissance music performed.

5. Researchers believe that secular choral music performed for the aristocracy in the court, such as chansons and madrigals, contained only one (and occasionally two) performer(s) on a part. Due to its difficulty, adolescents find it difficult to execute Renaissance literature with only one singer per part. Today, in most junior and senior high schools, teachers perform madrigals with at least three (and usually more) singers on each part.

Whenever directors choose a Renaissance piece, they should consider the performance site or location. Renaissance musicians performed in one of three places: a cathedral or chapel, a room (chamber), or outdoors. The composer wrote a piece with the acoustical properties of the performance area in mind. Madrigals, chansons, and the Elizabethan music of the period are chamber music. Most of the music of the fourteenth century sounds better in an intimate

---

[17] This is exclusive of the music performed in the Sistene Chapel, which was strictly a cappella.

hall or large room. Most music written for brass instruments as well as the sixteenth-century festival music from Florence were for outdoor performances. Plainsong, motets, and double choruses are for large halls with live acoustics.

Directors should be particularly careful to choose publications of Renaissance works edited by Renaissance authorities. Since some of the music was written in early notation (modern shapes of notes emerged around 1600), there were usually no tempo nor dynamic markings, and phrasing was never marked, it behooves directors to select a modern edition that will yield an authentic sound. Be careful about editions prior to 1960 because many contain markings that depict the nineteenth-century style and, if followed, will result in a very Romantic rendition. Any overedited edition limits the freedom of conductor interpretation.

Improvisation was an important part of a Renaissance performance. In fact, historians believe that if a choral group performs a selection exactly as it was written by the composer, it would not sound at all like what the listeners of the period heard. Choral singers of the sixteenth century received extensive training in improvisatory practices. Conductors who desire to incorporate the improvisatory component into their performances should study treatises by Giovanni Baptiste Ganassi, Diego Ortiz, Giovanni Bassano (instrumental ornamentation), Hermann Finck, and Lodovico Zacconi (vocal ornamentation). Robinson and Winold provide a brief summary of the instructions and rules found in these works.[18]

During the Renaissance the composer was usually present to rehearse the musicians before performance. The musicians understood the performance practices of the time, so it was not necessary for the composer to be precise in the original manuscript. Conductors today rely on their understanding of the style to interpret the music correctly. If they consider the acoustical properties of the piece, the limitations and advantages of the voices or instruments, and the character of the texture, then they should be able to rely on the text and mood of a piece to interpret it.

Music of the Renaissance did not embody the principle of regular accents as dictated by bars and measures that are important in most music from the Baroque period to the present. Therefore modern notation misleads choral singers today since bars and measures are a necessary component of the system. In Renaissance music, the text determines the phrasing, dynamics, and to some extent the tempo of the music, although the prolation of the beat and accepted practices (the *tactus*, or established beat, was from 48 to 80 semibreves per minute) influences the tempo the most.

Each phrase is an entity in itself; therefore it should depict a life of its own. Except in the dance music of the period, teachers should use the *legato mode* (see "Modes of Choral Singing" described earlier in this chapter) and, since much of the music is polyphonic, each section should peak together as predetermined by the director.

Most junior and senior high school choral directors may determine that to

---

[18] Robinson and Winold, *The Choral Experience*, pp. 356–60.

achieve good tone production (see Chapter 10) and to execute the music in the proper mode with good choral technique may be as close to Renaissance authenticity as they can attain. Others should admire and emulate choirs who have achieved that much authenticity.

Twentieth Century (1900 to Present)

Next to the Renaissance period, directors will probably find more choral music that addresses the needs of adolescents from music composed since 1900 than any other period. The many varied performance styles from this period are derived from the way the composers wrote the music, not from how the choirs perform it. Relative to tone production, all the different styles must be performed with good vocal technique (see Chapter 10) and directors must choose the mode of singing that best relates to the style and mood of each piece.

Art music of the period includes impressionistic, expressionistic, atonal, twelve tone (serial), chance (aleatory), neo-Classic, neo-Baroque, post-Romantic, nationalistic, primitive, pandiatonic, and electronic styles, much of which are too difficult for most adolescent choir members particularly if stark dissonances, extended pitch retention, and exceptional vocal range and prowess are involved.

Since 1960 art music performed with prepared electronic tape has become a leading twentieth-century choral idiom, although its popularity waned during the 1980s. Many of these pieces are well within the capabilities of secondary school choir members primarily because of the improvisatory (and dictated) aspects that give the students opportunities to produce a variety of timbres such as shouting, whispering, clicking the tongue, whistling, grunting, and howling. The unorthodox sounds required for many of the pieces intrigue most adolescent singers.

Other musical characteristics unique to this period are mixed meters, changing meters, complex rhythm patterns, nontraditional sound sources, extreme dynamic levels, specially devised systems of notation, highly complex musical scores, special dramatic effects, highly efficient vocal prowess, and new timbres for sundry types of smaller ensembles.

Creating musical tension is the impetus of much of this music. Often composers achieve this with unorthodox uses of the voice (yelling, screaming, grunting, and other throaty sounds). Understandably, since they spend so much time with adolescents developing beauty in choral tone, the possibility of vocal abuse and disruption of consistent tone production concerns some directors. For this reason some directors have been hesitant to embrace much of the music from this period, particularly for adolescents.

Through cautious selection, other directors find music from this period to be quite useful. They find the adolescent voice to be useful for works requiring exact tuning that can result from the absence of vibrato in the students' voices. Directors must train the students to sing disjunct, nondiatonic intervals with precision and they must preserve good vocal technique at all cost.

Another attribute of twentieth-century music for adolescents is the performance of folk, jazz, and media music (rock and roll, rock, soul, gospel, pop) as

prominent choral idioms (see Chapter 15). The singing of folk choral arrangements prevailed during the 1940s and 50s, but in the 1970s, arrangements of
music heard on radio and television (media music) became more popular. In
the 1980s vocal jazz enjoyed significant popularity.

Many directors choose to sing choral arrangements of media music. Singers
must develop a unique choral style to perform the music written for contemporary
pop ensembles. Special techniques like the glissando-portamento, doit, spill, plop,
shake, smear, turn, ghost note, fall off, and flip are necessary to perform this music
stylistically correctly. Students also must develop the ability to scat sing.[19]

Directors express concern when students sing media music that often emphasizes a raucous style of vocal production. Here again there is fear of vocal abuse
and a breakdown of traditional choral tone production. Leaders in the field assure
directors that when performed correctly, this style of vocal singing is not counter
to traditional choral singing because good breathing, resonance, and tone production are essential for both. They argue that the chance for vocal abuse is no more
likely than with traditional singing if the singers use good vocal technique.

Folk music represents the musical heritage of a culture. Tragically, students
in public and private schools no longer sing much of the authentic American
folk music. They sing very little of that brought with their ancestors from abroad
because teachers have replaced these great folk songs with media music. Each
generation that passes takes much of this music with them and it is disappearing
from the society because new generations are not learning it to pass it on. Some
of the most beautiful choral works in existence are the many published
arrangements of folk tunes. They should be part of every choral program. It is
music brought from the people, so directors and choirs have a responsibility to
return it to the people.

Baroque (1600–1750), Classical (1750–1820), and Romantic (1820–1900)

Some of the most magnificent choral music ever written came from the pens of
the Baroque, Classical, and Romantic composers. The performance practices
that surrounded these musical geniuses, which in many ways were a result of
the way they wrote, are examined in this section. To understand these specific
considerations fully, read the historical and stylistic information in Chapter 1.

Choosing Music from These Periods   Regrettably, the composers wrote most (not all,
but most) of the music for adults, some of whom were professional singers.
Articulation requirements, range, and tessitura demands place much of it beyond
the vocal prowess of adolescents.

---

[19] Gene Grier has published a series of chorals (octavos) that train the adolescent
how to develop the proper style. They are entitled *Warm-up Exercises* (H158), *Rhythmic
Exercises* (H159), *Articulation Exercises* (H160), *Improvisation and Scat Singing Exercises*
(H161), and *Baroque Scat* (H184) (501 E. Third St., P.O. Box 802, Dayton, Ohio: The
Heritage Music Press, 1978). Also, consult Chapters 7 through 10 of Doug Anderson's
Jazz and Show Choir Handbook (P.O. Box 470. Chapel Hill, N.C.: The Hinshaw Music,
Inc., 1978), pp. 42–72.

When selecting music from these periods, directors must be careful to choose works that their choir members are capable of singing well. Directors enjoy impressing their colleagues by teaching their choirs difficult music. It is impressive to sing difficult music well, but it is very embarrassing when choirs sing it poorly. In many cases when they perform it poorly, it is because the vocal demands of the music are beyond the students' maturity and capability. It is always vocally healthier for the students and more aesthetically pleasing to the listeners to sing less difficult music beautifully than to sing difficult music badly. Teachers should ask themselves the following questions as they choose music for their students.

1. *Does each part have high and low notes the singers cannot sing well?* The following illustration shows the extreme high and low notes directors should consider when they choose music for adolescents. There should be no more than one or two of these extremely high or low notes in the entire piece.

Extreme Ranges - Early Adolescents

Extreme Ranges - Older Adolescents

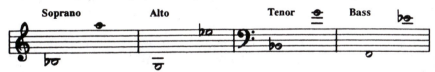

2. *Is the overall tessitura of the part too high or too low?* The comfortable singing range for most adolescents is shown below. If many of the notes in a part move outside of this area, students will probably experience vocal fatigue unless their technique is exceptional.

Comfortable Singing Tessitura - Early Adolescents

Comfortable Singing Tessitura - Older Adolescents

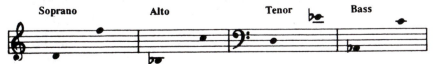

3. *What are the articulation and enunciation demands of the piece?* If the piece contains long melismatic passages, it will be difficult for adolescents to perform well. This is particularly true with early adolescents, but it also applies to older adolescents if they have not developed their vocal technique. Be very careful when choosing music from the middle and later Baroque period because some of the music contains long and difficult melismas. If the music requires awkward or wide leaps, some early adolescents will have difficulty executing them. When the text contains syllables and words on sixteenth and eighth notes at a fast tempo, some adolescents will have enunciation problems.

4. *Does the piece require penetrating resonance and mass volume?* Singers performed much of the music from the Romantic period in a loud, exciting, and intensive way. Adolescents do not have the vocal maturity nor the technique to supply the intensity these pieces require.

5. *Is the tempo so slow that the students will be required to sing long, well-supported vocal lines?* This is a gray area depending upon the vocal technique of the students. Some choirs are unable to keep the body of choral sound vital, alive, and supported if the tempo is extremely slow, or the piece contains multiple half and whole notes. The need to stagger the breathing weakens the choral intensity to the point that the body of choral sound does not withstand to the end of the line. If the students have good breath control and can sing a well-supported tone from the beginning of the phrase to the end, directors may choose pieces of this type. If not, they should wait until the vocal technique has developed before choosing to sing them.

Due to the large amount of choral music written during these periods, there is plenty of music that adolescents can sing if directors will take time to find it.

Performance Considerations for the Baroque Period   Consider the following performance practices when preparing music from the Baroque:

1. Composers used *word painting* in much of the music. Directors should be aware of the relationship between the text and the music. For instance, composers may set words such as *ascend, high, up, heaven,* and *resurrection* to an ascending vocal line or high notes. They may set words such as *hell, abyss, descend, low,* and *down* to a descending vocal line or low notes. Singers may color the voice or use other ways to emphasize the words to address their relationship to the music, but not in an exaggerated fashion.

2. Authorities characterize Italian music of the Baroque as passionate, impulsive, spontaneous, unrestricted, austere, and bizarre. It requires intensity and a forthright approach. The performer often determines how to execute the ornaments, articulation, dynamics, and figured bass symbols.

3. French music of the Baroque is characterized as even, constant, regular, steady, rational and tempered. It requires more of a sense of relaxation in performance. The composer often dictates how to execute the ornaments, articulation, dynamics, and figured bass symbols.

4. There were three practical types of music: church music, theatre music, and chamber music. Directors should be cognizant of their purpose, mood and how they differ.

5. At the beginning of the period two styles of composition flourished simultaneously: *stile antico* (modal, equal contrapuntal voice parts, and even-flowing

rhythm) and *stile moderno* (emphasis on the words, major-minor tonality, both strict and free rhythm, homophonic, and in most cases monodic). The *stile antico* usually applied to Catholic church music (German, French, and Italian) while the *stile moderno* applied to theatre music (mostly Italian opera and oratorio).

6. By the end of the period (the time of Bach and Handel) both homophonic (chorales) and polyphonic textures (motets and choruses in oratorio and opera) flourished. An obvious soprano line; a very active, equal bass line; and supporting, dependent, but less important inner parts characterized the polyphony.

7. Each selection establishes a specific mood (*Doctrine of Affections*) and maintains it throughout the work. The composer confirms the ritards by writing longer note values. In most cases directors should not change the tempo of the beat.

8. The same beat and tempo should persist throughout but not at the total expense of spontaneity of the performer.

9. The harpsichord, portative organ, or large organ are the principal accompanying keyboard instruments. The piano was not in use at that time. If an acoustical harpsichord is not available, at the chance of criticism from some quarters, teachers may consider using the harpsichord stop on a synthesizer instead of the piano.

10. There is little evidence to support singing German chorales and motets a cappella. Instruments apparently doubled the voices.

11. Choir members should execute Baroque pitch notation correctly, so directors must use choral music edited by competent authorities. However, most editions do not deal with the proper interpretation of Baroque rhythmic notation and ornamentation. To be absolutely correct, directors should study each thoroughly. An excellent source is *The Choral Experience*.[20]

12. Accompanists should be able to realize the figured bass if directors choose to sing a work where the editors have not realized it.[21]

13. Recommended tempos are *Presto*—160, *Allegro*—120, *Allegretto*—80, *Adagio*—40, and *Lento*—20. As with music in other periods, these may vary depending on the nature of the music, the abundance of fast or slow notes, the abilities of the performers, and acoustics.

14. Performers used *terraced dynamics* but not to the exclusion of crescendos and decrescendos, which they employed sensitively and in moderation.

15. The music portrays more warmth; however, this is not a license for singers to add extensive vibrato to the tone. They may use it in moderation but not as much as they can use it in the periods to follow. A wide vibrato will hinder the rhythmic drive of the music. Further, it is very difficult to sing articulate melismas, particularly with a group of singers, if they use vibrato.

Performance Considerations for the Classical Period   Authorities characterize music of the Classical period as being graceful, elegant, refined, balanced, symmetrical, simple, clear, objective, and traditional. It differs from Baroque music in form more than in performance practices. Use of terraced dynamics disappeared. Melismatic passages, particularly for choral singers, were minimal. Contrapuntal

---

[20] Robinson and Winold, *The Choral Experience*, pp. 381–401.
[21] Ibid., pp. 401–7.

writing, except in masses, was not as prevalent. Composers gave more consideration to vertical relationships with the inner parts becoming more important. Even though the music requires excellent vocal prowess, particularly with the solo singer, some of the choral music does not require so much intensity, agility, and range extension. As a result, some of the choral music of Haydn, Mozart, Gluck, and Cherubini is quite appropriate for adolescent singers. Consider the following performance practices:

1. Crescendos and decrescendos are more prevalent and slightly more extreme than in the Baroque period, but still not overdone.
2. Ornamentation is still prominent but not as excessive as in the Baroque. The improvisational aspect of the music has waned, with the composer taking more control by writing exactly how to perform the music.
3. Successive contrasting phrases with the first loud and the second soft or vice versa are used.
4. Tempos are moderate and never extreme. Accelerando and rallentando appear in the music. Conductors may include rubato with caution.
5. Music marked allegro or faster needs to have a dancelike quality. The *combination mode* (see "Modes of Choral Singing" described earlier in this chapter) is quite appropriate.
6. Expressive singing is important but certainly not overdone. Directors should be careful not to interpret the music in the same expressive fashion as they do Romantic music.
7. The piano appeared during this period, so directors may use it as an accompanying instrument without criticism.
8. Teachers should give careful attention to phrasing as dictated by the text. They should teach note separation when necessary to communicate the message of the words.

Performance Considerations for the Romantic Period Music from the Romantic period, when considered as a body of music, is probably the most inappropriate for adolescent singers because much of it is so vocally demanding and requires dynamic extremes, wide ranges, intense tone quality, and more use of the vibrato. However, teachers still may find works that adolescents can sing well.

Symphonic music and opera predominated. Most often, when composers wrote choral music it was with a large orchestra or part of an operatic scene that required highly trained, professional musicians. Only selected composers wrote a cappella music. When directors teach selected pieces from the Romantic period, probably only to the **Advanced Choir**, they should consider the following performance practices:

1. Romantic music is very expressive. Extremes are the norm from *pppp* to *ffff* and prestissimo to molto largo. Performers may apply rubato freely. Crescendos and decrescendos are so dramatic some may consider them to be burlesque. Accelerandos and rallentandos are abundant. Directors will desire to choose the *legato mode* (see "Modes of Choral Singing" described earlier in this chapter), which emphasizes peak phrasing and expressive singing.
2. Composers explore tone color to the fullest. They use chromaticism and

dissonance to achieve rich chordal sonorities that took precedence over highly contrapuntal approaches.

3. Mäelzel began to manufacture the metronome in 1816, so this allowed composers to dictate the tempos precisely.

4. The music requires warmth, depth, and fullness of tone, so singers use rich tone color and vibrato to achieve these qualities.

CONCLUSION

In this chapter we examined the choral components necessary for adolescents to sing well together. We looked at diction, choral tone, interpretive factors, and style. We considered the unique vocal characteristics of adolescents and how to apply the choral technique to those characteristics. I provided all of this with one thought: to help you become the best choral technician possible. I have done my job; now it is your turn to do yours.

Much of the enjoyment in teaching comes from *going through the process* of training our choirs to perform well, but for me, there is nothing more satisfying than leaning back in my easy chair and enjoying the fruits of my labor after the concert as I listen to the recording or watch the videotape. I know then that all the hard work and sacrifices the choir members and I encountered in that process was worth it all, and I am soon ready to begin again.

THOUGHTS FOR CONTEMPLATION AND DISCUSSION

1. Think about your favorite choral directors (without naming them). Which aspects of their choral technique were beneficial and which were not?

2. Is it necessary to be a style purist? Can performances of music from various periods still be beneficial to the performers and listeners without performing them stylistically correct? Why or why not?

3. Who should have more influence over the way a piece is performed, the conductor or the composer? How much liberty can a conductor take in interpreting a composer's music? How does one determine where to draw the line?

4. What speech patterns are prevalent from your part of the country that will have to be eliminated if your choirs are to have good choral diction?

5. If beautiful choral tone is the desired result of good choral technique, how does one justify singing texts that do not speak about beauty nor require beautiful tones?

6. How does choral tone reflect the musical style? Can a choir sing stylistically correct and use the same approach to tone production for all styles?

7. To you, which is the most important, the music or the text? Why?

8. Will you require your middle/junior and senior high school choir members to memorize their music? Why or why not?

9. Do you plan to conduct your performances by memory? Why or why not?

10. Is it always necessary to program period pieces chronologically? Why or why not?

11. Think about selections that have served as concert openers and closers. Why do you think they were chosen for those positions in the concert?
12. How will your choirs dress for performances? Why?
13. Relative to choral technique, compare the thought processes of a student who thinks like a musician with one who does not.
14. When singing a cappella, which is more important: (1) staying in tune within the group or (2) finishing the piece without lowering or raising the key?

BIBLIOGRAPHY

BARTLE, JEAN ASHWORTH. *Lifeline for Children's Choir Directors*. Toronto: Gordon V. Thompson, 1988. (Available through Oxford Press.)

BESSOM, MALCOLM E., ALPHONSE TATARUNIS, and SAMUEL L. FORCUCCI. *Teaching Music in Today's Secondary Schools*, 2d ed. New York: Holt, Rinehart and Winston, 1980.

COLLINS, DON L. *The Cambiata Concept, a Comprehensive Philosophy and Methodology of Teaching Music to Adolescents*. Conway, Ark.: Cambiata Press, 1981.

COOPER, IRVIN, and KARL O. KURSTEINER. *Teaching Junior High School Music*, 2d ed. Conway, Ark.: Cambiata Press, 1973.

DECKER, HAROLD A., and JULIUS HERFORD, eds. *Choral Conducting Symposium*, 2d ed. Englewood Cliffs, N.J.: Prentice Hall, Inc., 1988.

EDELSON, EDWARD. *The Secondary School Music Program from Classroom to Concert Hall*. West Nyack, N.Y.: Parker Publishing Co., 1972.

EILERS, JOYCE. *Dealing with "Uncertain Singer" Problems through Careful Selection of Music*. New Berlin, Wisc.: Jenson, 1979.

HEFFERNAN, CHARLES W. *Choral Music, Technique and Artistry*. Englewood Cliffs, N.J.: Prentice-Hall, Inc., 1982.

HOFFER, CHARLES R. *Teaching Music in the Secondary Schools*, 4th ed. Belmont, Calif,: Wadsworth Publishing, 1991.

JIPSON, WAYNE R. *The High School Vocal Music Program*. West Nyack, N.Y.: Parker Publishing Co., 1972.

LAMB, GORDON H. *Choral Techniques*, 3d ed. Dubuque, Iowa: Wm. C. Brown Co., 1988.

MARPLE, HUGO D. *Backgrounds and Approaches to Junior High Music*. Dubuque, Iowa: Wm. C. Brown Co., 1975.

MARSHALL, MADELEINE. *The Singer's Manual of English Diction*. New York: Schirmer, 1953.

MAY, WILLIAM; and CRAIG TOLIN. *Pronunciation Guide for Choral Literature*. Reston, Va: Music Educators National Conference, 1987.

MILLER, KENNETH E. *Vocal Music Education, Teaching in the Secondary Schools*. Englewood Cliffs, N.J.: Prentice-Hall, Inc., 1988.

MOE, DANIEL. *Basic Choral Concepts*. Minneapolis: Augsburg Publishing House, 1972.

NEIDIG, KENNETH L., and JOHN JENNINGS, eds. *Choral Director's Guide*. West Nyack, N.Y.: Parker Publishing Co., 1967.

PFAUTSCH, LLOYD. *English Diction for the Singer*. New York: Lawson-Gould, 1971.

RAO, DOREEN. *Choral Music Experience* (Twelve Volumes on Children's Choral Singing). Farmingdale, N. Y.: Boosey and Hawkes, 1987.

ROBINSON, RAY, and ALLEN WINOLD. *The Choral Experience*. New York: Harper's College Press, 1976.

ROE, PAUL F. *Choral Music Education*, 2d ed. Englewood Cliffs, N.J.: Prentice-Hall, Inc., 1983.

SCHMIDT, JAN. *Basics of Singing*. New York: Schirmer-Macmillan, 1984.

SINGLETON, IRA. *Music in Secondary Schools*, 2d ed. Boston: Allyn and Bacon, Inc., 1965.

STANTON, ROYAL. *Steps to Singing*, 2d ed. Belmont, Calif.: Wadsworth Publishing, 1976.

SWAN, HOWARD. *Conscience of a Profession*. Chapel Hill, N.C.: Hinshaw Music, 1988.

TRUSLER, IVAN. *The Choral Director's Latin*. Lanham, Md.: University Press of America, 1987.

TRUSLER, IVAN, and WALTER EHRET. *Functional Lessons in Singing*, 2d ed. Englewood Cliffs, N.J.: Prentice-Hall, Inc., 1986.

VENNARD, WILLIAM. *Singing, the Mechanism and the Technic*. New York: Carl Fischer, 1968.

WADE, ARCHIE, and CLARENCE SAWHILL. *The Anatomy of a Vibrato*, 16mm film, 12 min. with sound. Los Angeles: Radiology Department, Medical Center, University of California, 1960.

13

Getting the Most Out of Rehearsal

Most choral directors would like to have more class time to prepare their choral organizations for concerts. After concerts we have a tendency to say, "That concert was good, but if there had been a little more time to rehearse, it would have been great." Even though perfectionists (and there seem to be more perfectionists in the choral teaching profession than in many others) are never satisfied with the end product, the real problem with time is not *having* enough of it but understanding how to use it effectively. In business there is an adage, "time is money." When teaching choral singing, one might say "time is success," because effective use of time results in better performances and more productive classroom teaching.

In time management, the salient points are: (1) remain dedicated to the immediate task and (2) execute efficacious organization. It is not within the purview of this chapter to address how you learn to concentrate (stay on task) or to be tenacious, determined, and persistent. We do, however, want to help you learn how to organize your rehearsal so that you will not waste precious rehearsal time. Also, I will address several other aspects of rehearsal and teaching technique that will be helpful.

PREREHEARSAL ACTIVITIES

Before rehearsals begin, directors should have decided the method they will use to determine who the membership will be in each of their choirs. Many directors,

315

particularly in senior high school, audition the singers individually before enrolling them in class.

Students usually approach the audition with fear and trepidation and in some cases choose not to sing in a choir because directors require them to audition. For this reason, some directors decide not to have an official audition process, particularly for membership in the **Beginning Choir** (see Chapter 15) whether it is in middle/junior or senior high school. In fact, some never have an official audition. To them, an individual audition promotes musical "giftedness," which is counter to the idea of "music for every student." Once teachers enroll students in a sequential choral program (the **Beginning Choir** is open to everyone), through effective training the students move from one choir to the next without auditions. Since the directors teach the students daily, they notice all those factors the audition reveals, so there is no apparent reason to audition the students individually. The selectivity considered necessary for the **Advanced Choir** comes through the natural process of fulfilling the designated requirements of membership (see Chapter 15).

If there is no audition for the **Beginning Choir**, how do these directors deal with proper voice classification? Usually they employ some type of group classification process (see Chapter 8 under "Irvin Cooper's Cambiata Concept" for an example). Also, since developing musicianship and vocal-choral technique (activities that require individuals to sing for teachers daily) are the primary goals of the **Beginning Choir**, determining where to place the students in sections and how to deal with their specific voice types becomes clear.

Some directors want to have an audition, not because they plan to eliminate anyone from singing, but because the process of auditioning serves to communicate to the students the "specialness" of choral singing. Even though students dread the audition, once they complete it and receive notification of acceptance, their attitude and approach to the choral organization are more positive. Membership becomes a treasured asset.

Preparing for the Audition

Directors who audition their students do so because the audition helps (1) to determine for which choir they are best suited, (2) to choose the best singers for the organization (this applies primarily to the **Advanced Choir**), (3) to determine the singers' voice types, (4) to control the quantity of singers in each section of the choirs, (5) to get better acquainted with the singers, (6) to isolate musical strengths and weaknesses, and various other specified reasons.

Before the students come to the audition, directors should prepare data instruments so they will have a record of the information the audition yields. A simple audition index card, which directors may obtain commercially or may prepare for themselves, should be available for the student to complete. Information on the card should include: (1) name, (2) address, (3) grade level, (4) telephone number, (5) previous choral experience, (6) musical instruments played, and (7) grade point average. Teachers should instruct the students to list any special musical performances in which they have been a participant or special musical honors they have received. They may write this information on the back of the card.

Directors should prepare a second card for personal use that contains the results of the audition. How they use the categories entered on this card in the audition are explained later in this section. This card should include: (1) name of the student, (2) voice type, (3) pitch level (key) chosen on "My Country 'Tis of Thee," (4) results of the melody retention test, (5) results of the rhythm retention test, (6) results of the harmony differentiation test, (7) an evaluation of their basic tunefulness and intonation, (8) an evaluation of their basic voice quality (this also might include a response about how they approach the voice relative to resonance and freedom of singing), (9) an evaluation of their ability to express themselves orally, and (10) the directors' first response suggestion as to which choir each singer is best suited. Some directors devise a point system for evaluating the students' success in each area in which they are tested. On this data card directors record the total points earned, which gives some indication as to the students' musical strengths. After the audition, directors may put the information from both cards in a data-base computer program or file it for immediate procurement.

In choosing and preparing the audition rooms (one for waiting and one for singing), directors should (1) assure that the piano has been tuned, (2) assure that there is a comfortable area for the participants to sit while waiting, and (3) assure that the audition room is large enough for the singer to stand at least ten feet away on the opposite side of the piano keyboard. If possible, choose rooms that promote a cordial atmosphere so the students can relax and calm down from their audition jitters.

The Components of the Audition   Obviously, directors desire to determine the basic musical ability of the singer at the audition. More importantly, they also should desire to determine the ability of singers to assimilate information quickly and to adjust immediately. Often teachers judge singers at an audition strictly on their initial musical responses, which relate directly to their previous musical training. Inexperienced students may become excellent choir members if they respond well to instruction. Intelligent directors will give students an opportunity to correct a musical response (no matter how difficult it may appear or how poorly the students performed it initially) after instructing them about how to listen and analyze the musical example being played or how to manipulate their vocal instruments for success.

Begin the audition by greeting the students with a pleasant smile to ease their anxiety and to establish, in this first encounter with them, that they will have assistance in accomplishing what their interests, efforts, and abilities will allow. Ask the students to sing the first stanza of "America" ("My Country 'Tis of Thee"). All those who audition should sing the same selection so that directors can evaluate each student fairly when comparing the musical renditions. Do not give a beginning pitch from the piano and do not accompany them. Allow them to choose their own starting pitch. An a cappella presentation of this type should reveal to the directors: (1) the voice type, (2) the natural ability to "carry a tune,"

(3) the accuracy of pitch relationships, (4) memory, understanding, and the ability to communicate the words and music, (5) the natural flow of the breath, and (6) the smoothness and timbre of the voice.

After the students have completed the song, directors should choose the final pitch and play several two note intervals, five-note scales, and arpeggiated three-note chords on the piano. Ask the students to sing each example in the same manner as it was played (legato, staccato, loud, soft, fast, slow, and so forth). Do not play with them as they sing. Suggest that the students sing using the nonsensical word *LAH*. The *L* places the tongue in a relaxed position in the bottom of the mouth, and the *AH* vowel enables their voices to be heard more clearly due to the wider opening of the mouth. The auditioner should encourage them to "fill the room with their voices." If the students are unable to reach a note immediately, tell them to use "more energy" or "more breath" in singing. Sometimes it is advisable to request the students to sing softly on the word *LOO* to give them an opportunity to experience the head voice or falsetto. Also use major, minor, augmented, and diminished arpeggiated chords and close this section of the audition with the following more difficult musical motifs to test the students' melodic memory (tonal or pitch retention). Articulate the examples as they are marked. If the students are unable to remember the entire example after one hearing, divide the example into two parts, play one, then the other. After, ask the students to sing the entire example again. Conceiving it in two parts should improve the students' tonal memory. If the students sing it correctly the second time, that success is an indication of how quickly the students can learn.

Next, clap several rhythm patterns and ask the students to mimic them (clap back) as nearly as possible with the same strength and tempo as those they clapped. One hand should be used as a platform for clapping and the other hand to tap lightly against the base of the platform hand with three fingers only. This test shows not only the students' ability to recognize and remember rhythm patterns, but it is also indicative of their coordination. If at any time students have difficulty in repeating rhythmic or tonal patterns, ask them to close their eyes and listen carefully as the directors clap or play them again. Usually this helps prevent further distraction from the surroundings.

After the rhythmic test, play several different harmonic triads or four-part chords (all tones simultaneously): major, minor, diminished, and augmented. Ask the student to sing one of the three or four tones; directors should designate if they want to hear the highest, next to highest, middle, next to lowest, or lowest of the three or four tones. If the students are successful in doing so, then ask them to sing all three or four tones one after the other, beginning with the highest then moving downward to the lowest.

Finally, ask the students to read a paragraph from a textbook written for their grade level. This part of the test allows directors to observe speech and diction patterns, literacy level, and how expressively the students communicate.

Preparing the Rehearsal Area

Kurt Lewin points out the importance of the learning environment on student motivation (see Chapter 4). By use of attractive decor and furnishings, a rehearsal hall should say, "Come in, learning occurs here." If students are to take pride in their choral organization, the rehearsal hall should be one that helps them feel good about being there. Teachers should decorate bulletin boards attractively with information about music reading, vocal-choral technique, or well-known choral groups. They should display trophies and certificates proudly. Custodians should clean the room each day before the classes begin (that includes more than just sweeping the floor). There should be a place to hang all the coats and a place to lay the excess books and study materials. The choral library should be housed outside the room and out of view of the students. All storage areas should have doors on them to protect the stored materials, and they should be painted periodically to keep them looking clean. The windows should be cleaned often to promote the "sparkle" of an inviting room.[1] Carpet on the floor enhances the warmth of the room provided the ceiling is high and hard enough to promote supportive acoustical response to the choral sound.

At the beginning of the year, before the first rehearsal, the director will need to arrange the desks, chairs, and/or risers for the arrival of the students. Place a lock on the piano cover so that the keys will be unaccessible unless the pianist is playing it.

Assigning Music and Folders

When officers for the choir are elected (or appointed), teachers should make every effort to assure that the most reliable member of the choir be elected librarian. Librarian may not be the most prestigious office to hold, but it is certainly one of the most important. Officers for the new school year should be elected at the end of the previous year, and the librarian should be available

---

[1] Regrettably, some schools do not have enough custodial help to clean the rooms and windows and to paint areas that need painting nearly often enough. Although it is a distasteful responsibility for some teachers, sometimes they must be custodians as well as a teachers. If directors want the environment of their rooms to enhance the learning process, periodically teachers must ask the students to have a work day to "put the room in order." Their hands on involvement will deepen their pride in the organization.

before school begins to prepare the music folders for the first day of class. Teachers waste time in rehearsal if they distribute and retrieve the music daily. Members should have consecutively numbered individual folders (see Appendix A for names of suppliers of folders and cabinets to store them) containing the music, vocalises, sight-reading material, and any other supplies required in rehearsal (if funds are not available to purchase folders, directors may use $8\frac{1}{2}$-by-ll-inch envelopes). Sharing music contributes to misbehavior, particularly with early adolescents. Members should have the same number for music folders (each piece of music inside the folder should be marked with that number), robes (or other wearing apparel), and books.

Occasionally, choir members need to take music home to rehearse. Allowing them to take their folders home usually creates confusion if they fail to return with them for the next rehearsal. To alleviate this problem directors should have several extra unassigned folders of music that members may check out to be used outside the rehearsal hall.

Seating or Standing Formations

Middle/Junior High School If auditions have been held, directors should have prepared the seating or standing formation for the choir before the first rehearsal. Several practices currently prevail in the United States: (1) Some directors allow their students to sit in chairs or desks while singing. (2) Others allow them to sit in desks or chairs for all purposes other than singing; then they are requested to stand beside the desk when singing. (3) Some prefer no chairs at all in the rehearsal room. The students stand most of the time, but they are allowed to sit on the floor when they are not singing. (4) Some directors use still another approach (which is highly advantageous, if there is enough room), an area with desks for activities other than singing and a separate area (usually with risers) for standing to sing. Several considerations pertaining to standing or seating will facilitate maximum controlled participation with early adolescents:

1. Directors must attend to the needs of students with changing voices on a daily basis, therefore:
    A. Place the boys in front and center of the class and place the girls behind and on each side of them.
    B. Leave space between each boy so that directors can move among the boys as they sing.
2. If possible, arrange the students in such a fashion (probably in a semi-circle[2]) so that directors are within no less than two giant steps from each student. This configuration is very difficult to attain if the group is extremely large. For maximun vocal productivity, training, and motivation when working

---

[2] I believe strongly in the semicircle rehearsal formation. It is advantageous because (1) the director can hear all parts evenly, (2) the students can hear each other well, and (3) the students are easily accessible for the director to give them attention and assistance.

with early adolescents, one teacher should attempt to teach no more than twenty students (ten is even better). Although it is only an ideal and not a reality in American schools, a group of sixty students should have three to six choral teachers.

3. Leave enough aisles among the singers so that directors can move to each student quickly.

4. It is best not to succumb to the pleas of the students to allow them to stand or sit near their friends, although the practice does contribute to positive attitudes among the students. The primary goal is effective choral results and individual vocal advancement; therefore, teachers should place students where they will make the strongest contribution toward that goal. Explaining this to the students may also prompt positive attitudes.

5. Students should stand when singing so that they can effectuate control of the singing mechanism (particularly the breath-band area) for good vocal technique.

6. If there are girls who have developed a definite soprano or alto quality at this age (these are rare), directors should place them between the two female sections. With most early adolescent singers the girls should sing two equal parts; therefore, when directors use music that contains one part lower than the other (SA voicing), definite sopranos may always sing the high part and definite altos may sing the low one.

7. Boy trebles should stand or sit with the cambiatas (boys in the first phase of change) but near the girls so that they may sing a treble part.

8. Place the uncertain singers near secure, strong singers but at the edge of the choir. By doing so the uncertain singers will be able to hear themselves and the strong singers nearby and will not be bombarded with sound from all around, which may add to their uncertainty.

If directors are unfamiliar with the type voices present on the first day of class, they should meet the students at the door and tell all the boys to sit in front and the girls in the back. After voice classification (see Chapter 8), permanent seating may be arranged.

Following are suggested seating or standing plans for early adolescent singers. Several different ones are provided due to the various possibilities of voice types. Notice particularly where the aisles have been placed.

TWO-PART FORMATIONS

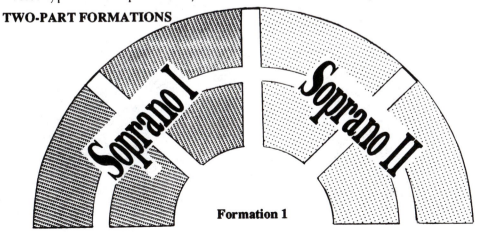

Formation 1

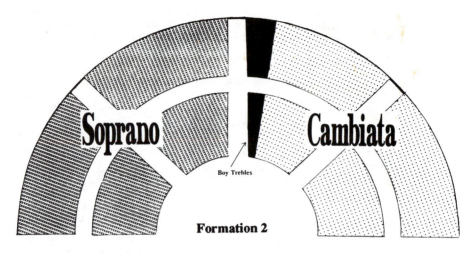

Boy Trebles

Formation 2

THREE-PART FORMATIONS

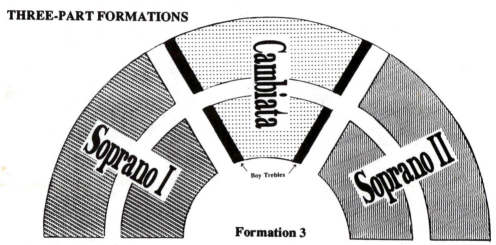

Boy Trebles

Formation 3

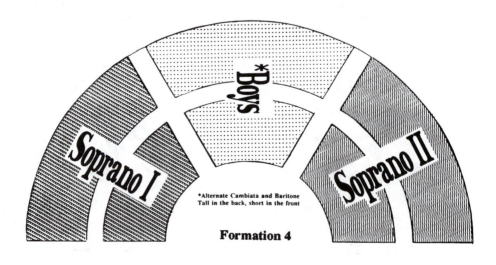

*Alternate Cambiata and Baritone
Tall in the back, short in the front

Formation 4

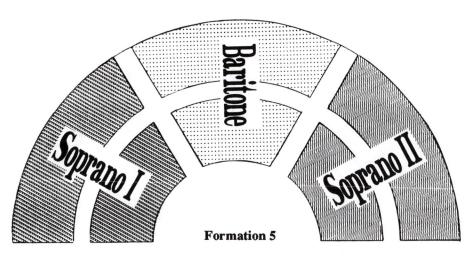

Formation 5

FOUR-PART FORMATIONS

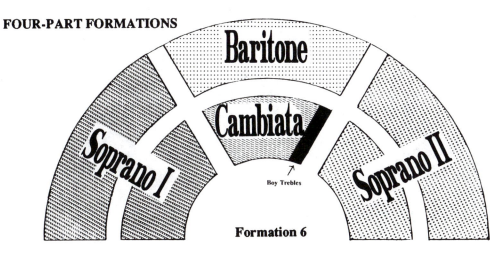

Formation 6

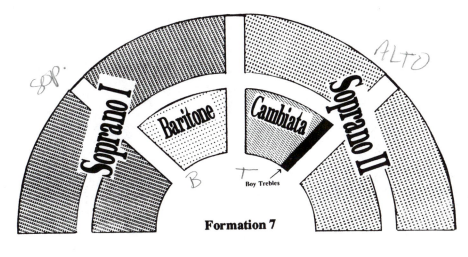

Formation 7

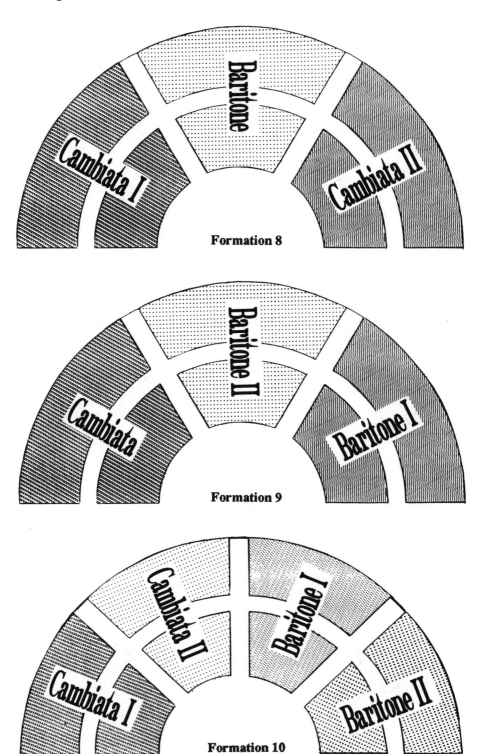

Formation 8

Formation 9

Formation 10

Senior High School

Before directors determine how members of their senior high school choir will sit or stand, they should determine the answer to several generic questions. Several seating or standing plans have been provided, and those that are best suited have been recommended. Relative to mixed choirs, the questions are:

1. Which sections are the largest? In **Beginning and Intermediate Choirs** there are usually more girls than boys. For the boys to balance the girls it is best to choose formation 5, 6, or 7. If the sections are equal as they may be in the **Advanced Choir**, directors might choose formation 1, 2, 3, 4, 8, 9, or 10.
2. Is the literature homophonic or polyphonic? If it is polyphonic, choose formation 1, 3, 4, 5, or 6 (definite sections). If the literature is homophonic, choose formation 8, 9, or 10 (scrambled).
3. Is the literature written for four or eight parts? If it is four parts, choose formation 4, 5, 6, or 7. If it is eight parts, choose formation 1, 2, 3, 8, 9, or 10.
4. Does the choir have difficulty tuning? To promote better intonation, choose formation 9 or 10.
5. Are most of the singers inexperienced? To help them bind together as sections, perform four-part music, and choose formation 4, 5, 6, or 7.
6. Do the Baritone and Tenor II need to sing with each other on occasions? Choose formation 3.
7. Do the Soprano II and Alto I need to sing with each other on occasions? Choose formation 3.
8. Do the Alto II and Tenor I need to sing with each other on occasions? Choose formation 3.
9. Do the boys need to sing together on one part (**Soprano, Alto, Boys** voicing)? Choose formation 4, 5, 6, or 7.
10. Do individual singers need to develop independence in singing? Choose formation 9 or 10.

EIGHT-PART FORMATIONS

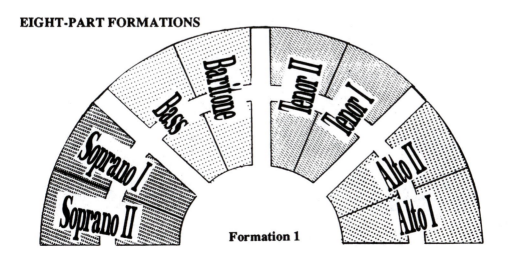

Formation 1

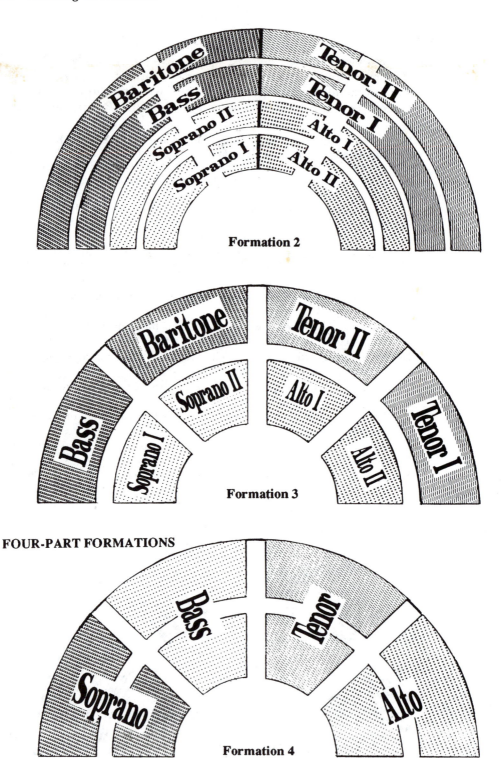

Formation 2

Formation 3

FOUR-PART FORMATIONS

Formation 4

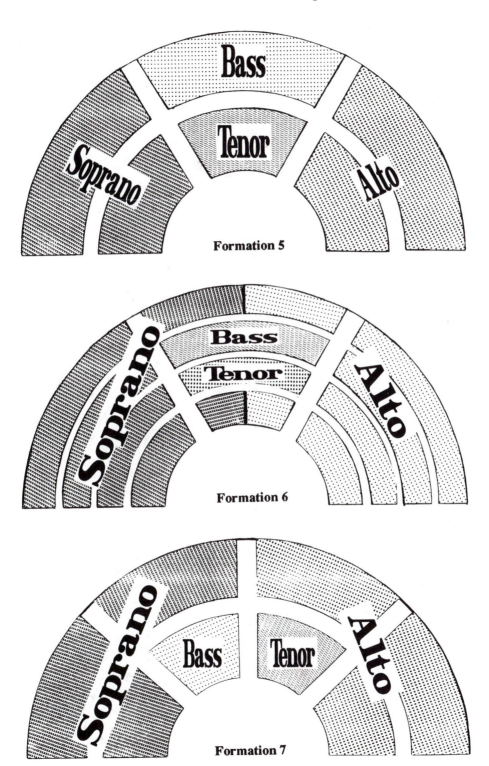

Formation 5

Formation 6

Formation 7

SCRAMBLED FORMATIONS

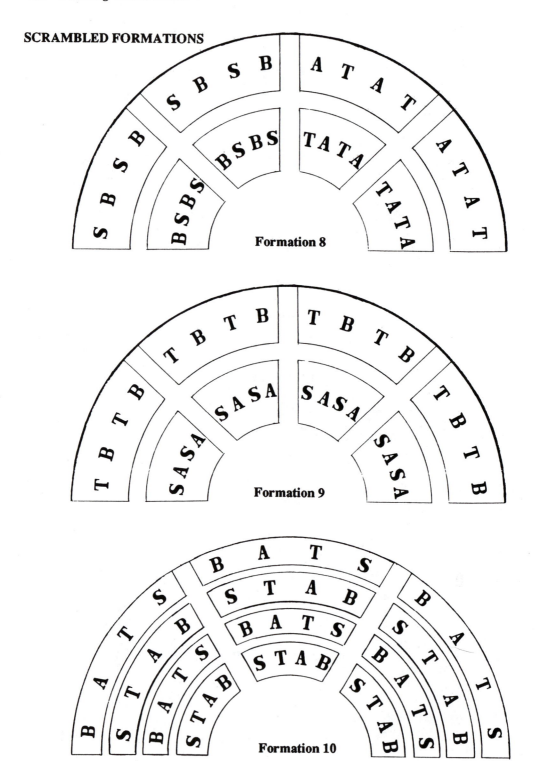

Formation 8

Formation 9

Formation 10

All-boys and all-girls senior high school seating formations are shown. Directors should choose the one that best suits their choral needs.

ALL-FEMALE FORMATIONS

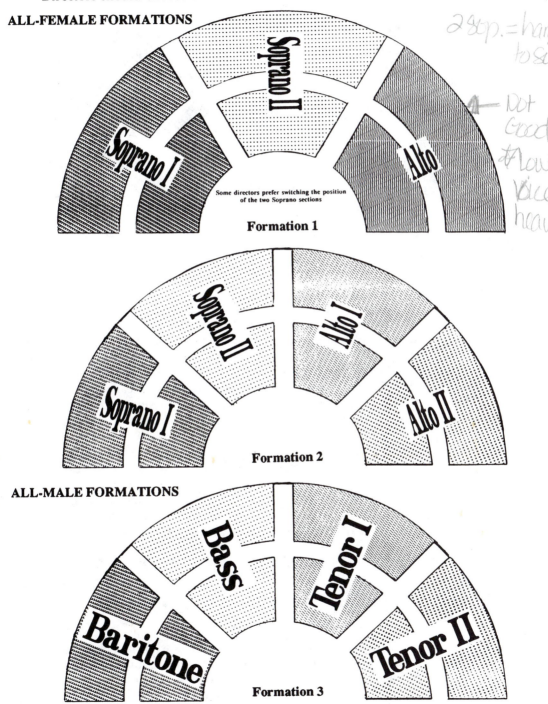

Formation 1

Some directors prefer switching the position of the two Soprano sections

Formation 2

ALL-MALE FORMATIONS

Formation 3

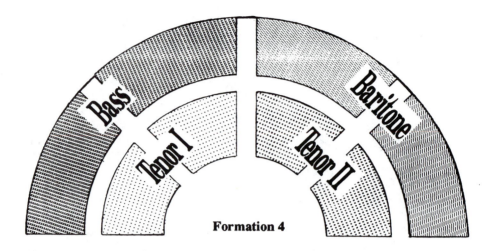

Formation 4

VOICE CLASSIFICATIONS

Voice Classifications in Middle/Junior High School

Chapter 9 addressed how to deal with early adolescent voices in the classroom. Please read and internalize that information before attempting to classify these voices in groups for choral singing. Keep in mind that the girls are neither true sopranos nor altos and the boys neither true tenors nor basses. It is recommended that directors divide girls arbitrarily into two sections called Soprano I and Soprano II and that directors allow each group to sing both the upper and lower female parts in the choral literature, alternating on different pieces. It is best to think about early adolescent boys as having one of four types of voices: (1) treble, (2) first-phase changing (cambiatas), (3) second-phase changing (baritones), or (4) changed voices (basses). When singing four-part music, place some trebles (be sure to read how to determine where to place the trebles) and cambiatas in one section and the baritones and basses in another.

Ranges (indicated by the whole notes) and comfortable singing tessitura (indicated by the quarter notes) for early adolescent singers are:

These ranges and tessitura relate to students who have never taken voice lessons, studied in a choir school, or received extensive musical training. Young singers who have studied and understand how to use the complete compass of the voice with ease will not be quite so limited.

Voice Classifications in Senior High School

If the **Beginning Choir** is a senior high school choir and not a middle/junior high school choir (see Chapter 15) directors will still have to be cognizant of the presence of changing voices. Depending on the type singers present, they might desire to use SSCB vocal classification. Probably, however, the students will be better suited to SATB voicing. Even so, directors should be very careful to select literature that administers to their changing voices.

Voicings for the **Intermediate and Advanced Choirs** will be SATB unless the Intermediate Choir is for all girls. If teachers classify these voices properly when listening to the entire section, they may be described as follows:

SOPRANOS:

These girls' vocal sound is light, airy, flutelike, sometimes breathy. They are inclined to be natural head singers. By the senior year some of the girls will begin to sound similar to adult lyric sopranos. A few of the girls will have strong lower tones (directors may place them on Soprano II part) but still have flexibility and agility in the upper voice.

ALTOS:

Very few girls in senior high school have true alto quality (a rich, dark, warm resonant sound). Adolescent altos may have a more mellow quality: the bright ring of the higher, lighter voice is not present in the voice. Directors tend to place the girls who are natural chest singers on the alto part. Be careful to vocalize these girls in the upper area of the voice regularly so that the full range of the voice will develop properly. In fact, it is a wonderful practice to allow the "altos" to sing the soprano part occasionally. They must never think about themselves as having "low" voices. Altos should have a mental image of being sopranos who can sing lower.

TENORS:

Adult tenors have a bright, ringing quality and may be able to carry modal voice phonation (with some "mixed" or "head" resonance) to high C (fourth space, treble clef actual pitch). Relative to adult tenors, one can think about all older adolescent boys (be careful not to confuse them with cambiatas who are first-phase changing voices) who sing tenor as being "high baritones." Some will have definite tenor brightness, but most will have less brightness with even a slightly "smoky" or "youthy" sound. Directors often ask them to sing tenor because they do not have the low notes necessary to sing bass. Since they will be singing adult literature, usually when they move above D or E flat (above middle C), they will need to use falsetto phonation (unless they have been taught excellent vocal technique at an early age) to keep them from developing bad vocal habits. Using the falsetto is very important at this age. If they are not taught to do so, they will sing with a protruded chin and will "grab" the upper tones (control the larynx with the same muscles that control swallowing) and produce a very tensive sound. Using the voice in this fashion creates habitually poor singing that will haunt them for years to come.

BASSES:

As with tenors, very few boys in senior high school have true adult bass quality. It is best to think about them as being low baritones. In fact, in reality most older adolescent male singers (both tenors and basses) have a baritone range (with the same "youthy" quality described above). Those boys chosen to sing bass have more security in the lower area. Encourage the singers not to try to "make" the lower tones be loud, but to "allow" them to emit freely with plenty of even breath flow. Adolescents are inclined to develop "bassitus" (an attempt to make the voice sound deep and dark, a covered effect). Directors should teach them how to develop the upper voice so that they sing with ease and brilliance. Some boys may need to employ falsetto phonation when tones move above middle C to keep them from developing poor singing habits.

Ranges (whole notes) and comfortable singing tessitura (quarter notes) for older adolescent singers are:

Soprano   Alto   Tenor   Bass

As with the ranges and tessitura delineated for early adolescents, those listed here represent untrained singers and are somewhat limiting when compared to the ranges of students with significant vocal training.

CHOOSING LITERATURE FOR ADOLESCENTS

In secondary choral classes, choosing literature that administers to the needs of adolescent voices and presents to the listener the best vocal attributes of each member in the choirs is a very important responsibility. Since discipline (controlling the class) is one of beginning teachers' concerns, believe it or not, choosing literature that adolescents are capable of singing well is one of the best ways to contribute to control in the classroom. If the music is within the comfortable singing tessitura of the singers' voices and they are pleased with the selections, they will have a positive attitude about choir that will cause them to be much more willing to cooperate and much less liable to disturb.

Directors may spend hours training their singers to be good musicians who sing with excellent vocal and choral technique, but in a desire to sing "impressive" literature some directors choose pieces that do not administer to the unique choral characteristics of their choirs, so the choirs do not sing well. All the hard work has been pointless. In this light, choice of literature may be the most significant contributor to the finished product of any choral organization.

Other than the unique limitations of adolescent voices, there are several important criteria directors should consider when choosing literature for their choirs (middle/junior and senior high school ages).

DIFFICULTY LEVEL

A basic principle directors should follow is "never choose a piece that is too easy nor one that is too difficult." Adolescents often judge the value of a selection by how difficult it is. If it is too easy, they may feel insulted, and if it is too difficult, they may give up. The music should challenge their ability and musicianship but never make them feel defeated. Factors to consider when judging difficulty are as follows:

*Rhythmic complexities—Are there meter changes and if so, how frequent are they? Are there many short notes to execute at a rapid tempo? How much syncopation does the piece contain and what is its complexity?

*Key changes— Are there frequent key changes? Are the modulations choral or instrumental? Does the tonality move to closely related or foreign keys?

*Harmonic complexities—How severe is the dissonance, particularly in regard to minor seconds? Do the dissonances resolve properly or do they remain unresolved? Is the harmony tonal, atonal, or polytonal? How fast is the harmonic rhythm?

*Melodic features—Do the melodies contain long melismatic passages? Do they contain frequent awkward leaps? Are they disjunct? Are there fast and frequent articulation requirements?

*Texture—How many parts are there? If it is polyphonic, are the choir's weak sections exposed? If it is accompanied, does the accompaniment support the voices? Is the vocal texture thick or sparse?

*Text—Is it to be sung in a foreign language? Are the words to be articulated rapidly?

SOCIOLOGICAL AND CULTURAL APPEAL

Appeal is particularly important to directors in a new position. They must consider the social and cultural influences on the school, community, and state when they choose the music the choirs will sing. Considerations about those who will be attending the concerts are:

*Location—Is the audience from a rural, suburban, or urban area?

*Socioeconomic level—Are those attending primarily professionals, from the business world, or blue-collar workers?

*Race—Will the listeners be mostly minorities? If so, which minority will predominate?

*Religion— What faiths will be represented?

*Musical background—Will the audience readily accept music with which they are unfamiliar? Will they prefer music of one specific type?

*Educational level—Will the audience be predominantly college and university graduates?

EDUCATIONAL VALUE

Directors must choose music that supports the educational goals they have set forth in musicianship training, their study of vocal-choral technique, and aesthetic education. Both a cappella and accompanied literature should be chosen. All the accompanied literature should not be for keyboard only; some should include various orchestral and band instruments (if not for full orchestra or band). After adolescents have completed their tenure in a fully sequential choral program, directors should have chosen music from all periods, large and small forms, folk music, spirituals, Broadway and contemporary popular music, and festival selections for them to study and sing.

AESTHETIC VALUE

When evaluating the text and music, directors should consider the "lasting" value of the selections. They should contemplate:

> *Text*—Is the text too mature or too childish? Does it wed well with the music? Do the two belong together?
>
> *Arrangement*—If the selection has been arranged, does the arrangement enhance or detract from the original style?
>
> *Time test*—Has it passed the time test? How long has it been part of the culture? (This is not to imply that all pieces chosen should be from periods of the past, but this should be a consideration.) Those pieces that have high cultural value are the ones students remember and continue to sing throughout their lives.

Special Considerations in Choosing Literature for the Middle/Junior High School Choir

In a sequential choral program the **Beginning Choir** will be the middle/junior high school choir, if possible (see Chapter 15). If the choral program cannot be sequential beginning in middle school and continuing through senior high school, the **Beginning Choir** may need to be the first choir in which the students enroll in senior high school.

   Choosing to sing literature written specifically for early adolescents is the most important decision choral directors make when working with this age singer.[3] **These young singers do not have adult voices, therefore they should not be singing music written for adults.**[4] **It does not administer to their unique vocal characteristics and limitations. Years ago directors of early adolescent choirs had no alternative but to attempt to sing music written for adults because publishers did not realize that early adolescent choirs needed a unique type of literature. Now, leading composers, arrangers, educators, and publishers recognize the importance of supplying music written specifically for**

---

[3] This statement is exacting and to the point. There is no question about its definity. You must understand that the topic of early adolescent choral literature is a very important aspect of teaching early adolescents. To this date, in almost 150 professional workshops in thirty-one different states, I have advocated strongly the tenets about which you are to read. I have spent almost twenty years preaching this gospel because I sincerely believe that choice of literature is the secret to success in teaching choral music to early adolescents.

[4] Difficulty is not the consideration here. I have conducted some early adolescent choirs who were capable of singing difficult music better than many adults I have conducted. The music the adolescents sang, however, was written or arranged for their unique vocal limitations.

choirs in middle/junior high school. Regrettably, they cannot agree about such important matters as (1) how to group the singers, (2) what to call the changing voices, (3) which clefs to use when writing the parts, and (4) how many parts early adolescent choirs should sing. Perhaps as our profession matures we will come to a consensus about these matters. Most of the music recommended currently for early adolescent choirs by American publishers is worthy of consideration.[5] Even though publishers recommend their music for adolescent singers, directors must be careful to evaluate each piece they choose: The piece may not fit the particular voices of the students they have in their choirs at that time.

How can we know if we are choosing music that will present our choirs in the best light? In the form of a question-and-answer dialogue I have presented important information relative to choosing music for early adolescent singers. Read it with care. Study and attempt to internalize it. It is some of the most helpful information you will receive from this book.

Which is best for choirs containing early adolescent voices—unison, two, three, or four parts? The answer to this question is illusive. The number of boys enrolled in the choir provides the answer. If there are twenty girls (or more) and only two boys, it is very difficult to perform four-part music. On the other hand, if there are twenty girls (or more) and at least four boys, directors may be surprised as to how successful the choir may be singing four parts. The inclination of some directors is to place all the boys (if there are as few as four) on one part and divide the girls into two groups (Soprano I and II), thinking that four boys can balance ten girls on each part better than two boys. If all four boys are cambiatas or if they are all baritones, that is sound logic; but if there are at least two cambiatas and two baritones, consider this reasoning. Examine the comfortable singing tessitura of both cambiatas and baritones provided in the section above ("Voice Classifications in Middle/Junior High School"). Notice that if they sing together *comfortably*, they must sing a part that has an overall compass of A (top line, bass clef) upward to D (above middle C), only an interval of a fourth. Directors may choose a part that is written with an overall compass of F (fourth line, bass clef) to F (above middle C), which represents a composite overall *range* capability of both voices, a full octave. In either case, there are problems when the boys sing the part together. The part will keep the baritones in the upper area of their voices all the time, which causes vocal tension, poor intonation, and unhealthy vocal results. The same part will keep the cambiatas in the lower area of their voices all the time, which does not allow them to use the most comfortable and best-sounding tones of their vocal instruments, the

---

[5] Alfred Publishing Company, Belwin Mills, Bourne Company, Broadman Press, Cambiata Press (publishes music only for early adolescents), Carl Fischer Music Publishers, Inc., Charles Hansen Music and Books, Cherry Lane Music Co., Inc., Choristers Guild, Columbia Pictures Publications, Hal Leonard Publications, Heritage Music Press, Hinshaw Music, Inc., Jenson Publications, Kendor Music, Inc., Lawson-Gould Music Publishers, Inc., Lorenz Corp., Oxford University Press, Plymouth Music Co., and Shawnee Press are the leading publishers that have music recommended specifically for the middle/junior high school market.

tones of D (above middle C) upward to G. Therefore, none of the boys will be able to sing in the best area of his voice. Putting them together hampers both cambiatas and baritones. If the two cambiatas and two baritones are allowed to sing two separate parts written specifically for them, ones that put into use the most comfortable singing area and best tones of each, two boys are more likely to balance ten girls than will four boys who are hampered by the part they must sing. For this reason, *early adolescent choirs almost always will function better singing four-parts rather than three*, provided those four parts are written to administer to their vocal limitations.

Singing in two parts (cambiatas and baritones on one part and the girls on another) creates the same problem described above because any time the cambiatas and baritones must sing together, neither can use the best tones of their singing instrument.

Unison-octave singing presents a similar problem if both cambiatas and baritones sing in the same octave. If directors find a unison piece that has an overall compass of D (above middle C) upward to A, the cambiatas can sing in unison with the girls and the baritones may sing an octave lower. Early adolescents cannot sing successfully in unison if the part moves above or below the D to A compass. Choosing to sing unison melodies with a range outside of the D to A compass usually causes the cambiatas to "flounder around," attempting to sing with the girls (a part that is too high) or to sing with the baritones (a part that is too low), neither of which allows them to be successful. They soon become altogether disenchanted with singing and start to disrupt the class because they realize that they are not making a significant contribution.

Is it possible to use SATB voicing with early adolescent singers? It is possible, but perhaps not practical. If directors are careful they can find SATB music that early adolescents can sing *successfully*, provided (1) the soprano part does not move above F (top line, treble clef), (2) the alto part does not move below B-flat (below middle C) and it has a relatively high tessitura, (3) the tenor part (which the cambiatas will sing) does not move below A (top line, bass clef) and it has a relative high tessitura, and (4) the bass part (which will be sung by the adolescent baritones) does not move below B-flat (second line, bass clef) nor above D or E-flat (above middle C). Notice that the term *successfully* was used in the sentence above. The more a piece of SATB-voiced music adheres to the strict limitations described above, the more successful early adolescents will be when they try to sing it. When using SATB voicing, it is important (if directors want to present their choirs at their best) for directors to scrutinize each part and select only music that adheres to the strict limitations described above. The best solution is to choose music written specifically for them. From this point of view, choosing SATB voiced music certainly is possible but may not be practical.

Is it possible for cambiatas to sing a part written for adult altos? It is possible, but again, perhaps it is not practical. Cambiatas will be quite comfortable singing an alto part that has a compass from A upward to A (below and above middle C). Directors must be careful not to choose a part that contains unison passages that requires the cambiatas to sing with the sopranos because it will likely move above the comfortable singing tessitura of their voices. The primary problem directors have with cambiatas singing alto does not relate to their ability to sing the part; it is a gender problem. Because publishers label the part *alto*, this communicates *female* to the cambiatas, so automatically they assume that they should not and cannot sing it. To them, that part was written for a girl. Interestingly enough, if directors ask girls to join them in singing a cambiata part in SSCB voicing, they do not object so ardently. They think about the part having been written for them; it is a *male* part even though the girls are helping them sing it. Cambiatas are capable of singing four-part music marked SSAB (one often finds this type voicing in music written for the Moravians) or three-part music marked SSA if the alto parts meet the limitations described above and if directors are successful in persuading them to sing a part originally intended for a female. Three, four, and five-part choral music from the Renaissance period (English madrigals are the most prevalent) have parts usually designated by editors as *alto* (originally countertenors may have sung it), which is perfect for cambiatas.[6] When examining this music, directors must be careful to choose an alto part with an A to A compass.

Will early adolescent singers be successful singing SAB music? The answer to that question depends on what the *B* means. If it means *baritone*, and contains a part written for adult baritones or boys in the second phase of change, there will be no part for the cambiatas to sing; the baritone part will be too low for them. They may attempt to sing the alto part if directors are successful in persuading them to do so and provided it is limited to a compass of A to A. If the *B* stands for *boys* and contains a part with a compass of F upward to D or E-flat (below and above middle C), then adolescent singers will be capable of singing it. The points of argument against all boys singing together (described in the latter part of the first question in this section) are germane to SABoys voicings as well.

There is music on the market labeled Parts I, II, and III. Is this music written for adolescent voices? If so, which parts are the cambiatas and baritones to sing? Music containing generic vocal designations are often written for adolescent voices but publishers use the nondescriptive labeling so that younger or older singers may sing them as well. Publishers are able to increase their octavo sales if they do not designate the parts for one specific type of clientele. Most of this music contains three parts (some of it has two or four parts). If the lower of the three parts is written in the bass clef, usually it is intended for all adolescent boys (cambiatas and baritones combined) with the same limited range and considerations described above for SABoys voicing. Quite often (if limited to the A to A compass) cambiatas and/or altos may sing Part II (the middle part), leaving Part III for the boys in the second phase of change (baritones).

---

[6] "Quam Pulchra Es" by John Dunstable (three part), "Come, Holy Ghost" by Christopher Tye (four part), and "Mother, I Will Have a Husband" by Thomas Vautor (five part) are examples of these published in the *Three Centuries of Choral Music* compilations, a series by Harold Flammer (distributed by Shawnee Press). These three are in the booklet *Renaissance to Baroque, Volume III, English Music.*

If Part III (the lower part) is written in the treble clef, the arrangement is usually intended for SSA or SSC voicing and should be sung by choirs without adolescent baritones unless they sing one of the upper parts an octave lower.

Is there a specific process that may be used to help analyze octavos as to how appropriate they may or may not be for early adolescent singers? Yes, as follows:

1. Look at each line of music in the octavo, determine to which group of singers that part should be assigned, then ascertain if it is within the overall *range* of those singers. If all parts are within range, the octavo may be sung by adolescent voices, but the upper notes may be tensive and the lower notes may be weak, particularly if there is an abundance of them.

2. Look at each line of music in the octavo, determine to which group of singers that part should be assigned, then ascertain if it is within the *comfortable singing tessitura* of those singers. If so, this octavo is highly recommended to be sung by adolescent voices if the text, difficulty, and articulation speed of the voices are appropriate.

3. If the octavo is designated to be for an SATB choir, assign the soprano part to the Soprano I section, the alto part to the Soprano II section, the tenor part to the Cambiatas, and the bass part to the adolescent Baritones and analyze it according to steps 1 and 2 above.

4. If the octavo is designated to be for an SSA choir, assign the soprano I part to the Soprano I section, the soprano II part to the Soprano II section, and the alto part to the Cambiatas. Do not consider it to be sung by a choir with adolescent Baritones unless they could sing the soprano 1 part one octave lower. Analyze it according to steps 1 and 2 above.

5. If the octavo is designated to be for an SA choir, assign the soprano part to all the girls and the alto part to the Cambiatas and analyze it according to steps 1 and 2 above. Obviously, the octavo may be sung by girls only, if it fits their voices.

6. If the octavo is designated to be for an SAB choir, assign the soprano part to the Soprano I section, the alto part to the Soprano II section, and the baritone part to all the boys. If the boys' part is out of range and tessitura for both Cambiatas and adolescent Baritones combined, consider the octavo in a different light. Assign the soprano part to all the girls, the alto part to the Cambiatas, and the baritone part to the adolescent Baritones, then analyze it according to steps 1 and 2 above.

7. If the octavo has no vocal designations and refers to the parts by numbers (parts I, II, and III) with all parts being in the *treble clef*, assign part I to the Soprano I section, part II to the Soprano II section, and part III to the Cambiatas and analyze it accordingly. This type octavo also may be sung by an all female-choir. Assign part I to the Soprano I section, part II to the Soprano II section, and part III to the Altos and determine if the parts are within the range and tessitura of adolescent girls.

8. If the octavo has no vocal designations and refers to the parts by numbers (parts I, II, and III) with part III being in the *bass clef*, assign part I to the Sopranos, part II to the Cambiatas, and part III to the adolescent Baritones. If the octavo is out of range and tessitura using these assignments, check to see if it will work if part I is assigned to the Soprano I section, part II to the Soprano II section, and part III to all the boys (Cambiatas and adolescent Baritones combined) and analyze it accordingly.

9. If the octavo has no vocal designations, refers to the parts by numbers, and has four parts (with part IV in the bass clef), assign part I to the Soprano I

section, part II to the Soprano II section, part III to the Cambiatas, and part IV to the adolescent Baritones and analyze it accordingly.

10. If the octavo is in unison, or has unison sections, its ease of use must be evaluated according to the composite unison-octave range (B-flat below middle C to C, one octave above) and tessitura (D to A above middle C) for changing voice singers. If the boys' parts move into unison, or if the cambiatas are asked to sing with the girls, consider the composite unison range and tessitura.

Choosing Literature for All-Male Choruses

In certain parts of the country all-male choruses are very popular both in middle/junior high and senior high schools. See Chapter 15 ("The All-Male or All-Female Chorus) for reasons to include them in the choral program. As indicated in Chapter 15, one of the difficulties with an all-male chorus in middle/junior high school is finding literature written specifically for their changing voices.[7] Even though some of these groups sing four-part music, the consensus of most directors indicates that three-part voicing is more advantageous. Depending on the age level and number of boys in various stages of change, either CCB or CBB voicing is the most popular. Recommended ranges for each of the parts are:

| Cambiata I | Cambiata II | Baritone I | Baritone II |

When choosing TTBB, TTB or TBB voicings, directors should be careful to determine if the arrangements were written for adolescents or adults. The adult tenor part may be too high for older adolescent tenors (senior high school) and the bass part may be too low for early adolescent baritones (middle/junior high school). Recommended ranges for senior high school all-male choruses are:

| Tenor I | Tenor II | Baritone | Bass |

Multicultural Influences

Many schools in the United States require a multicultural curriculum. Certain subjects and approaches to classroom content must include not only the predominant culture of the school, but representation of the various minority

[7] Cambiata Press (P.O. Box 1151, Conway, Arkansas 72032) has a special series for all-male early adolescent choirs, *The Sound of Singing Boys.* Write to them for reference copies.

cultures present as well. In general music, fine arts, and music appreciation classes, it is important to include units about the musical heritage and background of all the culturals represented in class. Teachers should choose a textbook that includes a multicultural emphasis.

The selection of choral repertoire should include compositions and arrangements by minority musicians and folk songs from many different cultures. Some music distributors are equipped to provide reference copies of octavos on consignment with whatever cultural emphasis directors might desire to program. When new releases come to the distributors from the publisher, necessary information about each title is entered into their computer allowing them to assemble a packet of single octavos for directors' perusal upon request. Consult the Music Retailers.[8] Many have Wide Area Telephone Service (WATS), toll-free for the directors' convenience.

SCORE PREPARATION AND PRESENTATION

If the truth were known, there may have been times that every director has stood before a choir unprepared to teach the selection on the music stand. On those occasions they probably tried to rationalize their incompetence by declaring to themselves that they were too busy to prepare the score. Some of the choir members may not have known that the director was unprepared, because after years of conducting and rehearsing, conductors become pretty adept at concealing their lack of understanding of the score and lack of knowing exactly how they were going to approach it.

Some of the finest conductors we know might have to make such a confession. Even though some of their choir members may not have known they were unprepared, *they* knew the circumstances and *they* understood the consequences. A director should never be proud of being unprepared, even though it occurs occasionally. The point is: It is remarkable how quickly and thoroughly choir members learn a piece when the directors are prepared as compared to when they are not. *Lack of conductor score preparation is probably the leading contributor to inefficient use of rehearsal time.* Beyond that, poor performances can be traced directly to lack of director preparation. When directors stand before choirs without understanding the score thoroughly and without knowing exactly where they are going with the rehearsal and how they are going to arrive, it is similar to driving an automobile blindfolded. The results may be calamitous.

As years of experience accumulate, master conductors devise special ways to mark their scores that relate to each conductor's distinctive needs and personality. The gamut of approaches run from the simple to the complex. Some conductors use very elaborate methods that include color-coded markings

---

[8] Malecki Music in Grand Rapids (4500 Broadmoor, SE, P.O. Box 150, Grand Rapids, MI 49501, 800–253–9692) and Council Bluffs (3034 S. Eleventh St., Council Bluffs, IA 51502) offer this service.

and specialized sets of symbols. Others more or less memorize the score as they study it so that it is "marked mentally" and not on the printed page. Most approaches fall somewhere between these two. Young, inexperienced conductors appear to require and exhibit a greater intensity of study and depth of analysis because they must write down everything to understand and remember it. The more experienced conductors become, the more intensely and in-depth they analyze their scores because they have more completely developed their interpretative and communicative skills. There is a greater need to understand fully everything the music has to offer the listener, even though they may not mark their scores so extensively. As young conductors, intensive score study is essential to develop these valuable interpretative and communicative skills. Mark the score thoroughly to assure that everything is communicated to the singers in rehearsal and through the conducting process.

Design

Initially, conductors should analyze the form or design of the piece (*binary, ternary, strophic, through-composed,* and so forth). The design dictates the overall rehearsal plan. If definite sections are apparent they might plan to rehearse the piece one section at a time. If the work is through-composed and follows the dictates of the text, they might desire to rehearse the whole.

The Text

The text provides valuable clues in understanding how conductors should interpret and execute the music. Read the text aloud. Examine every word to determine proper pronunciation (pure vowels and effective consonants). Look for trouble spots that need special consideration in rehearsal to assure the listener will understand the text (see "Diction—The Choir's Ability to Communicate the Text" in Chapter 12). If it is written in a foreign language, directors should study a precise translation so that they understand the exact meaning of each word. Be careful not to rely on a companion English text printed with the foreign text. It may not be a direct translation. Poor translations to English often result in the musical accents falling on the wrong syllable of a word. Occasionally, directors will need to reconstruct the English sentence to allow the accent to fall properly.

If the piece was written in the Renaissance or Baroque period, directors should look for *word painting* (a musical representation of specific textual images) and determine ways to emphasize or highlight these words. If the music is homophonic and the text *strophic* (one setting of music for all stanzas) or *through-composed* (new music for each stanza) the audience will not understand the text unless they can discern each word. Much of the polyphonic music (particularly that from the Baroque period) uses short important sentences that are repeated over and over so that the listener discerns the meaning of the text through repetition. Directors will need to spend more time perfecting the pronunciation of the homophonic, strophic pieces than the polyphonic ones.

The text is an indication of the mode of choral singing directors should choose (see "Modes of Choral Singing" in Chapter 12), although an analysis of the music is also important in determining the mode. If a composition is well-written, both text and music will communicate the spirit of the piece and the mode directors should choose will be obvious. The choice of mode will determine how the work is introduced to the choir.

Finally, look for places where closed vowels (*EE, IH,* and *OO)* occur on very high pitches, particularly in the soprano part (see "Vowel Color and Modification" in Chapter 12). These places will need special attention in rehearsal to alleviate tensive singing.

Voice Parts

Beginning conductors should play the voice parts on the piano (or have a pianist to play them as they listen) to establish the sound of the parts together before entering rehearsal. Play the parts in duets: soprano and bass, soprano and alto, soprano and tenor, alto and tenor, alto and bass, and tenor and bass. Be aware of strong dissonances and trouble spots so that the choir members may be alerted. Then play the accompaniment to determine how it relates to the voice parts. Look for places where the accompaniment doubles the voices, strongly supports the voices although it may not be an exact doubling, or moves independently from them.

Sing each of the parts. Look for awkward intervals, wide leaps, and areas of high or low tessitura. These will need special attention in the rehearsal. Determine places where voice parts relate to each other as well as ways various parts may cue off others. Directors should determine how to phrase each of the parts and mark the phrasing in their scores. Determine if the phrases in the parts all peak together or if each part peaks separately. Mark where each phrase peaks.

Observe the melodic characteristics of each part. Are the phrases regular (four or eight bars) or irregular? Look for sequences. Determine places where the parts outline triads, move in ascending or descending scales, and display unique melodic characteristics.

Directors should practice singing each part until they have developed performance proficiency by which to model necessary aspects for the choir.

Style

Study the life of the composer, the period in which the piece was written, and, if available, anything that might have been written about the piece itself. It is not necessary to "wax eloquently" during rehearsal when sharing this information with the singers, but a brief explanation is important in helping them to understand how to approach the piece. Determine the style of the piece (see "Style—The Choir's Authenticity" in Chapter 12). Directors should decide which of the four basic components of the music (melody, harmony, rhythm, or texture) predominates. Effective communication of proper style is arrived through emphasis of that predominating component.

Directors' approach to harmony will be different depending on the style of the piece. If it is a twentieth-century piece, they must determine if it is tonal, atonal, polytonal, twelve-tone, or whatever. They will need to determine the harmonic rhythm. If it is a Baroque chorale they should be cognizant of the fast harmonic rhythm. Folk songs and polyphony have a much slower harmonic rhythm. In traditional harmony, mark the nonchord tones and determine how to execute them. Determine how harmonic dissonance and resolution occurs and decide how to deal with it in rehearsal and performance. Examine key relationships and points of modulation, then mark those that might be atypical or difficult to learn and give them special attention.

Directors should point out rhythmic characteristics that might be unique to a piece, particularly with those pieces that are inherently rhythmic in nature. Look for rhythmic sequences or repetition of distinctive rhythm patterns and determine the most effective way to perform them. Determine the correlation between the rhythm complexity and tempo. Fast tempos often create problems in the execution of rhythm patterns that require distinct articulation. Mark triplets, duplets, mixed meter, and meter changes and indicate how these affect the rhythmic accents (in both pulses and beats). Practice conducting them for effective communication. In rehearsal directors will need to give attention to the accents so that the rhythmic drive will permeate execution of the piece. Examine each part for places singers will have difficulty reading and executing the rhythm. Mark them and plan to extract them for specific drill in the rehearsal.

Nontraditional notation such as that found in *aleatoric* or *chance music* will need special explanation. Since the composers explain this notation in each publication, directors must study the explanation thoroughly and teach it to the singers.

Actually, directors should consider the texture of the work before they choose to perform a selection. Directors should not choose to sing a work with texture that has more voices or instruments than are accessible. Conversely, neither should they consider singing a work in which the texture is so sparse that it exposes areas that certain sections are unable to sing well. For instance, some choirs should not attempt monophonic, unaccompanied music because their vocal technique is not sufficient to allow them to sing it in tune and in a perfect unison.

If texture appears to be the most important component in the selection such as in the polychoral works of Giovanni Gabrieli, directors need to assure that they have access to different choirs (instrumental and vocal) and that the choirs are sufficiently separated to simulate the acoustical environment of St. Mark's Cathedral where Gabrieli intended them to be sung. Due to the thick texture of polyphonic works, double chorus works, and some eight-part settings, directors should mark their scores and rehearse the choirs so those voice parts that should be heard will stand out above those voice parts that are less important.

A Checklist for Score Preparation

Whatever system is used to mark the score, beginning conductors will desire to consult the following checklist in preparing their score for rehearsal.

Relative to design:

1. What is the design (binary, ternary, strophic, through-composed, and so forth)?
2. What is the rehearsal approach? Shall it be rehearsed by sections or as a whole?

Relative to the text:

1. Read the text aloud. Which words need special attention for the purpose of clear communication?
2. Prepare an explanation about exactly what the text means. This is particularly important with adolescents.
3. If it is in a foreign language, what is the exact meaning of each word?
4. Does it include word painting? If so, be prepared to explain it to the choir.
5. Is the text strophic or through-composed? What means will be used to assure that the words are communicated?
6. Are there high pitches on closed vowels? How shall the singers deal with them?

Relative to the voice parts:

1. Play the voice parts together and in duets.
2. Is there a special seating or standing formation that will address special needs in the voice parts?
3. Where are the strong dissonances and trouble spots where the singers may need assistance?
4. Does the accompaniment double the voices? How does it relate to the voices?
5. Are the awkward intervals and wide leaps? Be prepared to help the singers initiate them accurately.
6. Are there areas of extreme high or low tessitura in the parts? Be prepared to deal with balance and vocal technique in these areas.
7. Are there places where one voice part may cue from another? Be prepared to alert the choir members.
8. Mark the phrasing of each part. Be prepared to instruct the choir to do the same.
9. Where do each of the phrases peak? When singing in legato mode, be prepared to alert the choir members of the direction of each phrase.
10. Are the phrases regular or irregular?
11. Do the phrases contain sequences?
12. Are there places where the vocal lines outline triads or ascending and descending scale lines?

Relative to style:

1. What is the historical style of the piece? How does it affect the rehearsal procedure and performance approach to the piece?
2. Prepare background information about the composer and the piece.

3. Which of the four basic components of music predominates (melody, harmony, rhythm, or texture)? Be prepared to build the rehearsal procedure, choice of mode of singing, and style around that component.

4. Is the piece tonal, atonal, polytonal, twelve-tone, and so forth?

5. If it has traditional harmony, what is the harmonic rhythm? Mark the nonchord tones and be prepared to teach the singers how to resolve them effectively.

6. Does the piece modulate? If so, how? What are the key relationships? Know how to approach teaching the modulation to the singers.

7. Are there difficult rhythmic patterns? Are there rhythmic sequences? Determine the most effective way to teach these to the singers.

8. Mark duplets, triplets, mixed meter, and rhythmic accents.

9. Does the piece contain nontraditional notation? If so, be prepared to explain it.

10. What is the texture of the piece? Choose the proper seating or standing formation accordingly.

REHEARSAL TECHNIQUE

Now that you have a basic understanding about preparing and holding an audition, preparing the rehearsal area, assigning music and folders, arranging the choir in their seats or on risers, classifying voices, determining how to choose appropriate literature, and preparing a choral score, I will deal specifically with ways of handling the rehearsal. Much of the information will apply specifically to the Intermediate and Advanced Choirs. To begin, however, let us look at some rehearsal techniques that relate specifically to the needs of the Beginning Choir.

The Beginning Choir Rehearsals

In Chapter 15 specific behavioral objectives and class activities for the Beginning Choir are delineated. Please read that information before proceeding further. That discussion discloses two basic goals for the membership of the Beginning Choir: (1) to master the fundamental principles of sound vocal-choral technique (see Chapters 10 and 12) and (2) to learn to read music (see Chapter 11 for specific methods) and develop basic musicianship.

Directors should address these two goals as they plan each of their rehearsals throughout the year. At the beginning of the year, before initiating a sequential sight-reading program, they will need to substitute rote teaching of *melody-part style* music until the students begin to feel comfortable singing four-part music. With some groups, directors will need to teach rote teaching only during the first three or four weeks; with other groups directors may need to address it for at least half of the first semester. At some point directors decide to wean the choir away from rote teaching and commence the sight-reading program. Both may thrive side by side until the students develop their sight-reading skills to the degree of sight-reading all the music during rehearsal.

Rote Teaching Melody-Part Style Music   When students are experiencing three and four-part music for the first time, they will have more success if the parts they are singing are melodies. It is very disconcerting for young singers when, upon trying to "harmonize" for the first time, they find themselves singing the established melody (probably the Soprano I part) or some part other than their own. They have difficulty "hearing" their part when it contains many repeated notes and no melodic contour. Directors will have more success with part singing in the Beginning Choir if they choose music written in melody-part style.

Common practice of rote teaching in most American schools is to pass the music out, and taking each section at a time, play the part on the piano and ask the students to sing what they hear. Often the instructor will sing the part as it is played. After several repetitions the alert adolescents are capable of listening to the piano and singing the part. With a few more repetitions they will have the part memorized. At this point, the students, particularly the boys, find very little purpose for the printed music and they set about using it to satisfy that insatiable desire they have to "piddle" with something. Eventually the corners will be torn off and it may be rolled up, stomped on, used as a paper airplane, or any other creative destruction their fertile minds can conjure up.

Consider an alternative approach to rote teaching. Two components in the above description are not essential: the printed music and the piano. Because adolescents develop a dependence on the piano that is detrimental to the learning process when teaching music reading, the practice of using it as a teaching instrument is discouraged; in fact, it slows the process. If the piano is used constantly to support the singers, soon they will depend on it for security in singing; if they are required to sing their parts without the piano, they soon learn to depend on their listening ability and voice for support. Since they do not know how to read the printed music, why give it to them? By teaching music written in melody-part style, why not sing the melody to them and ask them to sing it back? Since all the parts are melodies, the adolescents grasp them very quickly and are able to sing them correctly almost after one hearing. Further, by using line notation written on the board, on transparencies, or on teaching charts, the learning process can be greatly accelerated. Rote teaching in this fashion dictates that the instructors be able to sing each of the parts correctly, and line notation assists them as much as it does the students. Singing the parts together a cappella greatly quickens the students' ability to tune the chords and develop a sense of musical independence.

When teaching by rote, stand the singers in sections in four distinct areas of the room. Be sure there is enough separation between the groups to facilitate a slight isolation from each of the other groups. The melody each group is singing needs to predominate that area of the room. It is important that each group be able to hear the others but not as well as they hear themselves. The groups should be facing the board or area where the transparency is being projected. If teaching charts are used, place the chart for each group on a music stand in front of them. If there is a need to turn the charts in the middle of the arrangement, designate one of the less exuberant singers to that responsibility. Be sure the ones turning the charts are not the type who enjoy entertaining the other students or they will disrupt the choral process and make a production out of the turning process.

There is no set order in which the parts should be taught to the singers. The basic rule of thumb is to teach first the part that is the most melodious. If all the parts are equal, teach the baritone first to set the foundation for the tonality. Always teach the established melody last.

It is important that teachers know each part well and that they be able to sing it with confidence. During their preparation time, if one particular phrase or note seems difficult, they should be sure to master it completely before attempting to teach the singers. The students will sense any hesitation or insecurity on the part of the teacher and it will affect the students' sense of assurance as they sing the melody back to the teacher. Teachers should not dwell on chromatic tones or point them out. The singers do not analyze those tones' nondiatonic character and probably will not recognize them as being foreign to the key. They will recognize them as being at home in their melody and that is how they should be approached.

Analyze each part and determine if it should be taught as a whole, one phrase at a time, or more than one phrase at once. A phrase with a strong cadence point or one that is repeated should be taught alone. If a phrase leads to the following phrase, the two phrases should be taught together. There will be rare occasions when the melody should be taught as a whole.

After determining exactly how it should be taught, the instructors should sing the phrase(s) for the students and ask them to sing it back. Teachers may sing with the students to support them if they desire. Point to the line notation on the charts, board, or transparencies as the singing occurs. With simple songs a couple of times through the phrase(s) should be sufficient. Several repetitions may be necessary with more difficult songs. It is important, however, not to spend more than two or three minutes with each section. Spending more time than that will result in the other sections becoming restless. Teach the proper part to the first group, then the second part to the next group. Before moving to the third group, ask the first two to sing their parts together. After teaching the third part, combine the three. Finally, teach the fourth part, then combine all four.

As the adolescents sing, teachers may encounter one or two singers who are experiencing difficulty singing in tune (particularly if the process is being used in a general music class). The teachers should not stop the rehearsal to deal with the problem immediately. The primary purpose is to bring the students to experiencing a four-part song as soon as possible. Individual attention will impede progress toward that goal. It will be necessary to show them individual attention at another time that can be arranged by the teachers.

When male teachers teach the cambiata part (if used in middle/junior high school), it is essential that they sing it at actual pitch. They should not transpose it down an octave because the cambiatas will attempt to do the same with disasterous results. It might be necessary for male teachers to utilize their falsetto in teaching, for singing in the correct octave is essential to success when teaching cambiatas.

Female instructors occasionally have difficulty relating to the changing-voice baritones since the baritones sing one octave lower than the female. Baritones who just have entered the second phase of change usually are the ones who do not understand what to do because as trebles and cambiatas they sang at the same pitch level as the female. The solution to the problem is to request one of the established baritones to sing the part instead of the teacher until the *light baritones* understand the octave phenomenon. After a few sessions as a baritone the young men will begin to relate to the female voice.

Since training the adolescents to listen to the tonal sounds is the principle impetus of choral singing, the emphasis of rote teaching should be placed on the music, not the words. Therefore, no words should be included on the transparencies or charts. A neutral vowel such as *LOO, LAH,* or *LEH* should be used as the parts are being sung both by the teachers and the students. *LOO* is better for all parts except the first soprano. It promotes good choral tone and blend. Be sure the inside of the mouth is open and the teeth are parted as the students sing. Attempt to establish a good *buzz* above the gum ridge (see Chapter 10) and remind the singers to begin each phrase with a slight tug at the breath-band. The first soprano will be more comfortable singing the open *LAH* particularly when the part moves into the upper area of the voice. Remind them to keep the vowel bright, concentrating on placing it above the gum ridge. Do not allow them to "swallow" the vowel or produce it from the throat. A third choice that might work well for all voices is *LEH*, particularly if the voices are inexperienced and not grounded in good vocal technique. This vowel promotes forward placement that is essential to good vocal tone.

At this point, if time allows, one may consider teaching the words to each part. If there is not enough time to complete teaching the words, it is best to move to a different activity or reinforce what has just been taught and leave teaching the words to another session. Teaching the words is most easily done by writing them on the board and singing the part already taught with the correct text. An effective method for longer songs where the words easily can be confused is *lining out.* The teachers sing the words to one phrase and the students sing them back, the teacher sings the words to the second phrase and the students sing them back, and so forth. This is all done without stopping the beat in a very smooth, continuous fashion. Adolescents find this technique of teaching the words intriguing particularly if it is explained to them that lining out was used for several generations in the colonial church before song books were available (see "The Beginnings" in Chapter 2). Lining out is a technique that takes preparation by the instructor and practice by the singers, but it will be an effective teaching tool after it is mastered.

After the words have been taught to each group, directors should ask the groups to sing the parts together. The beauty of rote teaching is that a singing organization can be taught a simple arrangement and be able to perform it by memory in as little as twenty minutes after the teachers have become proficient at their responsibilities. Since no music is placed in the hands of the singers, their attention is directed to the teacher and the charts (or the projected transparency image) and their comprehension is greatly enhanced; thus faster learning occurs.

After the song has been taught, the piano may be added as an accompanying instrument. It is important to point out that rote teaching is not an end in itself. It only should be used in the interim period at the beginnning of the semester (or year) until the students have learned enough about music reading to place the printed music in their hands and expect them to understand its purpose and how they should function in response to it.

On the next page and following is an arrangement of "Silent Night" written in melody-part style. Even though it is arranged in four parts, any one, two, or three of the parts that are not the established melody may be combined with the established melody and the choral effect will be satisfactory. In other words, it may be used as two, three, or four-part music to fit the needs of any choir. Line notation is included for rote teaching. Directors may make transparencies from these pages, draw the lines on the board, or make homemade charts. When used with middle/junior high school students, assign part I to Soprano I, part II to Soprano II, part III to Cambiata, and part IV to changing-voice Baritones. When used with senior high school singers, assign part II to the Sopranos, part III to the Altos (and Cambiatas, if they are present), Part I to the Tenors (to be sung 8va lower), and Part IV to the Basses (and changing-voice Baritones, if they are present).

The First Rehearsal   The director's approach to the first rehearsal affects students both consciously and subconsciously. Directors must establish the ambience of the first rehearsal to communicate how they desire to conduct rehearsals for the remainder of the year. This presupposes, of course, that they know the type rehearsal they want to manage (beginning teachers may not have determined this; see Chapters 3, 5, 6 and 14). Students will consciously or subconsciously evaluate a director's personality, organizational skills, communicative skills, conducting skills, vocal skills, pride in the group, love for teaching, concern for students, love of choral music, and unendless other factors.

The suggestions that follow provide a safe model for beginning teachers, but as they gain teaching experience they will want to scrutinize the suggestions' value for their specific approaches to the rehearsal and determine which ones suit their personalities and philosophies better.

Directors should number the chairs before the rehearsal so that students can find their seat immediately. An alternate method is to put the students' names on the seats; however, numbers are better than names since numbers occur consecutively, making it easier to find the proper seat. When students have to search randomly throughout the room for their names confusion often results. Place their folders of music beneath each chair. Place a seating chart on the bulletin board for future reference as those students may forget where they sit.

Teachers should establish classroom control the moment students approach the door. Stand at the door and warmly greet the students by name as they enter (if directors have difficulty remembering names, a hefty "hello" will

Silent Night

Joseph Mohr

Franz Gruber
arr. by Don L. Collins

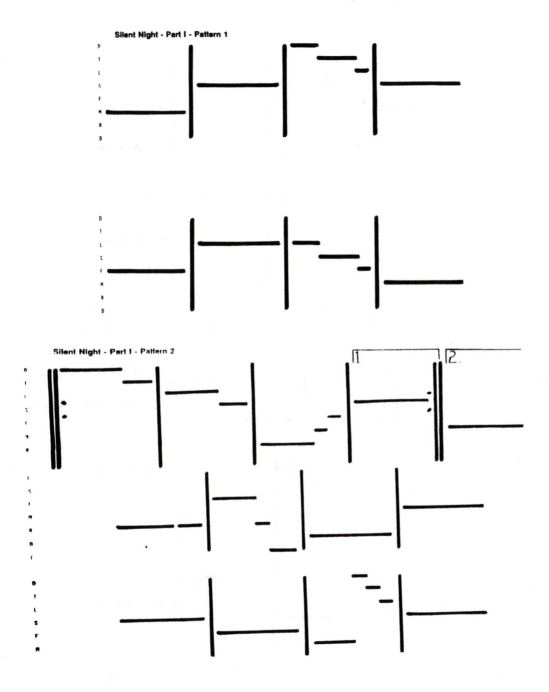

Silent Night—Part I—Pattern 1 - Silent Night—Part I—Pattern 2

Silent Night - Part II - Pattern 1

Silent Night - Part II - Pattern 2

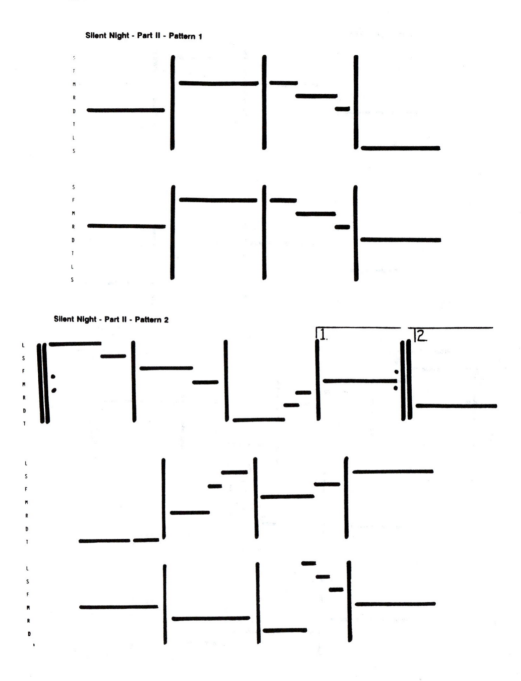

Silent Night—Part II—Pattern 1 - Silent Night—Part II—Pattern 2

Silent Night - Part III - Pattern 1 (last two phrases)

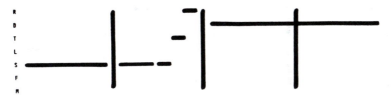

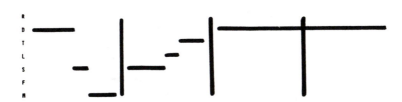

Silent Night - Part IV - Pattern 1

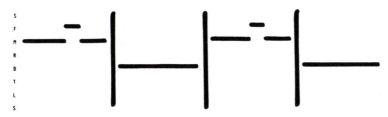

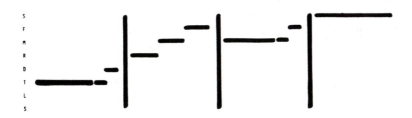

Silent Night—Part III—Pattern 1 - Silent Night—Part IV—Pattern 1

Silent Night - Part IV - Pattern 2

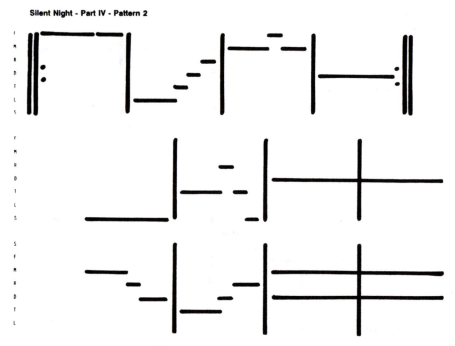

Silent Night—Part IV—Pattern 2

suffice). Directors may need to introduce themselves to new students if there has not been a formal audition. Show them where to place their books, coats, and so forth, inform them of their seat number and ask them to sit quietly until everyone arrives.

The first rehearsal is the place and time to challenge the students to the adventures of choral singing and to establish those regulations that will govern the choir throughout the year. This should be the first order of business as the rehearsal begins. "The Challenge and Rewards of Choral Singing" (Chapter 14) contains a suggested monologue that directors may deliver at the first rehearsal. It is designed for the Advanced Choir, but directors may use it with the Beginning Choir, or they may use it as a model to devise one that is more appropriate for the Beginning Choir. Since the students joined choir to sing, directors should limit this introductory time to no more than fifteen minutes.

Beginning Choir members probably will not have experienced singing four-part music. If they are able to learn a four-part song in the remainder of the first rehearsal, it will be an experience they will not soon forget. By rote teaching a simple melody-part style piece, directors can achieve that goal in about twenty minutes, if they use line notation and the process explained in the preceding section. If time allows, after they have learned the song directors may give a few tips relative to making it sound better, but it is important not to get involved with tedious aspects of choral technique at this time. The students will leave the first rehearsal very exciting about the prospects of choir for the remainder of the year.

Secondary students respond well to a piece chosen to be sung regularly (perhaps every rehearsal). It serves as a rallying supplication to bring the students together in one mind and voice. Students often remember it for years after graduation and it brings back pleasant memories of all they experienced in choir. Following the monologue in Chapter 14 is a brief choral selection entitled "Motto." Directors may use it with their choirs or they may select another that they deem more appropriate. It can be taught by rote in about ten minutes. If time allows, directors may teach the "Motto" at the end of the rehearsal. If there is not enough time, it may be taught in subsequent rehearsals.

Beginning Choir Rehearsal Procedure Directors should plan to spend regular segments of time in each rehearsal on three areas:

DEVELOPING SIGHT-READING SKILLS AND BASIC MUSICIANSHIP

After several weeks of rote teaching of melody-part style four-part music, a structured and sequential method of sight reading should begin. Directors will need to spend fifteen to twenty minutes of a fifty-minute period on developing these skills.

DEVELOPING PROPER VOCAL AND CHORAL TECHNIQUE

Fifteen to twenty minutes of a fifty-minute period should be spent developing these skills.

APPLYING EACH OF THE ABOVE TO THE CHORAL LITERATURE

Finally, ten to twenty minutes of a fifty-minute period should be spent on literature.

Directors should adjust these recommended intervals accordingly with periods longer or shorter than fifty minutes. The time increments above indicate that directors should place the emphasis during the rehearsal on training the students to be good musicians and to sing with proper technique over preparation for performance.

Directors should begin rehearsal with immediate singing (after the students have put away their books, coats, and materials, obtained their folders of choral music, and found their places on the risers or in their seats). Directors should handle announcements, checking roll, and necessary nonmusical responsibilities later in the rehearsal. If the administrative personnel require teachers to check the roll at the beginning of the period, sing for three or four minutes, then stop and check the roll. If possible, however, work for at least ten minutes before addressing these nonmusical matters. An even better approach is to assign an assistant (student leader, college or university student teacher, or teacher's aid) to check the roll without calling the students' names by observing if they are in their assigned places. This gives the director more time for musical matters.

Some directors begin each rehearsal with music that serves to bring the choir together in mind and purpose such as the "Motto" discussed previously. Others begin immediately with vocalises (if it is early in the day or right after lunch, some directors incorporate physical movements with the vocalises to awaken the body as well as the voice). Many directors believe the purpose of vocalises is to "warm up" the voices. In fact, they often refer to that period in the rehearsal as "warm-ups." Vocalises indeed may be used to warm up the voices, but they serve a much greater purpose, particularly with beginning singers. They are the means by which sequential approaches to individual vocal technique and cooperative choral technique unfold. Without them, there can be no cumulative, sequential approach to teaching. Study carefully the recommended usage of the vocalises delineated in Chapters 10 and 12 to train the students' voices and bodies in habitual response during the singing process. In Beginning Choir, directors should use the exercises (in proper order) described in Chapter 10 first and then move to those recommended for the Beginning Choir in Chapter 12. Occasionally when students are involved with the literature, directors will desire to incorporate an appropriate vocalise to address specific vocal-choral problems.

Some directors approach developing sight-reading skills by asking the students to "sight read" one piece during each rehearsal. This is a rather futile practice if they do not employ a sequential, cumulative, skill-building approach. Students are unable to respond effectively to all eight tones (or more) and the multiple combinations of rhythm complexities without first being trained to respond to them in small doses. Directors should use a specific plan to train the students to sight read in fifteen to twenty-minute segments each rehearsal throughout the year. Directors should continue the process with the Intermediate Choir (and possibly even with the Advanced Choir depending upon the background and commitment of the teacher and students) until they achieve their goals. Musicianship is a growth process. Remember, fast-food mentality cannot be applied to effective musicianship. It takes time.

Directors should spend a portion of the rehearsal applying the vocal and musical skills introduced in the vocalises to appropriate choral literature. At the beginning of the year after the students have learned the melody-part style four-part songs by rote, directors may begin to apply proper vocal and choral technique to the singing of them. Later, until the singers develop sufficient sight-reading skills, directors may teach by rote other appropriate choral literature and use it for training. The Beginning Choir may perform this literature in concert but directors should be mindful of the Beginning Choir's primary purpose—to train its members to be proficient musicians and vocalists—and directors should keep performance responsibilities in perspective.

Intermediate and Advanced Choir Rehearsals

The First Rehearsal   The preliminary procedure to be followed during the first rehearsal with the Beginning Choir should also be used with the Intermediate and Advanced Choirs. Follow the same procedure up through the delivery of the challenge to the adventures of choral singing (the model found in Chapter 14 is recommended for the Advanced and Intermediate Choirs).

The remainder of the first rehearsal should be devoted to singing. Selection of the repertoire for the first rehearsal is strategic because the singers should leave the rehearsal with a feeling that they have been successful as they sang. Most of the selections chosen to be sung at the first rehearsal should be pieces that do not offer an extreme challenge. It may be fine to attempt one difficult piece, but no more. Directors should have placed as many as ten different pieces (including the difficult ones) in the students' folders, even though they probably will not sing all of them during the first rehearsal. This allows the students the opportunity to peruse the folder to inform themselves about some of the music that has been chosen for the year. Directors may desire to list and briefly discuss each piece at the appropriate place during the introductory remarks at the beginning of the rehearsal.

The first rehearsal and all rehearsals that follow should move at a relatively rapid pace. Directors should be careful not to be too tedious when dealing with vocal-choral technique during the first rehearsal. The tedious work should come later. However, neither should they simply sing the songs without corrections. The singers should get a sample of the directors' rehearsal style. Further, directors should communicate to them from the beginning that rehearsal takes hard work and self-discipline and that the choir will be working for perfection.

The singing should begin with no more than three minutes of warm-ups. During the first rehearsal it is not advisable to continue the work on the sequential programs of vocal and choral technique (Chapters 10 and 12) begun with the Beginning Choir, even though they certainly should be part of all the regular rehearsals that follow. Choose a couple of the vocal exercises from Chapter 10 (consider exercises 13, 14, 15, 16, 19, or 20); they are all in unison and easy to sing) strictly to allow the singers to hear how the choir is going to sound and to warm up their voices.

Next, sing the Motto followed immediately by the easiest piece in their folder, possibly a unison piece or one that has several unison passages. It will be better if most of the students know the piece, but if they do not, let them sight-read it (see Chapter 11). If they have not been taught to sight-read well, choose one of the rote teaching approaches in the following "Presenting New Literature" section for teaching this piece.

Next, sing a more difficult, but familiar piece from last semester. The new students will have to rely on the older members to carry the parts, but it will be an enjoyable piece to sing. Singing a familiar piece will give the new members and opportunity to gauge the potential of the choir.

The most difficult piece of the rehearsal should follow. Either sight-read it or teach a portion of it by rote. This piece will give the students a sense of the type challenge they may expect in future rehearsals.

Other pieces may follow as time allows, but be sure to close the rehearsal with an up-tempo, exciting piece that is relatively easy for them to sing. A good arrangement of a folk song, spiritual, or contemporary popular piece usually serves well to finish the rehearsal. The students should leave the rehearsal looking forward to their return.

Presenting New Literature   After directors have studied the score thoroughly they must decide how they are going to present it to the choir. The score should be presented in a positive fashion to help the students accept it. Some directors are apologetic about presenting music they think the students might not enjoy singing. They present the piece by saying: "I know you're not going to like this but. . . ." Automatically the students presume it is a type literature that does not speak to them. It is much better to begin with: "All music we sing is important but this piece is particularly good because. . . ." If directors make statements of this nature the choir members feel that the piece is important to the director who is the authority in the class, so it is worthy of rehearsal. Making a few *brief* remarks about the composer, period, style, and work itself will intensify interest.

If it is possible to find a recording of other adolescents singing the piece, be sure to play it, particularly if it is a good rendition. Hearing other students their age sing it increases its value in their minds and gives them an overall concept of the piece. If the rendition is not extraordinary, directors might introduce the recording by saying "I believe we will be able to sing this piece better than the choir who recorded it" (they should withhold the name of the group) or "Listen to see if you can determine ways we might make our performance better than the one on the recording."

If a recording by adolescents is not available, choose one by college or university students or by a professional choral group. If none of these is available, choose an alternative to help the students form an overall concept about the work: Teach the song to a small ensemble and let them sing it to the choir or allow the accompanist to play the vocal score while the director sings the melody line(s).

At this point, the students are ready to sight-read the piece (see Chapter 11). It is to be hoped that members of the **Advanced Choir** sight-read well enough that it is not necessary to use rote teaching with them. If this is not the case, however, directors may approach rote teaching with the Advanced Choir in several ways. A description of each follows. In the **Intermediate Choir**, directors may choose to teach the rote methods recommended for either the Beginning Choir or Advanced Choir. No matter which of the following methods directors choose, if singing the rhythm, pitches, and text simultaneously proves to be too difficult for the students, it may be wise to allow them to chant or clap the rhythm first, then sing the parts on a neutral vowel (*AH* or *OO*, depending on the style of the piece), and finally, combine the music with the text.

ROTE TEACHING—METHOD 1

1. Play the bass part on the piano and have all sections sing it. The girls will sing the part one octave higher than the boys. Sopranos and Tenors may drop out on the few notes that may be too low.
2. Play the soprano part on the piano and have all sections except the Basses

to sing it. Basses may sing it if it is not too high for them. It is best for them not to sing it if it creates tension in their voices as they sing. Teach them to use falsetto phonation which will enable them to sing it without tension. The boys will sing the part one octave lower than the girls.

3. Sing the soprano and bass parts together. The Tenors and Sopranos may sing the soprano part and the Basses and Altos may sing the bass part.
4. Play the alto part on the piano and have all sections to sing it. Sopranos and Tenors may drop out on the few notes that may be too low.
5. Sing the three parts (Bass, Soprano, and Alto on their respective parts) together. Ask the Tenors to sing the soprano part.
6. Play the tenor part on the piano and ask the Sopranos and Altos (in the same octave as the Sopranos) and Tenors to sing it. Directors may allow Basses to sing falsetto, if they desire.
7. Sing all four parts combined, each sung by the appropriate voice type.

If the selection has several sections, teach the above process one section at a time. This particular method is good when the choir members have a tendency to talk. Since everyone is singing all the parts, there will be no time for them to talk. If sections sit and wait while other sections learn their part, it is easy for the nonsingers to talk and misbehave. Depending on the difficulty of the piece, directors will probably have to repeat the process for several rehearsals in succession before the choir can sing all the parts together correctly.

ROTE TEACHING—METHOD 2

1. Play the bass part on the piano and ask the Basses to sing it while the other choir members read the bass part silently.
2. Play the soprano part on the piano and ask the Sopranos to sing it while the other choir members read the soprano part silently, except the Basses who should read the bass part silently.
3. Ask the Sopranos and Basses to sing their two parts combined. As they do so, the Altos should read the bass part silently and the Tenors should read the soprano part silently.
4. Play the alto part on the piano and ask the Altos to sing it while the Tenors read the alto part silently and the Sopranos and Basses silently read their own parts respectively.
5. Ask the Sopranos, Altos, and Basses to sing their three parts combined. The Tenors should read the soprano part silently.
6. Play the tenor part on the piano and ask the Tenors to sing it while the other three voices read their own part silently.
7. Sing all four parts combined, each sung by the appropriate voice type.

Method 2 is particularly good for less-advanced singers. Having all singers sing every part, as in Method 1, may confuse those singers who have not had experience in part singing. Method 2 addresses that difficulty.

ROTE TEACHING—METHOD 3

Follow the procedure in Method 2 except that in the places where the students are asked to read the parts silently, they should be asked to hum or to sing the appropriate part on an *OO* vowel. This is a compromise approach between Methods 1 and 2.

ROTE TEACHING—METHOD 4

An excellent way to teach parts by rote is in sectional rehearsals. Each section goes to a separate location with a section leader and sings the parts as an accompanist plays them on the piano. In many secondary schools, this method is not practical because there are not four rehearsal areas available and, with a few exceptions, most secondary students are not mature enough nor musically proficient enough to serve as section leaders. When the choral programs in the middle/junior and senior high schools are team-taught with all three teachers working together at all three schools, or when college or university student teachers are available, Method 4 may be used with success. It is by far the best method to conserve time and make the rehearsal run efficiently.

Efficiency in the Choral Rehearsal Following are some cardinal rules for success and efficiency in choral rehearsal, regardless of the age level or type of choir:

PLANNING FOR SUCCESS

1. Always make long-range goals for the year. Never make day-to-day plans without a bird's eye point of view.
2. Go into a rehearsal with a specific plan but be willing to change the plan to meet the immediate needs of the moment. The goal of any rehearsal is not to work a rehearsal plan but to use the rehearsal plan to accomplish the goal of the rehearsal.[9]
3. Thoroughly study the music the choirs will sing and write specific short-range goals to be accomplished. Through analysis determine how to introduce and teach each piece of music. Directors waste rehearsal time learning the music as the choirs learns it.
4. Compare similarities and differences in each of the pieces to be rehearsed in one period, then devise ways of teaching similar passages that occur in separate works.

IN THE BEGINNING

5. Begin and end the rehearsal on time.
6. At the beginning of the semester, teach the singers how to respond to the director's important conducting gestures so they will respond without explanation throughout the year.
7. Write the names and the order of the pieces to be rehearsed on the board before the choir enters and train them to put their music in order before the rehearsal begins. Directors should teach the students to go through this process at the beginning of every period without being told. Plan to have

---

[9] The ambiguity of that statement is intentional. Think about it.

the most intense part of the rehearsal near the beginning while the students are fresh.

8. Before beginning to rehearse a piece, explain repeat bars, *al segno*, *dal segno*, and *da capo* sections. These are always difficult for young singers to understand and it will alleviate confusion later in the rehearsal.

DURING REHEARSAL

9. Develop the habit of giving instructions about where to start singing by giving the page, system (some people use the term *brace* or *staff*), measure, and beat in that order. Be consistent and insist that the choir members listen and concentrate when directors give these instructions. An alternative to this approach is to have the students number each of the measures in their music when they first receive it, then refer to specific measure numbers when instructions are given. This is a particularly useful approach because it trains the singers to deal with measure numbers, an approach that must be used when instructions are given at a combined rehearsal of band or orchestra and choir.

10. Give specific instructions and deliver them directly and briefly (with ten words or less, if possible). Keep the group singing. Learn to prompt the choir with acute, brusque three-to-five word ejaculations as they sing. When necessary, some directors can stop the singing, give corrective instructions, tell the group where to begin, then resume singing—all within the time value of one measure rest—without stopping the beat.[10]

11. Learn to analyze problems correctly on the spot. Do not waste rehearsal time trying to correct something that was not a problem in the first place.

12. Repetition of certain passages in the music is essential, but never repeat without purpose. Choir members must know why they are being asked to repeat a passage so they can work to improve the performance.

13. Vary rehearsal methodology and routine in order to alleviate boredom or frustration. When progress stops, be prepared to approach a problem from a different perspective. It may be necessary to delay addressing the problem until the next rehearsal so directors will have time to evaluate the situation and devise ways to solve it.

14. Sing for the choir (to demonstrate), but do not sing with it.

15. Take a break during the rehearsal (not at the very beginning) to handle the non-musical responsibilities such as checking roll and making announcements. This gives the singers a respite from singing and allows directors to establish control over the classroom as the students enter.

---

[10] There are times during a rehearsal in which directors should stop singing and talk to the choir. These periods should occur during a break or at the end of the rehearsal. There are several purposes for these heart to heart dialogues. (1) To evaluate the results of that particular rehearsal. (2) To indoctrinate (that term is used advisedly in a positive sense): Directors need to take time to explain why they do what they do. Students are more apt to trust directors and cooperate with them when they understand their motives for operation. (3) To inform: Psychologically students may reject unfamiliar musical styles and individual pieces so it is important that directors explain to the students about what to expect when they introduce the next pieces. Directors may even want to give them some *brief* historical information about the composer, style, and piece. (4) To build confidence: Students need to believe that they are capable and they need to be exposed to strong leadership so that they feel secure in following that leadership.

16. Always appear to have vitality and enthusiasm, even though by the end of the day that task becomes more difficult. Directors will be unable to motivate students to be excited about the music if they are not excited about it themselves.

17. Vocal-choral technique improves by telling singers when they have performed well, followed by ways they can become better. It seldom improves by telling them how badly they sing.

18. Be careful not to rehearse pieces with extreme range requirements or high tessitura until the voices are thoroughly warmed up. Also, alternate these type pieces with pieces that have comfortable ranges so that the voices can recuperate and the singers will be able to sing without vocal fatigue throughout the entire rehearsal.

19. On days when there are special events such as football games, pep rallies, school dances, and days that precede holidays, directors must realize that the students will have difficulty concentrating. It is best to accelerate the rehearsal pace, omit rehearsing parts, sing through pieces in their entirety, and incorporate more pieces into the rehearsal.

EVALUATION

20. Make videotapes and audiotapes of the rehearsals to improve all aspects of rehearsal technique.

21. Constantly evaluate how rehearsal time is wasted and try to decrease that wasted time in the next rehearsal.

Pacing the Rehearsal   To have success in choral singing, students must commit themselves to the singing process. Directors will alleviate much of the misbehavior if the rehearsal is paced well (however, some misbehavior will not be corrected by keeping the rehearsal moving; see Chapter 14). Following is a suggested rehearsal plan. As directors mature in their rehearsal technique, they will have to determine which parts are effective for them and those which are not.

1. When the students enter, they should put away their books, coats, and other materials (at a place provided for them), pick up their folders, move directly to their seats or places on the risers, and put the selections they are going to sing in the order they will be rehearsed (teachers should have the order on the chalkboard).

2. A student helper or college or university student teacher should check the roll according to the students' standing or sitting formations.

3. The rehearsal should begin with vocal and/or choral technique study (see Chapters 10 and 12). Attempt to keep this to fifteen minutes or less.[11]

4. It should continue with sight-reading study (see Chapter 11). Directors should keep this to fifteen minutes or less.

5. Before beginning work on the literature, directors should make the necessary

---

[11] When pressed for time, items three and four may be somewhat less than fifteen minutes in length, but it is advisable never to omit them completely. Doing so sends the wrong message to the choir members. They need constantly to be aware of the importance of sight-reading skills and vocal-choral technique, and omitting them makes them seem unimportant.

announcements and handle all choir business. They should train the students to hold all questions not related to the music, signing of slips, passes, and personal business until this time unless there is an emergency. Place this activity at different times in the overall rehearsal plan so that the students will not know when to expect it.

6. Place the most intense part of the rehearsal next. This is the time to be tedious and require perfection.

7. Next, sing the piece the students perform with the greatest ease. It should be the piece they know the best.

8. Introduce a new piece next. Unless it is relatively easy and short, teach only a portion of it. Continue to teach the piece in this time spot in the rehearsal until the students have learned to sing the notes correctly.

9. Teachers should leave the next spot in the order of rehearsal open to practice whatever the rehearsal dictates. They should choose the piece(s) to sing according to the mood of the choir members and their ability to continue to concentrate.

10. Close the rehearsal with a lighter, novelty type piece or the piece in the folder the students enjoy singing the most.

11. Be careful to maintain control of the class as they dismiss. Do not allow them to run, yell, or be excessively noisy as they put away their folders and gather their books, coats and other materials.

Directors should respond to rehearsals with spontaneity. There will be times when various parts of the rehearsal will be omitted on the spot or when something that was not planned must be added. Directors should teach to the needs of the choir and sometimes they are unable to plan for those needs. The needs arise in the rehearsal and so directors must address them in the rehearsal.

Rehearsals That Occur Immediately Before Performances   Preparing for performance can be particularly harrowing near the end. To free themselves from "busy-work" responsibilities, directors should have already finished much of the organizational work before entering into this special time. They should have (1) registered the time, date, and place on the official school calendar; (2) reserved the place of performance; (3) designed the program and tickets (if they are to be sold) and delivered them to the printer; (4) prepared news releases to be sent to the media at the appropriate time; (5) written personal invitations to friends, civic leaders, administrative personnel, and choir supporters, to be sent about one week before the performance; (6) chosen and asked the ushers and stage manager (if one is needed); (7) chosen and prepared all wearing apparel for the performance; and (8) prepared printed instructions for each of the choir members that delineate rehearsal and performance dates, times, places, and special instructions to assure smooth procedural activities.

As the time of performance approaches the goals and procedure of the last six to eight rehearsals change. Consider the following variables that will affect directors' rehearsal technique:

1. Attempt to assure that all parts are secure at least eight rehearsals before performance.

2. Concentrate on "polishing" the choral sound and working on interpretative responsibilities.

3. If the choir has not been accustomed to standing the entire rehearsal, they should do so during all the final rehearsals.

4. Rehearse in performance formation and in the performance hall several times before the performance. Once directors have heard their choirs in the performance hall, they may need to derive new performance formations for better blend and balance.

5. Tape every rehearsal and study the tape thoroughly to isolate points of concern before the next rehearsal.

6. To use time effectively, rehearse trouble spots that emerge from study of the audiotape rather than rehearsing entire pieces, except during the last two or three rehearsals, then assure that the choir sings completely through a piece before leaving it.

7. If the choir has not sung in performance dress thus far in the semester, about two or three rehearsals before the performance, ask them to do so. This will acquaint the students with the attire and it will allow time for alterations and changes that may need to be made to achieve uniformity of dress.

8. If the choir is singing with soloists or instruments on various pieces, they should be present for at least two rehearsals or more, if possible.

9. If the performance contains several choral ensembles, directors should have a combined rehearsal that emphasizes procedure (moving in and out of place, order of performance, and so forth) in the performance area. This rehearsal should not be immediately before the performance, however, because the directors need to have a time with each of the ensembles in which they can practice and review difficulties that might have emerged from the combined rehearsal.

10. The final rehearsal should be devoted to building confidence and reassuring the singers of their strengths. Directors should never be tedious, overbearing, fussy, or highly demanding during this rehearsal.

Choosing and Training Accompanists

Many directors are accomplished pianists and they find it difficult to move from the piano bench during rehearsals. Although there are a few pianists-directors who have achieved excellent reputations for their choirs, in most cases directors realize that conducting and dealing specifically with rehearsal technique are their primary responsibilities, so they replace the piano bench with the baton and the director's stand.

Since the director and choir must rely on someone else to serve as accompanist, they should find someone who is a competent player. Being able to play a concert piece well is not the best gauge to evaluate accompanists' skills. Excellent concert artists often do not make good accompanists. Neither is it absolutely necessary that the accompanist be a good sight reader. Directors should provide the music in advance of the rehearsal so that the accompanists may prepare it fully. Good accompanists should have the ability to relate well to the director and choir both musically and personally. Above all, they must be alert to directions given by the conductor and to the needs of the choir. They must be musically sensitive to the supportive role the accompanist plays.

Years ago, conductors relied heavily on the accompanist to assist in rehearsal activities, such as playing all the parts, taking sectional rehearsals and so forth. Nowadays, conductors have determined that working a cappella in the rehearsal pays dividends in better choral technique and musicianship, so they teach the students to sight-read (see Chapter 11) and vocalize a cappella, thus relieving the accompanist of so many rehearsal responsibilities. After the singers learn the choral parts, the piano accompaniment is added as a characteristically equal partner in the overall performance.

If directors use accomplished, professional accompanists, it may not be necessary for them to be present at all rehearsals. Depending on the rehearsal procedure of the directors, accompanists may be able to come in during the final rehearsals before performance.

Whenever possible it is advantageous to use student accompanists, if they are capable, because it strengthens the educational purposes of the choral program. Choosing two students to accompany allows both of them to sing and play, which does not negate their original choral obligations. One word of caution: If student accompanists are not capable of interpretative and expressive playing, it may be better to choose someone who is. Many sensitive choral performances have been destroyed with insensitive piano expressions.

When directors use student accompanists, they should be available at each rehearsal to sing or play. Also, it will be necessary to have separate rehearsals with them at the beginning of the semester so that they will know how to practice and prepare for their accompanying responsibilities. If directors desire accompanists to play for the vocalises during the vocal training section of the rehearsal, they should write out all the exercises and indicate how high or low to take the singers. Directors should also practice the exercises with the accompanists so that they will understand the correct rhythm, tempo, and modulations procedures.

Teachers should instruct accompanists to give pitches during the rehearsal beginning with the lowest pitch and playing a slow, arpeggiated chord to the highest pitch. Accompanists should be cognizant when pitches are needed so that they will give them automatically without instruction from the director.

After working in rehearsals for a while, a good accompanist should be able to analyze how a conductor gives instructions and anticipate starting places and other procedures that will facilitate effective rehearsal. Most of the time, a good accompanist will know inherently when to play voice parts, a reduced score, or the accompaniment according to the success the choir members are having in singing their parts. When playing voice parts, most students will not be able to read an open score (all four to eight voice parts at once), so it will be necessary to rewrite the voice parts in closed scoring or place two students at the keyboard simultaneously.

Student accompanists must realize the importance of their responsibilities. They should be seated at the piano ready to play as the rehearsal begins. They should notify the director if they are ill or must miss rehearsal. They must practice daily to prepare for rehearsal. Directors should inform them of these responsibilities at the beginning of the year and insist that they fulfill them dutifully. Also, directors should allow each of the accompanists to play with the choir at each performance so that their efforts will be rewarded.

CONCLUSION

In this chapter we have taken a rather detailed look at constructive techniques to get the most out of the choral rehearsal. As with many of the aspects of learning, to be an effective choral director, one learns best through hands on experience in the classroom. The difficulty some teachers have, however, is attempting to solve their daily problems without the assistance of informative books and the counsel of other master teachers. If you are a student now, you are spending considerable time reading and studying about how to teach choral music well. Most of what you have read in this chapter (and the other chapters in this book) will be much more helpful after you have had a few years of teaching experience. May I encourage you to keep this book on your desk in the choral room and refer to it often. It will become more helpful each time you read it.

THOUGHTS FOR CONTEMPLATION AND DISCUSSION

1. Think about your favorite choral teachers (without naming them). Which aspects of their rehearsal technique were beneficial and which were not?
2. How will your personal piano skills benefit or hamper your rehearsal capabilities as a choral teacher?
3. How will your personal theory background affect your analytical skills in preparing your score for rehearsal?
4. Will you have an auditioned approach to selecting the members in your Beginning Choir or will you open membership to everyone? Why or why not?
5. How many different seating or standing arrangements have you experienced in the choirs in which you have been a member? Which were the most beneficial? Which ones did you personally like the best?
6. Think of some selections you sang in middle/junior high school. Were they written for early adolescent voices? Did they fit the criteria delineated for early adolescent voices?
7. Think of some selections you sang in senior high school. Did they fit the criteria delineated for older adolescent voices?
8. Think of the selections you have sung in your college or university choir. Which ones are appropriate for middle/junior high school singers? Why or why not? Which ones are appropriate for senior high school singers? Why or why not?
9. How is the best way to get as many complimentary (reference) copies of octavos from music publishers?
10. Name all the different selections you have sung (or those with which you are otherwise familiar) from each of the major periods. Which ones of those selections are appropriate for early adolescent voices?

11. Think about the rehearsal room at your high school. How could you improve its appearance and utility?

12. Think about the first rehearsals of which you have been a part over the years. How could they have been improved?

13. Think of ways to justify to your principal why you should hire a rehearsal and performance accompanist if one is not available from the membership of your choirs.

14. Contemplate your high school choral rehearsals. Did your director waste rehearsal time? If so, what could have been done to have prompted more efficient rehearsals?

15. Think about the final rehearsals you have attended. How could they have been improved?

16. Do you think it is possible to spend too much time rehearsing your choirs for performance?

17. Think of the vocal timbre of each student in your class (without naming them). Which ones would you choose for your choir. Why?

18. Is it acceptable to cancel the performance of a selection during the final rehearsals? If so, how will the cancellation affect the choir members' attitudes? If not, how can you reconcile a poor performance of the piece?

19. Do you plan for the students to elect officers in the choirs you direct? Indicate the aspects of the choral operation in which will they have input. Name the aspects in which you plan to maintain complete control.

20. Do excellent soloists make good choir members? Why or why not?

BIBLIOGRAPHY

BESSOM, MALCOLM E., ALPHONSE TATARUNIS, and SAMUEL L. FORCUCCI. *Teaching Music in Today's Secondary Schools,* 2d ed. New York: Holt, Rinehart and Winston, 1980.

COLLINS, DON L. *The Cambiata Concept, a Comprehensive Philosophy and Methodology of Teaching Music to Adolescents.* Conway, Ark.: Cambiata Press, 1981.

COOPER, IRVIN, and KARL O. KURSTEINER. *Teaching Junior High School Music,* 2d ed. Conway, Ark.: Cambiata Press, 1973.

DART, THURSTON. *Interpretation of Music,* rev. ed. London: Hutchinson University Library, 1960.

DECKER, HAROLD A., and JULIUS HERFORD, eds. *Choral Conducting Symposium,* 2d ed. Englewood Cliffs, N.J.: Prentice Hall, Inc., 1988.

DROTLEFF, JOHN E. "Renaissance Music for Junior High School Singers." *Choral Journal* 16 (January 1976).

EDELSON, EDWARD. *The Secondary School Music Program from Classroom to Concert Hall.* West Nyack, N.Y.: Parker Publishing Co., 1972.

HAWKINS, MARGARET B., ed. *An Annotated Inventory of Distinctive Choral Literature for Performance at the High School Level.* Monograph No. 2. Lawton, Okla.: American Choral Directors Association, 1976.

HEFFERNAN, CHARLES W. *Choral Music, Technique and Artistry.* Englewood Cliffs, N.J.: Prentice Hall, Inc., 1982.

HOFFER, CHARLES R. *Teaching Music in the Secondary Schools,* 4th ed. Belmont, Calif,: Wadsworth Publishing, 1991.

JIPSON, WAYNE R. *The High School Vocal Music Program.* West Nyack, N.Y.: Parker Publishing Co., 1972.

KJELSON, LEE, and JAMES McCRAY. *The Conductor's Manual of Choral Music Literature.* Melville, N.Y.: Belwin-Mills Publishing Corp., 1973.

LAMB, GORDON H. *Choral Techniques,* 3d ed. Dubuque, Iowa: Wm. C. Brown Co., 1988.

LASTER, JAMES. *Catalogue of Choral Music Arranged in Biblical Order,* 2d ed. Metuchen, N.J.: Scarecrow Press, 1993.

MARPLE, HUGO D. *Backgrounds and Approaches to Junior High Music.* Dubuque, Iowa: Wm. C. Brown Co., 1975.

MILLER, KENNETH E. *Vocal Music Education, Teaching in the Secondary Schools.* Englewood Cliffs, N.J.: Prentice-Hall, Inc., 1988.

NEIDIG, KENNETH L., and JOHN JENNINGS, eds. *Choral Director's Guide.* West Nyack, N.Y.: Parker Publishing Co., 1967.

POOLER, FRANK, and BRENT PIERCE. *New Choral Notation.* Ft. Walton Beach, Fla.: Walton Music Corp., 1971.

ROBINSON, RAY. *Choral Music: An Anthology.* New York: W. W. Norton, 1978.

ROBINSON, RAY, and ALLEN WINOLD. *The Choral Experience.* New York: Harper's College Press, 1976.

ROE, PAUL F. *Choral Music Education,* 2d ed. Englewood Cliffs, N.J.: Prentice Hall, Inc., 1983.

SCHWARTZ, DAN. "A Selected Listing of SATB Gospel and Gospel Oriented Choral Arrangements." *Choral Journal* 24, (March 1984).

———. "Supplement #18 to A Selected List of Choral Arrangements." *Choral Journal* 26 (September 1985).

———. "Supplement #3 to A Comprehensive List of Medleys Published for SATB, SAB, SSA, and Two-Part Choirs." *Choral Journal* 24 (March 1984).

"Selective Music Lists." *Vocal Solos and Vocal Ensembles.* Reston, Va.: Music Educators National Conference, 1985.

SHROCK, DENNIS. "An Interview with Margaret Hillis on Score Study," *Choral Journal* 31, no. 7 (February 1991).

SINGLETON, IRA. *Music in Secondary Schools,* 2d ed. Boston: Allyn and Bacon, Inc., 1965.

ULRICH, HOMER. *A Survey of Choral Music.* New York: Harcourt Brace Jovanovich, 1973.

WHITE, J. PERRY. *Twentieth Century Choral Music: An Annotated Bibliography of Music Suitable for Use by High School Choirs.* Metuchen, N.J.: Scarecrow Press, 1982.

YOUNG, ALLEN, ED. *Choral Educators Resource Handbook.* San Francisco: Choral Resource Seminars, 1985.

14

Discipline Is a Discipline

Each year for over two decades Phi Delta Kappa has polled Americans about their attitudes toward education. One question always relates to what the public perceives to be the biggest problem with the public schools in their community. In most of the years since Gallup's first poll in 1969, the public has identified discipline (or the lack of it) as the most serious problem.[1] Recent studies show that 40 percent of new teachers leave the profession within the first three years, and the primary reason they give relates to discipline problems.[2] Teachers' inability to control classes causes extraordinary stress, which results in exhaustion, frustration, tension, high blood pressure, severe depression, and alcoholism.[3] The students in my methods classes invariably identify "how to control the class" as their primary concern.

Music students spend four to six years in undergraduate and graduate education preparing to teach choral music. They spend most of that time developing their musicianship and learning specific techniques, methods, and materials to aid them in teaching. Music is an important discipline (I use the

[1] Gallup, A., and D. Clark. "The 19th Annual Gallup Poll of the Public's Attitudes Toward the Public Schools," *Phi Delta Kappan*, 69, no. 1 (1987), 17–30.

[2] "Study Backs Induction Schools to Help New Teachers Stay Teachers," *Update*, 20, no. 4 (1987), 1.

[3] "Trends: Teachers Suffer Stress Around the World," *Today's Education*, 70 (1981), 6.

term *discipline* to mean "a broad field of study"), and it is the reason that most of us decide that we want to teach. We love music. We want to spend our lives making music and helping others discover the joys that music has given us. Almost half of the graduates never see that dream brought to fruition because they leave the profession before the end of the third year. This is a gross waste of time, money, effort, and labor. More tragically, it leaves psychological scars on those defeated individuals that take years to heal.

This does not have to happen to you. You do not have to be one of those 40 percent who will quit within the first three years of teaching (see "Being Successful in the First Position" in Chapter 18). In the following pages we examine ways that will keep you from being a statistic. We introduce you to a new discipline (again, I use the term to mean "a broad field of study"). That new discipline is discipline. This new field of study is as important as the field of music and will enable you to fulfill your dreams of "teaching the world to sing." You are going to find that as you teach music, so must you teach discipline.

Notice that I used the word *introduce*, not *teach*. I wish that I could "teach" you the discipline of discipline, but since I am not physically present with you now, that is impossible. This introduction, along with the efforts of your methods professor, should point you in the right direction to begin your study. To learn it well, it will take the same amount of time (four to six years) that it took you to learn the field of music. If you start now, it is to be hoped that you will be prepared before you finish that third year of teaching.

In the more than twenty years I have been teaching, I have always made this point to each class of students who have taken my methods courses: "You do not have the right to stop teaching until after you have taught for at least three years." It takes that long to learn the discipline of discipline. There may be mornings they would rather stay in bed than face the difficulties of the day, but as each year passes and as they hone their skills of teaching discipline, those early morning fears and frustrations gradually turn into feelings of satisfaction and pride. If they give up prematurely, they have relinquished a fundamental American right: the right to see their dreams fulfilled.

When students enter the choral classroom they expect to study choral music. The students are unaware that to become choral musicians they must first become artists, since musicianship is a highly sophisticated art. Becoming an artist entails mastering a very complicated system of behaviors. Students cannot master this complicated system of behaviors without discipline. In the beginning the teacher must impose this discipline, but eventually the students will impose it upon themselves.

Due to the limited life experiences of most secondary students, they will not know how to be disciplined individuals. When instructors teach the discipline of discipline they are teaching behavior. *Behavior* is "the way people act." It is the teacher's responsibility to "teach" (not "tell") the students how to behave from the minute they enter the classroom until they exit it. In this context, teaching them to behave does not mean keeping them from misbehaving. It means that teachers must train them how to act, in the same way they teach them how to sing. It means that teachers must be aware of every action and reaction of all the students, then train those actions and reactions to be beneficial to the singing process.

Teachers must teach the discipline of discipline just as they teach choral music (see Chapters 11, 12, 13, 15, and 16). They must have a structured, systematic method of teaching discipline (behavior). In this chapter, three approaches to teaching discipline are explained. Each is different, each has been proven effective both empirically and through research, and each is designed specifically for the choral classroom. Teachers must choose the approach that is most appropriate for their educational philosophy and personality. Before these methods are offered, some introductory remarks will set the stage for understanding them.

BEHAVIOR AND MISBEHAVIOR

Directors design a specific curriculum for teaching choral music (see Chapters 13, 15, and 16), but what is the curriculum for the discipline of discipline? This curriculum focuses on desirable classroom behavioral patterns and habits. Following is a list of proper behavior teachers should expect from each student. Teachers may desire to add to the list other types of student behavior that are appropriate for their particular situations or to delete those that do not apply.

1. To enter the room in an orderly fashion.
2. To hang or place their coats, books, and so forth in their proper places.
3. To find their music (or folders) and move to their seats or risers in an orderly fashion.
4. To speak to each other only in conversational tones and only when the teacher allows conversation.
5. To listen quietly for announcements or introductory information.
6. To stand on the risers or sit in the seats using proper posture.
7. To hold the music in such a fashion to be able to see both it and the director simultaneously.
8. To sing and participate with attention, maximum effort, and concentration.
9. To move from the singing position only with permission from the director.
10. To ask questions (except for those that pertain to the music or the lesson), make comments, or discuss disagreements with the director after the class has been dismissed.
11. To listen attentively when singing is not in progress.
12. To attempt with a positive attitude all the director requests.
13. To stand, sit, and move about (as requested by the director) expediently and quietly.
14. To keep the mouth and all other parts of the body free of any encumbrances that might limit effective vocal production.
15. To be dismissed in an orderly fashion, placing the music in its proper place, gathering books, coats, and so forth promptly and quietly, and speaking only in conversational tones.

For the most part, the approaches to teaching discipline described in this chapter emphasize training positive behavior rather than correcting inappropriate behavior. Misbehavior usually falls into five categories:[4] (1) aggression—physical and verbal attacks to teachers or other students, (2) immorality—cheating, lying, and stealing, (3) defiance of authority—refusing to do what the teacher requests, (4) class disruptions—talking, calling out, walking about the room, clowning, and tossing objects, and (5) goofing off—not doing the assigned tasks and daydreaming. The last two categories (four and five) generally require most of the teachers' attention in the choral classroom. Often the first three categories require professional assistance if the misbehavior becomes too severe.[5]

Following is a list of specific types of misbehavior that teachers should keep in mind as they devise their curriculum to teach the discipline of discipline:

1. Running when entering or leaving the classroom.
2. Excessive noise such as loud voices, inappropriate talking, or laughing.
3. Inattention to instructions from the director.
4. Unnecessary movement such as jumping, poking, or teasing.
5. Chewing gum or placing anything in the mouth that encumbers the singing process.
6. Destroying music and other teaching materials.
7. Displaying unkind behavior such as verbal or physical abuse to other class members.
8. Displaying rude conduct such as ridicule, sarcasm, bad manners, and tattling.
9. Walking around the room without permission.
10. Using inappropriate excuses (even lies) to obtain permission to leave the classroom.
11. Overtly refusing to sing or participate.
12. Arguing with the director or other class members.

THE CHALLENGE AND REWARDS OF CHORAL SINGING

Before any curriculum for teaching the discipline of discipline is adopted and introduced to the singers, directors must explain to them why choral singing is important. They must tell the students what to expect from their experience in choir, state the short-range and long-range goals and rewards, and close with a challenge. Any experienced teacher will verify how much easier teaching is if

[4] C. M. Charles, *Building Classroom Discipline from Models to Practice*, 3d ed. (New York: Longman, 1989), p. 2.

[5] In some schools (particularly those in urban areas) where discipline is affected by the use of drugs, broken homes, incarcerated parents, racial tension, and poor socioeconomic conditions, teachers should seek professional help in learning how to control and motivate these students. Beginning teachers whose first years are spent in this type of situation should be under constant supervision of the counselors and principals to assure that their training is complete. Outside assistance from social workers and the district school superintendent's office is usually needed and should be provided.

the students and teacher are pulling together rather than against each other. Most students will accept any curriculum on proper behavior if they understand why the director is requiring them to respond in a specific fashion. Following is a model for introductory remarks directors might make to their choirs at the first class meeting. It is designed to be delivered to the advanced choir, but directors may adapt it to conform to the needs of the beginning or intermediate Choir. They should deliver it with enthusiasm and sincerity, placing special emphasis on those statements in bold print.

You are about to begin an experience of a lifetime! (Pause, and let them think about that statement.) It will be an extraordinary experience, an experience that is different from any you have ever had. It may be so extraordinary that it will be different from any experience you ever will have again. I am going to be your guide through this wonderful experience. You will have to learn to follow me; you will have to learn to care for me; but most of all, **you will have to learn to trust me**. Without that commitment from you, the experience will only be ordinary. Together we can make it extraordinary.

In turn, I promise to care for you and guide you in the paths of those generations that have gone before us. I promise to give you full benefit of my four years of university education. I promise to give you the advantage of the years of training I have had in guiding others through this amazing experience. I promise never to lead you astray, and I promise that when you are older, you will remember and cherish this incredible experience. **In fact, it may be only** *then* **you will come to realize that is** *was* **an experience of a lifetime**.

There will be times when you may *not* feel the experience is extraordinary. In fact, occasionally you may think it to be downright impossible for, you see, extraordinary experiences only occur when we have learned how to sacrifice. It is through the sacrifice that we develop the fortitude to fashion the extraordinary. It is through the sacrifice that we become competent enough even *to recognize* the extraordinary. Without sacrifice our eyes are blind to the truly amazing.

Singing is the gift, discipline is the way, and making music is the art. This will be our motto for the year. It has been set to music so we will sing it often. Let me try to explain the meaning of these words.

We all have the ability to sing. We were born with it. Some say it is given from God. Others say we inherited it. That gift, however, is very much like an uncut diamond or crude oil. It has very little value in its original form. It must be forged, manufactured, and honed into something beautiful and useful.

That's where the second part of our motto takes effect. **Discipline is the way**. Only through discipline and sacrifice are we able to transform that gift of singing into something valuable that we can share with others or give back to God. We must take that simple gift of singing and apply to it choral technique, musicianship, and long hours of concentrated practice so that it will become valuable and useful to others.

Then, at that point, this wonderful gift, this magnificent process of making music, **becomes an art**. Art is our way of expressing life experiences in an extraordinary way. Artists have extraordinary experiences. When you become artists you, too, will have extraordinary experiences.

Beyond all this, you are going to be **choral artists**. Choral singers have a particularly unique way of expressing themselves because they become one big team and express themselves in a splendid, unified effort. In fact, there are very few teams in all society in which so many people join in such a superb, unified effort. There are very few teams that deal with such intricacies as do singers of choral music. Think of all the nuances and possibilities of the choral sound. The harmony, rhythm, melody, vocal color, dynamics, tempo, and text—all come together in one remarkable happening.

Beautiful, musically correct, and polished choral singing is surely as close as we will ever come, before death, to perceiving the truly ethereal.

So, let me guide you through a brief journey, a mere outline, of all that is in store for us this semester. (At this point, tell them some of the activities you have planned including those that are immediate as well as those planned for later in the year. Describe some of the music and tell them why you chose it. However, don't tell them everything because you'll want to keep some surprises for later.)

Finally, as I mentioned, we can only become artists through discipline and sacrifice. I am going to teach you how to be disciplined so that you will be able to experience the extraordinary. At first, I will impose upon you much of what you will learn, but eventually, you will take control and you will impose the discipline upon yourself: **you will become self-disciplined**. That will be our goal: to have a choir in which all the singers are highly motivated, well-trained, remarkable musicians.

This is our plan. (At this point you must describe your curriculum for teaching discipline. You may want to choose one of the approaches that follow, combine what you consider to be the best components of each, or devise one for yourself. The point is, discipline is a discipline!)

Directors should make remarks of this nature at the beginning of each semester with every choir they teach. In fact, if it is good, the same address may be made each time. When it is repeated, directors may preface it by telling the singers that they have heard these remarks before and they will continue to hear them at the beginning of each semester because they are very important. They serve to give the choir direction and purpose as they work. Repeating them only reinforces the remarks' meaning to the returning choir members. Occasionally choir members laugh and joke about "the speech" the director gives each semester, but, in reality, they are complimenting the director because they are acknowledging that the director really cares about them and about the progress they continue to make.

On the next page is a setting of the motto, "Singing is a gift, discipline is the way, and making music is the art." Directors should teach it by rote to each of their choirs. If they do not sing it each period, they should sing it at least twice a week. It will serve as a constant reminder of their purpose for being in choir.

THREE EXEMPLARY APPROACHES TO TEACHING DISCIPLINE IN THE CHORAL CLASSROOM

The point of controversy in deciding how directors should teach discipline in the choral classroom usually has to do with whether teachers should be predominately positive, predominately negative, or a combination of both positive and negative. Very few advocate a totally negative approach in which teachers base their entire system on a set of rules that begin with the word "don't" and the students are punished (sometimes severely) if the rules are broken. There are those, however, who point out how teachers used this approach in early American classrooms for generations (with, according to them, much success) before the advent of more psychologically oriented methods.

Conversely, there are several very impressive approaches based on a completely positive approach in which there is very little punishment and where

Cambiata Vocal Music Institute of America

Motto

Four-Part Variable Voicing
Acappella

Don L. Collins

teachers modify students' behavior by rewarding them through removal of distasteful requirements and by giving them both tangible and intangible positive reinforcement. Then there are those who use a combination of positive and negative reinforcement to achieve desired results. The approach teachers decide to adopt depends on the way their teachers and parents disciplined them, the successes and failures of previous attempts, and their inherent personality and philosophy of life.

The "Taking Charge" Approach[6]

Mrs. Kaster believes that she should insist on responsible behavior from her students. Experience has taught her that the students need this type of behavior, parents want it, the community at large expects it, and her teaching is ineffective without it. Each time her choir sang poorly at concerts and festivals she traced the performance back to her failure to maintain adequate classroom discipline.

She once mistakenly believed that good teachers could handle discipline problems on their own. At one time she thought that firm discipline caused psychological trauma to her students. She once operated on the idea that if she provided activities that met students' needs, her discipline problems would disappear. Some way or another she got the mistaken idea that misbehavior resulted from some deep-seated problem that was beyond the influence of the teacher. She observed how some directors in other schools believed that firm control is stifling and inhumane.

She now feels that a firm hand is indeed liberating. It is her responsibility to provide a singing environment where students can attain maximum success, so she must expect and require appropriate behavior from them. Furthermore, she expects help from the administration and parents when she needs it.

She realizes, however, that students have basic rights too. They have the right for her to help them limit inappropriate, self-destructive behavior. They have the right to choose how to behave with the full understanding that there are consequences following their choices. She protects these rights best by taking charge of the classroom. She clearly communicates her expectations and consistently follows with appropriate action, never violating the best interest of the students.

In learning to be a "take control" individual, she trained herself to act in an authoritative manner. Now she often willingly says "I like that" or "I don't like that." She is persistent in stating her expectations and feelings. She uses a firm tone of voice. She maintains eye contact. She uses nonverbal gestures in support of verbal statements. She uses hints, questions, and personal messages rather than making demands when requiring appropriate behavior. She always

---

[6] This approach is based on the tenets of Lee Cantor and Marlene Cantor and the plan they call "Assertive Discipline." For more detailed information consult Lee Cantor, *Assertive Discipline, a Take Charge Approach for Today's Educator* (Seal Beach, Calif.: Cantor and Associates, 1976); Lee Cantor, "Be an Assertive Teacher," *Instructor* 88 (1978), 60; and L. Davidman and P. Davidman, "Logical Assertion: a Rationale and Strategy," *Educational Forum* 48 (1984), 165–76.

follows through with promises set forth at the beginning of the term rather than with threats. When she has a confrontation with a student she states what she expects, delineates the consequences, and explains why her actions are necessary.

Several years ago, at the time Mrs. Kaster made the decision to take control of the classroom, she decided before the first day of class exactly the type of behavior she expected from her students. She determined the consequences for improper behavior then she took her list to the principal's office for approval and support.

When she met with her students for the first time she discussed the behavior she expected and she described the consequences for bad behavior, including the methods she planned to follow for punishment. The first time she made her list, it was much too long and specific and the singers could not remember all she expected. She since has learned to limit the list to five or six broad, all-encompassing expectations.

She stressed at the first meeting that she would not allow students to break the rules. She delineated exactly what would happen with the first offense, the second, then the third, and the fourth. Each consequence was more severe than the previous, with suspension from school being the most severe.

She asked each student to write the behaviors and consequences on a sheet of paper. She requested that the students in her middle/junior high school classes repeat orally the behaviors and consequences they had written. She also asked them to take the paper home and get their parent's signature. In senior high school she asked the students personally to sign the paper, make a photocopy for themselves, and give the original to her.

She explained thoroughly to the class why the rules were necessary, with the primary motive being to produce an excellent choir with trained, disciplined, and highly motivated personnel.

She prepared a short letter about the plan and sent it to the parents indicating the need for their support and her pleasure in collaborating with them for the benefit of the choir. Finally, she implemented the plan with the first meeting of each class and continued it throughout the year.

She uses both negative and positive consequences to achieve her goal of a controlled classroom. The negative consequences are gradual in their severity. In middle/junior high school, upon the first offense, the student's name is written on the board. The second offense adds a check by the name and results in a thirty-minute detention after school. The third offense requires the student to meet with the principal. The fourth offense reaps a visit from the parents and the students with the principal. The fifth offense results in suspending the students from school, with the principal, vice-principal, or counselor escorting them home.

In senior high school the offenses are more direct. First, she gives the students a verbal warning. Second, she gives them a one-hour detention. Third, the students and parents visit with the principal; and fourth, the administration suspends the students from class and escorts them home. With all the students who misbehave, she reinforces the understanding that she does not condone their actions by ignoring them, not looking at them, not speaking cordially to them, and not giving them special attention.

Consequences of good behavior are several. The students get special personal attention from the teacher such as greetings, short talks, compliments, acknowledgments, smiles, and friendly eye contact. Mrs. Kaster writes notes or makes phone calls to the parents of those who make significant contributions to the choir through commitment and concentration of thought and effort. In middle/junior high school, she gives special awards for high achievement and significant improvement. She also gives group parties for them. In senior high school she gives special privileges such as time to visit with friends at the end of the period. She also requests that parents give the senior high school students special privileges at home such as allowing them to come home an hour later than usual.

Everyone has not received her plan with open arms. Some of the teachers and a group of parents have complained that the approach is too harsh, too militant, too demeaning for the students, and too focused on suppressing bad behavior to the exclusion of reinforcing good behavior. On the other hand, many of her cohorts and parents highly applaud her. They feel that the students are accomplishing much more than they would under more liberal, less controlled conditions.

The "Meet Their Needs and Help Them Make Good Choices" Approach[7]

Mr. Gonzales believes that the most appropriate way to teach the discipline of discipline is for teachers to provide a classroom environment and curriculum that meet students' basic needs for belonging, power, fun, and freedom. He also focuses on helping students make proper choices relative to behavior that ultimately lead to personal success in singing.

He believes that students are rational beings. They are capable of controlling their behavior so they choose to act the way they do. Good choices produce good behavior and bad choices produce misbehavior. Mr. Gonzales makes every effort to see that his students make the good choices. Since he truly cares about his students, he accepts no excuses for their misbehavior and he provides reasonable consequences for both good and bad behavior. He believes choir rules are essential and they must be enforced, so he has "make proper choices" sessions during choral rehearsals in which he attends to matters about class rules, behavior, curriculum, and discipline.

Mr. Gonzales's rationale is rather rudimentary. For his students to choose

---

[7] This approach is based on "The Glasser Model" developed by William Glasser, a Los Angeles psychiatrist, and emphasizes that good behavior comes from making good choices and meeting the student's needs. For more information, please consult William Glasser, *Reality Therapy: A New Approach to Psychiatry* (New York: Harper and Row, 1965); William Glasser, *Schools Without Failure* (New York: Harper and Row, 1969); William Glasser, "Ten Steps to Good Discipline," *Today's Educator* 66 (1977), 60–63; William Glasser, "Disorder in Our Schools: Causes and Remedies," *Phi Delta Kappan* 59 (1978), 331–33; and William Glasser, *Control Theory in the Classroom* (New York: Perennial Library, 1985).

good behavior, he must make the results of their choices desirable. He forces them to acknowledge their behavior and make value judgments about it. When they make the wrong choice, he points out what would have been a better one.

He feels that the choral classroom is a place where students have a chance to be successful and to be recognized. In fact, for some students it may be the only place that offers opportunities that meet their needs in this way. Success as a singer produces a sense of self-worth and a productive identity that discourages aberrant behavior. For students to develop an identity that encompasses success, they must develop a good relationship with people who care. Mr. Gonzales cares.

Experience has taught Mr. Gonzales that some students resist entering into a quality relationship because they fear teachers, distrust adults in general, and receive positive reinforcement from other students who disdain authority figures. To help the students accept him, he has spent time developing a reputation as a person who really cares about them. He feels that his choir members cannot begin to make responsible choices until they become deeply involved emotionally with people who make good choices.

The reading and study Mr. Gonzales has done has brought him to believe that his student singers have four genetically inborn basic needs:

1. *The need to belong*, to feel accepted, to be a member of some group or class. He tries to make choir that class.
2. *The need to be in control of their lives*, to be competent singers and musicians. Choir membership supplies that need because singing offers the challenge to do excellent work and a way to display it. He also attempts to help them realize that it is difficult to live with other people and still be in total control.
3. *The need for freedom*, to become self-reliant without constant direction from others.
4. *The need for fun*, which in choral class includes enjoyment, pleasure, and satisfaction from singing.

Mr. Gonzales contends that it is impossible, when the choral curriculum and process do not address students' four basic needs, to keep them from misbehaving. He uses the analogy that it is "like asking someone who is sitting on a hot stove to sit still and stop complaining."[8] Therefore, he designs his choral curriculum and classroom approach to meet those needs.

It took Mr. Gonzales more than five years to develop his approach to teaching discipline. Each year of teaching contributed to the final product. Now he has cultivated it into seven basic tenets that serve as the core of his discipline curriculum.

Students Must Be Responsible   Mr. Gonzales keeps the students' responsibilities for making proper choices in the forefront. He accomplishes this with "making proper choices" sessions once a week or when needed that deal with the students'

---

[8] Glasser, *Control Theory in the Classroom*, 53.

responsibilities. The students sit in a tight circle with the teacher and discuss matters that concern the choir. In one session they may discuss what should be done about wasted rehearsal time. Several students make positive suggestions and the choir members decide to try one of them. In a later session the choir members may discuss the success of those recommendations with Mr. Gonzales, noting what he considers to be their strengths and weaknesses. From Mr. Gonzales's perspective, the follow-through session points out that (1) attention to the solution emphasizes that good behavior comes from good choices and (2) the message that he really cares about the students and their behavior.

Rules Lead to Success   Mr. Gonzales believes that students need and desire direction, particularly since the lack of it adversely affects the excellence of the choir. At the beginning of the semester during the first "making proper choices" session he and the choir members determine the rules. After emphasizing that choir members make rules to reinforce choral excellence through learning and participation, he allows the students to recommend those rules that will govern the choir. They discuss the chance of success and failure for each rule, how it will affect each member, how Mr. Gonzales will enforce it, and the possible consequences when students disregard it. After the students have suggested rules, Mr. Gonzales makes his suggestions. In subsequent sessions the choir members evaluate the rules to determine if they have been useful and if they should be continued or discarded.

There Are No Excuses   There are no excuses for breaking the rules. Once the students have made a commitment to good behavior, Mr. Gonzales never accepts excuses for their inability to live up to it. This includes anything that might have happened away from class as well as during the choral rehearsal. Students have a tendency to use family situations and trouble at home to justify misbehavior in choir. It is regrettable that certain home situations exist, but they do not give the students excuses to impose their problems on the choir through misbehavior. If Mr. Gonzales accepts excuses for breaking the rules, he is in effect saying that it is all right to break a commitment and that it is all right for students to harm themselves. If he is to be a caring teacher, he must not accept their excuses.

Make Proper Choices   When students misbehave, Mr. Gonzales asks them to make a value judgment about their behavior by asking the question, "Is the behavior helping you and the choir?" If the students do not feel threatened, they will probably answer "No." Mr. Gonzales's response at that point is, "What could you do that would help?" If the students are unable to determine the proper behavior, Mr. Gonzales suggests several appropriate alternatives, then allows the students to choose the best one. In this way, the students learn to make proper choices. Mr. Gonzales accepts no excuses for the students' failure to abide by the proper choice although, if the choice does not function well, he allows the students to choose another one.

The Consequences Should Fit the Behavior   Reasonable consequences must follow whatever behavior students choose. Positive consequences should reinforce good behavior just as negative consequences should result from bad behavior. Mr. Gonzales administers negative (unpleasant) consequences promptly without exception. The consequences are never physically punishing and he never uses caustic language, ridicule, or sarcasm. He attempts to make the positive consequences pleasant and personally satisfying.

Being able to choose proper behavior that brings positive consequences or negative behavior that reaps negative consequences gives the students a sense that they are in charge of their own lives and in control of their own behavior.

Be Consistent and Persistent The object of Mr. Gonzales's approach is to help students choose proper behavior all the time, not just when it is convenient. They must learn self-discipline. Commitment means constancy. This presupposes that Mr. Gonzales is also self-disciplined and consistent.

For the students to learn to be consistent, the teacher must be persistent. He never gives up no matter how unruly the student. When progress is slow he perseveres because he knows that consistency is the students' best hope for gaining maturity and respect.

Always Review To keep the students on task toward choosing proper behavior, the choir members must constantly review the progress in the "making proper choices" sessions. An individual session should have one of three outcomes: (1) It should help solve social problems that arise from the choir members working together in a group setting; (2) it should serve as a diagnostic session to improve choral technique, musicianship, and the learning process; or (3) it should allow the students to bring up specific concerns they might have. No matter what the object of the sessions, they always have two primary purposes: to identify problems and to find solutions. Mr. Gonzales does not allow the choir members to find fault with specific individuals, to place blame on anyone for problems the entire choir has, or to administer punishment. He tries to remain in the background during the discussion, offering suggestions to keep them on course toward a solution. He indirectly assures that his concerns surface for discussion as the sessions continue.

When students exhibit inappropriate behavior, Mr. Gonzales follows a specific sequence of events.

1. He asks the students in a nonthreatening tone, "What are you doing?" If the students do not feel threatened, they usually give an honest answer. Then Mr. Gonzales says, "Is that helping you or the class," to which the students obviously must answer, "No." Then he asks, "What could you do that would help?" At that point the students name a better behavior. If they can think of none, Mr. Gonzales suggests two or three appropriate alternatives and allows the students to choose.

2. When the answer is negative, hostile, or unacceptable, he responds, "I would like to speak with you privately at the end of the period."

3. At the private conference, he asks again, "What were you doing? Was it against the rules? What should you have been doing?" At that point the

4. If the misbehavior continues, Mr. Gonzales requests a second private conference. At that time he says, "We have to work this out. What kind of plan can you make so you can follow the rules?" The students might say, "I'll stop doing it," to which Mr. Gonzales replies, "No, we need a plan that says exactly what you will do. Let's make a simple plan you can follow. I'll help you."

5. If the students do not abide by their own plans, Mr. Gonzales isolates them. He removes the students from the rehearsal and places them in an area of isolation until such time they will commit to adhering to their own plans. If the students disrupt while in isolation, he sends them to the office. Mr. Gonzales always informs the principal about the possibility of visits from certain students.

6. If the students disrupt after rejoining the choir for rehearsal, Mr. Gonzales says, "Things are not working out here for you and me. We have tried hard. You must leave the class. As soon as you have a plan you are sure will allow you to follow the rules, let me know. We can try again, but for now, please report to the principal's office for suspension." Then the principal or another competent staff member accompanies them home. The principal may phone the parents and request that they pick up the students.

7. Mr. Gonzales asks the principal to refer students who are repeatedly suspended to an agency for professional help.

Over the years Mr. Gonzales has kept records on his choral students that reveal the success of the way he teaches the discipline of discipline. According to his records, about 25 percent of his students were still unproductive after having been in his chorus. He also determined that even the most productive students often lack self-discipline. They also show that even though his approach takes time and effort, he produces excellent singing organizations with members who feel that he really cares for them as individuals.

The "Behavior Modification" Approach[9]

Mr. Roscoe teaches the discipline of discipline by a systematic application of reinforcement. He bases his approach almost entirely on giving rewards for good behavior. Early in his career he tried to discipline students by being harsh and disagreeable and by using various types of punishment. The new approach allows him to maintain control in a warm, supportive, and positive manner instead of in a cold, harsh, and punitive way. He found that by using behavior modification not only was he able to control the students' misbehavior, but they also became much better singers.

[9] This approach is based on the tenets of B. F. Skinner and his disciples. For further study, please consult S. Axelrod, *Behavior Modification for the Classroom Teacher*, (New York: McGraw-Hill Book Co., 1977); G. Firth, *Behavior Management in the Schools: A Primer for Parents* (New York: Thomas Publications, 1985); and Charles Madsen, Jr. and Clifford Madsen, *Teaching Discipline, A Positive Approach For Educational Development*, (Raleigh, N. C.: Contemporary Publishing Company, 1983).

When he began to experiment with behavior modification, he did not believe that punishment was necessary at all. Experience had taught him that punishment had a dark side. By punishing the students he was successful in suppressing unwanted behavior, but he found that the punishment also produced side effects that sometimes overshadowed his ability to teach good choral technique. Some of the students saw punishment as unwarranted, malicious, or excessive and it created bad feelings that were very difficult to overcome. In some cases those bad feelings provoked retaliation against him and the other students or it caused the offenders to withdraw completely from participating in the rehearsal.

He soon learned that some students took advantage of him when he only rewarded good behavior and did not punish misbehavior, so he has found an effective middle ground. He tells them exactly what is expected, what will happen when they comply (they will receive a reward), and what will happen when they do not (there will be negative consequences). This approach helps the students realize that they are the ones who choose the punishment that invariably accompanies misbehavior.

Mr. Roscoe uses four types of rewards, which he calls reinforcers: social, graphic, activity, and tangible. The *social reinforcers* include words, gestures, and facial expressions. He has found that some students work very hard to get a pat on the back, a smile, or a kind word. He gives these rewards immediately when he observes good behavior.

The *graphic reinforcers* include marks of various kinds such as notes and special symbols. During rehearsal he makes a mental note of those students who worked hard and he slips a happy face or a complimentary note in their folders of music so that they will find it at the next rehearsal. He often places a frowning face in the folders of those who misbehave. He often sends a congratulatory letter to the parents.

Activity reinforcers consist of any activity the students enjoy doing while in school such as spending time with a friend, excusing them from singing in quartets when checking memory work, or assigning special rehearsal responsibilities they might enjoy.

The *tangible reinforcers*, which he has found to be the most effective, include tokens that students earn as rewards for desired behavior. At the beginning of each semester each student contributes a small fee (usually five dollars) or, as an alternative to the fee, during the semester they have a fund-raising activity (selling candy, fruit, Christmas cards, or whatever). That money is used to pay for an end-of-semester event (dance, house party, hamburger cookout) for all the students in Mr. Roscoe's classes. Throughout the semester Mr. Roscoe rewards the students for good behavior (which also includes working hard during the rehearsals) by giving them tokens that they cash in for merchandise, privileges, and food at the end-of-semester event.

For instance, there will be an entrance fee (which usually requires the most tokens). The students pay a token for a hamburger bun, another for mustard, another for the meat, chips, lettuce, and tomato when they buy food. They also must pay tokens for the privilege to dance with each other or to participate in whatever events are planned. Mr. Roscoe obtains complimentary items from downtown merchants that the students may buy with the tokens at the special event. When the students spend all their tokens they may continue to participate in the activities by spending real money. This allows those students who have not behaved properly throughout the semester to participate, if they desire.

In the classroom he uses what he calls the RRP (rules, reward, and punishment) method. At the beginning of the semester he specifically delineates the positive behavior that will earn the rewards (tokens, laudatory notes to parents, happy faces, special privileges). He also gives them a list of rules they must follow with a description of the resulting negative consequences if they are broken. The students receive the reward for the good behavior and they are punished for the misbehavior. He writes these lists (which may be similar to those behaviors listed at the beginning of this chapter) on a sheet of paper and gives them to each student. He also puts a copy on the bulletin board for those students who misplace the list.

He has found that his "behavior modification" approach clearly sets expectations, rewards, and punishments. The students consider it to be fair. They soon learn that they have the ability to choose consequences through their behavior and that they are responsible for that behavior. Other teachers and parents have accused him of manipulating the students but he does not see it that way. He feels that he is freeing them to behave in ways that bring success and positive recognition. Since he has been using it, his work is easier and more enjoyable. He truly believes it is the best way to teach the discipline of discipline.

CONCLUSION

Directors should teach discipline as if it were another subject that the students take. They should teach the discipline of discipline. It should have a curriculum that is organized and systematic, just as the discipline of choral music is organized, sequential, and systematic. In fact, the subject of discipline is more important in many ways than their choral music curriculum because if the students do not understand how to behave, they will be unable to learn how to sing effectively. Directors should plan for it to take at least three years for them to learn how to teach the discipline of discipline and to be experienced enough for it to be effective. Three approaches to teaching discipline were provided, each of which is different and all of which have been proven with research and empirical knowledge. Teaching choral music can be a very rewarding endeavor if the singers have been taught proper behavior. Teaching discipline as a discipline accomplishes that goal.

THOUGHTS FOR CONTEMPLATION AND DISCUSSION

1. What are your three greatest concerns about your ability to be a disciplinarian? After having read the chapter, how do you plan to deal with each of them?

2. Think about your favorite choral teachers (without naming them). Which aspects of their ability to discipline were beneficial and which were not?

3. How do you plan to rely upon your music supervisor and principal to assist you in controlling your classes, particularly during the first year of teaching?

4. Do you feel that teachers' age affects their ability to discipline? If so, what considerations should you give to the effect of your particular age? How can you use your age as an advantage? How will it be a detriment, and what will you do to compensate for it?

5. In view of the family life and societal factors in America today, express your realistic expectations in regard to productivity in your classroom. What should we as professionals be doing about upgrading and fulfilling all of our expectations?

BIBLIOGRAPHY

AXELROD, S. *Behavior Modification for the Classroom Teacher.* New York: McGraw-Hill Book Co., 1977.

BAKER, R. J., L. L. BARKER, and D. T. MILES. *Behavioral Objectives and Instruction.* Boston: Allyn and Bacon, Inc., 1970.

BESSOM, MALCOLM E., ALPHONSE TATARUNIS, and SAMUEL L. FORCUCCI. *Teaching Music in Today's Secondary Schools,* 2d ed. New York: Holt, Rinehart and Winston, 1980.

BOYLE, J. DAVID, and RUDOLF E. RADOCY. *Measurement and Evaluation of Musical Experiences.* New York: Schirmer Books, 1987.

CANTOR, LEE. *Assertive Discipline, a Take Charge Approach for Today's Educator.* Seal Beach, Calif.: Cantor and Associates, 1976.

———. "Be an Assertive Teacher." *Instructor* 88, (1978).

CHARLES, C. M. *Building Classroom Discipline from Models to Practice,* 3d ed. New York: Longmans, 1989.

COLLINS, DON L. *The Cambiata Concept, a Comprehensive Philosophy and Methodology of Teaching Music to Adolescents.* Conway, Ark.: Cambiata Press, 1981.

COOPER, IRVIN, and KARL O. KURSTEINER. *Teaching Junior High School Music,* 2d ed. Conway, Ark.: Cambiata Press, 1973.

DAVIDMAN, L., and P. DAVIDMAN. "Logical Assertion: a Rational and Strategy." *Educational Forum* 48 (1984).

DEUTSCH, DIANA. *The Psychology of Music.* New York: Academic Press, 1982.

EDELSON, EDWARD. *The Secondary School Music Program from Classroom to Concert Hall.* West Nyack, N.Y.: Parker Publishing Co., 1972.

FIRTH, G. *Behavior Management in the Schools: A Primer for Parents.* New York: Thomas Publications, 1985.

GALLUP A., and D. CLARK. "The 19th Annual Gallup Poll of the Public's Attitudes Toward the Public Schools." *Phi Delta Kappan* 69, no. 1 (1987).

GLASSER, WILLIAM. *Control Theory in the Classroom.* New York: Perennial Library, 1985.

———. "Disorder in Our Schools: Causes and Remedies." *Phi Delta Kappan* 59 (1978).

———. *Reality Therapy: A New Approach to Psychiatry.* New York: Harper and Row, 1965.

———. *Schools Without Failure.* New York: Harper and Row, 1969.

———. "Ten Steps to Good Discipline." *Today's Educator* 66 (1977).

HOFFER, CHARLES R. *Teaching Music in the Secondary Schools,* 4th ed. Belmont, Calif,: Wadsworth Publishing, 1991.

JIPSON, WAYNE R. *The High School Vocal Music Program.* West Nyack, N.Y.: Parker Publishing Co., 1972.

LAMB, GORDON H. *Choral Techniques,* 3d ed. Dubuque, Iowa: Wm. C. Brown Co., 1988.

MADSEN, CHARLES JR., and CLIFFORD MADSEN. *Teaching Discipline, A Positive Approach For Educational Development.* Raleigh, N. C.: Contemporary Publishing Company, 1983.

MARPLE, HUGO D. *Backgrounds and Approaches to Junior High Music.* Dubuque, Iowa: Wm. C. Brown Co., 1975.

MILLER, KENNETH E. *Vocal Music Education, Teaching in the Secondary Schools.* Englewood Cliffs, N.J.: Prentice Hall, Inc., 1988.

NEIDIG, KENNETH L., and JOHN JENNINGS, eds. *Choral Director's Guide.* West Nyack, N.Y.: Parker Publishing Co., 1967.

Roe, Paul F. *Choral Music Education,* 2d ed. Englewood Cliffs, N.J.: Prentice Hall, Inc., 1983.

Rossman, R. Louis, ed. *Tips, Discipline in the Music Classroom,* Reston, Va.: Music Educators National Conference, 1989.

Serafine, Mary Louise. *Music as Cognition.* New York: Columbia University Press, 1988.

Shuter, Rosamund. *The Psychology of Musical Ability.* London: Methuen and Co., Ltd., 1968.

Singleton, Ira. *Music in Secondary Schools,* 2d ed. Boston: Allyn and Bacon, Inc., 1965.

Sloboda, John A. *The Musical Mind.* Oxford: Clarendon Press, 1985.

"Study Backs Induction Schools to Help New Teachers Stay Teachers." *Update* 20, no. 4 (1987).

"Trends: Teachers Suffer Stress Around the World." *Today's Education* 70 (1981).

15

Classes with Emphasis on Performance

Traditionally, music in public and private schools of the United States has followed one of two directions. From elementary school through middle school (or junior high school in some parts of the country), music has been and continues to be taught in what are commonly referred to as *general music* classes that, for the most part, have been taught from a *vocal* or *singing* point of view. General music class customarily has been an essential part of the school curriculum to be taken by all students. Secondary schools (which includes most junior high schools), for the most part, have been and continue to be characterized as having a *choral* emphasis for the vocal music activity with classes being offered in the form of select and nonselect choirs, glee clubs, choruses, and other singing organizations available as electives for musically interested students but not to be taken by everyone.

Recently there is evidence throughout the United States that both approaches are being nurtured at all levels. In some systems, particularly those with magnet schools, one can find general music classes offered for students from kindergarten through the twelfth grade. There is a strong contingent of music educators nationally who support and promote general music as a requirement for all secondary students. By the same token, for years one has been able to find elementary schools with strong and active choral programs, particularly for the upper grades. Further, there are many high schools offering classes with special musical emphases such as fine arts, music appreciation, humanities, music theory, and music history.

In this chapter we take a look at those courses in the choral music education curriculum that feature performance as a primary motivational factor in the education process. In Chapter 16 we examine those courses in the curriculum that may be taught by the choral music educator but that have educational values other than performance.

During the twentieth century, performance-oriented classes have dominated the music curriculum in U.S. secondary schools, particularly in high school. This practice was a result of a lack of qualified music specialists during the early part of the century when there was a rapid increase of students who remained in school for the entire twelve grades. By 1940 there were over seven times the number of students who stayed in school through the twelfth grade compared to school enrollments in 1910. Since music teachers were not available, school administrators hired professional musicians to teach choral music in the secondary schools. These professional musicians were available because they found themselves out of work due to the advent of talking motion pictures, which did not require live background music. The Depression of the 1930s also accelerated their unemployment. These professional musicians did not teach classes, they held rehearsals. They were not teachers, but directors, and they felt that their primary responsibility was to produce a well-polished performance. From their perspective, good performance technique was good teaching technique.

Even though most educators today realize that performance is not the only reason (and for many, certainly not the primary reason) that students are involved in choral organizations, the emphasis on performance has so permeated the curriculum that it would be very difficult to eradicate its influence even if there was a demand to do so. Certainly there are many educators who will defend its presence in the curriculum against all odds.

Performance-oriented classes are justified to be included in the curriculum because (1) students learn by doing, (2) students have a need to be recognized for their accomplishments, (3) performances serve as a primary motivator to learning, (4) students have a need to entertain, and (5) the process of preparation for performance teaches cooperation, esprit de corps, discipline, and many other positive social and intellectual virtues.

Those who argue against the emphasis on performance classes point out that (1) there is an exclusion of students who are not music makers from studying about music, (2) strenuous and time-consuming performance requirements minimize the necessary emphasis on academics, and (3) music performance is not a legitimate academic subject such as general music, fine arts, music theory, and other nonperformance classes.

As a choral teacher it will be (or is) your responsibility to determine the emphasis you place on performance in the curriculum. It is to be hoped that you will carefully contemplate the outcome of your decision and, while working with your administration, arrive at a balanced curriculum that includes both performance and nonperformance classes.

THE CHORAL CURRICULUM—A SEQUENTIAL PLAN

The study of how students learn found in Chapter 4 has highlighted the need to approach the curriculum in a structured, sequential fashion. "The current philosophy of learning emphasizes that beneficial and purposeful learning can be attained and used if it is acquired through a program organized around the basic structure of a subject."[1] This basic approach applies to the specific structuring of each class as well as to the overall sequential structuring of the classes in relation to each other. It is particularly important when choral classes are established for the first time. A comprehensive high school choral curriculum should include a Beginning Choir, an Intermediate Choir, and an Advanced Choir. Directors in even the smallest schools should consider a Beginning Choir for training purposes and an Advanced Choir with performance responsibilities. It is best if this class structuring can begin in junior high school, giving the directors six or seven years to train their singers in sight-reading skills and performance practices through an organized sequential system. Empirical knowledge and research supports the notion that instantaneous musicianship, "fast-food" musicianship à la Madison Avenue, does not exist. Students can become good musicians only through years of rehearsal and study that are persistent, consistent, organized, structured, and sequential in nature. The music-reading program and the vocal technique program should be applied consistently to all literature that the choirs sing. Kodály once said that singers can perform a program with some "quick fixes," but it is comparable to building a house on quicksand. If a secure foundation is not there, the whole structure will crumble. Building a choral program is rather like building a Gothic cathedral (another great work of art), which often took several decades. Both require years of careful attention to detail, assuring that each step along the way is secure. In reality, students literally grow into being good musicians.

The information that follows describes an ideal sequential program. As a beginning teacher you will probably have to accept the structure already designed for the choral program when you take your first position. In most cases it will be far from ideal. This does not mean that the program absolutely has to remain structured the same throughout your tenure. It is the teacher's responsibility to set about structuring the choral program so that it will be the most productive. Your challenge will be to determine how you want the program structured (depending upon that particular situation) and convincing the administration to support you as, through your expertise, you lead them.

The Beginning Choir

In developing a sequential program, if it is possible to coordinate the program through both junior high and high school, it is highly advantageous for the Beginning Choir to be a choir that combines all the grades in the junior high

---

[1] Robert Evans Nye and Vernice Trousdale Nye, *Music in the Elementary School* (Englewood Cliffs, N.J.: Prentice Hall, Inc., 1985), 43.

school. This is possible if the same director is responsible for both junior high and high school programs or if there is a spirit of cooperation and coordination between two directors. An even more desirable situation is for both junior high and high school directors to team teach in both schools.

The grade combination will vary according to the structure of the junior high school. Possible combinations with two grades might be sixth and seventh, seventh and eighth, or eighth and ninth. Some junior high schools include three grades. Under those circumstances the possible combinations might be sixth, seventh, and eighth or seventh, eighth, and ninth. When three grades are involved, because of different maturation levels, it might be best to have a sixth-grade choir and a seventh-and-eighth-grade choir or a seventh-and-eighth-grade choir and a ninth-grade choir. Combining at least two grade levels (or possibly three) is advantageous over single-grade-level choirs because of the presence of changing voices. Combining the grade levels allows the choir membership to include boys with unchanged, changing, and changed voices; therefore, the directors have more flexibility in the literature they choose. Generally, combined choirs have the potential of performing four-part music, whereas single-grade level choirs are limited to two or three-part music.

If the Beginning Choir is in junior high school there is also an advantage to dividing the groups into two combined grade-level choirs, one for all girls and another for all boys. Empirical knowledge supports the idea that during early adolescence, girls and boys seem to operate better when they are separated. This is not to say that they cannot be trained together. There are certainly some very fine mixed choirs in junior high schools throughout the United States. Dividing the sexes proves advantageous particularly when working with the boys. Dividing the boys into three or four vocal sections administers to the needs of their changing and maturing voices much better than when they are divided into only the two male groups present in mixed choirs. The availability of three or four parts allows the boy to be assigned to a part that is uniquely suitable for him as his voice gradually lowers. Since girls generally mature earlier than boys, dividing the sexes promotes compatibility among various individuals.

If the Beginning Choir is in high school, it is usually either a ninth-or-tenth-grade group or a group of ninth and tenth graders combined. No matter what the grade level or combination, the curriculum for the Beginning Choir is basically the same. The rate in which the group progresses might be slightly faster with ninth and tenth grade than sixth and seventh graders.

When working in a sequential choral program there is a tendency to exempt the more talented students and those with outstanding leadership qualities from the beginning group and place them in one of the more advanced groups, a practice that generally reaps more negative results than positive. It is best to allow all the students to progress through the sequence together. To pad the top group with younger, talented students is discouraged because:

1. It puts those students in a vulnerable position with their peers.
2. It deprives the younger groups of leadership examples.

3. If the program is really sequential, jumping a class will leave gaps in the student's education in basic areas.

4. It undermines the emotional involvement of most of the singers who get to the top group too early. Each year they experience a terrific letdown as they subconsciously draw comparisons between the current first of the year group and the previous year's final polished efforts.[2]

Occasionally, upper-level students transferring into a new school will not have had the necessary training or choral experience to succeed in the advanced groups. It becomes necessary to place those students in a beginning or intermediate group of younger singers. At the audition, it is important to explain the design and progressive learning process of a sequential system to transfer students and point out that it is necessary for them to spend a period of time in preparation for the more advanced groups. If upper-level beginning singers work hard, sometimes it is possible to accelerate their pace by allowing them to remain in the beginning or intermediate group for one semester only.

Directors should have two basic goals for the membership of the Beginning Choir: (1) to learn to read music and develop basic musicianship and (2) to master the fundamental principles of sound choral technique. Specific behavioral objectives might be:

1. To develop vocal skills.
2. To learn to sing in tune with good tone quality.
3. To develop sufficient skill in reading music to carry a part independently.
4. To learn to use and understand basic music terms.
5. To perform a wide variety of suitable, artistic music within the range and textual understanding of the students.
6. To develop a sense of how to sing in harmony first through melody-part style music (polyphonic) then through music with harmonic structure (homophonic).
7. To gain a knowledge and understanding of choral works.
8. To identify basic musical forms.
9. To develop discrimination in listening.
10. To develop a degree of refined artistic interpretation of the different musical styles and moods.

Activity in class should include:

1. Teaching a structured, sequential method of sight-reading based on numbers or syllables without the assistance of the piano.
2. Teaching a structured, sequential method of vocal technique that is supported with proper vocal exercises.
3. Initially teaching literature that is written in a melody-part style and then moving to literature that has harmonic orientation.
4. Singing choral literature (preferably four parts, if possible) designed for

[2] Wayne R. Jipson, *The High School Vocal Music Program* (West Nyack, N.Y.: Parker Publishing Co., 1972), 16.

adolescent voices that supports the principles of good choral technique and promotes good vocal health for both male and female singers.

5. Stressing in-tune singing by using proper vocal exercises and by using a cappella literature to reinforce the tunefulness.

6. Developing precision in attacks and releases and work for clear, distinct diction, proper balance, and blend.

7. Developing skill at subordinating an inner or supporting part of another line in music.

8. Frequently testing boys' voices to determine proper classification and to diagnose and correct any difficulties.

9. Listening discriminately to students' voices for tone quality, pitch, articulation, and ability to blend.

10. Using ensemble work (octets and quartets) to strengthen students' independence in singing.

11. Providing solo opportunities for selected students.

12. Introducing the principles of Latin diction and reinforcing the correct Latin vowel sounds with vocal exercises.

13. Teaching musical sensitivity and awareness of dynamics, tempo, phrasing, style, and mood.

The Beginning Choir, whether it is in junior high school or high school, is composed of singers with unique voices. Both males and females will be in various stages of puberty (before, during, and after). Their voices are changing and maturing. It is important to consider the range and tessitura limitations of their voices in all aspects of their choral experiences during these years. Proper voice classification is essential to successful singing with these young students. Directors should be very careful not to designate the girls as being true sopranos or altos but to allow them to vocalize throughout the entire compass of the voice and interchangeably sing both soprano and alto parts in the literature.

Pertaining to scheduling, there are those who suggest that the Beginning Choir should meet only twice weekly or every other day. Much can be accomplished with such a meeting schedule and it still affords the singers opportunities to explore other areas of the curriculum. However, the Beginning Choir truly is the training organization of the sequential program and it is important that as much musical foundation building transpire during the year as possible. If scheduling will accommodate it, daily classes are recommended.

In devising a seating plan for the Beginning Choir (see "Seating and Standing Formations" in Chapter 13), it is important to consider placing the singers in sections according to the phases of their voice change. Treble boys (unchanged) are seldom happy sitting with the girls even though they might be singing the same part. It is best to place them with the cambiatas (boys in the first phase of change) but near the girls with whom they will be singing. Because it is necessary always to be aware of the progression of the boys' vocal mutation, directors should place the boys in sections (trebles, baritones, tenors, and cambiatas) in front and center of the choir so that the directors can move among them as they sing. The girls may be placed behind and to each side of them.

Whether or not the Beginning Choir serves as a performing organization is optional depending upon the desires of the director and the occasions that might be available. Performance should not be a priority goal of the members of the Beginning Choir. It should be used only to motivate the students to learn to sing well and become good musicians, and it should be limited to one or two occasions during the year.

Teachers seem to look forward to the period in the day when they work with their advanced group. It is very easy to cultivate the attitude that the advanced groups are more important than the beginning and intermediate groups. Doing so is very detrimental to the success of a sequential choral program. In reality, the Beginning Choir could be considered to be more important because it is during that time that the directors teach the most important aspects of good choral technique and musicianship. Because of their dedication to the Beginning Choir they are able to reap the great satisfaction and musical rewards from the advanced groups. Students will sense any attitude of partiality shown to the advanced groups and it will hamper their progress with the Beginning Choir. Singers in the beginning group will feel second best. Master teachers will make the group with whom they are working at any period in the day feel that they are the most important group in the choral program.

The Intermediate Choir

If the Beginning Choir is a junior high school choir, the Intermediate Choir, composed of ninth graders, tenth graders, or ninth and tenth graders depending on the structure of the school, will be the first high school choir in which the students will be enrolled. If the Beginning Choir is a ninth-or-tenth-grade high school choir, depending upon the school structure, the Intermediate Choir will be a tenth, or possibly even an eleventh-grade choir. In school systems where there is a dearth of male singers, it might be necessary for the Intermediate Choir to be an all-girls choir particularly in the beginning years of a sequential program. After a few years, however, the all-girls group can usually be changed into a mixed group if directors will work hard to recruit boys.

It is often difficult to persuade second or third-year high school students who might have transferred or missed the first year because of scheduling problems to be in a class that is predominately comprised of first-year students. Here again, the promise of accelerating them through the program if they work hard usually solves the problem. Although there are obvious drawbacks, teachers may choose to allow talented and highly motivated second and third-year students to skip Beginning Choir if the teachers spend the first several weeks in the Intermediate Choir reviewing the Beginning Choir curriculum and building strong foundations.

Most of the objectives of the Beginning Choir are continued in the Intermediate Choir except in a more intense and expanded fashion. Some of the objectives might be:

1. To continue to develop vocal skills.
2. To continue to develop sight-reading skills.

3. To continue to teach the students to sing in tune with good tone quality.
4. To continue to perform a wide variety of suitable, artistic music within the range and textual understanding of the students.
5. To continue to develop a degree of refined artistic interpretation of the different musical styles and moods.
6. To continue to gain knowledge and understanding of choral works of different styles and moods.
7. To prepare and attend at least one festival or contest during the year.

Activity in class should include:

1. Continuing to teach sight-reading through a structured, sequential system of syllables or numbers. More attention should be given to applying the sight-reading skills to the literature. Reading hymns and chorales with numbers or syllables is an excellent means of building sight-reading skills with the Intermediate Choir.
2. Continuing to teach vocal technique through a structured, sequential system but expanding the amount and types of vocal exercises to improve articulation, increase vocal range, and develop confidence in singing.
3. Making a conscious effort to associate the vocal technique to the choral literature from the standpoint of teaching the students how to make their vocal instrument respond properly to the problems they encounter in the literature.
4. Choosing choral literature that will administer to the needs of adolescent voices.
5. Continuing to teach the choral skills delineated in activities five through twelve in the previous section about the Beginning Choir.
6. Applying the students' understanding of Latin pronunciation and purity of vowels to the literature by singing several pieces in Latin.
7. Introducing the students to the fundamental pronunciation skills of the German, Italian, French, and Spanish languages.
8. Spending more time singing good choral literature and preparing for performance opportunities.

There will be fewer changing voices in the Intermediate Choir, but all the voices will still be settling and maturing. It is important to find literature within the range and vocal limitations of their voices and still be challenging and gratifying when they sing. The girls should continue to vocalize throughout the full compass of their voices even though they may be settling in on a specific voice part. As the boys become very conscious of the masculine characteristics of their voices, basses will often display "bass-itus," which is an unnaturally heavy and stressed tone production. Tenors will have difficulty with notes in the upper area of their chest (modal or full) voice (around E and F above middle C). Directors should be particularly careful to stress proper vocal technique when the tenors are singing in this upper area and insist on the use of falsetto production when the literature is too high for free and unencumbered modal phonation. When singing SATB literature, the tenor section may be composed of a few cambiatas, several adolescent baritones (boys in the second phase of vocal change), and one or two true tenors (as recognized in the adult sense). Because adolescent baritones are further along in their vocal maturation, they often have more difficulty in singing tenor than the boys who sang the tenor or cambiata part in the Beginning Choir. Their voices are more constrained and less flexible at this stage. If there are only a few boys in the Intermediate Choir, a better balance may be achieved by singing SSCB literature in which the boys whose voices have changed (tenors and basses) or are in the second phase of change (adolescent baritones) all sing the baritone part. The cambiatas and girls who are definite altos sing the cambiata part, and the remaining girls sing the two soprano parts.

In seating the boys it might be well to place those in the second phase of change (adolescent baritones) between the basses and the tenors. When singing SATB literature this allows them to sing tenor on the lower notes of the tenor part and bass on the upper notes of the bass part. This practice necessitates placing all the boys in the center of the choir with the strongest section (probably the basses) seated in the rear (see the seating charts in Chapter 13).

In many high schools throughout the country there are often twice as many girls singing in the choral programs than there are boys. This unfortunate occurrence necessitates that the Intermediate Choir be an all-girls group. It is difficult to justify why boys, some of whom obviously have less vocal ability and technique than many of the girls, are moved from the Beginning Choir to the Advanced Choir. Directors who require the Advanced Choir to have an equal number of voices in all parts intensify the problem because that practice limits the number of girls in the advanced group. Generally, depending on the method of vocal technique taught by the director, boys at this age have more vocal strength than girls, so the director may choose for the Advanced Choir to be one of aural balance rather than numbers balance. This enables the Advanced Choir to contain more girls than boys and still be aurally balanced. It also solves the problem of having to deny so many girls the opportunity to sing in the Advanced Choir.

During the students' tenure in the Intermediate Choir those who have extraordinary vocal aptitude seem to begin to blossom. This phenomenon is particularly difficult for the other students because those with lesser talent may be working just as hard (or harder) yet displaying less ability. Directors have the responsibility of allowing the highly talented to take positions of leadership while still keeping the hard-working, less talented students interested, motivated, and continuing to grow. Directors must help every student to understand and accept their own performance capabilities. The challenge should be for all students to achieve their best within the limitations of their own potential.

It is also during their tenure in the Intermediate Choir that some of the singers begin to think they might pursue a career in music. They often seek the director's advice. Here again, directors must encourage everyone to maintain a lifelong interest in music without leading the unexceptionally talented ones down the primrose path. Directors could give those students who seek advice a music aptitude test such as the Gordon Musical Aptitude Profile[3] then let the result speak for itself.

Rehearsals should be held on a daily basis unless the administration absolutely forbids it due to scheduling difficulties.

The Advanced Choir

This group is often referred to as the A cappella Choir or the Concert Choir. The beauty of this organization lies in its training and ability. After the students (usually eleventh and twelfth graders) have grown up through a structured, sequential program, they are capable of singing almost any choral literature except that which only should be attempted by very mature, adult voices. No longer is it necessary to restrict the selection of the music because of extreme vocal and maturation limitations. The challenge, instead, is to choose music that is worthy of study with a well-trained and talented group of singers. Jipson "hits the nail on the head" when he says:

> History is alive and well, and living in the Advanced Choir classroom. Music students have the rare opportunity of reliving the past; of recalling, at will, the beautiful sounds of any era of notated music. The teacher of Advanced Choir has an opportunity to bring all of this to his students. He also has an obligation to include the sounds of today. This should involve music from all aspects of the local culture and reach as far beyond that as possible. Stylistic and tonal aspects become identifiable as to historic and, sometimes, geographic placement.[4]

The one primary objective of the Advanced Choir is to prepare (using proper choral technique and all aspects of good sight-reading skills and good musicianship) and perform (as stylistically correctly to the extent that adolescent voices are capable) great choral literature from all periods of music history (including music of today) in a highly polished and well-rehearsed fashion displaying proper blend, balance, purity of tone, articulation, enunciation, pronunciation, and all other musical attributes befitting the aesthetic qualities of the choral art.

Activity in class should include:

1. Vocal exercises that reinforce all aspects of a structured, sequential program of choral technique.
2. Daily exercises in sight-reading of choral literature that contains various textural, rhythmic, melodic, and harmonic complexities.
3. Preparing choral literature from all periods of music history (including contemporary) in various languages including Latin, German, Italian, French, and Spanish.
4. Singing in small ensembles such as quartets and octets to continue to develop musical independence.
5. Sitting in different seating arrangements, particularly using unsectioned,

---

[3] Edwin Gordon, *Musical Aptitude Profile* (Boston: Houghton Mifflin Co., 1965).
[4] Jipson, *The High School Vocal Music Program,* 45.

scrambled, or quartet mixtures that help the students to develop independent singing and to experience the sound of all the music instead of just the sound of their own parts.

6. Providing solo opportunities for those students with extraordinary vocal aptitude.

7. Using recordings, guest performances, and encouragement of attendance to outside choral concerts to help develop the mental image of outstanding choral performances.

8. Stressing good stage deportment including entering with good posture, paying attention to the director, maintaining pleasing attitude and facial expressions, and displaying the ability to cover mistakes.

9. Preparing for and attending at least one choral festival or contest each semester.

10. Preparing and performing at least one choral concert for the student body and parents.

11. Performing for community and civic organizations whenever the opportunity is provided.

Deciding if the membership in the Advanced Choir should or should not be limited is an important and difficult decision for most choral teachers. They certainly want the members of the Advanced Choir to be as good as possible and to be exposed to the finest literature; therefore, the tendency is to limit the membership so these goals may be assured. On the other hand, consideration should be given to including as many students as possible as a reward for their dedication, hard work, and tenacity in moving through the sequential program. If limitation is decided upon, what criteria should be used to choose the membership? Tradition supports a selected membership through audition or director preference. Possibly deliberation should be focused on a quasi-limited membership in which all students who have progressed through the sequential program be considered. There would be only two criteria that would limit membership: (1) Choral balance must be maintained within the organization, and (2) no member be admitted who brings anything less than a positive contribution. This approach would allow directors to include more girls (of whom there is an over-supply) than boys as long as the aural balance was preserved. It would also allow less-talented students to be members as long as they demonstrated a positive, progressive attitude and did not restrict the group as a whole in achieving musical excellence.

It is standing practice in high schools throughout the United States for the Advanced Group to practice daily. In view of the amount of literature that should be covered for both performance and study, daily classes are imperative.

EXTRACURRICULA CHORAL ACTIVITIES

So far we have discussed a sequential choral program with choirs that are scheduled as part of the daily classroom curriculum. We now consider those performing groups that, in most cases, must be scheduled as extracurricula

activities before or after school or at a special time that can be found by the director, such as during study hall or at the end of the lunch hour. The Chamber Ensemble (may be called Madrigal Singers) is one of these.

The Chamber Ensemble or Madrigal Singers

The terms *madrigal* and *chamber* are often used interchangeably. They are used loosely to designate a group of select voices of from five to twenty-five singers. Their repertoire often includes music from every historical period (including folk music). While they sing madrigals, they are not limited to such. Because the groups are small, the repertoire they are capable of performing is limited to some extent.

The core of the group's repertoire will be the four and five-part sixteenth century madrigal that may be voiced SATB, SA(Countertenor)TBB, SSATB, or SATBB. Originally these works were performed with one person on each part, but with adolescent singers the demands of the literature make this practice very difficult. There should be at least two students on a part and generally, as far as blend is concerned, three singers on a part is best. Various instruments such as the harpsichord, recorder, lute, rebec, and guitar can be used to add variety, color, and authenticity to the repertoire.

Small ensembles that perform chamber music from all periods serve several important functions. They provide a place for the highly advanced and gifted student to be challenged. They serve as an excellent source of musical fulfillment for the directors. They present a very professional image for the school they represent and are well suited to perform at civic and professional meetings. Because the group is small, transportation and traveling expenses are kept at a minimum. If a quasi-limited approach to membership for the Advanced Choir is used, the chamber ensemble may serve as that "super-select" organization that is open only by strict audition and limited to the most talented and dedicated singers. It is important, however, that only members of the Advanced Choir be allowed to audition. This strategy is necessary to preserve the status and clout that membership in the Advanced Choir deserves.

Because of the close working relationships required of members of the chamber group, teachers need not only look for good singers; they should also look for well-rounded, socially adjusted individuals. Another important personality ingredient to be found in the singers is intellectual curiosity. Specific characteristics to look for might include:

1. *Interest*—The student must be particularly interested in music of this type and in singing with a small group.
2. *Adaptability*—Even the world's best musicians are out of place in a chamber ensemble if they cannot conform to the collective wishes of director and the group as a whole.
3. *Alertness*—The ability to learn quickly, to react instantly, and to enjoy the association with other intelligent, alert young people is essential.
4. *Keen Ear*—Members must have a well-developed sense of pitch.
5. *Good Voice*—Not necessarily a "great" voice. Blend is extremely important,

therefore the voice must be very flexible, even if not of outstanding solo quality. (Reject the great soloists who cannot or will not blend.)

6. *Style*—The ability to imitate, to respond, and to react to the spoken, sung, or even felt, suggestions of the director and the other members is essential.[5]

Directors must have some knowledge about how to costume these groups tastefully. Madrigals and Renaissance music often are performed in costumes of Elizabethan style. Students can be led to research and make their own costumes. Contemporary formal dress is suitable for presenting other types of repertoire.

One of the responsibilities of the membership of Madrigal Singers is to present a Madrigal Dinner at Christmas or a Renaissance dinner in a nonseasonal time of the year. An event of this sort is very popular with both audiences and performers because of the unique setting and occasion. In fact, on many secondary campuses it has become the premiere social event of the year. On college and university campuses it often serves as a very successful fund-raising project because its formal and aesthetic social structure is suited exactly for inviting guests of influential social and financial standing. From an educational standpoint it has several advantages:

1. It provides an opportunity to perform madrigals in a quasi-authentic setting of pleasant surroundings, in authentic decor and dress, and accompanied by a good meal.

2. It is a perfect opportunity to sing quality literature to an audience who might not be inclined to come to a formal concert.

3. It allows for a variety of performance options: vocal solos, duets, quartets; recorder consorts; brass ensembles; instrumental chamber groups; harpsichordists; dancers; jugglers; and gymnasts.

A madrigal feast may be as simple or elaborate as directors may choose. A very simple presentation might include the entrance of the Madrigal Singers after which they sing several selections, serve the meal, then sing a few more selections before leaving. A more elaborate festivity might include: (1) a recorder or brass ensemble playing while the guests are seated (the guests may be announced in a formal fashion such as "My Lord and Lady John and Jane Doe," if desired), (2) entrance of the madrigal singers (preceded by brass fanfare), (3) entrance of the lord and lady of the manor (this may be the school principal and spouse or special guests whom the director desires to honor), (4) welcome by the court jester, (5) wassail toast (often preceded by a brass fanfare and including "original" toasts written to highlight the presence and personalities of various guests), (6) singing of a group of madrigals, (7) playing by a recorder consort (or they may play background music during the meal), (8) first course of the dinner (may be preceded by brass fanfare), (9) another group of madrigals

[5] Rose Marie Grentzer, "The Chamber Ensemble," *Choral Director's Guide*, edited by Kenneth L. Neidig and John W. Jennings (New Nyack, N.Y.: Parker Publishing Co., 1967), 61.

or a dance of the period), (10) second course of dinner (may be preceded by brass fanfare), (11) solos, duets, quartets, (12) a processional presenting the boar's head and singing of "Boar's Head Carol," (usually preceded by brass fanfare), (13) main course of the dinner, (14) presentation of gymnasts, jugglers, another dance, another group of madrigals, or instrumental group, (15) processional presenting the flaming plum pudding (may be preceded by brass fanfare), (16) final group of madrigals, and (17) the exit of the madrigal singers.

The entire festivity is most effective when presented entirely by candlelight. The madrigal singers may enter and exit while singing and holding candles. The court jester serves as the master of ceremonies. The part should be well written, memorized, and humorous. Depending on the type of audience present, the court jester often feigns a progressing degree of inebriety as the evening advances. Other "small, but nice, touches can be brought to this event such as spreading of flower petals as the ladies of the madrigal [feast] enter, ballad singers going table to table, well-trained and costumed servers, herald trumpets, English-style hall banners, homemade candles, and a well-designed souvenir program."[6]

It is not within the purview of this chapter to include other specific, detailed instructions pertaining to this event, but useful books and articles have been included in the bibliography of this chapter to assist choral directors if they should desire to undertake such a project.

The All-Male or All-Female Chorus

Historically, unisex choirs predate mixed choirs. Initially, liturgical choirs were all male. English glee clubs of the latter part of the eighteenth century were all male. Before 1750 women were restricted to singing in secular music and to occasions where females performed only with other females. All-male and all-female choruses were prevalent in Vienna and other parts of Europe during the latter part of the eighteenth and most of the nineteenth centuries.

> Why were there no mixed choirs before the middle of the 18th century? Most of the significant choral music up to that time was composed for and performed at court or church. (Theater or opera music was largely a function of the courtly aristocracy and oriented primarily towards the vocal solo.) Thus, the answer to this must be found by analyzing separately the needs of each institution.
>
> The amateur singing societies, which were the first important mixed choirs, were an outgrowth of an educated middle class interest in music beginning in the 18th century. Previous to this time political, social, and economic forces prevented the growth of a large educated middle class. Also, the choirs of the aristocratic courts were composed primarily of professional and student singers; and, historically, women have usually been prevented or discouraged from pursuing professional careers and career-oriented education and training. Thus, these choirs were male-dominated.[7]

[6] Gordon H. Lamb, *Choral Techniques,* 3d ed. (Dubuque, Iowa: Wm. C. Brown Co., 1988), 223.

[7] Timothy Mount, "Treble Voices in Choral Music," *The Choral Journal* 17, no. 5, (January 1976), 26.

History shows that there are obvious aesthetic and social purposes for singing in segregated groups. One reason they were so popular with preceding generations, to provide camaraderie and enjoyment of singing among members of the same sex, is the same reason they may be organized and enjoyed in the secondary classroom today. It is indeed a unique singing opportunity not experienced in a mixed group.

In recent years in the United States all-male and all-female choirs have not been as popular as mixed groups for a couple of reasons: (1) the movement among women for equal rights has discouraged segregation and (2) the dearth of men who desire to sing has forced, through necessity, most men to sing in mixed choirs. Although very difficult to find in other cultures, the pioneer heritage and spirit during America's developmental years has fostered an attitude among the populace that singing is not masculine and should be relegated strictly to women. This "pseudo-machismo" is unfortunate indeed because so many American men and boys never fulfill the aesthetic needs in their lives that allow them to become truly self-actualized individuals (see "Abraham Maslow's Needs Theory" in Chapter 4).

Often another reason that directors must include all-male and all-female groups in the curriculum is born out of necessity. In a structured, sequential choral program it has been mentioned that directors might desire to divide the Beginning Choir into two groups, one of which is all-male and the other all-female, particularly if the Beginning Choir is in junior high school. Along with the several reasons delineated previously, consideration for the maturation level of the students is the primary reason for separating the girls from the boys. It was also pointed out that in some school systems, the Intermediate Choir may need to be an all-female organization simply because there may not be enough boys enrolled in the choral program to support three levels of mixed choirs.

One of the principle problems with all-male choirs in middle/junior high school is the difficulty directors encounter in finding literature for them to sing in which the range and tessitura limitations of their changing voices is considered. Until there is a greater demand for the literature, publishers are unwilling to invest in such a product, and since there is limited literature, directors are reluctant to organize all-male choruses. It is a dilemma. Bobby Siltman, fine arts coordinator for the Abilene (Texas) Public Schools and an expert in dealing with early adolescent male voices, suggests that directors should arrange their own music. He wrote three excellent articles that instruct directors in this fine art of arranging.[8] Because of his twenty-five-year crusade, he has been able to persuade several publishers to release music written specifically for all-male middle/junior high school singers.

There is a similar problem with all-male high school groups, even though it is not as severe. Four-part TTBB compositions and arrangements intended

[8] Bobby Siltman, "Breaking the Vicious Circle," *Choral Journal* 18, no. 3 (November 1978), 9–10; Bobby Siltman, "Arranging for the Boys' Chorus," *Choral Journal* 18, no. 4 (December 1978), 11–14; Bobby Siltman, "Literature for the Junior High Male Chorus: More Than Singing," *Choral Journal* 18, no. 5 (January 1979), 18–20.

for adult singers are much easier to find but may be quite inappropriate for adolescent voices. Since many of the boys' voices are either changing or at least settling after the adolescent growth spurt, the extremely high notes of the Tenor I part and the low notes of the Bass II part are very difficult for some boys to produce. If TTBB compositions are used, it is best for the Tenor I part to be carried by cambiatas whose voices are in the first phase of change. If young changed-voice tenors or adolescent baritones (boys in the second phase of change) are asked to sing the Tenor I part, it is absolutely essential that they produce the upper notes of the part in falsetto phonation to prevent vocal problems that have the potential of haunting them the remainder of their lives. It might be necessary for directors to edit the Bass II part of some adult-oriented compositions and arrangements for adolescent basses to sing them. In some instances directors might find TBB- or TTB-voiced arrangements more appropriate for their high school all-male choruses.

The Society for the Preservation and Encouragement of Barber Shop Quartet Singing in America (SPEBSQSA) has been very active in promoting barbershop singing in schools in recent years, particularly through the Music Educators National Conference (MENC). Both junior high and high school adolescents are often intrigued with barbershop singing because of the challenging harmonic structure and the nineteenth-century American singing tradition it promotes. If directors are selective, they can find barbershop arrangements that are quite apropos for adolescent voices published by the society.[9]

Traditionally, all-female choruses have suffered from a feeling of low prestige when compared with the all-male chorus or mixed chorus. The most common explanation for this standing is that "the treble choir possesses limited dynamic and vocal ranges and that the absence of men's voices leads to a monochromatic sound."[10] Even the eminent choral conductor and composer Archibald T. Davison in his book *The Technique of Choral Composition* stated that "twenty minutes of unaccompanied singing in this medium [women's chorus] will lead most hearers, I believe, to yearn ardently for the presence of a bass voice."[11] Nonetheless, there are a number of leading American music educators, many of whom are men, who feel that there is a definite place for the all-female chorus in the school curriculum and who heartily defend their existence.[12] The chapter bibliography contains a listing of several articles that espouse their importance.

[9] The Society for the Preservation and Encouragement of Barber Shop Quartet Singing in America, Inc., 6315 Third Avenue, Kenosha, WI 53141.

[10] Raymond Sprague, "Literature of Quality for the Treble Choir," *Choral Journal* 24, no. 2 (October 1984), 5.

[11] Archibald T. Davison, *The Technique of Choral Composition* (Cambridge: Harvard University Press, 1966), 135–136.

[12] To name five: Gregory Vancil, assistant professor of music and director of choral activities at Trinity University in San Antonio, Texas; Al Skoog and David Niederbrach, director of choral activities and associate professor of voice respectively at Arkansas State University, Jonesboro; Raymond Sprague, professor of music and conductor of choirs at Saint Mary's College, Notre Dame, Indiana; and Betty Jane Grimm, professor of music at Florida State University, Tallahassee.

Here again, one of the problems encountered by directors of all-female choruses in junior high and high school is in fulfilling the needs of their young voices. It is very rare to find a true, natural alto among adolescent singers. Directors are inclined to place those students who are good readers on the inner and lower parts. Girls who are relegated to the lower parts consistently will never develop the upper (head voice) part of the range and soon will be complaining that they cannot sing high. It is important to vocalize the girls throughout the full compass of the range, which often takes them up to a high B-flat or C (above the treble clef).[13] Further, it is advisable to switch parts on some of the literature so that the "altos" will have an opportunity to use the upper regions of the voice. Directors must be very careful to select literature that does not keep the lower voices around middle C or below all the time. Choose literature that includes some unison singing so that all the girls can sing throughout the full compass of their ranges.

The Swing Choir, Show Choir, and Vocal Jazz Ensemble

Perhaps one of the most significant occurrences in choral music education within the last twenty-five years has been the advent of the swing choirs, show choirs and the vocal jazz ensembles. Like any new movement, these groups have had their strong advocates as well as critics and, in reality, the verdict is still out as to the movement's lasting significance. Even though they are still quite popular in various parts of the country, in the latter 1980s the number of these groups had decreased and changed in character and their future is somewhat in question. During this period, schools in every part of the country have added these types of choral groups to their existing programs. Many choral directors were inclined to develop these groups because their sound proved appealing to the students and they increased the attention being given to the choral department. When properly incorporated and structured into the overall choral program, they caused the other choral offerings to grow in participation and importance.

The various approaches to these contemporary ensembles emerged in different parts of the country. Most vocal jazz ensembles began in the Northwest, most show choirs in southern California, and the swing and staged choirs surfaced in the Midwest. The East and Southeast also have jazz ensembles, but more often they have swing or show choirs.

The Swing Choir   The swing choir is the oldest of the three. In the 1940s directors formed small choral groups to perform popular music in addition to madrigals. The singers were usually accompanied by piano and sometimes by an added string bass and drums. The choir generally numbered twelve to sixteen singers, stood in a semicircle, sang Broadway show tunes and other pop tunes (some of which might have been arranged by the director), and were not electronically

---

[13] This is not to infer that literature which includes these tones should be performed particularly by junior high school singers.

amplified. With the presence of television in most homes by the 1950s, such shows as "Hit Parade" and "Sing Along with Mitch" influenced these school ensembles to incorporate more energy into their singing, to swing and sway to the beat, and to communicate with their faces during the performance. They abandoned their semicircle and staged their presentations using stools, boxes, or layered stages and risers to present a less-formal atmosphere. In the 1960s choreography was added to the performance with professional groups such as the Johnny Mann Singers and Fred Waring and the Pennsylvanians serving as models.

By the 1970s and early 1980s, swing choirs saw the Fifth Dimension, The Young Americans, Up with People, the Jackson Five, The Carpenters, The Association, The First Edition, Now Singers, Free Design, and the Pointer Sisters as their prototypes and gained inspiration from these professional groups. During that time swing choirs were usually sixteen to thirty-two in number with about the same number of boys and girls to facilitate staging and choreography. Most often they were accompanied by a basic four-piece combo of piano, electric bass, guitar, and drums with added wind instruments (usually brass) as needed. They usually performed on a flat-surfaced stage area for the choreographed pieces then took positions on stools or boxes for the mellow selections. Since amplification of the voices was essential, strategically placed stand, hanging, or floor microphones were used. If the group was small enough, they may have used individual hand microphones. The technology of cordless microphones had progressed to the point that some groups purchased them for the soloists and others who were in the forefront or who displayed particularly complex choreography. Their outfits (costumes, in some cases) were colorful and color-coordinated with the stage setting.

Most high school swing choirs sang in what was commonly referred to as the *modern* or *contemporary* style, which were all-encompassing terms. The pieces were generally arrangements of tunes that were currently on the Top Forty listing. The melodies were usually easy to remember, the words spoke to the students, the harmony was attractive and close, and the rhythm was quite inventive. Special attention was given to shading of notes and phrases. "Bending," "slurring," and "scooping" were typical singing techniques utilized in the style (techniques that were certainly prohibited in a conventional chorus).

Occasionally, the swing choirs would include a section of their programs that was nostalgic in nature. They would sing tunes from the Forties, Fifties, and Sixties using arrangements similar to those made popular by Percy Faith, Ray Coniff, Ray Charles, Anita Kerr, and Norman Luboff. A few country or gospel tunes such as "Put Your Hand in the Hand," "Proud Mary," and "Take Me Home, Country Roads" worked their way into the repertoire of swing choirs calling for a special treatment of the diphthong, straight tones, and different tonal colors.

By the late 1980s the term *swing* began to disappear even though these choirs were still prevalent throughout the country. There seemed to be a tendency (possibly an emerging trend) for these contemporary groups to include more conventional selections on their pop programs. The groups displayed a much wider versatility in style, singing everything from madrigals to contemporary pieces. They were influenced principally by the King Singers and the New Swingle Singers whose genius lies in their wide range of repertoire and stylistic ability.

The Show Choir With the refined television productions of the 1970s and 1980s came the advent in educational circles of the show choir. In reality these groups were swing choirs with a different name. Although there were some differences, the similarities were more common. The primary difference was directly related to the part of the country from which they sprang, southern California and the West Coast as opposed to the Midwest. The influence of the Las Vegas shows and "commercial" studios resulted in a very high-energy production with a great emphasis on choreography, colorful backgrounds, multileveled staging, and lighting effects. Doug Anderson explains it this way:

> The show choir is similar to the swing choir except all aspects of its characteristics are embellished. It too is most commonly composed of 24 singers, with an equal number of boys and girls. They are often accompanied by a small combo with complete instrumentation. There are also groups which perform with the accompaniment track on a tape prepared in a studio by the finest school or professional musicians available. The program presented is often one continuous show, with one number smoothly blending into the next during the applause. The performance area is usually on a stage. Since the boxes and stools of the swing choir would interfere with the movement, these are usually eliminated, but more use is made of colorful backgrounds, multileveled staging, and lighting effects. The outfits are very showy and are often equal to the wild creations seen in professional shows. The movement is much more elaborate than that used by the swing choirs and, since the singers are so mobile, it is difficult to amplify them. Many groups do use a sound system, however, to highlight solo parts and by the use of sophisticated microphones are able to pick up the whole group for amplification in large performance areas.
> The strength of the show choir lies in its high energy performance gaining a high energy response from the audience. The weakness is often in the musical part of the presentation. Many times members are chosen on their ability to dance rather than superior vocal ability and the group becomes a "dancing group that sings." The vocal arrangements, though challenging rhythmically, often lack complete harmonies and a high desire for singing excellence does not seem to be present.[14]

The Vocal Jazz Ensemble When comparing the vocal jazz ensemble with the swing or show choir, one distinctive characteristics is their origins. The vocal jazz ensemble was uniquely an organization that had educational beginnings rather than professional roots. Even though the jazz ensemble had professional predecessors, such as the Hi-Los, they were not choral organizations as were the Pennsylvanians who preceded the swing groups. It is well known that jazz has its roots in the black African culture and through an evolutionary process has manifest itself educationally through the instrumental jazz band (often called the stage band), which has been part of the school band scene for many years.

---

[14] Doug Anderson, *Jazz and Show Choir Handbook* (Chapel Hill, N. C.: Hinshaw Music, Inc., 1978), 7–10.

The National Association of Jazz Educators (NAJE) was organized in 1968 and is an affiliate organization of MENC. Its official magazine, the *NAJE Educator* includes beneficial information for anyone interested in working with a vocal jazz group. Since its inception in 1968, the Northwest Vocal Jazz Festival at Mt. Hood Community College in Gresham, Oregon has grown to the point that there are over 100 vocal groups participating in its sessions each year.

The first vocal jazz ensembles appeared in the Northwest in the 1960s and were a result of groups who actually sang some of the stage band charts of Buddy Rich and other big band leaders. The idea of using nonsense syllables for words and applying them to instrumental music had been introduced earlier by Ward Swingle and the Swingle Singers when they recorded instrumental master works such as fugues and overtures with voices. Ultimately, specific vocal arrangements emerged (using both words and nonsense syllables) with similar harmonies and rhythms as the band charts, and the vocal jazz ensemble movement was born.

Of the three contemporary ensembles discussed here, the vocal jazz ensemble fits the definition of a choir better than any other because the emphasis is placed on the vocal sound rather than the visual aspects. However, this is not to say that jazz performers stand perfectly still—they do not—but the movement is not choreographed and is a result in the natural expression of the phrases and rhythm in the music. The movement is usually limited to standing space or a small proximity thereabouts. Like the swing or show groups, the size of most jazz ensembles is limited to between sixteen to thirty members. A larger number of singers will adversely affect the intonation as well as the sense of "snap" (energy and precision) necessary to initiate the highly syncopated rhythmic figures that are so prevalent in the idiom.

Another characteristic of vocal jazz work is the improvisation element. Many arrangements contain an improvised vocal solo using *scat* syllables (scat singing), which is performed in the style demonstrated in the recordings of Mel Torme or Ella Fitzgerald. "This is one of the strengths of a jazz choir— the tremendous creativity developed through spontaneous improvisation and unusual challenging vocal arrangements."[15]

Vocal jazz ensembles are usually amplified. Larger groups will have several microphones in strategic places not only to balance the voices with the instruments but also to give amplified color to the sounds. Smaller groups may use individual hand microphones. The singers' outfits may be color-coordinated or styled individually according to the desires of each singer. Accompaniment is usually provided by the basic jazz trio (piano, bass, and drums). Occasionally a rhythm guitar and an incidental wind instrument such as a flute may be added. Another option for accompaniment may be a six-piece jazz combo that includes piano, bass, drums, trombone, trumpet and saxophone.

Including Contemporary Ensembles in the Curriculum   Because of their immense popularity among students, one of the problems choral directors have encountered

---

[15] Ibid., 9.

when including these contemporary "pop" ensembles in the choral curriculum is the difficulty they experience in maintaining students' interest in the traditional choral offerings such as the chamber singers and Advanced Choir, which are considered by many to have lasting aesthetic and educational value. If choral directors intend to include these ensembles in their curriculum, it is important to choose their membership from those students enrolled in the traditional classes (particularly the Advanced Choir) so that these select students will be committed to the core of the program and will receive the necessary vocal and musicianship training essential to be successful in the select groups.

It is important that the students conceive these special ensembles as choirs, not as adolescent versions of their favorite recording groups. Because they are choral in nature and include more than one singer on each part, the students should not expect them to sound like their favorite recordings. The only similarity may be the title and melody of the tunes. Even the arrangements are different. Although a different style of singing is used with these contemporary choral groups than with the traditional groups, it is *not* the same style used by the recording stars. It is a choral style developed specifically for these unique choral sounds. The choral technique still requires the same fundamentals of singing (proper breathing and a resonated, free, and unrestricted vocal tone) as they have been taught to use when singing in their traditional groups.

Since the singing style for each is different, directors must have special knowledge and training to be successful with these groups. If choreography is used, they must have special training in applying it to choral singing that allows the singers to present a pleasing visual image without destroying good vocal production. They must be trained in the proper use of microphones in choral singing. Directors may find summer workshops that assist them in attaining the necessary training.[16] Three helpful books on dealing with proper style and choreography are Doug Anderson's *Jazz and Show Choir Handbook,* Kirby Shaw's *Vocal Jazz Style,* Carl Strommen's *The Contemporary Chorus,* and Sally Albrecht's *Choral Music in Motion.*[17]

Some directors have chosen an alternative to incorporating these contemporary ensembles as classes into their curriculum by attempting to include a visual aspect to their traditional choral ensembles by the use of *choralography,* a term coined by Frank Pooler, professor of music at California State University in Long Beach. In *Choralography*[18] he describes ways of adding simple body movements such as leaning, turning, bending, bowing, and using the hands, arms, and head to add a visual dimension of expression to the text and music of traditional choral music. The singers usually stand in one place on risers. Choralography is nothing as elaborate as choreography.

[16] Write Gene Grier, 'PoP'pourri Unlimited, P.O. Box 307, Drayton Plains, MI 48020 for information about summer workshops and a multitude of ideas pertaining to these contemporary ensembles.

[17] See the chapter bibliography to obtain the publication information for each of the books.

[18] Frank Pooler and Gail L. Shoup, *Choralography* (New York: Walton Music Corp., 1971).

The School Musical

To include the school musical as part of the choral curriculum is controversial. The strongest points of argument put forth by directors who are against including it are:

1. It is not a choral medium and should be part of the drama department.
2. The type vocal production it requires is counter to that used in choral music. It is generally hazardous to the vocal health of adolescent singers.
3. It requires too much time and energy for a successful production. That same time and energy produces much greater results if applied directly to the choral program.

Directors who feel the musical should be a part of the choral curriculum proffer the following points in its behalf:

1. The musical is, and has been, an accepted part of our culture since the beginning of the twentieth century. To ignore it is neither realistic nor fair to the students.
2. Contrary to the beliefs of many, the musical can be done with an emphasis on musical values.
3. The musical can serve as the perfect bridge for the often discussed generation gap. The music contains many aspects of both classical and pop writings.
4. The musical can be a catalyst for the entire music department. It can create an enthusiastic drive for a common goal throughout an entire school.
5. The musical will serve to draw into the choral program students who might otherwise not become involved. The teacher then has the opportunity to broaden their musical horizons.
6. If the director handles it correctly, the musical can be kept in proper perspective in relation to the rest of the choral program.[19]

It is recommended that the musical be placed under the auspices of the choral department but that directors attempt to incorporate teachers in drama, dance, manual arts, physical education, band, home economics, and art to make it truly an all-school production. This alleviates so much of the responsibility for the production usually taken by the choral teacher and fosters a sense of cooperation among the faculty of the entire school.

At the beginning of the semester the choral teacher who should be the Director of the Show may form a committee that includes the teachers in the disciplines delineated above to choose the musical (it is a good idea for the choral teacher to have several musicals in mind that are within the vocal capabilities of adolescents), to determine the audition process, and to put all rehearsals including the technical rehearsal, dress rehearsal, and the performance(s) on the master calendar. The committee should consider dividing the responsibility of the production in the following manner:

[19] Jipson, *The High School Vocal Music Program*, 171.

1. Preparation of the singers: the choral teacher
2. Preparation of the orchestra: the band or orchestra director
3. Acting: the drama teacher
4. Choreography: the dance teacher or the physical education teacher who trains the cheerleaders or drill team
5. Set: the art teacher
6. Staging and lighting: the manual arts instructor (or a staff member who has had this experience)
7. Costuming: home economics teacher (or show pictures of the type costumes desired and let each student be responsible for procuring his or her own costume)
8. Stage properties: a properties person (or have the leads be responsible for their own properties and a chorus member in charge of special chorus items)
9. Discipline: when the rehearsals begin, the director of the show should provide written instructions to everyone pertaining to behavior while on set
10. Makeup: the drama department or drama club
11. Publicity, tickets, and programs: the art department or art club
12. Money matters: the school business office
13. Scheduling: the school principal or school musical committee

The director of the show will be responsible for announcing the show and cast. The director is also responsible for blocking rehearsals, establishing how the leads and chorus will be amplified (microphones), bringing all the areas (orchestra, acting, singing, dancing) together, and running the technical rehearsal, the dress rehearsal, and all the performances.

THOUGHTS FOR CONTEMPLATION AND DISCUSSION

1. What is the best time of the day to have the Beginning Choir rehearsal? Intermediate Choir rehearsal? Advanced Choir rehearsal? Why?
2. How will you approach singing music several centuries old with early adolescents who only claim to like current media music?
3. If you were to find it difficult to schedule extracurricula ensembles, such as chamber singers or a jazz choir, should you forgo organizing them? If not, how will you deal with the problem?
4. Do you plan to organize contemporary popular ensembles in your choral program? Which type? How do you plan to choose the members? How do you plan to keep it in perspective with the other ensembles and choirs?
5. Think about conducting five or six rehearsals daily. How can you protect yourself against burnout? How can you develop the stamina to remain active and positive throughout the entire day?
6. How much input do you think students should have in setting the standards of quality for the choral music program?
7. Suppose you were a senior high choral director whose program is fed by excellent middle/junior high school programs. Will you choose only the "cream of the crop" for your choirs? If so, how will you justify ignoring the music education of those who are not chosen?
8. In your capacity as a secondary choral teacher, if you inherit a small, quality

program, will you concentrate on containing the size and quality of the program or will you branch out to recruit many untrained students creating a larger but less quality-oriented program? Why or why not?

9. How will you justify not allowing your middle/junior high students to sing contemporary popular style on traditional choral music?

BIBLIOGRAPHY

AITKEN, GENE. "Individual Miking." *Jazz Educators Journal* 17 (February–March 1985).

———. "Individual Miking the Set-Up and Rehearsal." *Jazz Educators Journal* 18 (October–November 1985).

———. "Rehearsal Techniques." *Jazz Educators Journal* 16 (February–March and April–May 1984).

———. "Vocal Jazz Techniques." *Jazz Educators Journal* 17 (October–November 1984).

———. "Vocal Jazz Vibrato." *Jazz Educators Journal* 17 (October–November 1984).

Alabama Department of Education. *Vocal Music Curriculum Guide, Grades 5–12*. Montgomery, Ala.: State Department of Education, 1986.

ALBRECHT, SALLY. *Choral Music in Motion*. East Stoudsburg, Penn.: Music in Action, 1984.

ALTHOUSE, JAY, ed. *The School Choral Program* (Conversations with Besig, Nygard, Albrecht). E. Stroudsburg, Penn.: Music in Action, 1987.

ANDERSON, DOUG. "A Conversation with Jack Kunz." *Pop, Jazz and Show Choir Magazine* 1 (Fall 1984).

———. *Jazz and Show Choir Handbook*. Chapel Hill, N.C.: Hinshaw Music, Inc., 1978.

———. "The Phil Mattson School." *Pop, Jazz and Show Choir Magazine* 2, (Spring 1985).

———. "Vocal Jazz for Your Choir." *Choral Journal* 17, no. 2 (October 1976).

Arkansas Department of Education. *Survey of Fine Arts, Arkansas Public School Course Content Guide*. Little Rock: Department of Education, 1988.

BEGLARIAN, G. *Comprehensive Musicianship: an Anthology of Evolving Thought*. Reston, Va.: Music Educators National Conference, 1971.

BESSOM, MALCOLM E., ALPHONSE TATARUNIS, and SAMUEL L. FORCUCCI. *Teaching Music in Today's Secondary Schools*, 2d ed. New York: Holt, Rinehart and Winston, 1980.

COLLINS, DON L. *The Cambiata Concept, a Comprehensive Philosophy and Methodology of Teaching Music to Adolescents*. Conway, Ark.: Cambiata Press, 1981.

Commonwealth of Massachusetts. *Music Curriculum Guide, Grades 7–12*. Boston: Department of Education, 1982.

COOPER, IRVIN, and KARL O. KURSTEINER. *Teaching Junior High School Music*, 2d ed. Conway, Ark.: Cambiata Press, 1973.

COSMAN, MADELAINE PEINER. *Medieval Holidays and Festivals: A Calendar of Celebrations*. New York: Charles Scribner's Sons, 1981.

CRYDER, JOHN. "Getting the Most from a Sound System." *Pop, Jazz and Show Choir Magazine* 2 (Spring 1985).

DAVISON, ARCHIBALD T. *The Technique of Choral Composition*. Cambridge: Harvard University Press, 1966.

DWIGGINS, ROSE R. "One Step at a Time for Show Choirs." *Music Educators Journal* 70 (February 1984).

EDELSON, EDWARD. *The Secondary School Music Program from Classroom to Concert Hall*. West Nyack, N.Y.: Parker Publishing Co., 1972.

EDWARDS, JIM. "How to Mike Jazz, Swing, and Show Choirs." *Pop, Jazz and Show Choir Magazine* 1 (Fall 1984).

FISSINGER, EDWIN. *The Madrigal Concert: Choral Music for the Madrigal Dinner, Renaissance Fest and Madrigal Concert*. Milwaukee, Wis.: Jenson Publications, Inc., 1981.

FREDRICKSON, SCOTT. "Vocal Improvisation: A Practical Approach." *Pop, Jazz and Show Choir Magazine* 2 (Spring 1985).

GARRETSON, ROBERT L. *Conducting Choral Music*, 6th ed. Englewood Cliffs, N.J.: Prentice-Hall, Inc., 1988.

GORDON, EDWIN. *Musical Aptitude Profile*. Boston: Houghton Mifflin Co., 1965.

GRENTZER, ROSE MARIE. "The Chamber Ensemble." In *Choral Director's Guide*, edited by Kenneth L. Neidig and John W. Jennings. New Nyack, N.Y.: Parker Publishing Co., 1967.

GRIER, AUDREY. "Choreography for a Large

Ensemble: A Checklist." *Pop, Jazz and Show Choir Magazine* 2 (Spring 1985).

GRIER, GENE. "Recommended Music for the Jazz and Show Choir." *Choral Journal* 16, no. 8 (1986).

GRIER, GENE, and AUDREY GRIER. "Female Show Choirs." *Pop, Jazz and Show Choir Magazine* 3 (Fall 1985).

HABERLEN, JOHN, and STEPHEN ROSOLACK. *Elizabethan Madrigal Dinners.* Champaign, Ill.: Mark Foster Music Co., 1978.

HAMMER, RUSSELL A. *Pragmatic Choral Procedures.* Metuchen, N.J.: Scarecrow Press, 1984.

HASS, GLENN. *Curriculum Planning, a New Approach,* 3d ed. Boston: Allyn and Bacon, Inc., 1980.

Henry County Public Schools. *Music Curriculum Guide, Grades 9–12.* Paris, Tenn.: Murray State University, Henry County Public Schools Teacher Corps Project, 1982.

HOFFER, CHARLES R. *Teaching Music in the Secondary Schools,* 4th ed. Belmont, Calif,.: Wadsworth Publishing, 1991.

HOLST, IMOGEN. *Conducting a Choir: A Guide for Amateurs.* New York: Oxford University Press, 1973.

JACOBSON, JOHN. *Dance Warm-Ups and Workouts for the Show Choir.* New Berlin, Wis.: Jenson Publications, 1984. (Booklet and LP Recording).

JIPSON, WAYNE R. *The High School Vocal Music Program.* West Nyack, N.Y.: Parker Publishing Co., 1972.

JONES, PERRY. "The History of Women's Liberation in Choral Music." *Choral Journal* 16, no. 6 (1975).

KOWALL, BONNIE C., ed. *Perspectives in Music Education, Source Book III.* Reston, Va.: Music Educators National Conference, 1966.

LAMB, GORDON H. *Choral Techniques,* 3d ed. Dubuque, Iowa: Wm. C. Brown Co., 1988.

LAMBLE, WALTER. "Choral Music's New Kid on the Block: The Swing Choir." *Choral Journal* 17, no. 3, (November 1976).

LEHMAN, PAUL R. *Music in Today's Schools: Rationale and Commentary.* Reston, Va.: Music Educators National Conference, 1987.

LEONHARD, CHARLES. *A Realistic Rationale for Teaching Music.* Reston, VA: Music Educators National Conference, 1985.

MARK, MICHAEL L. *Contemporary Music Education,* 2d ed. New York: Schirmer Books, 1986.

MARPLE, HUGO D. *Backgrounds and Approaches to Junior High Music.* Dubuque, Iowa: Wm. C. Brown Co., 1975.

MCKELVY, JAMES. *A Christmas Madrigal Dinner at the Home of Charles Wesley.* Champaign, Ill.: Mark Foster Music Co., 1980.

MILLER, KENNETH E. *Vocal Music Education, Teaching in the Secondary Schools.* Englewood Cliffs, N.J.: Prentice Hall, Inc., 1988.

MOUNT, TIMOTHY. "Treble Voices in Choral Music," *Choral Journal* 17, no. 5 (January 1976).

Music Educators National Conference. *The School Music Program: Descriptions and Standards,* 2d ed. Reston, Va.: Music Educators National Conference, 1986.

NEIDIG, KENNETH L., and JOHN JENNINGS, eds. *Choral Director's Guide.* West Nyack, N.Y.: Parker Publishing Co., 1967.

NYE, ROBERT EVANS, and VERNICE TROUSDALE NYE. *Music in the Elementary School.* Englewood Cliffs, N.J.: Prentice Hall, Inc., 1985.

POOLER, FRANK, and GAIL L. SHOUP. *Choralography.* New York: Walton Music Corp., 1971.

RINZLER, PAUL. "Does Vocal Jazz Really Hurt the Voice?" *Jazz Educators Journal* 18 (October–November 1985).

ROACH, DONALD. *Complete Secondary Choral Music Guide.* West Nyack, N.Y.: Parker Publishing Co., 1989.

———. *Handbook for Children's and Youth Choir Directors.* Garland, Tex.: Choristers Guild, 1987.

ROE, PAUL F. *Choral Music Education,* 2d ed. Englewood Cliffs, N.J.: Prentice Hall, Inc., 1983.

SALANTIEN, JOHN J. "An Early American Alternative to the Traditional Elizabethan Madrigal Dinner." *Choral Journal* 17, no. 2 (October 1976).

SCHWARTZ, DAN. "Resources for the Jazz and Show Choir Through November, 1983." *Choral Journal* 24 (February 1984).

SHAW, KIRBY. "Arranging for the Jazz Choir." *Choral Journal* 17, no. 5 (January. 1977).

———. *Vocal Jazz Style.* Milwaukee, Wis.: Hal Leonard, 1976. (Manual, books, tape)

SILTMAN, BOBBY. "Arranging for the Boys' Chorus." *Choral Journal* 18, no. 4 (December 1978).

———. "Breaking the Vicious Circle." *Choral Journal* 18, no. 3 (November 1978).

———. "Literature for the Junior High Male Chorus: More Than Singing" *Choral Journal* 18, no. 5 (January 1979).

SINGLETON, IRA. *Music in Secondary Schools,* 2d ed. Boston: Allyn and Bacon, Inc., 1965.

SPOLIN, VIOLA. *Improvisation for the Theatre.* Evanston, Ill.: Northwestern University Press, 1963.

SPRAGUE, RAYMOND. "Literature of Quality for the Treble Choir." *Choral Journal* 24, no. 2 (October), 1984.

STROMMEN, CARL. *The Contemporary Chorus.* Van Nuys, Calif.: Alfred Publishing, 1980.

Wisconsin Department of Public Instruction. *A Guide to Curriculum Planning in Music Education,* Bulletin No. 6268. Madison, Wis.: Wisconsin Department of Public Instruction, 1986.

———. *Music Curriculum Guide K-12,* Bulletin No. 159. Madison, Wis.: Wisconsin Department of Public Instruction, 1986.

16

Classes without Emphasis on Performance

In the early part of the nineteenth century, American educators, unlike many of their European counterparts, decided that music should be included in the curriculum for everyone to study and should not be offered just for the "musically gifted." This basic tenet has permeated the thinking of music educators on the elementary level and directed their actions for all these years, but, in reality, secondary music educators never have been completely committed to such an idea. Classes for adolescents, for the most part (except in some middle/junior high schools), have been scheduled to be elected by those who really desired to pursue educational endeavors in music. Seemingly, there always has been a contingent of secondary music educators who have espoused the "music for everyone" tenet but were unsuccessful in persuading the majority to commitment. Recently, due to the national revision of the secondary curriculum to strengthen basic education as a whole, many states have added a required fine arts course in senior high school and a required general music class in middle/junior high school. This revived interest in new required courses has also regenerated the argument favoring senior high school general music. In this section we look at these two nonperformance type of courses (general music and fine arts) that are recommended for everyone. We also examine other nonperformance courses designed specifically for the interested music students, particularly those desiring to major in music at the college or university level.

TEACHING GENERAL MUSIC TO ALL ADOLESCENTS:
THE DEFINITIVE CHALLENGE

Most secondary music teachers have been trained to teach either band, orchestra, or choir, and, therefore, may find the definitive teaching challenge in a general music or fine arts course. Some specialists resist the idea of music classes for everyone because they are too busy identifying and teaching the talented (or getting ready for contest). Others resist because they seem to have little interest teaching dull, unmotivated students who are piqued because they have been forced to enroll in class, who will receive no reward through performance, and who have a universal proclivity for listening to some sort of popular music. Still other teachers resist because they believe that developing a senior high school fine arts or a junior/senior high general music class will be a gigantic, unworthy task. This argument is based primarily on there being very few published course materials to serve as a developmental source or textbook.

When given the opportunity to teach these classes, most master teachers overcome these reluctancies by seeking for the rewards inherent in each course, thus developing a positive attitude as they meet their task at hand. A much greater challenge looms over them, however, and it is manifested in the struggles of the family and the society as a whole. A brief demographic look at the attitudes of typical American adolescents and how they spend their leisure time demonstrates the magnitude of this challenge. One study indicates that the average graduating high school senior will have spent around 18,000 hours watching television but only 12,000 hours in the classroom.[1] The average American adolescent will have viewed approximately 250,000 commercials by the time of graduation from senior high school.[2] The manner in which adolescents spend their leisure time and their desire to have money in their pockets to buy the things they see advertised profoundly affects their attitudes about attending school and being involved in their classwork. In some senior high schools, more than half of the juniors and seniors each day leave school early for work. To them, taking a course in fine arts or general music certainly will not enhance their ability to find a job and make more money.

Robert Hampel reports on one study that shows "most students cared primarily about friendships, sports, sex, television, and music [the popular music to which they listen]."[3] When given the opportunity to choose what they liked best about school, they chose the category designated as "nothing" over either of the categories designated "teachers" or "classes I'm taking."[4]

Over the last twenty years, while observing student teachers working

---

[1] Robert Benenson and Sandra Stencel, "Pressures on Youth," *Education Report Card: Schools on the Line* (Washington, D.C.: Congressional Quarterly, 1985), 152.

[2] Larry A. Tucker, "Television, Teenagers, and Health," *Journal of Youth and Adolescence* 16, no. 5 (1987), 415–25.

[3] Robert L. Hampel, *The Last Little Citadel: American High Schools Since 1940* (Boston: Houghton Mifflin, 1986), 151.

[4] Ibid.

with junior/senior high school pupils, the effect of the demographic conditions described above has become apparent to me. I have watched these young prospective teachers attempting to motivate pupils who obviously desired to be some place other than in a general music class. This challenge is certainly beyond the ability of a student teacher and, I am fearful, as demographic studies indicate, it is beyond the ability of many of our seasoned professionals.

What can be done about the situation? How can educators design a curriculum that will meet the needs of the students? What teaching techniques can be developed to capture their attention? These are perplexing questions and certainly ones that deserve the attention of America's best minds in the field of education.

There was a period of time during the 1970s in which educators attempted to add what they considered to be a more attractive set of elective courses to the overall curriculum, particularly in the areas of language arts and social studies. There were courses of a low-level intellectual challenge with "youthy" titles such as "Girl Talk," "What's Happening," "Personal Relations," Man to Man," and "Troubleshooter."[5] Similar courses even permeated the music curriculum in some schools. In most cases time has proven that they have not created a stronger interest in school attendance and study than has the traditional curriculum. If anything, these courses have caused the students to view the curriculum as having even less value and they have enhanced the students' attitudes of unconcern.

Some educators feel that one of the goals of general education is to help students become better informed "consumers" of music, and they have used this approach in teaching general music. Diane Ravitch believes that this approach, too, has resulted in watering down the music curriculum because too many compromises have been made to capture students' attention:

> The guiding principle, it seemed, was to give students what they wanted; in this way, they would stay in school longer, have higher motivation to learn, and cause less trouble while there, while adults could compliment themselves having met the needs of their students without using coercion.[6]

It is very difficult to bridge the gap from the music that students like to that which they do not accept when more emphasis is placed on the music to which they are already listening than is placed on the music that they do not understand.

Timothy Gerber makes some very insightful suggestions in attempting to devise ways to reach today's students. First, he suggests "it is crucial to determine what a music course uniquely can offer that is not available on the street."[7] Second, "if the ultimate trick of teaching high school [and junior high school]

---

[5] Philip A. Cusick, *The Egalitarian Ideal and the American High School* (New York: Longmans, 1983), 69.

[6] Diane Ravitch, *The Schools We Deserve: Reflections on the Educational Crisis of Our Time* (New York: Basic Books, 1985), 69.

[7] Timothy Gerber, "Reaching All Students: The Ultimate Challenge," *Music Educators Journal* 75, no. 7 (March, 1989), 38.

is to challenge and interest everyone enrolled, then teachers themselves must be equally challenged and interested in the courses they teach."[8] He points out that most music teachers are usually more interested in their performing groups than they are in teaching general music. It has been his experience that in most cases unmotivated students are a result of unmotivated teachers. To him, "there is no good reason why teaching music in nonensemble settings cannot be just as challenging or rewarding as teaching performing groups."[9]

Third, he feels that students learn less from listening to teachers talk than any other method of teaching. "[S]tudents respond most favorably to learning situations that provide concrete, activity-oriented experiences. Moreover, students often prefer courses that develop tangible musical and analytical skills. Courses featuring active learning ... produce greater enthusiasm among adolescents than do relatively passive courses.... [D]rab formality of most college lectures, still a vivid memory for many teachers, is hardly a model for reaching today's ... students!"[10]

Finally, according to Gerber, "we need to push students to ask and answer questions that seek more than factual information, ... we must have the courage and creativity to ask students to think critically, to analyze, to synthesize, and to make reasoned judgments for which they may be held accountable [Bloom's taxonomy of educational objectives; see Chapter 5]."[11]

General Music in Middle/Junior High School

In view of the previous remarks, a middle/junior high school general music curriculum is presented here which is based on three basic tenets: (1) Music is a discipline and should be taught as such, (2) the most important purpose of general music is to teach music literacy, and (3) students learn through active participation, not by sitting and listening.[12]

Throughout the years, the complexion of general music in middle/junior high school has changed as easily as the color of the chameleon, instantaneously and at will. The most casual method of presenting a general music lesson consists of playing recordings, with no consideration to a cumulative plan of learning. Whatever is topical at the moment becomes a subject for interpretation through the medium of the cassette or disc. Every listening lesson is a separate experience and there is no continuity of music learning envisioned in the course.

There was a period during the 1950s when the general music period was

---

[8] Ibid., 38–39.

[9] Ibid., 39.

[10] Ibid.

[11] Ibid.

[12] This approach to teaching general music in the middle/junior high school is based on tenets of the *Cambiata Concept* as instituted by Irvin Cooper and promulgated by Don L. Collins. It is described in detail in Cooper's book *Teaching Junior High School Music*, (Conway, AR: Cambiata Press, 1973) or Don L. Collins's book, *The Cambiata Concept, a Comprehensive Philosophy and Methodology of Teaching Music to Adolescents*, (Conway, AR: Cambiata Press, 1981). In fact, some of the material presented here is taken directly from these books.

used as a supplement to the social studies class. The music teacher consulted with the social studies teacher to determine what aspects of geography or history were being taught and engaged in personal research to discover appropriate songs the class might sing (irrespective of whether or not the melodic range was compatible with the restricted vocal ranges of the adolescents) or recordings of folk dance music that supported those lessons. Advocates of the *core* curriculum supported this type of general music program because it contributed to the social studies lessons and also had some musical value when regarded as an introduction to further music experiences. When teachers realized that this brief interlude may well have been the terminal organized school music activity for these children, it became evident that this procedure scarcely constituted the kind of instruction that led to understanding or loving music.

By the latter 1960s there was a significant trend away from social studies as a basic influence for the general music program. A different basis was found in humanities, which, although never accepted on a wide scale, could have led to further dilution of the general music program to the point where it eventually might have lost its unique identity. Correlation between the various components of the humanities concept presupposed the presence of previously acquired information about the components to be correlated. Such information concerning music, art, literature, architecture, philosophy, and religion had not yet been acquired in sufficient depth by middle/junior high school students to constitute even the flimsiest base for use in an integrated humanities program. The notion, however, presented a tempting solution for scheduling problems faced by the school principal, who could telescope a number of mislabeled "frill" subjects into one near schedule package designated "humanities," a culturally persuasive title.

The *project* type of general music program had considerable support in some quarters. A class would, for instance, engage in an Indian project for which feathers would be collected and painted, a wigwam constructed, Indian songs discovered and learned, and Indian pictures collected and pinned to the bulletin board, all in the name of music.

The *committee* program was one in which the class split up into sets of committees. Each had its own appointed area of busy work and reports were made frequently at full class sessions. On occasions an exercise in democracy followed, during which the class voted to approve or to disapprove the committee's report.

Another kind of program encouraged creative music in the middle/junior high school, which on the whole was (and is) a good idea but in reality accomplished little for the class in terms of lasting musical growth (although it might have assisted a few individuals). There were no reports of these classes producing any great composers, and the hours spent in extracting note after note from various members of a class and careful editing by the teacher produced a class song of dubious musical value.

Singing, which has been the backbone of general music class in the elementary school *ad infinitum*, fell in disrepute in the middle/junior high school general music class during the first part of the twentieth century because of the problems encountered in dealing with boys' changing voices. Nowadays, however, when the range and tessitura limitations of these adolescent voices are understood and literature is chosen that administers to their particular needs, it is accepted practice for singing to be the foundation upon which the general music program is built.

Teaching general music can be a most challenging and engrossing activity if a stand is taken for the intrinsic values of music. Adolescents deserve and have a right to be taught to understand, to enjoy, and to love music throughout life for its own sake and not because it is a fringe benefit to geography, history, or other subjects. The general music course can provide teachers with continuous and enjoyable experiences while they carry out their obligations to the various classes they meet.

To accomplish this goal, consider the following suggested general music curriculum: (1) singing, (2) music reading, (3) ear training—listening, (4) music history, and (5) written work (theory). These activities should be carried out not in the typical college or university lecture format but in a structured, sequential, challenging, and active technique of teaching. Further, they must be initiated by master teachers who truly love children and are excited about teaching lasting, intrinsic musical values to them. Whether teaching this music curriculum or any other that might be chosen, success is dependent upon highly motivated teachers who have a strong commitment to teaching.

Singing is the Core Activity　Singing should be the core of the middle/junior high school general music program. Vocal expression is our instinctive medium of communication. In moments of exultation, happiness, unhappiness, sorrow, anguish, or any moment of stirring emotional experience, personal feeling is reflected in vocal expression. Deep personal emotion can on occasion transcend the immediate environment so completely that mere words are inadequate for communication, but through music or words wedded to music a more satisfying expression of the emotion becomes possible.

In singing, the performers are able to achieve an experience even more sublime than in listening because they are actively participating. There is also great satisfaction in expressing oneself directly with the voice, a satisfaction greater perhaps than through the secondary medium of a mechanical instrument. Middle/junior high school boys, noisily articulate about anything else, are often very inarticulate about their deeper emotions that, when expressed, are often considered unmanly. Choral music in the classroom provides the ideal vehicle for self-expression. Girls and boys experience the emotions reflected in their various songs and through them express themselves. The frequent defense of the teacher of a nonsinging general music class that "boys often dislike singing so they should not be compelled to sing" is difficult to accept. Certainly they have little taste for the childish musical fare that is sometimes offered them and resent being considered juvenile.

Singing is not merely a quasi-therapeutic activity. It is the most natural and spontaneous of all media of musical expression, and through this simple medium, particularly in three- and four-part music, it is possible for participants to realize personal musical expression of rare beauty. The lasting beneficial influences of such experiences are incalculable. Every adolescent should be brought to participate in singing and not solely on an elective basis, for they are much too young to understand the values of music in their own lives or its implications for an aesthetically richer adult life.

Successful singing in middle/junior high school is impossible if literature is chosen that is not written with consideration to the specific limitations of adolescent voices. Teachers should be sure to consult Chapters 8 and 9, which recommends music for early adolescent singers before embarking upon a singing voyage with singers of this age.

Music Reading   The objective of music reading in the general music curriculum is to teach adolescents to understand music notation and to develop their skills in reproducing vocally what they see on the printed page. Here again, the secret to success is choosing a music-reading method which is structured and sequential. Often, particularly on the college or university level, learning to read music by sight becomes a series of tests during which the singers are given new music to read in no sequence.

There are those who advocate that students can learn to read music through the literature. Learning to read music through song or octavo singing is a completely unorganized process wherein specific technical reading difficulties appear by chance. There are methods on the market that combine skill-building exercises and literature reading. The primary motivation for the students using literature and not just exercises is the success they have when teachers place music (a complete piece) in their hands and they are able to apply the skills they have learned in singing the piece.

The process of learning to read music cannot be accelerated. As in so many areas of musicianship development, there is no "fast-food" approach. Teachers should set easy-to-reach goals for each lesson. It is sometimes advisable to spend several lessons on the learning and mastering of one technical difficulty. Teachers should consult Chapter 11 for more information pertaining to teaching musicianship.

Ear Training—Listening   The essence of music is *sound*; the beautiful sound of melodic, harmonic, and rhythmic progressions constantly moving through tranquil, climatic, and anticlimatic phases to an inexorable final cadence, as exemplified in compositions written by great masters of the past and present. Without the sound there is no music, there would be no theory of music, no history of music, and no pedagogy of music. The sound, therefore, should be the center of all music learning, from which should radiate all other associated aspects of music instruction. While the school chorus, orchestra, and band are highly commendable organizations, participation in these groups is not enough in itself to ensure that the students will absorb the sonorities and sensitive subtleties of the music being performed, nor does it ensure their future musical literacy. They also need vast exposure as a *listener* not involved in any other manner with the performance.

Teachers cannot impart to their students a love of music, a concept of sound, or a knowledge of the fine music literature unless those teachers possess these attributes and this knowledge. Teachers need constant musical refreshment. A reservoir cannot continue to dispense its supply of water without being resupplied continuously from some natural source. By the same token, a music teacher cannot pour music instruction and, more importantly, stimulation without running dry unless they recharge regularly by listening to performances of great music literature; not as a background for some other involvement but as a total involvement in the music itself. In other words, teachers should thoroughly enjoy music listening and should want to develop an intimate acquaintance with the best literature and pass on some of this to their students; otherwise, they should not be in this vocation.

Ear training should be considered to be an integral part of the overall general music curriculum and should not be isolated from other aspects of music learning. The purpose of ear training is to teach students to listen attentively, to interpret what they hear, and to give their opinion of it. It is not an end in itself but is a preparation for engaging with keener aural perception in music activities either as performers or consumers of music. It is also a means for developing discriminating taste in the choice of the musical menu to be enjoyed. The structured, sequential approach is essential here also. To be effective, ear training must be a cumulative process starting with the simplest of musical phenomena and leading gradually to the more complex. Student response must constantly be solicited to ensure total class participation and interest.

The ear-training curriculum should evolve from, and closely parallel, the music-reading curriculum. Organized ear-training activities should take place during every music period immediately following the music-reading activities. For example, suppose the class has been drilling to develop their ability to sing three pitches; so, la, and mi. After they have finished their music-reading exercises in which these three pitches have been used, the teacher should move to the board and write four short melodies (composed on the spot, if desired) containing only these three pitches, numbering the melodies one through four. At this point, the students should be asked to take out a sheet of paper. The teacher will lead the class in singing each of the four melodies using whatever method (tonic sol-fa, numbers, and so forth) they have been taught. Then, using the neutral vowel *loo*, the teacher will sing one of the melodies. The students are then asked to listen and compare the melody just sung with the first one written on the board. After a few seconds, the teacher should sing the same melody again and ask the students to compare it with the second melody on the board. This process should be used for all four melodies. Then the teacher should ask the students to write on the sheet of paper the number of the melody that is identical to the one that was sung by the teacher. This ear training process may be used at all levels of complexity as the students proceed through the music-reading curriculum.

A structured process of music listening is part of the ear-training curriculum as well. In this process the students are taught to recognize the sound of all the band and orchestra music instruments and various types of human voices and choral ensembles. They also should be taught to determine which component in music (rhythm, harmony, or melody) predominates a selection and to recognize the basic form (ternary, binary, rondo, sonata-allegro, minuet/trio/minuet, theme and variations, and so forth) of a piece. After the basic components of music have been introduced, the listening curriculum should include selections that parallel the music history part of the curriculum.

Since the music-listening part of the curriculum requires the students to sit and listen, it may be difficult to motivate some middle/junior high school students to pay attention and to concentrate in this activity. It is important to devise ways to keep the activity interesting. One way is to make a cassette tape containing a short portion of several of the melodies the students might have encountered in their listening lessons and then have a contest (similar to a spelling bee or current television game-shows) in which the musical example is played and the students attempt to recognize it by name. As new listening repertoire is introduced in class, add the themes from these works to the cassette tape and play the game quite often. The competition will maintain interest in the listening portion of the curriculum and it will help them to remember the main themes of great literature so that they will recognize them when they encounter them later in life.

Music History   Parallel with the listening program should be a broad, uncompli- cated review of the development of music that includes pertinent information concerning master composers who have contributed to this growth, such as Palestrina, Bach, Handel, Mozart, and Beethoven. The lives of minor composers should be given brief mention if their works are to be used in the listening lesson.

Almost without exception, the study of music history begins with early music. Each successive development is described and, eventually, the music of today is revealed as the culmination of an evolutionary process. Such an approach is systematic and logical for the more mature student. However, this usual approach to the history of music contains certain difficulties for the adolescent since the music that is the most difficult to understand and appreciate is studied first. Gregorian chant certainly is not the best medium to interest the adolescent in art music. The tendency is to begin with music that is currently popular and to segue into music with which the students are unfamiliar. The trick is to make that segue skillfully and proceed through uncharted territory without allowing the students' interest to sag. However, there comes a point where the students realize that current popular music is not the total content to the story of music, and teachers are faced with the problem of convincing the students that there is value in studying music history and listening to music of all ages.

One might want to consider an alternate approach. Before the listening and music history curriculum is begun, teachers might consider making a statement to the class similar to this:

The time has come for us to consider why music today sounds the way it does. We are very familiar with that sound because we spend several hours each day listening to our favorite pieces. Even I have favorite pieces to which I listen that are not "classical" in nature. Does it surprise you that I listen to pop music too? My favorite pieces may not be the same as yours, just as Jon's are not the same favorite pieces as Karen's, but I do like today's music. It is interesting to note that I don't have to inform you about the musical characteristics and lyrics of your favorite songs. You know more about them than I. In fact, you probably know as much or more about today's music as I because we are living and listening together. We would be wasting our time if I spent the music class periods telling you about and listening to today's music. After all, aren't we in school to learn about that which we don't know? It is also interesting to note that there is a great deal of "classical" music written in the recent past that sounds very similar to today's music. It has many of the same rhythmic, harmonic, and melodic characteristics. Because we are able to relate to this type music (it sounds similar to today's pop music), we will begin with it and take a walk back through time. When we get to the beginning you will be able to see, in reverse, the evolution of music, which is the reason why it sounds the way it does today.

By taking this approach, teachers face the impending problem (convincing the students about the value of art music) initially and put it to rest. Further, they do not compromise their belief in the value of art music and their love for it by endorsing rock, rap, heavy metal, punk, soul, gospel, and country through its introduction into the classroom. It is to be hoped that the students will accept the teacher's position and they can move forward together. As a reminder, information previously presented in this chapter indicates that the basic problems in motivating adolescents are not found in choosing curriculum that is challenging and which has eternal values as much as are found in the attitude and teaching technique of the teacher and the social and family endeavors of the students.

The music of Gershwin, Stravinsky, Prokofiev, Bartók, Bernstein, Copland, and Dello Joio should be selected for relating the current sounds of popular music to those of the recent past. It is important that teachers point out those characteristics that are present in both.

Written Work   Finally, a general music program is not complete without sufficient theoretical written work to implement the sight-reading and listening portions, to the extent that students will be able to interpret basic music symbols found on the printed page.

The fundamentals of music are the scientific side of music. Adolescents have the right to ask why they should study music fundamentals. Sometimes the best way to answer a question is by asking one. Why study the reading and writing of words? Why not just listen to others talk and repeat what they have said? The answers to these questions are the same, whether the problem is one of music or words. People learn to read words or music in order to acquire information and knowledge. Each individual must be able to read to be sure that information and knowledge are correct. People must be able to read if they wish to be able to write. Finally, people must be able to read and write in order to communicate successfully with others: to buy and sell things, to make a living, to protect themselves, and to be good citizens in a civilized society. Briefly stated, what we hear, we can say; what we say, we can write; what we write, you can read; and what others write, we all can read. Perhaps this is a magic formula for living in a civilized world! The average individual interested in music as a pleasurable experience seldom cares to do more than to just enjoy it. This attitude does not warrant severe criticism, but if these people were told that their interest in music could yield more pleasure and satisfaction than they are presently deriving, they would doubtless be interested in knowing how. Understanding the fundamentals of music is one of those ways.

General Music in Senior High School

If general music is continued in senior high school after having been studied in middle/junior high school, it is important to continue the music values, skills, and parts of the curriculum discussed in the preceding section on middle/junior high school general music with the idea of graduating the most musically literate and aesthetically aware individuals as possible. If the students are basically musically illiterate when taking general music in senior high school, it is suggested that teachers use the same curriculum suggested for junior high pupils except teach it in a way that would relate to senior high school students.

There are teachers in the United States who do not believe that music literacy is the principle goal for the study of general music. They are more inclined to promote the enjoyment of music making and music listening without the need to master skills necessary to be able to read and write it. They desire to use current popular music as a vehicle of expression and study in order to reach as many senior high school students as possible (we'll refer to them as "popularists" for lack of a better term). To those educators who strongly believe in the intrinsic value of music, who accept the need of a vital music heritage, and who understand the effect the two can have on persons' lives (we'll call them "traditionalists"), this approach is a "cop out," to say the least. The traditionalists are convinced that the popularists have taken this compromise approach because the idea of a musically literate and aesthetically aware society is an impossible consideration. The popularists seem to be satisfied with sharing a little musical knowledge rather than what they consider to be the obvious alternative, none at all. It is not within the function of this chapter to argue the pros and cons of these approaches. The traditionalists' approach to general music already has been provided. In the remaining discussion several different approaches to general music in senior high school are presented, most of which fall within the domain of the popularists.

One educator suggests that teachers can begin to relate to general music classes by finding ways to teach elementary music skills through using the songs that adolescents hear daily.[13] He further suggests that teachers take advantage of their desire to create music quickly by teaching them the two chords (tonic and dominant seventh) needed to accompany many simple songs, a principal

[13] Hunter C. March, "Expanding Experiences for Choral Directors," *Music Educators Journal* 75, no. 7 (March 1989), 48.

that may be used with the electronic keyboard or guitar. When appropriate, the teacher can teach meter signatures, key signatures, new chords, and other music fundamentals. He suggests that in guided critical listening to music they enjoy, students can be taught form, harmonic structure, meter, melodic development (or lack thereof), instrumentation, and texture. To him this can be a bridge to get them to listen to standard literature.

One choral music teacher initiated a general music class in this way:

A diverse group of students with many different musical preferences elected the course. The teacher decided to emphasize listening and, as a first assignment, asked the students to listen to one of their favorite selections and list four qualities that would be found in all music. She was quite surprised by their response. She explained, "Those four qualities were obvious to me, but, oh my, the answers I got ranged from risqué to non-musical."

She then discussed the elements of rhythm, pitch, timbre, and dynamics and asked the class to listen to their selections again with these concepts in mind. "Everyone played a pop tune ranging from rap to punk." The students were surprised when the teacher played her choice, a vocal jazz selection, not the "long-haired classical stuff" they expected. She established the rule that students could not make comments about likes or dislikes of any music selected. Discussion centered on the elements found in the music. She listened to her students' choices without making judgmental comments and asked students to do the same with the selections she played.

Recently, one of her students prepared a presentation on the rock group Kiss. The student played examples of the group's music, beginning with early recordings and concluding with the most recent releases. The teacher was pleased that her student talked about the influence of blues and Bach, and she was heartened that those influences could actually be heard in the recordings the student selected to share with the class.

As she approaches the final weeks of the school year, this teacher is already planning for next year's class. She admits that she has learned a great deal about teenagers and about music. She will have to plan different activities and select new musical examples for the course next fall because many students plan to repeat the class. Four other students have decided to sing with the school choir.[14]

Another teacher approaches a course entitled "Introduction to Music Performance" with lessons planned around such activities as listening; performance on rhythm and percussion instruments, recorder, some keyboard; and composition. He now devotes time to "helping students develop skills in evaluating movies, concerts, plays, recordings, and videotapes."[15] After teaching the course for two years the teacher has learned that he must be extremely flexible to maintain student interest. He has realized the importance of using a variety of activities and examples. He has found that popular music provides opportunities for teaching about musical elements. He believes that the time he has spent discovering the different learning styles of students has made him a more effective teacher.

Another music educator teaches general music exclusively. Two of the courses are geared strictly for the career-oriented music students but others are

[14] Ibid., 49.
[15] Ibid., 50.

open to everyone and include electronic music, advanced electronic (computer) music, guitar, and piano. In the guitar class she teaches chords and strumming first so that the students may experience immediate success. Music notation and reading are introduced later as the need arises. It is very important to her that students develop a positive attitude about music, especially during the early weeks of the course.

Another teacher has as one of his goals in general music to "give the students the language they need to make value judgments about the music they listen to as well as the music that others may prefer."[16] His process is as follows:

> My first step in approaching this task was to make an excerpt tape to play in class. I selected twenty compositions from styles that included rock, pop, jazz, classical, and country. I chose some selections that were current popular tunes and some that were as obscure as possible to these young people. I recorded about fifteen to twenty seconds of each selection, arranged the excerpts "back to back," with no time lapses, and alternated periods, tempi, styles, and media (between vocal and instrumental works). The resulting tape is a musical montage that is both entertaining and challenging to the students.
>
> As the tape is played in class, I ask the students to write the name of the selection and the composer or performer if they can. In addition, I ask them to include a few comments to describe their reactions to the music. I do not coach the students on what to write; instead, I let each person use his or her own words. The reactions are usually predictable, but there are a few surprises now and then.
>
> This exercise serves as a point of departure for subsequent lessons in the language of criticism. In their comments on the taped montage of examples, many students may indicate a preference for jazz but know very little about its form. Perhaps the opening theme of John Williams's "Star Wars" is powerful and familiar to them, but they are unaware of the theme and variations technique the composer has used in structuring his composition.
>
> The next section of discussion centers around slightly longer music examples of two to three minutes. . . . For this second listening experience, the students must write short essays about the selections played. At this point I *do* coach the students by telling them they must support their criticisms with "believable" remarks. They are not allowed to write things like "that's dumb" or "that's boring" (even if it is!); they must explain *why* it is boring. The usual result is evidence that students lack skill in handling the language of music criticism. This exercise serves as a pretest, providing a point of departure from which the teacher can launch into a study of form, texture, or numerous other music concepts and better equipping the teacher to help the students become more intelligent performers and consumers of music.[17]

Since developing listening skills should be a goal for students in senior high school general music, an assistant professor of music education at one of the leading universities suggests a unique way to achieve that goal.[18] She created four modules fashioned to teach the design of music, each of which consists of an instructional booklet, a cassette tape, and pretests and posttests to measure

[16] Brian N. Lanier, "High School General Music in Action: Music Criticism," *Music Educators Journal* 75, no. 7, (March 1989), 51.

[17] Ibid., 51.

[18] Barbara Brinson, "High School General Music in Action: Developing Listening Skills," *Music Educators Journal* 75, no. 7 (March 1989), 51–52.

learning gains. The first module serves as an introduction to unity and variety in music and includes aural comparison of phrases and melodies. The three remaining give the students the chance to learn about and to discriminate aurally between theme and variations, ternary, and rondo forms. The modules are designed for individual use rather than for a large group. Instructional time allows for different reading rates as well as for the need for additional review. Students have the option of rewinding the tape to listen to musical examples again.

Another approach suggested by a graduate assistant includes teaching students the basic listening skills necessary to understand the concepts of simple improvisation and variation. To assure interest he examined the traditional theme and variation form of "classical" literature and compared it to various renditions of contemporary jazz pieces that contained improvised solos. It became obvious to the students that each improvised solo was simply a variation of the original theme.[19]

Teaching general music in senior high school certainly may prove to be the ultimate challenge, but with ingenuity, creativity, and attention to the challenge, there can be many satisfying rewards to this most essential responsibility.

THE FINE ARTS COURSE IN SENIOR HIGH SCHOOL

Because of legislation enacted as part of educational reform, a fine arts course is now required curriculum in several states for senior high school students. As a result, it may be well within the obligation of choral teachers to be prepared to teach it. Such a required course has provided principals with several challenges. The course curriculum always includes music and the visual arts, and in some states it will include drama, dance, literature, and architecture in any combination. Therefore, in this age of specialists, it is difficult to find an individual teacher who is qualified to teach all areas of the fine arts. Principals deal with this problem in several different ways. By omitting drama, dance, literature, and architecture either the visual arts teacher or the music teacher may be qualified to teach such a course. If all areas or a combination of any of the areas are included, most principals make it a team-taught course in which each area is taught by the most qualified faculty member. It will probably continue to be handled in this fashion until there are teachers being graduated from colleges and universities with a major in fine arts who are qualified to teach all disciplines.

An examination of the *Curriculum Guide for the State of Arkansas*, one of the states with a required fine arts course that includes music, visual arts, theater arts (drama), and dance, reveals a general survey approach to each of the

---

[19] James W. Coons, "High School General Music in Action: Variation and Improvisation," *Music Educators Journal* 75, no. 7 (March 1989), 54.

subjects. It is recommended that the instructor cover the basic fundamentals and elements of the discipline, including appropriate terminology, followed by a reverse chronology of the historical evolution of the art form.

Wisconsin's *Music Curriculum Guide, K-12,* recommends a course in the allied arts that is a "combined-area approach to broadening and deepening the student's aesthetic response to and intellectual curiosity about works of art from the fields of music, visual arts, literature, theater, dance, and architecture and developing the student's understanding of their inter-relationships."[20]

RELATED SECONDARY MUSIC EXPERIENCES

Music appreciation, music history, and music theory are related nonperformance courses for the general education of senior high school students. Music history and theory are courses recommended for students who are preparing to major in music in college or university. Music appreciation is a course for any student who is interested in the art of music, particularly from the listener's point of view.

Usually the objective of teachers of music appreciation classes is to develop perceptive listening through the application of musical understanding to enhance aesthetic responses. Most courses include the stylistic characteristics of the music eras from ancient times to the present, composer's lives with reference to the culture in which they lived, and a brief history of musical performance. The course may be organized in units from a period approach but not necessarily in chronological order. Other areas related to the core curriculum might include attending live performances of recitals, concerts, and performances by various school organizations. Certain television and radio programs are often recommended.

Music history can be similar to music appreciation, with a greater emphasis on the actual history of music and less emphasis on style and listening. In most cases the study unfolds in chronological order from ancient times to the present.

Music theory in senior high school usually takes the form of a study of the basic fundamentals (rudiments) of music in preparation for college or university theory classes. Depending upon the progress of the class, the study may include: (1) the science of music including pitch, quality, harmonic series, dynamics, and acoustics; (2) the symbols of music including pitch names, staves, clefs, keyboard pitches, and pitch dictation; (3) the rhythm of music including beats, pulses, meter, meter signatures, bar lines, measures, notes, rests, simple and compound meter, and rhythmic dictation; (4) scales in music including diatonic major and minor scales, the circles of keys, playing scales on the piano, and the chromatic, whole-tone, and pentatonic scales; (5) melodic and harmonic intervals through dictation and keyboard experiences; (6) transposition and modulation; (7) chords

[20] Wisconsin Department of Public Instruction, Bulletin No. 159 *Music Curriculum Guide, K-12.* (Madison: Wisconsin Department of Public Instruction, 1987) 37.

including inversions; (8) cadences and basic progression of chords; and (9) harmonizing simple melodies.

CONCLUSION

Even though most secondary music educators view themselves as being choral, band, or orchestra teachers, this chapter has dealt with those parts of the curriculum that are not encompassed within those three domains but might well be the teaching responsibility of the choral instructor. It is to be hoped that if teaching nonperformance classes is to be among your responsibilities, you will envision the challenge and fulfillment from doing so and contribute significantly to the satisfaction of those students under your tutelage.

THOUGHTS FOR CONTEMPLATION AND DISCUSSION

1. Suppose you are a senior high choral teacher. You would like to offer a section of general music. Your principal tells you that the students interested in music will choose to be in band, orchestra, or choir; therefore, there is little reason to offer the class. How will you persuade the principal that it is an important class?

2. If you had the opportunity but were limited to recommending only one course, would you recommend a fine arts class or a general music class for students in senior high school? Justify your choice.

3. Do you believe that singing should be the core activity of middle/junior high general music? If so, why? If not, describe the curriculum you plan to use.

BIBLIOGRAPHY

Alabama Department of Education. *Vocal Music Curriculum Guide, Grades 5–12*. Montgomery, Ala.: State Department of Education, 1986.

Arkansas Department of Education. *Survey of Fine Arts, Arkansas Public School Course Content Guide*. Little Rock: Department of Education, 1985.

BEGLARIAN, G. *Comprehensive Musicianship: an Anthology of Evolving Thought*. Reston, Va.: Music Educators National Conference, 1971.

BENENSON, ROBERT, and SANDRA STENCEL. "Pressures on Youth." *Education Report Card: Schools on the Line*. Washington, D.C.: Congressional Quarterly, 1985.

BESSOM, MALCOLM E., ALPHONSE TATARUNIS, and SAMUEL L. FORCUCCI. *Teaching Music in Today's Secondary Schools*, 2d ed. New York: Holt, Rinehart and Winston, 1980.

BRINSON, BARBARA. "High School General Music in Action: Developing Listening Skills." *Music Educators Journal* 75, no. 7 (March 1989).

COLLINS, DON L. *The Cambiata Concept, a Comprehensive Philosophy and Methodology of Teaching Music to Adolescents*. Conway, Ark.: Cambiata Press, 1981.

Commonwealth of Massachusetts. *Music Curriculum Guide, Grades 7–12*. Boston: Department of Education, 1982.

COONS, JAMES W. "High School General Music in Action: Variation and Improvisation." *Music Educators Journal* 75, no. 7 (March 1989).

COOPER, IRVIN, and KARL O. KURSTEINER. *Teaching Junior High School Music*, 2d ed. Conway, Ark.: Cambiata Press, 1973.

CUSICK, PHILIP A. *The Egalitarian Ideal and the*

American High School. New York: Longman, 1983.

EDELSON, EDWARD. *The Secondary School Music Program from Classroom to Concert Hall.* West Nyack, N.Y.: Parker Publishing Co., 1972.

GERBER, TIMOTHY. "Reaching All Students: The Ultimate Challenge." *Music Educators Journal* 75, no. 7 (March 1989).

HAMPEL, ROBERT L. *The Last Little Citadel: American High Schools Since 1940.* Boston: Houghton Mifflin, 1986.

HASS, GLENN. *Curriculum Planning, a New Approach,* 3d ed. Boston: Allyn and Bacon, Inc., 1980.

Henry County Public Schools. *Music Curriculum Guide, Grades 9–12.* Paris, Tenn.: Murray State University, Henry County Public Schools Teacher Corps Project, 1982.

HOFFER, CHARLES R. *Teaching Music in the Secondary Schools,* 4th ed. Belmont, Calif,: Wadsworth Publishing, 1991.

JIPSON, WAYNE R. *The High School Vocal Music Program.* West Nyack, N.Y.: Parker Publishing Co., 1972.

KOWALL, BONNIE C., ed. *Perspectives in Music Education, Source Book III.* Reston, Va.: Music Educators National Conference, 1966.

LAMB, GORDON H. *Choral Techniques,* 3d ed. Dubuque, Iowa: Wm. C. Brown Co., 1988.

LANIER, BRIAN N. "High School General Music in Action: Music Criticism." *Music Educators Journal* 75, no. 7 (March 1989).

LEHMAN, PAUL R. *Music in Today's Schools: Rationale and Commentary.* Reston, Va.: Music Educators National Conference, 1987.

LEONHARD, CHARLES. *A Realistic Rationale for Teaching Music.* Reston, Va.: Music Educators National Conference, 1985.

MARCH, HUNTER C. "Expanding Experiences for Choral Directors." *Music Educators Journal* 75, no. 7 (March 1989).

MARK, MICHAEL L. *Contemporary Music Education,* 2d ed. New York: Schirmer Books, 1986.

MARPLE, HUGO D. *Backgrounds and Approaches to Junior High Music.* Dubuque, Iowa: Wm. C. Brown Co., 1975.

MILLER, KENNETH E. *Vocal Music Education, Teaching in the Secondary Schools.* Englewood Cliffs, N.J.: Prentice-Hall, Inc., 1988.

Music Educators National Conference. *The School Music Program: Descriptions and Standards,* 2d ed. Reston, Va.: Music Educators National Conference, 1986.

RAVITCH, DIANE. *The Schools We Deserve: Reflections on the Educational Crisis of Our Time.* New York: Basic Books, 1985.

ROE, PAUL F. *Choral Music Education,* 2d ed. Englewood Cliffs, N.J.: Prentice-Hall, Inc., 1983.

SINGLETON, IRA. *Music in Secondary Schools,* 2d ed. Boston: Allyn and Bacon, Inc., 1965.

TUCKER, LARRY. "Television, Teenagers, and Health." *Journal of Youth and Adolescence* 16, no. 5 (1987).

Wisconsin Department of Public Instruction. *A Guide to Curriculum Planning in Music Education,* Bulletin No. 6268. Madison, Wis.: Wisconsin Department of Public Instruction, 1986.

Wisconsin Department of Public Instruction. *Music Curriculum Guide K-12,* Bulletin No. 159. Madison, Wis.: Wisconsin Department of Public Instruction, 1986.

17

Teaching Music Is Not Just Teaching Music

It would be great if the only responsibilities teachers had were to direct their choirs and to sing. These activities drew most of us to the profession. The organizational and promotional aspects of our responsibilities are not greeted so warmly, particularly when we are beginning our careers. As we get older, these aspects sometime provide much satisfaction when we have developed the skills to conquer their demands. In fact, the intricacies that frustrated us when we first began teaching later in our careers become the challenges that keep us professionally vital and aware.

This chapter is provided to help you face the challenges of your nonmusic responsibilities and to conquer them. I must warn you that many highly gifted conductors and teachers have fallen along the wayside because they failed to develop their organizational, management, and interpersonal skills. Although you often dread these nonmusical aspects, it behooves you to approach them with a willing spirit. The proper attitude will help you overcome their complexities, and the success will boost you down the road to being a master teacher.

RECRUITMENT IS ALL IN THE IMAGE

If all of society, and the teaching profession in particular, viewed the discipline of choral music as a required academic study, it would not be necessary to recruit students nor so zealously to apprise the school faculty, administration, school board and general public about the activities of the choral organizations. Since such is not the circumstance in America now, music educators need to be both super salespersons and public relations executives to survive. I believe that there are very few professional choral teachers who have never secretly longed (and sometimes even openly declared) for a time when all they had to do was to teach music. Concerns about the security of their position based on the number of students they have enrolled, whether the school board will allocate money for a choral music instructor next year, the parent's critical response to their last program, the choirs' ratings at the last contest, and so forth enervate them and sap them of energy, strength, and stamina that they should allot to the business of teaching. Due to current conditions and the image of music education in the American mind, I must advise young educators to train themselves in the crafts of sales, public relations, and publicity. Those who fail to address those issues soon find themselves in a different profession.

Directors should never give up in their quest to help everyone understand that the study of choral music is an academic discipline. It is not solely an entertainment entity. It is not an extracurricula activity. It is not a time for a break so that the students can get away from the "real" disciplines. It is just as important to life as math and science. Without it and the other arts, one would not be a totally fulfilled individual (see "The Challenge" in Chapter 4). In the meantime, until society understands this, it is necessary for us to be super salespersons and public relations experts. We must help the public to see the importance of music and to understand why our teaching responsibilities are essential to fulfilled living.

Helping Singers to Choose Choir

One may relate the ability to recruit fine singers directly to the image the directors and their choirs portray to the general student body. It does very little good to beseech individuals to sign up for choir if they do not have an earnest desire to do so. Directors must create that compelling yearning within the students by helping them to perceive their choral involvement as "the thing to do," just as a campaign manager directs the public to perceive a candidate as the one who is right for the job. It is strictly a public relations challenge. That compelling yearning to be involved in choir must be greater than the yearning to be involved in industrial arts, visual arts, athletics, or any of the many options (elective courses and activities) open to the students.

Peer pressure to conform and the need to be part of the "in crowd" are two of the strongest drives adolescents experience (see Chapter 7). With several options available to students, directors must ensconce choral singing as the best class to elect. Once choir has that image the number of students who will enroll will take care of itself. Usually the challenge is extended beyond the perimeters of the secondary campus. That students do not participate in choral music may be due to parents' negative attitudes (they may characterize singing as being effeminate, which will discourage boys to sing, or they may instill other similar misconceptions) or students may not participate because singing was unacceptable in the elementary grades and this attitude carries into secondary school. As a result, directors will have to begin to create that compelling yearning to be in choir before the students reach secondary school. Thus, for future security, image building begins (1) at their place of current employment for immediate enrollment and (2) in the home and in the elementary schools for future enrollment.

How, then, do directors create in students that compelling yearning to be in choir? Consider the following sequential procedure:

1. Create a choral situation and environment which will be appealing to adolescent singers. This can be done by:
   A. Developing the best performing organization possible with the singers now enrolled. Adolescents do not want to be in a choir that is not good.
   B. Singing some literature (but not *all* literature) that will appeal to adolescents who do not understand choral music. Deal with developing their music appreciation after they have enrolled. Directors must first capture their attention with the music they already appreciate. However, do not mislead them into believing that all the music the choir performs is of that type.
   C. Placing pertinent information about choir and choir members on bulletin boards throughout the school (including those in the choir room). Directors must design this information to capture the attention of the adolescent. Use adolescent means of expression by choosing words that are in vogue. Include attractive artwork in the style of popular cartoon strips and characters.
   D. Giving choral music awards to the singers at the annual awards assembly. The choral program should have equal status with athletics and other elective subjects.
   E. Making announcements (at least every week or two) during the morning announcement period. This will keep the choral program in the minds of the students. Write the announcements in the current language of the adolescent. Be innovative and clever.
2. Clear the way for the students to enroll in choir. Meet with the principal and head counselor and schedule a time for each of the choirs, and particularly the Beginning Choir, that will present the least number of conflicts for students who want to choose choral music. Do not expect to find a time in which there are absolutely no conflicts. Those generally do not exist.
3. To use public relations terminology, once the directors have "softened the market" and set the stage, they should be ready for an overt recruitment campaign. Initiate the following steps:
   A. Determine the top ten girls and top ten boys (or twenty, depending upon the amount of time directors have to recruit) who are the most popular in the school. In senior high school these may be the ten "couples." Some may be athletes, but not all. Athletes commit to athletics and may show no interest in choir. Obtain their home addresses and telephone numbers. Whether they have had singing experience is not a priority, but be sure to include all those who are known singers. Once the directors enroll the popular students in choir, then they may concentrate on auditioning the best singers in the student body.

> B. Plan for the choirs to present a "command performance" concert for these top twenty (or forty) students.
>
> C. Call each of them on the telephone. After the necessary introductions, request a time that the director may visit in the home with them and their parents. Do not invite them to the command performance on the telephone. A direct visit is best to set up a personal relationship with the prospective student.
>
> D. Visit in the homes of the students with the parents. The directors should take a couple of the currently enrolled choir members with them. Tell the prospective students about the choir and the directors' goals and aspirations for the program. Invite the students (not the parents) to the command performance and encourage them to bring a date, if they desire. If possible, during the visit in the home, try to get a commitment from them to come to the performance. Emphasize that the command performance is exactly that, a special program given just for them.

4. Go back to the counselor and principal and examine with them the forthcoming semester's schedule for each prospective student and try to have the counselor to rearrange the schedule so that they will be free to enroll in choir. If it is impossible with one student, choose a different student who does not have conflicts.

5. Announce the command performance to the entire student body. Invite any student interested in joining choir to attend. Those students whom the directors and choir members did not visit personally should feel they also have a special invitation to the performance.

6. Give the command performance for the prospective students. Make it as entertaining as possible. Above all, make them feel special to have been invited to attend. After the performance invite those students who want to sing in choir next semester to set up an appointment with the director (it may be better not to call it an audition, because that term often scares inexperienced singers). Tell the students not to concern themselves with scheduling conflicts because the directors can deal with those at their appointment.

7. Once the students have enrolled in choir, make a congratulatory announcement that includes each of the new members' names to the entire student body. All the students must know that the popular ones are enrolling in choir. Invite anyone else who would like to make an appointment to do so.

8. Directors should use this approach to recruitment for several years until the choirs have reached the desired enrollments.

9. To assure that those students in elementary school know and understand about the choral programs in secondary school, directors should plan for different choirs to sing at the elementary schools at least once a year. These are good performance opportunities for the Beginning and Intermediate Choirs because the audience will not be too critical and it allows these choirs to be beneficial to the entire choral program. At those concerts, directors should describe their choral programs to the children and explain what they must do when they reach middle/junior high school to choose choir as an elective.

Because every teaching position in secondary school has its own set of limitations, directors may find that they will be unable to work the above plan in their own teaching situation for one reason or another. This plan of recruitment will work, and work well, if directors have the freedom to use it. If they do not, it should serve as a model by which they can devise a plan that will work for them. The point is that directors will not be successful in recruiting students to their choral programs unless they devise a specific recruitment plan. Further, the plan must be a structured, sequential plan of approach.

Other hints that will help directors in recruitment are: (1) to determine which students might have been in choir in middle/junior high school but have not enrolled in senior high school and to contact them; (2) to rely upon current students to supply names of interested singers; (3) to build the image of an active choral department by sending news releases to all radio stations and newspapers about students who have been involved in newsworthy events such as All-State Choir, musical productions, special programs, and special social events involving the choirs; (4) to send out news releases about choral students who have received scholarships, who plan to major in music in college, or who plan careers in music; (5) to attend extra-curricula school functions and to take time to visit with the students while there; (6) to determine which students sing in their church choir and to contact them; and (7) always to smile and to be friendly in the halls, to speak to the students as they pass, and to build the image of a caring teacher.

Recruiting Boys to the Choral Program

As delineated earlier (see Chapters 8, 9, 12, and 15), American choral organizations have always had to put special effort into recruiting boys. The future undoubtedly will provide many extracurricular activities that will vie for students' time, so it is unlikely that those who will be teaching choral music then will be relieved of the responsibility of cajoling boys to participate in choir. Many believe that men are more successful at recruiting boys than women, but certainly there are many fine programs directed by women throughout the United States that have plenty of boys enrolled.

In certain parts of the country some still consider singing to be effeminate, an image that directors must strive to destroy. Often boys are not aware of the many very masculine role models who are singers. Wise directors will assure that the boys in their school know about them.

Boys who attempt singing for the first time in middle/junior high school may become discouraged because of the frustrations they encounter due to changing-voice problems. These frustrations do not have to occur, particularly if the directors understand the changing voice and select choral literature that administers to their needs (see Chapters 9 and 13).

Further, in middle/junior high school, empirical knowledge verifies that boys are more inclined to consider singing if the choir in which they enroll is all male. There are some very fine mixed choirs in middle/junior high schools, but many of these are a result of strong, well-established programs. Teachers beginning new programs will have more success recruiting boys if they place them in a group together instead of mixing them with the girls.

Adolescent boys are inclined to enjoy choral music more if directors treat them as if they were men (even though directors know there are numerous occasions when they revert to their childhood behavior). Directors should be careful to choose language that promotes masculinity. Talk about masculine topics and be positive and authoritative when relating to them. Choose literature that relates to their masculinity. Certainly men should learn to relate to the finer, more artistic, and more aesthetic aspects of life, but possibly this should be a growth process that begins with young singers after they feel confident in their masculinity and after they have committed themselves to the choral program.

PROMOTING THE CHORAL PROGRAM

Two fundamental areas need attention when promoting the choral program: (1) the school faculty and administration and (2) the public at large. Since the administration may view choral directors as public relations arms of the school and since directors are in the limelight more than other faculty members, the two (faculty and administration) often relate differently to the choral personnel. Further, the parents and entire community have yet a different concept of choral music directors. In short, choral directors must wear many hats and must be careful to tip them properly according to whom they are speaking.

Principals often relate to choral directors in light of their budget because, next to athletics and instrumental music, choral music is one of the most expensive areas to operate. Principals customarily expect to "get their money's worth" and to be paid back in favorable comments and goodwill generated from within the community. Principals expect the choral department to make the school look good. This puts extra pressure on choral directors to spend more time than they should developing and maintaining the public relations part of their program. If the choral area becomes too visible and receives too much emphasis, directors run the risk of falling into disfavor with the rest of the faculty. The faculty may have difficulty understanding why the choral director and the choral program get so much attention. Choral directors often find it very difficult to walk the fine line of pleasing both administration and faculty.

When choral directors relate to other faculty members and the administration, they should be careful to show that they are not trying to exploit students for personal gain. They must help the faculty to understand that performance is a natural outgrowth from the study of music. Directors must lead the faculty to an understanding of the value of performance to students.

Time is always at a premium, but every minute invested in developing good relationships with other faculty members pays large dividends in support of the choral program. Ways in which choral directors can generate support from the rest of the faculty are as follows: (1) Invite them to drop in on the choral rehearsal during their break. Since the activity is so different from the more cognitive disciplines, they usually find it very enlightening and enjoyable. (2) In return, ask permission to visit in their classes. Show genuine interest in the other departments and their activities. (3) Be sure to give recognition to faculty, administration, and staff who assist the choral program in any way. Print their names in the programs, give them credit in the news releases, and recognize them publicly at concerts or events. (4) Volunteer to help them in their special efforts. Directors should always make other faculty members feel that they can request their assistance any time it is needed. (5) Directors should keep a stack of thank-you notes on their desks. It only takes a moment to express gratitude for assistance. Everyone likes to be appreciated. Notice how willing they will be to aid when asked again later.

Parent organizations are usually founded to assist in fund-raising for a choral organization, but they often serve a greater purpose. Parent meetings provide wonderful opportunities for directors to extol the hard work and commitment of their children to the choral program. They also provide a chance to describe activities of the year and delineate future plans. Directors must always remember that parents are the choir's greatest supporters because their children receive the most benefit from the efforts. Informed parents multiply the voice of the director many times over. They are the most beneficial public relations component of the department.

Positive relations with the news media is vital to the public image of choral music. Directors should take time to become acquainted with the program directors of the local radio and television stations and the editors of newspapers. If directors do not take time to meet them personally and share some of their aspirations for their school and choral program, they should not expect to receive favorable coverage when they send them news releases. The news media are much more likely to assign a bigger headline and appropriate a better place on the radio or position in the newspaper if they know the director personally. People flood them with public service requests that they relegate to an established time and place for such without giving them special attention. The personal acquaintance gives the director the edge of priority.

Officers in music clubs and service organizations are important people to know. They deal daily with the public and can be helpful in promoting choral music, particularly if directors apprise them of their activities and aspirations.

Other methods of publicity for specific choral events include: (1) placing posters in highly frequented places in the community; (2) placing handbills on cars and doors; (3) sending news releases to public service, radio, and television programs; (4) writing personal invitations, and (5) calling important people whom directors would like to see at the programs.

Following is a sample news release. It is important to use a format that is accepted by the media. This adds credibility to the choral department and entire school. It should be printed on the school's letterhead stationery.

In smaller communities, it is appropriate to include the names of the participants (in the case of the previous announcement, of course, that would be impossible) and a list of all the music that will be presented. Large media companies in metropolitan areas usually will not print such information.

SPECIAL ON- AND OFF-CAMPUS CHORAL ACTIVITIES

Since performance is inherent to choral singing and since it is one of the main reasons students enroll in choir, directors should plan several performances

News Release: Junction City High School, 200 N. Market St. Junction City, ME 72015

Contact: Mr. Jim Johnson, Jr., Choral Director, 1806 Bruce St., River Valley, ME 72032

Phone: (501) 222-2222 (high school) or 333-3333 (home)

Date: October 20, 2007

Subject: *THE OCTOBER FESTIVAL OF CHOIRS*, October 30, 2007, 7:00 p.m., in the Junction City High School Auditorium

---

The Choral Department of Junction City High School will present *THE OCTOBER FESTIVAL OF CHOIRS* at 7:00 p.m., October 20, in the school auditorium. Twelve different outstanding senior high school choirs from throughout the city will be featured performing great festival music from throughout the ages. Over 900 students will participate. Some of these selections, all of which were written by master composers such as Bach, Beethoven, and Brahms, will be accompanied by a forty-piece symphonic orchestra composed of members from the Capitol City Symphony. Tickets may be obtained from John's House of Music, 2100 Broadway, Junction City, from members of each of the choruses, or from the Choral Department at Junction City High School. Reserve tickets by calling 222-2222.

during each semester. Various types of concert opportunities are presented and discussed in this section.

Contests

Region, district, and statewide choral adjudication contests (where choirs earn ratings of I through IV against an accepted standard of excellence) have been part of the secondary choral music scene for several generations. When they first appeared, faculty and administrations praised them highly for their value in recruiting new students to the choral program, motivating the students to stay on task during rehearsal, and improving choral sound, among many reasons. Over the years they became so important to many choral directors that they were often the center of concentration in their daily musical activities. To have a choir that received sweepstakes (straight I ratings in all areas of competition) at contest became the ultimate symbol of success. Getting sweepstakes year after year possibly meant that the director would be offered one of the most prestigious senior high school choral positions in the state, being revered as a superb choral technician by the directors' peers, or having to work less diligently to recruit talented singers to their choral program. Some senior high school choirs have spent an entire semester polishing the same three selections first for region, then district, and finally state contests. There are also privately funded national contests with lucrative amounts of prize money given to the winner, although they have a slightly different purpose and approach than the public school contests sponsored by various professional music teachers' associations described previously.

In recent years some educators have disapproved of the amount of time and attention given to choral contests by many directors. They have questioned the educational soundness of spending so much time in preparation of a few selections and thereby limiting the exposure to more and varied literature. They have questioned the motives of the directors with the inference that they were engaging in contests more for self-aggrandizement than for educational purposes. To the opponents, contests have become the proverbial "tail wagging the dog."

Proponents proffer several persuasive reasons for engaging in choral contests: (1) Contests motivate students to better performance practices due to the challenge of competition. (2) They prepare students for the competitive nature of life experiences. (3) The results of the contests serve to alert administrators to the effectiveness of the school choral program. (4) The students receive constructive criticism from judges who are usually recognized choral experts. (5) While attending the contest students can hear other secondary groups comprised of students of the same age.

Opponents argue: (1) Clinics and other festive activities motivate students as effectively as contests, and they remove the dimension of competition that sets director against director and school against school. (2) Clinics also allow the students to be critiqued by a choral expert, without the dimension of a rating that can be discouraging to some groups. Clinicians critique choirs through verbal and musical expression instead of completing an adjudication form as is the practice of the judge at contest. They also work directly with the singers to improve their choral technique. (3) Competition should be reserved for athletic competitions. The fine arts serve a different purpose in society. (4) Directors should teach a varied curriculum in the choral classroom, such as exposing choir members to many different types of literature, developing aesthetic awareness, and singing in varied choral settings (with orchestra, band, opera choruses, or on the musical stage) that are ignored due to the time spent in preparation for contests. (5) Administrators must judge a choral program and its director on the results of competition rather than on quality teaching and sound educational principles.

Whether or not beginning directors participate in choral contests depends on their experiences in senior high school as contest participants, the amount of emphasis placed on contests by their administration and professional school music associations, and if the choral program where they teach has a tradition of participating in contests. If directors decide to participate in contests, it is advisable for them to keep their choir's involvement in perspective. Contests should be only one aspect of a multifaceted choral program. Obviously, they can be helpful when they are allowed to serve the purposes for which they were intended. On the other hand, they supercede sound educational tenets when directors involve their choirs to the extreme.

If directors choose to take their choirs to contests, they should consider the following tips to promote success both for the entire choir and the individual singers involved.

1. Since the choirs will be adjudicated, they should prepare to make a high rating. If they go just for the experience or for a day of fun and participation, the occasion may be more detrimental than beneficial to the overall choral program. Not taking the contest seriously and returning with a poor rating negates the purpose of the contest. The process of preparing for a I rating, both psychologically and musically, and returning with a high rating (even though it may not be a I) is what makes the event beneficial.

2. Study the rules of the contest thoroughly. Directors should not arrive and find they have prepared the wrong type of music or have made plans to leave after their choirs have sung, which may be violating the contest rules.

3. Selecting the proper music is most crucial. Directors should study many different scores to find the piece that is best suited for their choirs. Music that is too difficult, too simple, too high, too low, written in a style that their choirs have not previously experienced, or written in a style that is inappropriate for that particular type of contest, and so forth will place their choirs at a disadvantage even before the rehearsals begin. Directors should determine the best qualities of their choirs and find music that highlights those qualities.

4. Begin rehearsals five or six weeks in advance of the contest. If the ensemble does not have a regularly scheduled time to rehearse, find a time that all the singers can rehearse. Students missing rehearsals can be devastating to the success of the ensemble. One absentee negatively affects the ensemble's sense of unity and the ultimate outcome. If necessary, choose the personnel according to their accessibility for rehearsal as well as their musicianship and vocal talent.

5. Plan the schedule so that the music is memorized entirely when the students commence the final week of rehearsals. During the final week rehearsing the contest music should fall in small time increments. Rehearse the contest music at the beginning of the rehearsal, put it away, and return to it at the end.

6. Rehearse details. Work for perfection. Do not let any incorrect happening pass without attention. Be consistent in the process, and do not make a major change at the last moment.

7. During the last week of rehearsal, be positive. Telling them how badly they are performing only breaks down their confidence. They must enter the day of the contest believing that they are fully prepared psychologically and musically.

8. Rehearse the contest numbers in several different environments, if possible. Change of acoustical situations can be devastating to a group if they are not prepared for it.

9. Record the music each time it is rehearsed, evaluate the recording before the next rehearsal and make the necessary corrections. It is probably best for the group not to hear the recordings, even if the director feels that they are good. Singers need to develop a mental image of how they sound from

each individual's perspective. Changing that perspective may be negative psychologically.

10. Practice the visual aspects of the performance including the proper singing attire and how to walk, turn, and stand. Practice the overall demeanor of the choir so that the members will communicate a pleasant appearance when they are not singing and the appropriate expressions when they are singing.

11. If during the five- or six-week preparation period the director decides to cancel one of the groups participation in the contest, it should be done early. Try not to cancel during the last week because by then the singers have become psychologically ready for the contest. Removing the event at that time may destroy the groups morale and commitment for the rest of the year.

12. During the final week, meet with all the accompanists, go over the contest schedule, and help them to arrange their music in proper order for each group. Give them specific instructions when and where they are supposed to be.

13. During the final week, arrange the music for the judges in the order of performance. Attach any instructions pertaining to changes (such as transposition of keys and so forth) to each of the judge's copies.

14. Assure that the students and parents know when and where the bus is leaving, when and where the students should meet for warm-ups, when and where they will sing, and when and where they will depart. Do this *before* everyone leaves for the event.

15. During the warm-up for the performance, remind the singers of common mistakes and problem areas, then sing the music without stopping. Do not be critical at that point. Be positive, relaxed, and pleasant. Encourage the singers to relax and enjoy the performance. Having an enjoyable performance is most important to success. They have paid the price of sufficient rehearsal. They are well-prepared; therefore, they will perform better if they are having a good time.

All-Region, All-District, and All-State Choirs

Most states have all-state choirs for senior high school students. A few have all-state choirs for middle/junior high school students, but usually participation for early adolescents is limited to all-region or all-district choirs. In most cases, all-state choir rehearses and performs in the spring while the teachers attend professional activities sponsored by various professional music teachers associations. Usually, all-state choir performs on the same program with the all-state band and all-state orchestra at the end of three days of rehearsals and activities (usually on Thursday, Friday, and Saturday).

Students are chosen for all-state choir by audition. The local choir directors prepare the students who want to audition (they customarily audition on the music they will perform), and the best are chosen for membership. Having been chosen to sing in all-state choir becomes quite important to serious music students because it routinely means that they will be offered a music scholarship to one or more leading university in the state, particularly if they are first-chair selectees.

The choir will have a guest conductor from out of state. In most cases the conductor will be a national choral leader from a prestigious university. Each participant learns (and sometimes memorizes) the music before the rehearsals begin. The situation is unique because the best young singers in the state singing under the direction of an eminent choral authority provides an occasion the singers will remember throughout their lives.

All-region and all-district choirs are handled in a similar fashion except they are more localized and the conductor may be one of the leading university directors within the state. It is a standing practice to encourage middle/junior high school students to participate in All-Region or All-District Choirs in preparation to be involved in All-State when they attend senior high school. However, some states have All-Region and All-District Choirs for senior high school students as well.

Festivals and Clinics

Other special on- and off-campus activities include festivals and clinics, terms that are used interchangably for different types of activities. For example, several choirs may be invited to participate in an all-day activity where they perform individually and as a mass choir on a closing concert. Each of the choir directors conduct their own groups on the concert, and a guest director is brought in to rehearse and conduct the mass choir.

For another approach, individual directors may invite a guest conductor to come to their schools and have a day of special rehearsals. The guest conductor may work with the Beginner, Intermediate, and Advanced Choirs separately or the choirs may be put together for a mass rehearsal. Sometimes this clinic occurs about a month before contest and the guest conductor rehearses the music each of the choirs will sing for adjudication.

In both types of activities it is important for the choir members to have learned the notes before the guest conductor arrives. If they do not, the occasion will not be beneficial to the individual singers because the guest conductor will spend most of the time teaching the notes before choral technique can be rehearsed. Teaching good choral technique should be the primary reason for the guest conductor's invitation.

Some directors believe that these special clinic and festival activities are as important as all-region, all-district, or all-state choirs because they involve all the students in a local school situation whereas auditioned choirs are directed only to the best singers. Special festival activities are particularly important to those students who may not be completely committed to choral music, because it provides an expanded choral happening that they may not experience in their day-to-day involvement.

Singing for Parents and the School Assembly

When choral music is an accepted and revered part of the school curriculum and when a large percentage of the student body has been taught music in elementary school and is enrolled in various music classes (band, orchestra, choir, music appreciation, fine arts, and so forth), singing for school assembly can be a joyous and rewarding experience. The choir members look forward to displaying the results of their hard work to an appreciative audience of their peers. Conversely, if choral music is a misunderstood and poorly accepted discipline with only a small percentage of the general student population participating in music organizations, singing for the student body may be a harrowing experience. When choir members must endure snide remarks about their performance and their membership in the choir, and when students shout and jeer (or even display boredom by sleeping or talking) during the performance, the occasion becomes dreaded and unfruitful.

Directors working in a school environment in which choral music is misunderstood and unappreciated should be very careful about exposing their choir members to situations where they are not warmly accepted. There are many performance opportunities where singers are appreciated without exposing them to any type of overt ridicule. If the administration requires directors to have their choirs perform for school assembly under adverse circumstances, it is best to prepare an entertaining, youth-oriented selection (or small group of pieces, not more than five to eight minutes of singing) and perform them at the beginning of the assembly. Directors should never consider performing a full, traditional choral concert for such an unappreciative audience.

Singing for the parents of the choir members is completely different. They are usually very appreciative because their sons and daughters are the participants. At least once a semester, directors should plan a special evening for the parents (or sing for the parent-teacher organization) in which the choir sings and the directors demonstrate their teaching technique and explain their goals and future plans for the choir.

Another approach is to join with the band and orchestra for a combined concert for the parents and friends. Each musical organization may perform individually and then they combine for a mass choral selection accompanied by band and/or orchestra to close the concert.

Miscellaneous Off-Campus Performances

Some administrators and choral directors believe that the choral department should serve as a publicity arm of the school. There is some controversy about choirs functioning in this way. Those who disagree contend that it minimizes the true educational purposes of the department and maximizes the image that choral music in the schools is primarily an entertainment entity. The detriment of such an image becomes evident when there are too many off-campus performances and too much literature chosen that may be characterized as strictly entertaining and not educational in nature. The students neglect their studies because of their choral responsibilities. They have to miss their regular classes when they are off campus. They begin to view themselves as semiprofessional entertainers instead of students.

Indeed, performance is a vital part of choral music, but overindulgence is the culprit. If directors choose those performance opportunities that allow them to sing music that supports the educational purposes of the program and when they limit the number of performances each semester, concertizing becomes a vital and positive part of the student's education. Suggested performance opportunities that support sound educational principles include: (1) exchanging concerts with other senior high school choirs, (2) singing for local music clubs, (3) performing in university and college departments of music, (4) singing in worship services (this if often difficult since students may need to be in their own churches or synagogues during worship), and (5) singing at regional and national Music Educators National Conference (MENC), American Choral Directors Association, and other similar professional music conventions (these performances are invitational through audition only; directors should consult their district supervisor of music for the audition process in their area).

NONBUDGETARY FINANCIAL SUPPORT

It is estimated that two out of every three dollars acquired for music education in secondary schools in the United States is a result of fund-raising efforts of the students and staff. Only one-third of the revenue comes from taxes. As with recruitment, the need to participate in fund-raising activities is a result of society not viewing music as a truly academic discipline. They perceive music to be for a special few; therefore, this special few must raise money to support their program. To be fair, however, some departments spend money on aspects of the music program that, some would say, fall outside the realm of academics, such as tours and trips for special performances beyond the local community. One must make the point, too, that some schools buy music, materials, and equipment that their districts do not provide from tax revenue.

Many music educators are not comfortable with the role of fund-raiser because it takes time and energy away from their primary responsibility of teaching. Fund-raising also requires students to give time and effort that they should give to practice and study. Since some people in the community never see choir members except in their role as fund-raisers (constantly the students are knocking on their door asking them to buy something or to give them a donation), the activity either camouflages or hides completely the beneficial aspects of choral music education. This further promotes the concept that music is not a true discipline.

Once choral directors plan and activate annual comprehensive and successful fund-raising campaigns, administrators begin to view the choral department as self-supporting; tax revenue once provided for it is designated to other budgetary needs in the school. If directors plan to embark upon fund-raising activities, it is extremely important to establish ground rules with the administration about their purposes and how the money is to be spent. Administrators should understand that they must never enter these funds as a standard budget item for support that tax revenue traditionally provides.

Directors usually form parent booster organizations, or "choir clubs" as they are often called, to facilitate the fund-raising activities, among other reasons. The parents soon realize that the fund-raising bandwagon is a treadmill from which they cannot disembark. Perhaps it would be much more sensible philosophically to encourage a parent organization to serve as a lobby to the administration, school board, and even the state legislature to seek ways for increasing tax revenue or designating current taxes to music education in the schools. If parents expended as much time and effort in lobbying as they spent fund-raising, more than likely they would be as successful. When organized properly by professionals, lobbying will yield excellent dividends in support of education.

Since the prevailing practice for getting nonbudgetary resources is fund-raising, teachers who desire to participate should contact a fund-raising organization to help them plan and initiate the activity. These professional companies have elaborate plans for assuring that the endeavor will be successful. Some of them even will send a representative to the school to train the students and the staff how to be successful. They will provide all the merchandise the department will handle and they will recommend the items (fruit, candy, cookies, clothing accessories, nuts, Christmas cards) that yield the most profit and are the easiest for the students to sell.

Easy recruitment is one of the results of having the extra money for choir travel. Secondary students are eager to join active and thriving choirs who have attractive outfits and who perform out of state regularly. Directors should be careful to use the money to benefit the entire choral program (which includes the training choirs). All enrollees in the choral program should participate and all should benefit. The choral department, not just one specific choir, should sponsor the fund-raising activities.

EVALUATION OF STUDENTS

I have had secondary students tell me, "My parents don't care about the grade I get in music." In conferences, parents may say, "Oh, that's music class, it doesn't count." These statements are exemplary of some attitudes about the study of music. As indicated earlier in this chapter (see "Recruitment, It's All in the Image"), they do not consider it a discipline. Teachers of subjects other than music often perceive it as a fun time for their students, a time to relax and certainly not to be taken seriously.

Of the many reasons why people perceive music in this fashion, one is because for years many teachers of music did not evaluate (give grades) that were demonstrative of a true discipline. They used attendance and participation as the primary criteria for grade determination, so most of the students made A's in choir. This promulgated the contention that music is not a "real" subject and certainly not one that should be characterized as a true discipline of study. Before the general public can understand the true character of the study of music, teachers must treat it seriously. They must devise a significant method of evaluating music learning and apply it consistently and fairly to all their students.

Evaluation in Performance-Oriented Classes

Evaluation (giving grades) should be a natural outgrowth of a teacher's overall teaching strategy. In Chapter 5, a strategy for teaching choral music that included identifying student needs, delineating instructional goals, devising teaching strategies, and assessing the progress was proposed. Assessment, the final step of a productive teaching strategy, should include a structured method of determining each singer's grade based on a specific set of criteria of evaluation.

Clearly, teachers want to measure what the students have learned (basic facts and skills) in the class, but there are several considerations unique to the discipline of music to contemplate before determining the criteria for proper student evaluation. (1) Aesthetic growth (the deepening of appreciative sensitivities) is certainly unique to the study of music and the arts. (2) All music students do not begin study on an equal standing because their innate vocal instruments are not the same. The inherent vocal quality of some students is unquestionably better than others. (3) Musical aptitude (raw talent) varies among students. (4) The maturation level of secondary age students (particularly in middle/junior high school) varies significantly among students.

A comprehensive system should measure progress in the cognitive, affective, and psychomotor domains and learning should penetrate to the more comprehensive levels of response (see Chapter 5) in each domain. The system also should measure the extent to which students attain the behavioral objectives delineated in the directors' teaching strategies for each student and a class as a whole.

Probably it is impossible to devise a grading system in which teachers give equal value and consideration to the unique musical variables and criteria described in the previous paragraphs, but they should try. Since every director formulates teaching strategies to meet their own students' needs, a model for evaluating how *all* students satisfy requirements cannot be presented here, although definite approaches to teaching musicianship (Chapter 11) and vocal and choral technique (Chapters 10 and 12) have been provided. Following is an evaluation form designed to measure the students progress in the areas described in these chapters. This form should serve as a model for evaluation forms that teachers could design to meet their specific needs. If teachers desire to give their forms a more objective dimension by assigning points or a percentage to each of the areas, they may do so. How much each area (vocal, choral, musical, maturation, and aesthetic progress) should affect the final grade has not been suggested. Teachers must determine that according to their own value system and student profiles.

Further, teachers must decide how the results from this form should integrate with tests and other grade-earning activities. Other options for grade input that teachers may combine with the grade assessed on the evaluation form are: (1) Grades given from tests that evaluate the cognitive considerations of the course. (2) Grades given for the number of points earned as a result of inside and outside classroom activities. For instance, teachers may give points for each rehearsal attended, each solo sung, hours of practice outside the classroom, private lessons, and so on. (3) Grades given as a result of group auditions where the students perform the literature on which they have been working. This may be done privately, as part of a regular rehearsal, or through a taping session. (4) Teachers may consider amalgamating a grade into the final appraisal in which the students make a self-assessment of their own work and progress. (5) Finally, as mentioned previously, teachers should complete the following form or a similar instrument for an evaluation of each student as part of the final grade.

The teacher should share the final average of all the grade sources with the student and the student's parents. So that students may receive maximum benefit from the evaluation, if the task is not insurmountable, teachers should have a conference with every student and parent. The conference may serve as a vehicle for understanding past work and for motivating future work. It also communicates to both students and parents the importance of the study of the art of music and how disciplined one must be to become an accomplished singer.

Grading in Nonperformance Oriented Classes

Grading in nonperformance classes such as fine arts, music appreciation, music theory, and such will probably be more traditional in the evaluation process since these disciplines are dominated by the cognitive domain. Cognitive testing is the basis of evaluation in the American school system. Most teachers have taken many cognitive tests over the years, thus they feel that they are experts in devising these tests for their students. However, teachers should exercise caution when designing these tests to formulate an instrument that is both valid (it tests the material it was designed to test) and reliable (it is written so that the students understand how to give the correct answer, when they know it).

The *essay* question or examination gives the students the freedom to organize their responses and express their own ideas. Grading the test can be a problem because graders vary in their assessment of the answers. Graders may even vary in their own assessment from one time to another. It is also very time-consuming to grade an essay test; therefore, often it is not feasible to use it when the class is large. Finally, the test may discriminate against students who are less articulate than others.

True or false questions are very suspect. In fact, many feel that they are completely unsatisfactory. It is difficult to devise questions that minimize the effects of chance (since there are only two choices for answers, the students have a fifty-fifty chance of being correct) and ambiguity.

For *completion* (fill in the blank) questions to be reliable they must request an answer that is very precise. Teachers also run the risk of ambiguity with a question such as "an important musical form of the Classical period is _____." Obviously, several answers would be correct.

Multiple-choice questions are the most common and the most valid and reliable if devised properly. Teachers should take care that the original statement (called the *stem*) is brief and to the point, and they should vary the position of the correct choice (called the *foil*). Using multiple-choice questions allows the

STUDENT PROGRESS EVALUATION FORM

MUSICAL PROGRESS	Exceptional	Satisfactory	Needs Improvement
VOCAL PROGRESS			
Posture			
Breathing			
Humming			
Vocal exercises			
Application of technique to the literature			
Freedom in singing			
Range development			
Vowels			
Consonants			
Articulation			
Sigh (breath support)			
Sigh (phrasing)			
Dynamics			
CHORAL PROGRESS			
Blend			
Balance			
Vowel color			
Intonation			
Vibrato			
Ensemble precision			
Modes of singing			
Appearance			
Facial/body language			
Style			
PROGRESS IN MUSICIANSHIP			
Sight-reading (tonic sol-fa)			
Sight-reading (rhythm)			
Understanding of form			
Sensitivity			
MATURATION			
Ability to concentrate			
Attention span			
Attitude			
Application of knowledge to singing			
Assertiveness			
Social behavior			
Attendance			
AESTHETIC PROGRESS			
Practice outside of class			
Outside concerts attended			
Performing in other groups			

examiner to probe a particular subject when several questions approach the subject from different perspectives. Using "all of the above" and "none of the above" requires the students to have more than a cursory knowledge of the subject. Several questions can be formed from a quoted musical example or paragraph.

Matching and *listing* questions are good for examining knowledge of several components in a given category. Students often consider listing questions to be difficult because they require long, memorized lists of category components. Studying for matching questions helps students to place information into mental compartments and promotes organization in study.

A FRIEND IN NEED IS A FRIEND INDEED

In the complicated routine of teaching, conducting, administering, counseling, disciplining, motivating, and all the other facets of being a choral director in a secondary school, many times you may feel that you are "in need" of professional help. There is "a friend" to whom you can turn. That person is your music supervisor. For a "friend in need," he or she is truly a "friend indeed."

In an age of specialization a typical school system may have an elementary specialist (music teacher) in each of the elementary schools, instrumental (one for orchestra and one for band), choral, and general music specialists in each of the middle/junior and senior high school. The person who coordinates all the programs and works with each of these educators is the *music supervisor*. Music supervisors must: (1) supply perpetuity throughout the system at all levels, (2) diagnose problems and attempt to improve the situation, (3) counsel and motivate the teachers, and (4) facilitate the procurement of all teaching literature and materials. They, too, are specialists but in all the teaching areas: instrumental, choral, and general.

Most urban and suburban school districts have full-time music supervisors. One of the music teachers (usually the senior high school choral or band director) may serve as a part-time music supervisor in the smaller districts. Very small districts (one to ten schools) may not have a supervisor at all.

There are also supervisors of music on the state level (employees of the state Department of Education) who serve primarily as consultants to the music programs throughout the state. They are available to the schools to aid in organizing and developing the music programs, to provide in-service courses for the music faculties, and to suggest ways to build and improve music facilities.

Most choral directors will find that their "friend indeed" will more than likely be the local, district, or county supervisor who is most directly responsible for their immediate needs.

Responsibilities and Duties of the Supervisor

The local board of education hires the supervisors; the supervisors ultimately are responsible to them. The supervisors usually answer directly to the school superintendent. Supervisors are of most assistance to the music teachers and their principals.

According to Malcolm Bessom, music supervisors have five main areas of activity: (1) curriculum organization and development; (2) provision of materials, equipment, buildings, and space; (3) direction and improvement of the teaching-learning situation; (4) professional growth; and (5) evaluation and interpretation.[1]

Curriculum organization and development includes (1) formulating objectives and policies such as surveying and evaluating the present program's strengths and weaknesses, outlining the purposes of the programs, and coordinating the objectives with the educational philosophy; (2) planning activities and courses of study; and (3) coordinating and articulating instruction that includes meeting with the teachers to help coordinate activities within individual classes.

Provision of materials encompasses (1) selecting texts, music, and recordings for regular courses and for special programs and activities; (2) providing lists of available instructional material and supplementary material such as bulletins and guides; (3) determining the best means of distributing materials; (4) planning budgets for long-range and emergency purchases; and (5) appraising materials currently in use. Provision of equipment involves (1) appraising equipment presently owned by the schools; (2) determining new equipment the educators may need and devising long-range plans for purchases and replacement; (3) preparing specifications for equipment; and (4) providing for repair of instruments and other equipment. Provision of buildings and space includes (1) determining the spatial requirements of the music programs; (2) providing storage facilities for materials and equipment; and (3) advising the board of education on plans for new buildings.

Direction and improvement of the teaching-learning situation involves (1) making recommendations for employment of music personnel; (2) improving staff relations and working conditions; (3) providing an active and complete in-service program such as workshops, teacher meetings, conferences, and demonstrations; and (4) encouraging enrollment in extension courses, summer clinics, and so forth.

Professional growth encompasses (1) attending and participating in meetings of local, regional, state, and national professional organizations; (2) serving on educational committees; (3) participating in surveys and research studies; (4) conducting experiments on instructional problems; and (5) keeping informed about new publications in music and education.

Evaluation and interpretation of the various music programs entails (1) maintaining accurate records about inventory, student enrollment, students in special programs, and proposed and present musical activities; (2) devising a fair and comprehensive program of how to evaluate teachers, programs, students, and systems and developing and promoting the music-testing and advising program in all areas such as strings, bands, general, choral, and theory; and (3) keeping teachers, principals, the administration, the board of education,

---

[1] Malcolm E. Bessom, *Supervising the Successful School Music Program* (West Nyack, N.Y.: Parker Publishing Co., 1969), 9–12.

the media, and the community informed about plans, programs, buildings, evaluations, concerts, and all vital areas of the school music programs.

Teacher evaluation is one of the most difficult, yet important, areas of music supervisors' responsibilities. Beginning music teachers often fear their supervisors because the evaluations usually include critical recommendations to the principals. This fear may be amplified when there are basic philosophical differences between the two. Conversely, due to the supervisors' many years of experience, they can be a tremendous help to beginning teachers, if the teachers are secure enough within themselves to rely upon their expertise. Further, the music supervisor may serve as a liaison between them and their principals. Music supervisors (because they are both administrators and musicians) usually can be more persuasive in helping principals understand the problems of the music teachers than the teachers can be when dealing with the principals alone. Good music supervisors have developed the knack for making the music teacher feel uninhibited about depending on them. Music teachers should feel comfortable with their supervisors, view them as helpers, not hurters, and rely on them in all problem-solving situations.

PROFESSIONAL ETHICS

Professional ethics refers to the conduct of teachers in their relationships to those with whom they work. Teachers must have standards for themselves as the entire profession should have standards to guide the teachers. Included here are two different codes of ethics: the Code of Ethics of the Education Profession as adopted by the National Education Association and the Code of Ethics and Standard Practices for Texas Educators. The first speaks primarily to the relationship of teachers with students and the teachers' relationship to the profession. The second speaks to the relationships of teachers to each other, to the students, and to the parents and community at large. Every teacher (or prospective teacher) should study these thoroughly. The future of the profession depends upon teachers' desire to uphold and support them.

Code of Ethics of the Education Profession[2]

Preamble The educator, believing in the worth and dignity of each human being, recognizes the supreme importance of the pursuit of truth, devotion to excellence, and the nurture of democratic principles. Essential to these goals is the protection of freedom to learn and to teach and the guarantee of equal educational opportunity for all. The educator accepts the responsibility to adhere to the highest ethical standards.

The educator recognizes the magnitude of the responsibility inherent in

---

[2] *NEA Handbook, 1990–91*, copyright 1990, National Education Association. Reprinted with permission.

the teaching process. The desire for the respect and confidence of one's colleagues, of students, of parents, and of the members of the community provides the incentive to attain and maintain the highest possible degree of ethical conduct. The Code of Ethics of the Education Profession indicates the aspiration of all educators and provides standards by which to judge conduct.

The remedies specified by the NEA and/or its affiliates for the violation of any provision of this Code shall be exclusive and no such provision shall be enforceable in any form other than one specifically designated by the NEA and its affiliates.

Principle I—Commitment to the Student   The educator strives to help each student realize his or her potential as a worthy and effective member of society. The educator therefore works to stimulate the spirit of inquiry, the acquisition of knowledge and understanding, and the thoughtful formulation of worthy goals.

In fulfillment of the obligation to the student, the educator:

1. Shall not unreasonably restrain the student from independent action in the pursuit of learning.
2. Shall not unreasonably deny the student access to varying points of view.
3. Shall not deliberately suppress or distort subject matter relevant to the student's progress.
4. Shall make reasonable effort to protect the student from conditions harmful to learning or to health and safety.
5. Shall not intentionally expose the student to embarrassment or disparagement.
6. Shall not on the basis of race, color, creed, sex, national origin, marital status, political or religious beliefs, family, social or cultural background, or sexual orientation, unfairly:
   A. Exclude any student from participation in any program;
   B. Deny benefits to any student;
   C. Grant any advantage to any student.
7. Shall not use professional relationships with students for private advantage.
8. Shall not disclose information about students obtained in the course of professional service, unless disclosure serves a compelling professional purpose or is required by law.

Principle II—Commitment to the Profession   The education profession is vested by the public with a trust and responsibility requiring the highest ideals of professional service.

In the belief that the quality of the services of the education profession directly influences the nation and its citizens, the educator shall exert every effort to raise professional standards, to promote a climate that encourages the exercise of professional judgement, to achieve conditions which attract persons worthy of the trust to careers in education, and to assist in preventing the practice of the profession by unqualified persons.

In fulfillment of the obligations to the profession, the educator:

1. Shall not in an application for a professional position deliberately make a

false statement or fail to disclose a material fact related to competency and qualifications.

2. Shall not misrepresent his/her professional qualifications.
3. Shall not assist entry into the profession of a person known to be unqualified in respect to character, education, or other relevant attributes.
4. Shall not knowingly make a false statement concerning the qualifications of a candidate for a professional position.
5. Shall not assist a non-educator in the unauthorized practice of teaching.
6. Shall not disclose information about colleagues obtained in the course of professional service unless disclosure serves a compelling professional purpose or is required by law.
7. Shall not knowingly make false or malicious statements about a colleague.
8. Shall not disclose information about students obtained in the course of professional service, unless disclosure serves a compelling professional purpose or is required by law.

Code of Ethics and Standard Practices for Texas Educators[3]

Adopted in 1971 and revised in 1988, the Code of Ethics and Standard Practices for the Texas Educators states: (1) The Texas educator should strive to create an atmosphere that will nurture to fulfillment the potential of each student. (2) The educator is responsible for standard practices and ethical conduct toward students, professional colleagues, parents, and the community. (3) The Code is intended to govern the profession, and interpretations of the Code shall be determined by the Professional Practices Commission. (4) The educator who conducts his affairs with conscientious concern will exemplify the highest standards of professional commitment.

Principle I—Professional Ethical Conduct The Texas educator should endeavor to maintain the dignity of the profession by respecting and obeying the law, demonstrating personal integrity, and exemplifying honesty.

1. The educator shall not intentionally misrepresent official policies of the school district or educational organization and shall clearly distinguish those views from his personal attitudes and opinions.
2. The educator shall honestly account for all funds committed to his charge and shall conduct his financial business with integrity.
3. The educator shall not use institutional or professional privileges for personal or partisan advantage.
4. The educator shall accept no gratuities, gifts, or favors that impair or appear to impair professional judgment.
5. The educator shall not offer any favor, service, or thing of value to obtain special advantage.
6. The educator shall not falsify records, or direct or coerce other to do so.

[3] Used with the permission of the Teachers' Professional Practices Commission of Texas.

Principle II—Professional Practices and Performances   The Texas educator, after qualifying in a manner established by law or regulation, shall assume responsibilities for professional teaching practices and professional performance and shall continually strive to demonstrate competence.

1. The educator shall apply for, accept, offer, or assign a position or a responsibility on the basis of professional qualifications and shall adhere to the terms of a contract or appointment.
2. The educator shall possess mental health, physical stamina, and social prudence necessary to perform the duties of his professional assignment.
3. The educator shall organize instruction that seeks to accomplish objectives related to learning.
4. The educator shall continue professional growth.
5. The educator shall comply to written local school board policies, Texas Education Agency regulations, and applicable state and federal laws.

Principle III—Ethical Conduct Toward Professional Colleagues   The Texas educator, in exemplifying ethical relations with colleagues, shall accord just and equitable treatment to all members of the profession.

1. The educator shall not reveal confidential information concerning colleagues unless disclosure serves professional purposes or is required by law.
2. The educator shall not willfully make false statements about a colleague or the school system.
3. The educator shall adhere to written local school board policies and legal statutes regarding dismissal, evaluation, and employment processes.
4. The educator shall not interfere with a colleague's exercise of political and citizenship rights and responsibilities.
5. The educator shall not discriminate against, coerce, or harass a colleague on the basis of race, color, creed, national origin, age, sex, handicap, or marital status.
6. The educator shall not intentionally deny or impede a colleague in the exercise or enjoyment of any professional right or privilege.
7. The educator shall not use coercive means or promise special treatment in order to influence professional decisions of colleagues.
8. The educator shall have the academic freedom to teach as a professional privilege, and no educator shall interfere with such privilege except as required by state and/or federal law.

Principle IV—Ethical Conduct Toward Students   The Texas educator, in accepting a position of public trust, shall measure success by the progress of each student toward realization of his potential as an effective citizen.

1. The educator shall deal considerately and justly with each student and shall seek to resolve problems including discipline according to law and school board policy.
2. The educator shall not intentionally expose the student to disparagement.
3. The educator shall not reveal confidential information concerning students unless disclosure serves professional purposes or is required by law.

4. The educator shall make reasonable effort to protect the student from conditions detrimental to the following: learning, physical health, mental health, or safety.

5. The educator shall endeavor to present facts without distortion.

6. The educator shall not unfairly exclude a student from participation in a program, deny benefits to a student, or grant an advantage to a student on the basis of race, color, sex, handicap, national origin, or marital status.

7. The educator shall not unreasonably restrain the student from independent action in the pursuit of learning or deny the student access to varying points of view.

Principle V—Ethical Conduct Toward Parents and Community   The Texas educator, in fulfilling citizenship responsibilities in the community, should cooperate with parents and others to improve the public schools of the community.

1. The educator shall make reasonable effort to communicate to parents information which should be revealed in the interest of the student.

2. The educator shall endeavor to understand community cultures and relate the home environment of students to the school.

3. The educator shall manifest a positive role in school public relations.

High Faculty Morale and Job Satisfaction

Principals often consider the faculty lounge as the "den of iniquity" because it is where faculty members complain to each other about administrative policy. Faculty often see the faculty lounge as a "haven of consolation" because it is where they meet to console each other (sometimes to the disparagement of others) in facing the difficulties of the day. In fact, the faculty lounge should be neither of these. It should be a place where faculty members may go to relax, partake of physical refreshment, engage in professional, academic, or casual conversation, and revive themselves for the remainder of the teaching activities of the day. Using the faculty lounge for reasons other than these is counterproductive to quality teaching and administration. Often it is a place that reinforces low faculty morale, but such should not be the case. Instructors should leave there boosted to better performance in the classroom.

High faculty morale is absolutely essential to productive teaching. Providing and enjoying job satisfaction is a two-way street. Administrators must be very adept in human relations to create an atmosphere where faculty morale remains high, just as faculty members must try to maintain a positive attitude and support the administration.

Faculty members should discuss all points of dissatisfaction in a formal open forum (the faculty meeting). This is the time for verbal disagreement and a time to seek solutions. Each faculty member should enter into the decision-making process, and once they have made the decision, they should abide by it and support it. They should reserve any further discussion with their colleagues (in the faculty lounge or wherever, and particularly if they have not expressed themselves openly in the faculty meeting) until the next open forum.

If there is dissatisfaction with the principal's policies or procedures, the faculty and administrative staff should discuss it in the formal open forum. If the faculty cannot receive satisfaction or settlement, they should follow the specific protocol (as delineated in the faculty school or district handbook) to approach the immediate supervisor. Everyone should go through the chain of command. They never should go directly to the top. If the immediate supervisor cannot help, the member should proceed up the line until they have contacted the right person.

Faculty members should attempt to maintain a positive attitude about their work. If they need counseling, they should seek professional help or counsel with someone who is not directly involved in the situation. It is usually an unfruitful practice to discuss personal problems and job dissatisfaction with fellow faculty members or to attempt to build a personal relationship with members of the administration who serve as their supervisors. Professional (not personal) relationships with students, administration, and other faculty members promote good mental health and high faculty morale.

Faculty members should be courteous and cordial with their colleagues and administrative personnel. They should refuse to listen to gossip and unkind or untrue statements about others. They should suggest to their troubled colleagues that they initiate a discussion in the open forum that will deal with the dissatisfactions.

Faculty members should never discuss faculty and administrative business with the students or the parents. They should never make disparaging remarks about their students, the administration, or their colleagues. If they feel that certain faculty members are not good teachers, rather than talk about them in private, they should attempt to see that the entire faculty enacts stipulations that will improve faculty performance. Teachers should try to solve the problem of poor student classroom performance by devising ways to motivate, encourage, and change the students instead of giving up on them and making remarks that cause them to appear unfavorable in the eyes of other faculty members.

Faculty members should always keep the administration fully informed about plans and activities, particularly if they are giving consideration to implementing major changes. They should present requests and proposals in a logical and factual fashion. They should accept the decisions of the faculty or administration, but they may desire to study their proposal carefully, revise it with additional supporting information as evidence, and to bring the matter before the open forum again to seek a new decision. It is quite acceptable to lobby faculty members on a one-to-one basis in seeking support for various proposals, provided it is done in a professional and unthreatening manner.

Administrators' jobs are made easier when teachers read memoranda carefully, follow instructions, complete all forms correctly, and respond to them on time. It should not be necessary for the principal to have to write a second memorandum or telephone the faculty member to get a response.

Teachers should never cultivate intimate or highly personal relationships with students. Students generally do not seek that type of friendship from faculty members; they seek knowledge and guidance. Faculty members should always be cordial and helpful yet always speak with calm, firm authority. They should refrain from counseling students on subjects, needs, and problems outside the area of music. Almost every school has part-time or full-time counselors who are trained to deal with personal problems. They should report abnormal student behavior patterns to the counselors.

PROFESSIONAL ADVANCEMENT

Most of us as teachers do not have the forethought, particularly when we are young, to plan our careers, that is, to set long-range goals that will help us accomplish whatever we want with our lives. We usually set a series of short-range goals and, as the doors open, we walk through them. If they do not open, we walk in another direction. For instance, after we receive our baccalaureate we either decide to take a teaching position or to do further graduate study. If we decide to teach, we work for a few years and when the opportunity to go back to school to do graduate work occurs, we take advantage of it or we decide to continue to teach. If positions outside of teaching become available to us, we think about them, then decide to leave the profession or stay in it. If the chance for a more prestigious and higher-paying teaching position becomes accessible, we investigate it, weigh the pros and cons, and accept or reject it. So go our lives, living short-range goals one after the other and accepting or rejecting opportunities as they occur.

It may be that this is the best approach to life because if we set lofty goals for ourselves that we may not attain, we arrive at the end of our careers disenchanted with the results of our efforts. It is important to most of us to feel that what we have done professionally has been worthwhile; therefore, we hesitate to gamble with our future by setting goals we may not attain. We must understand, however, that the risk is there with or without planning because if we do not plan, we may be disenchanted at the end of our careers and feel that we wasted the time.

For those who feel that they must have control over their lives, I recommend long-range planning. Overall, one accomplishes much more in a lifetime and, surprisingly enough, the human spirit has a marvelous way of reconciling, justifying, and rationalizing failures. If one day you would like to be a published Ph.D. on the faculty of a prestigious university with national recognition in your area of expertise, devise a plan to attain the goal, and then set about working the plan.

The First Teaching Position

During their professional semester (student teaching) the soon-to-be graduates begin to give serious consideration to finding a permanent teaching position. They begin to ask questions and to meet with people who can assist them. The process can be exasperating, yet exciting.

The first step is to prepare a professional dossier that includes a personal vita, a photograph (not essential), letters of recommendation, and a transcript containing a list of the courses (and grades) and the final grade point average. Students should put a copy of the dossier in their professional file at the college or university placement office. If their state maintains a placement office with the state teacher association, students need to have their dossier on file there as well. Another option is to place it with a professional placement agency[4] (they usually charge a percentage of the first year's salary for their fee). Students should take advantage of all means for finding the appropriate position that suits their skills and desires.

The next step is to write letters of inquiry to all the school districts in which the graduates have an interest, asking for an application form and requesting the staff to notify them if there is a vacancy. Then graduates should contact all acquaintances in the field of music education such as college or university faculty, colleagues, and previous teachers, to tell them of their impending graduation and to ask them to apprise the graduates of any vacant positions. If graduates personally know the principals of schools where they would like to teach, it is quite acceptable to write or call to inform them of their availability.

When graduates notice vacant positions that interest them, they should write a letter of application (the applicant may include a supporting recommendation letter from someone who knows the principal personally, if they think it to be appropriate) and send their credentials. They may call the principal of the school personally if they desire, but they should keep the call short and to the point. Briefly inquire about the position with a simple, general statement such as, "Please tell me about the position." The principal will volunteer what he or she wants the applicants to know. Do not ask specific, detailed questions at that time. When waiting for an interview, applicants might desire to find out as much about the position as possible from friends, colleagues, or other school personnel who might be willing to inform them.

Since the letter of application is the applicant's first contact with a prospective employer, it should be prepared well. The applicant should write it with a word processor or type it (be sure the format is correct) and assure that it is free of errors, neat, concise, and grammatically correct. A professional person (maybe a university professor) should proofread it before the student sends it. The applicants should keep a copy for their files.

Applicants should include the following information in the letter (in this order): (1) a statement naming the vacant position and how the applicant became aware of it; (2) a brief statement about the applicant's educational background that indicates preparation for requirements of that specific position (if there are unique aspects to the position, be sure to give qualifications that address them); (3) a statement that acknowledges the applicant's availability for a personal interview; and (4) the applicant's address and phone number (if not included on the letterhead). Note the following example application.

After the principals (or administrative assistants) have received all the applications (or the date for applying has passed), they will select those they

---

[4] Lutton Music Personnel Service, Inc., P.O. Box 13985, Gainesville, FL 32604 (904–376–9055) is one of the oldest and well-established (since 1913) national agencies that locates positions for music teachers and performers.

Rufus R. McClanahan

1121 Acclamation Avenue
Apartment 7B
Lucas Landing, North Dakota 12345

April 4, 2002

Dr. Jimbo Jenkins, Principal
Nobpoppy High School
Lewcindy, Wyoming 54321

Dear Dr. Jenkins:

My advising professor, Dr. Leland Leftland, indicated to me that Nobpoppy High School is seeking a Director of Choral Music for the 2002/03 academic school year. Please accept this letter as official application for the position.

I will graduate with the Bachelor of Music Education degree in secondary choral music from Lucas Landing University in May. State teaching certification will be awarded the following July. Dr. Leftland indicated that one of the classes included teaching a recorder choir, and since I have been playing the tenor recorder for fourteen years, he felt that I was particularly well qualified for the position. I have enclosed his personal letter of recommendation.

I have instructed the placement office to send you a copy of my credentials and university transcript. I am available for a personal interview, so please contact me when you set up interviews for the position, if you feel I am qualified. You may contact me at 987-654-3211 or at the above address at any time except June 17-24 when I will be away on vacation. I anxiously await your call.

Respectfully,

Rufus R. McClanahan

enclosure
/rm

want to interview. Some administrators will hold two sets of interviews, one for all applicants and then another for the finalists. If they schedule preliminary interviews, they may not allow the applicants to ask extensive questions (some will allow no questions at all). The purpose of the preliminary interview is to determine which applicants suit the position best. They design the final interview so that the administrative staff can become fully acquainted with the finalists and to allow the applicants the opportunity to become fully acquainted with the details of the position and to meet members of the administration (music supervisor, vice-principals, principal, and even the superintendent).

When administrators invite applicants to interview for a position, applicants should use the following checklist to assure that the interview goes well:

1. Do the applicants understand exactly when and where to go?
2. If interviewers ask about their background, do they know exactly how they plan to answer? Do they know how many hours they have in their major and minor areas?
3. If interviewers ask about their philosophy of music education, have they determined exactly what they should say?
4. If interviewers ask about their philosophy about how to discipline the students, do they know exactly what they should say?
5. If interviewers allow them to ask questions, are they prepared to ask questions that will inform them about:
    A. teaching schedule?
    B. budget?
    C. available equipment and materials?
    D. performance responsibilities?
    E. salary?
    F. choir room or teaching area?
    G   performance area?
    H. students' extra curricular activities?
    I. noncurricular responsibilities?
    J. availability of the students for after-hours rehearsals?
    K. the administration's philosophy about specific concerns?
    L. others areas of interest?

Following are some helpful hints that will help applicants make a good impression:

1. Dress fashionably. Do not overdress or underdress. Wear clothes that are professionally acceptable. Be careful about clothes that make a negative sociological or philosophical statement.
2. Do not be late, but do not arrive more than five minutes early. Come alone; do not bring friends, spouses, or children unless the interviewers have told the applicants to do so.
3. Be pleasant, cordial, and friendly. It is best not to relate jokes or funny stories (unless they are very brief and directly related to the conversation). Try not to laugh gregariously.
4. Shake hands firmly.
5. Look the interviewers directly in the eyes when engaging in conversation (unless, due to the interviewers' nationality and background, it is culturally unacceptable to do so).
6. Allow the interviewers to direct the conversation.
7. Listen carefully and concentrate on what the interviewers are saying. Answer all questions succinctly and to the point. Do not elaborate unless there is a definite reason for doing so.
8. Ask questions when invited to do so. Ask only relevant questions and listen carefully to the answers. Observe the attitude of the interviewers when they answer the questions. Did they answer them (1) flippantly, (2) seriously, (3) with interest, (4) uncaringly, or (5) enthusiastically?

9. Observe the interviewers' attitudes about the present choral program and those of the past.
10. Once the interview is over, do not linger. Express gratitude for the opportunity to interview and leave.

After the interview, applicants should take time to write down all the responses the interviewer made to their questions in case they have several interviews. They should not run the risk of getting the interviews confused. They should evaluate the interviewers' attitudes about the subject matter of each question (particularly if one of the interviewers was the principal or music supervisor) because the interest that principals show in a particular subject relates directly to the support they will give to it. The success of a choral director's program will depend on the administration's support. If they have a casual, uninterested attitude or if they have not supported the choral program in the past, it is unlikely that they will support future ones.

When principals extend an offer of employment, applicants should accept or decline it within about ten days. Whenever graduates hold several interviews in succession, the tendency is to wait for the best offer. If a principal offers them employment at one of the schools that is not their first choice, they may need to decline or accept the position before they know the results of the interview at the one they like best. This may be an agonizing decision, but they must decide, particularly if it is late in the season. Principals need prompt decisions so that they will have time to offer the position to other applicants if their first choice declines.

Being Successful in the First Position

Most people will agree that the first three years of teaching are the hardest. During these years you learn so much from your teaching experience. You have more intense preparation for your classes during the first year since you are doing it for the first time. Teaching becomes easier each successive year because you learn how to organize so that you become more efficient with your time; you learn how to motivate the students so that discipline ceases to be such a great challenge; you begin to understand and learn how to work within the system to accomplish what you want; and you learn how to deal more successfully with the administration, parents, and the school board. Many other responsibilities become easier with experience as well.

Most beginning teachers contemplate quitting at least once during the first three years they teach and some think about it almost every day. Their rationale is that if teaching is going to be so stressful there is no way that they can spend the remainder of their lives doing it. There will be times that you will not want to get out of bed and face the day. I have one very sound bit of advice to offer. Stick with it for at least three years, and then if you wake up every morning wishing you were dead, look for another profession. Chances are, if you have not learned to love it in three years, you never will. On the other hand, you are being completely unfair with yourself if you "cash it all in" before you give yourself time to "learn the ropes". When you consider the years of study, time, and investment you have made in your preparation and the number of family, friends, and students who are depending upon your success, it seems foolish not to give it your best effort.

Students who graduate with a music teaching degree but fear their first job also should heed this advice. Often they look for different employment that does not offer such a challenge. Here again, if you are in this category, you are being unfair to yourself. Most teachers who make it through the first three years usually become very happy and make a career of teaching.

PROFESSIONAL COMMITMENT—TO STAY OR TO LEAVE, THAT IS THE QUESTION!

In traveling and holding workshops throughout the United States, it has become apparent to me why private schools are proliferating on a daily basis like growth cells in a newborn. There are many public schools, particularly in large cities, whose personnel are doing very little teaching because they are buried in bureaucracy or cannot function due to a multitude of problems. Some parents feel that if their children are to receive an education, they must pay for it and demand results from their investment.

One of the biggest problems is flight to the suburbs and neighboring communities. The primary reason for the flight is that the parents do not feel that the schools are educating the students. They feel that teachers are wasting the taxpayers' money. They also feel that the primary reason so little teaching occurs is because there is inadequate discipline in the classroom. The principle reason students go to school—to learn—simply does not happen.

Why cannot the teachers control their classes? Many of the solutions to the problems, regrettably, are out of the teachers' hands, although some parents perceive the teachers as the basis for the problems. They feel that the teachers are more interested in the weekend than the week. They think that teachers treat their work as a job, not as a profession. Perhaps teachers do not enjoy their work and they want to get away from it. Parents also feel that many teachers have never been taught how to teach. Parents conceive teachers to have been educated under the philosophy that holds that the students should have the right to total self-expression when, in reality, some parents feel that students cannot express themselves if they do not know themselves. To be able to teach, in many ways, is an inborn trait, but to be a master teacher takes developing special techniques learned from other master teachers. Some parents feel that teachers are not willing to pay the price it takes to become master teachers.

Further, the parents often feel that the students do not respect the teachers because the students do not sense that the teachers are truly concerned about their well-being. The parents accuse the teachers of not taking full advantage of the opportunities they had as students while in college. Ostensibly, as college students they spent four years earning grades and getting a degree instead of an education.

Teachers' jobs have changed dramatically over the last twenty-five years.[5] The public not only asks teachers to provide a good education but also to address significant, complex, and diverse social problems. Drugs, sex, violence, broken homes, and poverty manifested in the classroom mirror the affliction of all of society. Because two-earner couples head most middle-class homes, the children suffer from lack of attention without time from their parents to assist in homework or to attend PTO meetings. Moreover, the rapidly growing population of students from non-English-speaking households compounds the problem. P. Michael Timpane, president of Teachers College of Columbia University, supports the teachers in the struggle: "Society has taken the position that teachers ought to succeed with everybody: the economically disadvantaged, racial minorities, and the handicapped. No one took those issues seriously a generation ago."[6]

Working material and equipment are battered or nonexistent in many school systems, a situation tolerated in no other profession. One can only imagine the response of the public if doctors, lawyers, or other professionals asked them to use similar equipment. If those professionals rendered their services in an environment resembling that of the public schools, the public would be outraged.

Psychologists now classify teaching as a high-stress profession. Coffee breaks, a full hour for lunch, and a few moments to chat leisurely with colleagues are privileges of the past in some school situations. It is not unusual for teachers to arrive at 7:00 A.M. and leave at 3:00 P.M., during which time they teach six classes, grade papers, prepare lessons, have a round of hall duty, grab a sandwich at their desk, and call parents to discuss discipline problems or schoolwork. This daytime schedule, often followed by two hours of work at home at night, is so hectic that there are days when the last-period bell rings and they realize that they have yet had time to go to the bathroom.

Burnout is rampant. Over half of all new teachers leave the profession within three years. The percentage is higher among minorities who frequently work in schools with the most complex social and academic problems. Many students who graduate with a teaching major never even bother to get a teaching certificate, and from those students who do certify and begin teaching, only about a third of them teach a second year.

Low salaries cause some teachers to leave the profession and prevent others from choosing to join it. During the 1970s salaries in many professions soared upwardly but teachers actually lost about 15 percent of their overall earning power. In the late 1980s some states' starting salaries were as low as $13,000 yearly. Some teachers' salaries were somewhat better with earnings of nearly $50,000 after thirty years, but that was still less than their children's starting salaries if they were engineers.

---

[5] Some which follows in this section is a summary of information taken from the excellent article by Susan Tifft (reported by D. Blake Hallanan, San Francisco; Michael Mason, Tunica; and Janice C. Simpson, New York), "Who's Teaching Our Children?" *Time* 132, no. 20 (November 14, 1988), 58.

[6] Ibid., 59.

Another contributor to the poor status of American public education is the administrative structure of most systems. Many decisions affecting school operations are still made from the top. Some administrators make it clear that teachers should hold back students only once and then promote them to the next grade, regardless of performance. Due to bureaucratic encumbrances there are days in which students languish in unsupervised classrooms waiting for the staff to find an authorized substitute. Some students completely disappear before a substitute arrives. Dealing with this inept bureaucratic confusion makes some teachers feel completely powerless in their ability to take control of their teaching responsibility.

Some states have enacted tougher training requirements for teachers, including minimum college grade point averages. While many teachers applaud these changes with the hope that they will help attract higher caliber students to the profession, some veteran educators feel that standardized competency tests, such as the National Teachers Examination, cannot predict success in the classroom. To many teachers, this additional teacher testing shows the weakness of a system that makes all the major decisions at the top, in some cases as high as the state legislature. Ernest Boyer, president of the Carnegie Foundation for the Advancement of Teaching said: "Whatever is wrong with America's schools cannot be fixed without the help of those inside the classroom."[7]

The loss of teachers from the profession is further compounded by the high retirement rate of teachers, expanding career options for college graduates, more rigorous certification requirements, and competency testing of professionals already teaching.

Many college and university music departments have declined in enrollment even though statistics indicate that Americans love music and are avid consumers of the art. Almost half of all American households contain at least one amateur musician. To keep music an effective discipline in public schools, universities, and colleges, teachers must adapt their curriculum to fit the needs of the public.

Unless choral directors teach in the inner city or in a rural area where poverty is severe, they may never have to face some of the extreme conditions in American public schools. There are more subtle, persevering difficulties, however, with which most choral directors contend on a daily basis that constantly affect the progress of quality teaching and learning. Many of these concerns are persistently chipping away at the aspects of the choral process that many directors cherish. These are topics of conversation in the teachers' lounge or around the coffee table at state conventions and meetings that almost everyone would like to change, but few, as individuals, have the power to do so.

The general status of choral music in the schools concerns many choral directors. In general, there appears to be a lack of interest in the history of our culture and very little respect for art or for the lessons we learned from the past. There is fear concerning the trend away from the use of traditional choral literature such as music of master composers and authentic folk-song arrangements that incorporate the accepted four-part voicing and sound. The

[7] Ibid.

trend appears to be toward arrangements that use current popular music styles of writing and voicings that do not provide what many teachers consider to be the "beautiful choral sound" that has been a part of the tradition since the Middle Ages. Entertainment, not education, is the primary motivation for the choral programs of many choral directors. Costumes, sound equipment, lighting, software, and fund-raising dominate the exhibit areas at the MENC conferences. Since publishers must make a profit to stay in business, they are flooding the market with new issues of current, popular media-music. Due to lack of storage space and a slower return for their investment, they are unwilling to keep the slower-selling, older copyrighted, more traditional music in stock. The philosophy of placing entertainment practices over educational goals and the problem of publishers' persistent search to seek new and different pieces to capture the attention of their clientele constitute the two main influences that are effecting change from traditional practices.

The declining participation of the male singer in choral groups throughout the country is also a concern. Some young men discontinue participation in vocal music when they enter middle/junior high school because of the prevailing idea that music is for girls and they do not want "to blow their macho image" by being in choir. There are directors who feel that the teaching field no longer attracts enough men. The only teachers some boys have are female, a situation that compounds the problem of male participation, particularly in choral music.

Television, compact discs, and tape cassettes bombard young people with Madison Avenue glitz to the point that attending a live amateur music concert no longer seems to be appealing. Subsequently, presenting and participating in live amateur choral concerts at school, in the church, or on choir tour apparently do not have the appeal to today's young singer as in the recent past. The number of touring senior high school and church choirs has declined significantly over the last twenty years primarily due to the lack of interest in membership in these groups (particularly in church youth choirs). Some directors feel that the spirit of volunteerism and altruism is waning in our society. The "don't get involved" syndrome that once pervaded the society, particularly in the large cities, has affected the participation of young people in worthwhile community, school, and church organizations.

Increased interest in athletics is of vital concern to many choral directors. "Spectator emphasis, competition, need of an outlet for aggressive feelings, and Super-Bowl mania all contribute to young men [and young women] thinking that the only way to excel is through sports."[8]

In many quarters, the arts have suffered financially. The federal government has cut back in support, expecting state governments to take up the slack, but many state governments have not done so. Through private donations, some corporations, businesses, and individuals have been helpful, but not nearly enough to equal the strength of art's support in the recent past.

Some choral teachers believe that in the remedial policies to improve

[8] Leonard Van Camp, "Current Status of U.S. Secondary and College/University Groups and Male Participation," Part 2, *Choral Journal* 29, no. 5 (December 1988), 6.

education, reformers have overlooked the arts. The national thrust to improve Scholastic Aptitude Tests (SAT), American College Testing Program (ACT), and other standardized test scores places such strong emphasis on intellectual/verbal skills that teachers of the arts feel the importance of the emotion/feeling/appreciation aspects of the individual will be ignored.

Why, then, under the conditions I just described, would you as a prospective teacher (or practicing professional) desire to teach choral music? Believe it or not, I have not painted this dismal picture to discourage you, not at all! Rather, I have presented this description of the way things really are to challenge you. The current negative public image, low professional esteem, and lack of high regard for the teaching profession does not have to continue. I challenge each of you to commit your youth, vitality, energy, and intellect to changing the perilous direction of American public education. You have the power to change it. All you need is the desire!

Believe it or not, your job may be easier, in many ways, than it was for those who went before you. Teachers' salaries have always been low when compared to other professions. Classroom control has always been a problem to some teachers. The effect of society's ills has always influenced the teachers' workplaces (granted, those ills certainly are more severe than in the recent past). In most cases, teachers have never had enough money to equip the classroom properly for maximum results. The buildings and working environment, in many places, have always been substandard when compared to other professions. Generally, Americans have always supported capitalism over education. There is, however, one condition that existed until now with which, according to current trends, you may not have to deal—and it has been as big, if not a bigger problem than all the woes described thus far: apathy! Until now, very few really cared!

The situation has finally deteriorated to the point that Americans are realizing something must be done. Therefore, your job will be easier because you do not have to awaken the sleeping giant. He is already yawning. From all accounts, you may be living and working in a time in which great change and innovation may occur. Furthermore, you may be in a position in which you may be able to effect that change tremendously.

What I have described represents the extremes of what is wrong with the society and public education. It is still possible to find excellent teaching environments in many parts of the country, places where the educational process is superb and where teachers as well as students are making significant contributions to all of knowledge. One cannot, however, afford to soft-pedal the situation. It is a fact that the condition of public education is precarious.

There are times in the lives of each teacher when we soberly have asked ourselves the question, why teach? As promising young educators, you, too, will ponder that question several times in your career. At times nothing will have gone well, times when the students have asked ten thousand useless questions that you have answered a million different ways already, times when you feel that you will pull out your hair if they miss that same group of notes just one more time, times when you feel the pressure of contest or that spring concert and there are not enough hours in the day to get the job done, and times in which you have dealt with many of those problems previously described in this chapter. Why teach? Why submit yourselves to such physical discomfort?

Many of the great rewards from teaching are certainly intangible. Those intangible remunerations, however, drew us to the profession and keep us committed to it. Why teach? We know the answer to the question when, at the end of the term, we sit down in that easy chair and contemplate the accomplishments of the year. We think about how much the young singers have grown. We remember on the first day of class we greeted a cute, sandy-haired boy soprano or a curly-haired, dark-skinned boy alto who on the last day of class said goodbye in a crackling, but soon to be resonant, baritone voice. We think about the personal problems many of the students encountered and how they overcame them. We think about how many notes that were taught and how many that were missed. Then we truly know the answer to the question.

I submit to you as teachers and future teachers of adolescent singers that your responsibility is more than teaching notes. It is more than teaching music. Parents have entrusted to you the lives of their adolescents during the most strategic periods of their development. Even though their bodies and voices are developing, they are developing attitudes, attitudes that will remain with them the rest of their lives.

In the first part of this section rather harsh accusations were levied against some of America's teachers. They were accused of being more interested in the weekend than the week, of thinking about their teaching as a job rather than a profession. It should have been obvious why many of these perspectives abide as we have examined the condition of American public education. If we take the responsibility to develop wholesome, positive attitudes within our own students, we will possibly be well on our way to alleviating many of the negative attitudes prevalent today by the next generation.

As a prospective teacher or practicing professional, how can you counter-act the degeneration of the public's image of the teacher? Here are a few suggestions:

1. Be vitally concerned with the well-being of your students.
2. Be willing to give 100 percent to your profession.
3. Attempt to improve your teaching technique daily.
4. Realize that you do not have all the answers and that you must rely on master teachers to find the answers.
5. Take the teaching responsibility as a divine calling; that is, realize that teaching is your purpose for living, that, literally, you have been born to teach.

If, as we have examined the perils, problems, and challenges of the teaching profession, it has been difficult for you to feel comfortable with the responsibilities that it will take for you to be a good teacher and to contribute to the profession, I suggest you reexamine the reason you chose to teach. More than anything, the profession needs committed teachers. We need for the public to restore the trust that at one time was such a vital part of our profession, so that when people pass us on the street they will say; "There goes a master teacher!"

To those of you now enrolled in a college or university course of study preparing to be teachers of choral music, please allow me to make some suggestions to set the stage for your later success as a teacher:

1. Arrive on time each day expecting to be taught, yes, even begging to be taught.
2. Expect to feel cheated if you cannot attend every class period.
3. Realize that the professor is the authority in the class, having paid the price of years of preparation and experience, and that he or she is there to help you be the best teacher you can possibly be.
4. Ask when you do not know.
5. Be prepared for class in whatever way is explained to you.
6. Expect to take every class seriously as if your life depended upon it because, in reality, your professional life indeed does.

As the sleeping giant of education begins to sit up, stretch, and flex his muscles, one of the most exciting times in the history of education is about to unfold. It is easy to contemplate all the problems of the profession and become disillusioned. On the other hand, when we consider the possibilities that the future undoubtedly holds due to this "great awakening," it is also easy to become very excited about being a part of it. That which should prompt the flow of adrenalin in your veins is that you can contribute significantly to the final results. Yours is going to be an exciting time. Relish every experience.

THOUGHTS FOR CONTEMPLATION AND DISCUSSION

1. What problems do you foresee in planning a one-week tour with your Advanced Choir? With the administration? With the parents? With the students?
2. Think about the contests in which the senior high choir with whom you sang participated. Now that you are older, do you feel that they were beneficial? Why or why not?
3. Is it possible for adjudicators in contest to be completely objective in their attempt to evaluate the choirs they judge?
4. Think of as many ways as possible to investigate a school system before applying for a position there.
5. What responsibilities and obligations do you have as a choral director to the entire profession at large?
6. If the system where you will teach has a teacher's union, do you plan to join? Why or why not?
7. Do you think the grades you will give your students will affect your popularity

as a teacher? If so, what are the problems inherent in the grading process? How do you think the profession should deal with these problems?

8. Do you plan to advise students relative to their personal problems? To their vocational choices? If so, since you are a choral teacher, how do you plan to justify that type of counseling to the school counselor? To the principal? To the students' parents? If not, how do you justify not taking a responsibility for the personal well-being of your students?

9. Do you feel that students should be charged special fees to cover nonbudgeted departmental needs? If so, will you eliminate students from the choral program who cannot afford the fee? If you would not eliminate them, how would you deal with the problem?

10. How will you deal with students who cannot attend performances because they must work?

BIBLIOGRAPHY

BESSOM, MALCOLM E. *Supervising the Successful School Music Program.* West Nyack, N.Y.: Parker Publishing Co., 1969.

BESSOM, MALCOLM E., ALPHONSE TATARUNIS, and SAMUEL L. FORCUCCI. *Teaching Music in Today's Secondary Schools,* 2d ed. New York: Holt, Rinehart and Winston, 1980.

BOYLE, J. DAVID, and RUDOLF E. RADOCY. *Measurement and Evaluation of Musical Experiences.* New York: Schirmer Books, 1987.

COLLINS, DON L. *The Cambiata Concept, a Comprehensive Philosophy and Methodology of Teaching Music to Adolescents.* Conway, Ark.: Cambiata Press, 1981.

COLWELL, RICHARD. *The Evaluation of Music Teaching and Learning.* Englewood Cliffs, N.J.: Prentice Hall, Inc., 1970.

COOPER, IRVIN, and KARL O. KURSTEINER. *Teaching Junior High School Music,* 2d ed. Conway, Ark.: Cambiata Press, 1973.

DEUTSCH, DIANA. *The Psychology of Music.* New York: Academic Press, 1982.

EDELSON, EDWARD. *The Secondary School Music Program from Classroom to Concert Hall.* West Nyack, N.Y.: Parker Publishing Co., 1972.

GALLUP, A., and D. CLARK. "The 19th Annual Gallup Poll of the Public's Attitudes Toward the Public Schools." *Phi Delta Kappan* 69, no. 1 (1987).

HOFFER, CHARLES R. *Teaching Music in the Secondary Schools,* 4th ed. Belmont, Calif,: Wadsworth Publishing, 1991.

JIPSON, WAYNE R. *The High School Vocal Music Program.* West Nyack, N.Y.: Parker Publishing Co., 1972.

KOWALL, BONNIE C., ed. *Perspectives in Music Education, Source Book III.* Reston, Va.: Music Educators National Conference, 1966.

LAMB, GORDON H. *Choral Techniques,* 3d ed. Dubuque, Iowa: Wm. C. Brown Co., 1988.

LEHMAN, PAUL R. *Music in Today's Schools: Rationale and Commentary.* Reston, Va.: Music Educators National Conference, 1987.

LEONHARD, CHARLES and ROBERT W. HOUSE. *Foundations and Principles of Music Education,* 2d ed. New York: McGraw-Hill Book Co., 1972.

MARPLE, HUGO D. *Backgrounds and Approaches to Junior High Music.* Dubuque, Iowa: Wm. C. Brown Co., 1975.

MILLER, GEORGE A. *Communication, Language, and Meaning.* New York: Basic Books, 1973.

MILLER, KENNETH E. *Vocal Music Education, Teaching in the Secondary Schools.* Englewood Cliffs, N.J.: Prentice-Hall, Inc., 1988.

NEIDIG, KENNETH L., and JOHN JENNINGS, eds. *Choral Director's Guide.* West Nyack, N.Y.: Parker Publishing Co., 1967.

ROE, PAUL F. *Choral Music Education,* 2d ed. Englewood Cliffs, N.J.: Prentice Hall, Inc., 1983.

SERAFINE, MARY LOUISE. *Music as Cognition.* New York: Columbia University Press, 1988.

SHUTER, ROSAMUND. *The Psychology of Musical Ability.* London: Methuen and Co., Ltd., 1968.

SIGMAN, MATTHEW. "A Serious Look at Serious Music Publishing." *Music Educators Journal* 74, no. 7 (March 1988).

SINGLETON, IRA. *Music in Secondary Schools,* 2d ed. Boston: Allyn and Bacon, Inc., 1965.

SLOBODA, JOHN A. *The Musical Mind.* Oxford: Clarendon Press, 1985.

STRIKE, KENNETH A., and JONAS F. SOLTIS. *The Ethics of Teaching.* New York: Teachers College Press, Columbia University, 1985.

"Study Backs Induction Schools to Help New Teachers Stay Teachers." *Update* 20, no. 4 (1987).

TIFFT, SUSAN. "Who's Teaching Our Children?" *Time* 132, no. 20 (November 14, 1988).

"Trends: Teachers Suffer Stress Around the World." *Today's Education* 70 (1981).

VAN CAMP, LEONARD. "Current Status of U.S. Secondary and College/University Groups and Male Participation, Part II." *Choral Journal* 29, no. 5 (December, 1988).

18

The Choral Environment: Building and Buying for Learning

Americans tend to equate quality in any endeavor with the state of a program's environment. Relative to choral music education, if choral directors have a fine choral room with plentiful materials and equipment, the perception is that they must have a first-class program. We all know that the people in the program are the chief contributors to quality teaching and learning. However, fine facilities and equipment certainly enhance directors' chances of developing and providing a quality choral program. Students tend to take greater pride in their choral organizations if they are housed in good facilities and if the teachers have enough equipment to support quality teaching.

Beginning teachers often feel uncomfortable approaching their principal with a wish list of equipment and materials. Such should not be the case because principals generally understand the importance of sufficient materials and equipment for effective teaching. If requests are denied it is usually because principals are not allotted the budgetary means by the school board to provide everything directors desire, not because the principals think that the requests are unnecessary.

PREPARING THE MUSIC BUDGET

Each school district determines how their funds will be distributed, so teachers must become acquainted with that process before they can prepare their first

472

budget. Many large districts have a central music budget under the control of the music supervisor. Others have individual school music budgets under the auspices of each school principal. Principals in small, rural districts may not even have a special line item for music, so the music teachers must inform the principals of their needs and the principals are responsible for finding the money to make the purchases. If beginning teachers obtain their first job in such a small, rural district, it is their responsibility to help the principal understand the importance of establishing a music budget (no matter how small).

Since the Depression, inflation has been an accepted entity in budget preparation. If over several years, directors do not request an annual increase to offset inflation, they will find it more and more difficult to operate on their allotted funds. It is important to gather current sales prices for everything directors must purchase to account for inflation. It is better to increase the budget in small increments annually than it is to stay even year after year and to expect a large increase at some future point.

Directors must realize that no one has all the money they desire to operate any department in public or private education. Therefore, it is essential that directors operate the choral department in an efficient, prudent, and businesslike manner. Staying aware of the budgetary needs, showing sufficient justification of purchases (how they benefit the students and the entire educational process), and making long-range plans will facilitate efficiency. Nothing succeeds like success, and administrators are aware of this. They tend to support the choral department if the directors have successful programs.

Budgetary items fall into two categories: those items that must be purchased each year and those items that are only purchased occasionally. Annual budgetary needs include (1) new music for each member of the choirs and other ensembles; (2) sight-reading and vocal-choral technique materials, filmstrips, audiotapes, videotapes, and compact discs; (3) cleaning and maintenance of singing attire; (4) tuning and maintenance of the pianos and other instruments; (5) professional dues and fees for directors and ensembles (conferences, workshops, festivals, clinics, and so forth); and (6) travel. Budgetary items to be purchased over several years are (1) choir folders and storage cabinets; (2) choir robes and other singing attire; (3) choir room performance and rehearsal equipment such as risers, chairs, bulletin boards, music stands, chalkboards, and choral shells; (4) audio and video recording and playback equipment; and (5) pianos and other classroom instruments. Directors should devise long-range plans for supplying and replacing these items over several years.

Consult Chapter 17 ("Nonbudgetary Financial Support") for information about obtaining funds for the choral department when they are not forthcoming from tax revenue.

PHYSICAL FACILITIES AND EQUIPMENT

Teaching materials and equipment necessary to run a successful choral department were delineated in the preceding section on preparing the music budget. Following is a guide for ordering these materials and equipment. After the guide, I have provided necessary information for building facilities to house a choral department. This will be helpful information when directors have the responsibility of making such recommendations to a building planning committee.

A Guide for Ordering Music, Materials, and Equipment

The Music Industry Conference (MIC), an auxiliary of the Music Educators National Conference, is one of the choral teachers' best friends because the organization serves as a liaison between music educators and the manufacturing and publishing firms that supply music, materials, and equipment for music education. The leading manufacturing and publishing firms in the industry are members of the MIC which they support with their membership dues.

The Business of Publishing Educational Music   Compared to most other industries, educational music publishing is very small. Even though many of the companies have gross sales of several million dollars annually, they are indeed small when one compares them to some U.S. corporations whose gross sales are in the billions of dollars. Recently, as it has been with several other facets of the music education profession, the music industry has suffered financially because of the shifting of school and governmental funds away from arts and education. Extensive growth of technology-intensive industries such as computer and photocopy machine manufacturing also has contributed to publishers' problems to the extent that some publishers have gone out of business or have been acquired by larger corporations. Nonetheless, there is still a significant amount of educational publishing occurring. In fact, over the last several years publishers have released more new issues of choral music each year than at any other time in the history of music education. Most publishers of serious choral music are privately owned and operated and experience only marginal profit. In spite of their profit-making status, publishers of serious music usually see themselves as existing not simply to make money but to be guardians and propagators of the choral art with the role of protecting composers' and arrangers' livelihood and preserving their talent. Most publishing executives are trained musicians who care about their product, who love music, and who often feel more compensated by the quality of their product than their paycheck.

For years choral music publishers were located on the East Coast, particularly around New York. Serious choral music has been the primary product from such companies as Theodore Presser, Belwin-Mills, G. Schirmer, Carl Fischer, C. F. Peters, Boosey and Hawkes, Lawson-Gould Music Publishers, Galaxy Music Corporation, Oxford University Press, and others for several generations. Because of xerography millions of illegal copies of music are photocopied each year and because of the prevalence of choral arrangements of media-music or music with a contemporary popular sound, these great landmark publishing institutions either (1) have been acquired by larger conglomerates, (2) have curtailed their operations significantly, or (3) have begun to rely on distributing music for other publishers, performance music rental, or retail sales to remain solvent. On the other hand, publishers who emphasize a more commercial product such as Hal Leonard Publications (Milwaukee), Jenson Publications, Inc. (New Berlin, Wis.), Columbia Pictures Publications (Miami, Fla.), Shawnee Press, (Delaware Water Gap, Penn.), and the Lorenz Corporation (Dayton, Ohio) have experienced phenomenal growth and now dominate the print music sales in the choral market.

All publishers depend upon a network of retailers such as J. W. Pepper and Son, Inc. (Valley Forge, Penn.), Southern Music Company (San Antonio), and Malecki Music (Grand Rapids, Mich.), to name just three of many, throughout the United States to assist in getting their music to choral directors for review. Before the mid-1960s most music sales were handled through a music retailer. The publishers tried to assure that a copy of all their new issues were in the browse boxes of dealers, large or small, throughout the land, and most major retailers stocked multiple copies so that directors could buy them while in the store. In the early 1970s the number of educational choral music publishers began to proliferate and existing publishers began to release larger amounts of new issues each year. Due to lack of space for storage and limited funds to invest in products that often sold very slowly, soon it became impossible for the retailers to stock multiple copies of such a mass amount of music. Gradually the system of distribution began to change. Some publishers began sending directors complimentary copies of their new releases and bypassed the retailer by promoting retail sales directly from the publishers themselves. The mail-order discount distributer emerged. These were retailers who did not stock the music of the publishers nor maintain facilities for doing so, but sold the music at ten to twenty percent off list price and had it sent to the choral director directly from the publisher. During the 1980s competition became even more aggressive. Many publishers, particularly those who sold arrangements of media-music and contemporary church music, recorded their new releases on cassette tapes or records and either distributed them through special membership or library plans or by sending complimentary recordings and score booklets through the mail to choral directors. Companies with the more competitive means of distribution have emerged as leaders in the sales of educational music. Tragically, many of the publishers of the more serious, art music have been unable to meet the demands of such competition and thus the market is flooded with arrangements of media-music (or original compositions with similar sounds), leaving a dearth of new releases of the more stable, traditional types.

When one considers the number of years many of these traditional publishers have been in business and the contributions they have made to the profession, it seems almost cataclysmic to think that they may be disappearing or that the role they have played for generations may be changing. Even more tragic is that their quality product may disappear as well. Matthew Sigman, assistant editor of *Symphony Magazine*, examines this trend in detail in a fascinating article published in *Music Educators Journal*.[1] It would behoove all serious music

---

[1] Matthew Sigman, "A Serious Look at Serious Music Publishing," *Music Educators Journal* 74, no. 7 (March 1988), 39–48.

educators to read the article to learn about the background, status, and tradition of these giants of the industry and the repercussions of their dilemma.

Helpful Suggestions When Ordering Music Materials and Equipment[2]   To receive full benefit of the services of any company in the music industry, choral directors' names, addresses, and schools must appear on the companies' mailing lists. Whenever directors take a new position, they should write to the music publishers and ask that their names be placed on the publishers' mailing lists. Addresses and phone numbers of the companies my be obtained from the Music Industry Conference by contacting MENC headquarters in Reston, Virginia. It is quite acceptable to use a form letter, but directors should attempt to use school stationery whenever possible. This assures the company that the position is legitimate. Directors should include the following information in the letter: (1) the director's full name, home address, Zip Code, and telephone number (i.e., Courtney LeeAnn Kelly, 1111 Ashdown Place, Narrow Gap, Maine, 76543-0404, 101-202-3030); (2) the full name, address, Zip Code, and telephone number of the school (i.e., Red Lobster High School, 2222 Mapleup Curve, Wider Gap, Maine, 75432-0505, 101-303-4040); (3) the director's position title (Director of Choral Activities, Supervisor of Music, General Music Instructor); (4) the place of the director's previous employment (formerly located at Jones High School in Jonesville, Idaho); (5) the name of the previous director at the current position (successor in Wider Gap to Zackory Allen Kelly); (6) special interests (choral music, instruction booklets, robes, risers, general music class materials); and (7) an indication if the company should send application forms for a personal or a school charge account. Soon the director will start receiving the basic tools needed for purchasing: catalogs, price lists, information about new materials, and complimentary copies of music, cassettes, or records.

It is also good to become personally acquainted with representatives from the favorite companies. On occasions, directors may desire to make an order by telephone; many of the companies have Wide Area Telephone Service (WATS lines). At that time, directors may take the opportunity to get better acquainted. Most of the members of the MIC maintain exhibit booths at state, regional, and national Music Educators National Conference and American Choral Directors Association conventions. Directors should visit their booths to meet the representatives and become better acquainted with their products. Technology changes and trends emerge very quickly in today's society, so a brief visit to an exhibit often can pay high dividends in improving classroom teaching technique.

When corresponding with businesses, to expedite better service directors should remember: (1) type the letters whenever possible; (2) letters that are legible, concise, and well organized receive immediate attention, while office workers may set aside letters requiring deciphering or further correspondence,

---

[2] These helpful hints are provided by the Music Industry Conference, an auxiliary of the Music Educators National Conference, 1902 Association Drive, Reston, VA 22091; 703-860-4000 and are published in a special supplement in the *Music Educators Journal* 74, No. 7 (March 1988), S3–S31.

often creating a service delay of several days; (3) use personal professional letterhead or school stationery (for business purposes) whenever possible; (4) whenever letterhead stationery is unavailable, directors should include their full name, city, state, Zip Code, and official position; (5) directors should always sign letters in the same fashion each time they correspond; and (6) avoid multipurpose letters in which they include several unrelated items of business in a single communication such as a rush order, a payment on account, and a request for information about other materials; three brief memoranda in one envelope, each addressed to the proper department such as Order Department, Correspondence, or Cashier, will assure that workers complete all three transactions.

Directors often do not receive prompt service because they do not follow proper ordering procedures. To avoid frustrating delays, directors should consider the following:

1. Refer to the company's catalog. Give the catalog number, specifying exact page(s) where they may find the item.

2. Music and materials are not immune to price changes. It is wise to obtain the latest price change whenever possible. This usually eliminates confusion and delays when the school accounts office attempts to pay the bill. If the catalog the director is using is not current, it might be well to give the company a call to get up-dated prices.

3. List and check titles and names carefully.

4. If the director's school or school system has a purchasing department or specifically requires administrative approval of orders, directors should notify the company to that effect. The director should use proper purchasing procedures and provide the purchasing department with complete and correct purchasing information.

5. Directors should be specific in the shipping instructions. They should include exactly where and to whom the company should send the materials, where and to whom they should send the bill, if it is different from the receiver of the materials, and the carrier (parcel post, United Parcel Service, or other methods) they should use.

6. Occasionally a firm will have three or more charge accounts for one individual (for example, a school account, a personal account, and a church account where he or she might serve in a part-time capacity). Directors should be very specific as to which account they are using.

7. Often directors desire to see the merchandise before ordering. This necessitates an on-approval order. Directors should be just as specific with these orders as they are when they dispense permanent orders. If directors do not know exactly what they want to see, a phone call may be better because they can describe their needs and ascertain exactly what is available from the company.

8. After the approval materials arrive, directors should decide as soon as possible what they desire to purchase. Materials sent for inspection remain on approval for only a specified length of time. Companies charge the materials to the customer's account but they do not send a bill until after the approval period has elapsed. Companies credit the materials returned within the specified period and do not send the customer the bill.

9. Unlike printed materials, when customers return some items such as recordings or cassettes, the company cannot resell them commercially. They have to destroy them and charge the customer; therefore, customers must ask what materials may or may not be available on approval.

10. If directors receive approval material from several different sources simultaneously, they must keep the materials separated. Confusion results when companies receive returned material which does not belong to them.

11. Following is a list of instructions directors should follow when returning material to a company:[3]

    A. Check with the supplier or manufacturer about procedures, authorizations, requirements, and special instructions for returning merchandise. Pack it well so that the material may reach its destination without damage or loss.

    B. Address the package plainly and accurately. Be sure to include a return address on the package so that the company will know exactly who made the shipment and from where it came.

    C. If directors charge the material to their account, they should write the name (and number, if they know it) of the account on the package so that the company will properly identify it and make the correct adjustment.

    D. When they send the package they should write a letter telling the receiver (a) what the package contains, (b) why they are sending it, (c) what they want the company to do about it, (d) the date they are sending it, and (e) the carrier they are using.

    E. They should not enclose any written correspondence in a parcel post package. According to strictly enforced postal regulations, written communication of any kind automatically requires the full first-class rate for the entire package. The following three suggestions refer, in one application or another, to this rule.

    F. Customers may mail printed and manuscript music, phonograph recordings, tapes, and books at special rates if they clearly mark the package as "educational material" and if it contains no correspondence.

    G. A simple way to have a letter accompany the package to which it refers is to address, seal, and stamp it exactly as one would for a separate first-class mailing, then paste or cement it firmly to the outside of the package. The stamp must represent first-class postage for the letter alone; the package carries its own lower-rate postage.

    H. Enclose the original invoice or a copy of the invoice in the return package or include a copy in a first-class letter with any information that is important to the transaction.

    I. Companies recommend insurance on parcel post packages and adequate valuation of United Parcel Service and freight shipments as a worthwhile safeguard.

Choral Music   When ordering choral music, be sure to include the voicing (SATB, SAB, SSCB, and so forth). When ordering from a source that carries publications of more than one publisher, do not order by number only: give the title,

---

[3] Ibid., p. S7.

composer, voice arrangement, arranger, number, and publisher. Customers should order larger works that require orchestral accompaniment according to the type that is available from the publisher. Some publishers sell the accompaniments outright; others make them available through rental only. Directors should specify keys of solo voice selections (high, medium, or low designations). Sometimes distributors erroneously report music out of print. It is best to check directly with the publisher if directors receive such a message.

Robes and Other Singing Attire When ordering choir robes or special travel or performance uniforms, it is best to call the manufacturer or the regional representatives who can provide the director with the requirements and specifications for their product. They also can provide catalogs and other beneficial literature. Directors should determine if the firm they choose will continue service after the first big order. Some firms do not want fill-in orders. It is a good idea to take the sample product to a reputable tailor in the community and request an unbiased evaluation of the quality of work and material.

Since uniform and robe manufacturing is a very specialized business with fluctuating costs, most manufacturers price their uniforms and robes from their home office. Purchasers should write out detailed specifications that will allow several manufacturers to bid on the same robe or uniform. Purchasers should request a stock sample as close to their specifications as possible and one they can examine for quality of construction and best price. After directors make their decision, they can ask the manufacturer of their choice to submit a special sample of their exact specifications. Then they can place the order contingent on the purchaser's approval and acceptance.

Keyboard Instruments When purchasing keyboard instruments (usually pianos), in most cases, directors must determine their choices by the exact function the instrument must fulfill (rehearsals, concerts, orchestra accompaniment, and so forth) and the funds available for its purchase. Important in the directors' purchase plans are: (1) payment schedules, either lease, with or without purchase option, or installment purchase (with interest charges separately disclosed); (2) written minimum warranty with Underwriter's Laboratory approval on electrical items; (3) installation, service, and maintenance facilities; (4) cost and availability of local contractual service and maintenance; (5) delivery schedule and total transportation and delivery charges; and (6) consultant services.

In the purchase of pianos, local dealers are important. They will be the contact with the manufacturer, a source of service, and often a source of experienced advice. When bids specify a group of proprietary features, they always should include the invitation for substitute bids for equal products. It is always wise to send a copy of the bid to the manufacturer or dealer whose product is specified. Alternate bids submitted in this way can offer advantages not contemplated in early considerations.

Computer Hardware and Software[4]   Rapidly developing technology makes ordering computer hardware and software very difficult. Directors must keep abreast of today's hardware technologies and software development. They must be in communication with the computer specialist in their school and make periodic trips to the local computer outlets in their area. Reviewing new software is as important as looking for new performance music. Software products are available for review at conferences and at many music stores. Some music dealers will allow directors to review products at their own school, and many programs have preview diskettes available. Directors should be specific and accurate in making their orders. Allow plenty of time for the software to arrive. Possibly, because of the fast growing technology, dealers may have to special order what directors need.

Recordings, Cassettes, and Compact Discs   Another rapidly changing technology which requires directors constant attention to stay informed is the recording business. Only a few years ago monophonic and stereophonic records were the primary media for recorded educational music. Now stereo cassettes, representing the largest sales of all sound reproduction, have taken over the market. However, compact discs are rising fast and according to most accounts will be the leading technology of the future. In any case, last year's catalog is obsolete. Directors must refer to current catalogs to be fully cognizant of the latest offerings in this field. When placing an order, be sure to include the manufacturer's name, catalog number, title, and performing artist for positive identification. Allow plenty of time for their arrival.

Rehearsal and Performance Equipment   When directors need to purchase music equipment for the rehearsal or performance area, they must plan to allow time for catalogs from the various manufacturers to arrive. Write or call for catalogs in the spring before ordering in the summer for arrival of the merchandise in the fall. Consider the following when ordering this equipment:

1. **Portable risers**—*Considerations*: weight, stability, quietness, storage requirements, separate parts, portability, indoor or outdoor use, and number of performers per unit.

   Standing chorus: materials (plywood, plywood and steel, plywood and aluminum, aluminum); construction (folding, rollaway, modular, three-step, separate step); style (semicircular, rectangular); depth of step (13″, 16″, 18″); elevations (8″, 16″, 24″); and covering (plastic, rubber, or rubberlike tread, carpet, spray-on finish).

---

[4] Often teachers are not trained sufficiently to apply computer technology to the music classroom. Computer technology is very useful in teaching music fundamentals, composition, choral arranging, music appreciation, fine arts, and general music and in administrative, library, and office work. Please consult the entries in the chapter bibliography for necessary information about the use of computers in the music classroom.

Seated chorus: materials (aluminum, plywood, steel); construction, (folding, rollaway, modular); style (semicircular, rectangular); depth of step (32″ to 36″); and elevations (8″, 16″, 24″).

2. **Music cabinets and racks**—*Considerations*: conservation of space, systematic handling, quick and easy transfer from permanent file to folio and back, and protection of music.

   Specifications: type (storage, sorting, handling); materials (steel, wood); construction (rollaway, stationary but movable); styles (shelf type with separate compartments for each arrangement or regular steel file, letter or legal); and sizes (band, orchestra, chorus).

3. **Robe or uniform storage**—*Considerations*: whether uniforms or robes will be taken on trips, whether they will be worn only for performance, sturdiness, weight, and mobility.

   Specifications: materials (wood, metal) and construction (rollaway, movable).

4. **Conductor's furniture**—*Considerations*: stability; size; adjustability; quietness; portability; and attractiveness.

   Podium: materials (wood with plastic or carpet tread); construction (permanent, two-step or folding, for travel); and size (about 30″ by 8″ folding or 36″ by 16″ two-step).

   Conductor's stand: materials (steel, wood, aluminum); construction (adjustable height and tilt, mechanical or friction); desk size (14″ by 21″ to 19″ by 31″); and variations (with or without shelves and light, combination conductor's stand and rollaway folio cabinet).

   Conductor's chair: materials (steel and wood); construction (adjustable height, depth, back): style (with or without built-in podium and foot ring); and upholstery (leatherette in colors, foam cushions).

5. **Music stands**—*Considerations*: sturdiness, stability, adjustability, and portability.

   Specifications: material (steel, aluminum, fiberboard); construction (permanent, folding); styles (permanent, adjustable height and tilt); mechanical or friction; finish (plated, enameled, chrome); and color (charcoal, black, or other).

6. **Rehearsal chairs**—*Considerations*: sturdiness, stacking, weight, posture, and ability to remove.

   Specifications: materials (steel, wood, steel and wood); construction (permanent nonfolding, folding) and style (posture folding and unfolding, regular, or lowback).

7. **Acoustical shells**—*Considerations*: acoustical effectiveness, storage requirements, portability, adjustability, ease of setup and takedown, and attractiveness.

   Specifications: materials (wood, plastic); construction (portable or rollaway, modular, adjustable wings and canopy); and style (with or without overhead panels, with or without wings).

8. **Portable practice rooms**—*Considerations*: sound isolation, acoustical environment, self-contained, can be relocated, ease of supervision, and ease of setup.

   Specifications: materials (steel and glass, wood and glass, plastic and glass); construction (modular and demountable); size (approximately thirty square feet to ninety square feet); lighting (fluorescent fixtures, in excess of seventy foot-candles); ventilation (maintain ambient temperatures within the module); and sound qualities (minimum noise reduction module to module, approximately thirty-one to eighty-five decibels over frequencies 125 to 2000 Hz).

9. **Music folders**—*Considerations*: size (for octavos, booklets, or both); usage (rehearsal, performance, or both); pockets (with or without, size, place for pencil); attachments that hold the music (with or without, metal, elastic string); color; and material (vinyl, plastic, or leatherette).

The Choral Classroom

In both junior and senior high school, a choral suite should be built that contains a rehearsal hall, several practice rooms, an ensemble room, directors' office, and the choral library. The rehearsal hall should be designed specifically for choral rehearsals, although it may double for a classroom where general music, music appreciation/history, music theory, or fine arts are taught. The hall should be large enough to have an area for seats equipped with desks for writing (portable desks that will stack are recommended so that they may be moved to make room for physical activities) and a separate area for risers when standing to sing is required. The ceiling should be sixteen to twenty feet high, and there should be ample storage space (with doors) for texts, recorded materials, classroom instruments, and audiovisual equipment and a double-entry door. The hall should be equipped with a minimum of forty square feet of chalkboard (a large portion of which contains permanent music staff lines) and approximately twenty-four square feet of corkboard for bulletin board display.

Adjacent to the rehearsal hall should be one or more ensemble rehearsal rooms of at least 400 square feet and several individual practice rooms. The directors' office should be at least sixty square feet and should have a telephone and individual semiprivate office area for each teacher.

Due to the sound component of choral music, the suite should be located in an area away from the other classrooms and the instrumental suite and treated acoustically for proper sound dispersement and control. Each wall should have a sound transmission classification (STC) of fifty or more. Noise criterion (NC) levels of lighting and ventilating systems should not exceed NC25 for the rehearsal hall and NC30 for the smaller practice areas.

The School Auditorium

The school auditorium should be close to the choral suite. It should have a stage large enough to accommodate seated risers that will hold the combined membership of all the choirs and instrumental ensembles in the school. If this is not possible, the stage area (stage, orchestra pit, behind the orchestra pit, and floor level) should be designed to accommodate these groups (standing and sitting) for a massing of all participants in a musical festival. The auditorium should be designed for adjustable acoustics for music and speech requirements; stage lighting including a sufficient number of proscenium lights, footlights, floodlights, and spots; and appropriate ventilation and lighting systems not to exceed NC20. The stage should be equipped with numerous overhead nondirectional microphones (for both amplification and recording) evenly distributed to alleviate dead spots (places where sound will not be picked up).

THE CHORAL LIBRARY

Keeping a choral library organized in such a way that the music is accessible is often very time consuming. Since directors seldom have time to do all they desire, maintenance of the choral library may occupy a low position in their list of priorities, so all they do is purchase boxes or envelopes, write the names of the octavos on them, and put them away in alphabetical order. This process is highly disadvantageous if: (1) they need to choose a piece written by a specific composer, (2) they need a particular type of music (Christmas, Easter, sacred, secular, folk, madrigal, chamber work, pop, and so forth), or (3) they need a specific voicing (SA, SATB, SSCB, and so on); they will have to search through all the octavos in the library to find the one they desire. Thus they spend more time looking for music than it would take them to organize the library. Further, directors must move all the old music to make room for newly purchased pieces to add to their alphabetized music.

The best way to organize music is to place it in boxes (they take more room than envelopes but will hold more pieces), number them consecutively, and place them on shelves with doors (nothing makes a choir suite look more cluttered than boxes of choral music on open shelves). Indicate on the outside of each door the numbers found on each of the boxes therein.

The best way to keep track of the music is to enter the title, composer, arranger, voicing, type, and number of copies available into a computer program specifically designed for libraries. Several computer programs are available for the Commodore, Apple, IBM, and other personal computers.[5] If a computer is not available, a library filing card should be prepared in each of the above categories for each octavo in the library. This process will yield five different card files: title, composer, arranger, voicing, and type.

After directors have set up the filing system, the student librarian, if the choirs have officers, should be responsible for placing all the music in the boxes, numbering them, typing the library filing cards, and placing them in the proper file or entering them into the computer.

Copying Music

For many years American music educators and church musicians photocopied (Xeroxed) multiple copies of octavos and booklets because they did not realize that it was illegal to do so. Now, however, most educators understand the copyright law, yet some still persist in copying music illegally. Not only is it illegal, it is ethically and morally wrong! To do so is to rob the artists (composers and arrangers) and the publishers of money that is rightfully and legally theirs. In America, artists are paid for their creative work by receiving royalties from

[5] Check with the dealers and/or refer to these articles for valuable information about computer programs for the choral library: Doug Skerritt, "Choral Library for Computer File," *Choral Journal* 27, no. 2 (September 1986), 21–27; and Bob Dingley, "Choral Music Library Computer File for IBM and Compatible PC Version," *Choral Journal* 27, no. 10 (May 1987), 33–37.

each copy of music sold. When educators photocopy music and do not buy it, creative artists are deprived of their just recompense. Penalties for violating the revised Copyright Law of 1979 include a fine from $250 to $50,000, or two years in prison, or both. According to that law, the following practices are prohibited without written permission from the copyright owner:

1. Copying music to avoid purchase,
2. Copying music for any kind of performance (see exceptions that follow),
3. Copying without including the copyright notice,
4. Making an arrangement or adaptation of a copyrighted work,
5. Copying music to create anthologies or compilations,
6. Copying classroom material such as workbooks, standardized tests, and answer sheets, and
7. Making a transparency, slide, or filmstrip of copyrighted music (projecting an image of a purchased copy of music on an opaque projector is permissible).

A detailed study of the law is recommended, but it appears that directors may copy music under the following stipulations without permission:[6]

1. In an emergency, directors may copy music for an impending performance when for some reason they cannot obtain purchased copies, provided that replacement copies are purchased immediately following the performance.
2. For academic purposes other than performances, excerpts of works may be copied provided they do not constitute a performable unit such as a section, song, or movement. In no case can directors copy more than 10 percent of a whole work. Only one copy per student is permissible.
3. Directors may edit or simplify purchased copies of music provided the basic character of the work is not changed. Original texts (lyrics) may not be added to nor changed in any way. One cannot add lyrics if they do not exist.
4. For evaluation purposes, teachers may make single copies of recordings of copyrighted music of student performances and place them in the school library. Also, they may make a single copy of a sound recording of copyrighted music to provide aural exercises or examinations for their students. Consult the copyright law for lifting excerpts to be used for aural exercises and examinations from copyright protected professional recordings.

THOUGHTS FOR CONTEMPLATION AND DISCUSSION

1. Have you ever duplicated copyrighted music with a photocopy machine? What was your rationale for doing so? Does your rationale justify your having done so?

[6] Directors may consult these useful descriptions and interpretations of the copyright law: *The United States Copyright Law: A Practical Outline* (New York: Music Publishers Association); and *The United States Copyright Law: A Guide for Music Educators* (Reston, Va.: Music Educators National Conference). For a strict presentation of the law, write to: write: Copyright Office, Library of Congress, Washington, DC 20559.

2. How does illegal copying affect the production of new material for the choral market?

3. How does illegal copying affect the creative output of composers and arrangers?

4. What can we, as a profession, do about the illegal copying of copyrighted material in the public schools?

BIBLIOGRAPHY

BLACKMAN, J. M. "The MIDI Potential." *Music Educators Journal* 73, no. 4 (1986).

CHOPP, J. M. "The Computer: Integrating Technology with Education." *Music Educators Journal* 73, no. 4 (1986).

DIEHL, N. C. "Computer-Assisted Instruction and Instrumental Music: Implications for Teaching and Research." *Journal of Research in Music Education* 19, no. 3 (1971).

DINGLEY, BOB. "Choral Music Library Computer File for IBM and Compatible PC Version." *Choral Journal* 27, no. 10 (May 1987).

HAIR, H. I. "Teaching Music with the Computer: Guidelines for Teachers." *Update: The Application of Research in Music Education* 3, no. 2 (1985).

HOFSTETTER, F. T. *Computer Literacy for Musicians.* Englewood Cliffs, N.J.: Prentice-Hall, Inc., 1988.

———. "GUIDO: An Interactive Computer-Based System for Improvement of Instruction and Research in Ear Training." *Journal of Computer-Based Instruction* 1, no. 4 (1975).

McGREER, D. M. "The Research Literature in Computer-Assisted Instruction." *Update: The Applications of Research in Music Education* 3, no. 1 (1984).

MOOG, R. "M.I.D.I. (Musical Instrument Digital Interface)—What it Is, What it Means to You." *Keyboard Magazine,* (July 1983).

PETERS, G. D. "Vibrato via Video." *Electronic Education* 5, no. 2 (1987).

PLACEK, R. W. "Choosing the Best Software for Your Class." *Music Educators Journal* 72, no. 1 (1985).

ROBINSON, R. L. *Uses of Computers in Music Education, Composition, and Performance.* Drexel Hill, Penn.: Unsinn Publications, 1984.

RUDOLPH, T. E. "Technology for Teaching: Selecting a Personal Computer." *Music Educators Journal* 76, no. 1 (1989).

SHRADER, D. L. "Microcomputer-Based Teaching." *College Music Society* 21, no. 2 (1981).

SIGMAN, MATTHEW. "A Serious Look at Serious Music Publishing." *Music Educators Journal* 74, no. 7 (March, 1988).

SKERRITT, DOUG. "Choral Library for Computer File." *Choral Journal* 27, no. 2 (September, 1986).

STRAUSBAUGH, W. B., and W. R. HIGGINS. *Techniques of Applesoft Programming.* Scottsdale, Ariz.: Gorsuch Scarisbrick Publishers, 1985.

WITTLICH, G. E., J. W. SCHAFFER, and L. R. BABB. *Microcomputers and Music.* Englewood Cliffs, N.J.: Prentice Hall, Inc., 1986.

Appendix A

Choral Literature for Middle/ Junior High School Choirs

The music listed in Appendix B has been evaluated and is recommended for early adolescent singers. Directors should keep in mind that even though this music may be sung by early adolescents, it is still necessary to evaluate each arrangement as to how well it is suited for their particular choral group. Literature needs in middle/junior high school change from year to year, so that which was suitable for one year's group may not be appropriate for a different group (see Chapters 8, 9, and 13 to understand how to select proper literature). SAB voicing may or may not be appropriate for early adolescent singers due to their range and tessitura limitations; therefore, none of the selections listed here is marked SAB. Consult Chapter 13 for proper criteria to use in choosing SAB voicing for early adolescent singers.

Many selections written for SATB voicing are appropriate for middle/ junior high school voices if they fit the range and tessitura limitations of early adolescent voices (see Chapter 13 for the criteria). A few of these are listed as examples of the type SATB selections recommended for early adolescent singers. The remainder of those listed here are four-part selections written specifically for early adolescent voices.

All the music listed for all-male early adolescent singers has been evaluated and adheres to the range and tessitura limitations of their voices. In many ways, early adolescent boys operate better when singing three- and four-part all-male settings because there are more part options from which to choose and the likelihood of finding a part that suits individual voices is greater.

There are hundreds of outstanding treble works, but some of them are not appropriate for early adolescent female singers because the ranges are too extreme or the comfortable singing tessitura is too high or too low. Also, there may be musical complexities that are too difficult for them to produce well. The music for treble voices listed has been evaluated and is recommended for early adolescent singers.

All Christmas selections are marked with an asterisk (*). Those recommended by Anthony Barresi (see "Anthony Barresi on Adolescent Voice" in Chapter 8) are marked with a plus sign (+).

MIXED VOICING

Two-Part

All for One World Collins Cambiata ARS980151 SC
Blest Are They Whose Spirits Long Handel/Hopson Choristers Guild CGA183 SB
Christmas Is a Time for Joy* Kirk Cambiata T979129 SC
Clap Your Hands Moore Heritage HS700 SC or SB
Come, Lord, Quickly Come Handel/Edwards Coronet CP277 SB
Come Thou Almighty King Italian Hymn/Yarrington Cambiata U485195 SB
Come, Thou Fount of Every Blessing Southern/Collins Cambiata T983174 SC
Gentle Mary* Ferris Gray GCMR3311 SB
Glory to God in the Highest* Pergolesi/Collins Cambiata D983175 SC
He's Got the Whole World in His Hand Spiritual/Cooper Cambiata S117695 SC
Hear This Ker General Words/Kjos GC55 SB
It's Good Bye Liza Jane, O American/Ehret Cambiata T981160 SC
Joy That Knows No Bounds* Genevan/Springfield Cambiata L97438 SC
Let Us Now Praise Famous Men Finzi Boosey and Hawkes 1919 SB
Listen with an Open Mind Hughes Lorenz 5768 SB
Lord Is Near, The Joncas/Causey Coronet CP300 SB
Lord of All Most Holy Hopson Flammer EA5002 SB
Lord of Life, King of Glory Grancini G.I.A. Pub G2357 SB
Not Every One Hutson Plymouth JR501 SB
O, My God, Bestow Thy Tender Mercy Pergolesi/Hopson C. Fischer CM7974 SB
One Way Collins Broadman 455147 SC
O Worship the Lord Handel/Causey Beckenhorst BP1235 SB
Peace/Just Light One Candle Cox Cambiata T485196 SC
Poor Man Laz'rus Spiritual/Suerte Cambiata S17675 SC

Praise to the Lord arr/Goodman Presser 31241220 SC
Prayer for Right Now Kirby Cambiata L17673 SC
Pray Tell Me, O Please Tell Me* Mexican/Collins Cambiata U117696 SC
Psalm 103 Russian/Knight Cambiata T180137 SC
Rise Up, O Youth of God Kirby Pro Art 2570 SB
Roundelay Lovelace Hope A478 SB
Simple Gifts Quaker/Cooper Cambiata T978116 SC
Spacious Firmament on High, The Tallis/Cooper Cambiata I979132 SC
Stan' Still Jordan Spiritual/Dodds Cambiata T180136 SC
The Lord is a Mighty God Mendelssohn/Hopson Hope A540 SB
Three Proverbial Loves Collins Cambiata ARS980150 SC
Tomorrow Artman Hal Leonard 08598202 SC
Trains Fitch Cambiata T978117 SC
Two Christmas Partner Songs* Medley/Ashton Cambiata T483172 SC
Waltzing Matilda Australian/Cooper Cambiata U117451 SC
Watchman, Tell Us Mason/Cooper Cambiata I979132 SC
Wondrous Love Southern/Collins Cambiata S97685 SC
Ye Servants of God arr/Young Kjos 5277 SC

Three-Part

Alleluia Mozart/Ehret Cambiata M979124 SAC
Alleluia* Brenclley Shawnee D260 SAT
Alleluia* Eilers Hal Leonard 08540200 SAT
All For One World Collins Cambiata ARS980151 SCB
All My Trials Spiritual/Cooper Cambiata S980145 SCB
Angels We Have Heard On High* Trad/Cooper Cambiata I97678 SCB
Aren't You Glad That It's Christmas* Hoover Cambiata A978118 SAC/B
Balm in Gilead Spiritual/Cooper Cambiata I978102 SCB
Begin Today Tanzer Cambiata A982164 SAC/B

Bell Toll Eddleman Silver Burdett SAT/B

Best Day of My Life, The Butler Hal Leonard Variable Voicing

Bile Them Cabbage Down Willet Heritage HV131 Variable Voicing

Brennan on the Moor arr/Freed McAfee DMC8120 Variable Voicing

Brighten My Soul With Sunshine Eilers Hal Leonard 0854100 Variable Voicing

Bring a Little Joy Kirk Cambiata A979128 SSC

Bring Your Torches* arr/Wasner G. Schirmer 8791 SAT

Cherish Kirkman Hansen C505 Variable Voicing

Ching-A Ring Chaw arr/Van Wyatt Pro Art 2850 Variable Voicing

Christmas Cha Cha, A* Ashton Cambiata A485190 SSC

Christmas Is a Time for Joy* Kirk Cambiata T979129 SCB

Come Ye Thankful People Come Elvey/Cooper Cambiata I978106 SCB

Confitemini Constantini/Kirk Pro Art Ch3002 SAT

Drill, Ye Terriers, Drill! arr/Freed McAfee DMC8124 Variable Voicing

Eveningtime Medley Medley/Ashton Cambiata U483173 SSC

Fairest Lord Jesus Trad/Cooper Cambiata I97681 SCB

Footlights and Fame Poorman Hal Leonard 08602855 Variable Voicing

For All the Saints V. Williams/Cooper Cambiata I978103 SCB

For the Freedom of Man North Cambiata P978111 SAC/B

From Scotland with Love Kirk Pro Art CH3003 Variable Voicing

Fum, Fum, Fum* Spanish/Springfield Cambiata U117211 SSC

Glory to God in the Highest* Pergolesi/Collins Cambiata D983175 SCB

Goodbye Eilers Hal Leonard 08543500 Variable Voicing

Good Christian Men, Rejoice* Trad/Covert Cambiata U97561 SSC

Green Grow the Rushes, Oh arr/Kirk Pro Art 2775 SAC

Hallelujah, Amen Handel/Taylor Cambiata M17312 SAC/B

Hand Chapin Silver Burdett SAT/B

Hang in There, But Hang Loose Collins Cambiata L117323 SSC

He's Got the Whole World in His Hand Spiritual/Cooper Cambiata S117695 SCB

Hitch Your Dream to the Morning Star Butler Hal Leonard Variable Voicing

Holiday Time* Thygerson and Iams Heritage 86501 SAT

How Firm a Foundation Trad/Cox Cambiata U485193 SCB

I Have Done arr/Cooper Fischer CM6584 SSC

I'm A-Headin' Home Gallina Jenson 41509040 Variable Voicing

I'm Comin' Back Norred Jenson 41209020 Variable Voicing

Immortal, Invisible Trad/Cooper Cambiata I180140 SCB

In That Great Gettin' Up Morning arr/Harris Pro Art 2773 Variable Voicing

It's Time for Christmas* Vance Schmitt 7652 SAC

I've Got the World on a String Arlen/Koehler Belwin 6 Variable Voicing

Jesus, Jesus, Rest Your Head/Gentle Jesus* Spiritual/Cox Cambiata U982169 SCB

Jesus Christ Is Risen Today Trad/Cooper Cambiata I978104 SCB

Joshua Fit the Battle of Jericho arr/Willet Heritage HV108 Variable Voicing

Joy in Judea* Davenport Richmond Press TEV61 Variable Voicing

Joy That Knows No Bounds* Genevan/Springfield Cambiata L97438 SCB

Just a Bit of Sunshine Eilers Hal Leonard 085443000 Variable Voicing

Just a Little Sunshine Besig Jenson 41810010 Variable Voicing

Kum Ba Yah African/Roach Cambiata U180136 SSC

Kyrie Eleison Ashton Cambiata C979125 SAC

Let Your Love Fly Free Emerson Jenson 40212030 Variable Voicing

Lift Thine Eyes (from **Elijah**) Mendelssohn/Kirby Cambiata M117322 SCB

Liza Jane arr/Harlow Heritage H6508 SAT

Love Divine Pritchard/Cooper Cambiata I180139 SCB

Love Is the Way Olson Fischer CM8060 SAC

Marching Saints, The Thygerson Heritage H6504 SAT

Mary, Where Is Your Baby, O* arr/Kalbach Silver Burdett SAT

May the Road Rise to Meet You Irish/Kirby Cambiata C982165 SAC

Michie Banjo arr/Freed McAfee DMC8121 Variable Voicing

My Lord arr/Eilers Hal Leonard 08545500 Variable Voicing

New River Train arr/Kalbach Silver Burdett SAT

Nine Hundred Miles arr/Kalbach Silver Burdett SAT

Non Nobis Domine Byrd/Weck Somerset SAT

October Cox Cambiata C485194 SCB

O Freedom arr/Artman Hal Leonard 08595500 Variable Voicing

Old Ark's A-Moverin', The Spiritual/Ehret Cambiata S97205 SCB

Old Joe Clark arr/Eilers Jenson 42315030 Variable Voicing

One Small Boy* Middlemas Cambiata C485188 SSC

One Way Collins Broadman 455147 SCB

Petals arr/Cooper Fischer CM6583 SSC

Poor Man Laz'rus Spiritual/Suerte Cambiata S17675 SCB

Power and the Glory, The arr/Eilers Jenson 40216010 Variable Voicing

Praise the Lord Carter Hope JC285 SAT

Praise the Lord with Joyful Song Hopson Jenson 43316010 SAT

Praise to the Lord Gesanbuch/Cooper Cambiata I978105 SCB

Praise Ye the Lord of Hosts* Saint Saëns/Eilers Jenson 40216020 SAT

Prayer for Right Now, A Kirby Cambiata L17673 SCB

Psalm 103 Russian/Knight Cambiata T180137 SCB

Riddle Song, The arr/Freed McAfee DMC8122 Variable Voicing

Risin' Out of My Soul Eilers Jenson 40218010 Variable Voicing

River, Sing Your Song Butler Richmond TEV54 Variable Voicing

Saints Bound for Heaven Spiritual/Suerte Cambiata S97560 SSC

Sanctus Butler Fischer CM8156 SAT

Sanctus (from **German Mass in F**) Schubert/Weck Somerset SP767 SAT

Saviour, Hear Me, O Von Gluck/Taylor Cambiata M17672 SAC

Send Down the Rain Eilers Jenson 40219030 Variable Voicing

Shady Grove Appalachian/Nichols Cambiata U981157 SSC

Shepherds, Come a Runnin', O* arr/Avalos Pro Art CH2995 SAC

Simple Gifts arr/Freed McAfee DMC8126 Variable Voicing

Simple Gifts Quaker/Cooper Cambiata T978116 SCB

Sing! Robertson Jenson 40919020 Variable Voicing

Sing a Happy Song Avalos Pro Art 2776 Variable Voicing

Sing a Happy Song Granito Alfred 7037 SAT

Sing and Shout arr/Thugerson Heritage HV103 SAT

Sing and Shout arr/Thygerson Heritage HV103 Variable Voicing

Sing Me a Song of the Land I Love Wilson Jenson 40919020 Variable Voicing

Sing of Love and Peace, Alleluia Jacobe Cambiata C180141 SACB

Sing of Love and Peace, Alleluia Jacobe Cambiata C180141 SAC

Sing to His Name, for He Is Gracious Cambiata Butler SAC

Sinner Man, O Spiritual/Suerte Cambiata S17430 SSC

Smile Can Make a Difference, A Mallow/Stelly Coronet CP324 SAC

Someone Must Care Kelley Cambiata A982166 SCB

Spacious Firmament on High, A Tallis/Cooper Cambiata I979132 SCB

Stan' Still Jordan Spiritual/Dodds Cambiata T180136 SCB

Steal Away to Jesus Medley/Quiett Cambiata S982168 SCB

Take in the Sunshine Loper Cambiata A982167 SSC

Thanksgiving Song Davis Warner W71009 SAT

There Is a Ladye Collins Cambiata ARS980152 SCB

Those Good Ole Days Freed Hansen C833 Variable Voicing

Three Novelty Choruses arr/Thygerson Heritage H56500 SAT

Three Proverbial Loves Collins Cambiata ARS980150 SCB

To Friendship, Right On, Man! Collins Cambiata L17313 SSC

Tomorrow's Here Tsuruoka Belwin Mills OCT2454 SAC

Twenty-Third Psalm, The Trad/Taylor Cambiata U17556 SAC

Two Chorales from Christmas Oratorio* Bach/Weck Somerset SP774 SAT

Up, O Shepherds* arr/Schroeder Concordia 982066 SAT

Veni Jesu Cherubini/Weck Somerset SAT

Wabash Cannonball, The arr/Freed McAfee DMC8118 Variable Voicing

Wade in the Water arr/Emerson Jenson 40223050 Variable Voicing

Wait for Love arr/Thygerson Hal Leonard 08603800 Variable Voicing

Wake Up the World to Rhythm Ramseth Coronet CP216 Variable Voicing

Walloon Carol, The* arr/Kirk Pro Art CH3008 Variable Voicing

Waltzing Matilda Australian/Cooper Cambiata U117451 SCB

Watchman, Tell Us Mason/Cooper Cambiata I979132 SCB

We Like to Sing! Hoem Fischer CM7782 SAT

Welcome the Day Wilson Jenson 40923010 Variable Voicing

When Jesus Christ Was Born* Trad/Cooper Cambiata I97679 SCB

While Shepherds Watched Their Flocks* Trad/Cooper Cambiata I97680 SCB

Whoa, Mule, Whoa! arr/Rowen and Simon Fischer CM6973 Variable Voicing

You Must Fly Eilers Jenson 40225010 Variable Voicing

Four-Part

Adolescence Collins Cambiata L97558 SSCB

Adoramus Te, Christe (from **The Seven Last Words**) Dubois/Richison Cambiata M17797 SSCB

Adoramus Te, Christe (from **The Seven Last Words**) Dubois/Richison Cambiata M17797 Variable Voicing

Adoramus Te, Christe Mozart/Collins Cambiata D978120 SSCB

Adoramus Te, Christe Palestrina/Farrell Cambiata M485187 SSCB

Adoramus Te, Christe Palestrina/Farrell Cambiata M485187 Variable Voicing

Agnus Dei Gabrieli/McCray Cambiata M97682 SACB

Agnus Dei Gabrieli/McCray Cambiata M97682 Variable Voicing

Allegiance to Liberty Collins Cambiata P47435 SSCB

Alleluia + Bach/Emerson Jenson 40301000 SATB

All From the Same Clay Pool Cambiata C117569 SSCB

All Praise to Thee + Tallis/Stone Belwin Mills 2223 SATB

Amazing Grace arr/Eddleman Silver Burdett SACB

Appalachian Lament McCray European American B-355 SSCB

Aren't You Glad That It's Christmas* Hoover Cambiata A978118 SACB

Arrow and the Song, The Cooper Fischer P47435 SSCB

At Last Cooper Fischer CM6814 SSCB

Au Clair De La Lune + Lully/Stone Belwin Mills 2156 SATB

Ave Verum Mozart/Lyle Cambiata M17552 SACB

Ave Verum Mozart/Lyle Cambiata M17552 Variable Voicing

Ave Verum Corpus Byrd/Collins Cambiata D978121 SSCB

Battle Hymn of the Republic, The arr/Cooper Bourne C503 SSCB

Battle of Jericho Spiritual/Knight Cambiata S97440 SSCB

Battle of Jericho Spiritual/Knight Cambiata S97440 Variable Voicing

Begin Today Tanzer Cambiata A982164 SAC(B)

Behold the Lamb of God (from **Messiah**) arr/Beal Cambiata M17427 SSCB

Bingo German/Riley Cambiata U17676 SSCB

Blessed Is the Man Butler Cambiata C97203 SACB

Blessed Is the Man Butler Cambiata C97203 Variable Voicing

Blow the Wind Southerly + arr/Vance Belwin Mills 2168 SATB

Campfire Blues Gustafson Fischer CM6863 SSAB

Carol of the Bells* Leontovich/Knight Cambiata U983176 SSCB

Carol of the Bells* Leontovich/Knight Cambiata U983176 Variable Voicing

Cast Thy Burden Upon the Lord (from **Elijah**) Mendelssohn/Farrell Cambiata M980143 SSCB

Chantez, Chantez Gamse/Field/Carlyle Plymouth SCC2001 SACB

Cherubim Song + Bortniansky/Collins Cambiata D978119 SSCB

Clap Your Hands Newbury Kjos GC68 SACB

Climbin' Up the Mountain + arr/Ehret Studio PR SACB

Climbin' Up Those Golden Stairs + Wiley Pro Art 2997 SSCB

Colorado Trail, The American/Lyle Cambiata U17316 SACB

Colorado Trail, The American/Lyle Cambiata U17316 Variable Voicing

Come Thou Almighty King Italian Hymn/Yarrington Cambiata U485195 SS/CB

Consider Yourself Bart/Carlyle Plymouth SCC2016 SACB

Da Pacem Domine Franck/Pardue Cambiata M979126 SSACB

Deck the Halls* + Welsh/Knight Belwin Mills ProCh2988 SACB

Dunderbeck arr/Ehret Studio PR SSCB

En La Fuenta De Rosel + Vasquez Lawson-Gould 51376 SATB

English Street Cry English/Kicklighter Cambiata U978110 SSCB

Exposition Cooper Fischer CM6815 SSCB

Ezekiel Saw the Wheel + arr/Ehret Studio PR SACB

Fa Una Canzona + Vecci Lawson-Gould 556 SATB

Feelin' Good + Myers/Rodman Celebration Press G3666 SATB

Follow, Follow* arr/Kirk Kjos GC84 SSCB

For the Freedom of Man North Cambiata P978111 SSC(B)

Foster Mania Foster/Ashton Cambiata U485184 SSCB

Friends with You Danoff/Nivert/Fry Cherry Lane 8157 SSCB

Fum, Fum, Fum* arr/Nightingale Fischer CM7105 SSAB

Fum, Fum, Fum* Spanish/Springfield Cambiata U117211 SSC(B)

Fum, Fum, Fum* Spanish/Springfield Cambiata U117211 Variable Voicing

Git on Board, Little Chillen' arr/Grant Belwin Mills 1688-6 SSCB

Give Me Liberty or Give Me Death Collins Cambiata P47434 SSCB

Gloria (from **Gloria Mass**)* Vivaldi/Collins Cambiata M117207 SSCB

Gloria (from **Gloria Mass**)* Vivaldi/Collins Cambiata M117207 Variable Voicing

Go and Tell John + arr/Wiley Belwin Mills ProCh2976 SACB

God Rest Ye Merry Gentlemen* Lovelace Cambiata C117324 SACB

Goin' Down the Road Eisman and Winston Silver Burdett SSCB

Gonna Build a Mountain + Bricusse/Newley/Carlyle Plymouth SCC2002 SACB

Good Health, All Gathered Here! Burger Heritage H7022 SSAB

Good Time Singers, The Wilson/Riley Cherry Lane 8169 SSCB

Go Tell It On the Mountain* Spiritual/Springfield Cambiata S117325 SSCB

Green Grow the Rushes, Oh English/Suerte Cambiata U97206 SSCB

Hail the King of Heaven* Polish/Ehret Cambiata U97441 SAC/B

Hallelujah Baptismal Shout/Collins Cambiata S485192 SSCB

Hallelujah (from **Messiah**) Handel/Richison Cambiata M97317 SS/CB

Hallelujah (from **Messiah**) Handel/Richison Cambiata M97317 Variable Voicing

Hallelujah, Amen Handel/Taylor Cambiata M17312 SSC(B)

Hang in There, But Hang Loose Collins Cambiata L117323 SSC(B)
Harmony Simon/Kaplin/Carlyle Plymouth SCC2008 SACB
Herzegovina Dance Song arr/Kirk Kjos GC76 SACB
He Watching Over Israel (from **Elijah**) Mendelssohn/Collins Cambiata M97557 SSCB
Hold On Spiritual/Knight Cambiata S177100 SSCB
Home for the Holidays Stillman/Allen/Carlyle Plymouth SACB
Hosanna Gregor/Lyle Cambiata M979135 SA/SSCB
How Can I Leave You Again Denver/Curtright Cherry Lane 8153 SSCB
How Lovely Is the Rose Medley/Crocker Cambiata U485189 Melody-Plus
How Lovely Is the Rose Medley/Crocker Cambiata U485189 Variable Voicing
I Believe Drake/Carlyle Plymouth SCC2015 SACB
I Climbed the Mountain Kirk Cambiata A983178 SSC/B
I Come to This Hallowed Hour + Artman Studio PR V7921-2 SATB
If I Had a Hammer Hays/Seeger/Carlyle Plymouth SCC2003 SACB
I Got Shoes Spiritual/Melton Cambiata S980156 SSCB
I Got Shoes Spiritual/Melton Cambiata S980156 Variable Voicing
I Heard the Voice of Jesus Say English/Collins Cambiata L17798 SSCB
I'm Goin' to Be There Someday Williams/Ascher/Fry Cherry Lane 2411 SSCB
I'm Gonna Walk Eddleman Silver Burdett SSAB
Impossible Dream, The Leigh/Riley/Schwartz Cherry Lane 3799 SACB
Infant Joy + Moore/Blake Beckenhorst BP1089 SATB
It's a Grand Night for Singing Rodgers and Hammerstein/Ehret Williamson W830750363 SSAB
It's a Wonderful Thing to Be Me! Besig Shawnee D170 SSAB
Jesu, Priceless Treasure Cruger-Bach/Collins Cambiata M982170 SSCB
Joseph Dearest, Joseph Mine German/Ehret Cambiata U117326 SAC/B
Joy Fills the Morning Lotti/Farrell Cambiata M983177 SSCB
Joy Fills the Morning Lotte/Farrell Cambiata M983177 Variable Voicing
Laudate Dominum + Pitoni/Wiley Pro Art 2893 SACB
Let It Snow, Let It Snow, Let It Snow Cahn/Styne/Carlyle Plymouth SCC2013 SACB
Let Love Come Near Roberton Fischer CM7916 SSAB
Let Your Smile Be Your Umbrella Fain/Wyatt Belwin Mills 64434 SACB
Liberty Tree Collins Cambiata P47436 SSCB
Life Is Burroughs Cambiata L97318 SACB
Lincoln Log, A Butler Hal Leonard 08041950 SSAB
Little Chilun + Spiritual/Beal Cambiata S17315 SSCB

Long Years Ago Over Bethlehem's Hills* Vick Cambiata C97684 SACB
Lovely Guitar Wink and Wink Kjos GLC78 SSCB
Lovers Love the Spring Pfautsch Kjos GL69 SSCB
Lully, Lullay, Thou Little Tiny Child* + arr/Tappan Studio PR SACB
Mark Well, My Heart Vick Cambiata C117209 SACB
Masters in This House + Morris/Vance Belwin Mills 2249 SATB
Maxwell's Silver Hammer Lennon and McCartney/Esposito Cherry Lane SSCB
May Day Carol + arr/Vance Belwin Mills 20022-7 SATB
May the Road Rise to Meet You Irish/Kirby Cambiata C982165 SAC(B)
Moonscape Boyd Kjos GC74 SSCB
My Lord, What a Morning Spiritual/Knight Cambiata S485185 SSCB
My Lord, What A Morning Spiritual/Knight Cambiata S485185 Variable Voicing
Nelly Bly Foster/Cooper Cambiata U117571 SSCB
New Day McCray Cambiata A978130 SSCB
New Day McCray Cambiata A979130 Variable Voicing
Night Song + Harley Fischer CM4710 SATB
Nobody Knows the Trouble I've Seen Spiritual/Collins Cambiata S97320 SSCB
Nothing Can Stop Me Now Bricusse/Newley/Carlyle Plymouth SCC2017 SACB
Now Let the Heavens Adore Thee Bach/Collins Cambiata D978122 SSCB
Now Thank We all Our God arr/Cooper Bourne C510 SSCB
Ob-la-di, Ob-la-di Lennon and McCartney/Fry Cherry Lane 8156 SCB
O Bone Jesu + Palestrina Pro Art SATB
O Come, Emmanuel* arr/Niles Fischer CM6751 SSAB
O Occhi Manza Mia + Di Lassus/Ehret Walton 800463 SATB
Oh, Freedom Terri Kjos GC73 SSCB
Oh Sinner Won't You Listen? + Spevacek Jenson 47315010 SSAB
Old Ark's A-Moverin', The Spiritual/Ehret Cambiata S97205 SAC/B
One Small Boy* Middlemas Cambiata C485188 SSC(B)
On Independence Collins Cambiata P47433 SSCB
On This Blessed Merry Season* American/Ehret Cambiata U97686 SAC/B
Our Savior on Earth Now Is Born* + arr/Ehret Studio PR SSCB
Passing By + Middlemas Cambiata A180142 SSCB
Pirate Don Durk of Dowdee, The Peninger Cambiata C17674 SACB
Plenty Good Room Spiritual/Melton Cambiata S983279 SSCB
Plenty Good Room Spiritual/Melton Cambiata S983179 Variable Voicing
Praise God in His Holiness + arr/Kirk Belwin Mills ProCh2978 SACB

Praise Thee, Lord Collins Cambiata L17553 SSCB

Praise the Lord All Ye Nations Kirk Cambiata C117694 SSCB

Praise to Thee, Thou Great Creator Bach/Coggin Pro Art 3012 SSCB

Psalm 98 Bavicchi Kjos GC72 SSCB

Rainbow Connection, The Williams/Ascher/Fry Cherry Lane 2428 SSCB

Rest in the Lord (from **Elijah**) Mendelssohn/Knight Cambiata M117567 SSCB

Ride the Chariot Spiritual/Melton Cambiata S117450 SACB

Ride the Chariot Spiritual/Melton Cambiata S117450 Variable Voicing

Sail On, O Ship of State Roff Cambiata P978112 SACB

Saints Bound for Heaven Spiritual/Suerte Cambiata S97560 SSCB

Saints Bound for Heaven Spiritual/Suerte Cambiata S97560 Variable Voicing

Sakura arr/Nightingale Fischer CM6694 SSCB

Send Out Thy Light Farrell Cambiata C980149 SSCB

Set Down Servant+ arr/Ehret Tetra Music Corp AB428 SATB

She Believes in Me Gibb/Esposito Cherry Lane 8165 SSCB

She Walks in Beauty Brahms/Hokanson Cambiata M117447 SACB

Sing a Song of Happiness Kirk Kjos GC77 SACB

Sing a Song to the Lord Kirk Cambiata C978107 SSCB

Sing a Song to the Lord Kirk Cambiata C978107 Variable Voicing

Sing of Love and Peace, Alleluia Jacobe Cambiata C180141 SAC(B)

Sing to His Name, for He Is Gracious Cambiata Butler SAC(B)

Sing to the Lord+ Wilson/Foster Studio PR V7917 SATB

Sing to the Lord of Love arr/Wiley Belwin Mills ProCh2930 SACB

Sing to the Lord Who Reigns Above+ Hadley Belwin Mills ProCh2975 SACB

Sinner Man, O Spiritual/Suerte Cambiata S17430 SSC(B)

Somebody Cares for Me Rowen and Simon Fischer CM7078 SSAB

Someone Must Care Kelley Cambiata A982166 SSC/B

Sourwood Mountain+ arr/Ehret Lawson-Gould 653 SATB

Spread Your Wings and Fly Eilers Jenson 40119124 SSAB

Square Dance Cooper Bourne C507 SSCB

Stand Up and Sing Davis Cambiata C97319 SSCB

Star-Spangled Banner, The Smith/Collins Cambiata D978123 SSCB

Summertime Gershwin/Ehret Chappell 5565023-36309 SACB

Take Me Home, Country Roads Denver/Curtright Cherry Lane 8159 SSCB

Teacher, Help Me Spencer Cambiata ARS980154 SSCB

Teacher, Help Me Spencer Cambiata ARS980154 Variable Voicing

Tenebrae Factae Sunt Ingegneri/Collins Cambiata D981155 SSCB

There Is Something to Sing About Kirk Pro Art 2998 SSCB

They Call the Wind Maria Lerner and Loewe/Ehret Chappell 593003-36309 SSAB

This Is Our Land Burroughs Kjos GC71 SSCB

This Land Is Your Land Guthrie/Carlyle Plymouth SCC2004 SACB

Those Magic Changes Casey/Jacobs/Winston Silver Burdett SSAB

Thou By Whom We Come to God, O Peninger Cambiata C17554 SACB

Thou by Whom We Come to God, O Peninger Cambiata C17554 Variable Voicing

Three Easter Songs Medley/Collins Cambiata U485191 SSCB

Three Sacred Christmas Songs* Medley/Collins Cambiata MP983171 Melody-Plus

Three Sacred Christmas Songs* Medley/Collins Cambiata MP983171 Variable Voicing

To Friendship, Right On, Man! Collins Cambiata L17313 SSC(B)

Tribute of Carols, A* arr/Gordon Warner W7-1014 SACB

Tune in Our Time, A Tierney/Richar/Esposito Cherry Lane 1866 SSCB

Turn, Turn, Turn Seeger/Carlyle Plymouth SCC2005 SACB

Twenty-Third Psalm, The Trad/Taylor Cambiata U17556 SAC(B)

Two Christmas Carols* arr/Nightingale Fischer CM7987 SSAB

Wade in the Water Spiritual/Lyle Cambiata S117570 SACB

We Sing with Grace in Our Hearts Collins Cambiata C117449 SSCB

What Do All of These Things Mean?* Kirby Cambiata L117208 SACB

When I'm Sixty-Four Lennon and McCartney/Esposito Cherry Lane 1856 SSCB

When It's Love Kirk Cambiata A981159 SSCB

Where Are the Flowers Ashton Cambiata A485186 SSCB

While Shepherds Watched Their Flocks By Night* arr/Collins Broadman-455127 SSCB

Who's a Loser? Matthews Kjos GC70 SSCB

Wonderful Day Like Today Bricusse/Newley/Carlyle Plymouth SCC2007 SACB

Words Fitch Cambiata C17799 SSCB

Worship Christ the Newborn King*+ arr/Ehret Studio PR SACB

Young and Old Cooper Fischer CM6813 SSCB

Young Love Joyner/Carter/Simeone Shawnee D171 SSAB

MALE VOICINGS

Two-Part

Freedom, Freedom Siltman Southern SC119 TB
Gadie, The Scottish E.E. Schirmer 586 TB
Gallant Men Siltman Southern SC155 TB
Goodbye, My Lover, Goodbye arr/Siltman Southern SC72 TB
Hark, the Vesper Hymn Is Stealing arr/Siltman Southern SC67 TB
Holly and the Ivy, The* arr/Collins Cambiata L97688 CC
Noah's Ark arr/Siltman Southern SC71 TT or TB
Sing Out Young Voices (Four Songs, Vol. 1) arr/ Swanson G. Schirmer 12328 TB
Toot, Toot, Tootsie Kahn/Artman Hal Leonard 08598205 TB
Zion Hears the Watchman Singing Buxtehude E. C. Schirmer 538 TB

Three-Part

Alleluia Bach/Siltman Cambiata M486198 CCB
Alleluia Spiritual/Siltman Southern SC70 TTB or TBB
America Carey/Siltman Cambiata P486197 CBB
America the Beautiful Ward/Siltman Cambiata P980147 CBB
Captain, The Van Wormer Kjos GC44 TBB
Christmas Medley* Medley/Swenson Cambiata U97566 CBB
Down the River American/Green Cambiata U485182 CCB
Dream of a Nation, A Siltman Southern SC156 TTB
Drink to Me Only with Thine Eyes English/Siltman Cambiata U985181 CCB
Emmanuel's Birth* Medley/Siltman Cambiata U982161 CBB
Fairest Lord Jesus Willis/Lawrence Cambiata U983180 CBB
Girls! Lucas/Houston Studio PR V7939 TTB
Goodbye, My Lover, Goodbye arr/Siltman Southern SC72 TTB or TBB
Hark, the Vesper Hymn Is Stealing arr/Siltman Southern SC67 TTB
Holly and the Ivy, The* English/Collins Cambiata L97688 CCB
Jesu, Joy of Man's Desiring Bach/Siltman Cambiata M97687 CBB
Junior High Collection for Male Voices (thirty-two songs) arr/Wheeler and Wadsworth Associated TTB
Lady of Liberty Siltman Southern SC118 TTB
Li'l Liza Jane American/Swenson Cambiata U979134 CCB
Live in Peace Siltman Southern SC154 TTB
Mary and Martha Spiritual/Siltman Southern SC117 TTB
Medley for Christmas* Medley/Siltman Cambiata U978115 CBB
Music for Chorus 6 (five songs) arr/Siltman Silver Burdett TTB

Noah's Ark arr/Siltman Southern SC71 TTB or TBB
Poor Wayfaring Stranger arr/Johnson Jenson 44616011 TTB
Salty Dog American/Siltman Cambiata U485183 CBB
Scarborough Fair English/Swenson Cambiata U97691 CCB
Sea Song Swenson Cambiata C981158 CBB
Sing, Boys, Sing (eight songs) arr/Cooper Fischer 4029 CCB
Sing Unto the Lord, O Swenson Cambiata S982163 CCB
Spiritual Trilogy Medley/Siltman Cambiata S980148 CBB
Steal Away arr/Siltman Southern SC69 TTB or TBB
This Train American/Siltman Cambiata U978114 CBB
Three Christmas Carols* Medley/Swenson Cambiata U979133 CBB
Vive L'Amour College Song/Siltman Cambiata U980145 CBB
Who Came to See?* Baker Cambiata C485181 CBB
Won't You Sit Down, Oh Spiritual/Lawrence Cambiata U982162 CBB

Four-Part

Blessed Is the Man Butler/Rich Cambiata C97564 CCBB
Brother, Show Us the Way Beal Cambiata C97444 CCBB
Didn't My Lord Deliver Daniel? Spiritual/Springfield Cambiata S97445 CCBB
Integer Vitae (Father Almighty) Flemming/Johnstone Cambiata M97562 CCBB
Poor Lonesome Cowboy American/Giles Cambiata U97446 CCBB
Together We'll Make the Journey Beal Cambiata L97563 CCBB
What Do All of These Things Mean?* Kirby/Rich Cambiata L97443 CCBB
Where'er You Walk Cram Cambiata C978113 CCBB

FEMALE VOICINGS

Two-Part

Above the Clear Blue Sky Martin Fischer
Again to Thy Dear Name Fauré/Ferguson Music 70 (Plymouth)
Ah, Holy Jesus* Cruger/Jennings Augsburg
All Glory Be to Thee Handel/Kirk Pro Art
All the Pretty Little Horses arr/Artman Studio 224 (Columbia)
All Things Bright and Beautiful Rutter Hinshaw
An Die Nachtigall Schumann (English or German) National Music Publishers
And You Are Not Alone Duson Kjos
Antiphonal Hosanna Smith Hope
Ave Verum Corpus (from **Sing Joyfully**) Saint-Saëns Walton

Baloo, Baloo Rhein G. Schirmer
Be Like the Bird Frackenpohl Kjos
Blessed Be That Maid Mary* Williams Jenson
Boat Song Grieg/Platt/Lewis Plymouth
Buttermilk Hill Bacon Boosey and Hawkes
Cancion de Cuna (Spanish Lullaby) Posegate (Spectrum of Music 7, Spanish or English) Macmillan
Carol for the King* arr/Crocker Southern
Ca' the Yowes Goetze Boosey and Hawkes
Charlotte Town Crocker Jenson
Cockleshells (from **Three Folk-Songs**) Broude (Plymouth)
Come and Follow Me Pierce Plymouth
Come and Sing Together (from **Rounds for Everyone from Everywhere**) arr/Terri Lawson-Gould
Come, Jesus, Holy Son of God* Handel/Hopson Flammer
Creator of the Stars of Night arr/Pasquet (Spectrum of Music 7) Macmillan
Dance of the One-Legged Sailor Pierce Plymouth
Da Pacem Domine Franck/Goetze Boosey and Hawkes
Dearest Jesu of My Heart Harmon Plymouth
Der Morgenstern (The Morning Star) Schubert (Juilliard Repertory Library, Vocal 2, English or German) Canyon Press (Kerby)
Drunken Sailor, The arr/Crocker Jenson
Expandi manus (Juilliard Repertory Library, Vocal 2) Lassus Canyon Press (Kerby)
Father, Holy Father Land Plymouth
First and Seconds ed/Apple and Fowler (nine songs) Oxford
From Heaven Above to Earth I Come Pasquet Elkan-Vogel (Presser)
Fugue Fux (Silver Burdett Music, Level 8) Silver Burdett
Glockchen Kling/Kirk Pro Art
Go Ye, My Canzonets Morley (Silver Burdett Music, Level 7) Silver Burdett
Gute Nacht arr/Kjelson (Spectrum of Music 7, English or German) Macmillan
Hasten Shepherds On* arr/Pable Fredonia Press
Herrick's Carol* Neufel/Herrick Aberdeen Music (Plymouth)
Hodie, Nobis De Caelo Grandi (Latin or English) Fostco Music Press (Mark Foster)
How Brightly Shines Yon Morning Star* Pratorius (Juilliard Repertory Library, Vocal 5, German or English) Canyon Press (Kerby)
Hush, My Baby* Kovdelka/Bacon G. Schirmer
I Have Touched the Face of God Goemanne Kjos
In Dulci Jubilo Pratorius (Juilliard Repertory Library, Vocal 8) Canyon Press (Kerby)
In the Meadow arr/Krone Kjos
I Walk the Unfrequented Road Kjelson Belwin Mills
Joyful Song, A Kirk Kjos
Lamb, The DeWell Coronet
Lamb of God Decius/Pooler Augsburg
Lamb of God Rein/McCray European American (J.W. Pepper)
Like a Rose in the Summer arr/Crocker Southern
Lord Is My Shepherd, The arr/Pfautsch Summy-Birchard

Loving Shepherd of the Sheep arr/Lenel Concordia
Lowly of Heart Pasquet Elkan-Vogel (Presser)
Lullaby Jesu* arr/Gordon Presser
Music in the Air Norton Boosey and Hawkes
Night Song Hester Shawnee
Panis Angelicus Franck/Siltman (Silver Burdett Music, Level 7) Silver Burdett
Pasternoster (from **Bicinia Hungarica I**) Kodály/Russell/Smith Boosey and Hawkes
Pick a Bale of Cotton arr/Bertaux Boosey and Hawkes
Praise the King Handel/Kirk Pro Art (Columbia)
Praise the Lord Adler Oxford
Prepare Thyself, Zion Bach/Hurt Hinshaw
Psalm 150 Britten Boosey and Hawkes
Rejoice and Be Merry Pasquet Elkan-Vogel (Presser)
Rejoice Norton Boosey and Hawkes
Schon Blumelein Schumann (English or German) National Music Publishers
Shepherds, Tune Your Pipes Purcell/Kirk Pro Art
Shepherds Saw a Star, The* Pasquet G. Schirmer
Simple Gifts Copland/Fine Boosey and Hawkes
Sleep, Gently Sleep* Brahms/Harris (English or German) Jenson
Song of Evening Thiman J. Curwen and Sons (Hal Leonard)
Sound the Trumpet, Praise Him Handel/Hopson Coronet
Spring Song Paulus Fischer
Three Songs Grieg/Tappan Hinshaw
Thy Spirit Ascending Purcell/Rodby Ply-mouth
Tree Toad, A Henderson Gordon Thompson
Two Roses (from **Two Thoughts for Children's Chorus**) Bartok/Suchoff Alfred
Verdant Meadows Handel/Platt Plymouth
We Came to the Manger* Caldwell Fischer
Wenn Ich ein Voglein War Schumann (English or German) National Music Publishers
We Wait for Thy Loving Kindness, O God Elvey/Pascall Oxford
What Sweeter Music Butler Curtis House of Music (Kjos)
Where Go the Boats? Copley Shawnee
Where Go the Boats? Rinker Music Corp. of America (Hal Leonard)
Will You Walk a Little Faster? Carroll/Carter J. Fisher (Columbia)
Yak, The Henderson Gordon V. Thompson
Ye Watchers and Ye Holy Ones arr/Siltman (Silver Burdett Music, Level 7) Silver Burdett

Three-Part

Across the Sea Mendelssohn Gentry
Autumn Song Crocker Southern
Candu De Cesare (English or Spanish) Ludwig
Confitemini Domino (from **The Seventh Chester Book of Motets**) Constantini J. and W. Chester (Magna Music)
Early One Morning arr/Bacak Jenson
Echoing Song, The Crocker Southern

Folk and Spiritual Time Iams/Thygerson Heritage Music Press

Four Noels* Oldham Oxford

Girl Merrily Was Dancing, A (from Three Songs from Sweden) arr/Hallstrom Shawnee

Give Way, Jordan arr/Goetze Boosey and Hawkes

Great Gettin' Up Morning arr/Goetze Boosey and Hawkes

Hares on the Mountain arr/Holst Novello (Presser)

Infant Jesus* Goetze Boosey and Hawkes

It's All I Have to Bring Today Kennedy Belwin Mills

Jesu Rex Admirabilis (from The Seventh Chester Book of Motets) Palestrina J. and W. Chester (Magna Music)

Maiden's Song* Crocker Southern

Make a Joyful Noise Unto the Lord Knowles Jenson

My Heart's in the Highlands Wagner Heritage

Old Joe Clark arr/Goetze Boosey and Hawkes

Over the Sea and Skye arr/Wagner Shawnee

Rainbow Comes and Goes, The Land Southern

Rocking Carol* arr/Shearer Southern

Shepherd's Cradle Song, The* Leuner/Lane Presser

Tanzen und Springen Hassler (Juilliard Repertory Library, English or Spanish) Canyon Press (Kerby)

Though My Carriage Be But Careless Weelkes National Music Publishers

Time Schultz G. Schirmer

Tua Jesu Dilectio (from The Seventh Chester Book of Motets) Palestrina J. and W. Chester (Magna Music)

Two Vignettes McLaughlin Belwin Mills

We Are the Music Makers Crocker Southern

When to Her Lute Corrinna Sings Shearer Southern

Where the Wind Blows Larson Somerset

COLLECTIONS

Accent on Singing (1955) arr/Cooper Hansen

Adolescent Reading Singer, The arr/Collins Cambiata

Cambiata Contempora! arr/Kirk Kjos

Cambiata Easter Hymnal (1955) arr/Cooper Hansen

Cambiata Hymnal (1954) arr/Cooper Hansen

Cantate Deo (1960) arr/Cooper Fischer 04149

Choral Music for Changing Voices (1969) arr/Cooper Fischer 04785

Choral Time arr/Ehret Lawson-Gould

Descants for Junior High Singing (1962) arr/Cooper Fischer 04244

Familiar Christmas Carols arr/Hardin Cambiata

Festival Processional arr/Cooper Fischer 04490

For Youth Only, Book 1 comp/Raymer Broadman

General Music Singing (1956) arr/Cooper Hansen

Hymns for Teentime (1957) arr/Cooper Fischer 04037

Junior High Choral Concert, The (1964) arr/Cooper Fischer 04454

Junior High Collections for Male Singers (1958) arr/Wheeler and Wadsworth Associated Music Publishers

Let's Sing Parts (two volumes) arr/Staples Mills Music

Living with Music (two volumes) arr/Richardson and English Witmark

More Tunetime for Teentime (1962) arr/Cooper Fischer 04228

Music for Chorus 6 arr/Siltman Silver Burdett

Patterns in Songs arr/Richardson and Frackenpohl Witmark

Secular Christmas Songs (melody-part style) arr/Collins Cambiata

Sing! Schott et al. Hinshaw Music (Choose selections for Jr. High School)

Sing, Boys, Sing (1957) arr/Cooper Fischer 04029

Singing Teens, The (1952) arr/Cooper Gordon V. Thompson

Sing Praises arr/Ehret Broadman

Sing One, Sing All (1954) arr/Cooper Bourne

Something New to Sing About G. Schirmer

Something to Sing About, Vol. 1 G. Schirmer

Songs for Pre-Teentime (1956) arr/Cooper Fischer 03953

Songs for Sight-Singing SAB ed/Whitlock Southern B376

Songs for Sight-Singing SATB ed/Whitlock Southern B375

Songs for Sight-Singing Tenor-Bass ed/Whitlock Southern B374

Songs for Sight-Singing Treble ed/Whitlock Southern B373

Teen-age Songs (1942) arr/Cooper Fischer 03360

Tunetime for Teentime (1952) arr/Cooper Fischer 03814

Unison Songs for Teen-age Boys (1953) arr/Cooper Gordon V. Thompson

World of Choral Music Hausmann et al. Silver Burdett and Ginn (Choose selections for Jr. High School)

Young Folk Sing arr/Gwyneth Cooper Bourne

Yuletime for Teentime (1954) arr/Cooper Fischer 03881

Appendix B

Choral Literature for Senior High School Choirs

OCTAVOS

Mixed Voicing

Ach, Arme Welt Brahms/Klein (German) G. Schirmer SATB

Achieved Is Thy Glorious Work Haydn/Mason (from **The Creation**) Walton SATB

Adieu, Sweet Amarillas Willbye Lawson-Gould 51865 SATB

Adoramus Te Palestrina E. C. Schirmer 2985 SATB

Adoramus Te Christe Palestrina E. C. Schirmer 1760 SATB

Advent Motet Schreck/Christiansen Kjos 5083 SSAATTBB

African Noel (Liberian) arr/Lewis Plymouth PCS 38 SATB

African Noel Kauffmann Elkan-Vogel 362-03288 SSATBB

Aftonen (Evening) Alfven Walton W2705 SATB

Afton Water Pierce Plymouth BP-113 SATB

Agnus Dei Kallinikof/Rye Belwin Mills 848 SATB

Agnus Dei Lotti Mercury 352-00475 SATB

Agnus Dei Morley/Greyson Bourne SATB

Agnus Dei Persichetti Elkan-Vogel 362-001173 SATB

Ah, Holy Jesus Petrich Oxford SATB

Ah, May the Sun Palestrina/Greyson Bourne AP 513 SATB

Ah, My Beloved Jesus Child Scheidt/Granville Sam Fox FXCM SSATB

Ahrirang DeCormier Lawson-Gould 51540 SATB

Ain'-a That Good News Dawson Kjos T103-A SATB

Ain't Got Time to Die Johnson G. Schirmer 10301 SATB

Air Is Moving, The Duson Kjos SATB

Alleluia Bach/Ramsey Kjos 5381 SATB

Alleluia (from **Cantata 142**) Kuhnah (Bach)/McKelvy Mark Foster MF 544H SATB

Alleluia Schein/Stone Tetra SAATBB

Alleluia Thompson E. C. Schirmer 1786 SATB

Alleluia! Sing Praise (from **Cantata 142**) Bach/Hirt C. Fischer CM7140 SATB

Alles hat seine Zeit Haydn C. F. Peters SATB

Alleluia, Amen Frackenpohl Shawnee A-1524 (Canon)

Alfred Burt Carols, The Burt Shawnee Set I A0449, Set II A-450, Set III A-451 SATB

All for Love Young C. Fischer SATB

All Glory, Praise and Majesty Bach (German) National SATB
All Hail the Power Vaughan Williams Oxford SATB
All My Trials Brunner Somerset SP778 SATB
All My Trials Luboff Walton 3065 SATB
Allon, Gay Gergeres Costeley/Shaw/Parker G. Schirmer SATB
All Praise to God Eternal Gaul Fisher/Belwin 5600 SATB
All Praises Be to the Lord Antes Boosey and Hawkes 5938 SATB
All Sing Loudly Brahms/Fettke Flammer A-5715 SATB
All Through the Night Wagner Lawson-Gould 659 SATB
All Ye That Cried Unto the Lord Mendelssohn National NMP-102 SATB
Alma Redemptoris Mater Palestrina Jenson SATB
Al Meine Herzgedanken Brahms Walton W700a SSATBB
Almighty and Everlasting God Gibbons Oxford TCM 36 SATB
Alouette Luboff Walton 3057 SATB
Also Hat Godt Die Welt Geliebt Schütz Hanssler-Verlag 20.380/5 SATB
Amazing Grace Valerio/Buchner Continuo AB943 SATB
Amen (from **Stabat Mater**) Pergolesi/Howorth Belwin Mills 1259 SATB
Americana (Folk Suite) Zaninelli Shawnee A-935 SATB
American Folk Trilogy Lojeski Hal Leonard 08200555 SATB
Andenken Mendelssohn/Richter Tetra AB-162-8 SATB
And I Will Exalt Him (from **Israel in Egypt**) Handel/Craig Plymouth Fs-103 SATB
And in That Day Beck Kjos GC 32 SATB
And the Glory of the Lord (from **Messiah**) Handel G. Schirmer 3829 SATB
Angelus ad Pastores Hassler (Latin) E. C. Schirmer SATB
Annie Laurie Frackenpohl Mark Foster 347 SATB
Apres De Ma Blonde Shaw/Parker Lawson-Gould 644 SATB
Arise, My Soul, Arise! Wood Sacred Music S-181 SATB
Arise and Let Us Sing Now Peuer/Field (German) Theodore Presser SATB
As Dew in Aprille (from **Ceremony of Carols**) Britten Boosey and Hawkes 1829 SATB
As Lately We Watched arr/Black Gray CMR 1358 SATB
As Pants the Heart Tye Concordia 98-2297
As Torrents in Summer (from **King Olaf**) Elgar Flammer 81068 SATB
At the Round Earth's Imagined Corners Spencer Shawnee SATB
Auf dem See Mendelssohn European American/National SATB

Ave Maria (Roch) Victoria/Wilhousky C. Fischer CM6581 SATB
Ave Maria Stravinsky Boosey and Hawkes 1832 SATB
Ave Maria Victoria Continuo SATB
Ave Vera Virginitas Desprez GIA G-565 SATB
Ave Verum Byrd AMP SATB
Ave Verum Corpus Byrd/Greenburg Associated Music Publishers SATB
Ave Verum Corpus Mozart G. Schirmer 5471 SATB
Awake the Harp (from **Creation**) Haydn/Neuen Lawson-Gould 51982 SATB
Away in a Manger arr/Sjolund Walton WW1023 SATB
Babe Is Born, A Diemer Sacred Music Press S61 SATB
Barbara Allen Willcocks Oxford 58.097 SATB
Basket of Wood (from **Four Pastorales**) Effinger G. Schirmer 11061 SATB
Beautiful Dreamer (S. Foster) Shaw/Parker Lawson-Gould 853 SATB
Beautiful Saviour Christiansen Augsburg 11-0051 SATB
Be Calm and Peaceful Bach/Kemmer Gray 1934 SATB
Be Thou Exalted, Lord My God Schütz/Ehret Flammer A05632 SATB
Beggar's Canon Offenbach Broude SATB
Behold, God Is My Help Hovhaness C. F. Peters 66190 SATB
Bella Bimba DeCormier Lawson-Gould 51256 SATB
Bells, The Ahrold Fisher SATB
Bells of Rhymney, The Seeger/Joyce Aberdeen 1036 SATB
Benedictus Es, Domine Purvis Gray 2043 SATB
Birds' Courting Song Harris Belwin Mills 64432 SATB
Birthday Greeting Kodály Boosey and Hawkes 312-40579 SATB
Blessed Are the Faithful Schütz/Shaw-Speer G. Schirmer 10114 SATB
Blessed Is the Nation Pasquet Elka SATB
Blessed Jesu, Fount of Mercy (from **Stabat Mater**) Dvorak G. Schirmer 4490 SATB
Blessed Lord Jesus Buxtehude/Hunter Marks MC4508 SSATB
Blessed Lord Jesus Buxtehude/Hunter Marks SSATB
Blessing, Glory and Wisdom Bach/Thach Kjos 5140 SATB
Bless the Lord Ippolitoff/Ivanoff/Clough-Leighter Presser 332-13770 SATB
Blow, Blow, Blow, Thou Winter Wind Rutter Oxford 52024 SATB
Born, Born in Bethlehem Wagner Somerset AD 2020 SATB
Bound for Jubilee Eilers Studio 224 SATB
Boy Was Born, A Britten Oxford X92 SATB
Boy Was Born in Bethlehem, A Barlow Novello 644 SATB

Break Forth, O Beauteous, Heavenly Light (from **Christmas Oratorio**) Bach Kjos 5002 SATB

Bright Star (from **Light of the World**) Dello Joio Marks 4567 SATB

Brother James's Air (Marosa) arr/Jacobs Oxford 763 SATB

By An' By Curtis Mark Foster 249 SATB

Call to Remembrance, O Lord Farrant/Shaw Gray GCME 1751 SATB

Calypso Christmas Sleeth Hope A0508 SATB

Canite Jehovae Canticum Novum Dering/Potter Presser SATB

Canon in D Pachelbel/Goemanne Flammer A-5833 SATB

Cantate Domino Anerio/Stephens G. Schirmer 11273 SATB

Cantate Domino Hassler/Greyson Bourne 2737-6 SATB

Cantate Domino Pitoni/Greyson Bourne ES5 SATB

Cantate Domino Schütz (Latin) Gordon V. Thompson/Concordia SATB

Cantate Sing to the Lord Goemanne Fostco SSATB

Canticle of Praise Beck Presser 312-40588 SATB

Cantique De Jean Racine Fauré Broude 801 SATB

Carol of the Bells Leontovich/Wilhousky C. Fischer CM4604 SATB

Carol of the Drum Davis B. F. Wood 568 SATB

Carol of the Russian Children arr/Gaul G. Schirmer 6770 SATB

Carol of the Sheep Bells Kountz Galaxy 1080 SATB

Carols Three: A Christmas Overture Zaninelli Shawnee A-1270 SATB

Cast Thy Burden Upon the Lord (from **Elijah**) Mendelssohn G. Schirmer 10015 SATB

Ce Moys De May Janequin/Contino R. Dean CA-106 SATB

Chantez Noel Mathews Kjos SATB

Charlottown arr/Bryan J. Fisher 8136 SATB

Charlottown arr/Christianson Curtis SATB

Cherubic Hymn, The Gretchaninoff/Matterling Kjos 7015 SSAATTBB

Cherubim Song No. 7 Bortniansky G. Schirmer 2560 SATB

Children Don't Get Weary Smith Kjos 1007 SATB

Children's Letters to God Shearer Southern SATB

Ching-a-Ring Chaw Copland Boosey and Hawkes 5024 SATB

Christ, to Thee Be Glory (from **St. Matthew Passion**) Schütz/Hilton Mercury MC375 SATB

Christ-Child, The Binkerd Boosey and Hawkes 5982 SATB

Christmas Bells arr/Rutter Hinshaw HMC-348 SATB

Christmas Carol, A Dello Joio Marks SATB

Christmas Carol, A Kodály Oxford 84.091 SATB

Christmas Carol, A Rorem/Sanburg Elkan-Vogel SATB

Christmas Chorale Schein/Boepple Mercury DCS 7 SATB

Christmas Collage Zaninelli Shawnee A-1345 SATB

Christmas Cradle Song of the 14th Century, A Bodenschatz C. Fischer CM173 SATB

Christmas Day (Solos, Orch. Parts) Holst Novello 29012903 SATB

Christmas in the Straw (Violin) Pfautsch Lawson-Gould 51587 SATB

Christmas Lullaby, A Brahms/Suchoff Sam Fox XPS 191 SATB

Christmas Parade Holden Broude WW18 SATB

Christus Factus Est Bruckner Summy-Birchard 5249 SATB

Christus Factus Est Pitoni Tetra AB757 SATB

Circles of Silence Williams-Wimberly/Collier Belwin Mills SATB

Cockles and Mussels Puerling Hal Leonard 07359067 SATB

Coffee Grows on White Oak Trees arr/Boyd Shawnee A1003 SATB

Cold December Flies Away Clausen Mark Foster 543 SATB

Collect Bassett Westwood SATB (with prepared tape)

Come, Let Us Start a Joyful Song Hassler Bourne ES-74 SATB

Come, Lovely Spring (from **Seasons**) Haydn/Shaw Lawson-Gould 52078 SATB

Come Again, Sweet Love Dowland E. C. Schirmer SATB

Come All You Fair and Tender Ladies Zaninelli Shawnee A-935 SATB

Come Let Us Sing a Song of Joy (Double Chorus) Gabrieli/Nordin Shawnee A-1243 SATB

Come Now Let Us Be Joyful Vecchi/Greyson Bourne ES 64 SATB

Come Thou, Holy Spirit Tschesnokoff/Tkach Kjos 6521 SATB

Come to Me, My Love Dello Joio Marks MC4609 SATB

Confirma Hoc, Deus Aichinger/Martens Walton 6016 SATB

Corpus Christi Young Hinshaw SATB

Country Style Simeone Shawnee SATB

Create in Me a Clean Heart O God Brahms G. Schirmer 7504 SATB

Creche Carol, The Hutson/Raymond Plymouth JR 100 SATB

Crucifixus Lotti/Damrosch G. Schirmer SSATTB

Dadme albricias, hijos d'Eva arr/Greenburg Associated NYPMA 9 SATB

Dance and Turn Jennings Curtis 8327 SATB

Dance to the Music of Time Leisy Lawson-Gould SATB

Das Benedicite und Vaterunser Schütz Tetra SATB

David's Lamentation Billings C. Fischer CM6572 SATB

Day By Day We Magnify Thee Handel/Barrie Lawson-Gould 797 SATB

De Glory Manger Schroth Kjos 5214 SATB Divisi

Deep Blue Sea DeCormier Lawson-Gould 51754 SATB

Deep River Ringwald Shawnee A-90 SATB

Deo La Venda Guerrero/Nin-Culmell Broude SSAT
Der Abden Brahms G. Schirmer 10134 SATB
Dere's No Hidin' Place Shaw/Parker Lawson-Gould 51110 SATB
Der Gluckliche Mendelssohn/Richter Tetra SATB
Der Tanz Schubert Hinshaw HMC 247 SATB
Dessus le Marche d'Arras Lassus/Erb AMP SATB
Did Mary Know? Averre Presser 312-40289 SATB
Didn't My Lord Deliver Daniel? Smith Kjos 1014 SATB
Die Mit Tranen Saen Schein/Porter Associated Music Publishers A-870 SATB
Die Nachtigall Mendelssohn/Robinson Hinshaw HMN 407 SATB
Dies Irae (from **Requiem**) Mozart G. Schirmer 10016 SATB
Dieu! qu'il la fair bon regarder! (from **Trois Chansons**) Debussy Durand SATB
Ding Dong Merrily on High arr/Alwes R. Dean/Heritage HRD 130 SSAATBB
Dixit Dominus (from **Vesperae Solemnes de Confessore**, K. 339) Mozart Lawson-Gould SATB
Dixit Maria Hassler J. Fisher SATB
Domine Fili Unigenite Vivaldi Belwin Mills/R. Dean SATB
Don't Be Weary, Traveler Seals R. Dean/Heritage HRD 133 SATB
Dona Nobis Pacem Clemens Non Papa/Van Camp Hope SSATB
Donde esta la Ma Teodora Nin/Culmell Rongwen Brothers SATB divisi
Down by the Sally Gardens Donovan Galaxy 555 SATB
Dry Bones Simeone C. Hansen 1977-260 SATB
E la don don, Verges Maria arr/Greenburg Associated NYPMA 8 SATB
Early One Morning Cain Presser 332-15147 SATB
Earth Adorned, The Ahlen/Jennings Walton WH-126 SSATB
Earthly Tree a Heavenly Fruit, An Byrd Stainer and Bell 2631 SATB
Ecco Mormorar l'onde Monteverdi Franco Colombo SSATB
Ego Sum Panis Vivus Byrd/Collins J. and W. Chester SATB
Ehre sei dem Vater Schütz/Stone Tetra SATB
Ehre sei dir, Christe Schütz/Shaw G. Schirmer SATB
Ein fauler Baum Franck/Richter Schott SATB
Elijah Rock Hairston Bourne S1017 SATB
En Natus Est Emanuel Praetorius/ Clough-Leighter E. C. Schirmer 2298 SATB
En Priere Fauré/Meyerowitz Broude SATB
Es Jagt Rin Jager Vor Dem Holz Lassus Schott AP510 SSATB
Es Steht Ein Lind arr/Ahrold Witmark W3616 SATB
Est Cor Meum (from **Two Motets from Cantica Sacra**, 1662) Dering/Potter-Ardens Presser SATB
Et in Terra Pax (from **Gloria**) Vivaldi/Martens Walton 2044 SATB

Et Misericordia Vivaldi/Kjelson Belwin Mills 2236 SATB
Evening Primrose, The Britten Boosey and Hawkes 1874 SATB
Every Night Vance G. Schirmer 12556 SATB
Every Night When the Sun Goes Down Williams G. Schirmer 52193 SATB
Every Time I Feel the Spirit Smith Kjos 1006 SATB
Every Valley Beck Beckenhorst BP1040 SATB
Ev'ry Time I Feel the Spirit Dawson Kjos T117 SATB
Exultate Deo Palestrina J. and W. Chester SAATB
Exultate Deo Poulenc Salabert SATB
Exultate Deo Scarlatti G. Schirmer 11001 SATB
Exultate Justi Viadana/Vene Franco Colombo/Chester SATB
Eyes of All Wait Upon Thee, The Berger Augsburg 1101264 SATB
Ezekiel Saw de Wheel Dawson Kjos T110 SATB
Ezekiel Saw the Wheel Simeone Shawnee A-130 SATB
Fable, A Dello Joio C. Fischer CM5299 SATB
Facta Est Cum Angelo Aleotti Broude SAATB
Fahr Hin, Guts Liedelein Hassler/Richter Schott SSATTB
Fahr Wohl Brahms/Klein G. Schirmer SATB
Fain Would I Change That Note Vaughan Williams Gray Mod 587 SATB
Fanfare for a Festival Nelson Boosey and Hawkes 5383 SATB
Fanfare for Christmas (2 Tpts, 2 Trbns) Pfautsch Flammer 84758 SATB
Fanfare for Christmas Day Shaw G. Schirmer 8745 SATB
Father William (from **Alice in Wonderland**) Fine Witmark 5-W3182 SATB
Fa Una Canzona Vecchi G. Schirmer 556 SATB
Feller from Fortune Somers Gordon Thompson WEI-1008 SATB
Festival Magnificat Pinkham C. F. Peters 6555 SATB
Festival Psalm, A Kauffmann Elkan-Vogel 362-3266 SATB
Fiddler Man (from **Three American Lyrics**) Rutter Hinshaw HMC815 SATB
Finale from The Gondoliers Gilbert and Sullivan E. C. Schirmer 356 SATB
Fine Knacks for Ladies Dowland/McCray Lawson-Gould 52121 SATB
Five Flower Songs Britten Boosey and Hawkes 1873 SATB
Five Secular Songs Schein Broude SATB
Five Traditional French Christmas Carols arr/Gaul Oliver Ditson 12377 SATB
Floral Fancy, A Tull Boosey and Hawkes SATB
Flower of Beauty Clements Galaxy 1-5024-1 SATB
Flower of Beauty Copland Boosey and Hawkes 5020 SATB
For All the Saints Vaughan Williams/Barthelson Plymouth HA9 SATB

For the Beauty of the Earth (Orch) Rutter Hinshaw HMN-550 SATB

For the Lord Is a Mighty God Mendelssohn/McKelvy Foster 233 SATB

For Tonight a King Is Born in Bethlehem Roberton Presser 312-41238 SATB

For Unto Us a Child Is Born (from **Messiah**) Handel G. Schirmer 3580 SATB

Four German Folk Songs Brahms/Robinson Hinshaw HMC 353 SATB

Four Madrigals to Poems of James Joyce Spencer Fostco SATB

Four Slovak Folk Songs Bartok Boosey and Hawkes 17658 SATB

Friendly Beasts, The Downing G. Schirmer 8714 SATB

From Heaven Above to Earth I Come Schein/Cramer Marks SSATB

Fruhlingsfeier Mendelssohn National SATB

Fruhzeitiger Fruhling Mendelssohn National SATB

Full Edition, A (from **A Set of Five**) Berger Kjos SATB

Full Fadom Five Fink Fostco SATB

Fum, Fum, Fum Vree Presser 312-40281 SATB

Galliard, A Staden/Howerton C. Fischer CM4705 SATB

Gaudete Omnes Praetorius, Dodd Tetra SSATTB

Gebet (Prayer) Hauptmann/Young Broude MGC37 SATB

Gentle Mary and Her Child arr/Lundquist (Finnish) Elkan-Vogel 1152 SATB

Gloria (from **La Fiesta de la Posada**) Brubeck Shawnee A-1365 SATB

Gloria (from **Misa Criolla**) Ramirez/Segade (Spanish) Lawson-Gould SATB

Gloria from Mass II Hassler G. Schirmer 9410 SATB

Gloria in Excelsis Gabrielli/Proulx GIA Publications G-2412 SATB

Gloria in Excelsis (from **Missa Brevis in C**) Mozart/Cramer Marks 4553 SATB

Gloria in Excelsis (from **Twelfth Mass**) Mozart G. Schirmer 3515 SATB

Gloria in Excelsis Deo (Brass) Cobb Gentry JG-502 SATB

Gloria in Excelsis Deo Vivaldi/Thomas R. Dean SATB

Gloria in Excelsis Deo Wilson Hope JW 7782 SATB

Glory and Worship Bach/Ehret Presser 312-40729 SSAATTBB

Glory and Worship Are Before Him Handel/Malin Belwin Mills 2435 SATB

Glory in the Highest Davis Galaxy 1092 SATB

Glory to God (from **Messiah**) Handel G. Schirmer 7217 SATB

Glory to God in the Highest Thompson E. C. Schirmer 2470 SATB

Glory to God in the Highest (from **Stabat Mater**) Pergolesi/Manney Belwin Mills 64046 SATB

Glory to the Father Pergolesi/McEwen Hinshaw HMN 685 SATB

Glory to the Son Butler (2 Tpts, Timp) Hope A-520 SATB

Go and Tell John Pfautsch Hope CY 3334 SATB

God of Wisdon, God of Mercy Schubert/Rodby Marks 4161 SATB

Go Down, Moses Cain G. Schirmer 7575 SATB

Go Forth into the World in Peace Sjolund Hinshaw HMN-511 SATB

Gold Fever arr/Ahrold Lawson-Gould 51999 SATB

Go Lovely Rose Stevens Mark Foster SATB

Go Lovely Rose Thiman Novello SATB

Go Now My First Love Costeley/Greyson Bourne ES127 SATB

Go Ye into All the World Butler C. Fischer CM7880 SATB

Grant Me True Courage, Lord Bach/Davison E. C. Schirmer 313 SATB

Grant Them Eternal Rest (from **Requiem**) Verdi/Howorth Belwin Mills 1348 SATB

Great Lord God! Thy Kingdom Shall Endure Handel/Carlton Presser 312-41125 SATB

Guide My Head Heath G. Schirmer 11868 SATB

Gypsy, The Hendrickson Mark Foster 3010 SATB

Haleluya, Haleli Nafshi Rossi Bourde SATB

Hallelujah DeCormier Lawson-Gould 51272 SATB

Hallelujah (from **Messiah**) Handel G. Schirmer 7217 SATB

Hallelujah, Amen (from **Judas Maccabeus**) Handel/Williams Broude 1042 SATB

Hallelujah Chorus (from **Mount of Olives**) Beethoven Presser 312-20978 SATB

Happy Christmas Comes Once More, The Weiss Shawnee A-1351 SATB

Hark, How, O Shepherds arr/Luvaas Birchard 840 SSAATTBB

Hark Ye! The Lord Comes with His Thousands Buxtehude/Granville Sam Fox CM23 SATB

Harp That Once Through Tara's Hall, The Hindemith Associated Music Publishers SATB

Hava Nageela Goldman Lawson-Gould 51270 SATB

He, Watching Over Israel (from **Elijah**) Mendelssohn G. Schirmer 2498 SATB

Hear My Cry, O God Kopyloff/Clough-Leighter Presser 332-13804 SATB

Hear My Supplication Archangelsky/Krone Witmark 5-W2727 SATB

Heavens Are Telling, The (from **Creation**) Haydn G. Schirmer 3521 SATB

Heavens Declare the Glory of God, The Beethoven Flammer 84802 SATB

He Hath Put Down the Mighty Pergolesi/McEwen Hinshaw SATB

He Knows Rhea Belwin Mills SATB

Here We Come A-Caroling arr/Jennings Curtis/Kjos C8421 SATB

Hide Not Thy Face Farrant/Hallagan Presser 312-40445 SATB

Hodie Christus Natus Est Gabrieli/Jergenson G. Schirmer SATB/SATB

Hodie Christus Natus Est Marenzio/Thomas Concordia SATB

Hodie Christus Natus Est Poulenc Salabert SATB

Hodie Christus Natus Est Sweelinck Presser 312-40155 SSATB

Hodie Christus Natus Est Wesley Broude 1022 SATB

Hol' de Light Johnson C. Fischer CM7104 SATB

Hold On Hairston Bourne SATB

Holly Carol arr/Fissinger Jenson 411-08024 SATB

Holy, Holy, Holy (from **Requiem**) Fauré FitzSimons 2119 SATB

Hor Che La Vaga Aurora Aleotti/Carruthers-Clemens Broude SATB

Hort Ich Ein Kuckuck Singen Eccard/Richter Schott AP508 SSATB

Hosanna to the Son of David Moe Mercury/Presser 352-00212 SATB

Hospodi Pomilui Von Lvov/Wilhousky C. Fischer CM5680 SATB

How Excellent Is Thy Name Butler Bourne 837 SATB

How Far Is It to Bethlehem? Christiansen Kjox 42 SATB

How Lovely Are the Messengers (from **St. Paul**) Mendelssohn G. Schirmer 3741 SATB

How Lovely Is Thine Own Dwelling Place Hammerschmidt/Malin Belwin Mills 2436 SSATB

How Lovely Is Thy Dwelling Place Brahms (from **German Requiem**) C. Fischer CM632 SATB

How Lovely Thy Place Kubik Gray CCS 16-(4) SATB

How Still He Rests Pierce Walton SATB

Hunter, The Brahms/Granville Choral Art SATB

I Am a Poor Wayfaring Stranger arr/Bratt Spire ED.ESE 978-8 SATB

I Beheld Her, Beautiful as a Dove Willan Oxford SATB

I Bought Me a Cat Copland Boosey and Hawkes 5024 SATB

I Can Tell the World Hairston Bourne SATB

Ich Freue Mich Im Herrn Homilius/Kaplan (German or English) Lawson-Gould SATB

Idden-Dem Mallida Makil/Gomez Lawson-Gould 52216 SATB

Ifca's Castle Harley/Aschenbrenner C. Fischer CM4708 SATB

I Got a Key Shaw/Parker Lawson-Gould 1105 SATB

I Got a Shoe Wilson Somerset JW7771 SATB

I Got Shoes Shaw/Parker Lawson-Gould 51116 SATB

I Got the Spirit Rodby WR1008 SATB

I Hear a Voice A'Prayin' Bright Shawnee A-335 SATB

Ihr Lieblichste Blicke Bach/Malin Belwin Mills SATB

Il Est Bel Et Bon Passereau/Fauré Editions Salabert SATB

I'll Never Turn Back No More Dett J. Fisher FE 4435 SATB

I'll Say It Anyway Certon/Hirt Hinshaw HMC 519 SATB

I Lost My Love in Scarlet Town Wilder G. Schirmer 11158 SATB

I Love My Love Holst J. Curwen 8117 SATB

I Love My Love Holst G. Schirmer SATB

I Love the Word of God the Father Costeley/Mochnick Broude CR28 SATB

I'm Goin' to Sing! Kjelson Belwin Mills 2061 SATB

I'm Gonna Sing Gardner Staff 499 SATB

Im Herbst Brahms Hinshaw SATB

Im Kuhlen Maien Hassler/Knight C. Fischer SATB (double chorus)

In Epiphania Domini Festa/Otten Unicorn SATB

In His Care-O Dawson Kjos T122 SATB

In Memoria Aeterna Vivaldi/McEwen Hinshaw HMC-179 SATB

In Music God Is Glorified Pfautsch Hinshaw HMC-403 SATB

In Natali Domini Praetorius Kjos 2007 SATB

Innsbruck, I Now Must Leave Thee Isaac/Howerton C. Fischer CM4704 SATB

In Nomine Jesu Handel J. and W. Chester SAATB

In Praise of Spring Mendelssohn Associated Music Publishers WHC 95 SATB

In Pride of May Weelkes/Porter Associated Music Publishers A-817 SSATB

In Steadfast Faith I Stand Bach/Heller Schmitt 1696 SATB

In That Great Gittin' Up Mornin' Heath G. Schirmer 11867 SATB

In the Beginning of Creation (Electronic Tape) Pinkham E. C. Schirmer 2902 SATB

In Thee, O Lord, Have I Trusted Handel/Ehret Mercury MC361 SATB

In These Delightful Pleasant Groves Purcell Witmark 5-W2641 SATB

Io Ti Verila Lassus G. Schirmer 11339 SATB

I Saw Three Ships arr/Harris Somerset AD 2015 SATB

I Saw Three Ships arr/Jennings Curtis 8323 SATB

Is This the Way to Bethlehem? Dickinson Gray 178 SATB

It Is Good to Be Merry Berger Kjos 5293 SATB

I to the Hills Lift Up Mine Eyes Berger Augsburg 110678 SATB

It Was a Lover and His Lass Kirk Shawnee SATB

I Want Jesus to Walk with Me Cram Fine Arts Music Press/S1261B SATB

I Will Give Thanks Unto Thee, O Lord Rossini/Fitzhugh Flammer 4058 SATB

I Will Greatly Rejoice Nystedt Hinshaw HMC-226 SATB

I Will Sing You a New Song Nysted Hinshaw SSAATTBB

I Wonder as I Wander (Appalachian) Niles-Horton Schirmer/8708 SATB

Jamaica Farewell House Sam Fox PS106 SATB

Jauchzet dem Herrn Pachelbel/Ruf Concordia SSAATTBB

J'ay Fait Pour Vous Cent Mille Pas de Sermisy/Robinson Hinshaw SATB

Jesu, Joy of Man's Desiring Bach/Riegger Flammer 84137 SATB

Jesu, the Very Thought of Thee Thiman Gray 1845 SATB

Jesu, Thy Blessings Give to Me Franck C. Fischer CM7505 SATB

Jesus, Blest Redeemer (from **Ave Maris Stella**) Grieg/Dickinson Gray SSAATTBB

Jesus, Jesus, Rest Your Head (Appalachian) Niles-Warren Schirmer 8302 SATB

Jesus, Jesus, Rest Your Head Vance New Music NMA143 SATB

Jesus, Sun of Life, My Splendor Handel-Bunjes Corcordia 98-1445 SATB

Jesus Walked This Lonesome Valley Krone Kjos 1032 SATB

Johnny Has Gone for a Soldier Dooley Franco Colombo FC2798 SATB

Johnny Has Gone for a Soldier Shaw/Parker Lawson-Gould 502 SATB

Johnny, I Hardly Know Ye Parker Lawson-Gould 51452 SATB

John Saw Duh Number Shaw/Parker Lawson-Gould 51109 SATB

Join Hands Ringwald Shawnee A-1257 SATB

Joseph Came Walking to Bethlehem Young Flammer A-5860 SATB

Joseph Dearest, Joseph Mine Walther Flammer A-5763 SATB

Joshua Fit the Battle of Jericho Dressler Agape 7128 SATB

Joyous Christmas Song, A Gevaert Gray GSC 11 SATB

Jubilant Song, A (Brass and Handbells) Pote Hope F979 SATB

Jubilant Song Dello Joio G. Schirmer 9580 SATB

Jubilate Deo Britten/Willcocks Oxford SATB

Jubilate Deo Walton Oxford 42-373 SSAATTBB

Jubilate Deo Omnis Terra Peeters Summy-Birchard SATB

Keep A Inchin Along Cain Boosey and Hawkes 1605 SATB

Keeper, The arr/Brandon Greenwood Press CE-1940-8 SATB

Keeping Holy Vigil Schroth Kjos 5185 SATB

Keep in the Middle of the Road Lewis Plymouth PCS-152 SATB

King Jesus Is A-Listening Dawson Fitzsimons 4025 SATB

King's Singers Folk Songs, The Hinshaw SATBBB

Kittery Billings G. Schirmer 10309 SATB

Komm, Heiliger Geise Hassler/Shrock (German or English) Hinshaw SATB

Kum Bah Ya Koepke Belwin Mills OCT02524 SATB

Kyrie (from **Mass in C Minor**) Schumann/Hines Chor Pub 30049 SATB

Kyrie (from **Missa Brevis Sancti Joannis de Deo**) Haydn/Hines G. Schirmer 11442 SATB

Kyrie (from **Missa Luba**) Haazen Lawson-Gould 51803 SATB

Kyrie Eleison Hassler/Harris Shawnee SATB

Lacrymosa (from **Requiem**) Mozart G. Schirmer 11564 SATB

Lamb of God Bizet/Ryder Oliver Ditson 12246 SATB

Lark in the Clear Air, The Cashmore Novello SATB

Lark's Song, The Mendelssohn/Greyson Bourne SATB

Lasciatemi Morire Monteverdi Recordi NY841 SATB

Lass Dich Nur Nicht Dauren Brahms/Klein G. Schirmer SATB

Last Words of David, The Thompson E. C. Schirmer 2294 SATB

Laudate Dominum Young Coronet CP 321 SATB

Lautrier Priay de Danser Costeley Kjos SATB

Lawd I Wanna Go Home Smith AMSI 305 SATB

Lebenslust Schubert/Gordon Tetra AB258-6 SATB

Lerchengesang Mendelssohn/Carl National SATB

Let All Mortal Flesh Keep Silence Edmundson J. Fisher/Belwin 8749 SATB

Let All Mortal Flesh Keep Silence (Band or Orch) Holst Galaxy 3.2309.1 SATB

Let All Mortal Flesh Keep Silence Holst Galaxy 1.5019.1 SATB

Let All the World in Every Corner Sing Roberton G. Schirmer 8721 SATB

Let Hearts Awaken Clokey Gray 1597 (Plainsong, Orch)

Let Me, God, Your Help Be Finding Mendelssohn Presser 312-41192 SATB

Let Nothing Ever Grieve Thee Brahms/Buszin/Soldan C. F. Peters 6093 SATB

Let Their Celestial Concerts All Unite (from **Samson**) Handel E. C. Schirmer 312 SATB

Let the People Praise Thee, O God Mathias Oxford SATB

Let the People Praise Thee Monhardt Augsburg SATB

Let Us Break Bread Together Beck Hope A447 SATB

Let Us Break Bread Together Terri Lawson-Gould 896 SATB

Let Us Celebrate God's Name Bruckner Augsburg PS 626 SATB

Let Your Eye Be to the Lord Moe Augsburg 110544 SATB

Liebeslieder Walzer, Opus 52 Brahms/Shaw (English or German) Lawson-Gould SATB (4-hand piano)

Lift Up Your Heads, Ye Mighty Gates Willan Concordia HA 2003 SATB

Lift Your Hearts and Sing Kirk C. Fischer CM8195 SATB

Light Divine Archangelsky/Walker Hal Leonard 08681500 SATB

Like as the Culver on the Bared Bough Stevens Associated Music Publishers SSATB

Linden Lea Vaughan Williams Boosey and Hawkes 1401 SATB

Listen to the Lambs Dett G. Schirmer SATB

Listen to the Lambs Watson Belwin Mills 1263 SATB

Little Jesus Came to Town Sojlund Hinshaw HMC-734 SATB

Little Talk with Jesus, A Rhea Bourne RSS1 SATB

Little Wheel A-Turnin' Pfautsch Lawson-Gould 547 SATB

Little White Hen, A Scandello/Greyson (German) Bourne SATB

Lo, A Voice to Heaven Sounding Bortniansky E. C. Schirmer 151 SATB

Lo, How a Rose E'er Blooming Praetorius/Baker G. Schirmer 2484 SATB

Locus Iste Bruckner G. Schirmer SATB

Londonderry Air Frackenpohl Mark Foster 354 SATB

Lonesome Valley Lynn Presser 312-40062 SATB

Lord, From Thee Comes Our Strength Caldara/Pauly E. C. Schirmer 3075 SATB

Lord, Give New Tunes (Harp, Tpts, Trbns, Timp) Wetzler C. Fischer CM 7772 SATB

Lord, I Want to Be a Christian Laster Augsburg 1101739 SATB

Lord, Make Me an Instrument of Thy Peace Rutter Hinshaw HMN-470 SATB

Lord Is a Mighty God, The Jothen Coronet CP 210 SATB

Lord Is My Shepherd, The Cain Flammer 84221 SATB

Lord Lead Us Still Brahms/Dickinson Gray GSC 60 SATB

Lord Shall Be Unto Thee, The Thompson E. C. Schirmer 2641 SATB

Lost in the Night Christiansen Augsburg 11-0119 SATB

Love Came Down at Christmas arr/McGlohon-Ringwald Glorysound/Shawnee A-5858 SATB

Love Came Down at Christmas (Handbells, C Inst.) Pote Hinshaw HMC-404 SATB

Love Came Down at Christmas Sowerby Fitzsimons 2054 SATB

Love Came Down at Christmas Wood AMSI 346 SATB

Love Me Truly Lefevre/Knight C. Fischer CM7561 SATB

Lover's Ghost, The Vaughan Williams Galaxy 1.5177.1 SATB

Love Songs Parker Hinshaw SATB

Lullaby on Christmas Eve Christiansen Augsburg 136 SATB

Lusty Month of May, The Clemens Non Papa Tetra AB 847 SATB

Madrigal Fauré Broude SATB

Magdalena Brahms (German) G. Schirmer SATB

Magi Viderunt Stellam Victoria Shawnee A-1355 SATB

Magnificat (Double Chorus) Pachelbel C. F. Peters 6087 SATB

Magnificat Anima Mea Porter Associated Music Publishers SATB

Maiden Is in a Ring, A Alfven Walton SATBB

Make a Joyful Noise Unto the Lord Mathias Oxford SATB

Make We Joy Robinson Oxford SATB

Man's Spirit Duson Kjos SATB divisi

Mary, Did You Know? Davenport Richmond MI-174 SATB

Mary and Martha Christiansen Schmitt 664 SATB

Mary Ann Hendrickson Mark Foster 3002 SATB

Mary Had a Baby Dawson Tuskegee 118 SATB

Mary Hynes Barber G. Schirmer SATB

Mary's Lullaby arr/Rutter Oxford X-272 SATB

Masters in This Hall arr/Black Gray 2710 SATB

Matona, Lovely Maiden Lassus C. Fischer 4637 SATB

Matthew, Mark, Luke and John (from **Five Childhood Lyrics**) Rutter Oxford SATB

Mayday Carol Taylor J. Fisher 4838 SATB

Minnedienst Binkerd Boosey and Hawkes 5980 SATB

Misericordias Domini (Double Chorus) Durante/Durand Walton 2193 SATB

Misericordias Domini Durante/Damrosch G. Schirmer SATB/SATB

Monday's Child (from **Five Childhood Lyrics**) Rutter Oxford SATB

Monday's Child Rutter Oxford SATB

Morning Trumpet, The Richardson Mark Foster 245 SATB

Musicks Empire (from **Tryptich**) Pfautsch Lawson-Gould SATB

Music Spread Thy Voice (from **Solomon**) Handel/Cramer Marks MC4132 SATB

My Dancing Day arr/Shaw/Parker Lawson-Gould SATB

My Gentle Harp Parker Lawson-Gould S-1409 SATB

My Heart Is Offered Still to You Lassus Lawson-Gould 563 SATB

My Lagan Love Erb Lawson-Gould 52134 SATB

My Lord, What a Morning Christiansen Choral Art SATB

My Shepherd Will Supply My Need Thomson Gray 2046 SATB

My Soul Is a Witness for My Lord Rhea Choral Art R142 SATB

Nach Gruner Farb Meine Herz Verlangt Praetorius Schott AP 513 SATB

Nachtens Brahms G. Schirmer 11799 SATB

Neckeriein Brahms National SATB

Neujahrslied Mendelssohn/Palmer National SATB

Never Tell Thy Love Bright Associated Music Publishers A-171 SATB

New Psalm, A Duson Kjos SATB

Nine Hundred Miles Ehret Frank Music F671 SSATB

Noe, Noe, Noe, Psallite Noe Mouton/Mochnick R. Dean SATB

Noel, Noel (Finger Cymbals, Tamb) Kirk Somerset AD 2005 SATB

Noel, Noel, Let Us Sing Merry Christmas Rodby and Roff Schmitt 8039 SATB

Noel Benedictus Charpentier/Ehret Shawnee A-1430 SATB

Notre Pere Durufle Durand 14075 SATB

Now It Is Christmas Time arr/Pooler Augsburg TC13 SATB

Now Thank We All Our God Pachelbel (English or German) Concordia SATB

O, No John Miller Presser 312-40506 SATB

O Be Joyful in the Lord Pfautsch Hinshaw HMN-445 SATB

O Bella Fusa Lassus E. C. Schirmer 11338 SATB

O Beloved Shepherds (O Ihr Lieben Hirten) Hammerschmidt/Mueller (English or German) Concordia SATB

O Bone Jesu Palestrina G. Schirmer 10022 SATB

Occhi Piangete Lassus/Herder Continuo SATB

O Clap Your Hands Rutter Oxford A 307 SATB

O Clap Your Hands Vaughan Williams Galaxy 1.500.1 SATB

O Come Little Children Schulz/Fritschel Himshaw HMC-148 SATB

O Domine Jesu Christe Palestrina/Walker Shawnee SATB

O Gladsome Light Arkhangelsky/Norden J. Fisher/Belwin 4332 SATB

O God, We Pray Arensky/Davison E. C. Schirmer 1126 SATB

Oh, No John arr/Southers Hinshaw SSATB

O How Blessed Bruckner Choral Art R154 SATB

Oh Rock-a-My-Soul Kubik Lawson-Gould 52013 SATB

O Lamb of God Franck/Gillette Summy-Birchard 1370 SATB

Old Abram Brown Britten Boosey and Hawkes 1786 SATB

Old Hundredth Psalm Tune, The (Orch) Vaughan Williams Oxford 42P953 SATB

O Lord, Give Thy Holy Spirit Tallis/Simkins Concordia 98-2249 SATB

O Lord, How Can We Know Thee? Nelson Boosey and Hawkes 5439 SATB

O Lord, My Heart Is Not Lifted Up Grantham Fostco SATB

O Lord Most Holy (Panis Angelicus) Franck Summy-Birchard 396 SATB

O Lord of Heav'n Lassus Marks 4062 SATB

O Lovely May (O Susser Mai) Presser 332-14456 SATB

O Magnum Mysterium Byrd Tetra SATB

O Magnum Mysterium Gabrieli Hinshaw SATB

O Magnum Mysterium Rorem Boosey and Hawkes 6006 SATB

O Magnum Mysterium Scarlatti/Brandvik Schmitt 1439 SATB

O Magnum Mysterium Victoria Broude CR 30 SATB

O Make Our Hearts to Blossom Clokey Summy-Birchard B-2065 SSAATTBB

Omnipotence, The Schubert/Spicker G. Schirmer 4346 SATB

On Christmas Night arr/Luvaas Kjos 2038 SSATBB

One and Twenty Heldman R. Dean SATB

On This Good Christmas Morn Cain Flammer 84177 SATB

Onward, Ye Peoples Sibelius Galaxy GM 938-10 SATB

Open Our Eyes MacFarlane G. Schirmer 7273 SSAATTBB

Open Thou Mine Eyes Rutter Hinshaw SATB

O Quam Gloriosum Est Regnum Victoria/Robinson Hinshaw SATB

O Rejoice, Ye Christians, Loudly Bach/Clough/Leighter E. C. Schirmer 367 SATB

O Rex Gloriae Marenzio Oxford SATB

O Salutaris Hostia Rossini/Zipper Broude SATB

O Sanctissima Shaw/Parker G. Schirmer 10194 SATB

O Saviour Sweet Bach/Dickinson Gray GSC 82 SATB

O Shepherds, Go Quickly arr/Fissinger Jensen 411-15014 SATB

O Sing Unto the Lord Purcell/Davison E. C. Schirmer 1103 SATB

O Sing Unto the Lord Sweelinck/Klein G. Schirmer 12102 SSATB

O Sing Ye to the Lord (Cantate Domino) Sweelinck G. Schirmer/Concordia SSATB

O Taste and See Vaughan Williams Oxford 43 SATB

O Thou Most High Scarlatti/Ehret Lawson-Gould 52105 SATB

Out of the Depths Charpentier/Lovelace Concordia 98-1521 SATB

O Vos Omnes Casals Tetra AB128 SATB

O Vos Omnes Croce/Kjelson Belwin Mills 2149 SATB

O Vos Omnes Jommelli/Hunter Belwin Mills SATB

O Vos Omnes Victoria/Klein GIA G-1525 SATB

O Waly, Waly Rutter Oxford 52.206 SATB

O Whistle and I'll Come to Ye (from **Three Scottish Folk Songs**) Wilberg Hinshaw SATB

O Worship the Lord Purcell/Hilton Mercury MC 396 SATB

Paratum Cor Ejus Vivaldi/McEwen Hinshaw SATB

Parsley, Sage, Rosemary and Thyme arr/Coates Shawnee A-1063 SATB

Pat-a-Pan (Burgundian) arr/Grundman Boosey and Hawkes 6038 SATB

Path of the Just, The Hystedt Augsburg 11-9333 SATB

Pavane Pour Une Infant Defunte Ravel Broude 100 SATB

People Know Thee Eberlin/Hilton Mercury 352-00471 SATB

Petite Nymphy Folastre Janequin/Klein G. Schirmer 11725 SATB

Pharisee and the Publican Schütz/Williamson G. Schirmer 7473 SATB

Pick a Bale of Cotton DeCormier Lawson-Gould 51375 SATB
Pick a Bale of Cotton Gardner Staff 1063 SATB
Pie Jesu (from **Requiem in C Minor**) Cherubini/Hall National WHC-46 SATB
Placido e il Mar Mozart/Wagner Lawson-Gould 841 SATB
Pleasure Awaits Us Mozart/Malin Belwin Mills 2403 SATB
Plenty Good Room Smith Kjos 1003 SATB
Plorate Filii Israel (from **Jeptha**) Carissimi Bourne/ E. C. Schirmer SSAATBB
Polly Wolly Doodle Kubik G. Schirmer 9854 SATB
Poor Man Lazrus Hairston Schumann S-1001 SATB
Poor Wayfarin' Stranger Richardson Mark Foster 251 SATB
Praise the Lord Goemanne Summy-Birchard M-5949 SATB
Praise the Lord, O My Soul Rorem Boosey and Hawkes 6105 SATB
Praise the Lord Who Reigns Above Stevens Mark Foster EH9 SATB
Praise the Name of God with a Song Koepke/Pooler Jensen SATB divisi
Praise Ye the Father Gounod G. Schirmer 3325 SATB
Praise Ye the Lord Ivanoff/Douglas Pro Art 1591 SATB
Praise Ye the Lord, Ye Children Tye Oxford SATB
Praise Ye the Lord of Heaven Pitoni/Gray Broude 1044 SATB
Praise Ye the Lord of Hosts (from **Christmas Oratorio**) Saint/Saëns/Jurey Belwin Mills 60597 SATB
Praise Ye the Lord of Hosts (from **Christmas Oratorio**) Saint Saëns/Walker Hal Leonard 08681662 SATB
Prayer Pfautch Lawson-Gould SATB 2 pt.
Pretty Saro Vance Belwin Mills 2336 SATB
Promised Land Richardson Mark Foster 255 SATB
Proposal, The Tubb Associated Music Publishers SATB
Psallite Praetorius/Greyson Bourne ES 21 SATB
Psalm 121 Kodály Boosey and Hawkes 5330 SATB
Psalm 148 Praise Ye the Lord Stevens Mark Foster EH2 SATB
Psalm 150 (Praise Ye the Lord) Franck Oliver Ditson 332-14082 SATB
Psalm 150 Schütz Presser SATB
Psalm Nineteen Marcello/Hopson Agape HH 3912 SATB
Psalm 96 Sweelinck/Boepple (French) Mercury SATB
Psalm Settings (Violin I, II, Cello) Telemann Concordia 97-4838 SATB
Psalm 61 Hovhaness C. F. Peters 6255 SATB
Quem Vidistis, Pastores Victoria G. Schirmer 11974 SSATBB
Quem Vidistis, Pastores Dering/Terry Gray 1594 SSATTB
Rainsong Bright Associated Music Publishers A-269 SATB

Red Bird in a Green Tree arr/Harris Belwin Mills 64428 SATB
Reflection Bright Shawnee A-609 SATB
Regina Coeli Suriano/Porter Associated Music Publishers SATB
Reincarnations: Mary Hymes; Anthony O'Daley; The Coolin Barber G. Schirmer 8908; 8909; 8910 SATB
Rejoice and Be Merry Butler Beacon Hill/Belwin Mills AN-6015 SATB
Rejoice and Sing (from **Christmas Oratorio**) Bach Kjos 20 SATB
Rejoice Exultantly (Freut euch und Jubiliert) Calvisius (German) Sam Fox SSATBB
Remember arr/Routley GIA G-2317 SATB
Rest Vaughan Williams Galaxy 1.2478.1 SATB
Riddle Song, The Rutter Oxford X230 SATB
Rise Up, My Love My Fair One McCray National WHC-77 SATB
Rise Up, My Love, My Fair One Willan Hinshaw HMC 218 SATB
Rise Up, O Men of God! Miles FitzSimons 2074 SSAATTBB
Rise Up Early Kountz Galaxy 1665 SATB
Rise Up Shepherd and Follow arr/McGlohon Broude 1026 SATB
Rising Sun, The (Aleatory) Pooler and Pierce Somerset CE 4328 SATB
Road Not Taken, The (from **Frostiana-Seven Country Songs**) Thompson E. C. Schirmer 2485 SATB
Roll De Chariot Along Worley Belwin Mills 1381 SATB
Roll Jordan Roll Gillum J. Fisher 8390 SATB
Rorate Coeli Palestrina/Petti Tetra SSATB
Rose Touched by the Sun's Warm Rays, A Berger Augsburg 11-0953 SATB
Run, Run, Run to Bethlehem (from **La Fiesta de la Posada**) Brubeck Shawnee A-1534 SATB
Russian Picnic Enders G. Schirmer 9544 SATB
Saboly: Touro-louro-louro! Shaw/Parker G. Schirmer 10167 SATB
Salvation Is Created Tschesnokoff/Ehret Bourne WE 8 SATB
Salve Regina Poulenc Salabert SATB
Salve Regina Schubert/Sisson Broude 969 SATB
Sanctus Haydn, Michael/Walker Hal Leonard 08681753 SATB
Sanctus (from **German Mass in F**) Schubert/Craig Plymouth DC-109 SATB
Sanctus (from **Missa Brevis in C**) Mozart Marks 4555 SATB
Sanctus and Benedictus (from **St. Cecelia Mass**) Gounod Presser 332-00114 SATB
Sancta Maria, Mater Dei (K. 273) Mozart Novello SATB
Savior from on High, A Paulus AMSI 339 SATB
Say, Love If Ever Thou Didst Find Dowland/Contino R. Dean HCA-108 SATB
Scarabella Desprez/Unruh Mark Foster 352 SATB
Scarborough Fair arr/Bock Gentry J6104 SATB

Seeds Grow to Plants (from **Canticles of America**) Rutter Bourne SATB

Sehnsucht Brahms/Klein G. Schirmer SATB

Selig sind die Toten Schütz/Shaw G. Schirmer SSATBB

Send Forth Thy Spirit Schuetky/Hilton Mercury 352-00280 SSATTBB

Send Out Thy Light Gounod Presser 332-00063 SATB

Sense of Kinship, A Duson/Frostic Kjos SATB

Set Down Servant Shaw Shawnee 7 SATB

Set It Down Montgomery Plymouth JR106 SATB

Shadrack Lee C. Fischer CM4670 SATB

She'll Be Comin' Round the Mountain Carter Somerset SP785 SATB

She's Like a Swallow Lock Shawnee SATB

Shenandoah Erb Lawson-Gould 51846 SATB

Shenandoah Smith G. Schirmer 11055 SATB

Shepherds' Christmas Song Dickinson Gray 7 SATB

Sicut Cervus/Anima Mae Palestrina Broude SATB

Sine Nomine Vaughan Williams C. Fischer CM6637 SATB

Sing and Be Joyful Graun/Craig Plymouth FS-101 SATB

Sing a New Song Schütz/Jennings Belwin Mills SATB

Sing Gloria Davis Remick 5-R3158 SATB

Sing Praise to Christ Bach Concordia SATB

Sing Praises to the Lord Handel/Malin Belwin Mills SATB

Sing to the Lord a Marvelous Song Butler Hope A-451 SATB

Sing to the Lord of Harvest Peninger Hinshaw HMC-364 SATB

Sing Unto God Fetler Augsburg SATB

Sing We All Noel! Besig Flammer A-6122 SATB

Sing We All Noel Young Somerset AD 1999 SATB

Sing We All Now with One Accord Praetorius G. Schirmer 7543 SATB

Sing We Merrily Green/Martens Walton W2300 SATB

Sing Ye Praises to Our King (from **Four Motets**) Copland Boosey and Hawkes 6021 SATB

Six Afro-American Carols Clark Piedmont/Marks/Belwin 15595-6 SATB

Six Folk Songs Brahms Marks 9 SATB

Sixty-Seventh Psalm Ives Associated Music Publishers A-274 (divisi)

Skip to My Lou arr/Bryan Peabody College SATB

Sleep, Holy Infant, Sleep (from **La Fiesta de la Posada**) Brubeck Shawnee A-1360 SATB

Sleep Now, King Jesus Child Peninger Hinshaw HMC-365 SATB

Slumber Song of the Infant Jesus Gevaert Gray 14 SATB

Somebody's Knockin' at Your Door North Coronet CP120 SATB

Sometimes I Feel Like a Motherless Child Burleigh Ricordi NY1707 SATB

Sometimes I Feel Like a Motherless Child Parks Hal Leonard 08603701 SATB

Sometimes I Feel Like a Motherless Child Smith Kjos 1013 SATB

Songs of Nature Dvorak/Zipper Broude SATB

Sons of Men Cadman Flammer 4038 SATB

Soon-Ah Will Be Done Dawson Kjos T102-A SATB

So Wahr Die Sonne Scheinet Schumann (English and German) National WHC 117 SATB

Spring Canticle (from **Three Seasonal Reflections**) Nelson Boosey and Hawkes 6073 SATB

Stars Shinin' By'n By DeCormier Lawson-Gould 51751 SATB

Steal Away Dawson Kjos T108 SATB

Steal Away Hall Rodeheaver 1945 SATB

Steal Away Luboff Walton 3061 SATB

Steal Away Rumery Thomas House C28-8419 SATB

Still, Still, Still arr/Luboff (Austrian) Walton 3003 SATB

Stomp Your Foot Copland (4-hand piano) Boosey and Hawkes 5019 SATB

Streets of Laredo Terri Lawson-Gould 694 SATB

Study War No More DeCormier Lawson-Gould 51477 SATB

Super Flumina Babylonis Palestrina J. Fisher SSATB

Surgens Jesu Philips National/J. and W. Chester SSATB

Surrexit Pastor Bonus Lassus/Deis G. Schirmer SATB (Latin)

Sweet Are the Thoughts Amner/Carapetyan Schmitt SATB

Sweet Day Vaughan Williams Galaxy 1.50.11 SATB

Sweet Was the Song Clausen Mark Foster 550 SATB

Tambur Bardos Boosey and Hawkes 6055 SATB

Tantum Ergo Fauré Walton SATB

Tantum Ergo in E-Flat Schubert G. Schirmer SATB

Te Deum Laudamus Willan Gray 224 SATB

Tenebrae Factae Sunt Ingegneri/Decker National NMP-140 SATB

Tenebrae in E-Flat Haydn, Michael/Strickling Schmitt 1536 SATB

Thanks Be to Thee (Cantata con Stromenti) Handel/Lefebvre Galaxy 1228-6 SATB

That's My Jesus arr/Ehret McAfee M1233 SATB

Thee We Adore Candlyn C. Fischer CM492 SATB

Then Shall a Star Come Out of Jacob (Christus) Mendelssohn Schmitt 1903 SATB

There Is a Balm in Gilead Dawson Kjos T105 SATB

There Is a Balm in Gilead Smith Plymouth LC101 SATB

There Shall Be a Star from Jacob Come Forth Mendelssohn Addington SATB

There Shall Be a Star Come Out of Jacob Mendelssohn Jensen SATB

This Is the Day (Double Chorus) Gallus/Thomas Concordia 98-1702 SATB

This Little Babe (from **Ceremony of Carols**) Britten Boosey and Hawkes 1830 SATB

This Little Light of Mine Thygerson Coronet CP266 SATB

This Sweet and Lovely Siren Gastoldi/Greyson Bourne ES-103 SATB

Thou Art the King of Glory (Utrecht Te Deum) Handel/Klein Kjos 5481A SATB

Thou Hast Turned My Laments into Dancing Pinkham Editions C. F. Peters SATB

Thou Knowest, Lord, the Secrets of Our Hearts Purcell/Morse Presser 14713 SATB

Thou Must Leave Thy Lowly Dwelling (from **Childhood of Christ**) Gray CMR 1898 SATB

Three Chansons Debussy Durant 7191-1, 2, and 3 SATB

Three Chansons Ravel Durant SATB

Three Christmas Carols Guerrero/Petti (Spanish) Tetra SSATB

Three Harvest Home Chorales (Orch) Ives Mercury 352-00361 SATB

Three Hungarian Folk Songs Bartok/Suchoff Boosey and Hawkes 5326 SATB

Three Hungarian Folk Songs Seiber G. Schirmer 10715 SATB

Three Irish Songs Frackenpohl Shawnee B-200 SATB

Three Kings, The Willam Oxford 43P214 SATB

Three Madrigals Diemer G. Schirmer 5417 SATB

Three Shakespearean Madrigals Baber Canyon SATB

Tomorrow Shall Be My Dancing Day Gardner Oxford SATB

To Thee We Sing Archangelsky/Tellep Schmitt 857 SATB

To Us Is Born Immanuel Praetorius/Baker G. Schirmer 2482 SATB

Tu Es Petrus Palestrina National/G. Schirmer SSATBB

Tumbalalaika DeCormier Lawson-Gould 51225 SATB

Tune, The Mechem E. C. Schirmer 2647 SATB

Tu Ne L'Enten Pas, La La La LeJeune Galaxy SATB

Tu Pauperum Refugium Desprez/Beveridge G. Schirmer SATB

Tu Solus Desprez E. C. Schirmer 2253 SATB

Turn Back O Man (Band or Orch) Holst Galaxy 1.5001.1 SATB

Turtle Dove, The Price Hinshaw SATB

Twas Here a King Was Born Franck/Haufrecht Sam Fox PS 158 SATB

Two American Folk Songs Ruter Plymouth BPX247 SATB

Two Choruses (from **Queen Mary's Birthday Ode**) Purcell/Malin Piedmont SATB

Two Motets Croce/McCray Shawnee A-1731 SATB

Two Motets Monteverdi Oxford SSATTB

Two Welsh Love Songs arr/Thomas Oxford SATB

Ubi Caritas (from **Quatre Motets**) Durufle Durand 312-41253 SATB

Upon This Rock Beck G. Schirmer 11467 SATB

Verbum Caro Factum Est Hassler/Richter Tetra SSATTB

Verdant Meadows (Alcina) Handel/Cain Schmitt 1061 SATB

Vere Languores Victoria/Henson Jenson SATB

Virgin Most Pure, A arr/Halter (English) Concordia 98-1237 SATB

Virgin Unspotted, A Billings/Dickinson Music Press MP-64 SATB

Von Himmel Hoch da Komm Ich Her Schein/Pinkham E. C. Schirmer 2722 SATB

Votre Beaute Plaisante Et Lie Gombert/Malin Belwin Mills 2327 SATB

Wade in the Water Clark Marks 830 SATB

Wade in the Water Hayden Shawnee A-1490 SATB

Wade in the Water Kirk C. Fischer CM8022 SATB

Walking on the Green Grass Hennagin Boosey and Hawkes 5443 SATTBB

Water Is Wide, The Zaninelli Shawnee A-616 SATB

Waters Ripple and Flow Taylor J. Fisher 5676 SATB

Wedding Ring, The Dvorak/Suchoff Plymouth PXW100 SATB

We Have Heard the Words (Psalm 44) Sweelinck/Aks Marks 86 SATB

We Pledge You Forever (from **Cantata 208**) Bach/Malin Belwin Mills OCT 2406 SATB

Were You There? Burleigh Belwin Mills FCC592 SATB

Were You There? Parks Hal Leonard 08603818 SATB

Werfet Panier Auf Im Lande Telemann/Kaplan Tetra SATB

We Shall Walk Through the Valley Moore Augsburg 110565 SATB

We Shepherds Sing Weelkes Kjos 5997 SATB

We Sing Our Praises Now to Thee Farrant/Davies Flammer 84411 SATB

We Turn Our Eyes to Thee (Double Chorus) Belwin Mills 268 SATB

We've Been a While A'Wandring (Yorkshire) Christiansen Kjos 5105 SATB

We Will Remember Thy Name and Alleluia Amen Handel/Malin Belwin Mills SATB

What Cheer Walton Oxford 84.090 SATB

What Child Is This? Shaw/Parker G. Schirmer 10199 SATB

What Is Gold Duson Jenson SATB

What Strangers Are These? Purvis Summy-Birchard 1447 SATB

What We Have Once Enjoyed Duson Lawson-Gould SATB

What You Gonna Call Yo' Pretty Little Baby arr/Ehret Schmitt 884 SATB

When Christmas Morn Is Dawning (German) arr/Luvaas Augsburg TC9 SATB

When David Heard Weelkes/Collins Associated Music Publishers SSATB

When Jesus Wept Billings Broude 995 SATB

When the Trumpet Sounds Thomas Mark Foster 261 SATB

While Shepherds Watched Their Sheep (Echo Carol) arr/Jungst Gray 103 SATB

White Dove, The Brahms/Ehret Boosey and Hawkes SATB

Who Hath a Right to Sing Pfautsch Lawson-Gould 52048 SATB divisi

Who Is at My Window, Who Russell Clark and Cruickshank SATB

Wie schon singt uns der Engle Schar Freundt/Richter (German or English) Schott SATB

Willie, Take Your Little Drum (Patapan) Coggin Kjos 5944 SATB

Winter Journeyings (from **Four Pieces After the Seasons**) Nelson Boosey and Hawkes SATB divisi

With a Voice of Singing (Orch) Shaw G. Schirmer 8103 SATB

Witness Thygerson Heritage H315-3 SATB

Wondrous Love arr/Christiansen Augsburg 11-1140 SATB

Wondrous News! Wetzler Kjos C8419 SATB

Wood (from **Four Pastorales**) Effinger G. Schirmer SATB

Woodland Cool, Thou Woodland Quiet Brahms G. Schirmer SATB

Written in De Holy Book Rodby Schmitt 1876 SATB

Ye Banks and Braes O'Bonnie Doon Pierce Plymouth BP115 SATB

Ye Watchers and Ye Holy Ones Davison E. C. Schirmer 1780 SATB

Younger Generation Copland/Swift Boosey and Hawkes 1723 SATB

Zigeunerleben Schumann/Kaplan Lawson-Gould W2708 SATB

Male Voicings

Abducted Shepherd, The Dvorak (English or German) G. Schirmer TTBB

Across the Western Ocean arr/Dougherty G. Schirmer TTBB

Adoramus Te Corsi/Cain Choral Art R1880 TTBB

Adoramus Te Palestrina Bourne ES16 TTBB

Adoramus Te, Christe Palestrina E. C. Schirmer TTBB

Advent Carol Pfautsch Lawson-Gould TTBB

Agincourt Song, The Dunstable Boston 12633 TTBB

Ain't-a That Good News Dawson Tuskegee 104 TTBB

Ain't Got Time to Die arr/Duey Boston 13010 TTBB

Alleluia Handel/Dawe G. Schirmer 9412 TTBB

Alleluia for St. Francis Binkerd Boosey and Hawkes 5686 TB

All Glory Be to God on High arr/Malin Summy-Birchard 1538 TTBB

All This Night Shrill Chanticleer (from **Four Carols**) Stevens Peer/Southern Organization TBB

All Through the Night Morgan Fisher TTBB

All Through the Night arr/Ringwald Shawnee C-21 TTBB

All Ye Saints Be Joyful Davis Remick TTBB

Almighty God, Who Hast Me Brought in Safety Ford/Wolff Concordia TTBB

Amo, Amas, I Love a Lass Bartholomew Mercury 352-001338914 TBB

A-Roving arr/Wagner Lawson-Gould 791 TTBB

As Beautiful As She Butler Warner Bros. W3771 3 pt.

As Beautiful as She Butler Witmark and Sons TTBB

Ash Grove, The Luboff Walton 1014 TTBB

At the River Copland Boosey and Hawkes 5514 TTBB

Aura Lee Poulton/Hauter Lawson-Gould 527 TTBB

Auxilium Meum Dressler/Stocker/Crockett G. Schirmer TTBB

Ave, Maris Stella Grieg/Pitcher Summy-Birchard 881 TTBB

Ave Maria Arcadelt/Greyson Bourne ES4 TTBB

Ave Maria Goemanne Kjos TTBB

Ave Maria Vene E. C. Schirmer 2137 TTBB

Ave Maria Victoria E. C. Schirmer 2515 TTBB

Avenging and Bright Parker Lawson-Gould TTBB

Ave Verum Corpus Christi Desprez E. C. Schirmer TTBB

Babe So Tender, A Mauton E. C. Schirmer 543 TTBB

Bachelor, The Kodály Boosey and Hawkes 1893 3 pt.

Battle Hymn of the Republic Steffe/Ringwald Shawnee TTBB 4-hand piano

Battle of Stonington arr/Brandon Lawson-Gould TB

Beat! Beat! Drums! Heath G. Schirmer 10344 TTBB

Beati Mortui (Blessed Are the Dead) Mead G. Schirmer 517807 TTBB

Beautiful Savior Christiansen/Wycisk Augsburg 263 TTBB

Been in the Storm arr/Whalum Lawson-Gould 52246 TTBB

Behold Man Nelson Boosey and Hawkes 5403 TTBB

Be Thou My Vision arr/Hunter Hinshaw HMC-375 TBB

Black Is the Color of My True Love's Hair Churchill Shawnee C-51 TTBB

Blow the Candles Out arr/Richardson Mark Foster 1061 TTBB

Blow the Man Down arr/Parker/Shaw Lawson-Gould 51055 TTBB

Boar's Head Carol, The arr/Parker/Shaw G. Schirmer 10179 TTBB

Boatmen's Dance, The Copland Boosey and Hawkes TTBB

Bound for the Rio Grande Crocker Jenson TTB

Bound for the Rio Grande Shaw/Parker Lawson-Gould TTBB

Break of Day Rosenhaus Bourne TTBB

Bring Us in Good Ale! Gilbert Novello TTBB

Brother James's Air arr/Davies Oxford TTBB

Brothers, Lift Your Voices Pfautsch Gray CMR 2556 TTBB

Brothers, Sing On Grieg/McKinney J. Fisher 6927 TTBB

By the Sea Schubert Belwin Mills 1145 TTBB

Call to Remembrance, O Lord Farrant/Wolff Concordia TTBB

Cantate Domino Hassler/Beveridge E. C. Schirmer TTBB

Carol of the Bells Leontovich/Wilhousky C. Fischer CM2270 TTBB

Chant Funebre (Dirge) Rossini Joseph Boonin 103 TTBB and Tenor Drum

Charlottown arr/Bryan Fisher TTBB

Ching-A-Ring Chaw Copland Boosey and Hawkes TTBB

Christ Has Arisen Gabrieli/Pantaleoni Concordia TBB

Christ Lag in Todesbanden Schein/Stone Tetra TTB

Christmas Hymn arr/Jungst G. Schirmer 1414 TTBB

Christmas Night Lovelace Fisher TTBB

Clic, Clac, Dansez Sabots Poulenc (French or English) Editions Salabert TBB

Climbin' Up the Mountain arr/Smith Kjos 1101 TTBB

Colorado Trail Luboff Walton 1005 TTBB

Come Peace of God Butler Sacred Music Press S-5017 TTBB

Come Sweet Death Bach G. Schirmer 8956 TTBB

Come Thou Holy Spirit Tschesnokoff/Tkach Kjos TTBB

Coventry Carol arr/Gilbert Oxford TTBB

Curtains of Night Niles Fostco TTBB

Dank Sei Unserm Herrn Anonymous/Bevridge E. C. Schirmer TTBB

De Animals a-Comin' arr/Bartholomew G. Schirmer 8046 TTBB

Didn't My Lord Deliver Daniel? arr/Heath G. Schirmer 11058 TTBB

Die Nacht Schubert R. Dean/Lawson-Gould TTBB

Die Rose Stand Im Tau Schumann/Stone Tetra TTBBB

Down Among the Dead Men Vaughan Williams Galaxy 1.5025.1 TTBB

Down in the Valley arr/Mead Galaxy TTBB

Do You Fear the Wind? arr/Sateren Schmitt, Hall, and McCreary TTBB

Drinking Song (Back and Side Go Bare) Vaughan Williams Oxford TTBB

Drinking Song Mendelssohn G. Schirmer 12034 TTBB

Drinking Song Vaughan Williams Oxford 2 and 3 pts.

Drink to Me Only with Thine Eyes Quilter Boosey and Hawkes 18078 TTBB

Drop, Drop, Slow Tears Beveridge E. C. Schirmer 2174 TTBB

Drummer and the Cook, The Shaw/Parker Lawson-Gould TTBB

Du, du liegst mir im Herzen Shaw/Parker Lawson-Gould TTBB

Edit Nonna Schubert/McKelvy (English or Latin) Fostco TTBB

Erie Canal arr/Bartholomew G. Schirmer 9222 TTBB

Erie Canal, The arr/DeCormier Lawson-Gould 52073 2 pt.

Evening Song Kodály Boosey and Hawkes 5798 3 pt.

Ev'ry Time I Feel the Spirit Dawson Tuskegee 125 TTBB

Fain Would I Change That Note Vaughan Williams Novello TTBB

Farmer's Boy, The Vaughan Williams Stainer and Bell 2078 TTBB

Fill the Flowing Bowl Churchill/Landlord Plymouth TTBB

Follow Your Star Wagner R. Dean TTBB

From Heav'n Above Luther/Duson Kjos TBB

Give Me the Love Butler Schmitt 255 2 pt.

Gloria (from **Missa Mater Patris**) Desprez G. Schirmer 11012 TTBB

Glory to God Gretchaninoff Marks 53 TTBB

Gloucestershire Wassail arr/Scott Words and Music/Kjos TTBB

Go and Tell John Pfautsch Hope TTBB

God Rest You Merry Gentlemen Krone Kjos 1117 TTBB

Good Fellows Be Merry (from **Peasant Cantata**) Bach Boston 12065 TTBB

Good Friday Holst Boosey and Hawkes TTBB

Good News Brown/Bary Studio PR V7707 TTB

Good Night, Ladies arr/Hunter/Shaw Lawson-Gould TTBB

Gospel Train, The arr/Arch Roberton Publications TTBB

Grant Them Rest Eternal Cornelius Music 70 Publishers TTBB

Grass Heath G. Schirmer 10118 TTBB

Gratias Agimus Tibi Hassler Lawson-Gould 782 TTBB

Great Is He the Lord the Lord Eternal Nicholas/Davies-Bryn Myrddin Roberton Publications TTBB

Green Grow the Rushes, O! arr/Roberton R. D. Row 519 TTBB

Guide My Head arr/Heath G. Schirmer 11868 TTBB

Hallelujah (from **Mount of Olives**) Beethoven G. Schirmer 10774 TTBB

Hava Nageela Goldman Lawson-Gould TTBB

Heavenly Light! Kopylov/Wilhousky C. Fischer CM611 TTBB

Hello My Baby arr/Howard/Emerson/Hicks Bourne TTBB

Herbstlied Mendelssohn National TB

He's Got the Whole World in His Hands arr/Heath G. Schirmer 10854 TTBB

Hide Not Thou Thy Face from Us, O Lord Farrant/Wolff Concordia TTBB

Hodie Christus Natus Est Lamb G. Schirmer TTBB

Honor! Honor! Johnson C. Fischer CM2182 TTBB

How Merrily We Live Este E. C. Schirmer 540 TTB

Hunter, The (from **Three German Folksongs**) Linn (German) Lawson-Gould TTBB

Hunter's Chorus (from **Der Freischutz**) Weber G. Schirmer 11689 TTBB

Hunting Song Mendelssohn (English and German) G. Schirmer 12074 TTBB

I Couldn't Hear Nobody Pray arr/Bartholomew G. Schirmer TTBB

If with All Your Heart Blakley Hinshaw HMC-342 TTBB

If Ye Would Drink Delight Butler Heritage 2871 TTBB

If You Should Go Away Dvorak (English or German) G. Schirmer TTBB

I Give You a New Commandment Shepherd Oxford TTBB

I Got Shoes arr/Bartholomew G. Schirmer 7144 TTBB

I Hear A Voice A-Prayin' arr/Bright Shawnee TTBB

I Love My Love Holst G. Schirmer 10967 TTBB

Inveni David Bruckner C. F. Peters 6318 TTBB

I Will Extol Thee Moe Augsburg PS623 TTBB

I Will Praise Thee, O Lord Nystedt Augsburg TTBB

J'ay le Rebours Certon/Forbes E. C. Schirmer TTBB

Jenny Kissed Me Korte E. C. Schirmer 2311 2 pt.

Jenny Kissed Me Mechem Boosey and Hawkes 5856 3 pt.

Jerusalem, My Happy Home Gerike Mark Foster 1002 TTBB

Jesus Christ, Our Blessed Lord Brumel/Adams (Latin) G. Schirmer TTBB

Jimmie's Got a Goil Persichetti G. Schirmer 9860 2 pt.

John Henry Kubik Lawson-Gould TTBB

John Peel arr/Andrews Gray 31 TTBB

Jubilate Deo Goemanne McLaughlin and Reilly 2366 3 pt.

L'Amour de Moy Shaw/Parker Lawson-Gould TTBB

Land-Sighting Durren G. Schirmer 1013 TTBB

La Pastorella (The Shepherdess) Schubert Lawson-Gould 512 TTBB

Last Night Binkerd Boosey and Hawkes TTBB

Last Words of David, The Thompson E. C. Schirmer 2454 TTBB

Laudate Dominum Charpentier/Hitchcock Marks TTB

Laudate Nomen Domini Tye/Sheppard Boston TTBB

Laura Butler C. Fischer CM7905 2 pt.

Let Nothing Ever Grieve Thee Brahms C. F. Peters 6009 TTBB

Let the Toast Pass Burnham Heritage Music Press TTBB

Let Thy Holy Presence Tschesnokov/Ehret Boosey and Hawkes 5022 TTBB

Let Thy Merciful Ears, O Lord Weelkes/Wolff Concordia TTBB

Liebe (Love) Schubert Mark Foster 1059 TTBB

Liebe Schubert/Haberlen Fostco TTBB

Light of the World, The Sjolund Walton 9002 TTBB

Like As A Father Cherubini Music 70 Publishers/ Summy-Birchard 3-pt.

Lindea Lea Vaughan Williams Boosey and Hawkes 1991 TBB

Little Innocent Lamb arr/Bartholomew G. Schirmer 9907 TTBB

Loch Lomond arr/Duson Kjos 5564 TTBB

Loch Lomond Vaughan Williams Galaxy 1.5215 TTBB

Long Day Closes, The Sullivan/King's Singers Hinshaw TTBB

Lord, Make Me an Instrument of Thy Peace Rutter Hinshaw TTBB

Lord Bless You, The Bach Concordia 98-1474 TB

Lord Is My Shepherd, The Cain Harold Flammer TTBB

Lorena Webster/Hunter/Parker/Shaw Lawson-Gould TTBB

Lotusflower (from **Three Songs for Male Chorus**) Schubert/Pfautsch Lawson-Gould TTBB

Love and Wine Mendelssohn G. Schirmer 12033 TTBB

Love Is Here to Stay Pelz New Music Co. 3001 TTBB

March of the Kings Shaw/Parker G. Schirmer TTBB

Marry a Woman Uglier Than You DePaur Lawson-Gould 543 TTBB

Mary Ann Hendrickson Fostco TTBB

Match Sellers, The Bouchieri Marks 4387 TTB

Mater Patris et Filia Brumel/Forbes G. Schirmer TBB

May God Smile on You Bach C. F. Peters TB

May Now Thy Spirit Schuetky/Treharne Willis 5641 TTBB

Minstrel Boy, The arr/Duey Boston 2947 TTBB

My Gift Chorbajian G. Schirmer TTBB

My Gracious Lord and Master Schubert/Malin (German) Piedmont TTBB

My Horn Shall Weight a Willow-Bough Brahms G. Schirmer TTBB

My Lord, What a Morning arr/Whalum Lawson-Gould 51917 TTBB

My Lord, What a Mornin' arr/Burleigh Franco Colombo NY1713 TTBB

My Love She Mourneth Weiss Music 70 Publishers TBB

My Spirit, Be Joyful (from **Cantata 146**) Bach E. C. Schirmer 983 TB (4-hand piano)

New Heart I Will Give You, A Beck G. Schirmer 11781 TTBB

New Song, A arr/Hustad Somerset TTBB

Night, The Schubert Brodt DC5 TTBB

Nine Carols for Male Voices Vaughan Williams Oxford TTBB

Nocturnal Serenade Schubert/Stroh and Red Walton TTBB

Noel, Noel Gevaert/Grayson Kjos 5513 TTBB

No Man Is an Island Mead G. Schirmer 52043 TTBB

Non Nobis, Domine Quilter Boosey and Hawkes MFS348 TTBB

Now Look Away Merrifield Boston 12774 TTBB

Now Thank We All Our God Cruger-Mendelssohn Boston 471 TTBB

O Blessed are the Dead Mendelssohn (English or Latin) Lawson-Gould TTBB

O Bone Jesu Palestrina Bourne ES45 TTBB

O Come, Let Us Sing unto the Lord Diemer C. Fischer CM8014 TTBB

O God of Jacob by Whose Hand Tye/Wolff Concordia TTBB

Oh, What Delight (from **Fidelio**) Beethoven C. Fischer CM2245 TTBB

Old Ark's A-Moverin' Bartholomew G. Schirmer TTBB

Ol' Dan Tucker arr/DeCormier Lawson-Gould TB
O Mistress Mine (from **Three Shakespearean Love Songs**) Washburn Oxford TTBB
Once to Every Man and Nation Mead Galaxy 1.2264.1 TTBB
O Sacrum Convivium Viadana E. C. Schirmer 78 TTBB
O Sacrum Convivium Victoria/Temperley Oxford TTBB
O Sacrum Vivium Victoria Oxford A232 TTBB
O Salutaris Hostia Mathias Oxford TTBB
O Vos Omnes Casals Abingdon 242 TTBB
Parting Blessing, A Williams Shawnee TTBB
Parting Glass, The arr/Parker Lawson-Gould TTBB
Passing By Purcell Lawson-Gould 967 TTBB
Pasture, The (from **Frostiana**) Thompson E. C. Schirmer TTBB
Pasture, The (from **Frostiana**) Thompson E. C. Schirmer 2181 3 pt.
Peace I Leave with You Nystedt Augsburg TTBB
Pilgrims' Chorus (from **Tannhauser**) Wagner/Dawson Kjos 5490 TTBB
Polly Von Peterson Jenson 413-16011 TTBB
Polly-Wolly-Doodle Kubik G. Schirmer 9997 TTBB
Poor Lonesome Cowboy Luboff Walton 1007 TTBB
Poor Man Lazrus arr/Hairston Bourne 2653-7 TTBB
Praise Ye the Lord Saint-Saens/ Wilson/Ehret Boosey and Hawkes TTBB
Psalm 133 Sowerby Gray CMR 2982-4 TTBB
Quam Pulcra Es Dunstable/Shrock Hinshaw TTBB
Quatres Petites Prieres De Saint Francois D'Assise Poulenc Editions Salabert TTBB
Rebel Soldier, The Sheppard TTBB Boston TTBB
Rejoice, Rejoice, Ye Christians arr/Schroter/Malin Belwin Mills TTBB
Release Them Lord (Absolve Domine) Cornelius (Latin) Music 70 Publishers TTBB
Remember, O Thou Man Sheppard G. Schirmer TTBB
Remember Me Stevens Halsey Stevens/Mark Foster TBB
Ride the Chariot arr/Christensen National TTBB
Ride the Chariot arr/Smith Kjos 1102 TTBB
Ring de Banjo Foster/Parker/Shaw G. Schirmer TTBB
Round Around about a Wood Morley G. Schirmer 10745 TTBB
Ruins, The Kodály Boosey and Hawkes TTB
Ruins, The Kodály Presser 312-40595 TTBB
Sam Was a Man Persichetti G. Schirmer TB
Scarborough Fair Bock Gentry HMG-110 TTBB
Seeing Nellie Home Fletcher/Parker/Shaw G. Schirmer TTBB
Seek and You Will Find Sleeth Hinshaw HMC589 2 pt.
Selected Songs for Men Christiansen/Wysick Augsburg TTB
Set Down Servant arr/Shaw Shawnee C-26 TTBB
Shaver, The Shaw/Parker Lawson-Gould TTBB
She Is My Slender Small Love Thiman G. Schirmer 10671 TTBB
She Walks in Beauty Gibbs Oxford TTBB

She Walks in Beauty arr/Rhea Ludwig TTBB
Shenandoah arr/Shaw Lawson-Gould 51062 TTBB
Shenandoah arr/Wagner Lawson-Gould 848 TBB
Sigh No More, Ladies arr/Washburn Oxford 95.109 TTBB
Simple Gifts Copland Boosey and Hawkes 1093 TTBB
Singer's Creed, A Rathgeber (English or German) Oxford TTBB
Sing for Joy Pote Hinshaw HMC-517 TTBB
Sing Praise to Our Glorious Lord Schuetz/Lenel Concordia TTBB
Sleep of the Child Jesus Gevaert-Lefebvre Franco Colombo NY773 TTBB
So Dense Lully G. Schirmer 8568 TTBB
Soldier's Chorus (from **Faust**) Gounod G. Schirmer 4283 TTBB
Soldier's Song (Tpt and Drum) Kodály Boosey and Hawkes 1892 3 pt.
Somebody's Calling My Name arr/Whalum G. Schirmer 51932 TTBB
Sometimes I Feel Like a Motherless Child arr/Heath G. Schirmer 10567 TTBB
Song of Peace Persichetti Elkan-Vogel 130 TTBB
Song of the Guerillas (North Star) Boosey and Hawkes 1729 TBB
Songs of a Young Man Nance Hinshaw TTBB
Soon-ah Will Be Done Dawson Tuskegee T101-A TTBB
Spirits of the Dead (with tape) Gatwood Tetra TTBB
Standchen (Serenade) Schubert Lawson-Gould TTBB
Standin' in the Need of Prayer arr/Bartholomew G. Schirmer 8050 TTBB
Stomp Your Foot (Tender Land) Copland Boosey and Hawkes 6136 TTBB
Stopping by Woods on a Snowy Evening (from **Frostiana**) Thompson E. C. Schirmer 2182 3 pt.
Stopping by Woods on a Snowy Evening (from **Frostiana**) Thompson E. C. Schirmer TTBB
Stouthearted Men Rombert/Scotson Harms 9-H1184 TTBB
Streets of Laredo arr/Hunter Lawson-Gould TTBB
Surely He Hath Borne Our Griefs Lotti Marks 15311-4 TTB
Swansea Town Holst Curwen 50615 TTBB
Sweet Love Doth Now Invite Dowland Bourne ES7 TTBB
Swell the Full Chorus (from **Solomon**) Handel Plymouth F0-300 TTBB
Tabernacle of God Is with Men, The arr/Fissinger Jenson TTBB
Tarantella Thompson E. C. Schirmer 560 TTBB
Tenebrae Factae Sunt arr/Davye (Latin or English) Associated Music Publishers TTBB
Testament of Freedom Thompson E. C. Schirmer TTBB
Thanksgiving to God for His House, A Burnham Heritage 2874 TTBB
Then Round About the Starry Throne (from **Samson**) Handel E. C. Schirmer 907 TTBB
There Is a Balm in Gilead Dawson Tuskegee 106 TTBB

There Shall a Star from Jacob Come Forth Mendelssohn Hinshaw TTBB
This Train arr/Heath G. Schirmer 11244 TTBB
Thou Didst Delight My Eyes Finzi Boosey and Hawkes 5456 TTBB
Thou Must Leave Thy Lowly Dwelling Berlioz Galaxy 2065 TTBB
Three Chansons for Men's Voices Desprez Broude TTB
Three Chanteys Bartholomew G. Schirmer TTBB
Three Early Christmas Carols arr/Powell Concordia TBB
Three Love Songs Daniels Music 70 Publishers TTBB
Three Old American Songs Foster G. Schirmer 323 TTBB
Three Songs for Male Chorus Schumann/Pfautsch Lawson-Gould TTBB
Thy Word Is a'Lantern Heath G. Schirmer 11217 TTBB
To Thee, O Lord, Do I Lift Up My Soul Rachmaninoff/Hammer Lawson-Gould TTBB
Tumbalalaika arr/DeCormier Lawson-Gould TTBB
Turtle Dove, The Vaughan Williams Curwen 50570 TTBB
Two Liebeslieder Waltzes (Op. 52) Brahms E. C. Schirmer TTBB
Two Old English Airs: Shall I, Wasting in Despair and Drink to Me Only with Thine Eyes arr/Bartholomew G. Schirmer 7413 TTBB
Two Spirituals: Jesus Walked This Lonesome Valley and You Got to Reap Just What You Sow Dawson Warner Bros. C10783 TTBB
Two Spirituals: Old Ark's a-Moverin' and Steal Away arr/Bartholomew G. Schirmer 7756 TTBB
Vagabond, The Vaughan Williams Boosey and Hawkes 5454 TTBB
Veni Sancte Spiritus Janacek Universal 1678NJ TTBB
Vive L'Amour arr/Shaw G. Schirmer 51026 TTBB
Vocalise with Sop, Solo Chenoweth G. Schirmer 51041 TTBB
Wait for the Wagon arr/Hunter/Shaw Lawson-Gould TTBB
We Be Three Poor Mariners Ravenscroft Bourne 2587-5 TTBB
We Shall Walk through the Valley in Peace Appling World Library CE-2328 TTBB
What Shall We Do with a Drunken Sailor Bartholomew G. Schirmer TTBB
What Shall We Do with a Drunken Sailor Shaw/Parker G. Schirmer TTBB
When Allen-A-Dale Went A-Hunting Pearsall Modern Music Press 4152 TTBB
When Johnny Comes Marching Home arr/Heath G. Schirmer 10873 TTBB
Why So Pale, Fond Lover Butler Hal Leonard 08071575 TTBB
Widerspruch (Contradiction) Schubert (English and German) Lawson-Gould 513 TTBB
Wir Danken Dir, Herr Gott Schütz/Biester Lawson-Gould TTBB

With All My Spirit Duson Jenson TTBB
With a Voice of Singing Shaw G. Schirmer 10454 TTBB
Yes Sir, That's My Baby Donaldson/Kahn/Hicks Bourne TTBB
You, My Only Light (from **Five German Folk Songs**) Brahms/Pfautsch Lawson-Gould TTBB
You're the Flower of My Heart, Sweet Adeline Armstrong/Gerard Society for the Presentation and Encouragement of Barber Shop Singing in America TTBB
Zion's Walls Copland Boosey and Hawkes 6072 TTBB

Female Voicings

Ach Gott, von Himmel sieh darein Distler Foreign Music Distributors SSA
Adoramus Te, Christe Corsi/Scott Choral Arts Publications SSA
Adoramus Te, Christe Lassus E. C. Schirmer 890 SSSAA
Adoramus Te, Christe Palestrina/Glaser E. C. Schirmer 2510 SSA
Agnus Dei Schubert/Ehret Marks 4598 SSA
Ahi, Che Si Parti Monteverdi R. Dean CA-109 SSA
Alfred Burt Carols Burt Shawnee SSA
Alleluia Diemer C. Fischer CM7289 SSA
Alleluia Thompson E. C. Schirmer SSAA
All in Green My Love Came Riding Diamond Peer/ Southern Organization SSA
All in the April Evening Roberton G. Schirmer 9564 SSA
All Praise to Thee, My God, This Night Tallis/Harris Plymouth PCS-222 SSA
All the Pretty Little Horses Owen Presser 312-40518 SSA
And Back Again Duson Jenson SSAA
Angels and the Shepherds Kodály Universal 312-40593 SSA divisi
Angelus Mathias Oxford SSAA
Angelus ad Pastores Ait and Hodie Christus Natus Est Monteverdi Mercury 352-000-24 SSA
Angelus Ad Virginem Spencer Frank Music Corporation SA
Annunciation Pfautsch Lawson-Gould SSAA
Apres Un Reve Fauré Lawson-Gould 52162 SSA
As Costureiras Villa Lobos G. Schirmer SSAA
As Fair as Mourn Wilbye Stainer and Bell M 7-5 SSA
Ash Grove, The Smith G. Schirmer 11203 SSA
At the Gate of Heaven Allen Summy-Birchard 1570 SSA
At the River Copland Boosey and Hawkes 5512 SSA
Autumn Night Nelson Boosey and Hawkes SSA
Ave Maria Arcadelt Bourne ES-3 SSA
Ave Maria Brahms G. Schirmer 4 SSAA
Ave Maria (Op. 12) Brahms C. Fischer SSA
Ave Maria (double chorus) Holst Gray SSA
Ave Maria Kodály Universal 312-40592 SSA
Ave Maria Pinkham Associated Music Publishers SA
Ave Maria (from **Dialogues of the Carmelites**) Poulenc Ricordi SSA

Ave Verum Desprez Bourne ES 88A SSA

Ave Verum Corpus Poulenc Salabert RL 12532 SSA

Awake and Arise Gibbons Chappell Music Co SSA

Away in a Manger Terri Lawson-Gould 666 SSA

Balulalow (from **Two Lullabies** in **Presser Choral Collection**) Bennett Theodore Presser SSA

Beautiful Yet Truthful Pfautsch G. Schirmer LG549 SSA

Beauty Gilbert Oxford SSA

Benedictus (from **O Admirabile Commercium**) Palestrina/Woodworth G. Schirmer SSAA

Benedictus Victoria Belwin Mills 2040 SSA

Benedictus Vittoria/Vene Franco Colombo SSA

Black Is the Color of My True Love's Hair arr/Goldsmith Plymouth SSA

Bless Ye the Lord Ippolitov-Ivanoff C. Fischer 639 SSA

Blest Is the Man Lassus Augsburg PS603 SSA

Bought Locks Mennin C. Fischer CM6484 SSA

Bring a Torch, Jeannette, Isabella Nunn E. C. Schirmer 496 SSA

Bury Me Beneath the Willow Palmer National SSA

Call of the Shepherds, The Malin B. F. Wood 826 SSA

Cantate Domino Pitoni Flammer 89181 SSA

Carol of the Italian Pipers Zgodava Shawnee B321 SSA

Carol of the Rose Thomasponn E. C. Schirmer 2800 SSA

Ceremony of Carols, A Britten Boosey and Hawkes SSA

Charlottown Bryan Fisher 7993 SSA

Chiapanecas Marlowe Huntzinger 2039 SSA

Child in the Manger Duson Somerset Press SSA

Child Is Born to Us, A Davye Associated Music Publishers SSA

Child Said, A McCray National SSAA

Christ-Child, The (Piano or Harp) Binkerd Boosey and Hawkes SSA

Christ Is Born Robert C. Fischer 7455 SSA

Christmas Carol, A Dello Joio Marks 4323 SSAA

Christmas Carol, A Diemer C. Fischer SSA

Christmas Carol, A Kodály Oxford SSA

Christmas Hymn Jungst G. Schirmer 9890 SSA

Cold Wind, The Schroth Volkwein Bros. SSAA

Come, Let Us Start a Joyful Song Hassler Bourne ES 74A SSA

Come, Ye Gay Shepherds Costeley/Cramer Marks 4482 SSA

Come Hither, You That Love Diemer Marks MC4614 SSA

Come In (from **Frostiana**) Thompson E. C. Schirmer SSA

Come Shepherd Swains Wilbye/Greenberg Associated Music Publishers SSA

Czechoslovakian Dance Song Row R. D. Row 234 SSA

Dancing Song Kodály Oxford 54.942 SSA

Dancing Song Kodály Oxford SSAAA

Danny Boy Duson Kjos 6171 SSAA

Deo Gracias (from **A Ceremony of Carols**) Britten Boosey and Hawkes SSA

Desde el fondo de mi alma Santa Cruz Peer/Southern Organization SSA

Deux Chants de Carnival Ibert Heugel and Company SSA

Die Boten Der Liebe Brahms National SA

Domine Deus, Rex Coelestis (Latin or English) Borri/Boyd Lawson-Gould SSA

Domine Fili Unigenite Palestrina Belwin Mills SSA

Donna Il Vostro Bel Viso Weelkes National SSA

Down by the Sally Gardens Donovan Galaxy 555 SSA

Duo Seraphim Victoria Tetra SSAA

Early One Morning Scott Shawnee SSA

Elijah Rock Hairston Bourne S1025 SSA

El Niño Divino Nace Santa Cruz (English or Spanish) Peer/Southern Organization SSA

Exultation Scott Hinshaw SSAA

Exult You Now, Raise to the Skies (Frolocket min, erhebet hoch) Schein/Malin (German) Belwin Mills SSA

Facts Berger Presser 312-40632 SSA

Father William Fine Warner Bros. 2-W3204 SSAA

Fire, Fire My Heart Morley Bourne 9S65A SSA

Five Canons Mozart G. Schirmer 2620 SSA

Five Japanese Love Poems Watson G. Schirmer SSA

Four Carols Diemer Elkan-Vogel SSA

Four Cummings Choruses Persichetti Elkan-Vogel SSA

Four Little Foxes Henderson Gordon V. Thompson SSA

Four Noels Oldham (French) Oxford SSA

Four Sacred Songs for the Night Bright Shawnee SSA

Four Songs (Op. 17) Brahms C. F. Peters SSA

Four Songs for Treble Voices Brahms (German) Shawnee SSA

Fragments from the Mass Diemer Piedmont SSAA

Girl's Garden, A Thompson E. C. Schirmer 2540-5 SSA

Give Thanks to the Lord Staden/Thompson G. Schirmer SSA

Gloria in Excelsis Taverner Continuo Music Press SSAA

Glory to God in the Highest Pergolesi Flammer 89041 SSA

Gute Nacht McKelvy Mark Foster SSA

Hag, The Phillips C. Fischer CM6486 SSAA

Hallelujah, Amen (Judas Macabbeus) Handel/Whitford E. C. Schirmer 1915 SSA

Happy the Lovers Anerio/Malin Belwin Mills SSA

Hear Me, O Lord Schütz (English or German) McAfee SSA

Heare the Voyce and Prayer of Thy Servaunts Tallis/Herrmann Concordia SSAA

Hear My Prayer James G. Schirmer 8943 SSA

Heart We Will Forget Him Mulholland National SSAA

Heaven Haven Barber G. Schirmer SSAA

He Is Born, the Child Divine Ehret Sam Fox CC-17 SSA

Helas Mamour Clemens (English or French) C. Fischer SSA

Herbstlied Mendelssohn National SA
Herbstlied Schumann/Hall National SA
He's Gone Away (Three Mountain Ballads) Nelson Elkan-Vogel 362-03075 SSA
Heute Ist Christus der Herr Geboren Schütz/Klein G. Schirmer SSA
Hodie Apparuit Lassus G. Schirmer 11783 SSA
Hodie Apparuit in Israel Lassus E. C. Schirmer 1285 SSA
Hodie Christus Natus Est Monteverdi/Boepple Mercury SSA
Hodie Christus Natus Est Palestrina/Gronquist Tetra SSA
Holy Infant's Lullaby, The Dello Joio Marks 4392 SSA
How Excellent Thy Name Hanson C. Fischer SSA
How Merrily We Live Este Sam Fox EA6 SSA
Hymn to the Dawn Holst Belwin Mills SSAA
Hymn to Vena Holst Novello SSAA
I Am in Love, I Dare Not Own It Parker Hinshaw HMC457 SSA
Ifca's Castle Harley and Aschenbrenner C. Fischer 5223 SSA
If I Had a Hammer Hays/Seeger/Leyden Ludlow S-9011 SSA
If It Be Love Hilton Belwin Mills/National SSA
I Gave My Love a Pretty Little Ring Davis Summy-Birchard B-140 SSA
I Got Shoes Cain Flammer 83206 SSA
Il Est Bel et Bon Passereau Bourne ES9A SSAA
I'm Gonna Sing Gardner Staff 569 SSA
In Meinem Garten Schumann/Klein (English or German) G. Schirmer SSA
In Paradisium Krenek Rongwen Bros. SRM 3510 SSA
Japanese Christmas Carol Lee Gray GCMR-2948 SSA
Jesu, Joy of Man's Desiring Bach/Treharne G. Schirmer 8388 SSA
Johnny Has Gone for a Soldier Churchill Plymouth CH-200 SSA
Juchholla! Freut Euch Mit Mir! Schein Belwin Mills 2465 SSA
Knave's Letter, The Fine G. Schirmer SSA
Kum Ba Yah Palmer Alfred 6214 SSA
Lacrymosa (from **Requiem**) Mozart C. Fischer CM 6325 SSA
Ladybird Kodály Boosey and Hawkes 5674 SSA
La La and La Kennedy Boosey and Hawkes SSA
Lambs to the Lamb, The Creston C. Fischer SSA
Lass from the Low Countree, The Niles G. Schirmer 11206 SSA
Laudamus Te (from **Gloria**) Vivaldi/Martens Walton SS
Laudate Dominum Hollander/Gries Lawson-Gould SSA
Laudate Pueri Mendelssohn Marks AJ81 SSA
Laughing Song Pfautsch Lawson-Gould SSAA
Let All the World in Every Corner Sing Lekberg G. Schirmer SSAA
Libera Me Tubb (English or Latin) Lawson-Gould SSA
Lift Thine Eyes (Elijah) Presser 332-00820 SSA

Like As a Father Cherubini Summy-Birchard SSA
Linden Lea Vaughan Williams Boosey and Hawkes MFS219 SSA
Little Bird Grant Belwin Mills 1723 SSA
Little David, Play on Your Harp Cain Flammer 83178 SSA
Lo, A Voice to Heaven Sounding Bortnianski E. C. Schirmer 1079 SSA
Lobster Quadrille, The Fine Warner Bros. 2-W3205 SSA
Lord, For Thy Tender Mercies' Sake Farrant E. C. Schirmer 1890 SSA
Love Came Down at Christmas Duson Kjos 6184 SSA
Love Learns by Laughing Morley Stainer and Bell MIB-23 SSA
Lullaby (from **This Day**) Vaughan Williams Oxford 44.603 SSA
Lullaby of the Duchess Fine Warner Bros. 2-W3026 SSA
Madonna and Child Donata Boosey and Hawkes SSA
Magnificat Haydn/Pauly G. Schirmer SSA
Make Me a Fanciful Song Vecchi/Malin (Italian) Belwin Mills SSAA
Mass Techrepnin C. F. Peters SSA
May Day Carol Taylor J. Fisher 4872 SSA
Memory, Hither Come Pinkham E. C. Schirmer SA
Mi Lagerno Tacendo Mozart G. Schirmer 11850 SSA
Minnie and Winnie Berger J. Fisher 9169 SSA
Mock Turtle's Song, The Berger Presser 312-40633 SSA
My Dearest, My Fairest Purcell Gentry G-236 SSA
My Heart's in the Highlands Wagner Heritage SSA
My True Love Hath My Heart Land Plymouth SSAA
New Year Carol, A (Friday Afternoons) Britten Boosey and Hawkes 5848 SSA
Nightingale, The Butler Heritage SSA
Nightingale, The Weelkes Bourne ES66 SSA
Nigra Sum Casals Broude 120-8 SSA
Non Vos Relinquam Orphanos Donati Oxford SSA
Nova, Nova, Ave Fit ex Eva Spencer National SSA
Now I Lay Me Down to Sleep Thompson E. C. Schirmer 1985 SSA
Now Is the Month of Maying Morley Oxford SHM54.927 SSA
Now Is the Summer Springing Hilton Belwin Mills SSA
Now It Is Christmas Time Pooler Augsburg TC17 SSA
O Can Ye Sew Cushions? Britten/Holst Boosey and Hawkes 5213 SSA
O Dear! What Can the Matter Be? Kubik G. Schirmer 9995 SSA
Oh, My Love Luboff Walton 5001 SSAA
O Jesu Mi Dulcissimi Anerio Belwin Mills NY2183 SSA
O Jesu Sweet Bach/Greer (German) C. Fischer SSAA
O Lieber Herre Gott Schütz/Boepple Mercury SSA
O Lovely Catalina Guerrero/Seay Ludwig SSA
O Magnum Mysterium Morales/Goodale G. Schirmer SSAA

Once More the Flowers Bloom Schein/Malin (English or German) Belwin Mills SSA
Only Tell Me Bartok Boosey and Hawkes 1670 SSA
On the Nativity of Christ Butler Somerset SP727 SSA
Orpheus with His Lute Vaughan Williams/McDowell Hinshaw SSAA
O Sacrum Convivium Bell Gordon V. Thompson SSA
O Sacrum Convivium Victoria European American SSAA
O Sleep Fond Fancy Morley SB 23 SSA
O Tannenbaum Bohn Kjos 6177 SSA
Over the Sea to Skye Wagner Shawnee SSA
Parsley, Sage, Rosemary and Thyme Coates Shawnee B-332 SSA
Pars Mea Dominus Palestrina Belwin Mills NY 2186 SSA
Pastoral Holst Stainer and Bell/Part Songs 62 SSA
Pat-a-Pan Krone Kjos 1236 SSA
Patres Nostri Peccaverunt Palestrina/Rossini J. Fisher SSA
Pavanne for Spring Butler Hal Leonard SSA
Petite Voix Poulenc Salabert 7 SSA
Pleni Sunt Coeli (from **Pange Lingua**) Desprez/Boepple Music Press, Inc. SA
Praise Ye the Lord Bach/Trusler Plymouth TR-103 SSA
Praise Ye the Lord of Hosts Saint-Saens Belwin Mills 698 SSA
Prayer of Thanksgiving Kremser G. Schirmer 6812 SSA
Pretty Vines and Roses Weelkes/Greyson (Italian) Bourne SSA
Psalm 150 Kodály Oxford W-72 SSA
Psalm 150 Willcocks Gordon V. Thompson SSAA
Psalm Twenty-Three Duson Kjos 6182 SSAA
Pueri Hebraeorum Thompson E. C. Schirmer SSA (double chorus)
Rain, The Land Plymouth SSA
Random Thoughts Revicki Boosey and Hawkes SSA
Rejoice, Holy Mary Malin Belwin Mills 693 SSA
Rejoice in the Lord Always Purcell/Davis E. C. Schirmer 1875 SSA
Rejoice Now, Rejoice with Me (Juchholla! fruet euch mit mir) Schein/Malin (German) Belwin Mills SSA
Repleti Sunt (double chorus) Hand/Boepple Mercury SSA
Rise Up, My Love, My Fair One McCray National WHC-44 SSA
Rocking Carol Shearer Schmitt SSA
Sanctus Schubert Plymouth DC-201 SSA
Scarborough Fair Archibeque National SSA
Scarborough Fair Palmer Alfred 6222 SSA
Scherzo for Spring Washburn Oxford 95P400 SSA
See the Gipsies Kodály Oxford SSAA
Send Out Thy Light Balakirev Boosey and Hawkes 1924 SSA
Seventh Chester Book of Motets J. and W. Chester Ltd. SSA
Shenandoah Goetze Boosey and Hawkes SSAA
Shepherds Awake Hallstrom Shawnee SSA

Shepherd's Carol Billings Gray 3024 SSA
Shepherd to His Love, The Diemer Marks 97 SSA
Short Alleluia, A Fine Music Corporation of America SSA
Shy Love Boberg Kjos 6088 SSAA
Sigh No More, Ladies Vaughan Oxford 54.143 SSA
Sing a New Song Mendoza New Wind Music Company SSAA
Sing, Sing a Song for Me Vecchi Bourne ES53A SSA
Skeleton, A (from **Three Riddles**) Bertaux Boosey and Hawkes SSA
Slumber of the Infant Jesus Gevaert/Davis E. C. Schirmer 1088 SSA
Soldier, The Davis Galaxy 1.1698 SSA
Something Beyond Duson R. Dean HCB 809 SSA
Song of Innocence Binkerd Boosey and Hawkes 6988 SSA
Songs (from **The Morike Lieder**: Er Ist's and Jagerlied) Wolf National WHC-19 SSA
Songs (from **The Tempest**) Spencer National SSA
Songs of Late Summer Baksa Shawnee SSA
Sound Sleep Vaughan Williams Gray SSA
Spin, Spin Barthelson Marks MC-4012 SSA
Spring Bartok Boosey and Hawkes SSA
Spring Things Vehar Shawnee SSA
Still, Still, Still Eilers Hal Leonard 08547300 SSA
Surely He Hath Borne Our Griefs Lotti/Hunter Marks 4457 SSA
Surrexit Pastor Bonus Mendelssohn/Stone Tetra SSA
Susanni Collins C. Fischer R-6118 SSA
Suscepit Israel (Magnificat) Bach E. C. Schirmer 813 SSA
Swallow That Leaves Her Nest, The Holst J. Curwen and Sons SSA
Sweet Day Jordahl Belwin Mills 2420 SSAA
Sweet Was the Song Britten G. Schirmer 11639 SSAA
Swing Low, Sweet Chariot Burleigh Ricordi 116469 SSA
Tambourinschlagerin Schumann Leeds Music L-428 SSAA
Tantum Ergo Fauré E. C. Schirmer 861 SSA
Tantum Ergo Liszt/Hines Lawson-Gould SSAA
Teach Me Thy Way Hovhaness Broude (Plymouth) SSA
There Is No Rose of Such Virtue McCray National SSA
This Is the Garden Persichetti C. Fischer CM6652 SSA
This Land Is Your Land Guthrie/Ehret Ludlow S-9003 SSA
This Little Babe (from **Ceremony of Carols**) Boosey and Hawkes 5138 SSA
Though My Carriage Be But Careless Weelkes Sam Fox EA2 SSA
Though Philomela Lost Her Love Morley SB 23 SSA
Three Choral Pieces Berger Kjos 6081 SSA
Three Choruses for Female Voices Smetana R. Dean HRD 110 SSA
Three Emily Dickinson Songs Hennagin Walton SA
Three Excerpts from the Peasant Cantata Bach Witmark W-3445 SSA

Three Highland Airs Best Shawnee B-158 SSA
Three Hungarian Folk Songs Bartok/Suchoff Boosey and Hawkes 5488 SSA
Three Irish Songs Frackenpohl Shawnee B-200 SSA
Three Sacred Choruses Brahms Broude 136-1 SSA
Three Sacred Choruses Brahms (Latin) C. F. Peters SSAA
Three Songs from Sweden Hallstrom Shawnee B-215 SSA
To Be Sung on the Water (Op. 42, No. 2) Barber G. Schirmer SSAA
Tomorrow Shall Be My Dancing Day Rutter Oxford SSA
Toquen Arpas y Guitarras Santa Cruz Peer/Southern SSA
Tota Pulchra es (from **Quatre Motets**) Durufle Durand Company SSA divisi
To Those Who See Duson R. Dean HCB-807 SSA
Travelog Pierce Walton 9274 SSA
Trilogy for Women's Voices Bright Shawnee SSAA
Triolett Schumann/Heilberg Music Corporation of America SSA
Twelve Songs of Romance: Set I Brahms Marks 105 SSA
Two and Three-Part Choruses for Women's Voices Schubert C. F. Peters 4639 SSA
Two Madrigals Diemer Hinshaw SSA
Two Old Spanish Carols arr/Whitecotton Galaxy SSAA
Two Psalms Lassus National SSA
Two Songs of Longing Crocker Jenson SSA
Veni Creator Spiritus Berlioz Marks 13 SSA
Veni Domini Mendelssohn Broude 166-10 SSA
Vier Gesange (Op. 17) Brahms (English or German) C. F. Peters SSA
Virgin's Slumber Song, The Reger (German) Associated Music Publishers SSA
Von dem Rosenbusch Schumann G. Schirmer SA
Vreneli Lester Belwin Mills 1830 SSA
Wassail Song Davis E. C. Schirmer 1066 SSA
Water Is Wide, The Zaninelli Shawnee B-222 SSA
Waters Ripple and Flow Taylor J. Fischer 5065 SSA
Weg Der Liebe Brahms/Hall National SA
We Sing to Spring (Salut Printemps) Debussy (English or French) Hinshaw/C. F. Peters SSA
What You Gonna Call Yo' Pretty Little Baby Ehret Schmitt 334 SSA
When Love Is Kind Trinkans C. Fischer 6139 SSA
When Soft Voices Die Harris/Music National SSAA
When Spring Is on the Meadow Bright Shawnee SSA
Who Has Seen the Wind? Kreutz Kjos SA
Wild, Beautiful, and Free Duson Kjos G179 SSA
Willow Song, The Reed Marks MC4666 SSA
Wir eilen mit schwachen, doch emsigen Schritten Bach (English or German) E. C. Schirmer SSA
Wisdom and Understanding Newbury Somerset SSA
Wolcome Yole! (from **Ceremony of Carols**) Boosey and Hawkes 1755B SSA
Wooing of a Girl, The Bartok Boosey and Hawkes SSA

You Lovers That Have Loves Astray Hilton Marks 4333 SSA

COLLECTIONS

Mixed Voicing

ABC Choral Art Series, Vols. 1, 2, 3, 4 (Mixed, Treble, and Male Voices) American Book Company
A Cappella Singer, The Clough-Leighter E. C. Schirmer SATB
Album of Hymns and Motets Victoria Belwin Mills 6495 SATB
Bach Chorales McKelvy Mark Foster SATB
Carols for Choirs, Vols. I, II, III Jacques, Willcocks, and Rutter SATB
Choral Art for Mixed Voices Kirk General Words and Music/Kjos SATB
Chorales and Motets Lundquist Summy-Birchard SATB
Choral Music Through the Centuries Buszin Schmitt, Hall, McCreary SATB
Choral Perspective Malin Marks SATB
Choral Program Book, Vols. 1 and 2 Christiansen Augsburg SATB
Choral Program Series, Books 5 and 6 Wilson Silver Burdett SATB
Choral Sounds, Vols. 1, 2, 3, and 4 (Mixed, Treble, Male Choruses) Red Holt Rhinehart Winston
Christmas Chorales and Motets G. Schirmer SATB
Concord Anthem Book, The Davison and Foote E. C. Schirmer SATB
European Madrigals Kraus G. Schirmer 2601 SATB
First Motet Book, A Thomas Concordia SATB
Five Centuries of Choral Music Hartshorn, et al. G. Schirmer 2529 SATB
Golden Age of the Madrigal, The Einstein G. Schirmer SATB
Invitation to Madrigals, Vol 2 Dart Galaxy SATB
Invitation to Madrigals, Vol. 6 Scott Galaxy SATB
Invitation to Madrigals, Vol. 7 Scott Galaxy SATB
Joy to the World: Fifteen Sacred Carols and Christmas Hymns Rutter Hinshaw SATB
Madrigals and A Cappella Choruses Cain Schmitt, Hall, McCreary SATB
Madrigals and Motets of Four Centuries Associated Music Publishers SATB
Medieval Motet Book, A Tischler Associated Music Publishers SATB
More European Madrigals Kraus G. Schirmer 2837 SATB
O Holy Night: Thirteen Sacred Carols and Christmas Hymns Rutter Hinshaw SATB
One Hundred and One Chorales Harmonized by Johann S. Bach Buszin Schmitt, Hall, McCreary SATB
One Hundred Carols for Choirs Willcocks and Rutter Oxford SATB
Oxford Book of Carols, The Dearmer, Vaughan Williams, and Shaw Oxford SATB
Oxford Book of English Madrigals Ledger Oxford SATB

Oxford Book of Italian Madrigals Harmon Oxford SATB
Rediscovered Madrigals Malin Marks SATB
Renaissance Choral Music Malin Marks SATB
Renaissance to Baroque, Vol. 1: French-Netherlands Music Engel Flammer SATB
Renaissance to Baroque, Vol. 2: Italian Music Engel Flammer SATB
Renaissance to Baroque, Vol. 3: English Music Engel Flammer SATB
Renaissance to Baroque, Vol. 4: German Music Engel Flammer SATB
Renaissance to Baroque, Vol. 5: Spanish Music Engel Flammer SATB
Second Concord Anthem Book, The Davison and Foote E. C. Schirmer SATB
Selected Choruses for SATB Lawson-Gould/G. Schirmer SATB
Sing (Text and Literature for Treble, Male, and Mixed Chorus) Schott et al. Hinshaw
Sixty Chorales Bach/Goetschius Oliver Diston/Presser SATB
Something to Sing About, Vols. 1, 2, and 3 (Selected Octavos from Texas ACDA Lists for Sr. High Mixed, Treble, and Male Chorus) G. Schirmer
Songs for Sight-Singing ed/Whitlock Southern B370 Treble
Songs for Sight-Singing ed/Whitlock Southern B372 SATB
Songs for Sight-Singing ed/Whitlock Southern B371 TB
Songs for Sight-Singing ed/Whitlock Southern B376 SAB
World of Choral Music (Text and Literature for Treble, Male, and Mixed Chorus) Hausmann et al. Silver Burdett and Ginn

Male Voicings

Anthems for Men's Voices Vols. 1 and 2 Oxford Press TTBB
Birchard Choral Collection, No. 1 Vandevere and Hopkin Birchard TTBB
Caroling, Caroling Luboff Walton (12 Carols for Male Chorus)
Chapel Choir Anthem Book, The Holler Gray TTBB
Choral Program Series, Book 3 Wilson Silver Burdett TB, TTB, TTBB
Christmas Carols for Male Voices Strickling Schmitt TTBB
Eight Folksongs and Spirituals Johnson Augsburg TTB
First Steps in Part-Singing Weil G. Schirmer TTBB
For Boys Only Wheeler/Wadsworth Associated Music Publishers
Four Folksongs and Spirituals Johnson Augsburg TTBB
Gentlemen Songsters Gearhart and Hoggard Shawnee TB, TTB, TTBB
Harvard Glee Club Collection Davison E. C. Schirmer TTBB

Hymn Anthems for Male Voices Hansen Kjos TTBB
Hymns for Men Cassler Augsburg (48 hymns for TTBB)
Invitation to Madrigals, Vol. 4 Dart Galaxy TB
Library of Song for Male Voices (Books 1-5) Follett Pro Art/Belwin Mills
Men's Get-Together Songs Lorenz TTBB
Music, Men Ades Shawnee TTBB
Rise Up, O Men of God! Vols. 1 and 2 Johnson Sacred Music Press TTBB
Salute to Music Wilson/Ehret Boosey and Hawkes Unison, TB, TTB, TTBB
Schirmer's Favorite Two Part Choruses for Boy's Voices G. Schirmer TB
Selected Songs for Men Christiansen/Wycisk Augsburg
Songs for Boys Cain Harold Flammer TBB
Songs for Young Gleemen Morgan Schmitt, Hall and McCreary TTBB
Strictly Barbershop (20 songs for barbershop chorus) SPEBSQSA

Female Voicings

A Cappella Singer, The Davis E. C. Schirmer SSA
American Folksongs for Young Singers Matteson G. Schirmer Unison, SA, SSA
Anthology of Polyphonic Masters, Book 2 G.I.A. 640 SA/SSA
Art Songs for Treble Voices Hood Belwin Mills Unison, SA, SSA
Carols for Choirs, IV Willcocks and Rutter Oxford SSA, SSAA
Choral Program Series, Book 1 Wilson Silver Burdett SA, SSA, SSAA
Choruses and Carols Marsh Summy-Birchard SA
Christmas Carols for Treble Choirs Martin Schmitt SA, SSA
Christmas Carols for Treble Voices Presser SA
Christmas Singing Bee, A Gearhart and Ades Shawnee SA
Concert Choral Collection G. Schirmer SSA
Concert Time for Treble Voices Pooler SSA
Descants on Sixteen Traditional Songs Pooler G. Schirmer SA
Duets Schumann C. F. Peters 2392 SSA
Duets (Op. 20, 61, 66, and 75) Brahms C. F. Peters 3909 SA
Duets for Two Parts Mendelssohn C. F. Peters 4747 SA
European Madrigals Kraus G. Schirmer (Equal Voices)
Festival Song Book, The Vol. 1 Belwin Mills Unison, SA, SSA
Fifteen Two-Part Christmas Carols Geer Shawnee SA
First and Seconds Appleby-Fowler Oxford SA
Friday Afternoon Britten Boosey and Hawkes SA
Galaxy Junior Chorus Book, The Davis Galaxy SA
Girls Book, The Hood Ginn SSA

Green Hill Junior Choir and Duet Book Davis E. C.
  Schirmer SA
**Green Hill Three-Part Sacred Music for Women's
  Voices, The** Davis E. C. Schirmer SSA
Invitation to Madrigals, Vol. 4 Dart Galaxy SSA
Medieval and Renaissance Choral Music Stevens
  McLaughlin and Reilly (Equal Voices)
More First and Seconds Appleby-Fowler Oxford SA
Musical Masterpieces for Young Voices Rossi MCA
  Music Unison, SA, SSA
Presser Choral Collection, Vol. 2 Hartshorn Presser
  SSA
Schirmer's SSA Program Collection Bradley G.
  Schirmer SSA
Seconds and Thirds Appleby-Fowler Oxford SSA
Sing by Threes Rorke Presser SSA
SSA Carols for Christmas (Optional Handbells)
  Strickling Abingdon SSA
SSA Chorale Book, The Thomas Concordia SSA
Sugar and Spice Ades Shawnee SSA
Thirteen Spirituals Hancock Gray SA
Twelve Motets Lassus Mercury SSA
Twelve Songs and Romances (Op. 44, Set I) Brahms
  Marks 105 SSA
Two and Three Part Choruses for Women's Voices
  Schubert C. F. Peters 2639 SSA
Two Part Canzonets Morley C. F. Peters H-1998 SA
We Sing in Harmony Ehret Belwin Mills SSA
Youthful Chorister, The Ehret Marks SA

EXTENDED WORKS

Mixed Voicings

Alice in Wonderland Suite Fine Witmark SATB
Brazilian Psalm Berger G. Schirmer SATB
Carmina Burana Orff Schott SATB
Carol Cantata I, II, III, IV Bennett G. Schirmer
  SATB
Ceremony of Carols Britten Boosey and Hawkes
  SATB
Cherubic Hymn Hanson C. Fischer SATB
Chichester Psalms Bernstein G. Schirmer SATB
Childe Jesus Clokey and Kirk Summy-Birchard/
  Fred Bock
Childhood of Christ Berlioz G. Schirmer (Gray
  Abridged Ed.) SATB
Choruses from Gloriana Britten Boosey and
  Hawkes SATB
Christ Lay in Death's Dark Prison (Cantata #4)
  Bach G. Schirmer SATB
Christmas Cantata Charpentier E. C. Schirmer
  SATB
Christmas Cantata (Brass) Pinkham Robert King
  Music SATB
Christmas Oratorio Saint-Saens G. Schirmer SATB
Christmas Story, The Schütz G. Schirmer SATB
Christus Mendelssohn G. Schirmer SATB
Creation, The (Rock Cantata) Bobrowitz and Porter
  Walton SATB
Crucifixion, The Stainer G. Schirmer SATB
Elijah Mendelssohn G. Schirmer SATB

Fancies Rutter Oxford SATB
Fantasia on Christmas Carols Vaughan Williams
  Galaxy SATB
Festival Te Deum Britten Boosey and Hawkes SATB
For Us a Child Is Born (Cantata #142) Bach Galaxy
  SATB
Frostiana Thompson E. C. Schirmer SATB
German Requiem, A Brahms G. Schirmer SATB
Gloria Pfautsch G. Schirmer SATB
Gloria Poulenc Salabert SATB
Gloria Rutter Oxford SATB
God with Us: Christmas Cantata Pfautsch Lawson-
  Gould SATB
Good Christian Men, with Joy Draw Near Buxteh-
  ude Concordia SATB
Hear My Prayer Mendelssohn G. Schirmer SATB
I Know That My Redeemer Lives (Cantata #160)
  Bach Galleon SATB
In the Beginning Copland Boosey and Hawkes
  SATB
Jepthe Carissimi Ricordi SATB
Jesu, Joyous Treasure Telemann/Conlon Augsburg
  SATB
Jesu, Meine Freude J. S. Bach C. F. Peters SATB
La Fiesta de la Posada: Christmas Carol Pageant
  Brubeck Shawnee SATB
Liebeslieder Walzer Brahms/Shaw (4-hand piano)
  G. Schirmer SATB
Many Moods of Christmas I, II, III, IV Shaw/Ben-
  nett G. Schirmer SATB
Mass in C (Op. 86) Beethoven Broude SATB
Mass in F Major Schubert G. Schirmer SATB
Mass in G Major Schubert G. Schirmer SATB
Messiah Handel G. Schirmer SATB
Midnight Mass for Christmas Charpentier Elkan-
  Vogel SATB
Missa Brevis in D Mozart Arista SATB
Missa Brevis in F Mozart G. Schirmer SATB
Missa Luba (Mass in Congolese Style) Haazen G.
  Schirmer SATB
Mystic Trumpeter, The Dello-Joio G. Schirmer
  SATB
Nanie Brahms G. Schirmer SATB
Now Thank We All Our God (Cantata #192) Bach
  G. Schirmer SATB
Nun Danket Alle Gott (Brass) Pachelbel Robert King
  Music SATB
O Beloved Shepherds Hammerschmidt Concordia
  SATB
O Sing Unto the Lord Handel G. Schirmer SATB
Peaceable Kingdom, The Thompson E. C. Schirmer
  SATB
Peasant Cantata, The Bach Pattersons Pub. Ltd.
  SATB
Prince of Peace Is Come (Moravian Christmas Can-
  tata) Gregor/Kroeger C. Fischer SATB
Psalm 90 Ives Presser SATB
Rejoice, Earth and Heaven Buxtehude C. F. Peters
  SATB
Rejoice in the Lamb Britten Boosey and Hawkes
  SATB
Requiem Durufle Durand SATB

Requiem Fauré H. T. Fitzsimons SATB
Requiem Rutter Oxford/Hinshaw SATB
Requiem Mass Mozart G. Schirmer SATB
Requiem Mass in C Minor Cherubini G. Schirmer SATB
St. Paul Mendelssohn G. Schirmer SATB
Seven Last Words from the Cross Mystedt Augsburg SATB
Seven Last Words of Christ, The Dubois G. Schirmer SATB
Shout for Joy (Suite of Christmas Spirituals) De-Cormier Lawson-Gould SATB
Sing to God the Lord Buxtehude Concordia SATB
Six Chansons Hindemith Schott SATB
Sleepers, Wake (Cantata #140) Bach Gray SATB
Song of Democracy Hanson C. Fischer SATB
Star of Love (Burt Carol Cantata) Burt/Merman Flammer SATB
Stronghold Sure, A (Cantata #80) Bach G. Schirmer SATB
Te Deum Haydn Associated Music Publishers SATB
Testament of Freedom Thompson E. C. Schirmer SATB
Three Choruses from Shakespeare Vaughan Williams Oxford SATB

Male Voicings

Alto Rhapsody (Alto Solo, Orch/Piano) Brahms J. Fischer 8559 TTBB
Ballad of Little Musgrave and Lady Barnard Britten Boosey and Hawkes 8599 TBB
Carnival Song (Brass or 4-hand piano) Piston Associated Music Publishers A-296 TTBB
Choruses from The Damnation of Faust (Orch/Piano) Berlioz Schott 567 TTB/TB
Demon of the Gibbett, The Hindemith Schott TTBB
Dirge for Two Veterans, A (Brass, Drums, Piano/Organ) Holst G. Schirmer TTBB
Entrance and March of Peers (from Iolanthe) Gilbert and Sullivan E.C. Schirmer TTBB
Four Songs for Men's Voices Washburn G. Schirmer TTBB
Four Welsh Songs (Orch/Piano) Hodinett Oxford 56.133 TTBB
Five Slovak Folksongs Bartók (English) Boosey and Hawkes TTBB
If You Can't Eat You Got To Bernstein Boosey and Hawkes TTBBBB
Mass in Honor of St. Sebastian Villa-Lobos Associated Music Publishers TTB
Missa Mater Patris Desprez Schott 2642 TTBB
Nachtgesang im Walde (Night Song in the Forest) (Four Horns) Schubert TTBB
Requiem in D Minor (Orch/Piano) Cherubini C. F. Peters S1 TTBB
Sketchbook for Men, A (Strings, Perc, Piano) Pitfield C. F. Peters H-268 TTBB
Song of Democracy (Orch/Piano) Hanson C. Fischer TTBB
Standchen Schubert Lawson-Gould TTBB with Alto Solo

Stopwatch and an Ordinance Map, A (3 Timp, Brass) Barker Schott 8799 TTBB
Testament of Freedom, The (Orch, Band, or Piano) Thompson E. C. Schirmer 2118 TTBB
Three Shakespearean Love Songs Washburn Oxford TTBB with Horn
Thy Will Be Done (Brass, Perc., or Piano) Nelson Boosey and Hawkes 557 TTBB
Two Motets Creston (Latin) G. Schirmer TTBB

Female Voicings

Blessed Damoiselle, The Debussy G. Schirmer SSA, A
Ceremony of Carols, A Britten Boosey and Hawkes SSA
Crucifixion, The Stainer Novello SSA
Emily Dickinson Mosaic, An Pinkham C. F. Peters SSA
Folk Songs of the Four Seasons Vaughan Williams Oxford SSA
Gloria Vivaldi Novello SSA
Magnificat Vaughan Williams Oxford SA, A
Mass in Honor of St. Sebastian Villa Lobos Associated Music Publishers SSA
Messe Basse (Low Mass) Fauré Broude SSA
Missa Brevis in D Britten Boosey and Hawkes SSA
Place of the Blest, The Thompson E. C. Schirmer SSAA
Psalm 150 Britten Boosey and Hawkes SA
Spring Cantata Persichetti Elkan-Vogel SSA
Stabat Mater Pergolesi G. Schirmer Sa, SA
Winter Cantata Persichetti Elkan-Vogel SSA

ELECTRONIC TAPE ACCOMPANIMENT

Alleluia, Acclamation and Carol (Timp) Pinkham E. C. Schirmer 2954 SATB
Amens Pinkham E. C. Schirmer 3016 SATB
Call of Isaiah, The (Organ) Pinkham E. C. Schirmer 2911 SATB
Collect Bassett Word Lib. Sacred Music CA2002-8 SATB
Evergreen (Opt. Insts.) Pinkham E. C. Schirmer 2962 Unison
Hymn of the Universe Felciano E. C. Schirmer 2944 SAB
In the Beginning of Creation Pinkham E. C. Schirmer 2902 SATB
In the Presence Trythall Marks 4495 SATB
I Saw an Angel Pinkham E. C. Schirmer 2973 SATB
Kyrie (Piano, Perc) Erb Merion 342-40026 SATB
Out of Sight Felciano E. C. Schirmer 2909 SATB
Pentecost Sunday Felciano World Lib. Pub. EMP1532-1 Unison Male, Organ
Sic Transit (Organ, Light) Felciano E. C. Schirmer 2807 SSA
Signs Felciano E. C. Schirmer 2927 SATB
Time to Every Purpose, A Trythall Marks 4586 SATB
Two Public Pieces: Cosmic Festival Felciano E. C. Schirmer 2938 Unison

Two Public Pieces: The Not-Yet Flower Felciano E. C. Schirmer 2937 Unison
Words of St. Peter Felciano World Lib. Pub. CA2093-8 (Organ) SATB

CHORAL SPEECH AND UNCONVENTIONAL NOTATION

Aleatory Psalm Lamb World Lib. Pub. CA-4003-8 SATB
All the Ways of a Man Nystedt Augsburg 119004
Anabathmos I Weinland Walton M-116 Strings, Woodchimes
Antiphona De Morte Slogedal Walton 2903 Speech Choir
Ave Maria Gaburo World Lib. Pub. MO-985-8 SATB A Cappella
Bilogy, A McElheran C. Fischer CM7802 4 pt. Chorus
Burst of Applause Mason Presser G-201 4 pt. Chorus
Canticle Schramm Capella Music, Inc. SATB
Chant and Jublication Hopson Flammer Organ, Drum, Speaking Chorus
Chortos I Browne Flammer A5629 Speech Choir
Down a Different Road Pierce Walton 2915 (Piano) SATB
Emperor of Ice Cream, The Reynolds C. F. Peters Piano, Perc, Bass, Multi-Media
Etude and Pattern McElheran Oxford SSAATBB
Etude and Scherzo McElheran Oxford SSAATBB
God Love You Now Erb Merion 342-40099 SATB
How Excellent Is Thy Name Butler Bourne 837 SATB, Speaking Chorus
Let the Floods Clap Their Hands Ludlow Flammer A-5673 3 pt. Speech and Percussion
Praise to God Nystedt Associated A-597 SATB, A Cappella
Praise Ye the Lord Read Lawson-Gould 51871 SATB
Prelude and Dance for Voices and Hands Pfautsch C. Fischer CM7803 SATB
Psalm 27, Part iii Karlen AMSI 160 SATB
Rising Sun, The Pooler and Pierce Somerset CE4328 SATB
Signposts Homberg G. Schirmer 11842 SATB A Cappella
Song of Hope Geomanne GIA G-1713 (Insts) Speech Choir
Sound Patterns Oliveros J. Boonin B-111 SATB, Speech Choir
Two Moves and the Slow Cat Kam Belwin Mills 2282 SATB
Unknown, The Hennagin Walton 2802 SSA Speech Choir
Valse Toch Belwin Mills A-112 SATB Speaking Chorus

BAND OR ORCHESTRA ACCOMPANIMENT

All Glory Laud and Honor Teschner/Cain Flammer SATB with Band or Orch

America Carey/Bennett G. Schirmer 51770 SATB with Orch
America, the Beautiful Ward/Bennett G. Schirmer 51771 SATB with Orch
American, Our Heritage Steele/Ades Shawnee SA, SSA, SAB, SATB with Band
And Thou America Butler SATB with Band
Battle Hymn of the Republic Steffe/Ringwald Shawnee SA, SSA, SAB, TTBB, SATB with Band or Orch
Battle Hymn of the Republic Steffe/Wilhousky C. Fischer SSATTBB with Orch
Break Forth, O Beauteous Heavenly Light Bach G. Schirmer SATB and Orch
Brigadoon Choral Selections Loewe and Leidzen Sam Fox SATB
Christmas Day Holst Gray SATB with Orch
Come Let Us Sing (95th Psalm) Mendelssohn G. Schirmer SATB with Orch
Elsa Entering the Cathedral (Lohengrin) Wagner/Duelzman C. Fischer SSAATTBB with Orch
Fantasy on Christmas Carols Vaughan Williams Galaxy SATB with Orch
Festival Song of Praise Mendelssohn/Wilson/Harris Bourne SATB with Orch
For the Beauty of the Earth Kinyon Alfred SA and Band
Give Me Your Tired, Your Poor Berlin/Ringwald Shawnee SA, SSA, SAB, TTBB, SATB with Orch
Gloria in Excelsis (Twelfth Mass) Mozart Presser SATB with Orch
Glory Rimsky-Korsakov Witmark SSAATTBB with Orch
Glory and Triumph Berlizo Mercury SATB and Band or Orch
Glory to God in the Highest Pergolesi/Houseknecht Kjos SATB with Band
God Bless America Berlin/Ringwald Shawnee SA, SSA, SAB, TTBB, SATB and Band or Orch
Hallelujah Chorus (from **Messiah**) Handel C. Fischer SATB and Orch or Band
Heavens Are Telling, The (from **Creation**) Haydn C. Fischer SATB with Orch
How Lovely Is Thy Dwelling Place (from **Requiem**) Brahms G. Schirmer SATB with Orch
Let All Mortal Flesh Keep Silence Holst Boosey and Hawkes SATB with Orch
Let There Be Peace on Earth Miller/Jackson/Ades Shawnee SA, SSA, SAB, TTBB, SATB with Band or Orch
Let the Trumpets Ring Kinyon Alfred 1635 SA and Strings
Mighty Fortress Is Our God, A Luther/Caillet Boosey and Hawkes SATB, TTBB with Band or Orch
O Clap Your Hands Vaughan Williams Boosey and Hawkes SATB with Brass and Percussion
Omnipotence, The Schubert G. Schirmer SSA, TTBB, SSAATTBB with Orch
Onward Ye Peoples Sibelius/Lefebvre Galaxy SSA, TTBB, SATB with Orch
Salute to America Kinyon Alfred 1205 SA with Band

Sing a New Song Bencriscutto Kjos B-407 SATB and Band

Sing Praise to Him Our Lord Christiansen Hal Leonard SATB with Brass Quartet or Band

Thanks Be to Thee Handel/Houseknecht Kjos SATB and Band

This Is My Country arr/Ringwald Shawnee SA, SSA, SAB, TTBB, SATB with Band

To Music Schubert/Wilson Schmitt SSA, SAB, SATB with Orch

Turn Back, O Man Holst Boosey and Hawkes SATB with Orch

We Shall Overcome arr/Ringwald Shawnee SA, TTBB, SATB with Band or Orch

With a Voice of Singing Shaw G. Schirmer SATB with Orch

Yuletide Overture Lang Belwin Mills SATB with Band

SWING, SHOW, AND JAZZ CHOIR

Ain't Gonna Grieve Artman Hal Leonard 2 pt.

Ain't Misbehavin' Cassey Belwin Mills SATB

Ain't Nobody Fredrickson Scott Music SATB

Alexander's Ragtime Band Berlin Shawnee SATB

All of Me Shaw Hal Leonard SATB

All the Things You Are Puerling Studio PR SATB

Anything Goes Porter/Rizzo Warner Bros. SATB

Anywhere the Heart Goes Kerr Jenson SAB, SATB

Aura Lee Shaw Hal Leonard SATB

Beautiful City (Godspell) Schwartz/Lojeski Hal Leonard SATB

Big Band Sing Shaw Hal Leonard SAB, SATB

Bluer Than Blue Kraintz Alfred SATB

Blues Down to My Shoes Shaw Hal Leonard SATB

Body and Soul Mattson Hal Leonard SATB

Brandy Lurie/Lojeski Hal Leonard SATB

Brothers and Sisters Shaw Hal Leonard SAB, SATB

Button Up Your Overcoat Puerling Studio PR SATB

Can't Help Lovin' Dat Man Mattson Studio PR SATB

Christmas Song Azleton Jenson SATB

Christmas Wishes Shaw Hal Leonard SAB, SATB

Circles Chapin/Lojeski Hal Leonard SATB

Come Go with Me Quick/Shaw Hal Leonard SATB

Come Rain or Come Shine Puerling Hal Leonard SATB

Corner of the Sky (Pippin) Schwartz/Cacavas Belwin Mills SATB

Crazy Rhythm Meyer and Kahn/Bretton Warner Bros. SATB

Da Lovely Fredrickson Scott Music SATB

Daybreak Manilow/Metis Kamakazi Music SATB

Deck the Halls Puerling Shawnee SATB

Doctor Jazz Shaw Hal Leonard SATB

Don't Get Around Much Anymore Kunz Jenson SATB

Don't Take Away the Music Tawney/Lojeski Hal Leonard SATB

Dream Your Dream Hannison Jenson SATB

Ease on Down the Road (Wiz) Small/Beard Shawnee SATB

Embraceable You Gershwin/Chinn Jenson SATB

Entertainer, The Joplin/Jojeski Hal Leonard SATB

Everybody Rejoice (Wiz) Vandross/Ades Shawnee SATB

Fifty-Second Street Allen/Shaw Hal Leonard SATB

Five Foot Two, Eyes of Blue Artman Hal Leonard 2 pt., SAB, SATB

For Once in My Life Shaw Columbia SATB

Forrest Shadows Perry Jenson SATB

Georgia on My Mind Puerling Studio PR SATB

God Bless the Child Herzog and Holiday/Kerr Marks SATB

Goodbye, Love Kraintz Scott Music SATB

Got to Get You into My Life Lennon and McCartney/Lojeski Hal Leonard SATB

Great Feelin' Fredrickson Hal Leonard 2 pt., SSA, SATB

He Gave Us a Love Song Drummond Glory Sound SATB

Here's That Rainy Day arr/Shaw Hal Leonard SATB

Hold Tight Brandow, Miller, and Spotswood/Rutherford Belwin Mills SATB

How Long Has This Been Going On? Mattson Jenson SATB

I Can't Give You Anything But Love Fields and McHugh/Rutherford Hal Leonard SATB

I Can't Stop Loving You Gibson/Shaw Hal Leonard SATB

I Got A Shoes Artman Hal Leonard 2 pt.

I Had a Dream Shaw Scott Music SATB

I Hear Music Lane/Lapin Warner Bros. SATB

I Left My Heart in San Francisco Puerling Studio PR SATB

I'll Never Smile Again Lowe/Kerr MCA Music SATB

I'm a-Headin' Home Gallina Jenson SAB

I'm Feeling Right Kraintz Scott Music SATB

I've Got Rhythm Kunz Jenson SATB

I've Got the World on a String Arlen/Rutherford Belwin Mills SATB

I've Got You Under My Skin Mattson Hal Leonard SAB, SATB

Jubilation arr/Shaw Hal Leonard 2pt., SAB, SATB

Laughter in the Rain Sedaka/Cassey Warner Bros. SATB

Let Me Be the One Nichols-Lojeski Hal Leonard SATB

Let There Be Love Rand/Shaw Hal Leonard SATB

Let the Sunshine In arr/Shaw Jenson SATB

Life Is Just a Bowl of Cherries Puerling Hal Leonard SATB

Lonesome Road arr/Shaw Hal Leonard SATB

Long Ago and Far Away Gershwin/Kern/Mattson Studio PR SATB

Lookin' for the Right Words De Miero Scott Music SATB

Love Is the Answer Hannison Shawnee SATB

Loving You Kunz Scott Music SATB

Magic to Do (Pippin) Schwartz/Fisher Belwin Mills SATB

Michelle Lennon and McCartney/Puerling Shawnee SATB

Mighty Clouds of Joy arr/Shaw Hal Leonard SATB

Mood Indigo Ellington/Rutherford Belwin Mills SATB

Mountain Dew Willet Heritage Press SAB

My Funny Valentine arr/Shaw Hal Leonard SATB

My Sweet Lady Denver/Lojeski Hal Leonard SATB

Night and Day Porter/Evans Warner Bros. SATB

Noah, Bring Your Children Olson Aberdeen SAB

Once Upon a Rainbow Carter Somerset SATB

People Need Love Anderson and Ulvaeus Hal Leonard SATB

Pippin Choral Medley Schwartz/Cassey Belwin Mills SATB

Place Where Lovers Dream DeMiero Somerset SATB

Raise a Ruckus Tonight Willet Heritage SAB

Reach for the Start G. Fry Belwin Mills SATB

Risin' Out of My Soul Eilers Jenson SAB

Salvation Train Schwartz Heritage SATB

Seems Like Old Times arr/Puerling Hal Leonard SATB

Side by Side Woods/Coates Shawnee SATB

Spread Your Wings and Fly Eilers Jenson SATB

Stayin' Alive Lojeski Hal Leonard 2 pt., SSA SAB, SATB

String of Pearls arr/Kerr Hal Leonard SAB, SATB

Summer Nights (Grease) Casey and Jacobs/Lojeski Hal Leonard SATB

Summer's Eyes Are Blue Kraintz Alfred SSAA, SATB

Summertime Gershwin/Shaw Hal Leonard SATB

Swing into Spring Schwartz Heritage 2 pt.

'S Wonderful arr/Mattson Jenson

Tangerine arr/Mattson Hal Leonard SATB

That Old Black Magic arr/Shaw Hal Leonard SATB

Theme from Ice Castles arr/Besig Studio PR SATB

This Is It! David and Livingston/Lapin Warner Bros. SATB

This Old Hammer Willet Heritage SAB

Through the Years arr/Lojeski Hal Leonard 2 pt., SAB, SATB

To Be in Love Kunz Hal Leonard SATB

Tuxedo Junction arr/Nowak Hal Leonard SAB, SATB

Way You Look Tonight, The arr/Knowles Jenson SATB

When I Fall in Love Young/Azelton Hal Leonard SATB

When Will I Find Love Kraintz Jenson SATB

Wonderful Day Like Today, A Bricusse and Newley/Leyden Musical Comedy Productions SATB

You Are So Beautiful Preston and Fischer/Lojeski Hal Leonard SATB

Index